Using BASIC

Second Edition

Using BASIC

Second Edition

Rich Didday

Information Tools

Rex Page

WEST PUBLISHING COMPANY

St. Paul New York Los Angeles San Francisco

Cover artwork: *Homage to M.C. Escher and Buckminster Fuller* by Mike Newman/ DICOMED Corporation, Minneapolis, Minnesota.

Using a DICOMED D38+ Design Station, a line program was applied to make one-fifth of a geodesic circle. Four consecutive duplications were made and rotated around the center 72 degrees to complete the circle. A completed geodesic circle was moved down to the bottom of the display terminal frame and squeezed into an elliptical shape. The computer interpolated the three shapes between the original at the top and the elliptical on the bottom. After color was added, the image was stored on a diskette and run through a D148SR Color Image Recorder onto 35 mm film.

50 West Kellogg Boulevard
P.O. Box 43526
St. Paul, Minnesota 55164

Printed in the United States of America

Library of Congress Cataloging in Publication Data

Didday, Richard L.
Using BASIC.

Includes index.

1. Basic (Computer program language) I. Page, Rex L.
II. Title
QA76.73.B3D5 1984 001.64'24 83-23430
ISBN 0-314-77885-3

In memory of
Richard Adrian Didday

Contents

Appendices

Preface

This is the second edition of *Using BASIC*. The changes fall into five main categories:

The enhancements described in Part III now follow the new proposed standards instead of (as in the first edition) representing our best guess as to the eventual standards.

The introduction of arrays is now clearer, and more properly implements our intent of using READ/DATA as a path toward understanding arrays.

Output formatting is now introduced earlier and more gently.

Old–fashioned flowcharts are no longer discussed.

We have cleaned up and added to the Review Exercises and Problems.

We thank our reviewers, users, and readers for your time and for your thoughts about how to improve *Using BASIC*. We hope we have implemented your suggestions well, because we received a great number of good ones.

The central theme of *Using BASIC* is **practicality.** This books presents

- a practical, systematic approach to program design
- pragmatic, useful programs solving problems which practicing programmers encounter time and again
- programs which interact with the user in a helpful, polite way, saving the user time and frustration
- portable programs which may be run on a variety of BASIC systems with minimal changes

With the explosion in sales of small computers to individuals and businesses in the last few years, there is a voracious demand for small-computer software. Virtually all recent computers provide an interactive BASIC system. Other languages are now beginning to become available, but the foothold that BASIC has notched out is not likely to erode — the investment in software and training is already too great. BASIC is the language used in most of the small-business software for microcomputers. Its syntax is easy to learn; input and output, the murky swamp that traps beginners in other languages, are natural and straightforward in BASIC; and arithmetic follows the principle of least astonishment (1/2 is .5, not zero, and 8/2 is 4, not 4.00000E+00.) Learning BASIC is of immediate practical value.

This book differs in several ways from other introductory texts on BASIC. First, it concentrates on a standardized form of BASIC — ANSI Minimal BASIC — and this encourages the development of programs which will run on a large number of systems instead of being specialized to one particular system. Until the passage of the 1978 ANSI standard for the programming language Minimal BASIC, portable programs for small computers were an impossible dream. (They have been a difficult dream, at best, for large computer systems because the other programming language standards — COBOL, FORTRAN, PL/I — fail to specify minimal configurations, and the programmer is left with no floor on which to base portability.) Now portability is a goal which can be met with a large variety of useful programs, and the first eleven chapters of this book demonstrate how it can be done.

Not all problems are easily solved within the confines of Minimal BASIC, however, so in later chapters we cover extended constructs in accord with the draft proposed American National Standard for BASIC (ANSI document X3J2/82-17, October 1, 1982). If the version of BASIC you are using incorporates the string enhancements (Chapter 16), we strongly suggest that you integrate them with earlier chapters. The problems at the end of Chapter 16 are designed to fit in with material in earlier chapters.

Does your version of BASIC conform?

Many older versions of BASIC fail to conform to the ANSI standards. Some (such as the "Tiny BASICs" or Apple Integer BASIC) are so different from ANSI Minimal BASIC that this book may not be of much use to you. Most of the others differ only in a few details. The most common deviation from the standards is in the treatment of FOR-NEXT loops, and places where such differences matter are marked (Chapters 8, 9, and 14).

A second difference lies in the emphasis on program design methodology. Programming, like any other complex task, benefits from careful planning and an esthetic concern for the finished product. Both by example and by instruction, we encourage the use of a range of design tools and practices. Each program in the text is preceded by a description of the problem (including input/output specifications) and a detailed design for the algorithm. The design is expressed and refined in the form of written plans. If you flip open this book, you will be within a few pages of such a plan.

We restrict ourselves to a few standard control structures for looping and selection, and we emphasize the use of these control structures in the text. In addition to the usual **IF-THEN-ELSE, select-case,** and **pretest** and **posttest** loops, we introduce (at a later point, after beginners have become comfortable with the concept of looping) a third type of loop, which we call a **search loop.** The practical necessity for a loop with two exits, one for normal termination and another for termination on some abnormal condition, has been discussed extensively and established empirically through the examination of large amounts of well-written code. *All our programs and plans are written within the confines of these five control structures.*

A third difference is the emphasis on practical applications. In fact, the text includes as examples a number of subroutines which have been used in major computer applications. These subroutines can be taken straight from the book and plugged into new programs being developed by readers of the text. Our emphasis on realistic, useful problems has one potential deleterious effect — in some cases there may not be enough time in a course to cover all the programs in detail. Chapters 9 and 11 contain fairly involved programs. Where appropriate, these may be treated in a "black box" fashion. That is, the instructor can provide the program directly to the students (on disk, cards, or via a time-sharing system), encouraging them to learn what it does and how it is used, without requiring them to become intimate with the internal details of the algorithms. In this way, students can gain valuable experience in using canned programs as building blocks in program development. (Situations where this approach is appropriate are marked "black box" in the table which follows.)

A fourth difference from other books is in the interactive, experimental approach to learning to program which permeates this text. The reader is encouraged to experiment with specially marked "experimental programs" to find out exactly what the computer will do in a variety of situations. This sort of directed experimentation contributes to the "learn by doing" attitude which novices must develop if they hope to become programmers.

The fifth difference is in the treatment of READ/DATA statements. We interpret the constants in DATA statements as *arrays of values* and use them in ways similar to *arrays of variables.* This smoothes the gap between simple variables and arrays, often a difficult transition for beginners.

The book has three parts. Part I is a self-contained, sequential introduction to programming in which the beginner progresses from no prior knowledge of computers to full knowledge of Minimal BASIC and a firm grasp of standard programming techniques. Part II contains a palette of different subjects treated independently and in deliberately different directions. Readers and instructors will want to choose from these chapters according to their own interests and requirements. Part III describes a number of enhancements of Minimal BASIC, with special emphasis on features that are necessary in large applications.

Appendix A (The World BASIC Lives In) may be covered at any time. It contains a brief description of computers and it indicates how a person can save, recall, and edit programs on a variety of different systems.

One note about the order of the presentation: Subprograms are introduced a bit earlier here than in most textbooks. They appear in Chapter 6 as a natural extension of the material on composing programs in Chapter 5, since they provide a clear way to express a hierarchical structure. If the instructor feels it wise, the sections on DEFined functions (Sections 6 4 and 6 5) can be delayed until much later in the course. However, subroutines are used from Chapter 6 on. Since, in BASIC, subroutines are extremely straightforward (no arguments), few students have trouble grasping the concept very early.

Three different audiences will find this text useful.

- **business programming:** students in business curricula who are specializing in computer applications and people who want to learn BASIC on their own and apply it to problems encountered in business (payroll, inventory, accounting, bookkeeping, statistical data, etc.)

- **general programming:** people who need to use computers in their work, such as students or professionals in the sciences, social sciences, or arts
- **general computer knowledge:** people who need to know what computers are used for and how they function in those applications

The following table suggests possible avenues through the book suited to each of these interest groups.

Possible Routes Through Using BASIC

business programming	*general programming*	*general computer knowledge*
introduction to programming (Ch. 1–8)	introduction to programming (Ch. 1–8)	introduction to programming (Ch. 1–8)
polite interaction with users (Ch. 9)	polite interaction with users (Ch. 9)	polite interaction with users (Ch. 9 — black box)
arrays (Ch. 10)	arrays (Ch. 10)	array (Ch. 10 — optional)
questionnaire program — an extended example (Ch. 11)	questionnaire program — an extended example (Ch. 11)	questionnaire program — an extended example (Ch. 11 — black box)
simulation (Ch. 13)	simulation (Ch. 13 — science orientation)	limitations of computers (Ch. 12)
sorting (Ch. 14 — black box)	sorting (Ch. 14)	simulation (Ch. 13 — black box)
strings (Ch. 16)	data structures (Ch. 15)	
input/output (Ch. 17)	input/output (Ch. 17)	
files (Ch. 18)	other enhancements (Ch. 19 — optional)	
other enhancements (Ch. 19 — optional)		

black box: treat the programs as routines to be "used" rather than "understood." Study their purpose, input, and output — not their internal details.

Acknowledgment

Special thanks to Dr. Spotswood D. Stoddard who
took what we had,
saw what we were trying to do, and
told us how to do it better.

Rich Didday
Rex Page

Winnemucca, Nevada

Notations

logo	*meaning*
	*a piece of cake (easy exercise or problem).* If you have trouble with this type of easy problem, take it as a sign that you have missed some important concepts and need to review the material in that section or chapter.
	*a tough nut to crack (hard exercise or problem).* This type of problem requires both a good understanding of the material in the section or chapter and some creative thought.
	*experiment:* Programs marked with this logo are testbeds for experimentation. Enter the program as shown and use it to discover strange and marvelous facts!

blanks: Although people rarely draw attention to them, blank characters are very important in written communications. A blank serves as an unobtrusive separator.

////Imagine/reading/a/sentence/like/this.////
Oronewithnoseparatorsatalllikethis.

You may not be used to thinking of a blank character as the same sort of thing as an "a" or "b" or "!". But on a printer (as on a typewriter) it takes a definite action to produce a blank just as it requires a definite action to produce an "a".

We have numbered sections in this book in a way which draws attention to the blank as a legitimate character.

A typical usage is "Figure 2 4 1," read "figure two four one," identifying the first figure in the fourth section of Chapter 2.

Part I consists of two intertwined threads. The first thread consists of the methods and techniques of program design, testing, and revision, and the reasons that make learning these techniques so important. The second thread is the specifics of the computer language Minimal BASIC.

Part I begins relatively slowly, since quite a few little "facts" must be learned before you can start writing serious programs. By the end of Part I, all the features of Minimal BASIC have been covered, and the two threads are brought together in a major example — the questionnaire analysis program of Chapter 11.

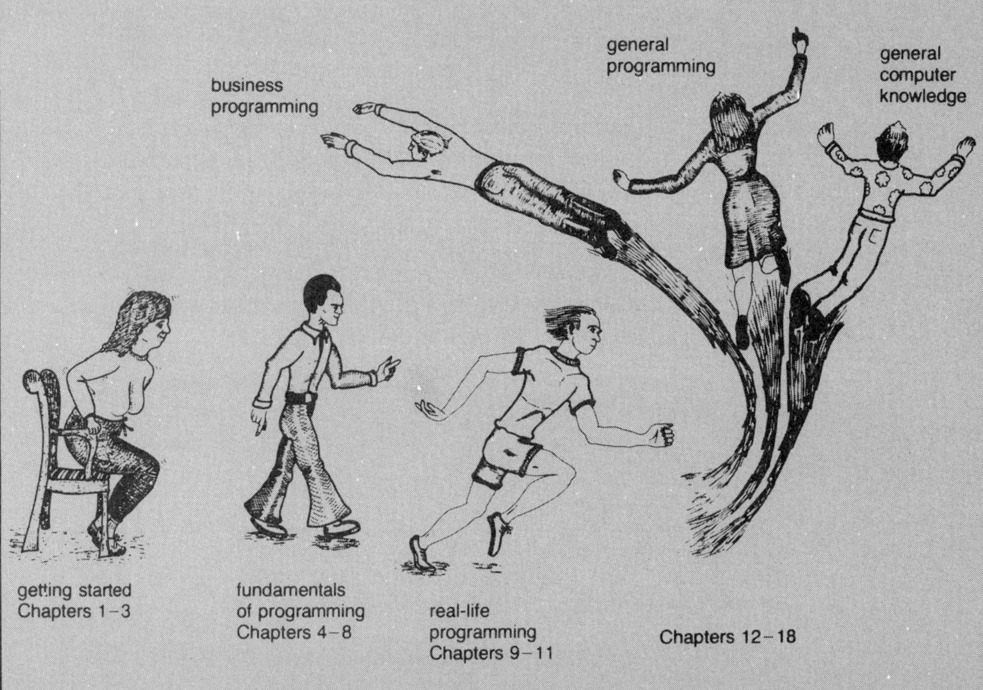

PART 1

ANSI Minimal BASIC

Chapter 1 **Basic BASIC Commands and Data Types**

Section 1 1

Getting Started

The best way to get started in BASIC is to experiment. If you have your own computer, or have access to a computer terminal that's not in heavy use, go there right now and start experimenting. Otherwise, read on and take notes in preparation for your first session with BASIC.

If you don't know how to "get in BASIC," that is, to get your system set up to accept statements in the BASIC language, ask someone. If there's no one in sight, look around. Maybe someone has scrawled what to do on the wall. If you have your own computer, look through the manuals that came with it.

When you "get into BASIC," the computer will print

```
READY
```

> The first part of Appendix A describes ways of "getting into BASIC" on several common systems.

or some similar *prompt* word indicating that it's ready for you to tell it what to do, using BASIC. If the word READY doesn't appear, ask someone for help before going on.

Once you're "in BASIC," we can begin. Type anything you feel like, and then hit the return key. On your keyboard, this key will probably be on the right-hand side, and it might be marked CR (for Carriage Return) or RETURN or ENTER. See what happens.

```
ANYTHING YOU WANT↵
ERROR-UNRECOGNIZED STATEMENT
READY
```

we'll underline things you type

we'll use this little curved arrow to denote hitting the "return" key

we won't underline things the computer types

Don't worry about hurting anything; you won't. You might not *accomplish* anything by typing whatever comes into your head, but you won't hurt anything.

Example

```
HELP! I DON'T HAVE ANY IDEA WHAT I'M DOING
ERROR-NOT A CONSOLE COMMAND
READY
```

> **Unavoidable fact of life**
>
> BASIC (like any other computer language) has a set of rigid conventions. If you don't follow them to the letter, the system will complain. The complaint takes the form of an **error message.** The specific error messages differ from computer system to computer system. Sometimes the message includes a phrase describing the problem; sometimes it's just a number. If your system gives error numbers, you'll need a manual to look up the meaning.

Type

```
PRINT "HELLO"
```

don't forget to hit the return key

and see what happens. If you get an error message (and you really typed exactly what's shown, with spaces, quotes, and everything), skip ahead to Section 1 2.

If your experiment came out like this

```
PRINT "HELLO"
HELLO
READY
```

look at it for a while. The important parts are the word PRINT (which is a meaningful word, a **keyword,** in BASIC) and the quotation marks around what you want to PRINT. Try some more — make them up.

Example

```
PRINT "BIX BEIDERBECKE'S HORN"
BIX BEIDERBECKE'S HORN
READY
```

Words aren't the only things you can PRINT. You can PRINT numbers.

Example

```
PRINT 2
 2
READY
```

And you can PRINT the results of computations.

Example

```
PRINT 2+3+4
 9
READY
```

Try some more. See what you can get the machine to do. Play around.

Section 1 2

What's a BASIC Program?

> **Unavoidable fact of life**
>
> A lot of specialized words are used in computing. Many of them are everyday words given special meanings. The first few times we use such a word, we'll put it in **boldface** type to warn you.

A **program** is a sequence of instructions which tell a computer to do something. A BASIC program consists of some number of **lines.** A **line** has two parts: first, a **line number,** and second, a **statement.** Each **statement** is a command to the computer, telling it to do some specific thing. A BASIC program is carried out one line at a time. After the computer has done the statement in one line, it goes to the next higher-numbered line and carries out the command it finds there.

In standard BASIC the last line in every program (the one with the highest line number) must be the command END. END tells the system that there are no more lines in the program.

Here's a BASIC program:

```
10   PRINT "HELLO"
20   END
```

To enter a line, just type it and hit the return key. Go ahead. Type the two lines and see what happens. Nothing, right? When you type a line (remember: a **line** is a **line number** followed by a **statement**), the BASIC system doesn't carry out the statement; it just stores the whole line. Specifically, it stores the line you just typed among the lines you've already entered (if any), in sequence according to the line numbers. That means it doesn't matter which of the two lines you type first — the result will be the same because the line numbers determine the sequence. To see the lines you've entered, in the order in which the computer has stored them, type LIST.

Example

```
LIST
10   PRINT "HELLO"
20   END
```

the machine carries out our command (LIST) by typing these lines

Notice that we didn't type a line number before LIST. We don't want the command LIST to be stored in our program; we want the computer to *do* it — right now. LIST is not part of our program.

There are two distinct phases in using a BASIC system. In one phase you enter (or perhaps correct) a program, one line at a time. In the other you allow the system to carry out a program. The system provides a number of features (like the LIST command) to help you in the program entry phase.

So far, we've entered two lines, and then LISTed them. At this point we can do several things. We can add another line — by just typing it.

Example

```
15    PRINT "THERE"
LIST
10    PRINT "HELLO"
15    PRINT "THERE"
20    END
READY
```

here's the line we added, right where it should be – after line 10 and before line 20

We can correct a line, or change it — by typing it over.

Example

```
15    PRINT "GOODBYE"
LIST
10    PRINT "HELLO"
15    PRINT "GOODBYE"
20    END
READY
```

Incidentally, if you are typing a line and notice before you hit the return key that you've made a mistake, there should be a way to back up and correct the mistake. If you don't know which key(s) to hit, type in part of a line incorrectly.

```
50    PRNIT
```

← don't hit the return key yet

and then try these:

a key marked BACKSPACE or BS

a key marked DELETE or DEL

a key marked RUBOUT or RUB

a key marked ←

hold down the key marked CONTROL and strike the x key

hold down the key marked CONTROL and strike the u key

hold down the key marked CONTROL and strike the h key

If you are using a video terminal, probably one of those keys will allow you to back up and retype the part of the line which you want to change. If your terminal prints on paper, then, most likely, the device won't physically back up on the paper, but instead will print a copy of each character you wipe out. For instance,

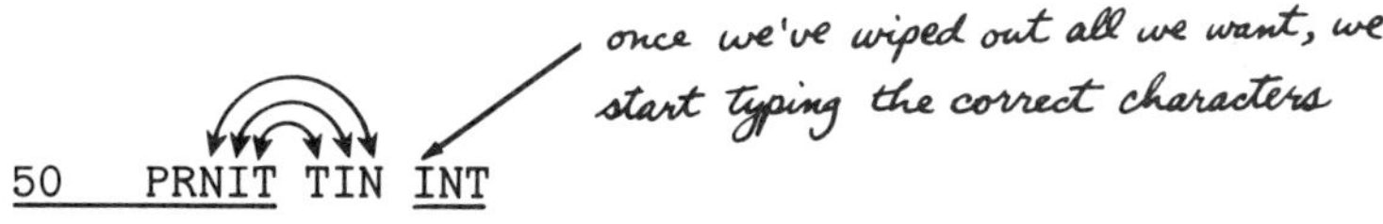

at this point we hit "rubout" — the system skipped a space, then printed the "T" we wiped out. Then we hit "rubout" twice more.

once we've wiped out all we want, we start typing the correct characters
50   PRNIT TIN INT

After you have corrected the line you can LIST it to see the corrected form. Type LIST plus the line number:

```
LIST 50
50    PRINT
```

Once you discover the right key(s) to hit, be sure to write it (them) in the diagram in Appendix F. You don't want to have to discover them all over again next time you use your system!

BASIC provides still more editing features. For instance, we can delete a line — by typing the line number and then hitting the return key.

Example

```
LIST
10    PRINT "HELLO"
15    PRINT "GOODBYE"
20    END
50    PRINT
READY
50
15
LIST
10    PRINT "HELLO"
20    END
READY
```

Not only can we delete specific lines, we can delete the entire program and start over with a clean slate. On our system the command happens to be NEW (which means, "I want to start developing a NEW program"), but on your system it might be NEW, SCRATCH, SCR, CLEAR, or something we never heard of. When you type the proper one for *your* system, you'll know it because

1 you won't get an error message, and

2 when you LIST the program, well, there won't be any program.

Example

```
NEW
READY
LIST
READY
```

So far, we've defined a program, added lines to it, taken lines out, and wiped it completely out. These are all aspects of the first phase of using a BASIC system — entering and editing a program. Finally, we can get to the exciting part — having the system carry out (RUN) our programs.

EXERCISES 1 2

1 Type in a program which you think should PRINT your name and address. Then LIST it.

2 Type in a program which you think should PRINT the sum of 45792 and 350999. Then LIST it.

3 Type in a program which you think should PRINT three blank lines. Then LIST it.

Section 1 3

RUNning a Program

To make the computer carry out a program you have entered, type RUN, then sit back and watch.

Example

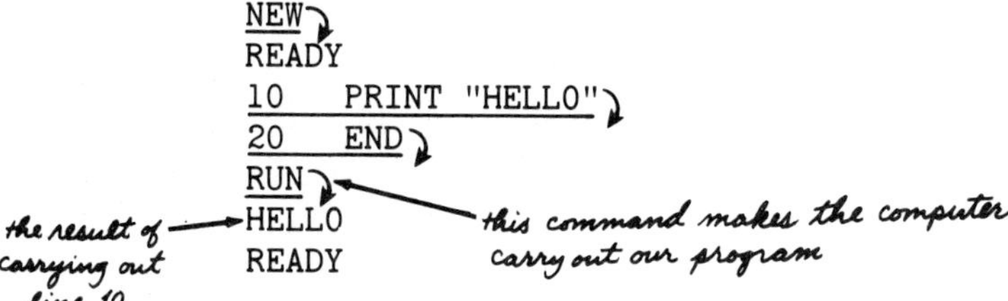

Programs are carried out in the order of their line numbers. Enter the program below, and you'll see what we mean.

Example

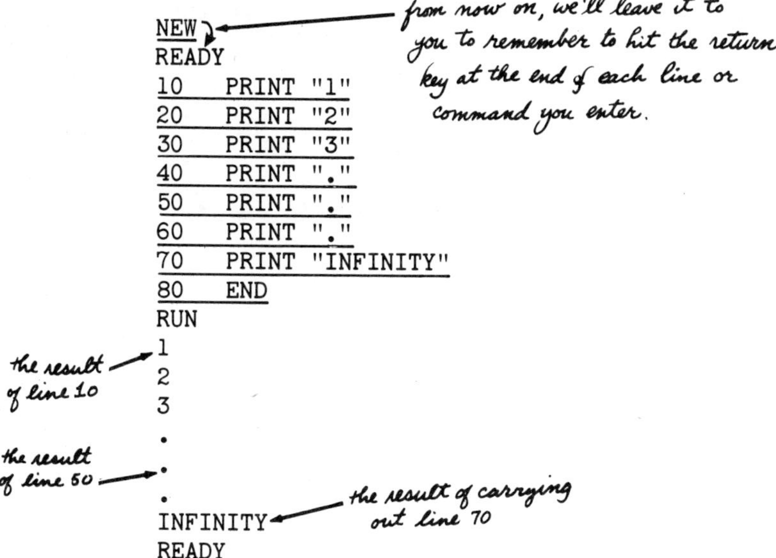

NEW
READY
10 PRINT "1"
20 PRINT "2"
30 PRINT "3"
40 PRINT "."
50 PRINT "."
60 PRINT "."
70 PRINT "INFINITY"
80 END
RUN
1
2
3
.
.
.
INFINITY
READY
from now on, we'll leave it to you to remember to hit the return key at the end of each line or command you enter.
the result of line 10
the result of line 50
the result of carrying out line 70

EXERCISES 1 3

1 What effect does adding this line

```
15 PRINT
```

have when you run the 1, 2, 3. . . infinity program?

2 Alter the above program so the 1, 2, 3, and the ellipsis (the three periods in a row that mean something has been left out) are lined up above the middle I in INFINITY. (Hint: " 2" isn't the same as "2".)

3 See how many quotation marks you can leave out of the program without getting an error message. (Hint: You really can leave out a *number* of them.)

4 Add two PRINT statements to the 1, 2, 3,. . . infinity program so it will leave blank lines above and below the ellipsis when it runs.

Section 1 4

"Things in Quotes" and Numbers

As you know from the programs you've RUN so far, when the computer carries out a line like this

```
70   PRINT "INFINITY"
```

it PRINTs (i.e., displays on your terminal) whatever follows the keyword PRINT. Two different sorts of things may follow PRINT. Things in quotes are called **strings** and are PRINTed **verbatim** — that is, everything which you enter between quotation marks, including punctuation marks and blank spaces, will be PRINTed. If a thing is *not* in quotes, it must be a number or a **numeric expression,** and its **value** is PRINTed.

Example

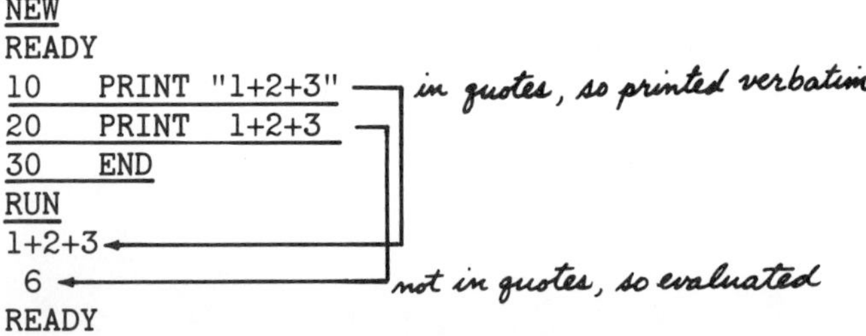

NEW
READY
10 PRINT "1+2+3"
20 PRINT 1+2+3
30 END
RUN
1+2+3
6
READY
in quotes, so printed verbatim
not in quotes, so evaluated

We'll cover the details of more elaborate **numeric expressions** in Chapter 2 — they can be rather complex. For now, it's enough to know that:

the operation of	*is denoted by*
addition	+
subtraction or negation	−
multiplication	*
division	/

Also, no two operators (+, −, *, /) may come in a row. Thus, such expressions as 2 + −2 are illegal and result in error messages.

Example

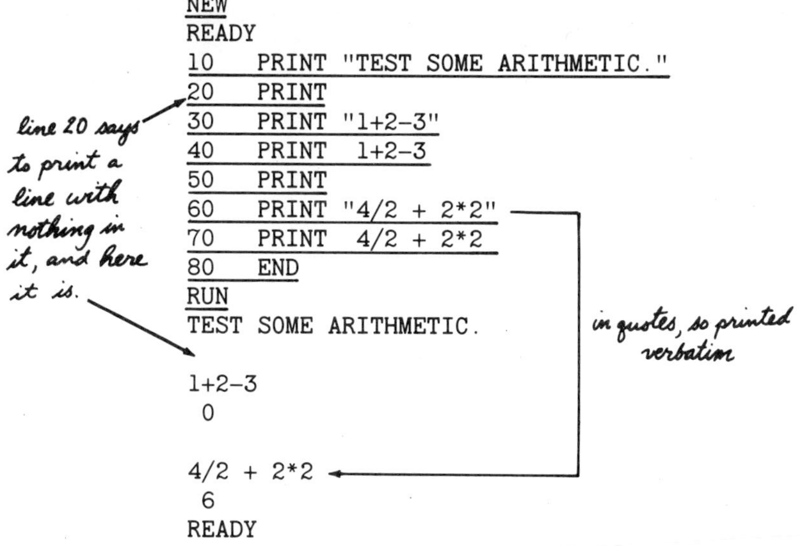

```
NEW
READY
10    PRINT "TEST SOME ARITHMETIC."
20    PRINT
30    PRINT "1+2-3"
40    PRINT  1+2-3
50    PRINT
60    PRINT "4/2 + 2*2"
70    PRINT  4/2 + 2*2
80    END
RUN
TEST SOME ARITHMETIC.

1+2-3
 0

4/2 + 2*2
 6
READY
```

line 20 says to print a line with nothing in it, and here it is.
in quotes, so printed verbatim

Write and RUN a BASIC program that tries out a number of numeric expressions. Watch out for surprises!

Be sure to try at least these statements in your program:

```
PRINT 1/2
PRINT 1/3 + 1/3 + 1/3
PRINT 0.01*100
```

EXERCISES 1 4

1 Write and RUN a BASIC program which (using just one PRINT statement) computes the sum of the first 10 numbers, i.e., 1+2+. . . +10.

2 Write and RUN a program which computes the product of the first 10 numbers, i.e., 1*2*. . . *10.

3 Suppose your checking account balance is $23.49, and this month you cashed two checks, one for $14.23 and one for $5.00. Write and RUN a program (using just one PRINT for the computation) which gives your new balance.

4 Enter and RUN this program and see if you notice any difference in the way the two PRINT statements are handled by the system.

```
NEW
READY
10    PRINT "        "
20    PRINT
30    END
```

Section 1 5

Programs Should Be Understandable

As you will soon discover, computer programs can be lengthy and, if you're not careful, hard to understand. We'll have a number of suggestions for making the program development process a rational, understandable one in later chapters. For now, let's concentrate on making programs, and the output produced by programs, easy to read and understand.

Perhaps you've noticed that in many cases inserting blanks in a program has no effect on what happens when you RUN it.

Example

```
NEW
READY
10           PRINT 1  +2
20   PRINT 1 + 2
30   END
RUN
 3
 3
READY
```

Of course, since strings (things in quotes) are PRINTed verbatim, inserting blanks there *will* make a difference.

Example

```
NEW
READY
10   PRINT "NOW"
20   PRINT "N O W"
30   END
RUN
NOW
N O W
READY
```

According to the standards, there may be no blanks before or within line numbers, and there must be a blank on either side of (but no blanks within) each **keyword** (such as PRINT or END). With those exceptions, blanks may be inserted (or left out) wherever you think it will make the program easier to read. It's doubtful that you'll get an error message if you ignore the above rules, as in

```
10PRINT1+2
```

or

```
35P RINT"RENT"
```

but doing so will make your programs very hard for you or someone else to read and understand, even if a computer can understand them without any trouble.

As your programs become more complex and more useful, you will want to *keep copies of them* for use at a later date, or to share with friends. Perhaps at a later date you will want to make small changes to your programs to make them easier to use. Perhaps a friend will want to figure out how one of your programs works. There are a number of reasons you or someone else might need to go over the statements in a previously written program. Anything you can do to make a program easier to understand will pay off many times over in the long run.

You can insert notes telling what certain parts of your program do, right in the program itself. Statements which begin with the keyword REM (which stands for REMark) can be used to include such notes. After the REM, you can type anything you like. When you LIST a program, the REM statements will be LISTed along with the others, allowing you to reread the notes you wrote. When you RUN the same program, the REM statements will have no effect, so they don't get in the way of what the program *does.*

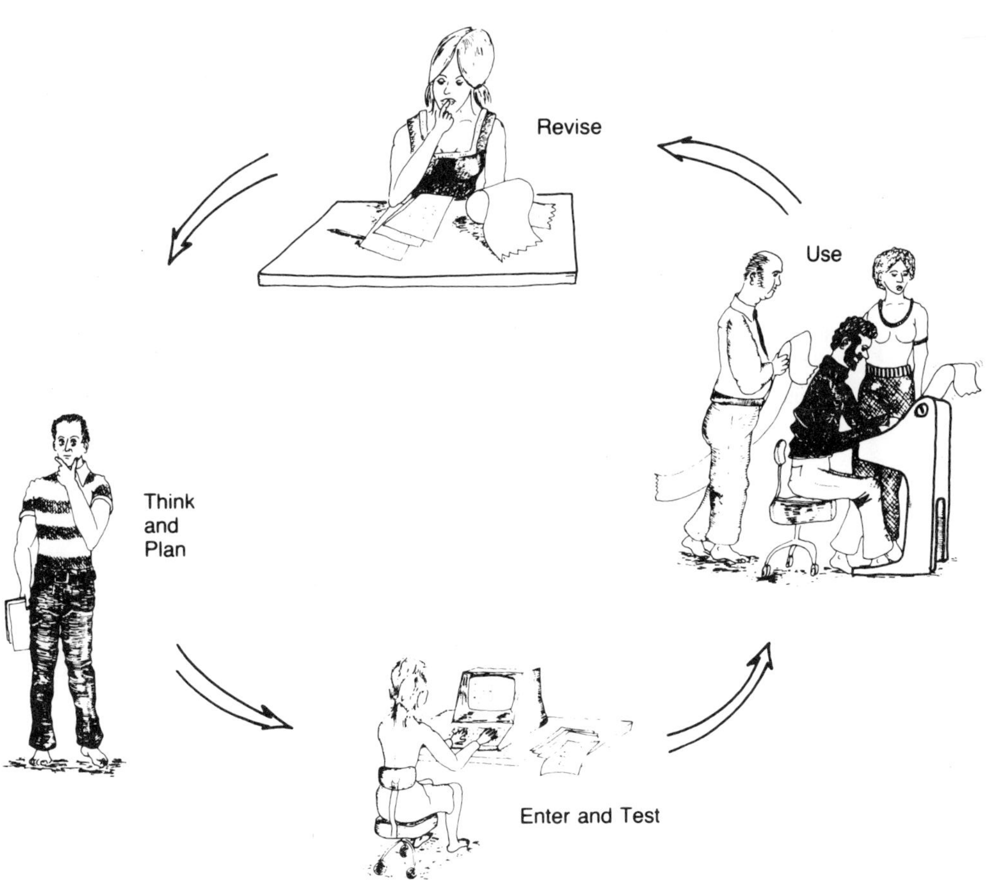

Example

```
NEW
READY
10 REM   TRY SOME SAMPLE ARITHMETIC
20       PRINT "THREE HALVES"
30       PRINT 3/2
40       END
RUN
THREE HALVES
 1.5
READY
LIST
10 REM   TRY SOME SAMPLE ARITHMETIC
20       PRINT "THREE HALVES"
30       PRINT 3/2
40       END
READY
```

the REMark doesn't affect what your program does

but it appears when you LIST the program, to help you understand what and why it does what it does

BASIC gives us quite a bit of control over the way things are PRINTed. For instance, you may include more than one item (i.e., more than one thing in quotes or number or computation) in order to get more than one thing PRINTed on one line. If you separate two items in a PRINT statement with a semicolon (;), the two values will be PRINTed next to each other. If you separate two items with a comma (,), the first value will be PRINTed, then the computer will skip over to the next (predefined) **PRINT zone** on the same line, and PRINT the second value. *If you stick a semicolon or a comma at the very end of a PRINT statement, the printer will stay on the same line when it does the next PRINT statement in your program.* Here are some examples. Try them, and play around with some of your own until you fully understand the effects of each form. That is, until you can impose your will on the system — making it PRINT values in exactly the form you desire.

Example

```
NEW
READY
10    PRINT "HALF OF 1 IS"; 1/2
20    END
RUN
HALF OF 1 IS .5
READY

10    PRINT "HALF OF 1 IS";
15    PRINT 1/2
RUN
HALF OF 1 IS .5
READY
```

re writing this line as these two doesn't change the output

```
NEW
READY
10    PRINT "VALUE", "SQUARE", "CUBE"
20    PRINT  1,  1*1,  1*1*1
```

```
30    PRINT  2,   2*2,   2*2*2
40    PRINT  3,   3*3,   3*3*3
50    PRINT  4,   4*4,   4*4*4
60    PRINT  5,   5*5,   5*5*5
70    END
RUN
VALUE         SQUARE        CUBE
 1             1             1
 2             4             8
 3             9             27
 4             16            64
 5             25            125
READY
```

start of the third print zone (arrow to CUBE)

second print zone (brace under SQUARE column)

EXERCISES 1 5

1 Here are two BASIC programs:

```
10    PRINT "HELLO", "THERE."      10    PRINT "HELLO ";
20    END                          20    PRINT "THERE."
                                   30    END
```

If you run them, which one will produce the output below?

```
HELLO THERE.
```

2 Here are two BASIC programs:

```
10    PRINT "HELLO "; "THERE."     10    PRINT "HELLO"; "THERE."
20    END                          20    END
```

If you ran them, which one will produce the output below?

```
HELLO THERE.
```

3 Devise, write, and RUN a program which will let you determine how wide the predefined PRINT zones on your system are. (The standards specify that the zones be at least 14 spaces wide, but they could be wider.) [Hint: You need to do two things here. First, PRINT a line that you can use to help you count column positions. Second, PRINT a line which has characters at the start of successive PRINT zones.]

4 Devise, write, and RUN a program which will PRINT the value of ½ (that is, the decimal value of the fraction, which means 1 ÷ 2) on the first line and the values of ⅓ and ⅔ in the first two PRINT zones on the second line, as shown below.

```
.5
.333333          .666667
```

5 What's the difference between using a REM statement and telling the computer to PRINT out something with a PRINT statement?

Section 1 6

Your Programs Can Ask You for Things

Computers are used to process information. The programs we have written so far have had all the information they processed embedded directly in the program. They have described fixed computations, unalterable once they start. There are few real problems which are solved by programs of this sort.

Most computations require that the information to be processed be supplied from outside the program. The computer collects the information, performs some computation involving the information, and prints the results. It is the nature of the computation itself that is fixed, not the data it operates on.

In BASIC the **INPUT statement** allows information to be supplied from outside the program. In the program below, an INPUT statement is used to get information from the person using the program — the **user.**

```
10  REM  THE "PERSONALIZED" HELLO THERE PROGRAM
20       PRINT "WHAT'S YOUR NAME";
30       INPUT N$
40       PRINT "HELLO THERE "; N$
99       END
RUN
WHAT'S YOUR NAME? FRED
HELLO THERE FRED
READY
```

When the computer gets to the INPUT statement, it prints a question mark and waits. (Take a look at the program. There is no question mark in the program, but there *is* one in the first line produced when we run the program.) After the INPUT statement produces the ?, the program waits for the person sitting at the keyboard to type something and hit the return key. In this particular case we typed FRED and then hit the return key. What happens to the string (FRED) that we typed? It has to be stored somewhere in the computer for later use, and our INPUT statement says to store it in the **string variable** named N$. There are 26 different **string variables** (A$, B$, C$,. . . , Z$) available for use in standard BASIC. We chose to use N$ because the N makes us think of "Name", which is what we wanted to store in N$.

Some people find it enlightening to think of string variables as containers or boxes. There are 26 such boxes in the computer, with the names A$, B$, C$,. . .,Z$. Each box can store a value called a **string** that's treated verbatim (like the things in quotes we've been using in PRINT statements). Our statement

```
30   INPUT N$
```

says to accept whatever the person at the keyboard types (before hitting the return key) and store it, verbatim, in the box with the name N$. Thus, after we typed

string: a sequence of characters. We denote strings by enclosing a sequence of characters in quotes. The sequence of characters making up a string may not contain any quotation marks because these mark the beginning and end of the string. A string may contain any characters other than quotation marks, including blanks. The possibility of having blanks in strings forces us to indicate exactly where strings start and end. Without starting and ending marks (quotes), we couldn't tell when a string starts or ends with a blank.

`"FRED"`	a string of four characters
`"A-1 SAUCE"`	a string of nine characters
`"HELLO "`	a string of six characters including a blank at the end

Remember! The quotation marks aren't part of the string — they just indicate where it starts and where it stops.

FRED and hit the return key, the boxes would look like Figure 1 6 1. We don't know (or care at this point) what's in any box except N$, which contains the sequence of characters FRED.

So the INPUT statement gives us a way to get information from the person at the terminal, and to store it away for the computer to use at a later point in the computation. In line 40,

```
40        PRINT "HELLO THERE"; N$
```

our program makes use of the value stored in box N$.

This is how the computer carries out PRINT statements: if an item is in quotes (e.g., "HELLO THERE"), the item is PRINTed verbatim; if an item is the name of a

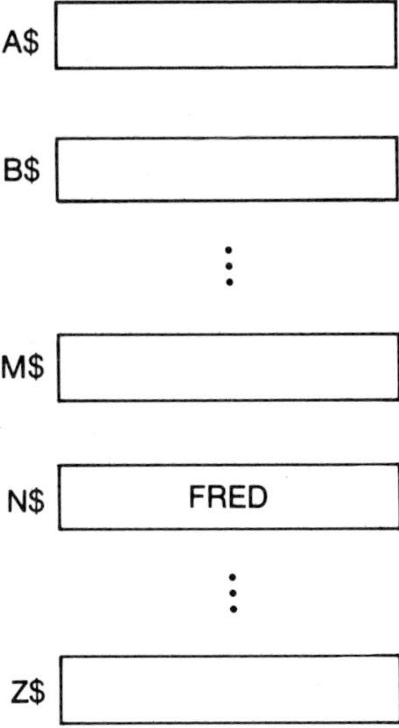

Figure 1 6 1 String variables are named A$, B$,. . .,Z$. Each may be thought of as a container for a string value. Here, variable N$ contains a string of four characters.

box (e.g., N$), whatever is in the box at that time is PRINTed. Since in our case, FRED is in box N$, line 40 PRINTs

```
HELLO THERE FRED
```

When we run our program, the computer PRINTs whatever name we type in when it asks for information (at the INPUT statement). In that sense the program is flexible — it does not have a single, fixed response.

```
RUN
WHAT'S YOUR NAME? ISABEL
HELLO THERE ISABEL
READY
```

or

```
RUN
WHAT'S YOUR NAME? RICO
HELLO THERE RICO
READY
```

or even

```
RUN
WHAT'S YOUR NAME? PIZZA
HELLO THERE PIZZA
READY
```

> **variable:** used for storing information. A **string variable** is denoted by a letter followed by a dollar sign (A$, B$,. . . Z$) and is used for storing a string, which may contain letters, certain punctuation marks, and blanks. A **numeric variable** is denoted by a single letter (A, B,. . . Z) or by a letter followed by a digit (A1, B1, Q0, Z9, etc.) and is used for storing numbers, which may be used in doing arithmetic.

As you know from the programs of Section 1 5, BASIC provides a way to deal with numbers as well as strings. To get a program to accept a number from the terminal, we can use an INPUT statement with a **numeric variable.** You can think of numeric variabes, like string variables, as boxes for storing information. But instead of letters, punctuation, and blanks, **numeric variables** contain numbers. A **numeric variable** (name of a "number box") is either a single letter or a letter followed by a single digit.

Example

```
NEW
READY
10  REM   ASK FOR A NUMBER AND THEN SQUARE IT.
20        PRINT "WHAT NUMBER DO YOU WANT SQUARED";
30        INPUT N
```

```
40        PRINT "OK, YOUR NUMBER IS"; N
50        PRINT N; "SQUARED IS"; N*N
60        END
RUN
WHAT NUMBER DO YOU WANT SQUARED? 12
OK, YOUR NUMBER IS 12
 12 SQUARED IS 144
READY
```

Figure 1 6 2 shows the numeric boxes after we entered the value 12 in response to the computer's question

```
WHAT NUMBER DO YOU WANT SQUARED?
```

We don't know (or care) what values are in any of the boxes except box N, and N contains the number 12. We chose to use N because it makes us think of Number, which is what our program is asking for. We could just as well have used box R, or T2, or Z8. The following version of the program uses the variable V1, but it does exactly the same thing as the version which uses the variable N.

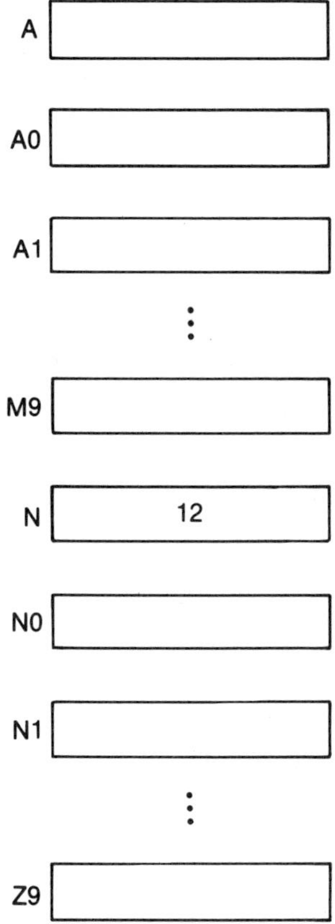

Figure 1 6 2 Numeric variables are named A, A0, A1,. . ., Z9. Each may be thought of as a "box" which contains a single numeric value. Here the numeric variable N is storing the value 12.

Example

```
NEW
READY
10  REM   ASK FOR A NUMBER AND THEN SQUARE IT
20        PRINT "WHAT NUMBER DO YOU WANT SQUARED";
30        INPUT V1
40        PRINT "OK, YOUR NUMBER IS"; V1
50        PRINT V1; "SQUARED IS"; V1*V1
60        END
RUN
WHAT NUMBER DO YOU WANT SQUARED? 11
OK, YOUR NUMBER IS 11
 11 SQUARED IS 121
READY
```

EXERCISES 1 6

1 Some of the following are names of string variables, some are names of numeric variables, and some are neither. Which are which?

```
N
N$
NOSE$
PRINT
V7
B29
M$
K
$K
```

2 There are 26 different string variables, A$ through Z$. How many different numeric variables, A through Z9, are there?

3 Write and RUN a program which asks for a person's name and then the person's age, and which PRINTs

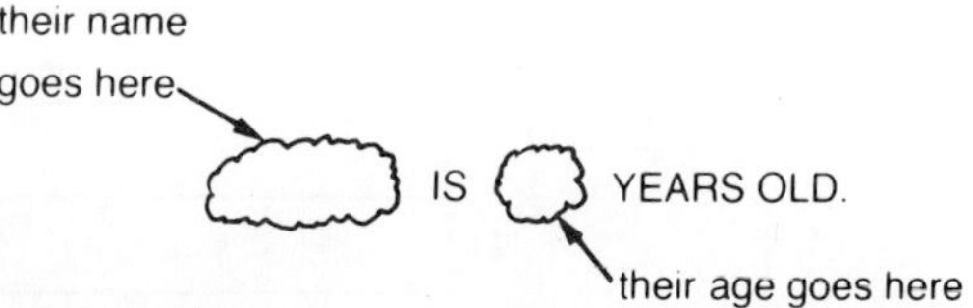

4 Do these two programs do exactly the same thing?

```
10   PRINT "WHAT NUMBER"          10   PRINT "WHAT NUMBER";
20   INPUT V                      20   INPUT N
30   PRINT "THAT'S"; V            30   PRINT "THAT'S"; N
40   END                          40   END
```

Section 1 7
Formalities

So far we've used four different BASIC statements: REM, INPUT, PRINT, and END. We've used two different types of values, one called **strings** (which are treated verbatim) and the other called **numbers** (which can be added, subtracted, multiplied, etc.). Let's review these things, taking a little more notice of the details. We'll also cover ways of having more control over PRINTed output.

A BASIC **program** is a sequence of **lines.** Each **line** has two parts, a **line number** (which identifies the line and determines its place in the program) and a **statement** (which specifies something that the computer is to do).

A **line number** has from one to four digits. It can't have a sign (+ or −), it can't have a decimal point or a fraction, and zero isn't allowed as a line number. This means that the numbers 1,2,3,4,. . .,9998,9999 are the only ones allowed as line numbers. Also, as we mentioned earlier, there can't be any blanks before or within a line number.

Programs are carried out in the order determined by the line numbers, so these two programs will produce the same result.

```
1   INPUT N$                  10   INPUT N$
2   PRINT "HELLO, "; N$       20   PRINT "HELLO, "; N$
3   END                       30   END
```

The reason we use line numbers as 10, 20, and 30 in our programs instead of 1, 2, and 3 is simple. If we suddenly realize that we forgot to include a statement as we're typing in a program, we can add it in the right position by giving it one of the unused line numbers (for instance, 15 will go after10 and before 20). If all the in-between line numbers were used up (as in the program to the left above), we'd have to renumber (and retype) all statements after the statement we wanted to add. (However, most versions of BASIC provide some form of RENUMBER command to help with this problem. See Appendix F.)

The second part of a line in a BASIC program is the **statement.** In standard BASIC each statement begins with a **keyword** which says what kind of statement it is. The keywords REM, PRINT, INPUT, and END identify four different types of statements.

The **END statement** can take only one form:

```
END
```

The purpose of the END statement is to mark the end of the program. It *must appear on the last line in the program.* From now on, we'll make it a practice to use the line number 9999,

```
9999   END
```

for the END statement. That way we'll always be sure that END is the last statement in our finished program, since there can be no number higher than 9999.

> **BASIC vs. Minimal BASIC:** Minimal BASIC is a standardized language which is available on a wide variety of computers. Most of these computer systems provide some extensions of Minimal BASIC and will accept commands outside the scope of Minimal BASIC. For example, many systems allow line numbers to have five digits instead of just four. Such extensions give the programmer extra flexibility, but there is a price: not all of the extensions are the same. They vary widely from one BASIC system to the next. We will stick with the standardized part of the language so our programs will work on almost any computer. The advantage for you is that your programs will still work when you change computer systems (something which happens more often than you might think) as long as you stay within Minimal BASIC.

The **REM statement** has the form:

REM *anything you can type on one line*

The REM (for REMark) statement is used to annotate programs. REM statements appear when you LIST your program but have no effect on what your program *does*. When you RUN your program and the computer gets to a REM statement, the computer ignores the statement and just moves on to the next higher-numbered line. Programmers use REM statements to make their programs more understandable to people reading them.

You can use as many REM statements as you want to type something which takes up more than one line. Just remember to start each line with REM again, so the computer will skip over it.

The **INPUT statement** consists of the keyword INPUT followed by one or more variables separated by commas. The variables in the list may be all numeric, all string, or some combination. Up to now, the "list of variables" has just been a single variable in our examples. For example,

```
20   INPUT N
```

will request the person at the computer to type in a number (and will complain with an error message if a nonnumeric item is entered), while

```
30   INPUT S$
```

will accept a string (verbatim) value. However, more than one value can be requested by a given INPUT statement. For example, the INPUT statement in line 20 in the following program asks for two values, one a string (which it will store in string variable N$), and the other a number (which it will store in numeric variable A).

Example

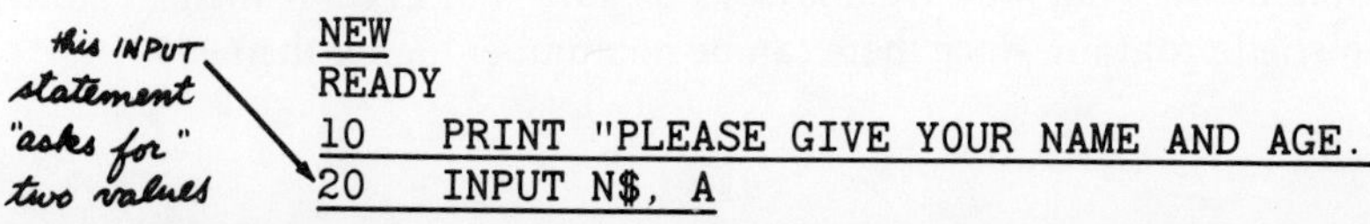
this INPUT statement "asks for" two values

```
NEW
READY
10   PRINT "PLEASE GIVE YOUR NAME AND AGE."
20   INPUT N$, A
```

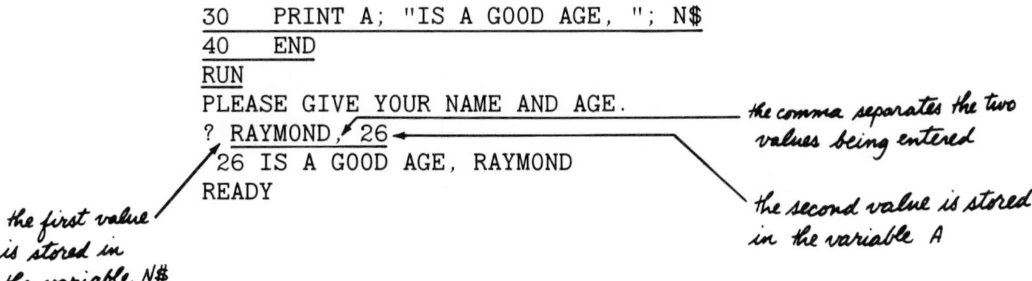
the comma separates the two values being entered
the second value is stored in the variable A
the first value is stored in the variable N$

```
30    PRINT A; "IS A GOOD AGE, "; N$
40    END
RUN
PLEASE GIVE YOUR NAME AND AGE.
? RAYMOND, 26
26 IS A GOOD AGE, RAYMOND
READY
```

Perhaps you can see that allowing the INPUT statement to ask for more than one value at a time can lead to some confusion. In our example above, line 20 is asking for two values, and it expects them to be separated by a **comma.** If the person at the keyboard enters too few or too many values or forgets the comma, some sort of error message will result. (A little experimentation with the above program should let you know how your system handles these errors. Try entering RAYMOND 26 with no comma. Then try SMITH, JOHN and see what happens.) This means that the PRINT statement preceding each INPUT must give the person at the keyboard a reasonably detailed description of what your program expects her or him to type in. But there are more problems — what if you want the person to type in her or his full name in the standard

Last Name, First

form? That is, sometimes you may want the person to enter a string value which *has a comma in it.* BASIC gives us two options in that case. Either we can use *two* string variables, one for the Last Name and one for First, as in this example:

Example

```
NEW
READY
10    PRINT "PLEASE GIVE YOUR LAST NAME, THEN A"
20    PRINT "COMMA, THEN YOUR FIRST NAME."
30    INPUT L$, F$
40    PRINT "THAT'S "; L$; ", "; F$
9999 END
RUN
PLASE GIVE YOUR LAST NAME, THEN A
COMMA, THEN YOUR FIRST NAME.
? LANGSFORD, RAYMOND
THAT'S LANGSFORD, RAYMOND
READY
```

notice: we put this comma here ourselves, in the PRINT statement

Or you may have the person at the keyboard enclose the entire entry in quotes, and your program will treat it as a single value — a string to be PRINTed verbatim — even if it has a comma within it.

Example

```
10   PRINT "PLEASE GIVE YOUR LAST NAME, THEN A"
20   PRINT "COMMA, THEN YOUR FIRST NAME, ALL"
30   PRINT "IN QUOTES."
40   INPUT N$
50   PRINT "THAT'S "; N$
9999 END
RUN
PLEASE GIVE YOUR LAST NAME, THEN A
COMMA, THEN YOUR FIRST NAME, ALL
IN QUOTES.
? "LANGSFORD, RAYMOND"
THAT'S LANGSFORD, RAYMOND
READY
```

all this gets stored in variable N$

in this case, the comma is stored in variable N$, along with the name

Again, a little experimentation on your part should make clear what's going on.

The **PRINT statement** is the other type of command we have been using in our programs. It has two different forms: the keyword PRINT followed by a **PRINT list,** and PRINT by itself, as shown in the statement below.

```
40   PRINT
```

In this form the PRINT statement tells the computer to go on to the next line in the output without PRINTing anything. The most common use of this type of PRINT statement is to leave blank lines in the output.

Where the keyword PRINT is followed by a list of things to be PRINTed, items in the list may be things in quotes (i.e., strings which are PRINTed verbatim), numbers or numeric computations (the value or result of the computation is printed), or string variables (the value stored in the "box" is PRINTed verbatim). Individual items in the **PRINT list** are separated by commas or semicolons, and the entire list *may* be followed by a comma or a semicolon.

> **program vs. output:** When thinking about PRINT statements, it is important to keep in mind the difference between the program and the output the computer PRINTs when you RUN the program. The program is the sequence of BASIC statements with their line numbers that you type in after the command NEW. It is what gets printed when you say LIST. The output, on the other hand, is what the computer PRINTs after you type the command RUN. It is all the characters and lines that your program tells the computer to PRINT.

A **semicolon** in a PRINT list means "Don't skip any spaces before printing the next value." A **comma** means "Skip over to the next (predefined) **PRINT zone** before PRINTing the next value." (See Exercise 1 5 3 for more on PRINT zones.) If there is a comma or semicolon at the end of the PRINT list, the computer stays on the same output line when it finishes PRINTing the values. Otherwise it moves on to the next line.

Each number that's PRINTed is automatically followed by a space. In addition, a space is PRINTed in front of a number if it is positive; if it's negative, a minus sign (−) is used instead of a space. Strings, on the other hand, are PRINTed verbatim — no extra spaces.

```
10   PRINT 1; 2; 3; 4
20   PRINT "SUZANNE"; "'S TURN."
9999 END
RUN
 1  2  3  4
SUZANNE'S TURN.
READY
```

blanks are automatically inserted before and after positive numbers

but no blanks around string values

It may seem that there are a lot of picky rules here. Maybe so, but the rules are chosen to make things happen in a reasonable way, without the programmer (you) having to worry too much. If you don't quite understand some specific aspect, be sure to try some experiments. Play around! Try all the things in Figure 1 7 1 and any other experiments that come to mind.

By using commas to change PRINT zones and strings of blanks to leave spaces on the line, you can format your PRINTed lines reasonably well. Sometimes, however, you may want things to line up in columns which don't correspond to the fixed PRINT zones. In that case you can use the TAB spacer.

Example

```
10   PRINT "A"; TAB(5); "B"; TAB(10); "C"
20   PRINT "AA"; TAB(5); "BB"; TAB(10); "CC"
30   PRINT "AAA"; TAB(5); "BBB"; TAB(10); "CCC"
9999 END
```

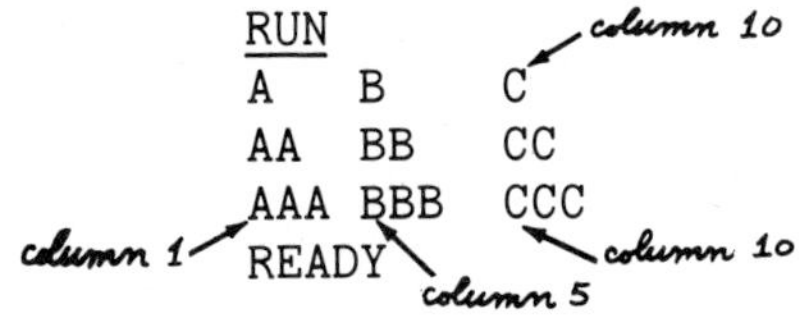

In general, TAB(x), where x is a numeric value, causes the computer to move to column number x before PRINTing the next item in the PRINT statement. (The columns are numbered from the left 1, 2, 3, . . .)

TAB( ) may appear *only* in PRINT statements, and the place you want to TAB to must be 1 or greater. If, by mistake, your PRINT statement says to TAB to a column that's already been PRINTed, the system will automatically go to that column on the next line.

Example

```
10   PRINT TAB(32); "PAGE"; TAB(35); "1"
9999 END
RUN
                                PAGE
                                  1
READY
```

it went to column 35 on the next line because the E in PAGE had already been printed in column 35

```
10   PRINT "EXPERIMENT 1"
20   PRINT
30   PRINT "BOTTOM LINE"
9999 END
```

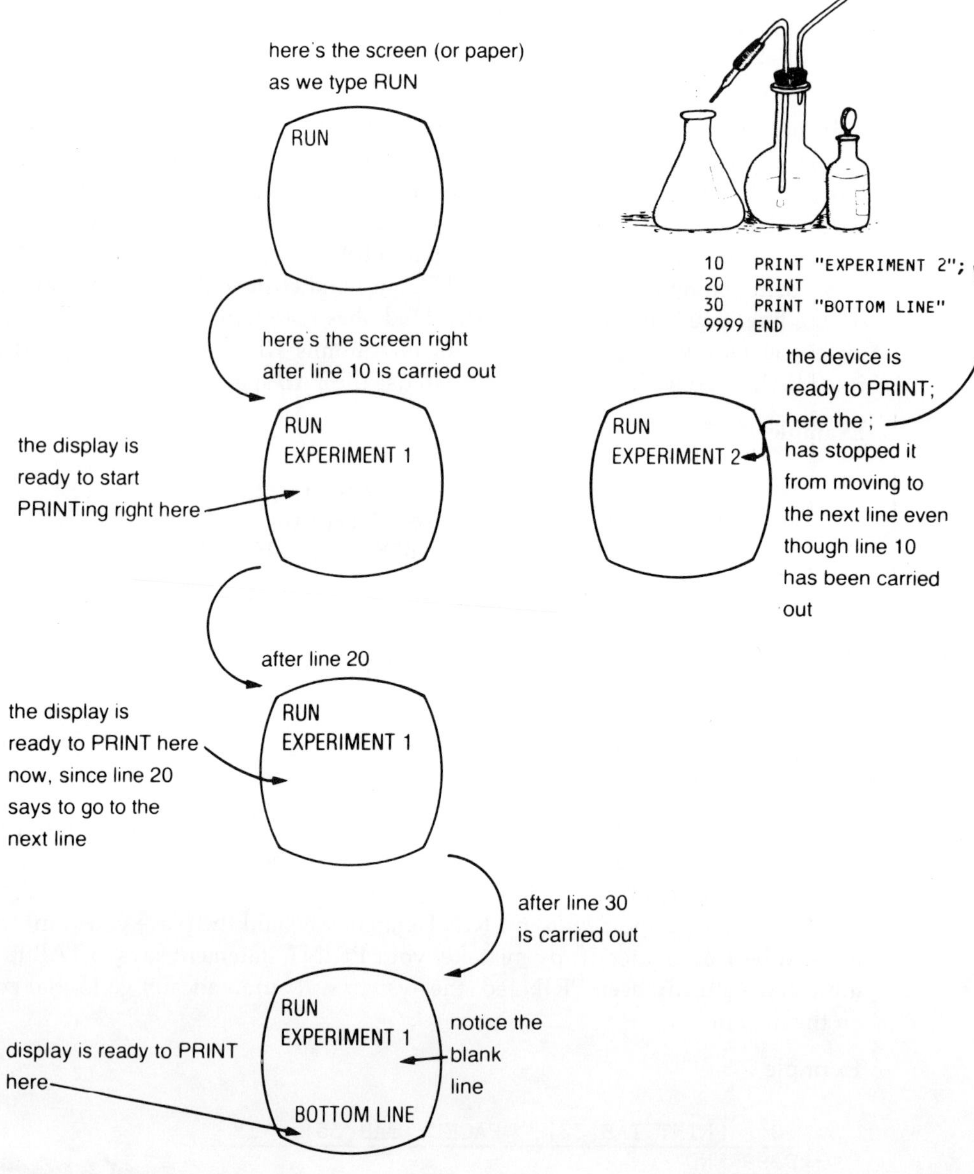

Figure 1 7 1 Experiments with PRINT Statements

If you try to TAB beyond the right-hand margin, the computer goes to the next line. It goes through some complicated gyrations to figure out which column to go to on the next line, but since you almost never try to TAB past the margin on purpose, there's no point in burdening you with the rules. See the MiniManual (Appendix C) if you ever need to know.

EXERCISES 1 7

1 What's wrong with this program?

```
10    REM  MULTIPLIER
20         PRINT "AUTOMATIC MULTIPLICATION"
30         PRINT "TYPE TWO NUMBERS TO BE MULTIPLIED."
40         PRINT "(BE SURE TO PUT A COMMA BETWEEN THEM)"
50         INPUT X Y
60         PRINT X; "*"; Y; "="; X*Y
```

2 Someone is trying to use the program below. What has happened?

```
10    REM  DIVIDER
20         PRINT "AUTOMATIC DIVISION"
30         PRINT "YOUR NUMBERS PLEASE";
40         INPUT X, Y
50         PRINT X; "/"; Y; "="; X/Y
9999       END
           RUN
           AUTOMATIC DIVISION
           YOUR NUMBERS PLEASE? 78
           ??<------ instead of going on with the program,
                     the machine printed these...
```

3 Write a program which asks the user's age and the current year and then PRINTs the year in which the user was born. (Don't worry about being off by one year if the user's birthday is later this year.)

4 Write a PRINT statement which will PRINT a dollar sign followed by the sum of $2 and $5.99. Can you get the computer to leave out the space between the $ and the number?

5 Write a program which uses PRINT zones to PRINT a table of three columns with five entries in each column. Column one should be the weekdays (Monday through Friday), and the other columns should be the times at which you got up and went to bed last week.

6 Will the following program line the numbers up in columns?

```
10    REM  COLUMNS OR NOT?
20         PRINT   1; "   ";   2; "   ";   3
30         PRINT 222; "   ";   9; "   "; 845
40         PRINT  92; "   ";  78; "   "; 327
50         PRINT  71; "   "; 707; "   ";  16
9999       END
```

7 If you were writing a program to keep track of your expenses, you might need variables for the amounts you spend on pencils, pizza, and popcorn. Think up appropriate names for the three variables.

PROBLEMS 1

1 Write and RUN a program which PRINTs your name in a box of asterisks, like this:

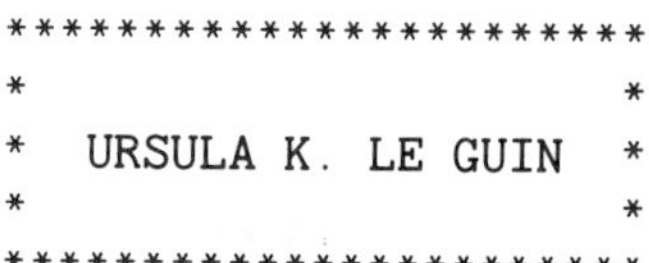

```
**********************
*                    *
*  URSULA K. LE GUIN *
*                    *
**********************
```

2 Write an RUN a program which PRINTs part of the multiplication table, like this:

```
    MULTIPLICATION TABLE
      1     2      3     4
--I-------------------
1 I 1     2      3     4
2 I 2     4      6     8
3 I 3     6      9     12
4 I 4     8      12    16
```

we're using I's to draw a vertical line. maybe you can think of something better

use the comma separator or TAB spacer in your PRINT statements to line the columns up

3 Write and RUN a program that uses a number of PRINT statements to produce a picture of the French flag. Use *'s for red, +'s for blue, and blanks for white.

4 Design a program to compute a car's gas mileage, which equals distance traveled divided by gallons of gas used. Use three INPUT statements to get the starting mileage, mileage at the end, and amount of gas purchased.

5 Write a program which asks for the length of the sides of a rectangle. Have your program PRINT the side lengths and the area of the rectangle.

6 Design a program which helps you visualize the effects of inflation. Ask for the inflation rate (for example, 0.06 if the rate is 6% per year) and PRINT

(a) the amount of money you will need in four years to buy what $1.00 will buy today (if the rate is 6 percent, then this is given by ($1.00*1.06*1.06*1.06*1.06).

(b) the amount of money you would have needed four years ago to buy what $1.00 will buy today ($1.00/(1.06*1.06*1.06*1.06)).

7 Write a program which figures out how long it will take to mow a rectangular lawn with a rectangular house on it. Your program should ask for the dimensions of the lawn and the house, and compute the area that's to be mowed. Assume you can mow at a rate of one hundred square feet per minute.

8 Do Problem 7 again, but include more accurate information about your personal mowing habits. In addition to the input data which allows you to compute the area to be mown, use these three input values:

(a) the width of your mower's out (e.g., 18 inches)

(b) your walking speed (e.g., 1.5 miles per hour)

(c) the fraction of the time you spend resting or drinking lemonade (e.g., 0.25 if you rest a quarter of the time).

9 Write a program which PRINTs the sum of the squares of the first ten numbers, $1^2 + 2^2 + 3^2 + \ldots + 10^2$. Don't PRINT just the answer — include enough text so that a person who looks only at what your program produces can tell what it has done.

10 Write a program which asks for a value in inches, and which PRINTs the equivalent length in centimeters (1″ = 2.54 cm).

11 If you are familiar with exponentiation, you will be interested to know that the operator "∧" can be used to raise numbers to powers. For example, PRINT 4∧3 prints the value of 4 raised to the power 3. Use this operator to expand the program of Problem 6. Have the user type in the number of years to be used in the computation as well as the inflation rate.

> **∧ or ↑**
> On some computers, the circumflex character ∧ appears as a small upward-pointing arrow ↑.

12 Write a program which prints a form you can use to list the things you have to do each day of the upcoming week. Here's one possible format:

```
     MON       TUE       WED       THU       FRI       SAT       SUN

1

2

3

4

5

6

7

8
```

Chapter 2 **The LET Statement**

Section 2 1
Uses for It

So far, the only way we have had to give a value to a variable is to list the variable in an INPUT statement, and to depend on the person at the keyboard to type the value when the program asks for it. Another way to give a value to a variable is by using a LET statement. Here's an example:

```
40    LET F = 400
```

When carried out, it will have the same end effect as if a person had typed the value 400 in response to a statement like

```
40    INPUT F
```

That is, it will store 400 in the numeric variable called F.

We can use the LET statement to define constants needed later in a program, as in this example.

Example

```
NEW
READY
10    REM  HOW MUCH PAINT WILL IT TAKE TO COVER A WALL?
20    REM  F  STORES THE NUMBER OF SQUARE FEET THAT
30    REM       ONE GALLON OF PAINT WILL COVER
40              LET F = 400
50    REM  GET WALL DIMENSIONS
60              PRINT "WHAT'S THE WIDTH OF THE WALL TO BE PAINTED";
70              INPUT W
80              PRINT "AND HOW HIGH IS IT";
90              INPUT H
100             PRINT "YOU'LL NEED"; W*H/F; "GALLONS OF PAINT."
```

the value stored in the variable F gets plugged into the computation here

```
110        PRINT "HAPPY PAINTING!"
9999       END
RUN
WHAT'S THE WIDTH OF OF THE WALL TO BE PAINTED? 20
AND HOW HIGH IS IT? 8
YOU'LL NEED .4 GALLONS OF PAINT.
HAPPY PAINTING!
READY
```

We can also use LET statements to express complex computations in small, more easily understood subparts, and to avoid repeating computations such as the area of the wall in this revision of the painting program.

Example

from now on, we'll leave it to you to remember to type NEW when you start a new program

```
10    REM  HOW MUCH PAINT AND TIME WILL IT TAKE
20    REM  TO PAINT A WALL?
30    REM  F  STORES THE NUMBER OF SQ. FT. PER GALLON.
40    REM  T  STORES THE TIME TO PAINT 1 SQ. FT.
50         LET F = 400
60         LET T = 90/400
70    REM  GET WALL DIMENSIONS
80         PRINT "HOW WIDE IS THE WALL YOU WANT TO PAINT";
90         INPUT W
100        PRINT "AND HOW HIGH IS IT";
110        INPUT H
120   REM  COMPUTE AREA OF WALL
130        LET A = W*H
140        PRINT "YOU'LL NEED"; A/F; "GALLONS OF PAINT,"
150        PRINT "AND IT'LL TAKE ABOUT"; A*T; "MINUTES,"
160        PRINT "NOT COUNTING SET-UP AND CLEANING TIME."
170        PRINT "HAPPY PAINTING!"
9999       END
```

it takes about 90 minutes to apply a gallon of paint, so 90 minutes per 100 sq. ft.

```
RUN
HOW WIDE IS THE WALL YOU WANT TO PAINT? 24
AND HOW HIGH IS IT? 8
YOU'LL NEED .48 GALLONS OF PAINT,
AND IT'LL TAKE ABOUT 43.2 MINUTES,
NOT COUNTING SET-UP AND CLEANING TIME.
HAPPY PAINTING!
READY
```

EXERCISES 2 1

1 Alter the first painting program so it makes clear to the person using it that the wall dimensions are to be given in feet.

2 Two of these programs have the same effect. Which two?

```
10 REM  -A-
20      LET F = 400
30      LET W = 10
40      LET H = 8
50      LET A = W*H
60      PRINT A/F; "GALS."
9999    END
```

```
10 REM  -B-
20      LET F = 400
30      LET W = 10
40      LET A = W*10
50      PRINT A/F; "GALS."
9999    END
```

```
10 REM  -C-
20      LET = 80
30      PRINT A/400; "GALS."
9999    END
```

3 Is it possible to write the second painting program without using any LET statements? If so, how?

4 What happens if the person using the painting program types in the wall dimensions in meters instead of feet?

5 Fill in the rest of the table showing the value that will be in variable N after each line of this program is carried out:

```
10   PRINT "N IS WHAT";
20   INPUT N
30   PRINT "AND NOW";
40   INPUT N
50   PRINT "N ENDED UP";N
9999 END
RUN
N IS WHAT? 1.0
AND NOW? -2.5
N ENDED UP-2.5
READY
```

AFTER LINE #	*VALUE IN N*
10	unknown
20	1.0
30	
40	
50	

Section 2 2
What It Does

Each LET statement is a command that says to give a specific variable a specific value. For instance, the LET statement

```
40        LET F = 400
```

says to give the numeric variable F the value 400. It puts 400 in the "box" named F.

Before your program puts a value in a variable, you can't be sure what's there, so it doesn't make sense to print the value of a variable before it has been given a value. Just to see what happens on your particular system, try this experimental program.

```
10 REM  I WONDER WHAT'S IN VARIABLE 'F'?
20      PRINT "F HAS THE VALUE"; F
9999    END
```

On some systems you'll get an error message telling you that F has no value. On some you'll get garbage (whatever number happened to be left in the box by some previous program). And on some systems you'll get zero.

Once a variable has a value, we can do a number of things with it. We can PRINT the value; we can use the value in a computation; or we can *change* the value by listing the variable in an INPUT statement or by putting it on the left side of the equals sign in a LET statement.

Example

```
        .
        .
        .
80    LET F = 4000
        .
        .
        .
150   LET F = 2*300
        .
        .
        .
```

A variable has room for just one value at a time, so when statement 150 stores the value 600 in F, the old value (400) is written over and lost.

The **LET statement** has this form:

Let *v* = *e*

where *v* is the name of a variable and *e* is an expression. The statement means, "First, compute the value of the expression *e* (whatever is on the right of the equal sign), and then store the resulting value in the variable whose name *v* appears to the left of the equal sign." Another way to say what a LET statement means is, "LET the variable *v* have the value computed in the expression *e*."

Since the value of the expression is computed *first*, there's no reason the current value of a variable can't be used to compute a new value for that variable; i.e., statements like

```
120        LET F = F*2
```

make sense, as you will see when you play around with the experimental program.

```
10    REM  EXPERIMENT WITH LET STATEMENTS
20         PRINT "GIVE ME A STARTING VALUE FOR F ";
30         INPUT F
40         LET F = F+1
50         PRINT "AFTER ADDING ONE, F IS ";F
60         LET F = F*2
70         PRINT "AFTER DOUBLING, F IS ";F
80         PRINT
9999       END

RUN
GIVE ME A STARTING VALUE FOR F ? 1
AFTER ADDING ONE, F IS 2
AFTER DOUBLING, F IS 4

READY
RUN
GIVE ME A STARTING VALUE FOR F ? 3
```

(program continued on page 32)

```
AFTER ADDING ONE, F IS 4
AFTER DOUBLING,   F IS 8

READY

RUN
GIVE ME A STARTING VALUE FOR F ? -1
AFTER ADDING ONE, F IS 0
AFTER DOUBLING,   F IS 0

READY
```

This same use of a LET statement to alter a variable, based on its current value, is made in this variation of the paint estimator program.

Example

```
10   REM  STILL PAINTING THAT WALL
20   REM  NOW TAKE THE SURFACE INTO ACCOUNT.
30   REM  NEED 1 GAL. TO COVER 400 SQ. FT.
40   REM  OF NORMAL WALL.
50        LET F = 400
60        PRINT "PLEASE ENTER A NUMBER BETWEEN 0.0 AND 1.0"
70        PRINT "INDICATING HOW ROUGH AND POROUS THE WALL IS."
80        PRINT "0.0 INDICATES AN EXTREMELY SMOOTH, HARD WALL."
90        PRINT "1.0 INDICATES A ROUGH, BUMPY, POROUS WALL."
100       PRINT "WHAT'S YOUR ESTIMATE";
110       INPUT E
120  REM  ADJUST FACTOR FOR WALL SURFACE
130       LET F = F/(1.0 + E)
140  REM  NOW GO ON AS IN ORIGINAL PROGRAM
150       PRINT "HOW WIDE IS THE WALL";
160       INPUT W
170       PRINT "AND HOW HIGH IS IT";
180       INPUT H
190  REM  COMPUTE AREA OF THE WALL
200       LET A = W*H
210       PRINT "YOU'LL NEED ABOUT"; A/F; "GALLONS."
220       PRINT "HAPPY PAINTING!";
9999      END
```

if E=0, we end up with the original value of F; if the value supplied for E is 1, we estimate that a gallon will cover only 200 sq. ft.

```
RUN
PLEASE ENTER A NUMBER BETWEEN 0.0 AND 1.0
INDICATING HOW ROUGH AND POROUS THE WALL IS.
0.0 INDICATES AN EXTREMELY SMOOTH, HARD WALL.
1.0 INDICATES A ROUGH, BUMPY, POROUS WALL.
WHAT'S YOUR ESTIMATE? .5
HOW WIDE IS THE WALL? 20
AND HOW HIGH IS IT? 8
YOU'LL NEED ABOUT .6 GALLONS.
HAPPY PAINTING!
READY
```

Let statements can also be used to assign values to string variables.

```
LET N$ = "BETTY"
LET P$ = "CAM SHAFT"
LET C$ = ","
LET E$ = "..."
LET B$ = "      "
```

After you've assigned a string value to a string variable, you can use the variable as a shorthand way of denoting the string. For example, if you want to print ellipsis (three dots) between a collection of input values, it will save typing if you assign the ellipsis string "..." to a variable, then use the variable wherever you need to print the ellipses.

```
10   REM  ELLIPSIS PRINTER
20        PRINT "TYPE IN 6 NUMBERS, SEPARATED BY COMMAS"
30        INPUT X1, X2, X3, X4, X5, X6
40        LET E$ = "..."
50        PRINT "THAT'S THE SEQUENCE:"
60        PRINT X1; E$; X2; E$; X3; E$; X4; E$; X5; E$; X6
9999      END
RUN
TYPE IN 6 NUMBERS, SEPARATED BY COMMAS
? 23,45,69,98,102,104
THAT'S THE SEQUENCE:
23 ... 45 ... 69 ... 98 ... 102 ... 104
READY
```

In a similar way you can use string assignments to lessen the typing involved in printing commas, strings of blanks, or other repeated characters in the output.

EXERCISES 2 2

1 What values will X and Y have after the following statements are carried out?

```
10   LET X = 9
20   LET Y = 4
30   LET X = X - Y
```

2 What values will A and B have after the following statements are carried out?

```
10   LET A = 15
20   LET B = 25
30   LET A = B
40   LET B = A
```

3 Write a LET statement which will add one to whatever number is in the variable C.

4 Write a single LET statement which will change the value of the variable T to the corresponding positive number if its value is negative and will change it to a negative value if it is positive.

5 Write a LET statement which will replace the value of the variable S with half of the square of its current value.

6 Write LET statements which will put the product of the numbers in the variables P and Q into the variable R and then put twice that number into the variable P.

7 What values will A and B have after the following statements are carried out? Compare the results with those of Exercise 2.

```
10    LET A = 15
20    LET B = 25
30    LET C = A
40    LET A = B
50    LET B = C
```

8 Write a program which asks the user to type four strings, then prints the strings with each separated from the last by five spaces.

Section 2 3

What Are Numeric Expressions?

We've used **numeric expressions** in PRINT statements

```
140      PRINT "YOU'LL NEED"; A/F; "GALLONS OF PAINT."
                              here
```

and in LET statements

```
                   here
130   LET F = F/(1.0 + E)
```

but we've never really said what numeric expressions (sometimes referred to as **arithmetic expressions**) are. Basically, they're exactly what you *think* they are, but there are a few details.

a **numeric expression** is either

a **constant** (e.g., 400)

a **numeric variable** (e.g., F)

a numeric expression preceded by a + or a − (e.g., +F)

two numeric expressions joined by an **operator** (e.g., A/F) or

a numeric expression surrounded by **parentheses** (e.g., (1.0 + E))

In addition, there is the rule that two operators may not occur in a row. So even though −F is a legitimate expression, and hence +−F is a numeric expression (namely, −F) preceded by a +, it's *not* legitimate because it has two operators in a row. If for some reason you need to write something like +−F, you can turn it into a legitimate expression by using parentheses: +(−F).

Anything you can get by following the rules is a numeric expression.

legitimate expressions	*illegitimate expressions*
`2`	`KGB`
`-F`	`--2`
`(1.0 + E)`	`1.0(+E)`
`(F + G)/A`	`(F) (G/A)`
`F+(-A)`	`F+-A`

No matter how complicated the expression is, if it's legitimate, it can be broken down into a number of applications of the rules. For example,

```
F/(1.0 + E)
```

is legitimate because it is formed by joining the two legitimate expressions F and (1.0 + E) with the operator /. (1.0 + E) is legitimate because it is formed by joining the two legitimate expressions 1.0 (a constant) and E (a numeric variable) with the operator +, and surrounding that expression by parentheses.

The arithmetic operators are the ones you're no doubt familiar with, even if you haven't used the same symbols (* for times, ∧ for raise-to-the-power) before.

operation	*standard symbols*	*examples*	*BASIC symbol*	*examples*
addition	+	$a + b$	+	A+B 1 + 1
subtraction	−	$a - b$	−	A−B 3−2
multiplication	×	$a \times b$	*	A*B 4*4
division	÷ — /	$a \div b$ $\frac{a}{b}$ a/b	/	A/B 10/2
exponentiation	superscript	a^b	∧	A ∧ B 2 ∧

Note: Some computer systems use the character ↑ instead of ∧

What we've described so far is the *form* that numeric expressions may take. Of course, it's also important to understand what they *mean.* Again, the meaning of BASIC expressions is pretty much what you'd expect, but there are a few rules. Each legitimate numeric expression has a **value,** and that value is computed according to these rules.

If the expression

is a constant, the value is that constant.

is a numeric variable, the value is the value stored in that variable.

is an expression preceded by a + or −, the value is the value of the expression multiplied by +1 or −1.

is two numeric expressions joined by an operator, the value is that obtained by (first) getting the value of each of the two subexpressions and then applying the operator.

is an expression surrounded by parentheses, the value is the value of the expression itself.

In most cases the interpretation given to arithmetic expressions will be easy to understand. What, however, about an expression like this?

8/4/2

Clearly, additional rules are required to interpret it, because it might mean, "Divide 8 by 4 and then divide that by 2," or it might mean, "Divide 4 by 2 and then divide 8 by that." BASIC specifies that expressions are evaluated in this order:

()	first	compute expressions within parentheses
∧	second	perform exponentiations on adjacent values
*,/	third	perform multiplications and divisions on adjacent values
+,−	fourth	perform additions and subtractions on adjacent values
	fifth	in case of ties, perform adjacent operations of the same category from left to right (i.e., 8/4/2*16 is performed left to right to get 2/2*16, then 1*16, then 16)

expression	*equivalent expression*	*another*	*value*
8−4+2	(8−4)+2	4+2	6
8/4/2	(8/4)/2	2/2	1
2∧2∧2	(2∧2)∧2	4∧2	16
8/4*2	(8/4)*2	2*2	4

As is true with most parts of BASIC, the rules correspond to what a "reasonable person" would expect. The oddball cases like

8/4/2

don't come up very often, and when they do, they can always be rewritten using parentheses to make the meaning clear.

(8/4)/2

Write and RUN a few experiments, and you should be ready for any eventuality.

> **Warning!**
>
> If you want to multiply two things together, you must always put a * between them. In BASIC, just writing two expressions together, like
>
> A(B+2) ← ooops!   AB ← ooops!
>
> **will** *not* cause the values to be multiplied together. It will either give you an obscure error message, or worse, have a confusing and wrong effect.

EXERCISES 2 3

1 Write LET statements to evaluate expressions equivalent to the ones written below.

(a) $\frac{x - y}{2}$

(b) $5x + \frac{1}{x - 1}$

(c) $a(b - c)^2$

(d) $\frac{az + b}{cz + d}$

(e) $\frac{x + y}{2} \cdot \frac{a^3}{xy}$

(f) $x - (ay - b)$

2 Write LET statements to evaluate expressions equivalent to the ones written below.

(a) $\frac{x + 3}{2x - 1}$

(b) $4pr^2$

(c) $\frac{4}{3}\, pr^3$

(d) $\frac{h}{3}\,(a + 4b + c)$

(e) $\frac{n(n + 1)}{2}$

(f) $\frac{n^2 - 3n + 1}{6}$

Section 2 4

Square Roots and More

We haven't told you the whole story on arithmetic in BASIC. You know about addition, subtraction, multiplication, division, and exponentiation. All of these operations are denoted by special symbols (+, −, *, /, and ∧), and **numeric expressions** are formed by placing the operator-symbols between the two numeric values involved.

Several additional mathematical computations can be carried out automatically. These include square root, absolute value, trigonometric functions, logarithms, and others. The notation BASIC uses for these operations is patterned after the function notation in mathematics, and as a result the operators are usually referred to as **functions.** However, in this text, as in mathematics, the terms **operator** and **function** are used more or less synonomously.

Minimal BASIC supplies eleven functions in addition to the five arithmetic operations +,−,*,/, and ∧. These are described in the MiniManual (Appendix C) so there's no need to go over all of them at this point. We'll just mention a few by way of illustration.

The square root of a number can be computed with **SQR function.** To compute the square root of 3, we would write SQR(3). Writing the operation in this form is typical of the eleven supplied functions. First comes a three-letter name designating the operation to be performed, then comes the number that the operation is to be applied to. This number must be enclosed in parentheses and may be a variable or even the result of another arithmetic computation. For example, SQR(X − 1) computes the square root of the number that is one smaller than whatever number is stored in X.

Supplied Functions (see MiniManual for details)

ABS	absolute value	RND	random number
ATN	arctangent	SGN	signum (+1, 0, −1)
COS	cosine		
EXP	exponential	SIN	sine
INT	greatest integer in	SQR	square root
LOG	natural logarithm	TAN	tangent

Here's an example of using the square root function SQR. When line 110 is carried out, the SQR operator produces the square root of whatever is stored in variable A (as long as the value stored there isn't negative!).

Example

```
10   REM  IF A BASKETBALL COURT WERE SQUARE INSTEAD
20   REM  OF RECTANGULAR BUT HAD THE SAME AREA,
30   REM  WHAT SIZE SQUARE WOULD IT BE, HE WONDERED?
40        PRINT "HOW WIDE IS A BASKETBALL COURT";
50        INPUT W
60        PRINT "HOW LONG IS A BASKETBALL COURT";
70        INPUT L
80   REM  AREA = LENGTH*WIDTH
90        LET A = L*W
100       PRINT "IF IT WAS SQUARE SHAPED,"
110       PRINT "EACH SIDE WOULD BE"; SQR(A)
9999      END

RUN
HOW WIDE IS A BASKETBALL COURT? 50
HOW LONG IS A BASKETBALL COURT? 94
IF IT WAS SQUARE SHAPED,
EACH SIDE WOULD BE 68.5566
READY
```

Since we'll be using some of these operators in later chapters, let's go over some of them in more detail.

The **ABS operator** doesn't do anything to positive values, but it strips the negative sign off negative ones to give the absolute value.

expression	*value*
ABS(10)	10
ABS(−10)	10
ABS(0)	0
ABS(7.0 − 7.2)	.2

One common use for the ABS operator is to tell how close one value is to another, without caring which number is the larger.

```
        .
        .
        .
210     LET D = ABS(Y - 2.0)
220     PRINT "YOU'RE WITHIN"; D; "OF THE ANSWER."
        .
        .
        .
```

The **INT operator** converts values which have fractional parts into ones which don't. Although what it does is easy to *say* ("INT(*e*) gives the largest whole number not greater than the value of *e*") it may take a few experiments to see what that *means*, especially when the number INT is operating on is negative.

expression	*value*
INT(1)	1
INT(1.5)	1
INT(5.78)	5
INT(−2)	−2
INT(−2.56)	−3 ← note: the result isn't −2 because −2 is greater than −2.56

Enter and RUN this experimental program until you see what's going on.

```
10   PRINT "GIVE ME A NUMBER";
20   INPUT N
30   PRINT "YOUR NUMBER IS"; N
40   PRINT "THAT PLUS A HALF IS"; N + 0.5
50   PRINT "INT("; N; ")="; INT(N)
60   PRINT "BUT ROUNDED OFF, IT'S"; INT(N + 0.5)
9999 END

RUN
GIVE ME A NUMBER? 1.75
YOUR NUMBER IS 1.75
THAT PLUS A HALF IS 2.25
INT( 1.75 )= 1
BUT ROUNDED OFF, IT'S 2
READY
```

The **SGN function** is referred to as the "signum function" in mathematics. It produces the sign of the number it operates on. If the given number is positive, then the SGN of the number is 1; if the number is zero, its SGN is zero; and if it's negative, the SGN is −1.

By using combinations of ABS, INT, and SGN, we can mutilate a numeric value almost any way we might want. We can rip the sign off with ABS, throw away the fractional part with INT, and segregate the sign itself using SGN.

The **RND operator** is different from all the others. The others compute some number based on a given number. The RND operator just produces a number out of the blue—one that's not related to anything in your program. If you use the RND operator more than once in a program, it produces a different value each time! We think of it as providing a *random number.* Each time you refer to RND, it supplies a number less than one and greater than or equal to zero.

Example

```
10 REM  LOOK AT A FEW RANDOM NUMBERS
20      PRINT RND
30      PRINT RND
40      PRINT RND
9999    END
```

(program continued on page 40)

```
RUN
.811635
.305003
.515163
READY
```

Are these numbers *really* random (whatever that really means)? Type RUN again, and you'll get the same numbers.

Example

```
RUN
.811635
.305003
.515163
READY
```

Why's that? Well, if you're developing a program that uses random numbers, you may well want to use the same numbers while you're trying to make the program work, so you can figure out what's going wrong. Once you're sure the program works, you'll want to use different random numbers each time. This is accomplished by inserting the command RANDOMIZE in your program.

Example

```
15       RANDOMIZE
LIST
10 REM   LOOK AT A FEW RANDOM NUMBERS
15       RANDOMIZE
20       PRINT RND
30       PRINT RND
40       PRINT RND
9999     END
READY
RUN
   .363751
   .984546
   .901591
READY
RUN
   .727313
   6.83401E-03
   .96943
READY
```

In many cases we'll want to be able to produce random numbers in different ranges. For example, to simulate flipping a coin, you would want to choose between two numbers, say 0 and 1, with each being equally likely. Or, if you want your program to simulate throwing a die, you probably would want to be able to create random numbers from 1 through 6. By combining the RND operator with the INT operator, we can do these things and more. Figure 2 4 1 shows how the following program works.

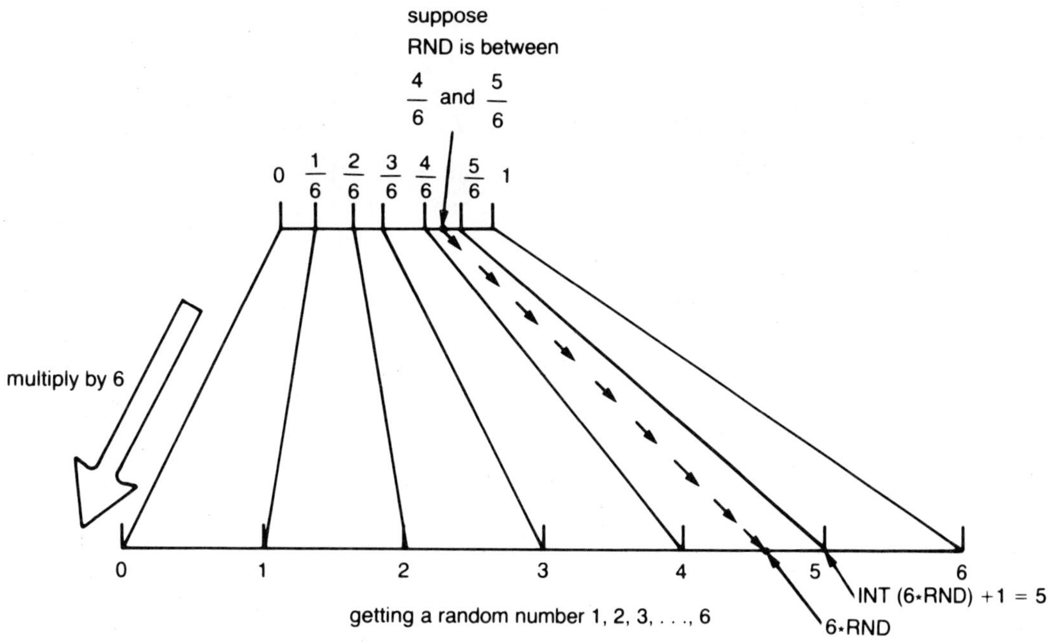

Figure 2 4 1 How does that work?

```
10 REM   PRODUCE A RANDOM NUMBER BETWEEN 1 AND 6
20       RANDOMIZE
30       PRINT INT(RND*6 + 1)
9999     END
RUN
 6
READY
RUN
 1
READY
RUN
 6
READY
RUN
 4
READY
```

EXERCISES 2 4

1 What are the values of the following BASIC expressions?

(a) SQR(2*3 + 10)
(b) INT(23/5)
(c) SQR(ABS(−4))
(d) 23 − 5*INT(23/5)
(e) SQR(12 − SQR(9))
(f) SNG(2∧3 − 3∧2)

2 What are the values of the following BASIC expressions?

(a) INT(3.9762*100 + .5)/100
(b) INT(66/12)
(c) 66 − 12*INT(66/12)
(d) ABS(INT(−5/4))
(e) SGN(SQR(2) −1)
(f) SQR(SQR(81))

3 Write a BASIC expression which truncates the number stored in X by eliminating the fractional part of the number, whether X is positive or negative. The value of the expression should be 3 if X is 3.2 or 3.8, and it should be −5 if X is −5.3 or −5.9.

4 Write a BASIC expression which rounds off the number in X to the nearest hundredth.

5 Write a BASIC expression which computes the number of whole feet in X inches. Write another expression which computes the number of inches left over.

6 Write a LET statement which stores a random number selected from the numbers 2,4,6,8, and 10 in the variable E.

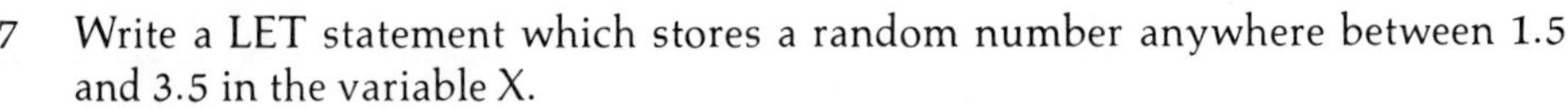

7 Write a LET statement which stores a random number anywhere between 1.5 and 3.5 in the variable X.

8 Which expression gives a random whole number in the range L, L +1, . . .,H?

(a) INT((H−L+1)*RND) +L
(b) INT((H−L)*RND) +L
(c) INT(H*RND) +L

Section 2 5

Details About Numbers

There are two different ways in which the little details about numbers can catch you napping. First, BASIC has a set of conventions about how numbers are printed, which may result in a number being printed in an unexpected form. Second, numbers in BASIC have a limited accuracy and a limited range, either of which may result in computations having unexpected values.

Numbers (numeric values) are printed in different ways depending on their size. A given numeric value will always be printed in the same form even though you may have entered it into your program in different ways.

For the next few pages, we'll be using this experimental program—it will be easier to follow what we're saying if you go to your computer, enter the program, and run each experiment as we come to it.

```
10 REM  EXPERIMENT WITH DIFFERENT FORMS OF NUMBERS
20      PRINT "YES";
30      INPUT N
40      PRINT "THAT'S PRINTED AS"; N
9999    END
```

If a value is small, with no fractional part, it is printed by itself, with no decimal point.

```
RUN
YES? 2
THAT'S PRINTED AS 2
READY
RUN
YES? 2.00000
THAT'S PRINTED AS 2
READY
```

If the value is small and does have a fractional part, it is printed with no trailing zeros.

```
RUN
YES? 2.500000
THAT'S PRINTED AS 2.5
READY
RUN
YES? 2.50010
THAT'S PRINTED AS 2.5001
READY
```

Large values are printed another way. Perhaps you've already used some large numbers while experimenting.

```
RUN
YES? 186000000000000
THAT'S PRINTED AS 1.86E+14
READY
```

Extremely small values are printed in a similar notation.

```
RUN
YES? .000000000001
THAT'S PRINTED AS 1E-12
READY
```

This is a form of "scientific notation" known, in BASIC, as the **scaled decimal notation**. Many pocket calculators use a similar notation for very large or very small numbers. The number following the E is a scale factor indicating a shift in the decimal point. In the first example it means that the actual value is obtained by shifting the decimal point 14 places to the right:

1.86000E + 14 means 1 86000000000000.

In the second example it means that the actual value is obtained by shifting the decimal point 12 places to the left ("+" means "to the right", and "−" means "to the left"):

1.00000E − 12 means .000000000001 00000

There are two good reasons for using the E form for very large and very small numbers. First, once you're used to the notation, the E form is easier to read (it's hard to count all those zeros yourself). Second, often you'll want to print nice, neat columns of numbers, and, because of the E notation, you always know how much room to leave for a number, no matter how large (or small) a value it might have.

You are free to use the E notation anywhere you want to, but a value will be printed in the E notation only when it's exceptionally large or small.

```
RUN
YES? 2.0E+1
THAT'S PRINTED AS 20
READY
RUN
YES? 1E-2
THAT'S PRINTED AS .01
READY
RUN
YES? 123.456E18
THAT'S PRINTED AS 1.23456E+20
READY
```

when a number is printed in the E notation, the decimal point is adjusted so the part in front of the E is from 1 to 9.99999

The second kind of little detail about numbers that can trip you up occasionally is that, in BASIC, they are stored to a limited accuracy, and they have a limited range. For one thing, the "boxes" that are used to store numeric values are of some-fixed size. Every version of BASIC that meets the standards provides variables with enough room to store values accurate to 6 decimal digits. Some versions of BASIC provide more accuracy. If a number has more digits than will fit, the last digit that fits is rounded off appropriately, and all the digits to the right are lost. You can see from the run below that on our system, numeric variables have room for 6 digits.

```
RUN
YES? 1.2345678901234567890
THAT'S PRINTED AS 1.23457
READY
```

N 1.23457 78901234567890

won't fit in the "box", so lost

rounded off, based on the part that's lost

As well as the limit on accuracy, each version of BASIC has a limit on the size of numbers. Versions which conform to the standards will allow at least values with scale factors from −38 up to +38. Some versions allow a wider range. If you enter a number outside the allowable range, you should get a warning message. Play around with the experimental program until you've discovered the range on your system.

```
RUN
YES? 1.0E+38
THAT'S PRINTED AS 1E+38
READY
RUN
YES? 1.0E+39
ERROR--OVERFLOW IN LINE 30
READY
```

Here are the specific rules for writing numbers. A number may be written as a sequence of decimal digits.

legal examples	*illegal examples*
0	0%
1234	1,234
033	#33

A number may have a + or − in front.

legal examples	*illegal examples*
+ 0	0+
− 128	128−

A number may include a decimal point.

legal examples	*illegal examples*
1.0	.1.
+0.5	5.+
−.3333	$4.95

A number may be any of the above forms followed by a **scale factor,** that is, an E followed by a whole number (i.e., with no decimal point in it.) A number written in this form is known as a **scaled decimal number.**

legal examples	*illegal examples*
1.0E34	1E34.0
37E02	2−E12−
−2.9E−12	3E1.7
16E8	

It's not terribly crucial for you to remember all these details. If you get an error message, or get confused about what a particular number means, you can always refer to this section. You shouldn't have much trouble—BASIC is designed to be reasonable.

EXERCISES 2 5

1 Write an experimental program to check out the process of adding numbers. Run the experimental program to see what happens when the following sums are computed.

(a) .7 + .3
(b) 1.0 + 1.0E−29
(c) 1.0E29 + 1.0
(d) .198653 + (−.198652)
(e) 1.0E38 + (−1.0E38)
(f) 10000.1 + (−0.1)

2 Write an experimental program to check out the process of division. Run the experimental program to see what happens when the following quotients are computed.

(a) 1/3
(b) 2/3
(c) 1.0/1.0E38
(d) 0.1/1.0E38
(e) 100001/100000
(f) 100001/0.1

3 What is the difference between 1.9*10∧1.7 and 1.9E1.7?

Section 2 6

Formalities About Strings

We have used **string values** in two different ways. We've used them in PRINT statements to specify things we want printed verbatim.

Example

```
10        PRINT "WHAT DO YOU WANT";
```

We've also asked for string values to be typed in response to INPUT statements.

```
20        INPUT W$
```

In the second case the string value which is typed is stored in a **string variable.** Like the "box" associated with a numeric variable, the "box" that goes with a string variable has a certain size—and there is a limit to how much a string variable can hold. In standard BASIC, string variables can hold at least 18 characters. Your system may allow more.

```
30        PRINT W$
9999      END
40
RUN
WHAT DO YOU WANT? CHESTER P. FARNSWORTHY
ERROR--STRING TOO LONG
?
```

only the first 18 characters will fit in the variable W$ on our system

the computer awaits a shorter string for W$

We'll be using the above experimental program again shortly. You might want to type it into your computer so you can follow along.

Since verbatim strings in PRINT statements *aren't* stored in string variables, the size of the "boxes" doesn't affect them. You are limited only by how much you can type up to the end of the line.

```
10        PRINT "CHESTER P. FARNSWORTHY"
9999      END
RUN
CHESTER P. FARNSWORTHY
READY
```

here the string isn't being stored in a variable, it's just part of the PRINT statement

In PRINT statements we always put strings in quotation marks, but the quotation marks don't get printed. That's because they merely serve to mark the beginning and end of a string. They're not considered to be part of the information *in* the string. When an INPUT statement asks for a string, we've been typing the strings without quotation marks. It is usually more convenient to type them this way, but the system allows the user to type the quotes around INPUT strings. In fact, for some strings the quotes are required. Try the experimental program again.

```
10      PRINT "WHAT DO YOU WANT";
20      INPUT W$
30      PRINT W$
9999    END

RUN
WHAT DO YOU WANT? "NUTS"   <- we can type the quotes on an INPUT string if we want
NUTS  <- they're not part of the string, though - just markers
READY

RUN
WHAT DO YOU WANT? "                    BLANKS"  <- we need the quotes here, otherwise the leading blanks would be ignored
                    BLANKS
READY   the blanks go into the string variable and so get printed

RUN
WHAT DO YOU WANT? FARNSWORTHY, C. P.  <- commas aren't allowed in INPUT strings without quotes — neither are any of these characters -> & ' , ! "
ERROR--TOO MANY DATA ITEMS
? "FARNSWORTHY, C.P."  <- comma is OK here
FARNSWORTHY, C.P.
READY

RUN
WHAT DO YOU WANT? 3.14159  <- digits are characters too
3.14159  <- the computer has printed a string, not a number, but it's hard to tell
READY

RUN
WHAT DO YOU WANT? 3.1415926535898
3.1415926535898  <- it's easier to tell here, because the string is obviously too long to be a number
READY
```

> **unquoted strings:** may be used in response to INPUT statements. If you don't type quotation marks around a string in response to an INPUT statement, the string stored in the variable will not have any leading blanks or trailing blanks—they will be ignored if you type them. In addition, you cannot type any of the following character within the string:
>
> & ' , ! "

For completeness we'll list all the operators in Minimal BASIC which work on string values. Here they are:

(there aren't any!)

(However, see Chapter 16.)

EXERCISES 2 6

1 Run the experimental program of this section to see how long a string you can store in a variable on your system.

2 What has happened in the computation below?

```
10 REM   SOMETHING BAD HAPPENS
20       PRINT "TYPE IN A NUMBER"
30       INPUT X$
40       PRINT 2*X$
9999     END
RUN
TYPE IN A NUMBER
? 2.76525
ERROR--WRONG TYPE IN LINE 40
READY
```

3 Here are some values to be entered in a single string variable via an INPUT statement (as in the experimental program in this section). Put a Q beside those values which would need to be entered surrounded by quotes. Put an X beside those which must not be entered in quotes.

(a) PIZZA
(b) MUSHROOM PIZZA
(c) A, B, AND C
(d) WOW!
(e) A, B, & C

PROBLEMS 2

1 The lawn mower problem (Problem 1 8) is very similar to the paint estimator problem in Section 2 1. In Section 2 2 we altered the painting program to account for the roughness and porosity of the wall being painted. Redo the lawn mower problem, adding a factor which depends on how overgrown and rugged the yard is.

2 Write a program which computes the area of a right triangle, given the lengths of the two legs.

3 Write a program which asks for a name and address, and prints a mailing label, like this:

```
CHESTER P. FARNSWORTHY
1704 MONDO VERDE LN.
FERNLY, NEVADA 89408
```

Remember the limitation in standard BASIC—a string variable can hold no more than 18 characters. Even if your system allows more, write the program so no variable will need to hold more than 18 characters unless the person has a very unusual name and address.

4 Write a program which asks for a number with a fractional part and rounds it off to an even number of dollars and cents. For example, when given 1.248, your program should print $1.25. If given the value 5.7311, it should print $5.73; and if given the value 2, it should print $2. (Hint: You can use the method for rounding a number we showed in Section 2 4 if you can figure a way to convert a dollar figure to cents and then back to dollars. Take a look at Exercise 2 4 2a).

5 Write a program which asks for a pair of numbers representing a fraction. The first number is the numerator, the second is the denominator. Print each fraction as a whole number followed by a proper fraction.

Examples:

if the input is	*your program should print*
2, 3	THAT'S 0 AND 2/3
7, 3	THAT'S 2 AND 1/3
23, 7	THAT'S 3 AND 2/7

(Hint: Exercise 2 4 5 illustrates a method of computing whole parts and remainders.)

6 Write a program which "undoes" problem 5. It asks for *three* values, and prints the equivalent improper fraction.

if the input is	*your program should print*
0, 2, 3	THAT'S 2/3
2, 1, 3	THAT'S 7/3
3, 2, 7	THAT'S 23/7

7 Mrs. Bigelsby has just purchased a ten-unit apartment building for $320,000. She paid $80,000 down, and makes mortgage payments of $1845 per month. During the first year, taxes are $3425, insurance is $450, power and gas cost $250, water and garbage cost $660, and repairs to the building cost $950. One of the units is provided free to the manger of the apartment. If Mrs. Bigelsby wants to make a 10% profit each year on her investment of $80,000, how much rent should she charge per apartment? (Note: These are real figures—the units have 2 bedroom, and 1 bath and are unfurnished except for stove and refrigerator.)

Your program should ask for the following: purchase price; monthly mortgage payment; yearly expenses for taxes, utilities, and repairs; number of apartments available to rent; and the desired yearly return on investment (e.g., Mrs. Bigelsby wants a profit of $8,000 the first year). Given these values, your program should compute the monthly rent required. Compare your results with apartments near you.

8 Write a program which solves this problem when you enter the appropriate numbers:

Generous Electric's 60-watt, 820-lumen, "long life" light bulbs cost $1.39 for 2, and last 1500 hours (each) on the average. Generous Electric's 60-watt, 855-lumen, "regular" light bulbs cost $2.13 for 4, and last about 1000 hours each. Assuming it costs you nothing to change a light bulb when it goes out, which type of bulb gives the most lumens*hours for the dollar? Which one gives you the most hours per dollar?

9 Find the number of half dollars, quarters, dimes, nickels, and pennies returned as change from one dollar. Have the user type in a purchase price (in cents, to make things easier) and print out how many pennies, nickels, etc., go into the change. (Hint: Exercise 2 4 5 illustrates a method of computing whole parts and remainders.)

10 Write a program to estimate the cost of siding for a house. Assume the siding comes in 4-foot-by-9-foot panels. Have the user tell you the cost of the siding per panel, and the length and width of the house. Assume that the house is a simple, rectangular, one-story ranch style house and that a 9-foot panel is long enough, placed vertically, to go from the foundation to the top of the exterior walls. Embellish the program, once it's finished, to ask the user how many stories the house has, and use his or her answer to multiply the price you figure for one story.

11 In a typical house with six inches of fiberglass insulation in the roof and none in the walls, 40% of the heating bill is for heat lost through the walls.

The insulating effectiveness of materials in indicated by the R-rating. A normal wall with no insulation in it has an R-rating of R4. Installing three-and-a-half-inch-thick fiberglass insulation increases the R-rating to R13. The R-rating is inversely proportional to the amount of heat flow through the material, so 4/13 as much heat is lost through an R13 wall as through an R4 wall.

It costs about $400 to buy enough insulation for the walls of a 200-square-foot house.

Write a program which illustrates the cost effectiveness of installing insulation in the walls. Your program should first ask how large the house is (in square feet), and what the average monthly heating bill is for a 2000-square foot house with uninsulated walls in this part of the country. Assume that heating bills, and cost of insulation are proportional to the area of the house. Print the monthly saving obtained by installing insulation in the walls.

12 Improve the program of Problem 11 in two ways. First, include figures based on both three-and-a-half-inch insulation and on five-and-a-half-inch insulation (in some areas, houses are being built with 2-by-6 framing members instead of 2-by-4's to allow thicker insulation). A wall with five-and-a-half-inch insulation has an R-rating of R21, and cost about $600 for a 2000-square-foot house.

Second, compare the monthly saving to the interest that would be earned on $400 or $600 if it were put in the bank at 10% interest instead of being spent on insulation.

13 Use the technique depicted in Figure 2 4 1 to write a program which simulates throwing a pair of dice. Each time you run the program, it should print the number of spots showing on each die. Remember to RANDOMIZE if you want fair dice!

Chapter 3 **Looping**

Section 3 1

Finding the Panic Button

All programs consist of a sequence of lines. Each line contains one statement or instruction. In the programs of the previous chapters the computer performs the task indicated in each line exactly one. We haven't been taking advantage of one of the best things about computers — their ability to do repetitive tasks. From now on, our programs will make more use of the individual lines by having some of them carried out over and over. That way, we'll be able to create programs which do big tasks a little bit at a time.

But before we write a program that does something over and over, we'd better make sure that we'll be able to stop it when we want to. Every system should have a special key or special symbol to type when you want to interrupt a program that's RUNning, but hasn't finished yet. If you don't know for sure *which* key, enter this program.

```
10 REM  FIND THE PANIC BUTTON!
20      INPUT A$
30      PRINT "DIDN'T FIND IT."
9999    END
```

As you can tell by looking at it, the above program tells the computer to print a ? and to wait for you to enter a value. Instead of entering a value, hit the key you suspect will terminate the program. If you hit the right key, the program will be stopped, and, depending on the kind of system you have, the system will type something like

```
BREAK IN LINE 20
READY
```

If you don't find the right key, either the system will just sit there waiting for you to hit the return key to end the input, or it will continue to completion, and print

```
DIDN'T FIND IT.
READY
```

Of course, if you see that message printed out, you know that you didn't manage to stop the program in the middle, and it ran to completion.

What key should you try? On many systems the ESC (for ESCape) key does the job. On some there is a key marked BREAK. On many systems you hold down two keys at once — the control key and the letter C. If none of these works on your system, you'll have to ask someone. In any event don't continue in this chapter until you have discovered how to stop a program that's RUNning — that is, until you've discovered the *panic button.*

If the terminal you use produces its output on paper (a **hard copy terminal**), read Section 3 2H, "Bookmark," next. If the terminal you use displays its output on a TV screen (a **video terminal**), read Section 3 2V, "Benchmark," next. Go to the appropriate section.

> **Warning!**
>
> Be sure you have found the **real panic button.** Some systems have several keys which act something like panic buttons but aren't. Find the key (or keys) which cause the computer to print READY (or whatever symbol your systems uses for READY).

Section 3 2H
Bookmark

It used to be a common practice for people to paste a little sticker in the front of their books. These stickers said "Ex Libris," which means "from the library of," plus the owner's name. We're not exactly sure *why* people used to use those little stickers* . . . but that's beside the point.

It's easy to write a program that prints a single sticker.

Example

```
10 REM  PRINT A BOOKMARK FOR RAYMOND LANGSFORD
20      PRINT "*******************************"
30      PRINT "*+++++++++++++++++++++++++++++*"
40      PRINT "*+ EX LIBRIS                 +*"
50      PRINT "*+                           +*"
60      PRINT "*+        RAYMOND LANGSFORD  +*"
70      PRINT "*+++++++++++++++++++++++++++++*"
80      PRINT "*******************************"
90      PRINT
9999    END
```

*In fact, now that we think of it, we can't remember what the little stickers are actually called. Probably not "bookmarks" — that's what you use to keep your place. Oh, well.

They're called "bookplates," Didday

Each time you RUN the program, you get a printed label which you can cut out and glue into a book. If you want a large number of them, though, it's boring having to type RUN for each one. By inserting one new statement into our program, we can have the program print one label after another until we decide to stop it. That is, until we hit the panic button.

By adding this line

```
100     GO TO 20
```

we convert the program from one which produces a single label to one which produces as many as you want. Now it will keep printing labels until you hit the panic button, or the paper runs out in the printer, or the computer catches fire.

Essentially our program now says to print labels forever! Why's that? Let's look over the program.

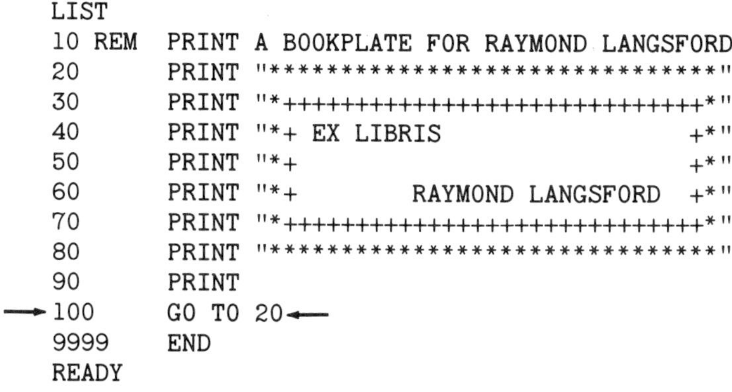

```
LIST
10 REM  PRINT A BOOKPLATE FOR RAYMOND LANGSFORD
20      PRINT "*******************************"
30      PRINT "*+++++++++++++++++++++++++++++*"
40      PRINT "*+ EX LIBRIS                 +*"
50      PRINT "*+                           +*"
60      PRINT "*+        RAYMOND LANGSFORD  +*"
70      PRINT "*+++++++++++++++++++++++++++++*"
80      PRINT "*******************************"
90      PRINT
→ 100   GO TO 20 ←
9999    END
READY
```

Line number 100 is the key. The number (20) after the keywords GO TO is a **line number.** When statement 100 is carried out, it tells the computer to take its next instruction from line 20. That is, it says, "Don't go on to the next line as usual; instead, GO TO line 20 and start up again there."

Let's trace through what happens when you run the program. When you type RUN, the computer starts carrying out the statement in the line with the lowest number. That, of course, is line 10. Since it's a REMark, the computer doesn't do anything except go on to the next higher-numbered line. Line 20 says to print something, so the machine does that, then goes on to the next higher-numbered line. 30 through 90 are all print statements, so they are carried out in order. Finally, the machine gets to line 100. It says to GO TO line 20. Line 20 says to print something, so the machine does that, then goes on to the next higher-numbered line. 30 through 90 are all PRINT statements, so they are carried out in order. Finally, the machine gets to line 100. It says to GO TO line 20. Line 20 says to print something, so the machine does that, then goes on to the...

EXERCISES 3 2H

1 What difference do you think it would make in the operation of our program if we had typed

```
100     GO TO 10
```

instead of

```
100     GO TO 20
```

?

2 Modify the bookplate program to produce bookplates with an underline in place of the person's name so that anyone can use them.

Skip over the next section; i.e., GO TO Section 3 3.

Section 3 2V

Benchmark

Every computer system has different characteristics. Some systems are especially efficient with one type of problem, and pathetically bad with others. So, when a company considers buying a new computer system (or subpart, like a terminal), it can't afford to just take the salesman's word that the new system will be better. The company has to test the new system, using a collection of programs that are typical of the uses it will make of its computer. Such programs are called **benchmark programs** — they serve to measure the effectiveness of the computer system. The company can make a reasonable choice by comparing the performance of different systems on a fixed set of benchmark programs.

One consideration of how useful a particular terminal will be is a simple one — how fast can the system fill a screen with text? If you want to use the system to help you edit manuscripts, and it takes too long to display a part of text, it will be awkward to scan through the manuscript looking for the place you want to correct. Some systems can fill the entire screen with text in a few thousandths of a second. Others take as long as three minutes.

You can find out how fast your system can fill the screen by designing a benchmark program to print a screen-full of characters and then timing the filling of the screen. For example, if your video terminal provides 16 lines, each of which contains 40 characters, the following program

```
10 REM  BENCHMARK--TEST TIME TO FILL SCREEN.
20      PRINT "++++++++++++++++++++++++++++++++++++++++"
30      PRINT "++++++++++++++++++++++++++++++++++++++++"
                          .
                          .
                          .
150     PRINT "++++++++++++++++++++++++++++++++++++++++"
9999    END
```

will do the job. To use the benchmark program, type it in, then type RUN and look at your watch just before you hit the return key. As soon as the screen is full, record the time it took.

But — before you actually do that — let's think about it. This program, while it serves the purpose, has some obnoxious features. First, it requires you to count the number of lines that fit on your screen, and how wide each line is. Worse, you have to do an inordinate amount of typing to enter the program.

It happens that by using a new statement we can devise a program with none of these undesirable features. We really want a program that will just keep printing a character, filling up line after line. Then we can watch, and record the time it takes to fill the entire screen.

To fill the screen, we want to keep performing this statement

```
PRINT "+";
```

over and over again. To do that, we'll start with a program which has that statement performed just once.

```
10 REM  BENCHMARK--TEST TIME TO FILL SCREEN
20      PRINT "+";
9999    END
```

By adding one more line, we can convert our program from one which prints just one character (+) into one which will print scads of +s. We'll add this line

```
30      GO TO 20
```

and now the machine will keep printing + until we hit the panic button. Essentially our program now says to print + forever! Why's that? Let's look over the program carefully.

```
LIST
10 REM  BENCHMARK--TEST TIME TO FILL SCREEN
20      PRINT "+";
→ 30    GO TO 20
9999    END
READY
```

Line 30 is the key. The number (20) after the keyword GO TO is a **line number.** When line 30 is carried out, it tells the computer to take its next instruction from line 20. That is, it says, "Don't go on to the next line as usual. Instead, GO TO line 20 and start up again there."

Let's trace through what happens when you RUN the program. When you type RUN and hit the return key the computer starts carrying out the statement in the line with the lowest number. In this program that's line 10. Since it's a REM statement, the computer doesn't do anything except go on to the next higher-numbered line. Line 20 says to print something, so the machine does that, then goes on to the next higher-numbered line. That's line 30. Line 30 says to GO TO line 20. Line 20 says to print something, so the machine does that, then goes on to the next higher-numbered line. That's line 30. Line 30 says to GO TO line 20. Line 20 says to print something, so the machine does that, then goes on to the next higher-numbered line. That's line 30. Line 30 says...

Now we have a program we can use to test the speed of our terminal. We measure the time it takes for the screen to fill up with +s. After you've written down the time it took, you'll have to hit the panic button to stop the program — if left to itself, the program would keep on spitting out +s forever. Or at least until the computer breaks, or somebody pulls the plug, or the sun goes nova...

EXERCISES 3 2V

1 What difference do you think it would make in the operation of our program if we had typed

```
30        GO TO 10
```

instead of

```
30        GO TO 20
```

?

2 Change line 30 as suggested in Exercise 1 and run the benchmark again.

Section 3 3

Conditional Repeating

The program you saw in the last section had this general form

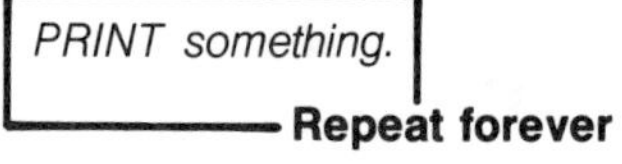

> **Note:** In the next chapter, we'll explain the notation we're using to describe programs. We hope it's clear what we mean—don't worry about the exact format for now.

The ability to repeat part of a program over and over is extremely useful, but it's rare to want to **repeat forever.** We depended on the person at the keyboard to hit the panic button at the right time, but that isn't a very satisfactory way to stop a program. Fortunately, it's possible to create **conditional repeats,** that is, statements which say to repeat under certain conditions and to discontinue the repetition under other circumstances. We often use the term **repeat IF** to describe these conditional repetitions. Here's an example.

Let's write a program that figures out how old people will be in the year 2000. Our program will take this form:

—how old in 2000 A.D.?—

Find out what year it is now.

Find out person's name and age.

Age in 2000 = 2000 − (current yr. − age).
PRINT answer for this person.

Ask if anyone else wants to know their age in 2000 AD.

Repeat IF *the answer was YES*

this means "repeat all the steps shown in the box if the user typed in YES"

Here's our program. Look it over carefully, or better yet, RUN it on your system.

```
10   REM   HOW OLD WILL PEOPLE BE IN 2000 AD?
20   REM   GET CURRENT YEAR.
30         PRINT "WHAT YEAR IS IT NOW";
40         INPUT Y
100 REM    TOP OF REPEAT LOOP
110             PRINT
120             PRINT "WHAT'S YOUR NAME";
130             INPUT N$
140             PRINT "AND HOW OLD ARE YOU NOW";
150             INPUT A
160             PRINT "WELL, "; N$; ", SINCE YOU ARE"; A
170             PRINT "YEARS OLD IN"; Y; ", IN THE YEAR 2000,"
180             PRINT "YOU'LL BE"; 2000 - (Y - A); "."
190             PRINT
200             PRINT "ANYONE ELSE WANT TO FIND OUT HOW OLD"
210             PRINT "THEY'LL BE IN THE YEAR 2000?"
220             PRINT "ANSWER 'YES' IF SO. WELL";
230             INPUT A$
240 REM            REPEAT IF THE ANSWER IS "YES"
250                IF A$="YES" THEN 100
9999        END
RUN
WHAT YEAR IS IT NOW? 1984

WHAT'S YOUR NAME? RAYMOND
AND HOW OLD ARE YOU NOW? 20
WELL, RAYMOND, SINCE YOU ARE 20
YEARS OLD IN 1984 , IN THE YEAR 2000,
YOU'LL BE 36 .

ANYONE ELSE WANT TO FIND OUT HOW OLD
THEY'LL BE IN THE YEAR 2000?
ANSWER 'YES' IF SO. WELL? YES
```

notice we've indented the lines in the loop to make the loop stand out

(program continued on page 58)

```
WHAT'S YOUR NAME? CELIA
AND HOW OLD ARE YOU NOW? 17
WELL, CELIA, SINCE YOU ARE 17
YEARS OLD IN 1984 , IN THE YEAR 2000,
YOU'LL BE 33 .

ANYONE ELSE WANT TO FIND OUR HOW OLD
THEY'LL BE IN THE YEAR 2000?
ANSWER "YES" IF SO. WELL? NO
READY
```

Line 250 is the one which performs the conditional repeat. It says to **repeat IF** the value stored in A$ (i.e., the person's answer) is equal to YES. Specifically, it says to repeat by branching (GOing TO) line 100. The statement in line 250 is an example of an **IF-THEN statement.** The IF-THEN is an extremely useful and powerful statement.

The general form of the IF-THEN statement is

IF *condition* THEN *line number*

and the meaning is, "IF the *condition* is true, THEN go to *line number.* IF it isn't true, then go on to the next line as usual."

The *condition* part of the IF-THEN in line 250 is

```
A$="YES"
```

which is true only if the user types YES exactly. If the person at the keyboard types anything else (NO, WHO CARES, Y, SURE, NO WAY, CERTAINLY,...) the *condition* is not true, and the repeat won't take place. Instead, the next higher line is carried out. In this program the next higher line is

```
9999        END
```

so the program stops.

EXERCISES 3 3

1 What would change if line 250 was written like this?

```
250        IF A$="Y" THEN 100
```

2 How would the program behave if line 250 looked like this?

```
250        IF A$="YES" THEN 120
```

3 Write a program to do multiplications forever (or until the user hits the panic button). Have the user type in two numbers and have your program print out their product. Then repeat.

4 Change the program of exercise 3 so that instead of repeating forever it asks the user if he or she wants to do another after each multiplication. If so, repeat; if not, stop.

Section 3 4
Conditions

In the preceding section the condition that determined whether the program would repeat was a test for **equality:**

```
A$="YES"
```

A program can use different kinds of comparisons, as Table 3 4 1 shows. *Conditions* may be expressed in the following forms:

any one of these is O.K. when numbers are being compared

numeric expression { = , < > , > , < , >= , <= } *numeric expression*

string expression { = , < > } *string expression*

only these two may be used with string values

Table 3 4 1 Conditions

	operator	*meaning*	*examples*
comparing strings	=	equals	A$ = "YES" "PIZZA" = B$
	< >	is not equal to, isn't the exact same thing	A$< > "NO" "PIZZA" < > "PIE"
comparing numbers	=	equals	N = 2 15 = 12 + 9
	< >	is not equal to	N< >0 2 < > 3 − B*C
	<	less than	X < 1 1 < Z ∧ 2
	>	greater than	Y > 2 15 > 600
	<=	less than or equal to	X <= Y − 1
	>=	greater than or equal to	Z2 >= 0

Using different types of *conditions*, we can write programs which repeat depending on a wide range of situations. For instance, we can alter the repeat conditions in the program in Section 3 3 so that the repeat occurs unless the person typed NO in response to our question.

250 IF A$< > "NO" THEN 100

Notice the difference that it makes — now the user has to type NO to stop the program. Anything else keeps it repeating. Before, the user had to type YES to make the program repeat. Anything else made it stop. (Of course, if we change line 250 to test against NO, we need to rephrase the question that the computer prints.)

Here's another example of repeating. It's a program which can serve as a building block for other programs. Whatever statements you insert in lines 120 through 970 will be repeated a specific number of times. The program counts how many times it has repeated the statements — that is, the number of *iterations* or repetitions — and it repeats again unless it has repeated the proper number of times. (See Exercise 3 below.)

—repeat a task R times—

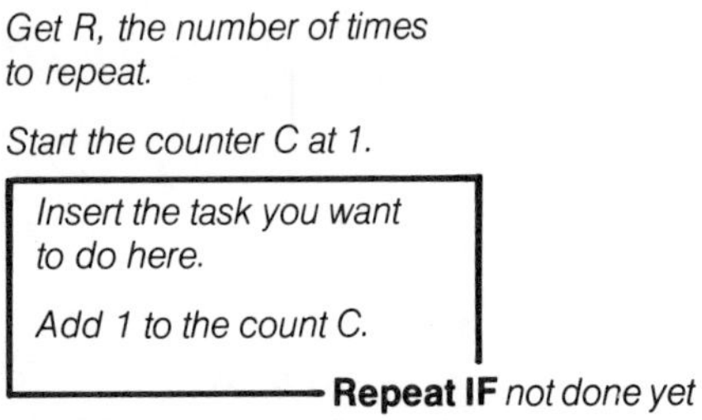

Get R, the number of times to repeat.

Start the counter C at 1.

Insert the task you want to do here.

Add 1 to the count C.

Repeat IF *not done yet*

```
10  REM  REPEAT A TASK R TIMES
10  REM  THIS IS A BUILDING BLOCK PROGRAM--
30  REM  ALTER IT TO DO THE TASK YOU WANT.
40       PRINT "HOW MANY TIMES SHOULD WE DO IT";
50       INPUT R
60  REM  START C OFF AT 1 AND COUNT UP TO R
70       LET C = 1
100 REM  EVERYTHING FROM HERE THROUGH LINE 1000
110 REM  WILL BE DONE R TIMES.
                 .
                 .
                 .      insert statements that do
                 .  <-- the task you want repeated
                 .      in here
                 .
980          LET C = C + 1
990 REM          REPEAT UNLESS WE'VE DONE IT R TIMES.
1000             IF C<=R THEN 100
1010 REM  FINISHED
9999      END
```

To test our building block program, we'll insert a trivial task.

```
500            PRINT "WE'VE BEEN HERE"; C; "TIMES"

RUN
HOW MANY TIMES SHOULD WE DO IT? 5
WE'VE BEEN HERE 1 TIMES
WE'VE BEEN HERE 2 TIMES
WE'VE BEEN HERE 3 TIMES
WE'VE BEEN HERE 4 TIMES
WE'VE BEEN HERE 5 TIMES
READY
```

EXERCISES 3 4

1 Which of these are legitimate IF-THEN statements? If not, why not?

(a) `IF A="YES" THEN 100`
(b) `IF F=2 THEN 200`
(c) `IF F*2 THEN 300`
(d) `IF N$="Y" THEN 400`
(e) `IF N$<="Y" THEN 500`
(f) `IF S2>=1+2+3+4+5 THEN 600`
(g) `IF A2=A2*2 THEN 700`

2 Under what conditions will the loop repeat?

```
       .
       .
       .
50     PRINT "BALANCE="; B
60     PRINT "CHECK=";
70         INPUT C
80         LET B = B - C
90         PRINT "ANY MORE CHECKS";
100        INPUT A$
110          IF A$<>"NO" THEN 60
       .
       .
       .
```

3 Insert statements in the "repeat a task R times" program to compute the interest on $1000 over a 12-month period at 1½% compounded monthly. To do this, start with the variable P (for principal) at $1000 and repeat the monthly interest calculation 12 times. (Hint: The monthly interest calculation can be accomplished by adding 1½% to the current principal via the statement LET P = P + .015*P.)

4 What (catastrophe ?) happens in the "repeat a task R times" program if we answer the question with a negative number?

```
RUN
HOW MANY TIMES SHOULD WE DO IT? -5
```

5 Make a plan for a program which computes the sum of the numbers 1, 2, 3,. . ., R after getting the value for R from the user.

6 Write the program you planned in Exercise 5. Does it work properly?

Section 3 5

Selecting Options

Any time a GO TO or an IF-THEN statement sends the computer back to a line that's been carried out before, we say the program has a **loop** in it.

You can always identify a loop in our programs because there will be a GO TO or IF-THEN statement (at the bottom of the loop) which contains a transfer back to a previous statement in the program. In the "how old will you be in the year 2000" program, line 250 contains a transfer back to line 100,

```
250            IF A$="YES" THEN 100
```

so you can tell that line 250 is the bottom of a loop. In our "repeat a task R times" program, line 1000 mentions a line number lower than 1000,

```
1000           IF C<=R THEN 100
```

so you can tell that line 1000 is the bottom of a loop. What happens if a statement says to jump *ahead* in the program — that is, what if a GO TO or an IF-THEN mentions a line number *greater* than the number of the statement itself? In that case we do not have a loop. Instead, a **selection** has been made. Let's see what that means.

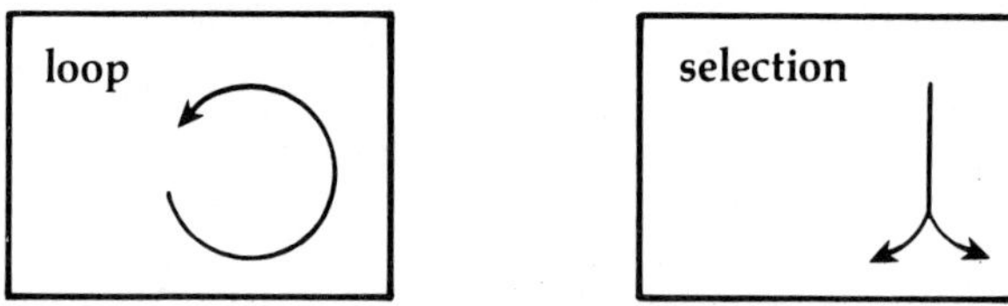

In the previous section we inserted this statement

```
500        PRINT "WE'VE BEEN HERE"; C; "TIMES"
```

in our "repeat a task R times" program. Recall that the numeric variable C stored the number of times our program had gone through the loop. When C has the value 1, the output looks sort of funny:

```
WE'VE BEEN HERE 1 TIMES
```

To use correct English, if C is 1, we want to say

```
WE'VE BEEN HERE 1 TIME
```

and for any other value of C (say 3), we want to use the plural, as in

```
WE'VE BEEN HERE 3 TIMES
```

That is, we want to select TIME or TIMES depending on the value of C. We can do that by splitting the PRINT statement

```
500        PRINT "WE'VE BEEN HERE"; C; "TIMES"
```

into three parts,

```
500        PRINT "WE'VE BEEN HERE"; C; "TIME";
530        PRINT "S";
540        PRINT
```

and then using the value of C to select line 530 when it's appropriate, as shown below.

—printing TIME or TIMES—

PRINT the first part of the phrase.

IF C isn't 1, THEN
PRINT an S to make TIME plural.


```
500        PRINT "WE'VE BEEN HERE"; C; "TIME";
510 REM    DO WE WANT THE "S" OR NOT?
520        IF C=1 THEN 540
530          PRINT "S";
540        PRINT
550 REM    CONTINUE ON OUR MERRY WAY.
               .
               .
               .
```

if C=1, the program skips past line 530

notice that we've indented the statement that gets selected (by two columns) to make it stand out

We use looping to get the computer to do a lot of work without typing a very long program, and we use selection among alternatives to make a program more flexible and adaptable to a variety of situations. These two notions, **looping** and **selection,** are among the most important concepts of programming. They are fundamental tools that we use again and again.

Here's another example of selection. The last time we were in Mexico, the peso has just been "floated" with respect to the dollar — the exchange rate changed each day. Each store was required to list their prices in Mexican pesos, and, if someone wished to pay in US dollars, to compute the price in dollars based on the exchange rate that day. We were fascinated to find that most stores had a pocket calculator which the clerks used to make the required conversions. We wondered if a government could have gotten away with demanding so much ongoing computation before the days of cheap computers and calculators. Today even small stores can afford a small computer. And virtually all the small computers come with a version of BASIC, so a store could seriously consider buying a small computer, entering the program shown below, running it each morning, and leaving it going all day to help with their monetary transactions.

Two different conversions need to be made (dollars to pesos/pesos to dollars), and the main part of our program is a selection between the two alternatives.

—pesos/dollars conversion—

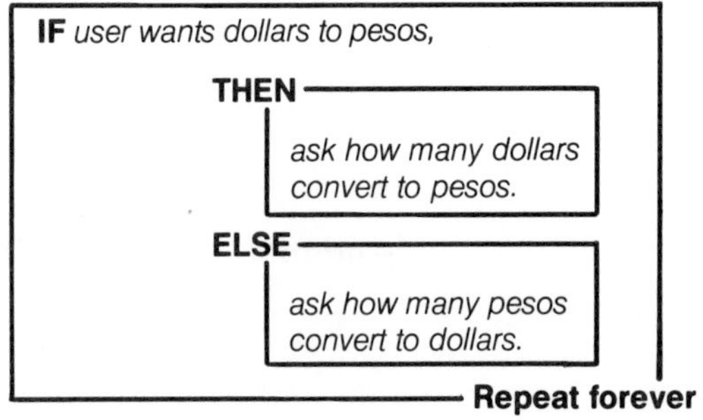

Get today's exchange rate.
IF user wants dollars to pesos,
THEN
ask how many dollars
convert to pesos.
ELSE
ask how many pesos
convert to dollars.
Repeat forever


```
              10   REM  SUPPORT YOUR NEAREST BORDER TOWN STORE.
              20   REM  THE EXCHANGE RATE IN THE MORNING IS
              30   REM  USED FOR THE WHOLE DAY'S TRANSACTIONS.
              40        PRINT "GOOD MORNING!"
              50        PRINT "HOW MANY PESOS PER DOLLAR TODAY";
              60        INPUT E
              100  REM  TOP OF REPEAT FOREVER LOOP.
              110           PRINT
              120  REM      DETERMINE WHICH OPTION TO SELECT
              130           PRINT "DO YOU WANT DOLLARS TO PESOS (TYPE 'D')"
              140           PRINT "OR PESOS TO DOLLARS          (TYPE 'P')"
              150           INPUT A$
              160  REM      THE NEXT STATEMENT PERFORMS THE SELECTION
              170           IF A$="P" THEN 300
            { 180  REM        DOLLARS TO PESOS
            { 190             PRINT "HOW MANY DOLLARS";
dollars to  { 200             INPUT D
  pesos     { 210             PRINT D; "DOLLARS="; D*E; "PESOS"
            { 220  REM        SKIP OVER THE OTHER OPTION
            { 230             GO TO 400
            { 300  REM        PESOS TO DOLLARS
pesos to    { 310             PRINT "HOW MANY PESOS";
 dollars    { 320             INPUT P
            { 330             PRINT P; "PESOS="; P/E; "DOLLARS"
              400  REM          REPEAT FOREVER
              410               GO TO 100
              9999      END
```

```
RUN
GOOD MORNING!
HOW MANY PESOS PER DOLLAR TODAY? 22.76

DO YOU WANT DOLLARS TO PESOS (TYPE 'D')
OR PESOS TO DOLLARS          (TYPE 'P')
? D
HOW MANY DOLLARS? 5.00
 5 DOLLARS= 113.6 PESOS

DO YOU WANT DOLLARS TO PESOS (TYPE 'D')
OR PESOS TO DOLLARS          (TYPE 'P')
? P
HOW MANY PESOS? 695.00
 695 PESOS= 30.536 DOLLARS

DO YOU WANT ...
```

Make sure you understand how the selection works. The IF-THEN statement in line 170 lets the program continue with line 180 (thus selecting the first option) unless the user answered P. In that case it transfers to line 300 (thus selecting the second option). Notice the GO TO statement in line 230. If it weren't there, when the user of the program wanted the first option (dollars to pesos) *both* options would be carried out!

In this section we've seen two examples of **selection.** In the first case we used an IF-THEN statement to determine whether to do something (PRINT "S") or to do nothing. In the second example we used an IF-THEN (and a GO TO) to select one of two alternatives. The second example is often called an **IF-THEN-ELSE selection.** *IF* the condition is true (if A$="P"), *THEN* the program does one thing, *ELSE (otherwise)* it does the other.

EXERCISES 3 5

1 Write a program to do addition or multiplication, as directed by the user. The program should ask for two numbers, then ask whether they are to be added or multiplied. Select one of two LET statements based on the answer to the add/multiply question.

2 The following program purports to quote Brown or Vonnegut, according to the taste of the user. What is wrong with it?

```
10 REM  BROWN VS. VONNEGUT
20      PRINT "DO YOU WANT BROWN OR VONNEGUT";
30      INPUT A$
40      IF A$<>"BROWN" THEN 60
50        PRINT "WE ARE ENTERING AN ERA OF LIMITS."
60        PRINT "SO IT GOES..."
9999    END
```

3 Discuss ways in which you could make the money conversion program more polite to the user. For example, if the user types PESOS instead of just P, what

happens? Is that polite? And shouldn't the program round the answer off to an even number of cents instead of making the user do it?

4 Write a program which computes products or squares. It should ask the user which to compute. Then, based on the answer, it should ask for two numbers (for products) or one number (for squares) and print the answer.

5 The following program purports to print a line or two from Aesop or Mother Goose, at the user's whim. What's wrong with it?

```
10 REM   AESOP OR MOTHER GOOSE
20       PRINT "DO YOU WANT AESOP OR MOTHER GOOSE";
30       INPUT A$
40       IF A$="AESOP" THEN 50
50         PRINT "IT IS THE POINT OF A WISE MAN TO BEAR WITH ";
60         PRINT "A MIGHTY COURAGE"
70         PRINT "THAT THING WHICH CAN IN NO WISE BE AVOIDED."
80         GO TO 9999
90         PRINT "JACK SPRAT COULD EAT NO FAT."
9999     END
```

6 Which of these statements are true in Minimal BASIC?

(a) One PRINT statement can cause many lines to be printed.

(b) One line can have been printed by many PRINT statements.

(c) One output line corresponds to one and only one PRINT statement.

(d) Spelling PRINT backwards causes the line to be printed from right to left.

(e) Once a PRINT statement finishes a line (has no comma or semicolon at the end), no subsequent statement can add to that line.

PROBLEMS 3

1 Redo the mailing label problem (Problem 2 3) so that your program keeps printing mailing labels until you hit the "panic button."

2 Here's one of our favorite programs for those days when nothing has been going right. Write it in BASIC.

```
PRINT "DON'T PANIC! ";
```
Repeat forever

3 Write a program to compute yards, feet, and inches when given a measurement in inches. (See Exercise 2 4 5 for a hint on how to do this.) Write a second program to go from yards, feet, and inches to inches only. Then combine the two programs into one that asks the user which way to go, then gets the input(s) and makes the appropriate computation.

4 Write a program which will help a person figure out how much cloth to buy to make a tablecloth for a rectangular table. Ask for the dimensions of the table, the length of overhang desired, and the width of the cloth that will be used. If the cloth is too narrow for a single width to cover the table, your program should assume that ⅝″ will be taken from the material on each side of each seam.

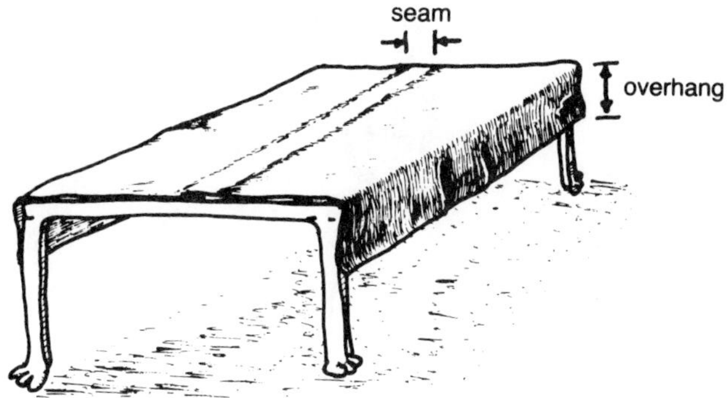

5 Use the "repeat a task R times" program from Section 3 4 to revise the bookplate program of Section 3 2H. Write a program which asks the user how many bookplates are desired, and then prints exactly that many.

6 Use the "repeat a task R times" program from Section 3 4 to revise the benchmark program of Section 3 2V. Write a program which asks the user how many +s to print, and then prints exactly that many.

7 Write a program which computes the first perfect square larger than 84,123. A perfect square is an integer which is the square of another integer (perfect square = *n***n*). Use a loop in your program. (An easy technique is to square each integer, starting at 1 and going up until you find a square larger than 84,123.)

8 One Denver Mint Tea tea bag makes one cup of strong, aromatic tea in eight minutes. Leaving the bag in longer than ten minutes has no further effect on the strength of the tea. If we say that strong (eight minutes) tea has relative strength 1.0, then the relative strength of tea steeped in a teapot for other lengths of time is

$$\text{number of bags} \;*\; \frac{\text{number of minutes}}{\text{number of cups}} \;*\; \frac{\text{1 cup}}{\text{8 minutes}}$$

if the steeping time is under ten minutes. For steeping times over ten minutes the relative strength is

$$\text{number of bags} \;*\; \frac{\text{10 minutes}}{\text{number of cups}} \;*\; \frac{\text{1 cup}}{\text{8 minutes}}$$

Write a program which asks for three values: (1) the number of bags used, (2) the number of cups of water used, and (3) the steeping time in minutes. Have your program compute and print out the relative strength of the tea. If the relative strength is less than 0.5, print HOPE YOU LIKE WEAK TEA, and if it's greater than 1.25, print HOPE YOU LIKE YOUR TEA STRONG.

9 Bobby's mom gave him a new bike for his birthday. The gear ratios on his bike are

gear	ratio
1	3.3:1
2	2.02:1
3	1.52:1
4	1:1

and the speed of his bike is given by the formula

speed (miles per hour) = .02* rpm/gear ratio

Bobby's New Bike

For example, his speed at 3300 rpm in low gear would be

.02 * 3300 * 1/3.3 = 20 mph

Write a program which asks for the rpm value where he shifts. For each shift point, have your program print out his top speed in each gear. If an rpm value over 6500 rpm comes in, print the message

```
BOBBY'S BIKE EXPLODED.
```

10 Redo the apartment building problem (Problem 2 7). Assume that one in twenty tenants defaults on one month's rent per year, and that all costs except mortgage go up by 10% a year. Print the rent per apartment the owner would have to charge each year over the next 10 years if she wants to continue making $8000 profit each year.

11 Redo Problem 2 7, assuming that the apartment building appreciates in value by 8% a year, and that the owner charges just enough rent to cover expenses. After 10 years, if the owner sells, paying a 6% sales commission, what will her average percentage profit per year have been?

Fahrenheit and Celsius

$$F = \frac{9}{5}C + 32$$

$$C = \frac{5}{9}(F - 32)$$

where F stands for Fahrenheit degrees and C stands for Celsius degrees

12 Write a program which could be used by someone who has lists of temperature readings to convert. On each pass through the main loop, ask whether the user wants FAHRENHEIT TO CELSIUS or CELSIUS TO FAHRENHEIT. Then accept a temperature reading, and make the appropriate conversion. [Hint: This program has the same basic organization as the border town store program in Section 3 5.]

13 Write a program to determine whether or not the three values of a set could represent the lengths of the sides of a triangle. If the three sides could make a triangle, calculate its area and print a message like

```
WHEN AB=3.00 AND BC=4.00 AND CA=5.00,
THE AREA OF TRIANGLE ABC IS 6.00
```

If *a*, *b*, and *c* are three side lengths, then the area is $\sqrt{[s(s-a)(s-b)(s-c)]}$, where *s* is the half perimeter $(a+b+c)/2$. (The formula is due to Hero, a mathematician of ancient times.)

If the three values in a set couldn't represent the sides of a triangle, print a message like

```
23.37,  19.51,  AND  9.37 COULD NOT POSSIBLY BE
                          THE SIDES OF A TRIANGLE.
```

> **a property of Hero's formula:** *If $s(a-a)(s-b)(s-c)$ is negative, then a, b, and c can't make a triangle.*

Here are some data values for your program.

23.37	19.51	8.37
57.46	40.06	27.57
42.09	35.78	61.65
8.63	15.74	12.38
61.94	78.07	10.87
19.56	23.54	33.28
84.37	61.98	15.93
37.80	49.24	23.51

Chapter 4 **Planning, Politeness, and Portability**

Section 4 1

The Life Cycle of a Program

There are several different stages in the life of a major computer program, and several different groups of people who will be affected by the program.

A program begins as an idea, as a desire to perform some computation. The person or persons who state the original problem often are not programmers, and in some cases may know virtually nothing about computers. It almost always takes a lot of effort to state the problem in a form that is meaningful to the person who is to program the solution.

A program starts to take shape when the programmer makes a **plan,** that is, writes down an abstract description of what the program is to do, and how it will go about the task. The programmer will study, amend, and **refine** the plan, making sure that it is reasonable and practical. Often a programmer will discover that the first thing that popped into mind isn't the best solution, and will scrap the original plan and write a new one. When the programmer is confident that the plan is correct, it is translated into BASIC—the actual program is written. (This step is often referred to as **coding,** since you're translating your solution into the "code" the machine uses—in this case lines of BASIC.)

Now the programmer tests the program, trying out all the options the program allows, and correcting those that don't work properly. It is most efficient to test and correct small subsections of the program before testing the whole thing. This phase is often called **debugging. (Bug** is computerese for "mistake.")

After the program works, most programmers go over it again, looking for small things that can be changed to make the program more convenient to use—in a word, more **polite.**

Once the program has been thoroughly tested, debugged, and refined, it is turned over to the **user** (who usually is not the same person as the programmer). The user, of course, uses the program. Most programs will be shared by a number of different users, and often will be sent **(transported)** to other computer systems to serve additional users. Transporting programs from one system to another is seldom easy, but if the program is written in a standardized language like Minimal BASIC, the job is much easier.

Even if the programmer has done a thorough job of testing the program, errors may crop up when the program gets to the users. Perhaps the users will use the program in ways unforeseen by the programmer—perhaps there are some cases the programmer just didn't think of. Or, after a while, the exact needs of the users may change. In any of these cases someone (perhaps the original programmer, perhaps another programmer) will have to alter the program. For this reason the program will have to be very clearly written and described. A programmer who hasn't looked at his or her program for some time will often find it hard to remember what it does. And, of course, the job is even harder for someone who didn't write the program in the first place. The job of keeping a program running properly is called **program maintenance.** The written material which describes how the program works, and how to use it, is called **documentation.**

Even if you don't intend to beome a professional programmer, learning some of the established program development tools and techniques will be of great help. The goal is to make the process of writing programs rational and efficient. And to keep you from tearing your hair out.

EXERCISES 4 1

1 Program development can be neatly divided (a little *too* neatly, really) into four stages. What are they?

2 The most important consideration in the design of useful programs is the correct production of the output the user wants. Name three other important considerations.

3 What is a portable program, and why is portability important?

4 What is debugging?

5 What is program maintenance?

6 How can programs be tested for correctness?

Section 4 2
Planning

If you don't really understand what each part of a program is supposed to do, how could you know if you've written it properly? How could you test a program that you didn't understand? Successful programmers develop their own guidelines and little rituals to ensure that they know what they're doing. Successful programmers don't just rush up to a terminal and type in whatever comes to their mind in a mad jumbled mess. No, sir.

Possibly you've been able to compose programs on the spot—flailing away at the keyboard. Soon, however, you'll be writing programs which have a number of interrelating subparts, programs which are so large that you can't keep all the necessary details in mind at once. Such programs will be very difficult to manage if you don't have a clear **plan** to follow and refer to.

But we're getting carried away here. Instead of blathering on in generalities, let's demonstrate what we mean by following through the program development process for a specific program.

First, we start with a vague idea, a rough statement of what we want to do.

Balancing a checkbook should be easy, but for some reason we never seem to get it right. Let's write a program that we can use to keep our checkbook in order.

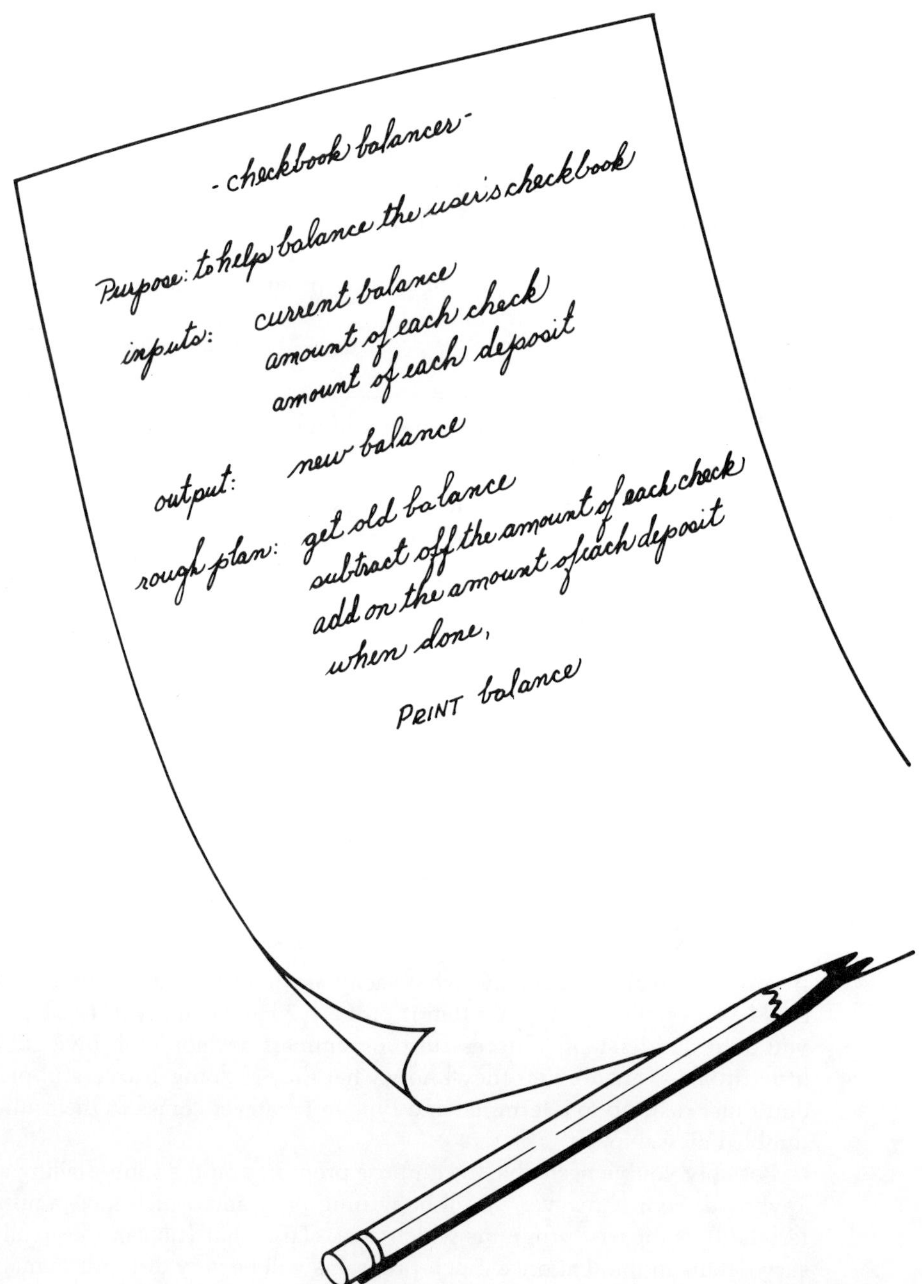

FIGURE 4 2 1 Preliminary plan for the checkbook-balancer program

Before we can even consider writing any BASIC statements, we've got to figure out what we want to do. Well, of course, we want to balance our checkbook, but what does that involve? It could mean anything from writing a trivial program that asks for two numbers and adds them together, all the way to designing a huge program that stores all our checking account activities for our whole life, keeping track of whom we paid how much for what, what's tax deductible, and so on.

We decide that we want a relatively simple program that will let us bring an account balance up to date. It won't keep any records itself. To use it, you'll enter your previous balance, then each check amount and each deposit, and it'll print out the new balance, which you copy into your checkbook.

OK. Now we can write something down. We'll write the main idea of the program, then a list of the values it needs to accept, and the value(s) it should produce.

But now, as we look at our rough plan (Figure 4 2 1), we realize that it's not very complete. What does "subtract off each check" really mean in terms of a computer program? Somehow our program has to know when it's through accepting checks, so it can start on deposits doesn't it? But do we really want it to go through all the checks first and *then* the deposits? In our checkbook (Figure 4 2 2) the checks and deposits are interspersed... Maybe we should have the program ask whether the next value is going to be for a check or a deposit. Or we could have the program ask the user how many checks will be entered, then use the "repeat a task R times" program from Section 3 4 to process exactly that many input values ...but that would be *rude* to the user, come to think of it. The user shouldn't have to count how many checks and deposits there will be. Mumble. Oh, wait! We can have the user type a C to mean the next value is going to be a check, a D to mean a deposit, and something else, maybe a Q for quit or an F for finished, to mean that there aren't any more transactions, and it's time to print the final balance.

Perhaps it sounds like we don't know what we're doing. That's true in a certain sense. In the first phases of designing a program, you have a rough idea of what you want the program to do, and maybe a few hunches about how it will do what you want. Unless for some reason you've written an identical program some time before, however, you *don't* know exactly what you're doing. Instead, you try out lots of alternative ideas in your head, or roughly on paper, attempting to come up with a good overall idea (or collection of ideas). There is always more than one way

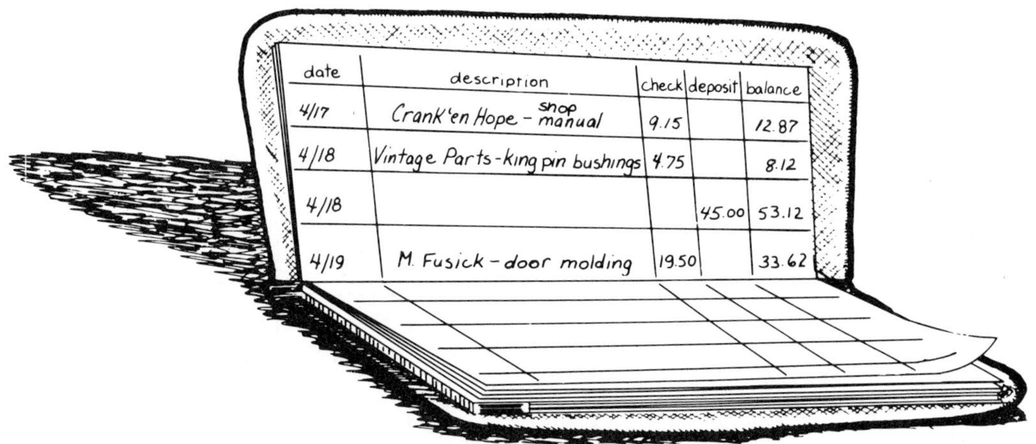

Figure 4 2 2 Our checkbook

Figure 4 2 3 Ideas are easy to change—programs are hard to change.

to solve a particular problem. The more alternatives you've considered in the early going, the more confident you can feel that your final solution will be a good one. Just think how much time we would have wasted if we'd sat down at the terminal and started typing the first BASIC statements that came into our head. This way, we've spent a little time puzzling over alternatives, are on the track of promising solution, and haven't wasted any time entering BASIC statements that we'd have to change later.

Here's the plan we're coming up with. To begin with, our program will ask the user for the current balance. Then we'll have our program accept either a C, a D, or some letter which means to quit. If the user entered a C, our program will then get the value of the check and subtract it from the running balance, and then repeat. If the user entered a D, our program will get the value of the deposit, add it to the running balance, and repeat. If the user entered an F (or whatever other letter indicates the end of the transactions) our program will print the final balance and quit.

Our plan is taking shape, but it's still pretty rough. To make sure our plan is adequate, we'll write it down in a neat, standardized form that will be easy to check for errors. In the next section we'll discuss the notations we use for plans. For now, we'll just write down the plan so you can see what we've come up with.

—balance a checkbook—

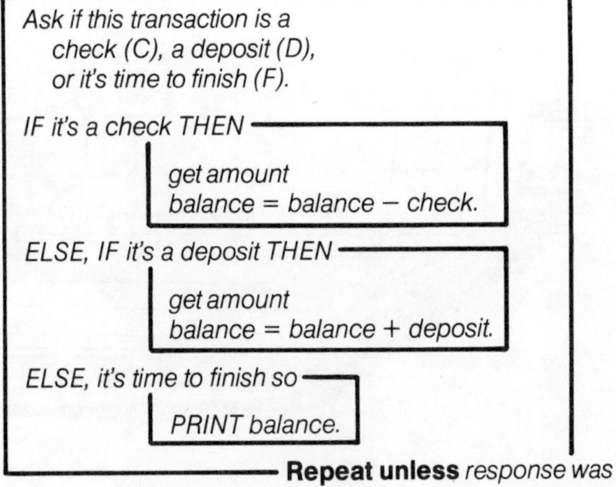

Get old balance.
Ask if this transaction is a
check (C), a deposit (D),
or it's time to finish (F).
IF it's a check THEN
get amount
balance = balance − check.
ELSE, IF it's a deposit THEN
get amount
balance = balance + deposit.
ELSE, it's time to finish so
PRINT balance.
Repeat unless response was F

Our plan is now concrete enough for us to spend some time going over it, making sure it will work properly, making sure that it covers every situation that might arise. Often at this stage you will realize that you *haven't* covered every reasonable situation, or (shudder) that your plan really won't work at all. In that case you just back up and come up with a new plan. Here we feel confident that our plan will work, so we're ready to begin coding it, that is, translating it into BASIC. We'll do that in Section 4 4.

Is this it?

Maybe we've made it seem as though once you settle on a plan, no further changes should ever be made in it. If so, we apologize. Making a reasonable plan is an important step in programming, but the first plan you come up with isn't sacred! In fact, we won't really know if you've hit on the best plan until we've used the finished program for a while. Perhaps after we've used this program, we'll discover that having to type C or D before each transaction is horribly boring. Perhaps we'll realize that we should include some way to handle service charges (some banks charge for each check you write). The main benefit of making a plan is that it helps us keep on top of what we're doing, so that once it's obvious that changes need to be made, we understand the program well enough to make those changes with minimal effort. The technical term for this approach to writing programs is **top-down design and iterative refinement.** First, we figure out what we think we want the program to do (i.e., make a plan). Then once we've got it working well enough to see if it's really what we want, we keep going back and tuning it until we're totally satisfied.

EXERCISES 4 2

1 Name three reasons for thinking and planning before writing BASIC code.

2 What does our plan for balancing a checkbook say about the case when the user types E by mistake instead of D?

3 How does the plan account for the possibility that the user might type in the wrong number for a check or deposit?

4 The initial plan you make for a program should have at least four principal parts. What are they?

Section 4 3
A Notation for Plans

Over the years, quite a few different notations for writing plans for programs have been used. We'll describe one which we like. There's nothing sacred about it —the important thing is for you to have a consistent, convenient, quick way to write your ideas down. Some way that's more precise than the way people "normally" think, yet not filled with the tiny, obscure details of computer programs.

Although our notation is more like English than BASIC, it is more precise and constrained than spoken English. We call it a **plan** or a **verbal description** of a program, yet it does contain some purely visual elements (the boxes which group related operations). Some people call such plans **pseudo code.**

In our notation there's a phrase for each important thing the program has to do, written in the order in which the thing is to occur. If a program is to do thing 1, then thing 2, then thing 3, we'd write

thing 1
thing 2
thing 3

If there's to be a loop in the program, i.e., if some part of the program must be repeated, we draw a box around that part. At the lower right of the box, we put the word *Repeat,* followed by a description of the conditions under which the material in the box is to be repeated. Here are two examples.

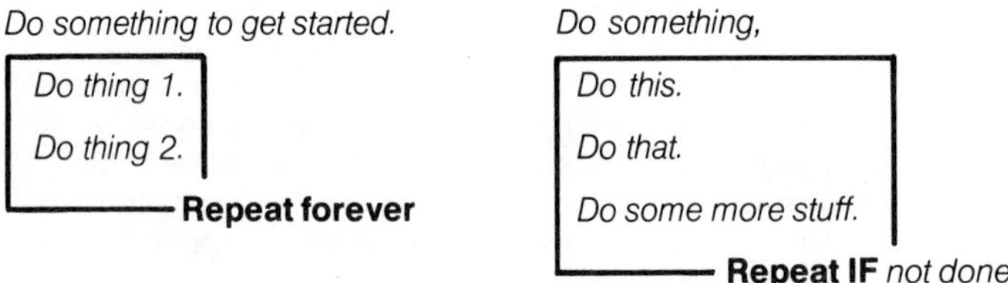
Do something to get started.
Do thing 1.
Do thing 2.
Repeat forever
Do something,
Do this.
Do that.
Do some more stuff.
Repeat IF not done

IF there's a selection to be made, we write a description of the test (the condition that determines which option to take). Following that is the word THEN, and, in a box (so we can tell at a glance what things happen), all of the things that are to be carried out when the condition is true. IF something else is to be done when the condition is false, we write the word ELSE (or *otherwise*) and include (in another box) all the things that are to be done in that case.

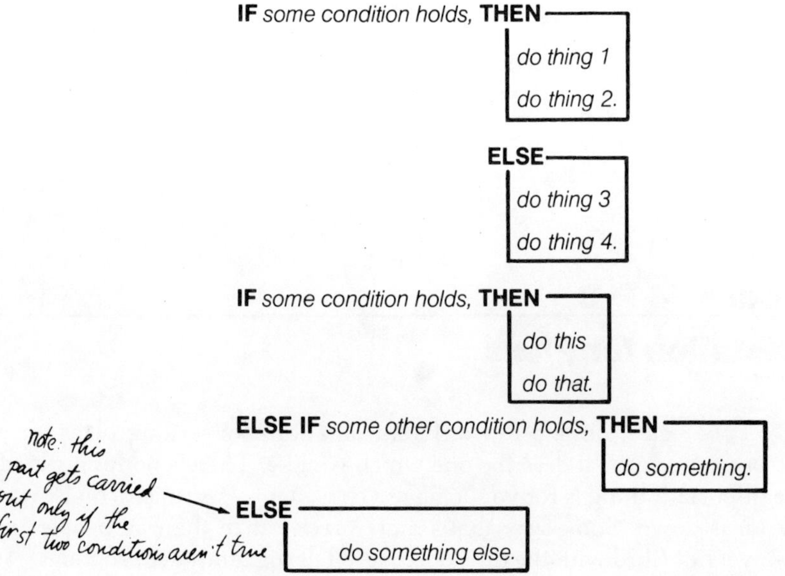
IF some condition holds, THEN
do thing 1
do thing 2.
ELSE
do thing 3
do thing 4.
IF some condition holds, THEN
do this
do that.
ELSE IF some other condition holds, THEN
do something.
ELSE
do something else.
note: this part gets carried out only if the first two conditions aren't true

Verbal plans are an intermediate stage between rough plans (general descriptions of what a program is suppposed to do) and the programs themselves. They are analogous to outlines that you might make before you write an essay or a book. Like outlines, they often get changed as the coding proceeds, and it's worthwhile to keep them up to date as you go along. Then, when the project is finished, you have a good, general description of the program that you can keep along with the other notes you've written (rough plans, special cases, alternatives considered etc.). This collection of notes and plans, plus a good write-up on how to use the program and a listing of its current form, should be kept in a **documentation package** for the program. This will be an enormous aid when the program needs to enhanced, fixed, or otherwise revised.

EXERCISES 4 3

1 Modify the plan in Section 4 2 for the checkbook-balancing program to make it print each C, D, F and each amount as it's entered. (This direct printing of input values is known as **echo printing** or **mirror printing.** Virtually every program should have some form of echo printing, especially in the testing and debugging stage.)

2 Write a plan for the problem of Exercise 3 3 3.

3 Write a plan for the problem of Exercise 3 5 1.

4 Write a plan for a program which will convert meters to feet or feet to meters, at the user's option. The program should ask the user which conversion to make, then ask for the length to be converted and print the results.

Section 4 4
Coding the Checkbook Program

In Section 4 2 we developed a plan for our checkbook program. Here it is again.

—balance a checkbook—

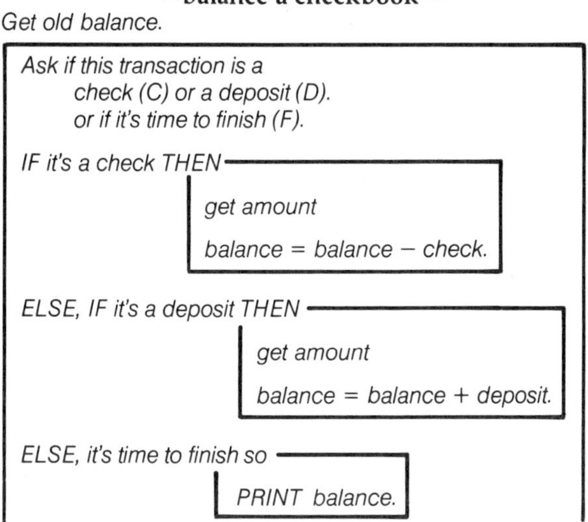

Get old balance.
Ask if this transaction is a
check (C) or a deposit (D).
or if it's time to finish (F).
IF it's a check THEN
get amount
balance = balance − check.
ELSE, IF it's a deposit THEN
get amount
balance = balance + deposit.
ELSE, it's time to finish so
PRINT balance.
Repeat unless response was F

Now we're ready to **code** our program, that is, to translate our plan into BASIC. We begin by entering REMark statements describing what our program does. If a month from now we have to look at our program (either to fix a mistake that's cropped up, or just to see if we want to use it), we don't want to have to fight our way through the whole thing to figure out what it does—we'll be able to get the general idea by reading just the first few lines.

```
10  REM  BALANCE A CHECKBOOK
20  REM  THIS PROGRAM COMPUTES THE NEW BALANCE,
30  REM  GIVEN THE VALUES OF CHECKS AND DEPOSITS.
```

Next, we'll enter a few REMarks that tell the names and meanings of the important variables. We decide to use numeric variable B to store the balance, C to store the value of the check being processed, and D the current deposit.

```
40  REM  VARIABLES--
41  REM    A$  OPTION SELECTOR--INPUT
42  REM    C   AMOUNT OF CHECK--INPUT
43  REM    D   AMOUNT OF DEPOSIT--INPUT
44  REM    B   RUNNING BALANCE
```

Now we can begin coding in earnest. The first thing our plan says to do is, "Get old balance."

```
50       PRINT "WHAT'S YOUR STARTING BALANCE";
60       INPUT B
```

Now we're getting into the heart of the program. We have a loop that repeats as long as there are still checks or deposits to be entered. To make it more obvious where the loop starts, we'll skip up to 100 for the next line number and put in a REMark.

```
100 REM  TOP OF RUNNING BALANCE LOOP
```

Next, we need to know what kind of transaction the user wants—check, deposit, or finished—so we'd better print a message telling the user what to do.

```
110          PRINT "TO ENTER A CHECK,   TYPE C"
120          PRINT "TO ENTER A DEPOSIT, TYPE D"
130          PRINT "IF YOU'RE FINISHED, TYPE F"
140          PRINT "WHICH";
150          INPUT A$
```

Now that we have the user's answer (stored in the string variable A$), we can start making the tests to determine what to do. If the answer wasn't C, we know the user isn't entering a check, so we want to skip to the next part of the test. By looking at our plan, we can see that we don't have too much to do for any of the options, so we can decide right now to place the test for deposit starting at line 300, the finished part at 400 and bottom of our loop at line 500.

```
160 REM       SELECT OPTION--CHECK, DEPOSIT, OR FINISHED.
170           IF A$<>"C" THEN 300
180 REM         THIS IS A CHECK.
190             PRINT "AMOUNT OF CHECK: $";
200             INPUT C
210             LET B = B - C
220             GO TO 500
```

Next, we need to see if the user typed D. If so, we need to get the amount of the deposit and add it to the balance.

```
300           IF A$<>"D" THEN 400
310 REM         THIS IS A DEPOSIT.
320             PRINT "AMOUNT OF DEPOSIT: $";
330             INPUT D
340             LET B = B + D
350             GO TO 500
```

And now we're left with the finished option. If the user didn't type C, and didn't type D, then he or she must have wanted the finished option, and typed F. The tests in line 170 and 300 will have both failed, sending the machine to line 400.

```
400 REM       FINISHED..
410             PRINT "YOUR NEW BALANCE IS $"; B
```

At last, we're at the bottom of our loop. Our plan says to *repeat unless* the user's response was F, and that's easy to do.

```
500 REM       REPEAT IF NOT FINISHED
510           IF A$<>"F" THEN 100
600       PRINT
610       PRINT "BYE"
9999      END
```

Now that we've **coded** our program, it's time to make sure it works properly.

```
LIST
10  REM  BALANCE A CHECKBOOK
20  REM  THIS PROGRAM COMPUTES THE NEW BALANCE,
30  REM  GIVEN THE VALUES OF CHECKS AND DEPOSITS.
40  REM  VARIABLES--
41  REM    A$  OPTION SELECTOR--INPUT
42  REM    C   AMOUNT OF CHECK--INPUT
43  REM    D   AMOUNT OF DEPOSIT--INPUT
44  REM    B   RUNNING BALANCE
50       PRINT "WHAT'S YOUR STARTING BALANCE";
60       INPUT B
100 REM  TOP OF RUNNING BALANCE LOOP
110          PRINT "TO ENTER A CHECK,    TYPE C"
120          PRINT "TO ENTER A DEPOSIT, TYPE D"
130          PRINT "IF YOU'RE FINISHED, TYPE F"
```

(continued)

```
140           PRINT "WHICH";
150           INPUT A$
160 REM       SELECT OPTION--CHECK, DEPOSIT, OR FINISHED.
170           IF A$<>"C" THEN 300
180 REM         THIS IS A CHECK.
190             PRINT "AMOUNT OF CHECK: $";
200             INPUT C
210             LET B = B - C
220             GO TO 500
300           IF A$<>"D" THEN 400
310 REM         THIS IS A DEPOSIT.
320             PRINT "AMOUNT OF DEPOSIT: $";
330             INPUT D
340             LET B = B + D
350             GO TO 500
400 REM       FINISHED.
410             PRINT "YOUR NEW BALANCE IS $"; B
500 REM       REPEAT IF NOT FINISHED
510           IF A$<>"F" THEN 100
600       PRINT
610       PRINT "BYE"
9999      END
READY
```

EXERCISES 4 4

1 Why do we always put a REMark at the beginning of a program?

2 Why does a statement in a plan like "get old balance" always translate into two or more BASIC statements in the program?

3 Redo our plan so it incorporates the PRINT statements at the end of the program.

4 If the user wanted the running balance printed after each transaction, where would you change the plan? Where would the changes appear in the program?

Section 4 5

Debugging

In the previous section we made it sound as if the process of translating our program into BASIC and entering it into our computer went without a hitch. Not true. Actually, we ran into a few problems.

A variety of problems await the unwary programmer. In this section we'll go over the problems we had and recreate the process we went through to track them down.

One of the most common sources of error is simple typing mistakes. Typing mistakes are easy to fix, once you notice them—you just retype the line, spelling things correctly. If you misspell a word in a REMark statement, or you misspell part of a string in a PRINT statement, of course you won't get an error message. But if you misspell one of the keywords, your system should complain. For instance, we got to typing too fast, and entered

ooops!

```
410                PIRNT  "YOUR NEW BALANCE IS $"; B
```

When we hit the return key at the end, our system responded with

```
ERROR-UNRECOGNIZED STATEMENT
```

It took us just a second to see what we'd done. We retyped the line.

```
410                PRINT "YOUR NEW BALANCE IS $"; B
```

> Typos often occur in **groups.** When you find one, look for others nearby.

A more insidious error is caused by mistyping a variable name. If we accidentally hit a V instead of a B,

```
410                PRINT "YOUR NEW BALANCE IS $"; V
```

the statement has the legal form of a PRINT; it just prints the wrong value, with no error message. It's a good idea to list your program, and go over it carefully, looking for little slip-ups.

> **LIST** your program and look it over for misspelled variable names, wrong line numbers, and other **typos.**

We listed our program and looked it over. It seemed OK, so we started testing it. Unfortunately, there were still a couple of errors in it at this point. Can you spot them in Figure 4 5 1?

The next step in program development is to test your program. Here, as in all aspects of programming, it's crucial to limit what you have to think about at any one time. We need to come up with a method for testing the program which will help us concentrate on one part of the program at a time, which will help us find the errors by narrowing the regions of the program which might be causing any observed improper behavior.

Looking at our plan and our program, we notice that the process of getting the user's selection of C, D, or F is extremely important. If that doesn't work right, then nothing else will work. So before we start checking the details of how the program processes a check or a deposit, we'd better make sure our variables are getting reasonable values when the program tries to select the right thing to do.

> Put in **debugging PRINT statements** to check values of key variables.

We insert some debugging PRINT statements right before the selection starts.

```
156  PRINT "TESTING-- BALANCE="; B
157  PRINT "TESTING-- USER'S CHOICE="; A$
158  STOP
```

```
10   REM  BALANCE A CHECKBOOK
20   REM  THIS PROGRAM COMPUTES THE NEW BALANCE,
30   REM  GIVEN THE VALUES OF CHECKS AND DEPOSITS.
40   REM  VARIABLES--
41   REM    A$  OPTION SELECTOR--INPUT
42   REM    C   AMOUNT OF CHECK--INPUT
43   REM    D   AMOUNT OF DEPOSIT--INPUT
44   REM    B   RUNNING BALANCE
50        PRINT "WHAT'S YOUR STARTING BALANCE";
60        INPUT B
100 REM   TOP OF RUNNING BALANCE LOOP
110           PRINT "TO ENTER A CHECK,    TYPE C"
120           PRINT "TO ENTER A DEPOSIT, TYPE D"
130           PRINT "IF YOU'RE FINISHED, TYPE F"
140           PRINT "WHICH";
150           INPUT A$
160 REM       SELECT OPTION--CHECK, DEPOSIT, OR FINISHED.
170           IF A$<> "C" THEN 400
180 REM         THIS IS A CHECK.
190             PRINT "AMOUNT OF CHECK: $";
200             INPUT C
210             LET B = B + C
220             GO TO 500
300           IF A$<>"D" THEN 400
310 REM         THIS IS A DEPOSIT.
320             PRINT "AMOUNT OF DEPOSIT: $";
330             INPUT D
340             LET B = B + D
350             GO TO 500
400 REM       FINISHED.
410             PRINT "YOUR NEW BALANCE IS $"; B
500 REM       REPEAT IF NOT FINISHED
510           IF A$<>"F" THEN 100
600       PRINT
610       PRINT "BYE"
9999      END
```

Figure 4 5 1 The checkbook program as entered, before debugging

Now we run the program with the inserted test statements.

```
RUN
WHAT'S YOUR STARTING BALANCE? 1.25
TO ENTER A CHECK,   TYPE C
TO ENTER A DEPOSIT, TYPE D
IF YOU'RE FINISHED, TYPE F
WHICH? C
TESTING-- BALANCE= 1.25
TESTING-- USER'S CHOICE=C

BREAK IN LINE 158
```

Now that we know the first part of the selection process is getting proper values, we can go on to make sure that each of the selections is made properly.

The difference between STOP and END

A STOP statement may appear anywhere in your program (except as the last line). An END statement must occur as the last line. Essentially the END is used by the system to tell how long your program is. A STOP just means to quit running. Most systems print some sort of message when a STOP is encountered, but not when END is encountered in running the program.

In standard BASIC there may be any number of STOPs in a program, but only one END.

Try these two programs.

```
10    STOP
99    END
RUN
BREAK IN LINE 10
READY
```

```
99    END
RUN
READY
```

We remove the STOP statement and run the program again. We'll run it three times, once specifying C, once D, and once F. We know by looking at our plan that in each case a specific thing should be printed which we can use to check that the program gets to the right place.

```
RUN
WHAT'S YOUR STARTING BALANCE? 1.25
TO ENTER A CHECK,    TYPE C
TO ENTER A DEPOSIT, TYPE D
IF YOU'RE FINISHED, TYPE F
WHICH? C
TESTING-- BALANCE= 1.25
TESTING-- USER'S CHOICE=C
AMOUNT OF CHECK: $?
```

At this point we can see that the check option is being chosen properly, so we type in any old number, hit return, and wait to see if the program completes the loop and gets back up to the top of the running-balance loop.

```
TO ENTER A CHECK,    TYPE C
TO ENTER A DEPOSIT, TYPE D
IF YOU'RE FINISHED, TYPE F
WHICH?
```

And it does, so we try the next option.

```
WHICH? D
TESTING-- BALANCE= 2.76
TESTING-- USER'S CHOICE=D
YOUR NEW BALANCE IS $ 2.76
TO ENTER A CHECK,    TYPE C
TO ENTER A DEPOSIT, TYPE D
IF YOU'RE FINISHED, TYPE F
WHICH?
```

we typed D for "Deposit", but our program gives the Finished option message!

Well! Obviously, something is seriously wrong here. We expected to see the line

```
AMOUNT OF DEPOSIT: $?
```

at this point, but instead, somehow our program got to the finish option. And more, instead of finishing like our plan says, it went back to the top of the loop.

Check the program with the **plan.** They should match up.

Since we've taken care to start testing crucial parts first, we know that the problem isn't that our program is getting the user's response wrong. Our testing print shows us that the user's response (stored in string variable A$) is D. And, looking at our plan, we know that's supposed to select the deposit option. So there must be something wrong in the program somewhere after the top of the loop. It can only be in some part of the selection process. Looking at the program listing, we see that lines 170, 300, and 510 implement the selection of the option. Something must be wrong with one of those. Look at the listing of the initial, "buggy" version of the checkbook-balancing program and see if you can tell what the problem is, and why it would cause the behavior we saw. (If you can't find it, look at the answer to Exercise 7 at the end of this section.)

Once we're certain the selection of options works right, we can begin testing the options themselves.

It won't hurt anything to leave our debugging PRINT statements in place until we're completely done, especially since that way we can see if the balance is being maintained properly by the check and deposit options. Let's begin with the check option. First, we made up some data simple enough that we could tell what the right answer should be. (See Figure 4 5 2.)

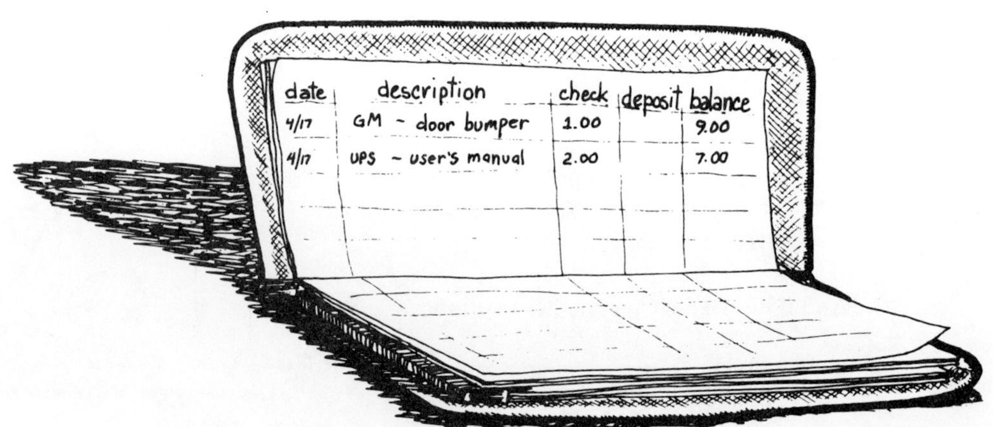

Figure 4 5 2 Test data for the check option

```
RUN
WHAT'S YOUR STARTING BALANCE? 10.00
TO ENTER A CHECK,    TYPE C
TO ENTER A DEPOSIT, TYPE D
IF YOU'RE FINISHED, TYPE F
WHICH? C
TESTING-- BALANCE= 10
TESTING-- USER'S CHOICE=C
AMOUNT OF CHECK: $? 1.00
TO ENTER A CHECK,    TYPE C
TO ENTER A DEPOSIT, TYPE D
IF YOU'RE FINISHED, TYPE F
WHICH? C
TESTING-- BALANCE= 11 <-------- ooops!
TESTING-- USER'S CHOICE=C
```

Obviously, there are still problems with our program! If our starting balance is $10.00 and we cash a check for $1.00, the current balance should be $9.00, not $11.00! But the problem is easy to find. We know that the selection process is working right, so it can't be that we're getting into the deposit option. We know we're actually in the check option.

There must be something wrong in the region of our program from line 180 through line 210. By testing things in an orderly way, we've reduced the area we have to look through to find the bug.

> Apply the **scientific method.** Formulate a hypothesis about what might be wrong, and design tests to check the hypothesis. Keep notes on which hypotheses you've checked.

After fixing the bug in the check option (exercise 8), we continue with the testing process, making sure each option works in isolation. The data shown in Figure 4 5 3 serves to test the deposit option. Once we've made sure that each option works in isolation, we can test a full-fledged case involving all the options in conjunction (i.e., use some test data involving both checks and deposits) to make sure

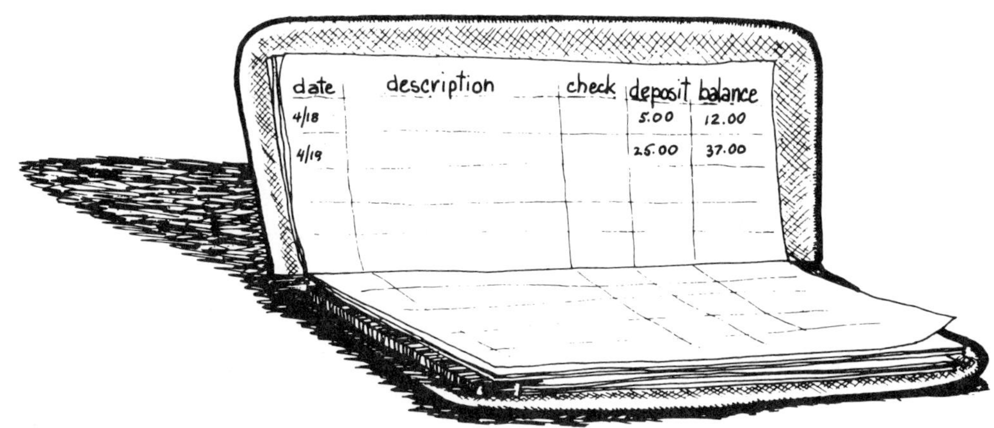

Figure 4 5 3 Test data for deposit option

that the interaction among subparts works properly. Only after having tested every aspect of the program do we feel confident enough to proclaim it ready for use.

In this particular case, by being patient and testing our program in an orderly way, we found our errors without much effort. We were fortunate—our plan was sound, and our mistakes were really minor ones. If we had discovered that our *plan* was at fault, we would have had to rethink it before continuing to test our program.

In harder cases, with large programs, it's not always so easy. You need to become a bit of a Sherlock Holmes, making and testing hypotheses, doing experiments on your program to determine what's going wrong. If you keep your plan by your side, and think in terms of it instead of in terms of the BASIC statements in your program, things will go more easily.

Program stubs

In more complicated programs it's common practice to write the top-level code (in this case the selection processes) and insert **stubs** for the detailed parts. A **stub** is extremely simplified program subpart. One common type of stub consists of a set of PRINT statements which tell the person doing the testing where in the program the computer has gotten to, and what the values of important variables are at that point. This way, the programmer can concentrate on one portion of the program, code it, make sure it works, and then go on to the next portion. Using this sort of top-down iterative coding and testing, programmers can code and test large programs without getting lost in a maze of details.

The key to successful debugging is to know exactly what each part of your program is *supposed* to be doing. You can know that only if you have a well-thought-out, clearly described plan before you start entering lines of BASIC.

The computer is a "great humbler." It seems that no matter how careful you are, there will always be bugs in your programs. Learning to avoid them requires great patience and great self-control. Like a master craftsman, a good programmer produces well-thought-out, finely finshed work.

EXERCISES 4 5

1 What is meant by the phrase, "The program shows improper behavior"?

2 What is a "debugging PRINT statement"?

3 Why should you use the scientific method to locate the more difficult errors?

4 Why doesn't the computer give an error message when you misspell a variable name?

5 Is there ever any need to refer to the plan after the coding is done?

6 It might help the user if the computer printed out the amount of each check and deposit so they could be checked for correctness. What needs to be added to the program to do this?

Printing everything the user types is called **echo printing** or **mirror printing.** It is almost always a good idea.

7 The first bug we found in the checkbook program was in the selection process. Which line is in error in the program in Figure 4 5 1, and what's the correct version of that line?

8 The second bug we found was in the check option. Which line is in error in Figure 4 5 1, and what's the correct version of it?

Section 4 6

Politeness

Programmers are not hired to write programs just for their own amusement. Almost always major programs will be used by people (users) who know less about computers than you do, and who *certainly* know less about your program than you do. Even if you do happen to write a program which only you will use, you will know much more about it at the time you write and debug it than you will a few months later when you want to use it again. After you've solved the hard parts of a program, and have it debugged—but before you forget the details of how it works—it's not a bad idea to go back over your program, adding explanatory REMarks and messages to the user, adding little touches to make it easier to use, more forgiving of user errors, that is to say, more **polite.** You've already done all these things, of course, but it doesn't hurt to add things you notice in a final pass.

Polite programming

Other common terms referring to what we call **politeness** in programming are

user-friendly

human engineered

fail-soft

error tolerant

Let's make another pass over our checkbook-balancing program to see if we can make it more polite to the person using it. To get started, we'll just look at the output our program produces, seeing if it could be more self-explanatory or easier to read.

It strikes us that the program's ouput is all crammed together, and that it's not easy to tell at a glance which lines really go together as part of one transaction. That's reasonably easy to solve—if each time our program is at the top of the loop it would print a blank line, each transaction would be separated from the next. We decide to enter

```
105          PRINT
```

to do the job.

Now that we think of it, our program seems to produce an awful lot of output. Lines 110 through 140 print four lines of output just to get one letter from the user. On the other hand, those lines do keep the user from forgetting what to do. On a video terminal it's probably OK to keep reprinting the instructions every time through the loop, especially since the user can see only the most recently printed lines. On a slow, hard-copy terminal it would probably be better to move the PRINT statements in lines 110, 120, and 130 out of the loop—to print them just once when the program is getting started. If the user forgets what to type when he or she is finished, it's still there on paper to look at.

There is a more serious breach of politeness in our program as it stands. What if someone accidentally, not paying close attention, types CHECK or CH instead of C? The test in line 170 will fail, sending the program to line 300. The test in line 300 fails, sending the machine to line 400—where there's no test. We assumed that if the user didn't type C or D, he or she must have typed F. Experience proves otherwise. Sooner or later, some users are bound to make a mistake. And if they do, our program behaves most confusingly. It prints a message about YOUR NEW BALANCE and then goes back to the top of the loop.

```
RUN
WHAT'S YOUR STARTING BALANCE? 10.00

TO ENTER A CHECK,    TYPE C
TO ENTER A DEPOSIT,  TYPE D
IF YOU'RE FINISHED,  TYPE F
WHICH? CHEQUE
YOUR NEW BALANCE IS $ 10

TO ENTER A CHECK,    TYPE C
TO ENTER A DEPOSIT,  TYPE D
IF YOU'RE FINISHED,  TYPE F
WHICH? WHAT ABOUT MY CHECK????
YOUR NEW BALANCE IS $ 10
          .
          .
          .
```

It would be more polite if the program would print a message telling the user it hasn't understood the input. Changing the plan and the program to issue this message is not difficult. We're not making any deep change in how our program works, just refining the way it interacts with the user. Of course, we will want to note the changes on our plans as well as making them in the program. We want to keep the plan as a permanent record of what the program does.

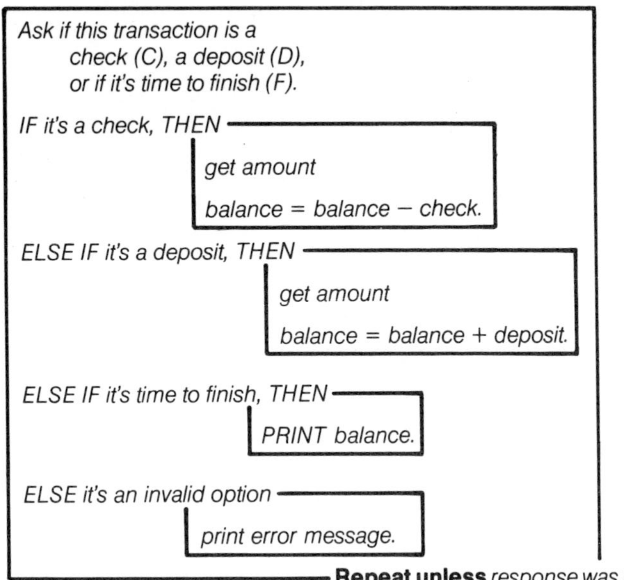

Get old balance.
Ask if this transaction is a
check (C), a deposit (D),
or if it's time to finish (F).
IF it's a check, THEN
get amount
balance = balance − check.
ELSE IF it's a deposit, THEN
get amount
balance = balance + deposit.
ELSE IF it's time to finish, THEN
PRINT balance.
ELSE it's an invalid option
print error message.
Repeat unless response was F

The program doesn't change much. To implement the extra option in the selection (the error option), we simply expand line 400. Now, instead of assuming the answer was F, the program will test for it. If it is F, take the finished option. If not, take the error option.

```
400          IF A$<> "F" THEN 450
410 REM        FINISHED
420            PRINT "YOUR NEW BALANCE IS $"; B
430            GO TO 500
450 REM        ERROR-- GIVE USER ANOTHER CHANCE
460            PRINT "SORRY, BUT "; A$; " ISN'T AN OPTION."
470            PRINT "PLEASE TRY AGAIN."
```

The rest of the program stays exactly the same.

EXERCISES 4 6

1 Why should you try to be polite to the user? Why not just depend on the user to keep things straight and figure out what to do?

2 Why should you look for places which need additional annotation via REMarks on a final pass through the program? Why aren't all the necessary REMarks there already?

3 What happens if the user types a negative number for a check or deposit? How can this be fixed?

4 Improve the politeness of the solution program Exercise 3 5 5.

5 Comment on the politeness of the system you run BASIC on. Do you feel it treats you politely? If not, in what way is it impolite?

Section 4 7
Portability

The computer system you're using right now will be obsolete within 5 years. Most major programs outlive the computer systems on which they were "born." Programs which are shared with or sold to other groups of users will face a variety of computer system environments.

A program that can be transferred to a wide variety of different computer systems with a minimum of effort is said to be **portable.** It takes extra effort to write portable programs.

The first two parts of this book emphasize a standardized form of BASIC, specifically, **ANSI Minimal BASIC.** (ANSI stands for American National Standards Institute. Minimal BASIC was defined by their Technical Committee X3J2 and adopted by ANSI in 1978. The language is described in the document *American National Standard for the Programming Language Minimal BASIC,* X3.60-1978, available from ANSI, 1430 Broadway, New York, NY.) The advantage of using a standard form of BASIC is that your programs will work properly on any computer system which provides a standard BASIC language processor, no matter what brand the computer is, no matter what the type of terminal, no matter where in the world your program is sent.

Not all computer systems provide a version of BASIC which conforms to the standard, but most do, and the number that don't is decreasing.

Some programmers don't like to write portable program because often it's a little extra work to express your plan in standard BASIC instead of using the fancy special statements most manufacturers provide with their versions of BASIC. You seldom get much help from the manufacturer's literature or manuals for your system either. Manufacturers aren't especially motivated to encourage program portability. After all, if your major programs are written in standardized languages, that is, if they are portable, then you're not locked in to any one type of equipment.

There is a fast-growing market in BASIC programs written for use by computer hobbyists and people with home computers. After you've finished this book, you will be able to write programs for sale to such groups. And programs written in standard BASIC will be usable by the widest range of people.

The *ideas* and programming *techniques* we cover in this book are applicable to any form of BASIC, but all the specific statements we show and use are standard ones. If you stick to the forms we show, you'll be in a good position in the future.

You may have discovered by now that on your system you don't face all the restrictions we've listed. Perhaps you've tried something, or forgotten something, and your program worked OK. We'll list some things here to make sure you know what we're talking about.

you may have noticed that on your system	*but in standard Minimal Basic*
it doesn't matter if your program has an END statement in it	the last line of a program must be an END
100L ETA = 40 works just as well as 100 LET A = 40	there may be no spaces within keywords or numbers, and keywords must be surrounded by spaces
string variable names like N1$ and V9$ work all right	string variable names consist of a single letter followed by a $
numeric variable names like NA, ST, or VQ work all right	numeric variable names consist of a single letter followed by nothing, or followed by one digit
IF X >0 GO TO 200 works the same as If X >0 THEN 200	only the second form is legal
IF A$ = "YES" THEN PRINT "OK" works the way it looks it should	the only thing that may follow the THEN is a line number

All the legal forms of ANSI Minimal BASIC are given in the MiniManual at the back of the book (Appendix C). If you're in some doubt about a particular construct, look it up.

EXERCISES 4 7

1 What is the name of the language the book emphasizes?

2 Why should a business which owns its own machine be interested in portable programs?

3 Find a feature available on your BASIC system which is not included in Minimal BASIC. (Start with the list above. Use the MiniManual as a reference for what is included in Minimal Basic.)

PROBLEMS 4

1 Design, write, and RUN a program which asks the user for a year, and then tells whether that year was (or will be) a leap year.

Although this won't be a lengthy program, it will require you to make a careful plan to express the necessary selection in a clear, correct manner, Here are the rules for leap years: If a year is evenly divisible by 4, then it's a leap year unless it's divisible by 100. If it's evenly divisible 100, it's *not* a leap year unless it's evenly divisible by 400, in which case it *is* a leap year. For example, 1984 is a leap year; 1900 was not a leap year; 2000 will be a leap year.

2 Design a program which presents clear instructions and then accepts either some number of inches or some number of centimeters. If the value was in inches, convert it to the equivalent number of centimeters, and vice versa.

3 Design a program which accepts measurements in sixteenths of an inch. Allow the user to enter as many measurements as he or she cares to, and keep printing the running sum. Print the sum with the fractional part a proper fraction of sixteenths. Use the format shown below, or devise a more polite one of your own.
Sample run:

```
START ENTERING MEASUREMENTS: INCHES, SIXTEENTHS
THIS TERM? 3, 3
SUM SO FAR IS 3 AND 3/16 INCHES.
MORE? Y
THIS TERM? 2, 1
SUM SO FAR IS 5 AND 4/16 INCHES.
MORE? Y
      .
      .
      .
```

4 Revise your solution to Problem 3 to make it print the fractional parts of an inch over the lowest common denominator. For instance, the second sum in the sample run should now print like this:

```
SUM SO FAR IS 5 AND 1/4 INCHES.
```

If your plan and program for Problem 3 are done properly, this change should affect only a small portion of each.

5 Alter the checkbook-balancing program in two ways. First, ask the user if he or she wants to see the running balance. If so, after each check or deposit is dealt with, have the program print the current value of B (with an appropriate message, of course).

Second, ask the user if there is a service charge on each check cashed, and if so, how much. Then, when your program handles a check, subtract both the amount of the check and the service charge from the current balance.

6 There must be a conspiracy: An even number of LP records never seems to fit on a tape no matter what length tape we buy. However, tha label on most LPs tells how long each cut is. "Song for My Father," by the Horace Silver Quintet, is 7:15—that is, seven minutes and 15 seconds long.

Design a program which a person could use to choose which cuts to put on a tape to most nearly fill it. Spend some time deciding what the most convenient-to-use program should do. Perhaps you will want to simply accept cut lengths and tell the user how much time they take up so far. Perhaps you will prefer a more elaborate strategy in which your program asks for the length of tape (in minutes), and prints the time remaining after each entry.

Remember: the next time after 7:59 is 8:00; and there is usually about a 5-second gap between cuts.

7 Design a program which could be left running all day at a golf course, and which will compute the handicap for any golfer who cares to type in the necessary data. Here are the rules for computing a golfer's handicap, according the USGA manual.

if the golfer has played this many games	*choose the best scores—this column tells how many to choose*
5	1
6	2
7	3
8 or 9	4
10 or 11	5
12 or 13	6
14 or 15	7
16 or 17	8
18 or 19	9
20 or over	choose the best 10 of the last 20

Now take the average of however many scores you selected (have the user tell your program how many games he or she has played; your program should then ask for the appropriate number of the best scores). Next, subtract the official course rating (this is listed on the score card of the course being played—get it from the user for each score). Next, multiply by 96%, and round the result to a whole number. The result is the player's handicap.

8 In Section 3 5 we developed a program for use in a border-town store. Go over that program very carefully, looking for ways to make it more polite and easier to use. Make at least these two improvements:

Guarantee that if the user types in PESOS, something reasonable happens (it doesn't as the program stands!).

Have the program round the converted figure to an even number of centavos or cents.

9 Design a program a person could use to estimate how much her car will cost her per year for the next five years. Ask for such items as original cost, miles driven per year, average gas mileage, and yearly cost of license and insurance. Assume that each year the car drops to 80% of its last year's value. Count the drop in value as a cost of owning the car. Assume the maintenance costs start at $100 a year and increase by 50% a year. Assume the price of gasoline will increase each year by 10%.

10 Problem 9 won't be of much use to a person who owns a classic car—such cars tend to *increase* in value each year. Revise the program so it asks the user for his or her estimate of the percentage change in value each year—negative if it loses value, positive if it gains in value.

Some cars go up in value

11 An electric guitar whose A string is plucked puts out this signal

$$\underbrace{11\sin(2\pi \times 220t)}_{\text{fundamental}} + 3(1 + s)\sin(2\pi \times 440t) + (1/2 + s)\sin(2\pi \times 880t)$$

where $s = 1$ if the switch is set to select the pickup nearest the bridge and $s = 0$ if the other pickup is selected.

One way to make the guitar sound less "pure" is to run the signal through a fuzz box. The fuzz box works by clipping its input signal.

$$\text{fuzz output} = \begin{cases} \text{input if } |\text{input}| \leqslant F \\ +F \text{ if input} \geqslant F \\ -F \text{ if input} \leqslant -F \end{cases}$$

where F is the fuzz setting on the fuzz box.

Write a program which prints out the signal every 1.0/4400.0 of a second for a total of 1.0/110.0 of a second (two cycles of the fundamental). Run the program and draw a graph of the results for each of the four combinations of the two switch settings and the two settings of the fuzz box at $F = 11$ and $F = 15$.

12H Redo the bookplate program (Section 3 2H). Now ask the user how many bookplates he or she wants. Then tell the user how many inches of paper that will require, and about how long it will take. Ask if the user really wants that many. If so, go ahead and print them; if not, ask again how many are required.

Get the number of inches of paper and time required for each bookplate by experimenting with the earlier form of the program.

Chapter 5 **More Loops, More Selection— Building Blocks**

Section 5 1

Testing at the Top of a Loop

Up to now, we've used just two types of loops — the *repeat forever* loop (which has a GO TO statement at the bottom that sends the computer back to the top of the loop, no matter what), and the *conditional repeat* loop (which has a test at the bottom, and *repeats IF* or *unless* some condition holds).

The *conditional repeat* is called a **posttest loop** since the test which determines whether to continue the loop occurs after the body of the loop has been carried out (*post* means "after"). That's fine if you're sure the statements that make up the body of the loop should always be carried out *at least once.* That may not always be the case; therefore, **pretest loops** are often preferable (Figure 5 1 1).

We can use a pretest loop to improve our paint estimation program (Section 2 1). As it stands, the program estimates the paint required to paint a wall by computing its area. However, if there are windows in the wall, their area should be subtracted from the wall area. The loop in the plan below subtracts the window area, one window at a time, using a pretest loop which does *no* subtraction if there are no windows.

—paint estimator (subtracts for windows)—

Get width and height of wall

*area = width * height*

Ask if there are any windows.

While *there are windows*

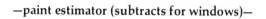

> *Get dimensions of one window*
>
> *Subtract window area from total*
>
> *Ask if there are any more windows.*

PRINT estimated amount of paint required.

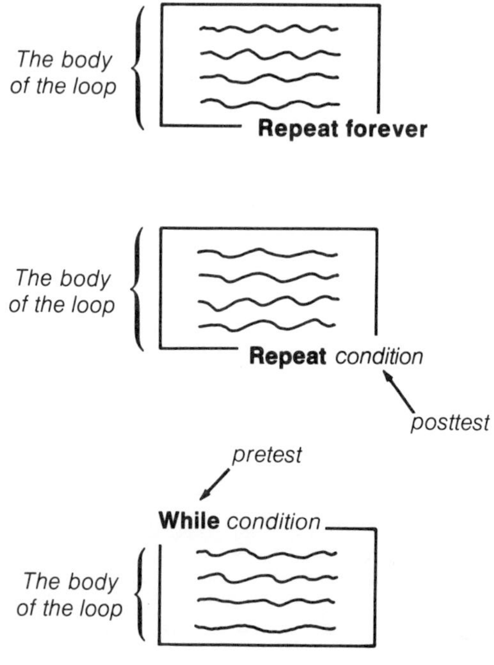

Figure 5 1 1 Types of loops

With this new sort of loop, our program will work sensibly no matter how many windows are in the wall — zero, one, two, three, or more. Here the test that determines whether the statements in the loop body are to be carried out occurs at the *top* of the loop, before the body. We'll call this pretest loop a **while loop. While** the condition is true, the statements in the body of the loop are carried out.

Here's the coded version of our plan.

be sure to find each part of the plan in the program listing

```
10  REM  HOW MUCH PAINT WILL IT TAKE FOR A WALL
20  REM  WITH WINDOWS IN IT?
30  REM  IT TAKES ABOUT 1 GALLON FOR 400 SQ. FT.
40       LET F = 400
50  REM  FIRST, GET WALL DIMENSIONS.
60       PRINT "WHAT'S THE WIDTH OF THE WALL";
70       INPUT W
80       PRINT "AND HOW HIGH IS IT";
90       INPUT H
100      LET A = W*H
110 REM  BUT OF COURSE YOU DON'T PAINT OVER WINDOWS.
120      PRINT "DOES THIS WALL HAVE ANY WINDOWS";
130      INPUT A$
200 REM  AS LONG AS THE USER DOESN'T ANSWER "N" OR "NO",
210 REM  CARRY OUT THE LOOP.  I.E., WHILE THERE ARE
```

```
220 REM  WINDOWS TO BE DEALT WITH, CARRY OUT THE LOOP.
230      IF A$="N"  THEN 500
240      IF A$="NO" THEN 500
250          PRINT "WHAT'S THE WIDTH OF THIS WINDOW";
260          INPUT W
270          PRINT "AND ITS HEIGHT";
280          INPUT H
290 REM      REDUCE THE AREA TO BE PAINTED BY WINDOW AREA
300          LET A = A - W*H
310          PRINT "ANY MORE WINDOWS";
320          INPUT A$
330          GO TO 200
500 REM  NOW WE KNOW THE AREA TO BE PAINTED, SO
510      PRINT
520      PRINT "YOU'LL NEED ABOUT"; A/F; "GALLONS OF PAINT."
9999     END
RUN
WHAT'S THE WIDTH OF THE WALL? 24
AND HOW HIGH IS IT? 8
DOES THIS WALL HAVE ANY WINDOWS? YES
WHAT'S THE WIDTH OF THIS WINDOW? 2
AND ITS HEIGHT? 3
ANY MORE WINDOWS? YES
WHAT'S THE WIDTH OF THIS WINDOW? 2
AND ITS HEIGHT? 3
ANY MORE WINDOWS? NO

YOU'LL NEED ABOUT .45 GALLONS OF PAINT.
READY
```

even though it takes 2 lines to express, we think of this as "the" test that controls the loop (lines 230–240)

the "body" of the loop (lines 250–330)

A always contains the "area-so-far"

Learning to identify and use the various kinds of loops and selections is both difficult and important. The distinctions are easy to see in our plans, but harder to see in our final programs. In our actual BASIC programs, pretest loops, posttest loops, and selections are *all* carried out with combinations of IF-THEN and GO TO statements. Since the distinctions depend on the way the BASIC statements are *used*, not on the statements themselves, it's hard to tell loops from selections after the code is written (which means that mistakes are *easy* to make, unfortunately). Take care.

EXERCISES 5 1

1 What assumption did we make in the checkbook-balancing program (Chapter 4) that allowed us to use a posttest loop instead of a pretest loop? Is that reasonable?

2 If we removed lines 130 and 320 and added

```
225      INPUT A$
```

what difference would it make in the way our program interacts with the user?

3 Two of these three programs print the same things. Which two?

```
100   PRINT "X"
110   INPUT Y
120   IF Y<0 THEN 9999
130       PRINT Y
140       PRINT "X"
150       INPUT Y
160       GO TO 120
9999  END
```

```
100   PRINT "X"
110   INPUT Y
120   IF Y<0 THEN 9999
130       PRINT Y
140       GO TO 100
9999  END
```

```
100   PRINT "X"
110       INPUT Y
120       PRINT Y
130       IF Y<0 THEN 100
9999  END
```

4 What happens in the painting program if the user types NONE in response to the INPUT statement at line 130 or the one at line 320? Should this be fixed?

5 What would be the effect of changing line 300 to read like this

```
300          LET A = A - ABS(W*H)
```

?

6 Exercise 3 shows three programs, each containing a loop. Write *post* by the program(s) with posttest loops; write *pre* by the program(s) with pretest loops.

7 If we were changing the paint estimator program to allow the user to add up several walls to be painted instead of just one, should we use a pretest loop or a posttest loop?

8 Getting your first driver's license is a loop: the body of the loop consists of taking the examination; the repetition test consists of seeing if you passed. Is this a pretest or a posttest loop?

Section 5 2

Another Example

Let's look at another example of a pretest loop. In situations where the user has to enter quite a few data values, the technique of asking whether there's more data before each value becomes obnoxious. In the program in Section 5 1, since it's safe to assume that no wall has very many windows in it, we didn't put too much of a burden on the user by making him or her type YES to get the program to accept the dimensions of each window. In other situations it is more polite to have the program make a multiple use of the data values the user enters. If the value is in one range, it's treated as a legitimate entry. If it's in another range, it's treated as a signal to stop the loop.

Let's develop a program which computes the user's gas mileage on a cross-country trip. To compute gas mileage, our program needs to know the distance traveled and the amount of gas used. We'll ask the user for the mileage and amount of gas purchased at each fill-up, and print the miles per gallon to that point. If the user enters a gas purchase that's less than or equal to zero gallons, our program will interpret it as a command to stop.

—running gas mileage—

Ask for the starting mileage.

Give user instructions for entering data.

While *gas purchased is greater than 0,*

> *Total gas = total gas so far + this purchase*
>
> *Get the mileage reading at this stop*
>
> *PRINT the gas mileage to this point.*

```
10  REM  RUNNING GAS MILEAGE COMPUTER
20  REM  VARIABLES--
30  REM    R0  ODOMETER READING AT START--INPUT
40  REM    R1  ODOMETER READING AT FILLUP--INPUT
50  REM    G   AMOUNT OF GAS AT FILLUP--INPUT
60  REM        (ALSO USED TO SIGNAL END OF DATA)
70  REM    T   TOTAL GAS PURCHASED
80  REM  NO GAS PURCHASED YET.
90       LET T = 0
100      PRINT "SO YOU'VE JUST COMPLETED A TRIP, EH?"
110      PRINT "I'LL FIGURE YOUR GAS MILEAGE."
120      PRINT "WHAT WAS THE MILEAGE ON YOUR CAR WHEN"
130      PRINT "YOU FILLED UP RIGHT BEFORE YOU LEFT";
140      INPUT R0
150      PRINT
200      PRINT "ALRIGHT.  TAKE YOUR RECORDS AND GIVE"
210      PRINT "ME THE AMOUNT OF GAS YOU BOUGHT AND "
220      PRINT "THE MILEAGE AT EACH STOP."
230      PRINT "I'LL SHOW YOUR CUMULATIVE MILEAGE"
240      PRINT "ASSUMING YOU FILLED UP AT EACH STOP."
250      PRINT "TO QUIT, TYPE 0 FOR THE AMOUNT OF GAS."

300 REM  WHILE THERE'S MORE DATA, KEEP PROCESSING.
310      PRINT "GALLONS OF GAS PURCHASED=";
320      INPUT G
330      IF G<=0 THEN 500
```

(program continued on page 100)

the "body" of the while loop

```
340          PRINT "MILEAGE AT THAT STOP";
350          INPUT R1
360 REM      KEEP TRACK OF TOTAL AMOUNT OF GAS.
370          LET T = T + G
380 REM      MILEAGE=(MILES DRIVEN)/(GAS USED)
390          PRINT "UP TO THAT STOP, YOU HAD GONE"; R1 - R0; "MILES,"
400          PRINT "AND HAD USED"; T; "GALLONS OF GAS."
410          PRINT "THAT GIVES"; (R1 - R0)/T; "MILES PER GALLON."
420          PRINT
430          GO TO 300
500      PRINT "BYE"
9999     END

RUN
SO YOU'VE JUST COMPLETED A TRIP, EH?
I'LL FIGURE YOUR GAS MILEAGE.
WHAT WAS THE MILEAGE ON YOUR CAR WHEN
YOU FILLED UP RIGHT BEFORE YOU LEFT? 79008.7

ALRIGHT.  TAKE YOUR RECORDS AND GIVE
ME THE AMOUNT OF GAS YOU BOUGHT AND
THE MILEAGE AT EACH STOP.
I'LL SHOW YOUR CUMULATIVE MILEAGE
ASSUMING YOU FILLED UP AT EACH STOP.
TO QUIT, TYPE 0 FOR THE AMOUNT OF GAS.
GALLONS OF GAS PURCHASED=? 7.3
MILEAGE AT THAT STOP? 79169.8
UP TO THAT STOP, YOU HAD GONE 161.094 MILES,
AND HAD USED 7.3 GALLONS OF GAS.
THAT GIVES 22.0676 MILES PER GALLON.

GALLONS OF GAS PURCHASED=? 6.4
MILEAGE AT THAT STOP? 79320.2
UP TO THAT STOP, YOU HAD GONE 311.5 MILES,
AND HAD USED 13.7 GALLONS OF GAS.
THAT GIVES 22.7372 MILES PER GALLON.

GALLONS OF GAS PURCHASED=? 8.0
MILEAGE AT THAT STOP? 79485
UP TO THAT STOP, YOU HAD GONE 476.297 MILES,
AND HAD USED 21.7 GALLONS OF GAS.
THAT GIVES 21.9492 MILES PER GALLON.

GALLONS OF GAS PURCHASED=? 6.1
MILEAGE AT THAT STOP? 79625.0
UP TO THAT STOP, YOU HAD GONE 616.297 MILES,
AND HAD USED 27.8 GALLONS OF GAS.
THAT GIVES 22.169 MILES PER GALLON.

GALLONS OF GAS PURCHASED=? 0
BYE
READY
```

EXERCISES 5 2

1 What would have to be changed in our program to avoid printing all the intermediate mileage figures and just print the overall mileage at the end?

2 What lines in the program correspond to "get the mileage reading at this stop" in the plan?

3 What lines in the program correspond to "give instructions" in the plan?

4 Write a plan for a program which gets three strings from the user (possibly the name, address, and city/state/zip for a mailing label), then asks the user how many copies of the strings to print and prints them as many times as indicated. (Hint: Use the "repeat task R times" program from Section 3 4.)

5 Make a plan for a program which computes batting averages. Ask the user how many times at bat in the game and how many hits. Allow the user to cover as many games as necessary, and print the overall batting average after each game.

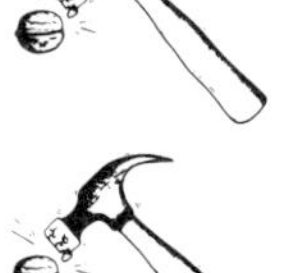

6 Modify the plan in exercise 4 to ask the user how many blank lines to put between the listings (0, 1, 2, . . .), then print the listings with that much space between each copy.

7 How could you modify the gas mileage program to print the one-tankful mileage at each stop instead of the cumulative mileage?

Section 5 3

Another Kind of Selection—ON-GO TO

When a selection must be made among more than two alternatives, you can always use a sequence of IF-THEN statements to carry it out. However, when a complicated multiple-path selection is done this way, the resulting maze of possible paths through the program is sometimes hard to follow and is prone to programmer error. When each option can be associated with a number, there is a statement in BASIC which allows us to express the selection very simply and clearly. Let's look at an example.

Suppose you are asked to compile some statistics on pay rates in a small company. You are given each employee's rate of pay, and you want a profile of the wages. That is, you'd like to know how many employees make between $2 and $3 an hour, how many make between $3 and $4 per hour, and so on, up through the maximum range of $6 to $7.

Our plan is to write a program which accepts each employee's rate of pay, one at a time. We'll use a variable to count the number of employees in each pay range, adding one to the appropriate variable for each pay rate the program gets. The key to our solution is being able to select the variable, given each pay rate. Here's our plan.

—pay rate statistics—

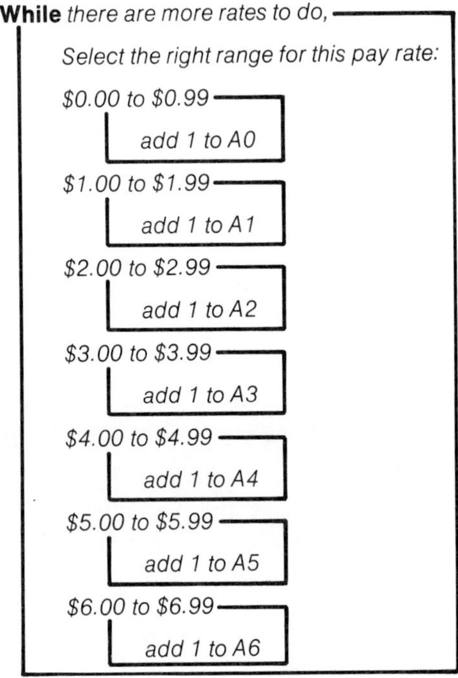

Set each counter variable to 0.
While there are more rates to do,
Select the right range for this pay rate:
$0.00 to $0.99
add 1 to A0
$1.00 to $1.99
add 1 to A1
$2.00 to $2.99
add 1 to A2
$3.00 to $3.99
add 1 to A3
$4.00 to $4.99
add 1 to A4
$5.00 to $5.99
add 1 to A5
$6.00 to $6.99
add 1 to A6
PRINT the number of employees in each range.
PRINT the total number of employees.

Let's concentrate on the selection process. If the pay rate the user enters is between 0.00 and 0.99, we want to add one to counter variable A0, to indicate that the program has just seen one more employee whose pay is in that range. If the pay rate is from 1.00 to 1.99, we want to add one to A1, and so on. The way we'll make the selection involves two steps. First, we'll convert the pay rate into a whole number: the number 1 if the pay rate is from 0.00 to 0.99; the number 2 if the pay rate is from 1.00 to 1.99; and so on. Then, we'll use that whole number along with a new BASIC statement (the ON-GO TO) to select the proper part of the program.

We've done things like the first step a number of times already. To convert all the numbers from 0.00 to 0.99 to the number 1, and all the numbers from 1.00 to 1.99 to the number 2, and so on, we can use an assignment statement like this:

```
290          LET P = INT(P) + 1
```

To make the actual selection, we can use an ON-GO TO statement like this:

```
300          ON P GO TO 400, 500, 600, 700, 800, 900, 1000
```

The statement means, "GO TO one of the listed line numbers, depending on the value stored in P. If P is 1, GO TO the first line number in the list (400); if P is 2, GO TO the second line number in the list (500); etc."

We could have gotten the same effect by using seven IF-THEN statements, like this:

```
300          IF P=1 THEN 400
301          IF P=2 THEN 500
302          IF P=3 THEN 600
                  .
                  .
                  .
307          IF P=7 THEN 1000
```

We think you'll agree that the ON-GO TO statement is cleaner (besides being much shorter to type).

As you go through our finished program, make sure you understand all the details of how the selection works. Go through a few test cases by hand to make sure you see how it works.

```
10   REM  PAY RATE STATISTICS
20   REM  TABULATE NUMBER OF EMPLOYEES IN
30   REM  EACH RATE CATEGORY.
40        PRINT "GREETINGS"
50        PRINT "I WILL COUNT THE NUMBER OF "
60        PRINT "EMPLOYEES IN EACH PAY CATEGORY"
70        PRINT "FROM $0.00 TO $0.99, $1.00 TO $1.99"
80        PRINT "UP THROUGH $6.00 TO $6.99"
90        PRINT
100       PRINT "ENTER THE HOURLY PAY OF EACH EMPLOYEE."
110       PRINT "WHEN YOU'RE THROUGH, ENTER A 'PAY' LESS"
120       PRINT "THAN 0 AND I'LL GIVE YOU THE SUMMARY."
130       LET A0 = 0
140       LET A1 = 0
150       LET A2 = 0
160       LET A3 = 0
170       LET A4 = 0
180       LET A5 = 0
190       LET A6 = 0
200  REM  AS LONG AS THE USER KEEPS GIVING PAY VALUES,
210  REM  CONTINUE THE LOOP.
220       PRINT
230       PRINT "PAY RATE=$";
240       INPUT P
250       IF P<0 THEN 2000
260       IF P>=7 THEN 2000
270  REM  CONVERT RAW PAY RATE INTO AN INTEGER
280  REM  FROM 1 (FOR $0.00 TO $0.99) TO 7
290           LET P = INT(P) + 1
300           ON P GO TO 400, 500, 600, 700, 800, 900, 1000
400  REM        RATE IS FROM $0.00 TO $0.99
410             LET A0 = A0 + 1
420             GO TO 1500
```

we think of this as "the" test at the top of the loop

(program continued)

```
500  REM        RATE IS FROM $1.00 TO $1.99
510             LET A1 = A1 + 1
520             GO TO 1500
600  REM        RATE IS FROM $2.00 TO $2.99
610             LET A2 = A2 + 1
620             GO TO 1500
700  REM        RATE IS FROM $3.00 TO $3.99
710             LET A3 = A3 + 1
720             GO TO 1500
800  REM        RATE IS FROM $4.00 TO $4.99
810             LET A4 = A4 + 1
820             GO TO 1500
900  REM        RATE IS FROM $5.00 TO $5.99
910             LET A5 = A5 + 1
920             GO TO 1500
1000 REM        RATE IS FROM $6.00 TO $6.99
1010            LET A6 = A6 + 1
1020            GO TO 1500
1500 REM      BOTTOM OF LOOP
1510          GO TO 200
2000 REM  DONE--GIVE SUMMARY
2010      PRINT
2020      PRINT "RATE RANGE   NUMBER"
2030      PRINT "----------   ------"
2040      PRINT "$0.00-$0.99   "; A0
2050      PRINT "$1.00-$1.99   "; A1
2060      PRINT "$2.00-$2.99   "; A2
2070      PRINT "$3.00-$3.99   "; A3
2080      PRINT "$4.00-$4.99   "; A4
2090      PRINT "$5.00-$5.99   "; A5
2100      PRINT "$6.00-$6.99   "; A6
2110      PRINT
2120      LET E = A0 + A1 + A2 + A3 + A4 + A5 + A6
2130      PRINT "# OF EMPLOYEES ="; E
9999      END
RUN
GREETINGS
I WILL COUNT THE NUMBER OF
EMPLOYEES IN EACH PAY CATEGORY
FROM $0.00 TO $0.99, $1.00 TO $1.99
UP THROUGH $6.00 TO $6.99

ENTER THE HOURLY PAY OF EACH EMPLOYEE.
WHEN YOU'RE THROUGH, ENTER A 'PAY' LESS
THAN 0 AND I'LL GIVE YOU THE SUMMARY.

PAY RATE=$? 3.35

PAY RATE=$? 4.70

PAY RATE=$? 5.10

PAY RATE=$? 4.33
```

```
PAY RATE=$? 4.33

PAY RATE=$? 2.53

PAY RATE=$? -1 ←— we're done

RATE RANGE    NUMBER
-----------   ------
$0.00-$0.99     0
$1.00-$1.99     0
$2.00-$2.99     1
$3.00-$3.99     1
$4.00-$4.99     3
$5.00-$5.99     1
$6.00-$6.99     0

# OF EMPLOYEES = 6
READY
```

EXERCISES 5 3

1 What part of the program corresponds to the selection of the appropriate range?

2 What would the pay rate summary program do (incorrectly) if we'd accidentally left out line 720?

3 Write an ON-GO TO statement to select line 100 if K is 1, 3, or 5 and line 200 if K is 2, 4, or 6.

4 Write an ON-GO TO statement to select line 100 if J is between 3 and 6, line 200 if J is 1, and line 100 if J is 2.

Section 5 4

Formalities About the ON-GO TO

The ON-GO TO statement has this form:

ON *numeric expression* GO TO *list of line numbers*

The numeric expression is evaluated and, if necessary, rounded to the nearest whole number. The computer transfers to one of the line numbers in the list. If the value of the rounded numeric expression is 1, the first line number in the list is selected; if it's 2, the second is selected; and so on.

If the (rounded) value of the expression is less than 1 or greater than the number of line numbers in the list, you get an error message. That means it's a good habit to verify that a value will be in the right range before your program carries out an ON-GO TO statement. If the number is out of range, have your program handle it in some reasonable way, possibly by printing a relevant error message. If you leave it up to the BASIC system, the program may blow up whenever the number is out of range and print some obscure, general-purpose error message.

You may put any of your program's line numbers in an ON-GO TO list, and the list may contain duplications. There is no restriction on the size of the list except that, like all Minimal BASIC statements, it must fit on one line in the program.

EXERCISES 5 4

1 What ON-GO TO statement will have the same effect as these three statements?

```
210     IF K=1 THEN 400
220     IF K=4 THEN 500
230     GO TO 600
```

Assume that the value of K will be from 1 up to 5.

2 What ON-GO TO statement will have the same effect as these statements?

```
700     IF T 5 THEN 730<
710     IF T 7 THEN 2000>
720       GO TO 1600
730     IF T=2 THEN 1400
740     GO TO 1200
```

Assume that T will have a value from 1 up to 9.

3 Use this experimental program to investigate what happens on your system when an ON-GO TO statement gets a numeric value for which there is no line number. Also, see if your system obeys the standards, and prints "SELECTION 2" when you give it values like 1.7654, 2.111, and so on.

```
10   REM  ON GO TO TESTER...
20        PRINT "OPTION #";
30        INPUT V
40        ON V GO TO 100, 200
50           PRINT "NO OPTIONS GO HERE"
60           GO TO 300
100  REM     FIRST OPTION
110          PRINT "SELECTION 1"
120          GO TO 300
200  REM     SECOND OPTION
210          PRINT "SELECTION 2"
220          GO TO 300
300  REM             REPEAT FOREVER
310                  GO TO 20
9999      END
```

Section 5 5
Sequence, Selection, Loops, and Nesting

All programs, no matter how large or small, are constructed from a small set of building blocks, using a few rules of combination. As a consequence, once you really understand looping and selection, the only thing keeping you from writing large, involved programs is finding a large, involved problem you're interested in.

In this section we'll go over the building blocks and the ways of combining them (also called **composition rules**). We have two purposes in mind. First, we want to show how larger programs are made from basic parts. Second, we want to show ways that make it easier to understand other people's programs — both the ones in this book and ones you'll come across in future programming activities.

Table 5 5 1 shows the basic building blocks of selection and looping. We've seen at least one example of each — now we want to point out ways of combining them.

	selection	*loops*
main idea	choose one thing to do instead of another (or others)	do one thing over and over
telltale signs in a BASIC program	a jump (THEN part of IF-THEN, or GO TO part of an ON-GO TO) specifies a higher-numbered line; part of the program is skipped when the jump is made	a jump (THEN part of an IF-THEN or a GO TO) specifies a lower-numbered line; you go *back* to a part of the program that's been carried out before
typical plan patterns	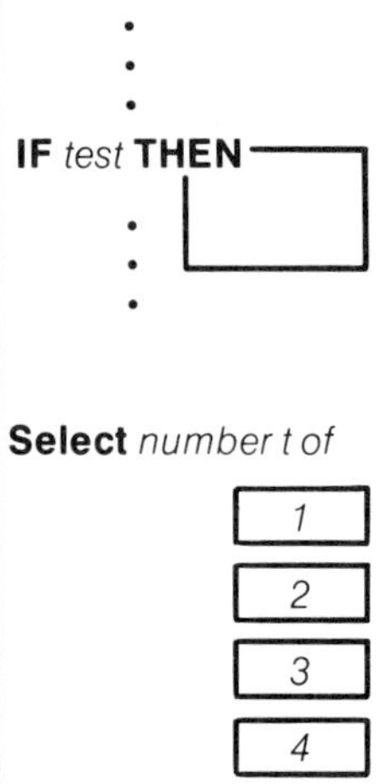 ⋮ **IF** *test* **THEN** [ ] ⋮ **Select** *number t of* [1] [2] [3] [4]	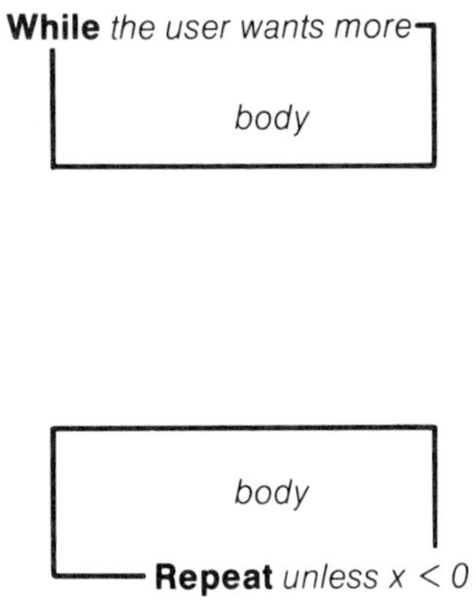 **While** *the user wants more* [*body*] [*body*] **Repeat** *unless x < 0*

Table 5 5 1 Differences Between Selection and Looping

The simplest way to make a more complex program out of two subparts is to do one part after another. We've been doing that ever since Section 1 2. This, of course, allows you to create a program which does **one thing, then another** — a **sequence** of actions. Nothing tricky here (Figure 5 5 1).

By using the selection building block, we can make a program which does **one thing instead of another** — a **selection** among alternatives. We've been doing that every since Section 3 5. Nothing tricky here (Figure 5 5 2).

By using the looping building block, we can make a program which does **something over and over — looping.** That we've been doing ever since Section 3 2. Nothing tricky here (Figure 5 5 3).

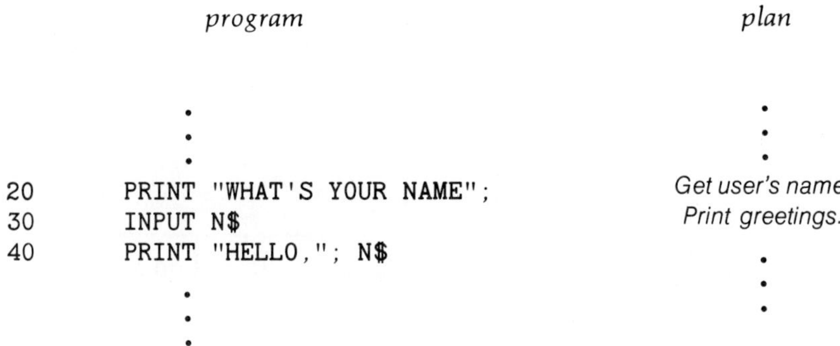

program
plan
20 PRINT "WHAT'S YOUR NAME";
30 INPUT N$
40 PRINT "HELLO,"; N$
Get user's name.
Print greetings.

Figure 5 5 1 One thing, then another — sequence

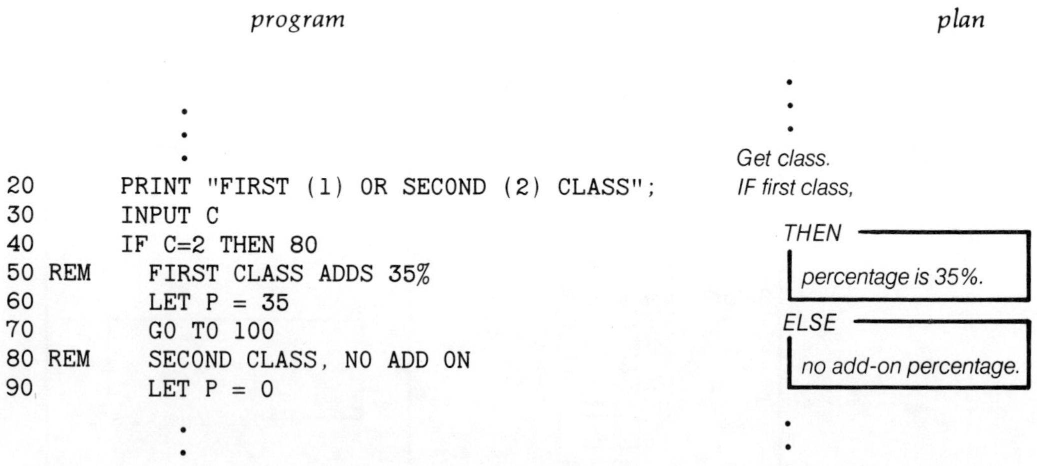

program
plan
20 PRINT "FIRST (1) OR SECOND (2) CLASS";
30 INPUT C
40 IF C=2 THEN 80
50 REM FIRST CLASS ADDS 35%
60 LET P = 35
70 GO TO 100
80 REM SECOND CLASS, NO ADD ON
90 LET P = 0
Get class.
IF first class,
THEN
percentage is 35%.
ELSE
no add-on percentage.

Figure 5 5 2 One thing instead of another — selection

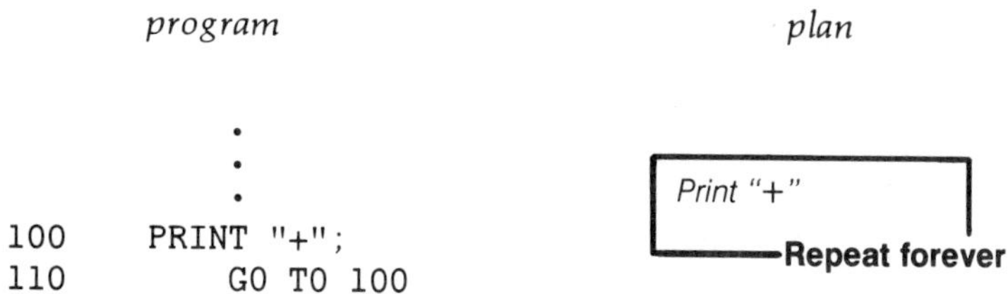

Figure 5 5 3 Do something over and over — looping

If anything is tricky at all here, it's in realizing the full implications of this: Each of the "things" we've been talking about follows the same rules. So when we said that selection allows us to create a program which does one thing instead of another, both things can be complex combinations made from the basic building blocks. We can have selections which choose among other selections, selections which choose among different loops, loops which repeatedly carry out selections, loops that repeatedly carry out loops which carry out selections, and so on. That is, in addition to being able to do one thing then another, one thing instead of another, and something over and over, we can do **one thing inside another — nesting.**

One of our first examples of nesting came in Section 3 5 in our program that converts dollars to pesos or pesos to dollars. There we have a selection inside a *repeat forever* loop. That is, the thing that is being done over and over happens to involve a selection (Figure 5 5 4).

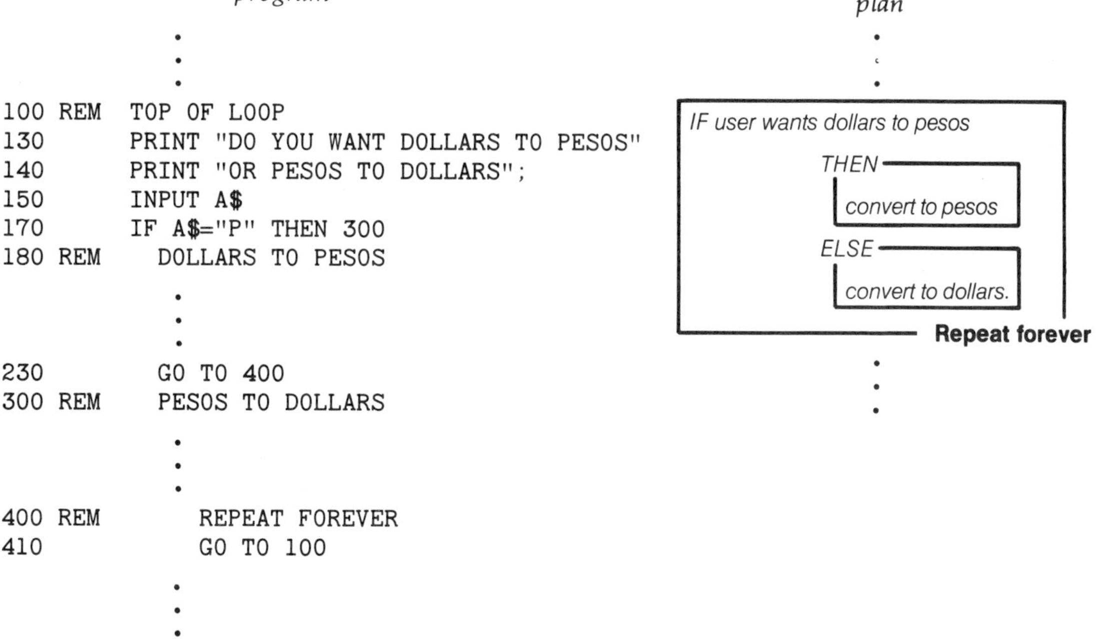

program
plan
100 REM TOP OF LOOP
130 PRINT "DO YOU WANT DOLLARS TO PESOS"
140 PRINT "OR PESOS TO DOLLARS";
150 INPUT A$
170 IF A$="P" THEN 300
180 REM DOLLARS TO PESOS
230 GO TO 400
300 REM PESOS TO DOLLARS
400 REM REPEAT FOREVER
410 GO TO 100
IF user wants dollars to pesos
THEN
convert to pesos
ELSE
convert to dollars.
Repeat forever

Figure 5 5 4 One thing inside another — nesting

EXERCISES 5 5

Each exercise below contains the skeleton of a plan. Describe the way the plan is constructed from the two building blocks (looping and selection) and the two rules of composition (sequence and nesting). For example, the skeletal plan below consists of an IF-THEN-ELSE selection nested inside an IF-THEN selection.

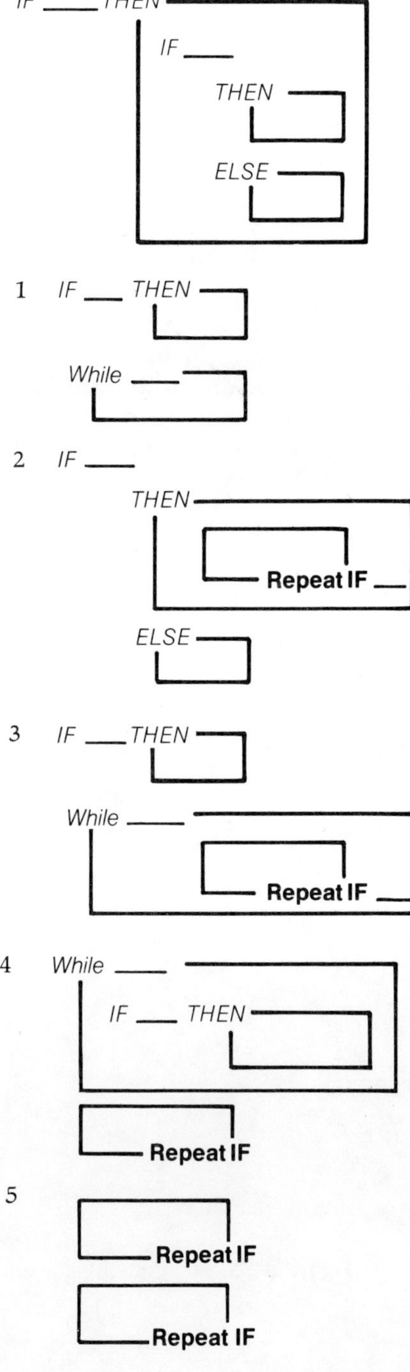

Section 5 6
Composing Programs—A Review

The key thing to learn is how to go from a problem description to a plan for solving it. That's the hardest part of programming. In order to do it, you need to know intuitively what the program structures do, and how to put them together in productive ways. Of course, it's something that takes practice — constant practice at all levels of the programming process. Look over the programs in the earlier part of this book, and study them until it's obvious how each plan fits with the problem description, and what parts of the final BASIC program correspond to what parts of the plan.

Here are some ideas that may help you focus on the creation of a plan from the description of a problem.

Ask yourself questions like this: What quantities or responses are you trying to obtain? What sort of values or user responses is the program to be given? Is there a simple mathematical or logical way to go from the inputs to the outputs? For example, if you're asked for the gas mileage, and you're given the distance traveled and the amount of gas used, then the plan must be to get the input values and combine them mathematically to get the result:

gas mileage = distance/gallons of gas

On the other hand, the quantity your program is to produce may not be so easily expressed, and it may be necessary to build it up a piece at a time. For instance, if you decide that to solve a problem, you need to compute the average of a list of numbers, then you need to know the sum of the values and how many values there are in the list. From the problem description you see that although the list of numbers will be entered into your program, neither the number of them, nor their sum is an input. So your program will have to compute them.

We can't write down a simple, fixed mathematical expression for the sum of a list of values, or for the number of values. We can, however, imagine a way to obtain those quantities, using the "something so far" method. Before our program sees *any* of the values in the list, we know that the sum so far is 0, and the number of values seen so far is 0. Each time our program receives a value, the sum so far is increased by that value, and the number of values seen so far is increased by 1.

Let *sum so far* = *sum so far* + latest value

Let *number seen so far* = *number seen so far* + 1

If we can get our program to carry out these two steps every time the user enters a value, then at the end, after the user has typed in all the values, the sum so far will be the sum of all the numbers, and the number seen so far will be the total number of values entered. And those were the exact quantities we decided our program would need to be able to compute the average.

Any time you are led to compute "something so far," you can be almost sure you will wind up with some sort of loop. Since there are only three major types of loops, it takes only a few questions to decide what type to choose. The *repeat forever* loop, obviously, is not the one to use to compute the average of a bunch of numbers — we know the user will enter a limited number of values, and the loop must terminate after the last one. To decide between a pretest loop and a posttest loop, we need to ask ourselves how the computer should interact with the user. In particular, how will the computer know when the user has entered the last value?

When your program has to get a number of values or responses from the user, there are several ways to determine when the last value has been entered. One way is to force the poor user to count how many values he or she will be entering:

```
HOW MANY WILL YOU ENTER?
```

This technique makes things easy for the programmer, but it is incredibly rude to the user. If the user has so few values to enter that it would be easy to count them, he or she would probably be computing the average by hand. The only situation we know of where it is reasonable for a program to ask how many values will be entered is when the user will be entering several lists of values, all the same length, and it would be helpful for the program to signal the user each time a list is completed. That's not the case here.

There are two reasonable methods of obtaining the list of numbers to be averaged. Either you ask the user after each number whether or not there are any more, or else you decide to use some special number (or range of numbers) as a signal that there is no more data. This second technique works fine as long as there is some range of data that you know will never come up in a legitimate computation, but in the general case of computing an average, we have to allow for any number to be input as data. We can't do as we did in the gas mileage program of Section 5 2 and use zero as a signal to stop.

That leaves the first technique — asking the user at each juncture whether there is more data. We've seen this technique used several times before. In the paint estimator program of Section 5 1, we were subtracting the area covered by the windows from the total wall area. On each iteration of the loop, we asked the user whether there were any more windows left to subtract. Since some walls have no windows, we had to write the loop so that there would be *no iterations* through the body of the loop in case the wall had no windows. This forced us to use the pretest loop because a posttest loop always goes through the body at least once.

Another place we've seen the "ask every time" technique is in the checkbook program of Chapter 4. In that program each iteration through the loop added another check or deposit into the current balance. We knew there would be at least one check or deposit to process; otherwise the user wouldn't be running the program. Relying on this knowledge of needing at least one pass through the loop, we implemented it with a posttest construction. Computing an average is a lot like the checkbook problem. We know there will be at least one number to average, so it makes sense to use a posttest loop like the one in the checkbook program. Once we have made this final decision, a plan comes easily.

The exact thought process you go through when you are composing a useful program will vary with the nature of the problem, but your general approach should always include the considerations we just went through. What kinds of constructions do you need? Loops? Selections? If loops, what kinds of loops? If selections, what are the cases?

Everyone and everything has limits. You, the programmer, can't keep every detail of the program in mind at once. The user of your finished program can't keep all the aspects of using your program in mind at once. And the computer can't perform

—computing the average—

Start counter for numbers at zero.

Sum so far is zero.

Get number.
Add to sum.
Increase count.
Ask if there are any more numbers.

Repeat IF *more*

operations with infinite precision, nor with instantaneous speed. Each of these limits affects the programming process. Write down your general plan, and then analyze the separate pieces and reduce them to programming constructions you know well and have used before. In this way you can focus on the problem at hand without worrying about an overwhelming mass of detail.

Turn back to a program earlier in the book that didn't quite make sense to you, and try to think through all the steps that we went through (but didn't write down) to get the plan. Then try the same thing on a program of your own that didn't quite make sense to you. As you go on, you'll get better and better at the process, until it becomes natural. Don't be discouraged if sometimes it seems as if we have magically gone from a problem to a plan for solving it. Even if we didn't write down all the considerations we went through, you can be *sure* we went through them. Programming isn't magic; it's hard work.

> "If a job is worth doing, it's worth doing well."
>
> *my father*

EXERCISES 5 6

1 Describe three ways of getting a list of data from the user.

2 What technique would you use to get the user to try to list the seven wonders of the world?

3 What technique would you use to get the user to enter a list of interesting Friday night TV shows?

4 Compose a plan for a program which gets a list of numbers from the user, then divides the smallest number by the largest.

Section 5 7

Reading Programs

As you become more familiar with the process of composing programs, you will begin to notice programming **idioms** — patterns of statements that express commonly occurring computations. Understanding how programs are built from these idioms will help you when you're writing your own programs. It is also of great help when you're trying to figure out someone else's program. One situation in which you have to do that is in reading this book. But here we show plans for each program, and we explain what the programs do. When you want to adapt a BASIC program from, say, a computer hobbyist magazine, or when at work you're asked to make a change to a program someone else wrote, you probably won't have so much help. Unfortunately, not all programs are written with ease of understanding in mind. Unfortunately, not all programmers provide copies of their plans. Unfortunately, programmers under time pressure sometimes leave out REMarks, thinking that they'll take time to put them in later (they usually don't). Unfortunately, some programmers never consider that other people might want to use and revise their programs, so they use idiosyncratic combinations of statements specially tailored to their computer system and their immediate needs, but which won't work in other situations. Programs like that are not easy to understand.

For practice, let's see if we can figure out a program that comes with no plans, no REMarks, and without the original programmer to tell us what the program does. Where should we begin? Let's start by skimming over the program to see if anything at all makes sense about it.

```
20  LET F = 400
30  LET A = 0
40  LET R = 1
50  PRINT "LENGTH AND WIDTH OF ROOM"; R
60      INPUT L
70      INPUT W
80      PRINT "CEILING HEIGHT";
90      INPUT H
100     LET A = A + 2*(L + W)*H
105     PRINT "ANY WINDOWS OR DOORS";
110     INPUT A$
120     IF A$="N" THEN 200
130         PRINT "HEIGHT AND WIDTH OF OPENING";
140         INPUT H
150         INPUT W
160         LET A = A - H*W
170         PRINT "ANY MORE OPENINGS";
180         GO TO 110
200     LET R = R + 1
210     PRINT "ANY MORE ROOMS";
220     INPUT A$
230     IF A$="Y" THEN 50
240 PRINT "TOTAL AREA"; A; "SQUARE FEET"
250 PRINT "YOU'LL NEED ABOUT"; A/F; "GALLONS"
9999 END
```

We begin by looking for patterns in the listing. The first thing we notice is the indentation. We're fortunate to have it. Some BASIC systems suppress the indenting, and some programmers don't use it even if they can. Without it, patterns of statements are harder to find.

From the indentation, it looks like there's some kind of pattern running from line 50 through line 230. Since line 230 contains a conditional jump back to line 50, we realize that the 50-230 pattern must be a posttest loop. On a separate piece of paper, we draw the outline of a large posttest loop. We'll fill in the details as we find them.

Now we have to figure out what's going on in the loop. To avoid distractions, we place sheets of paper over the rest of the program. Concentrating on the loop itself, we see that the program first asks the user for some information concerning the dimensions of a room (room number R, apparently). Then it computes a new value for the variable A from the user response. The formula for A adds the value 2*(L + W)*H, and we can guess from the PRINT statements that L, W, and H stand for length, width, and height. A little ingenuity leads us to the conclusion that 2*(L + W)*H is the area of the walls in a (rectangular) four-sided room. We add these discoveries to our plan sheet. Now we know that each time through the loop, the program adds the wall area of another room to A.

The next thing the program does is to ask about the existence of windows or doors, and we notice — from the indentation again — that there is some special pattern running from line 110 to line 180. The last statement in the pattern is an unconditional transfer back to the top, so it must be some kind of loop — either a *repeat forever* or a pretest loop. Looking at the top of the pattern, we see a test, so we're dealing with a pretest loop. We insert the outline of a pretest loop on our plan sheet (it now looks like Figure 5 7 1), and block the loop off on the program listing with the blank sheets of paper (Figure 5 7 2). The test at the top of the loop seems to be based on a yes/no answer to a question. After receiving anything but N, the program asks for more dimensional information (height and width), and subtracts the product from A. We conclude that it is deducting the area of the openings from the wall space in A. So at the end of the program, A will store the total wall area, less openings.

When all the openings have been deducted, the inner loop is exited, and the computer arrives at line 200, still within the outer loop. We move the blank sheets of paper to expose the outer loop, and notice that the value of R is increased by 1. That's an idiom — it's used in counting. R must be a **counter** of some sort which marks each iteration. Finally, the program asks whether there are any more rooms, and repeats the loop if there are. From the statement at the top of the loop, we can see that the variable R is being used to number (or count) the rooms; and from the rest of our analysis, we can deduce that A is being used to total the actual wall space, not including openings for windows or doors. We add these details to our developing plan.

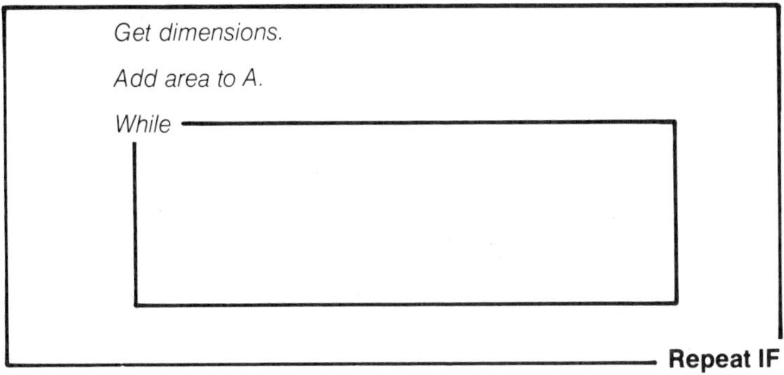

Figure 5 7 1 A partial plan for the mystery program

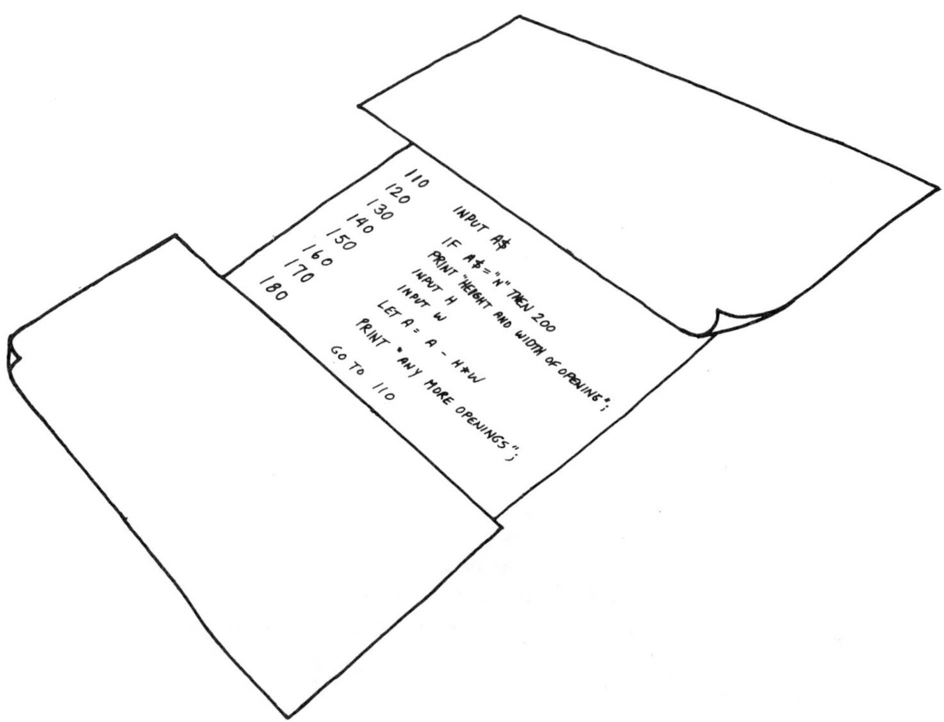

110 INPUT A$
120 IF A$="N" THEN 200
130 PRINT "HEIGHT AND WIDTH OF OPENINGS";
140 INPUT H
150 INPUT W
160 LET A = A - H*W
170 PRINT "ANY MORE OPENINGS";
180 GO TO 110

Figure 5 7 2 Using sheets of paper to concentrate on one building block at a time. Here only the while loop in the middle of the mystery program is uncovered.

The PRINT statement at 250 indicates that a quantity in gallons is being printed. This quantity is the area A divided by F. Since A/F is some number of gallons, and A is area, F must be in units of area per gallon. The program must be computing the number of gallons of some liquid (paint, disinfectant, wallpaper paste, or something) that it takes to cover the walls. The program is now fully outlined in our plan (Figure 5 7 3).

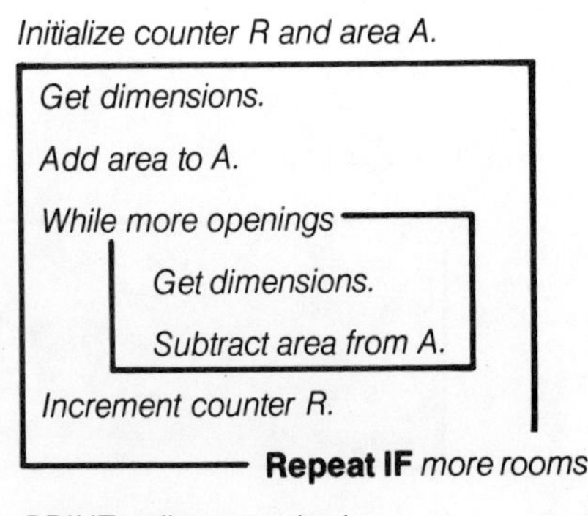

Initialize counter R and area A.
Get dimensions.
Add area to A.
While more openings
Get dimensions.
Subtract area from A.
Increment counter R.
Repeat IF more rooms
PRINT gallons required.

Figure 5 7 3 Outline of the mystery program

Assuming that the liquid is paint, we can put appropriate remarks in the program to make it easier for the next person to decipher.

```
1    REM  PAINTING A HOUSE
2    REM  ASSUMPTIONS--
3    REM     EACH ROOM IS RECTANGULAR;
4    REM     EACH WINDOW AND DOOR IS RECTANGULAR;
5    REM     THERE IS AT LEAST ONE ROOM TO BE PAINTED;
6    REM     THE WALLS ARE NORMAL, SO ONE GALLON
7    REM       COVERS 400 SQ. FT.
8    REM  VARIABLES--
9    REM     F    SQ. FT. PER GALLON OF PAINT
10   REM     A    WALL AREA TO BE PAINTED
11   REM     R    ROOM NUMBER (TO HELP USER KEEP TRACK)
12   REM     L,W,H  LENGTH, WIDTH, HEIGHT OF ROOM OR
13   REM            OPENING
```

Having new employees modify an existing program is a very common training method in computer companies. Most programmers we know were introduced to their jobs that way. The programs that new employees are given to modify tend to be horribly documented, poorly organized, and hideously obscure. We suspect it's a "sink or swim" test.

Before you can modify a program, you've got to understand roughly how the whole thing works, and you've got to understand in detail how the part you're to change works. To do that, you need to recapture the plan, decipher the structure of the program and figure out the meaning of the variables. In the example in this section, we've gone through all these steps for a very small program. Good luck when you have to do it on a three-thousand-line, undocumented program whose original author is long gone!

EXERCISES 5 7

Draw a plan and deduce the purpose of each of the program fragments below.

1

```
100 LET S = 0
110 PRINT "ANY NUMBERS";
120 INPUT A$
130 IF A$="NO" THEN 200
140 IF A$="N" THEN 200
150     INPUT N
160     LET S = S + N
170     PRINT "ANY MORE";
180     INPUT A$
190     GO TO 130
200 PRINT S
```

2

```
100 PRINT "NAME THE STATES"
110 LET S = 1
120 PRINT "STATE NUMBER"; S;
130     INPUT S$
140     LET S = S + 1
150     IF S<=50 THEN 120
```

3
```
100 PRINT "+ OR *";
110 INPUT A$
120 PRINT "OPERANDS";
130 INPUT X,Y
140 IF A$="*" THEN 170
150   LET S = X + Y
160   GO TO 200
170   LET S = X*Y
200 PRINT X; A$; Y; "="; S
```

4
```
100 PRINT "HOW MANY";
110 INPUT N
120 LET S = 0
130 LET C = 1
140 IF C>N THEN 200
150     LET S = S + C
160     LET C = C + 1
170     GO TO 140
200 LET P = 1
210 LET C = 1
220 IF C>N THEN 300
230     LET P = P/C
240     LET C = C + 1
250     GO TO 220
300 PRINT S, P
```

PROBLEMS 5

1 The board foot is a unit of volume used in lumber stores. One **board foot** is the volume of a board one inch thick, twelve inches wide, and twelve inches long. Write a program which asks for the dimensions of a piece of lumber, and which tells how many board feet that corresponds to.

2 Improve the lawn mowing time estimate program in Problem 1 9 so it would be of use to a commercial lawn mowing service. For example, they might be called on to mow a vacant low; or they might get a contract from a retirement village to mow a large area with a number of houses on it. Assume that all lots and all houses are rectangular.

3 Alter the gas mileage program (Section 5 2) so that in addition to the statistics it supplies, it also gives the miles per gallon for the most recent single tankful.

4 Write a program to help collect statistics on cars. The user sits at the terminal, looking through a window out onto a busy street. Every time a car goes by, the user types in a number indicating the manufacturer: (1) Ford, (2) General Motors, (3) Chrysler, (4) AMC, (5) German, (6) Japanese, (7) other, (8) quitting time. After quitting time, the computer prints the number of cars that were seen in each of the first seven categories.

5 Write a program which plays the old number-guessing game against the user. Here's a plan that shows the main idea.

Give instructions.

Let R = a random number from 1 to 100

Get user's guess

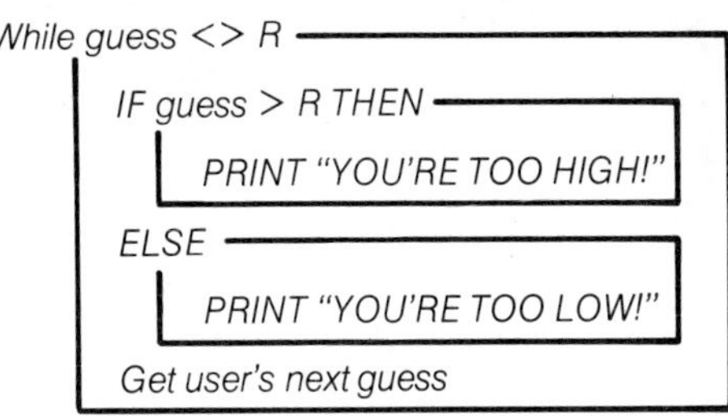

While guess <> R
IF guess > R THEN
PRINT "YOU'RE TOO HIGH!"
ELSE
PRINT "YOU'RE TOO LOW!"
Get user's next guess

PRINT "YOU GOT IT!"

6 Modify the number-guessing game (Problem 5) in at least two of these three possible ways:

(a) Instead of quitting when a game is over, ask the user

```
WANT TO PLAY AGAIN?
```

and if the user answers Y or YES, start a new game.

(b) If the user enters a number that isn't a whole number from 1 to 100, have your program complain and remind the user of the rules.

(c) Have your program count the number of guesses it takes the user to get the number. If the user takes more than 10 guesses, print "YOU CAN DO BETTER THAN THAT". If the user gets the right number in fewer than 7 guesses, print "YOU SURE ARE LUCKY!".

7 Design a program which will allow the user to estimate the heat loss through a window in a home in a cold climate.

There are two significant sources of heat loss through a window. First is the heat lost through the glass itself. This loss (in BTUs per hour) is given by the ratio.

$$\frac{\text{(Area of glass in square feet)*(Temperature difference in °F)}}{\text{R-rating}}$$

The R-ratings are

for a single pane of glass	0.885
for a double thickness of glass	1.54
for a storm window	1.80

Thus, to find the heat loss through a single 4-sq. ft. pane of glass when it's 70° inside and 28° outside, take

$$\frac{\text{(4 sq. ft.)*(70° − 28°)}}{0.885}$$

The second source of heat loss is air leakage. If the window is the kind that doesn't open, this isn't a significant factor. Otherwise there's a crack between the two sections of the window. If L is the length of the crack in feet, the heat loss is

(Air leakage)*0.075*0.24*(Temp. difference)*L ← *Leakage*

approx. density of air *specific heat of air*

Air leaking through crack in double-hung window.

Air leakage (in cubic feet per hour per foot of crack) is approximately

type of window	*air leakage*
wood frame	39
wood frame, weatherstripped	24
aluminum frame	72
aluminum frame, weatherstripped	32
storm window	13

The total heat loss is the sum of the two terms — the heat lost through the glass and the heat lost by air leakage. Take care in the planning phase here, as you consider ways of gathering the necessary information from the user.

8 In conventional loudspeakers the higher the frequency of the sound being reproduced, the more it tends to come out as a narrow beam along the axis of the speaker cone. If you walk around in conventional speaker, you'll notice that the bass notes don't change in intensity, but the highs are most pronounced when you're directly in front of the speaker. In less expensive speakers, the tendency is more pronounced. The relationship among intensity, frequency, and position is called the **dispersion pattern** of the speaker.

Intergalactic Stereo is a small chain of stereo stores that sells their own line of speakers. Their Hyper Realismo Model 55000 has a dispersion pattern given by the formula

relative intensity = 1 − |angle in degrees| *(frequency)^2*2.5E−11

Write a program which asks for the frequency at which the test is to be made, and then PRINTs the relative intensity level for directions from −180° to +180° in steps of 20°.

Use your program to plot a graph showing the change in speaker performance for frequencies of 100 Hz, 1000 Hz, 10,000 Hz, and 15,000 Hz. Note: In sales literature, the dispersion pattern is usually plotted as a circular graph. If you know how, plot your data that way.

9 In making fudge candy, a thermometer is handy. Unfortunately, accurate candy thermometers are difficult to find. The ones we've used have been off by several degrees. To test thermometers for accuracy, we use them to measure the temperature of boiling water, and compare their readings to the (known) temperature of boiling water.

At sea level water boils at 212°F. At higher altitudes it boils at lower temperatures. Use the computer to print out a table of boiling points at various altitudes: sea level, 500 feet, 1000 feet, 1500 feet, and so on in steps of 500 feet up to 15,000 feet above sea level. The boiling point changes by about 1°F for each 550-foot change in altitude. You can use the formula below to compute the boiling point in Fahrenheit degrees when the altitude is measured in feet above sea level.

$$\text{boiling point} = 212 - \frac{\text{altitude}}{550}$$

10 If your thermometer reads in Celsius (centigrade) degrees and you know your altitude in meters, the formula is

$$\text{boiling point} = 100 - \frac{\text{altitude}}{170}$$

Use the computer to print a table of boiling points as in problem 9, but in steps of 100 meters up to 5000 meters above sea level.

11 Write a program to count the votes in an election. There are three candidates: Milton P. Waxley (incumbent), Patricia Rhoder (progressive liberal), and Frederick "Red" Kemmeny (a reluctant candidate who filed at the last minute). Each voter makes his or her vote by entering a digit: 1 for Waxley, 2 for Rhoder, or 3 for Kemmeny.

At 7:30 p.m. an election official enters the value −1000000 to signal the end of balloting. Your program should print the election results. Note: Be sure to reject all mismarked ballots.

12 Do problem 11 and include the number of mismarked ballots in the output. Also PRINT a brief victory statement by the winner which includes the names of his or her worthy opponents.

This man has supported Milton P. Waxley in the last seventeen elections.

13 Design a program which PRINTs a rectangle of *'s of a size specified by the user. For example, if the user wants a rectangle that's 3 high by 7 wide, your program should PRINT

```
*******
*******
*******
```

If you like the appearance of such rectangles, alter the program so it also asks how far to indent the rectangle.

If you like Mondrian's paintings, you could also ask the user what character to use for the rectangle, and offer to print a number of them. By making a tasteful choice of characters and placing, you may be able to produce an interesting visual pattern.

14 The 324th Annual Pumpkin Growing Contest of the Future Farmers of Grand Fenwick has 16 entries this year. The weights of the pumpkins (in **tsernotecs,** the traditional measure of weight in Grand Fenwick) are shown below beside the names of the entrants.

Write a program which the judges could use to select the winner. Print a congratulatory message which lists the name of the lucky winner and tells how many tsernotecs the winning pumpkin weighs. (Thanks to the late Walter Orvedahl for this problem.)

Here's some sample data to try.

weight (tsernotecs)	*grower*	*weight (tsernotecs)*	*grower*
60.4	Hans Von Smong	69.4	Katy Klunz
86.1	Karl Schultz	78.8	Hans Von Der Door
63.9	Hans Von Neumann	85.3	Hans Schultz
71.2	Kristina Hampker	50.4	Hans Hanson
105.3	Karl Schmidthorst	67.3	Katy Kleinholter
54.7	Hans Von Laughen	57.9	Hans Bratworst
91.6	Karl Von Hausdorf	94.7	Kris Von Steinholder

Chapter 6
Subprograms

Section 6 1
Hierarchies and Modularity

Let's do an experiment. Up to this point we've covered eleven BASIC statements and commands — RUN, LET, END, PRINT, GO TO, INPUT, NEW, REM, LIST, ON-GO TO, and IF-THEN.

Put this book aside and try to write down the eleven statements and commands.

Probably you found it easy to write a half dozen or so of them as fast as you could write, with little mental effort. But you probably found that the rest of the words, if you could remember them at all, required more mental effort. Perhaps you resorted to some trick, like thinking back to the programs you've written, or trying to group the names in some way.

Let's try the task again, but first, organize the words into categories.

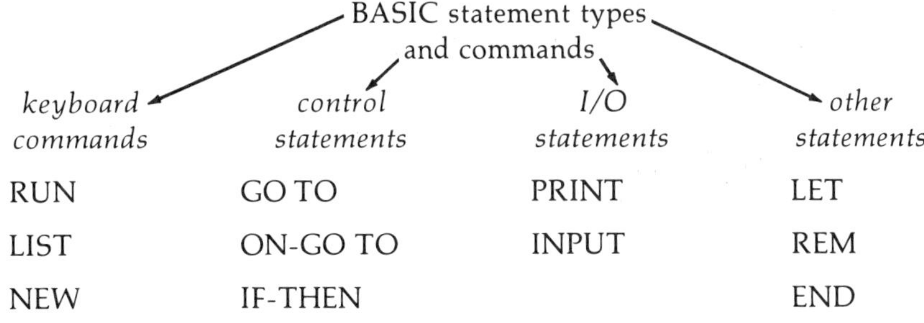

Read the category names and statements in each category aloud a couple of times. Then put the book down and try to write the eleven statements and commands again.

This time you probably found the task easy — it's easy to remember the four categories *keyboard commands, control statements, I/O (input/output) statements,* and *other statements.* And once you concentrate on a single category, it's easy to remember the two or three BASIC keywords in that category. They just seem to pop into mind.

But notice how strange this is. We've *added* four new items to the list of things to remember, yet we've made the task easier. By imposing a hierarchical organization, we can limit the number of things we have to remember or think about *at each point.* This appears to be a basic fact about the way the human brain works — we most naturally think, act, and plan in a way that results in about a half dozen ideas, considerations, categories, or possibilities being in mind at once.

> **7 ± 2:** the size of short-term memory. Most psychology texts discuss the idea that short-term memory is limited to about seven items (give or take two). This makes it difficult for people to remember long lists of things unless they have some way to group them into smaller lists. The classic paper on this topic is by G. Miller (1956), "The Magical Number Seven Plus or Minus Two," *Psychological Review,* 63, pp. 81–97.

Let's map out the two different ways of remembering the eleven keywords. First, we tried a simple list without any particular order:

Remember "RUN".
Remember "LET".
Remember "END".
Remember "PRINT".
Remember "GO TO".
Remember "INPUT".
Remember "NEW".
Remember "REM".
Remember "LIST".
Remember "ON-GO TO".
Remember "IF-THEN".

The second method, the organized or **structured** method, looks like this at the top level of the hierarchy:

Remember the *keyboard commands.*
Remember the *control statements.*
Remember the *I/O statements.*
Remember the *other statements.*

At the second level of the hierarchy, each task from the top level is divided into a small collection of subtasks (sometimes called **modules**), as shown below for the module control statement.

—remember the control statements—

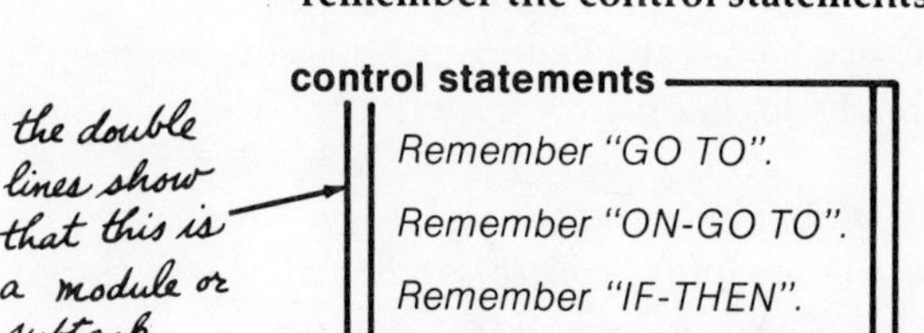
control statements
Remember "GO TO".
Remember "ON-GO TO".
Remember "IF-THEN".
the double lines show that this is a module or subtask

The psychological fact that thinking, remembering, speaking, and acting are most naturally carried out when the task is hierarchically structured, with about a half dozen things to keep in mind at each step, is so all-pervasive that most of us aren't even aware of it. Since computers *don't* share this constraint, it is possible to write programs which are acceptable to the computer, but which are incredibly hard for human beings to understand. A program which is hard for people to understand is very often a program which has errors buried in it, is difficult to debug, may be unwieldy to use, and, most likely, has caused the programmer grief and wasted time.

Creating large programs can be difficult — we have to make a conscious effort to make things easier for ourselves by giving our programs a clear, understandable organization. Of course, just chopping the problem up into arbitrary modules isn't enough — each module must be based on a logical view of the overall problem. (Figure 6 1 1 displays a useless decomposition of the remembering problem.)

A well-organized program can be thought about in a hierarchical way — at any point there are few enough subparts at the same level to be kept in mind at once. At any point the subparts should correspond to a natural way of dividing up the tasks to be done.

What isn't a module?

If a module is just a subpart of a program, then wouldn't you have a module if you took every other line of a program? No.

The most important characteristic of a module is that it corresponds to a specific, logical subpart of the overall task that the program is to do. In addition, we wouldn't think of something as a module unless it is reasonable to think of it as taking a definite (usually small) set of input values, producing a (usually small) number of specific output values, and performing an understandable operation on its input values to produce the output values. The benefit of designing your programs as collections of modules is that if you do it right, when you're working on one module, you don't have to think much about the rest of the program, because you can concentrate on how the module produces its specific outputs from its specific inputs. If you find that when you work on one part of your program, you have to think about very many other parts of the program, that's a sign that your plan is fouled up.

In this chapter we'll introduce statements which can help you to organize your programs. All our programs in the rest of the book will provide examples of using the organizational ideas. As we'll see in later chapters, the same principles can be used to help organize the way programs interact with their users, and the way data

A-IM	*IN-LI*	*LJ-RE*	*RF-Z*
END	INPUT	NEW	RUN
GO TO	LET	ON-GO TO	
IF-THEN	LIST	PRINT	
		REM	

Figure 6 1 1 A pointless division of the BASIC statements into modules is stored. In practice, huge programming projects are divided into subparts **(modules)** and assigned to programming teams which employ the same organizational principles. The structured, modular approach is used at every level of the professional programmer's world.

EXERCISES 6 1

1 What is the upper limit on the number of subtasks you should divide a top-level task into?

2 Why does short-term memory limit the number of parts a task should be divided into? Why not long-term memory?

3 Divide the problem of getting to work (or school) in the morning into a few logical subtasks.

4 Suppose your task is to apportion the phone bill for the month among four roommates. Divide your task into a few logical subtasks.

Section 6 2
Subroutines

Since our thoughts and plans are naturally hierarchical, it would be convenient if we could express programs themselves in a hierarchical manner. BASIC provides two features which give us some help.

This familiar statement

```
120     GO TO 5000
```

causes an unconditional transfer to line 5000. This similar-looking statement

```
120     GOSUB 5000
```

has a similar effect — at first. The "SUB" stands for **SUBroutine.** A subroutine is, as the name implies, a *sub*sidiary part of a program. (In the earlier days of computing, the word **routine** was more commonly used than it is now — it just means "program.") A subroutine is, in effect, a part of a program which supplies the details. The statement

```
120     GOSUB 5000
```

causes the computer to go to the subroutine which begins with line 5000. The statements in the subroutine are carried out, and when the subroutine is done — i.e., when the machine reaches a statement in the subroutine that looks like this —

```
5080    RETURN
```

the machine RETURNs and continues with the next statement after line 120.

By using subroutines, we can write programs whose structure is the same as a hierarchically organized plan. Here's an example.

Suppose we're given this problem: Our company wants a program which will print a nicely formatted bill, given the information from an invoice or order form. We are given a sample showing a typical invoice and a typical bill.

Sample input values:

customer:	Digital Solutions
product:	veeblefitzers
product code:	1200-7A
quantity:	144
unit price:	$1.05

Sample output:

```
*******************************************************
SOLD TO: DIGITAL SOLUTIONS
CODE        PRODUCT               QUANT UNIT COST TOTAL
1200-7A     VEEBLEFITZERS           144  $ 1.05   $ 151.2
                                  6% TAX--$ 9.07
                                                  --------
                                  PLEASE PAY      $ 160.27
*******************************************************
```

If we take the hierarchical approach, our first step is to make sure we understand the problem. Stating the problem in English is a good way to be sure we know what we're to do — if you can't express the problem in a few sentences, that usually means you don't understand it.

problem statement: Accept data describing a sale, and print a bill which includes the input information, a subtotal, sales tax, and grand total.

Our next step is to break the problem into reasonable subparts. In this case it seems that there are three main parts. First, we have to get the input values; next, we can compute the subtotal, tax, and grand total; finally, we need to print a bill in the desired format. Here's our plan.

—bill printer—

Get input values from the user.
Compute subtotal, tax, total.
PRINT nice-looking bill.

As we look over our plan, we wonder if the user will really want to do a sequence of bills rather than just one each time the program is RUN. It seems most likely that the user will want to do a bunch of bills, one after the other. Since we're still at a very high level in the program design, it's easy to change our plan.

revised problem statement: Accept data describing a sale, and print a bill which includes the input information, a subtotal, sales tax, and grand total. Repeat if there are more bills to do.

Get input values from the user.

Compute subtotal tax, total.

PRINT nice-looking bill.

Repeat IF *more to do*

Since we'll use a subroutine for each major subpart of our program, we can already write the main part of our program! It looks almost exactly like our plan.

```
10   REM  --BILL PROCESSOR--
100  REM  TOP OF REPEAT LOOP.
110  REM  REPEAT ONCE FOR EACH ORDER.
120  REM      FIRST, GET DATA ON THIS ORDER.
130           GOSUB 1000
140  REM      NEXT COMPUTE COSTS (SUBTOTAL, TAX, TOTAL)
150           GOSUB 2000
160  REM      FINALLY, PRINT BILL.
170           GOSUB 3000
180           PRINT "ANY MORE ORDERS";
190           INPUT A$
200             IF A$="YES" THEN 100
210             IF A$="Y"   THEN 100
220  REM  DONE
9999      END
```

> On a large programming project — one which is expected to take months to complete, in which different people will work on different modules — meetings are held at this point in the design process. Each person must have a complete understanding of what his or her module must do, how it fits into the overall plan, and what values it will get from other modules. Every hour spent clarifying the overall plan can save days of work later.

Now we can start in on the subtasks. The first is the one which gets the data. Of course, we realize that the other modules will need to use the data values, so we'll want to keep careful track of the names we give the variables that get the data. Looking back at the sample we were given, we can see what data items we need (Figure 6 2 1).

Our plan for this module is straightforward.

get input values

Get customer name.

Get product description.

Get product code.

Get quantity.

Get price per item.

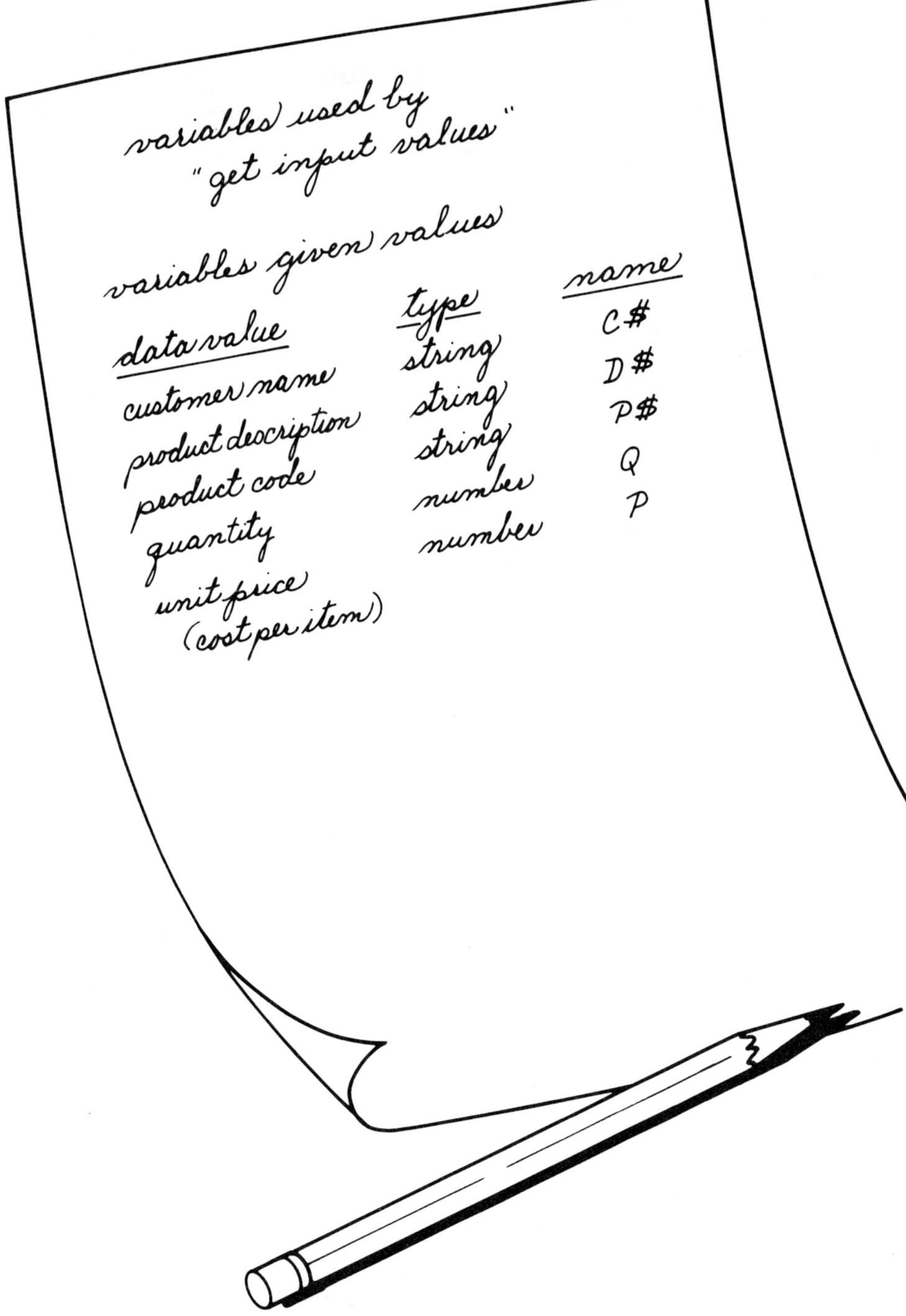
variables used by
"get input values"
variables given values
data value
type
name
customer name
string
C$
product description
string
D$
product code
string
P$
quantity
number
Q
unit price
(cost per item)
number
P

Figure 6 2 1

And the actual BASIC statements for the module follow directly from the plan.

```
1000 REM  MODULE 1--GET DATA
1010      PRINT
1020      PRINT "CUSTOMER NAME=";
1030      INPUT C$
1040      PRINT "PRODUCT DESCRIPTION=";
1050      INNPUT D$
1060      PRINT "PRODUCT CODE=";
1070      INPUT P$
1080      PRINT "QUANTITY=";
1090      INPUT Q
1100      PRINT "PRICE PER ITEM=$";
1110      INPUT P
1120 REM  HAVE ALL THE INPUT DATA.
1130      RETURN
```

Turning back to our top-level plan, we see that the second subtask is to compute the subtotal, tax, and grand total. Again, this is straightforward.

compute subtotal, tax, and total

*Subtotal = quantity * unit price.*

*Tax = subtotal * 0.06.*

Grant total = subtotal + tax.

As before, we'll write down the names and meanings of the variables we'll use, checking against our list from the first module to make sure that the uses are consistent (Figure 6 2 2).

We look over our plan for the second subtask, and everything looks OK. . . or does it? We're dealing with dollar-and-cents figures, not just arbitrary numbers. What if the grand total comes out to be something like $123.3333? That wouldn't be acceptable. We realize that we'll have to round the figures we get to two decimal places. Fortunately, that's something we've done before, so after jotting notes on our plan indicating that we need to round the numbers, we can write the BASIC version.

```
LIST 2000-2500
2000 REM  MODULE 2--COMPUTE SUBTOTAL, TAX, TOTAL
2010      LET CO = Q*P
2020 REM  ROUND TO DOLLARS AND CENTS.
2030      LET CO = INT(CO*100 + 0.5)/100
2050 REM  ASSUME FLAT RATE 6% SALES TAX.
2060      LET XO = CO*0.06
2070 REM  ROUND TAX TO AN EVEN NUMBER OF CENTS.
2080      LET XO = INT(XO*100 + 0.5)/100
2090 REM  TO = GRAND TOTAL
2100      LET TO = CO + XO
2110 REM  DONE COMPUTING COSTS.
2120      RETURN
```

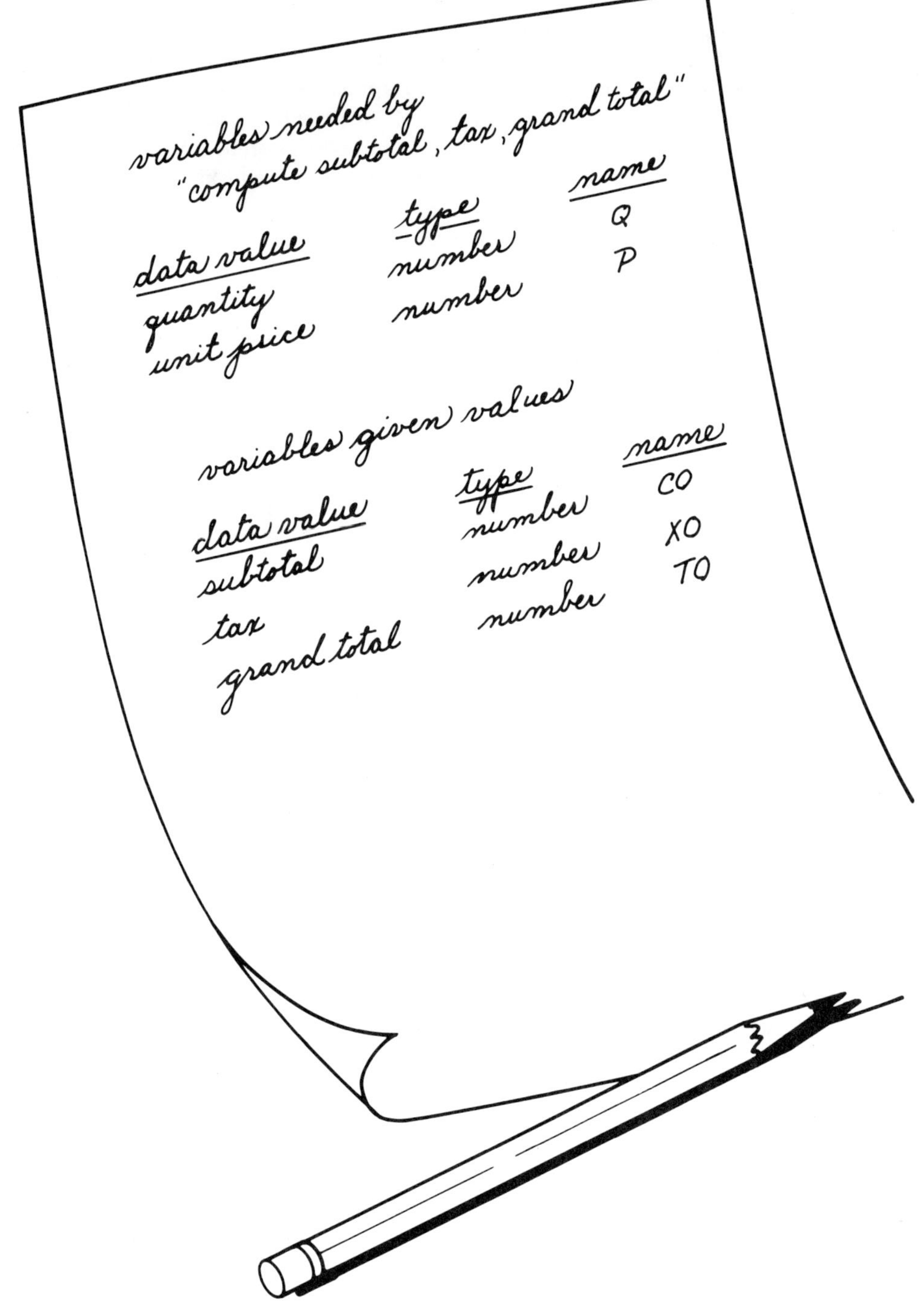
variables needed by
"compute subtotal, tax, grand total"
data value
type
name
quantity
number
Q
unit price
number
P
variables given values
data value
type
name
subtotal
number
CO
tax
number
XO
grand total
number
TO

Figure 6 2 2

The hardest part of doing the third subtask (print the bill) is figuring out the spacing. Let's focus on that problem. We have a sample of the desired output (near the beginning of this section), so we don't have to make any major decisions about what pieces of information should appear where. We'll need at least one PRINT statement for each line of the bill, so the only thing left to do is to determine where each item (heading or data value) should appear on its line. Here's how to do that:

Take a sheet of graph paper (or specially made **line spacing chart** paper, or a hand-drawn chart as in Figure 6 2 3), fill in the spaces with the headings you want, and mark where the data values should go. Once we've satisfied that the spacing looks OK, we can write the PRINT statements to implement the chart. We use TAB( ) spacers to make the printed output match our chart. For instance, we can see from our chart that we should TAB to column 12 before printing PRODUCT, then TAB to column 30 before printing QUANT. When we have to print a data value instead of a heading, we TAB to the appropriate column (read that from the chart), and then give the appropriate variable name. For that, we use our list of variables from the other modules. Without such lists, we'd get into trouble like this: We remember that we used C$ for one of the values, and so when we get to the place in this, the third module, where we want to PRINT out the code number of the product, we might think "Uh, code, right, that's stored in C$, of course." Not true. Our list shows that when we wrote the first module, we used C$ to store the customer name, and used P$ for product code.

```
3000 REM  MODULE 3--PRINT BILL
3010      PRINT
3020      PRINT "*****************************************************"
3030      PRINT "SOLD TO: "; C$
3040      PRINT "CODE"; TAB(12); "PRODUCT"; TAB(30); "QUANT"; TAB(36);
3050      PRINT "UNIT COST"; TAB(46); "TOTAL"
3060      PRINT P$; TAB(12); D$; TAB(31); Q; TAB(37); "$"; P; TAB(46);
3070      PRINT "$"; CO
3080      PRINT
3090      PRINT TAB(30); "6% TAX--$"; XO
3100      PRINT TAB(46); "--------"
3110      PRINT TAB(30); "PLEASE PAY"; TAB(46); "$"; TO
3120      PRINT "*****************************************************"
3130 REM  DONE PRINTING BILL
3140      RETURN
```

Now that we've worked out each of the subparts and expressed them as BASIC subroutines, we go back to our top-level plan and make sure everything still makes sense, checking to see if we've forgotten anything. Everything looks OK, so we RUN the program and test it.

```
RUN

CUSTOMER NAME=? DIGITAL SOLUTIONS
PRODUCT DESCRIPTION=? VEEBLEFITZERS
PRODUCT CODE=? 1200-7A
QUANTITY=? 144
PRICE PER ITEM=$? 1.05
```

(program continued on page 134)

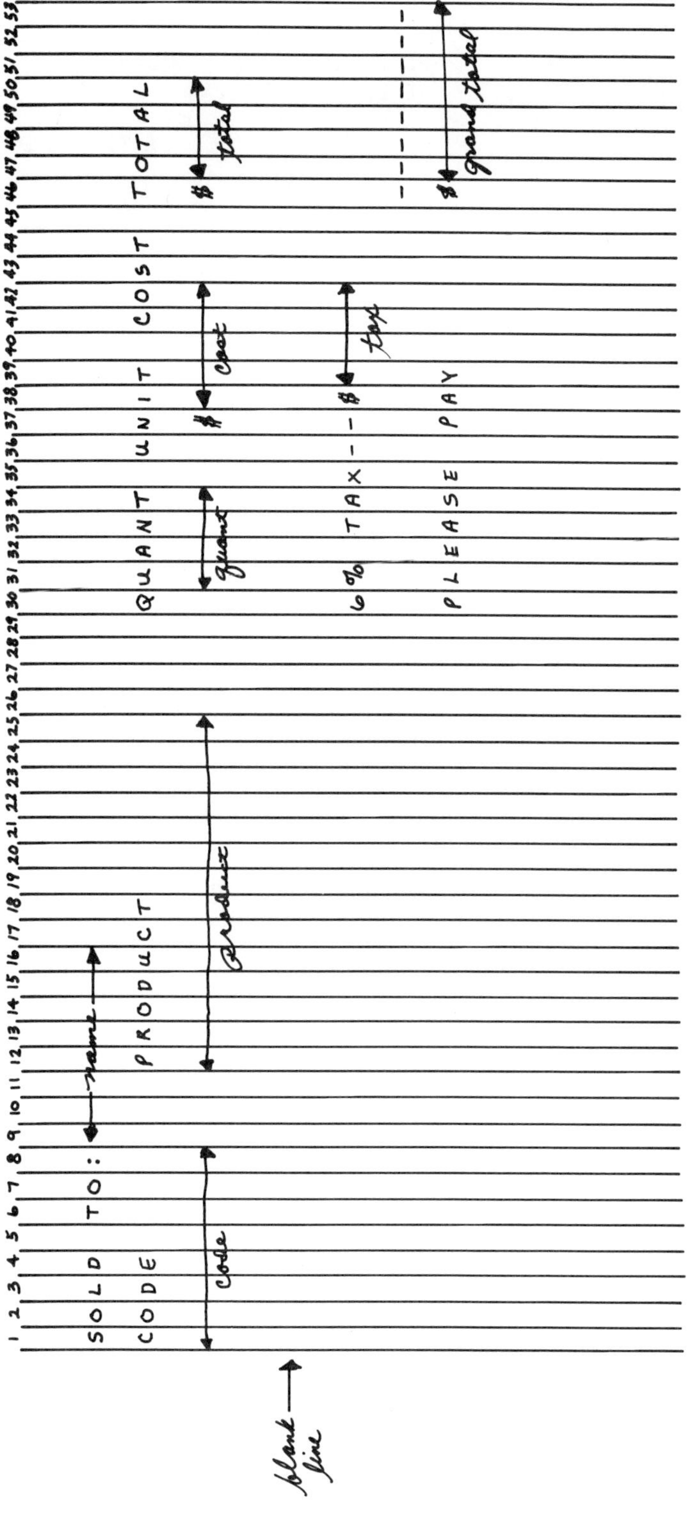

Figure 6 2 3 Figuring out the spacing.

```
*****************************************************
SOLD TO: DIGITAL SOLUTIONS
CODE        PRODUCT                QUANT UNIT COST TOTAL
1200-7A     VEEBLEFITZERS            144  $ 1.05   $ 151.2

                                   6% TAX--$ 9.07
                                                   --------
                                   PLEASE PAY      $ 160.27
*****************************************************
ANY MORE ORDERS? YES

CUSTOMER NAME=? ARNHOLDT CORP.
PRODUCT DESCRIPTION=? RANDOMIZERS
PRODUCT CODE=? 3304-9R
QUANTITY=? 12
PRICE PER ITEM=$? 19.95

*****************************************************
SOLD TO: ARNHOLDT CORP.
CODE        PRODUCT                QUANT UNIT COST TOTAL
3304-9R     RANDOMIZERS              12   $ 19.95  $ 239.4

                                   6% TAX--$ 14.36
                                                   --------
                                   PLEASE PAY      $ 253.76
*****************************************************
ANY MORE ORDERS? NO
READY
```

EXERCISES 6 2

1 Which subroutines would be affected if the company were to (a) add a blank line after "SOLD TO: customer name" in the bill; (b) add the date of the invoice to the printed bill?

2 Which subroutines would be affected if the state were to (a) raise the sales tax to 8%; (b) require a special tax on certain products?

3 Why do some of the numbers get printed with only one decimal place when we rounded to two decimal places?

4 Why do we keep a list of the variables that we use in each module?

5 Our spacing chart (Figure 6 2 3) shows that we planned to print the tax in a field starting right next to the dollar sign. But when we run the program, there's a space after the dollar sign. Why?

6 What column should we TAB to in line 3090 if our spacing chart had shown the tax dollar sign lining up with the unit cost dollar sign?

Section 6 3

Added Benefits

So far, we've seen how we can use subroutines to express programs in a way that's consistent with the way people naturally think about and plan complex tasks. That's one benefit of subroutines. There are more.

You don't want to keep re-inventing the wheel. Once you've gone through all the work involved in designing, refining, coding, and debugging a program which solves some problem, you don't want to have to go through it all again the next time you need to solve that problem. This idea applies within one program — if some subtask has to be performed in a number of different circumstances, you can use a subroutine to avoid having to repeat the gory details of the computation each time you need it. The idea also applies from program to program.

Professional programmers keep libraries of programs they've done, so that when the need arises, they can pull an old program out, dust it off, and use it again, thus saving time and mental anguish. It's most convenient to express such programs as subroutines, and to keep clear written records of what each subroutine does, what variables it uses, and what input and output values it needs and produces. Why as subroutines? Well, the kinds of programs that you use over and over are ones that perform common tasks usually needed as subparts of bigger tasks. By writing them as subroutines, and giving them line numbers that are high and nonoverlapping, you're most likely to be able to copy the helpful routine right into the program you're working on at the moment with no changes. And, of course, the fewer changes you have to make, the less room there is for error to creep in as you enter the routine.

> **saving programs:** Appendix A "The World BASIC Lives In," will give you some hints about how you can create libraries of programs on your system. Once you learn to do this, you can begin to make your computer system into a really useful tool, specialized to fit the type of work you do.

Here's a subroutine from our personal library of useful programs. We've used this very subroutine in every major business program we've written. It has to do with dates. Business people care more about what time it is and what day it is than most other computer users. Orders come in on certain days, billings have to be done on particular days, people get paid on specific days, and so on. Fairly often, programs we've written for business people have to ask for a date to be entered, usually in the familiar month/day/year format (e.g., 2/29/84). To avoid disaster, our programs have to check the date to make sure it's real. Too often, people don't quite get the date right. Nobody ever seems to give 31 days to September, but if yesterday was November 30, are you sure what today is? And leap years!

Eventually, we'll use the subroutine to add some useful features to the bill generator program we developed in the previous section. It's interesting in its own write, however. And, of course, it's consistent with our hierarchical program design principles for us to develop it in relative isolation, without getting bogged down in the details of *exactly* how the bill generator program will use it.

rough problem statement: Tell if a date is valid.

Now to tell if a date is valid, obviously the subroutine needs to know the date. So we'll assume the date is given by the values of three variables. M will store the month (by number), D the day, and Y the year. To report its decision after testing the date, our subroutine will have to communicate with the main program, so we'll say that the subroutine will store a 0 in variable E (for error), if the date is OK and a 1 if the date is unreal.

problem statement: The subroutine gets the month number in variable M, the day number in D, and the year in Y. If the date M/D/Y actually exists, the subroutine should store 0 in variable E (for error), indicating that there is no error. If the date doesn't exist, the subroutine should store a 1 in E. Some months have 30 days, some have 31. To tell if 2/29/Y exists, the subroutine will have to tell if Y is a leap year.

—test for valid date—

If day < 1, then date is illegal.

If year < 1752, then date is illegal.

If month < 1, then date is illegal.

If month > 12, then date is illegal.

Select based on month:

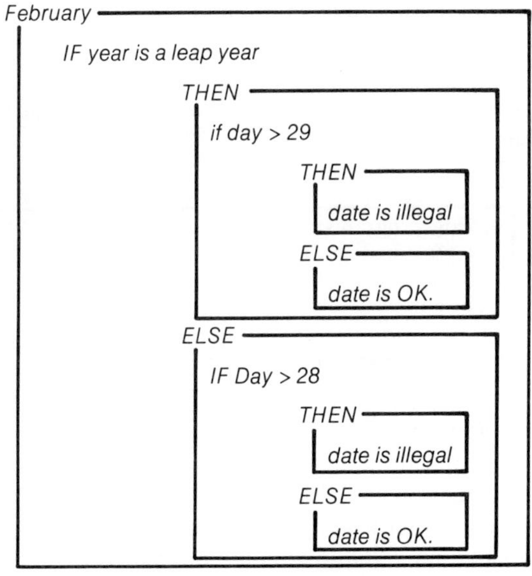

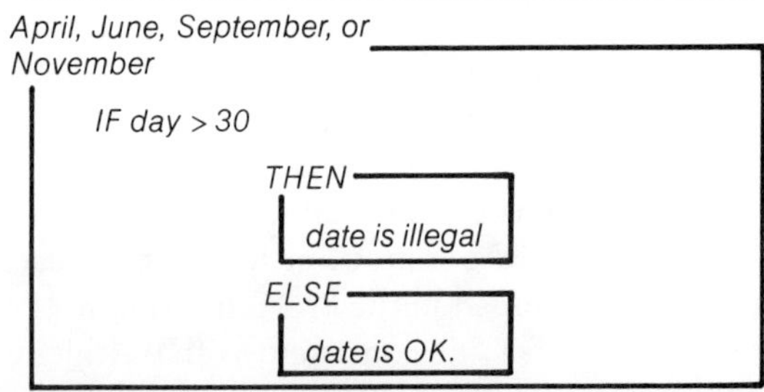

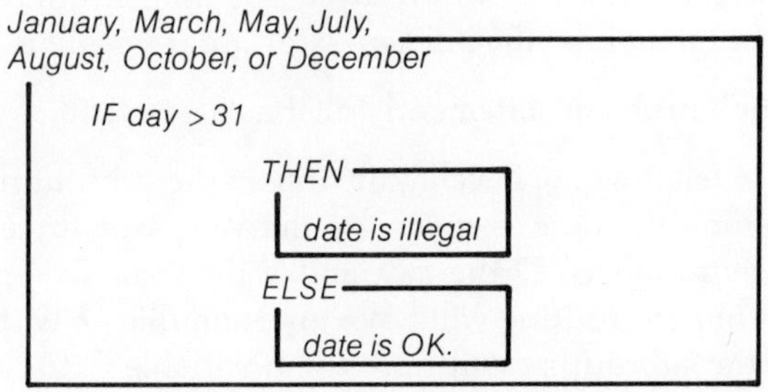

The plan should be easy to understand despite its abstruse details. Obviously, no day can be less than 1 and no month can be less than 1 or more than 12. The reason we plan to say any date before the year 1752 is illegal is more obscure. Basically, we don't want to risk accepting a year like 84 (no doubt the user has typed 84 to mean 1984), and calling any date with a year less than 1752 certainly protects against that. But why 1752 and not 100, which also protects against two-digit numbers? Because it happens that the Gregorian calendar was adopted by the British Empire in 1752, and our leap year computation is not valid before that time.

Once a date has passed the first tests, we need to check it in different ways for different months. If month has the value 9 (September), then day can't be more than 30, and so on. In February we need to know if year is a leap year. Problem 1 at the end of Chapter 4 gives the rules for leap years.

When we translated our plan into BASIC, we chose to start it at line 8000. The statements which handle February start at line 8200, the statements for months which have 30 days start at 8300, and those which have 31 days use the statements starting at 8400. We wanted to implement the selection of month with an ON-GO TO statement like this:

```
8120    ON M GO TO 8400,8200,8400,8300,8400,8300,8400,8400,8300,8400,8300,8400
                   ↑    ↑    ↑    ↑    ↑    ↑    ↑    ↑    ↑    ↑    ↑    ↑
                  Jan  Feb  Mar April May  June July Aug  Sept  Oct  Nov  Dec
```

but our computer gave us an error message! On our system no statement may have more than 72 characters in it. That's why we split the selection up into two ON-GO TO statements (see lines 8120, 8130, and 8140). [However, see Section 18 3.]

```
8000 REM  SUBR--TEST FOR LEGITIMATE DATE.
8010 REM  M  D  AND Y  GIVE MONTH, DAY, AND YEAR.
8020 REM  ON RETURN, IF  E = 0,  M/D/Y IS A LEGAL DATE.
8030 REM             IF  E = 1,  NOT A LEGAL DATE.
8040 REM  NO ERROR DETECTED YET, SO
8050      LET E = 0
8060      IF D<1    THEN 8500
8070      IF M<1    THEN 8500
8080      IF M>12   THEN 8500
8090      IF Y<1752 THEN 8500
8100 REM  NO OBVIOUS ERRORS, SO SELECT ON MONTH.
8100 REM  NO ROOM FOR ALL MONTHS ON ONE LINE, SO SPLIT THE TEST.
8120      IF M>6 THEN 8140
8130      ON M   GO TO 8400, 8200, 8400, 8300, 8400, 8300 ← June
8140      ON M-6 GO TO 8400, 8400, 8300, 8400, 8300, 8400 ← December
8200 REM  FEBRUARY HATH 28 EXCEPT UNDER BIZARRE CONDITIONS.
8210      IF INT(Y/4)<>Y/4 THEN 8270
8220      IF INT(Y/400)=Y/400 THEN 8240
8230      IF INT(Y/100)=Y/100 THEN 8270
8240 REM  Y  IS A LEAP YEAR
8250      IF D>29 THEN 8500
8260      RETURN
8270 REM  Y  IS NOT A LEAP YEAR
8280      IF D>28 THEN 8500
8290      RETURN
```

(program continued on page 138)

```
8300 REM  30 DAYS HATH SEPTEMBER AND ALL OTHER MONTHS THAT GET HERE
8310      IF D>30 THEN 8500
8320      RETURN
8400 REM  ALL THE REST HAVE 31
8410      IF D>31 THEN 8500
8420      RETURN
8500 REM  UH OH! DATE IS ILLEGAL.
8510      LET E = 1
8520      RETURN
```

Now that we have a subroutine to test for valid dates in our bag of tricks, there's no need to panic when we're asked to add a couple of things to the bill generator of Section 6 2. Suppose we're told to add a line telling the date the order was made, and a line giving the date our company promised to deliver the merchandise.

We need to make changes in the first and third modules. No change is necessary in the overall plan — and the second module, which computes costs and taxes, isn't affected.

Our new plan (shown below) for the "get input values" subtask includes the new requirement to get the date.

get input values

Get customer name.

Get product description.

Get product code.

Get quantity.

Get unit price.

Get date of order.

Get date delivery was promised.

Now we need to figure out how to implement the "get date" operations. In both cases we need to print a message, accept three numbers, check to make sure the numbers represent a legitimate date, and either return or, if the date wasn't valid, ask the user to correct it. Since both cases sound so similar, we might as well write one subroutine to do the bulk of the work. Before we go any further, we'd better update our list of variables that subtask 1 uses (Figure 6 3 1).

Now that we feel confident about what we're doing, we can write our new version of subtask 1.

```
1000 REM  MODULE 1--GET DATA
1010      PRINT
1020      PRINT "CUSTOMER NAME=";
1030      INPUT C$
1040      PRINT "PRODUCT DESCRIPTION=";
1050      INPUT D$
1060      PRINT "PRODUCT CODE=";
1070      INPUT P$
1080      PRINT "QUANTITY=";
1090      INPUT Q
```

(program continued on page 140)

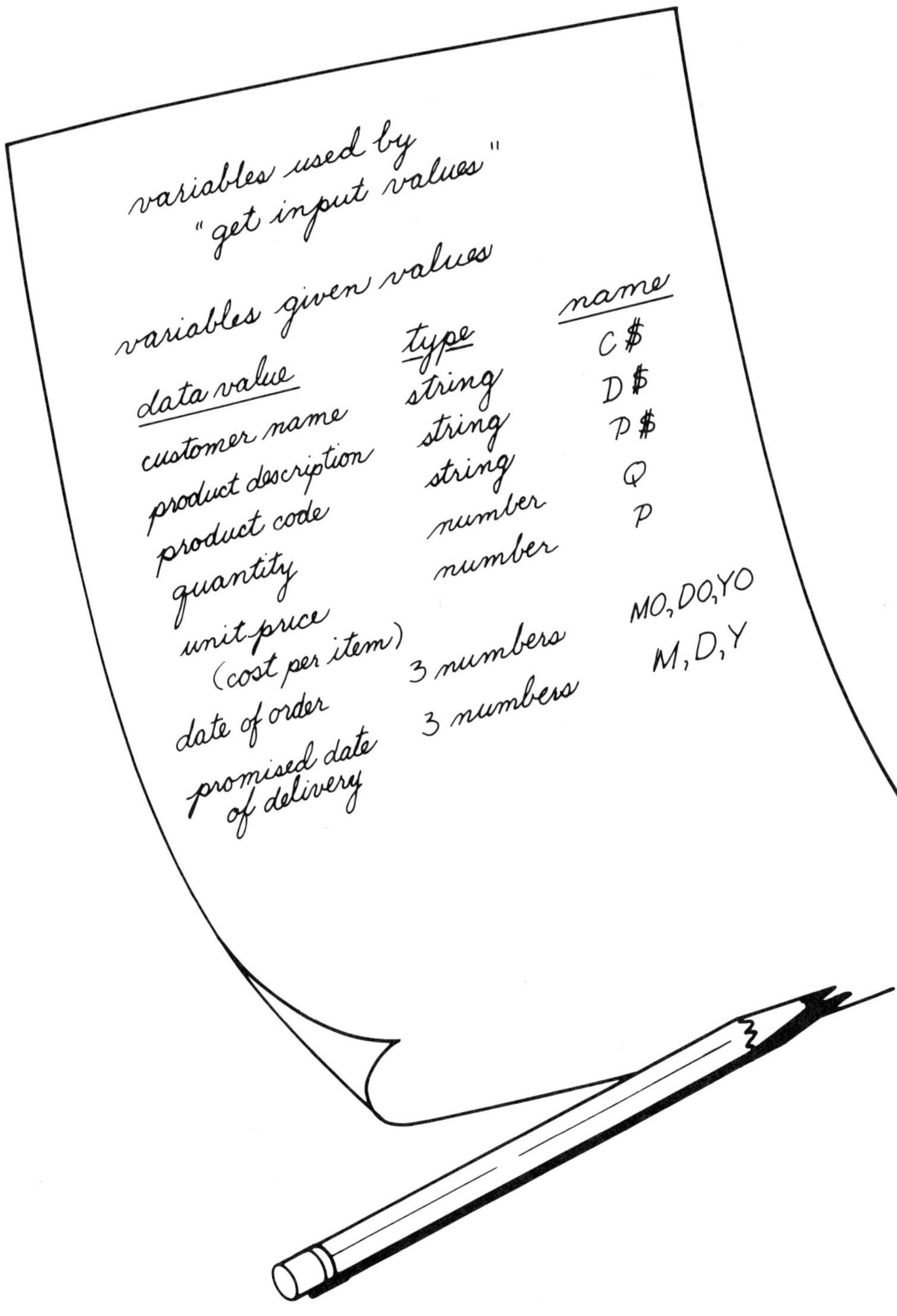
variables used by
"get input values"
variables given values
data value
type
name
customer name
string
C$
product description
string
D$
product code
string
P$
quantity
number
Q
unit price
(cost per item)
number
P
date of order
3 numbers
MO, DO, YO
promised date
of delivery
3 numbers
M, D, Y

Figure 6 3 1

```
1100      PRINT "PRICE PER ITEM=$";
1110      INPUT P
1120 REM  GET DATE OF ORDER
1130      PRINT "WHEN WAS THE ORDER PLACED?"
1140 REM  GET DATE AND VERIFY IT
1150      GOSUB 7900
1160 REM  SAVE DATE OF ORDER
1170      LET MO = M
1180      LET DO = D
1190      LET YO = Y
1200 REM  GET DATE MERCHANDISE WAS PROMISED
1210      PRINT "WHEN DID WE PROMISE TO DELIVER?"
1220 REM  GET DATE AND VERIFY
1230      GOSUB 7900
1240 REM  M  D  AND  Y  GIVE DELIVERY DATE
1250 REM  HAVE ALL INPUT DATA
1260      RETURN
```

Here's our plan for the "get date and verify it" subprogram.

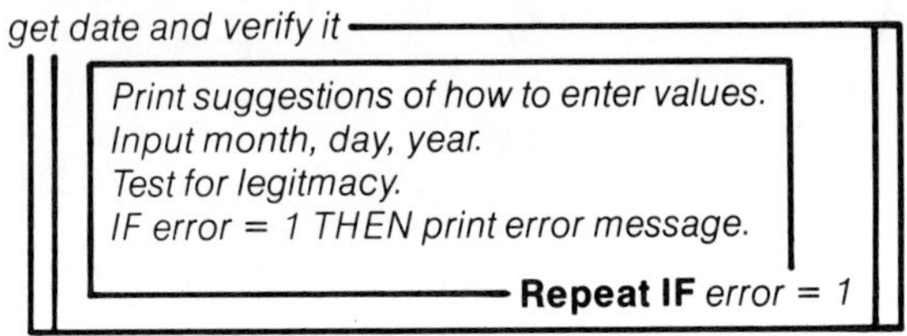

get date and verify it
Print suggestions of how to enter values.
Input month, day, year.
Test for legitmacy.
IF error = 1 THEN print error message.
Repeat IF error = 1

And here's our BASIC version.

```
7900 REM  SUBR--GET A DATE AND VERIFY IT
7910      PRINT "PLEASE GIVE THE DATE IN A FORM LIKE '9,28,1984'"
7920      INPUT M, D, Y
7930 REM  TEST FOR VALIDITY
7940      GOSUB 8000
7950      IF E=0 THEN 7990
7960        PRINT "BUT THAT DATE DOESN'T EXIST!"
7970        PRINT "PLEASE TRY AGAIN."
7980        GO TO 7910
7990      RETURN
```

try again (7910–7980)

this subroutine doesn't return unless the date represented by M, D, and Y is legitimate

To complete the process of adding the date features to our program, we need to add a couple of PRINT statements to our third module where we print the bill.

```
3032      PRINT "ORDER PLACED "; TAB(29); MO; "/"; DO; "/"; YO
3034      PRINT "DELIVERY PROMISED"; TAB(29); M; "/"; D; "/"; Y
3036      PRINT
```

look where we put them into module 3

Then we are finished with the revision of our program.

```
LIST
10   REM  --BILL PROCESSOR--
100  REM  TOP OF REPEAT LOOP.
110  REM  REPEAT ONCE FOR EACH ORDER.
120  REM      FIRST, GET DATA ON THIS ORDER.
130           GOSUB 1000
140  REM      NEXT COMPUTE COSTS (SUBTOTAL, TAX, TOTAL)
150           GOSUB 2000
160  REM      FINALLY, PRINT BILL.
170           GOSUB 3000
180           PRINT "ANY MORE ORDERS";
190           INPUT A$
200             IF A$="YES" THEN 100
210             IF A$="Y"   THEN 100
220  REM  DONE
230       GO TO 9999

1000 REM  MODULE 1--GET DATA
1010      PRINT
1020      PRINT "CUSTOMER NAME=";
1030      INPUT C$
1040      PRINT "PRODUCT DESCRIPTION=";
1050      INPUT D$
1060      PRINT "PRODUCT CODE=";
1070      INPUT P$
1080      PRINT "QUANTITY=";
1090      INPUT Q
1100      PRINT "PRICE PER ITEM=$";
1110      INPUT P
1120 REM  GET DATE OF ORDER
1130      PRINT "WHEN WAS THE ORDER PLACED?"
1140 REM  GET DATE AND VERIFY IT
1150      GOSUB 7900
1160 REM  SAVE DATE OF ORDER
1170      LET MO = M
1180      LET DO = D
1190      LET YO = Y
1200 REM  GET DATE MERCHANDISE WAS PROMISED
1210      PRINT "WHEN DID WE PROMISE TO DELIVER?"
1220 REM  GET DATE AND VERIFY
1230      GOSUB 7900
1240 REM  M  D  AND  Y  GIVE DELIVERY DATE
1250 REM  HAVE ALL INPUT DATA
1260      RETURN
2000 REM  MODULE 2--COMPUTE SUBTOTAL, TAX, TOTAL
2010      LET CO = Q*P
2020 REM  ROUND TO DOLLARS AND CENTS.
2030      LET CO = INT(CO*100 + 0.5)/100
2050 REM  ASSUME FLAT RATE 6% SALES TAX.
2060      LET XO = CO*0.06
2070 REM  ROUND TAX TO AN EVEN NUMBER OF CENTS.
2080      LET XO = INT(XO*100 + 0.5)/100
```

"main" program—same as before (lines 10–230)

getting the dates (lines 1120–1230)

main program: the part of a program which follows the top-level plan; i.e., everything but the subroutines.

(program continued on page 142)

```
2090 REM  TO = GRAND TOTAL
2100      LET TO = CO + XO
2110 REM  DONE COMPUTING COSTS.
2120      RETURN

3000 REM  MODULE 3--PRINT BILL
3010      PRINT
3020      PRINT "******************************************************"
3030      PRINT "SOLD TO: "; C$
3032      PRINT "ORDER PLACED "; TAB(29); MO; "/"; DO; "/"; YO
3034      PRINT "DELIVERY PROMISED"; TAB(29); M; "/"; D; "/"; Y
3036      PRINT
3040      PRINT "CODE"; TAB(12); "PRODUCT"; TAB(30); "QUANT"; TAB(36);
3050      PRINT "UNIT COST"; TAB(46); "TOTAL"
3060      PRINT P$; TAB(12); D$ TAB(31); Q; TAB(37); "S"; P; TAB(46);
3070      PRINT "$"; CO
3080      PRINT
3090      PRINT TAB(30); "6% TAX--$"; XO
3100      PRINT TAB(46);"--------"
3110      PRINT TAB(30); "PLEASE PAY"; TAB(46); "$"; TO
3120      PRINT "******************************************************"
3130 REM  DONE PRINTING BILL
3140      RETURN

7900 REM  SUBR--GET A DATE AND VERIFY IT
7910      PRINT "PLEASE GIVE THE DATE IN A FORM LIKE '9,28,1984'"
7920      INPUT M, D, Y
7930 REM  TEST FOR VALIDITY
7940      GOSUB 8000
7950      IF E=0 THEN 7990
7960        PRINT "BUT THAT DATE DOESN'T EXIST!"
7970        PRINT "PLEASE TRY AGAIN."
7980        GO TO 7910
7990      RETURN

8000 REM  SUBR--TEST FOR LEGITIMATE DATE.
8010 REM  M  D  AND Y  GIVE MONTH, DAY, AND YEAR.
8020 REM  ON RETURN, IF--E = 0,  M/D/Y IS A LEGAL DATE.
8030 REM                IF  E = 1,  NOT A LEGAL DATE.
8040 REM  NO ERROR DETECTED YET, SO
8050      LET E = 0
8060      IF D<1    THEN 8500
8070      IF M<1    THEN 8500
8080      IF M>12   THEN 8500
8090      IF Y<1752 THEN 8500
8100 REM  NO OBVIOUS ERRORS, SO SELECT ON MONTH.
8110 REM  NO ROOM FOR ALL MONTHS ON ONE LINE, SO SPLIT THE TEST.
8120      IF M<6 THEN 8140
8130      ON M   GO TO 8400, 8200, 8400, 8300, 8400, 8300
8140      ON M-6 GO TO 8400, 8400, 8300, 8400, 8300, 8400
8200 REM  FEBRUARY HATH 28 EXCEPT UNDER BIZARRE CONDITIONS.
8210      IF INT(Y/4)<>Y/4 THEN 8270
8220      IF INT(Y/400)=Y/400 THEN 8240
8230      IF INT(Y/100)=Y/100 THEN 8270
```

Margin notes (handwritten): "printing the dates" (beside lines 3032–3036); "subroutine that returns a legit date" (beside lines 7900–7990); "← June" (after line 8130); "← December" (after line 8140).

```
8240 REM  Y  IS A LEAP YEAR
8250      IF D>29 THEN 8500
8260      RETURN
8270 REM  Y  IS NOT A LEAP YEAR
8280      IF D>28 THEN 8500
8290      RETURN
8300 REM  30 DAYS HATH SEPTEMBER AND ALL OTHER MONTHS THAT GET HERE
8310      IF D>30 THEN 8500
8320      RETURN
8400 REM  ALL THE REST HAVE 31
8410      IF D>31 THEN 8500
8420      RETURN
8500 REM  UH OH!  DATE IS ILLEGAL
8510      LET E = 1
8520      RETURN
9999      END
READY
RUN

CUSTOMER NAME=? DIGITAL SOLUTIONS
PRODUCT DESCRIPTION=? VEEBLEFITZERS
PRODUCT CODE=? 1200-7A
QUANTITY=? 144
PRICE PER ITEMS=$? 1.05
WHEN WAS THE ORDER PLACED?
PLEASE GIVE THE DATE IN A FORM LIKE '9,28,1984'
? 11,1,1982
WHEN DID WE PROMISE TO DELIVER?
PLEASE GIVE THE DATE IN A FORM LIKE '9,28,1984'
?2,29,1983
BUT THAT DATE DOESN'T EXIST!
PLEASE TRY AGAIN.
PLEASE GIVE THE DATE IN A FORM LIKE '9,28,1984'
? 3,1,1983

**************************************************
SOLD TO: DIGITAL SOLUTIONS
ORDER PLACED                     11 / 1 / 1982
DELIVERY PROMISED                3 / 1 / 1983

CODE        PRODUCT              QUANT UNIT COST TOTAL
1200-7A     VEEBLEFITZERS          144  $ 1.05   $ 151.2

                                 6% TAX--$ 9.07
                                                 --------
                                 PLEASE PAY      $ 160.27
**************************************************
ANY MORE ORDERS? NO
READY
```

the get date and verify it subroutine won't "let go" until the user enters a legitimate date

EXERCISES 6 3

1 The bill processor program contains a main program and five subroutines, which we'll call "get data", "compute", "print", "get date", and "verify date".

Draw a chart (like a corporation's organization chart) indicating which parts of the program use which subroutines.

2 What part of the "get date" subroutine corresponds to the "test for legitimate date" in the plan?

3 Under what conditions is the statement in line 8420 carried out?

4 We have used subroutines mostly for organizational purposes in our programs. However, there is an additional advantage in having the "get date" section of the program written as a subroutine. What is it?

5 The error message from the "get and verify date" subroutine is potentially confusing. If the user enters 4/1/84, the routine says, "BUT THAT DATE DOESN'T EXIST." Make a plan for the "get and verify date" module that reports illegal year values with a separate error message.

Section 6 4

Formalities About Subroutines

The GOSUB statement has this form:

Note: GOSUB may also be written with a space like this: GO SUB. Use whichever seems clearer to you.

GOSUB *line number*

It means, "Transfer control to line [number], but keep track of the line this GOSUB is in, so an appropriate RETURN can be made."

The RETURN statement has this form:

RETURN

It means, "Transfer to the line immediately after the most recently activated GOSUB statement." (When a GOSUB is carried out, we say it is **active** until some RETURN statement is carried out which returns to the line after that GOSUB.)

These two statements are all that standard BASIC "knows" about subroutines. Thus, a burden is put on you, the programmer. There are no specific rules in Minimal BASIC which tell exactly what constitutes a subroutine. Since BASIC doesn't provide any way to isolate the lines or variables used in a subroutine, you will have to take a little care to be sure you know what you're doing.

Here are a few little experimental programs which have no purpose other than pointing out some of the advantages and some of the tricky points of subroutines.

First, obviously, this program doesn't make any sense:

```
10      RETURN
9999    END

RUN
ERROR--RETURN WITHOUT GOSUB IN LINE 10
READY
```

The first statement in the program says to transfer to the line immediately after the most recently activated GOSUB statement. But there are no GOSUB statements in the program at all, so there can *be* no "most recently activated" one. Of course, the system gives an error message when it tries to carry out line 10. And, of course, no one would write a program like that. . . at least, not intentionally. But this one results in the same error message.

```
10    REM  FIRST, CLEAR THE SCREEN.

20         GOSUB 3000
30         PRINT "HELLO."
              .
              .
              .
140   REM     REPEAT IF USER ANSWERED "MORE".
150           IF A$="MORE" THEN 10
160   REM
```

oops! →

```
3000 REM  CLEAR SCREEN BY PRINTING 24 BLANK LINES
3010      LET L = 1
3020 REM  TOP OF REPEAT LOOP
3030          PRINT
3040          LET L = L + 1
3050          IF L<=24 THEN 3020
3060      RETURN ←
9999      END
```

When line 20 is reached, it invokes the subroutine starting in line 3000. The subroutine clears the screen by PRINTing 24 blank lines, and then RETURNs to the line after the GOSUB, that is, line 30. Everything is fine so far. Lines 30 through 150 are then carried out, and if the user answers MORE, the program repeats, reusing the subroutine to clear the screen again. But what if the user is done, and doesn't answer MORE? Then line 160 comes next, and then (uh-oh) line 3000. Lines 3010 through 3050 cause the screen to be cleared again and then. . . And then the machine arrives at line 3070. At this point, there is no active GOSUB. We didn't get into the subroutine by means of a GOSUB statement, we just sort of fell into it. The system doesn't have any idea where to RETURN, so — error. We solve the problem by adding

```
170          GO TO 9999
```

that is, by skipping over the lines that make up our subroutine.

> **Unavoidable fact of life**
>
> You, the programmer, must insure that the only way your program can enter a subroutine is by means of a GOSUB statement.

Here's the other side of the problem: The rules of BASIC don't prevent you from having GO TO statements in a subroutine, but the only *sensible* way to have your program leave a subroutine is by means of a RETURN. Otherwise your program will be building up a stack of still active GOSUB statements, each waiting for a RETURN. You may be able to get your program to work, but it will be very hard to understand.

One last thing to keep in mind is that if you use a variable (say, N) in one part of your program, if you do something to that variable anywhere else in your program, even in a subroutine, the value stored in the variable changes. That may seem only reasonable, but the problem is that you may have forgotten that you were using N for one purpose in one part of your program when you write one of your subroutines. BASIC doesn't know what you're trying to accomplish — it just does what each line says to do. If a line in a subroutine says to store some value in N even though in another part of your program you were counting on variable N to store some important value, BASIC doesn't know or care. It's perfectly happy to wipe out that important value if your program tells it to.

Unavoidable fact of life

You, the programmer, must keep track of how your program uses its variables. It's up to you to avoid conflicting uses of the same variable.

Once you grasp the idea of subroutines in BASIC, you'll see that the warnings we've been giving are just common sense. And you'll discover for yourself the benefits provided by subroutines. Not only do subroutines enable us to write more hierarchical, hence more humanly understandable programs, they also make it possible to express larger, more complex computations with fewer statements.

First, as we've already seen, a given subroutine may be called upon time and time again. In the second experimental program in this section, for example, each time the user answers MORE, the program *repeats*, and uses the subroutine starting in line 3000 to clear the screen again.

Second, a given subroutine may be called upon by more than one GOSUB, as we saw in Section 6 3, where we used our "get date" routine twice.

Third, a given subroutine may have more than one RETURN statement in it. Each time a subroutine is carried out, it will use only one of the RETURNs to get back to the main program, but in different circumstances, different RETURNs can be used. For example, in the date verifier program at the end of the previous section, for our convenience in writing the program, we included five RETURN statements. Of course, we don't ever *have* to have more than one — we could replace the RETURNs in lines 8260, 8290, 8320, and 8420 with GO TO 8520, and the program would work the same. It's just easier to follow what's going on the way we did it.

Fourth, there's nothing preventing a subroutine from being entered at more than one point. As long as a GOSUB statement references a line which eventually leads to a RETURN statement, BASIC is perfectly happy to treat it as a legitimate subroutine call. You may come across an occasional BASIC program which uses this fact to some tricky advantage, and you may occasionally discover a hard-to-find bug caused by a mistyped line number. It's inadvisable to use this feature deliberately, because it makes programs hard to follow.

Fifth, one subroutine may call on others to do parts of its work for it. We saw that in the bill generator, too. The main program calls on the "get input data" subprogram.

```
130          GOSUB 1000
```

Within the "get input data" subroutine, we called upon the "get and verify a date" subroutine.

```
1150        GOSUB 7900
```

And the "get and verify a date" subroutine makes use of the "test for legitimate date" subroutine.

```
7930        GOSUB 8000
```

Remember that the RETURN statement sends control back to the line after the most recently invoked active GOSUB statement. Thus, when we're in the "test for legitimate date" subroutine, there are *three* active GOSUB statements. When we RETURN from the "test for legitimate date" subroutine, we go back to the latest active GOSUB. In other words, no matter which RETURN statement is carried out, it will cause a transfer back to the next line after

```
7930        GOSUB 8000
```

At that point there will be just *two* active GOSUBs. Once the "get date and verify it" subroutine has finished its work, its RETURN statement sends control back to the "get input data" subroutine, and there will be just *one* active GOSUB. And so on. In this particular program — since in certain circumstances there are three active GOSUBs — we say that the subroutine references are **nested** three deep. In standard BASIC, subroutine references may be nested no more than 10 deep, but it's best not to worry about this restriction until you run up against it.

EXERCISES 6 4

1 Which are valid subroutine calls, assuming that there really *is* a subroutine starting at line 9000?

(a) `120    GOSUB 9000`
(b) `120    GO TO 9000`
(c) `120    GOSUB 2*4500`
(d) `120    GO SUB 9000.0`
(e) `120    GOSUB TO 9000`

2 Which are valid RETURN statements?

(a) `RETURN 1`
(b) `RETURN NOW`
(c) `RETURN`
(d) `9100    RETURN`
(e) `9120    RETURN TO FOREVER`

Refer to this subroutine to answer Exercises 3–6.

```
9000 REM  COMPUTE MAX AND MIN
9010 REM  VARIABLES--
9020 REM    X, Y      INPUTS
9030 REM    M2, M1    OUTPUTS--MAX(X,Y), MIN(X,Y)
9040      IF X>Y THEN 9100
9050        LET M1 = X
9060        LET M2 = Y
9070        RETURN
9100        LET M1 = Y
9110        LET M2 = X
9120        RETURN
9130 REM  END OF MAX-MIN
```

3 Show a sample sequence of BASIC statements which use the MAX-MIN subroutine to print the larger of the two numbers stored in variables A and B.

4 What happens when the computer tries to carry out the program below?

```
10      REM  PRINT THE SMALLER PRICE PER OUNCE
20           PRINT "TYPE IN PRICE ($), QUANTITY (OZ.)";
30           INPUT P1, Q1
40           PRINT "PRICE AND QUANTITY FOR OTHER PRODUCT";
50           INPUT P2, Q2
60           LET X = P1/Q1
70           LET Y = P2/Q2
80           GO TO 9000
                 .
                 .
                 .
     Max-Min subroutine goes here
                 .
                 .
                 .
9900         PRINT M1
9999         END
```

5 The program fragment below is supposed to print the height of the taller of two mountains. What goes wrong?

```
100      PRINT "TYPE IN HEIGHT (FT) OF TWO SUMMITS";
110      INPUT M1, M2
120      GOSUB 9000
130      PRINT M2
140      GO TO 9999
             .
             .
             .
     Max-Min subroutine goes here
```

6 How could you modify the MAX-MIN subroutine so it would not only compute the maximum and minimum value, but would also indicate which variable contains the larger number?

Section 6 5
Your Own Numeric Operations

BASIC has several numeric functions with three-letter names like INT, SIN, TAN, RND, and so on (they're covered in Section 2 4). What if there's an arithmetic expression which appears frequently in a program you are writing, but which isn't one of the supplied functions? You'd like to have a shorthand way to refer to the expression, and you can get it by defining a special numeric operation.

The rules for defining your own numeric operations are rather strict in Minimal BASIC. For one thing, you don't have much freedom in giving names to your special operators. You must choose one of these 26 names: FNA, FNB, FNC, FND,. . .,FNZ. (The FN parts stands for FuNction.)

Once you have your special operations defined, you may use them freely in arithmetic expressions, just like the functions that BASIC provides. For instance, if you've defined a function called FNR which takes a number and rounds it off, you may use it in ways like these.

```
230   PRINT "OR, FOR INCOME TAX PURPOSES, THAT'S"; FNR(B)
```

or

```
450   LET R1 = FNR(R1)
```

or

```
666   LET A = SIN(FNR(D*180/3.14159))
```

To define your own operator, you must include a DEFine statement in your program:

```
10      DEF FNR(X) = INT(X + 0.5)
```

We could have used functions in some of our programs in previous sections. For instance, in our bill processor program (Section 6 2), there are several places where we round off values to two decimal places. Instead of repeating the rounding expression, INT (*value**100 + .5)/100, we can define a function to do the job. We need to do the rounding in the second module, so it makes sense to put the DEF statement at the beginning of the subroutine for module 2.

```
2000 REM  MODULE 2--COMPUTE SUBTOTAL, TAX, TOTAL
2010 REM  FNC(V) GIVES V ROUNDED TO NEAREST CENT.
2020      DEF  FNC(V) = INT(V*100 + 0.5)/100
2030      LET CO = FNC(Q*P)
2040 REM  ASSUME FLAT RATE 6% SALES TAX.
2050      LET XO = FNC(CO*0.06)
2090 REM  TO  GIVES GRAND  TOTAL.
2100      LET TO = CO = XO
2130 REM  DONE COMPUTING ALL COSTS
2140      RETURN
```

Our new version produces exactly the same values as the original one, but we've saved ourselves some typing, and, more important, the program is easier to understand.

Let's follow through an example of using our new operation. Suppose that when the subroutine is invoked, Q has the value 11, and P the value 0.035 (that is, we've received an order for 11 items at 3½¢ apiece). Line 2030 says

```
2030      LET CO = FNC(Q*P)
```

That's equivalent to

```
2030        LET CO = FNC(11*0.035)
```

or

```
2030        LET CO = FNC(0.385)
```

Now the machine "looks up" our DEFinition of FNC. The variable V matches up with the value of 0.385, so the DEF statement says that the value of FNC(0.385) is

```
INT(0.385*100 + 0.5)/100
```

That's the same as

```
INT(39)/100
```

or

```
0.39
```

Thus, FNC(Q*P) has the result 0.39 in this case. That value is assigned to CO, and on we go.

EXERCISES 6 5

1 Suppose apples are 59¢ a pound and you have bought 8.5 pounds. Write a single PRINT statement which uses the FNC function of this section to print the price (in dollars and cents, like $5.23) that you would have to pay for them, including 6% sales tax.

2 Write a DEF statement defining a function called FNR which rounds a value to the nearest whole number. For instance, FNR(0.8) is 1, and FNR(3.225) is 3.

3 Rewrite the FNC function so that it uses the FNR function from Exercise 2 in its computation.

4 If the bank pays you interest at a rate R (where R = .05 means 5%), then your money will double in log (2)/log (1 + R) years. Write a function FNT which computes how long it takes money to double when invested at a rate R.

5 Write a program to print how long it takes money to double at 5%, 6%, 7%,. . .,12%. Use the function from Exercise 4.

6 Define a function which will compute how long it will take $1 invested at an annual rate R to turn into a million dollars. (Hint: It will have to double twenty times.) Use the function FNT from Exercise 4 in your definition of this function.

Section 6 6

Formalities About DEFined Functions

We've already said that the only names you can use when you define functions are FNA, FNB, FNC,. . .,FNZ, and that you must provide a DEF statement for each one. But there are more rules.

The DEFine statement may have one of two forms: either

DEF FN*n* = *numeric expression*

or

DEF FN*n(parameter)* = *numeric expression*

In the previous section we used only the second form. The first form is used when the function doesn't need to be given a value to work on. You could use this type of operation to provide a commonly used constant

```
20     DEF  FNP = 3.14159
```

or, more commonly, to return a random number in some range. For instance, FND will give a random number between 1 and 52.

```
30     DEF  FND = INT(52*RND + 1)
```

The second form of the DEF statement includes a **parameter** enclosed in parentheses. A **parameter** looks just like a numeric variable name, but it has a different meaning. When the function is used in a program, it will be given some value to operate on. This value is known as the **argument** in the function reference. Wherever you use the parameter in the DEF statement, the value of the **argument** will be substituted for it in the computation. The *parameter* has no effect outside the DEF statement where it is used. In fact, the program may contain a numeric variable with the same name as the parameter, and that variable will have no direct connection with the DEF statement. Parameters are sometimes called **dummy arguments** because they stand for the actual values that will be used when the function is referenced.

The *numeric expression* in a DEF statement may be any legal arithmetic expression. It may refer to previously defined functions, but it may not refer to itself. That is,

```
40     DEF  FNF(N) = FNF(N - 1)
```

is *not* allowed.

The *expression* may also refer to numeric variables. For example, in the function definition.

```
50     DEF  FNL(X) = A*X + B
```

the variables A and B are ordinary numeric variables whose values will be looked up by the computer and used whenever FNL is evaluated.

Any function DEFined via the parameter-less form of the DEF statement is referenced by its name alone, as shown below for FNP and FND.

```
300    PRINT "PI="; FNP
```

or

```
510    LET C = FND
520    PRINT "YOU GOT CARD NUMBER"; C
```

A function DEFined with a parameter is referenced by giving its name and a numeric expression in parentheses:

a legal numeric expression

```
150    PRINT "THE SALE PRICE IS"; FNR( FNC( S/L )); "% LOWER"
```

this is a legal numeric expression too

The numeric expression in the reference to the function is evaluated first. Then its value is used wherever the parameter appears in the DEF statement which defines the function.

EXERCISES 6 6

1 What is wrong with the following function definition?

```
10    DEF  FNX(V + 1) = V + 2
```

2 What does the following function do?

```
10    DEF  FNX = 3.14159 / 2
```

3 Define a function to deliver a random whole number between 1 and N, where N is the parameter of the function.

4 Define a function to deliver the sum of two random numbers between 1 and 6, as if you were rolling a pair of dice. Use the function from Exercise 3 in your definition.

5 Which of the symbols D, D1, and D2 are parameters in the function below?

```
10    DEF  FNX(D) = D*(D1 - D2)
```

6 What does the function FNY below compute?

```
10    DEF  FNX(X) = X + X
20    DEF  FNY(X) = FNX( FNX( X) )
```

7 Using the functions of Exercise 6, what does the following statement print?

```
100    PRINT FNY(5); FNY(3); FNY(3 + 5)
```

PROBLEMS 6

Even if the particular problem you're working on doesn't mention subroutines or functions, be sure to make use of them if they are appropriate.

1 Write a program which asks the user for two baseball teams' names, the two starting pitchers, and each of their won-lost records. Have your program print that information in accord with this spacing chart:

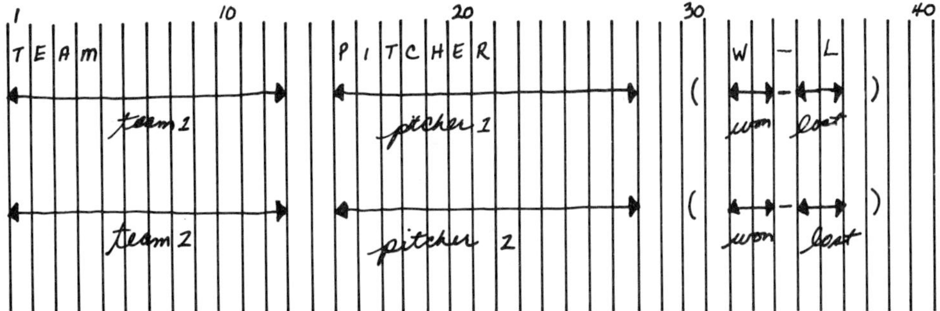

2 Write a subroutine which accepts a string A$, and which returns a value R with these values and meanings:

R = 0	The string in A$ means NO
R = 1	The string in A$ means YES
R = −1	Can't tell what A$ means

Design your subroutine so it will accept at least Y, YES, and YEP for a YES, and at least NO, N, and NOPE for NO.

Write a test program to demonstrate the operation of your subroutine.

3 Enter the date verification subroutine and use it to develop a program which, given today's date, prints tomorrow's date. (Hint: Add 1 to day; if that doesn't give a valid date, set day to 1 and add 1 to month. . . .) Use it to answer such exciting questions as, "What was the day after 2/28/1918?"

4 Revise the date entry subroutine so that if the user gives a year greater than 78 but less than 100, the subroutine adds 1900 to the value; if the user enters a value between 0 and 78, it adds 2000; if the user gives a value over 1752, it accepts the value as the year; otherwise it asks the user to repeat the entry.

5 Devise and test an operator called FNS (for sale) which rounds a value *up* to the nearest ¢. Use it in a program which a store could use to detemine the prices to mark on their merchandise for their annual ⅓-off sale. Your program should ask for the regular price and print the sale price.

6 The Good News Ice Cream Company sells 500,000 quarts of ice cream a year. The stores pay 85¢ a quart for each of Good News' 12 "natural" flavors. Raw materials cost 30¢ a quart.

Good News' research department reports that a new process has been developed that will cut the cost of raw materials by ⅓, to 20¢ a quart. However, the new process has the side effects of making the ice cream a little foamy and slightly less smooth.

The marketing department estimates that sales will be hurt by these changes. When pressed for figures, they say sales could drop by as little as 10% or by as much as 50% — they can't tell.

Assume that Good News still charges the stores 85¢ a quart, and that the conversion of the plant to handle the new process is paid for with a 10-year loan, with payments of $32,000 year. Write a program which, given the percentage loss of sales the user enters, shows the loss or gain that would result each year for the first 10 years if a switch to the new ingredients is made. (Note: The marketing department was wrong. Sales *increased* by 10%. Can your program handle sales increases if you give it a clever input?)

7 (Warning— don't do this problem unless you like puzzles.) Here's a perfectly legal BASIC program. It does a very simple thing, in fact. It just does it in a complicated way. What does it do? Note: This program isn't guaranteed to work on anything but very small whole numbers. If the second number is too big, the subroutine may be called too many times before any RETURNs are carried out.

```
10    REM  WHAT'S GOING ON HERE?
20         PRINT "GIVE ME A NUMBER";
30         INPUT N
40         PRINT "AND ANOTHER (BETWEEN 1 AND 10)";
50         INPUT M
60         LET M = INT(M)
70         PRINT "WHEN THE FIRST NUMBER IS"; N
80         PRINT "AND THE SECOND IS"; M
90    REM  GOSUB TO GET RESULT
100        GOSUB 1000
110        PRINT "THE RESULT IS"; N
120        GO TO 9999

1000 REM   WATCH CLOSELY NOW...
1010       IF M<=0 THEN 1050
1020         LET M = M - 1
1030         LET N = N + 1
1040         GOSUB 1000 <------- !
1050       RETURN
9999       END
```

8 Two cars are traveling down the highway at 55 mph, with the second car 70 feet behind the first. The first car suddenly slams on its brakes. Will the second car be able to stop in time to avoid ramming into the first? It will if its driver is able to slam on the brakes before the car has traveled 70 feet (right?). The time it takes the second driver to apply his brakes after seeing the brake lights on the car ahead is called his **reaction time.** People's reaction times depend on a number of factors, such as how tired they are, how distracted they are, how drunk they are, etc., so it seems reasonable to model the reaction time as if it were a random variable.

Use this operator to get each driver's reaction time.

```
10    DEF FNT = (RND + 1)/2.0
```

It gives a random number between 0.5 and 1.0 second each time it's used. Note: You might want to review the discussion of RND and RANDOMIZE in Section 2 4.

Given the reaction time, you can compute the distance the second car travels and from that, tell whether or not there was a wreck.

Write a program that simulates 100 emergency braking situations and outputs the 100 different distances, the number of wrecks, and the number of "close calls." If the second car stops less than one foot from the first but doesn't hit it, that's a close call.

9 This function

```
20     DEF  FND = INT( 52*RND + 1 )
```

returns a random whole number from 1 to 52. Use it to "deal" a card from a deck of playing cards. Develop and test a subroutine which, when given a card's number, prints out its *suit* and *value*. Use this representation:

Hint:
suit: INT((*card*−1)/13)
value: **card − 13*suit**

card number	*card*
1	2 of clubs
2	3 of clubs
.	.
.	.
.	.
13	A of clubs
14	2 of diamonds
15	3 of diamonds
.	.
.	.
.	.
26	A of diamonds
27	2 of hearts
28	3 of hearts
.	.
.	.
.	.
39	A of hearts
40	2 of spades
.	.
.	.
.	.
51	K of spades
52	A of spades

10 Design, write and run a program which "cuts" cards against the user. Use the subroutine from Problem 9 to "deal" the user and the computer each a random card, and add a subroutine that determines which of two card numbers is the highest-valued card. Suits don't count, only values. Aces beat Kings. Ties are possible: for example, Ace of spades ties with Ace of clubs.

11 Write a subroutine which accepts two dates in the m/d/y format and prints out the one which is later in time (in the sense that 12/13/1982 comes after 11/15/1982). Test your subroutine on the following pairs of dates:

12/13/1973	11/15/1973
01/04/1944	02/04/1944
07/04/1776	07/04/1976
02/12/1981	02/22/1981
09/27/1999	11/22/1999

12 Write a subroutine which will print the day of the week that a given date falls on, using the formulas below.

d: day of month

m: month number (Jan and Feb are considered to be the 13th and 14th months of the *preceding year,* while March through December are months 3 through 12 of the current year.)

y: year

$$N = 2 + 2m + \text{INT}\left(\frac{3(m+1)}{5}\right) + y + \text{INT}\left(\frac{y}{4}\right) - \text{INT}\left(\frac{y}{100}\right) + \text{INT}\left(\frac{y}{400}\right) + 1$$

N mod 7 = N − 7*INT(N/7) = 0 means Sunday
= 1 means Monday
.
.
.
= 6 means Saturday

Examples:

1 Jan 73

d = 1
m = 13
y = 1972

N = 1 + 26 + 8 + 1972 + 493 − 19 + 4 + 1 = 2486

N mod 7 = 2486 mod 7 = 1 = Monday

31 Dec 72

d = 31
m = 12
y = 1972

N = 31 + 24 + 7 + 1972 + 493 − 19 + 4 + 1 = 2513
N mod 7 = 2513 mod 7 = 0 = Sunday

13 Write a subroutine which will print a calendar for a given month in a given year. Use the formulas of Problem 12 to compute which day the month starts on, and use the techniques of the date-checker subroutine of Section 6 3 to compute the number of days in the months.

14 Write a program to print a complete calendar for a given year. Use the subroutine of Problem 13.

Chapter 7 The READ and DATA Statements

Section 7 1

A Bar Graph

Data which is plotted or graphed is easier to interpret, and has a more immediate impact, than the list of numbers used to make the plot. In this chapter we'll develop a program which takes weekly sales figures (from Tortilla Flats Shoe Store), and prints those figures in the form of a bar graph.

Figure 7 1 1 shows what we're after. For each week we want to print a number of peso signs ($) proportional to the sales during that week.

problem statement: print a bar graph from weekly sales data

It's not hard to see that for each bar in the finished graph, we need to (1) get the sales data for that week, (2) figure out how many $s should be in the bar, and (3) print that many, thus making the bar for that week. The only problem is, we'd like to get the sales data for *all* weeks before we print the bar graph. It wouldn't look

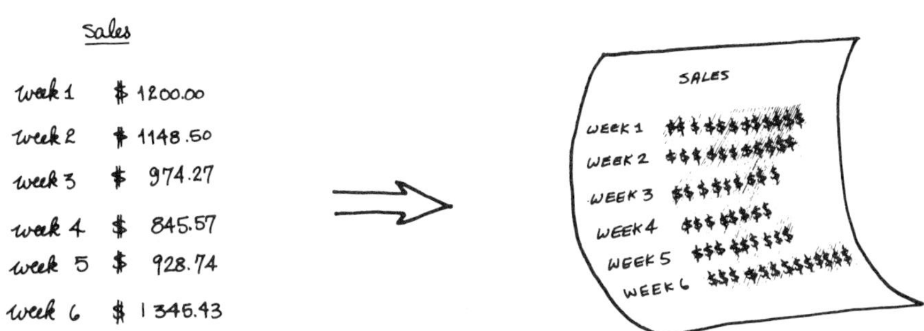

Figure 7 1 1 Trends are easier to spot in the graph

very good if the bars of the graph were interspersed with the PRINTs and INPUTs used to get the data:

```
SALES DURING WEEK 1 ? 1200
$$$$$$$$$$$$$$$$$$$$$$$$$$$$$$$$$$$$$$$$$
SALES DURING WEEK 2 ? 1145.50
$$$$$$$$$$$$$$$$$$$$$$$$$$$$$$$$$$$$$$$
SALES DURING WEEK 3 ? 974.27
$$$$$$$$$$$$$$$$$$$$$$$$$$$$$$$$$
                .
                .
                .
```

So we need to do something like this: First, get the sales data for all weeks. Then, taking one week at a time, and continuing while there are still weeks left to do, figure out how long the bar should be for this week, and print that number of $s.

There *is* a way to accomplish our goal using just statements we've seen already. But it is unwieldy. Suppose we want to plot a bar graph for six weeks' worth of data. Then this program will do the job.

```
10    REM  BRUTE FORCE BAR GRAPH PLOTTER
20    REM  GET THE DATA FOR ALL 6 WEEKS.
30         PRINT "SALES DURING WEEK 1";  } the pattern repeats
40         INPUT S1                      }   for each week
50         PRINT "SALES DURING WEEK 2";
60         INPUT S2
70         PRINT "SALES DURING WEEK 3";
80         INPUT S3
90         PRINT "SALES DURING WEEK 4";
100        INPUT S4
110        PRINT "SALES DURING WEEK 5";
120        INPUT S5
130        PRINT "SALES DURING WEEK 6";
140        INPUT S6
300   REM  FOR EACH WEEK, COMPUTE BAR LENGTH (SUBR 2000),
310   REM  THEN PRINT BAR (SUBR 3000) OF THAT LENGTH.
320        LET S = S1   }
330        GOSUB 2000   } the pattern repeats for each week
340        GOSUB 3000   }
350        LET S = S2
360        GOSUB 2000
370        GOSUB 3000
380        LET S = S3
390        GOSUB 2000
400        GOSUB 3000
410        LET S = S4
420        GOSUB 2000
430        GOSUB 3000
440        LET S = S5
450        GOSUB 2000
460        GOSUB 3000
470        LET S = S6
```

```
480          GOSUB 2000
490          GOSUB 3000
500   REM    DONE!
510          GO TO 9999

2000 REM     SUBR--COMPUTE LENGTH OF BAR FOR
2010 REM           SALES OF  S  PESOS.
2020 REM     ASSUMES BARS CAN TAKE UP TO  L  COLUMNS,
2030 REM     AND MAX SALES FIGURE IS  W .
2040         LET L = 64
2050         LET W = 1400
2060 REM     N  GIVES BAR LENGTH.
2070         LET N = INT(L*(S/W))
2080         RETURN

3000 REM     SUBR--PRINT BAR OF LENGTH  N .
3010 REM     NO PESOS SIGNS SO FAR, SO
3020         LET C = 0
3030         IF C>=N THEN 3070
3040             PRINT "$";
3050             LET C = C + 1
3060             GO TO 3030
3070 REM     DONE WITH BAR, MOVE TO NEXT LINE
3080 REM           ON PRINTER.
3090         PRINT
3100         RETURN
9999         END

RUN
SALES DURING WEEK 1? 1200.00
SALES DURING WEEK 2? 1145.50
SALES DURING WEEK 3? 974.27
SALES DURING WEEK 4? 822.25
SALES DURING WEEK 5? 928.74
SALES DURING WEEK 6? 1345.43
$$$$$$$$$$$$$$$$$$$$$$$$$$$$$$$$$$$$$$$$$$$$$$$$$$$$$$
$$$$$$$$$$$$$$$$$$$$$$$$$$$$$$$$$$$$$$$$$$$$$$$$$$$$
$$$$$$$$$$$$$$$$$$$$$$$$$$$$$$$$$$$$$$$$$$$$
$$$$$$$$$$$$$$$$$$$$$$$$$$$$$$$$$$$$$
$$$$$$$$$$$$$$$$$$$$$$$$$$$$$$$$$$$$$$$$$$
$$$$$$$$$$$$$$$$$$$$$$$$$$$$$$$$$$$$$$$$$$$$$$$$$$$$$$$$$$$$$
READY
```

this subroutine figures out how long the bar should be & stores that in N

depends on the width of your printer (LET L = 64)

depends on the sales figures (LET W = 1400)

this loop counts up to N peso signs printed

Our program needs some refinements to make the bar graph easier to interpret—probably we should print the week number and perhaps the actual sales figure at the base of the bar—but it does do the job. We've managed to separate the data-gathering phase from the bar-printing phase, so the graph comes out whole. But our progam isn't very general—it works for no more and no fewer than six weeks of data. Imagine how horrible it would be to rewrite it to produce a whole year's worth of sales figures! Fortunately, BASIC provides some features which make it much easier to write a general-purpose program like this.

So far, we have two ways to give a value to a variable. Either we name the variable in an INPUT statement

```
INPUT S
```

and allow the user to specify the value, or we use a LET statement

```
LET S = 1145.50
```

There's another way—by using a READ statement. Just as with an INPUT statement, you may list one or more variables after READ, as in

```
READ S
```

or

```
READ L, M, C1
```

and when the statement is carried out, values are stored in the variables whose names appear. The READ statement is like an INPUT statement, with one exception: instead of asking the *user* for the values as the INPUT statement does, the READ statement obtains the values from *within the program itself*. The programmer places the values to be READ in another new statement, the DATA statement. The DATA statement's sole purpose is to list values that READ statements can access. DATA statements have no other effect on the computation and may be placed anywhere in the program. Usually we'll put them at the end so they don't clutter up the rest of the program when we're looking it over. However, some people think it's clearer to put DATA statements near the READs that will use them.

There's no limit on the number of DATA statements that may appear in a program, nor is there a limit on the number of values that may appear in a given DATA statement (except the limit on the number of characters that fit on one line in your program). Each time a READ statement assigns a value to a variable, it takes the next available value from a DATA statement. The *order* of the values as they are listed in the DATA statements determines the order in which the READ statements will use them. Run the experimental programs, and you'll get the idea.

```
10    READ S
20    PRINT "FIRST VAL="; S
30    DATA 123
40    DATA -321
50    READ T
60    PRINT "SECOND VAL="; T
9999  END
```

```
LIST
10    READ S, T
20    PRINT "FIRST VAL="; S
30    PRINT "SECOND VAL="; T
40    DATA 123, -321
9999  END
```

Using READ and DATA statements, we can make a major improvement in our bar graph program. Now, instead of having to have a separate variable for each week's sales data (S1, S2, S3,. . .), we can get the next week's sales figure by just READing the next value from the DATA statements. Now we can write a program which can handle 52 weeks just as easily as 6. Here's our plan.

—bar graph—

Initialize (figure out scaling).

Week = 0

Read sales for first week.

While *there are more weeks to do*

> *Week = week + 1*
>
> *Figure out how many $s to print*
>
> *Print week number, then bar*
>
> *Read sales for next week*

To figure out the scaling factor, we need to know how many characters will fit on one line on the user's printer. We also need to know what sales figure should correspond to the longest possible bar. That depends on the largest sales figure. For now, we'll just ask the user.

As we continue refining our plan, we see that we don't have to worry about figuring out how many $s should be in a bar—our previous program did that fine. We'll just use subroutine 2000 as is. Printing the bar isn't hard—all we have to do is print the week number before doing what we did before in subroutine 3000.

The last thing we have to figure out is how the program is to know whether there are more weeks to do. Since we're working with sales figure (not profit), we know that no week will have a negative sales. And that means that we can adapt the "special data value to mark end of data" technique we used in the gas mileage program (Section 5 2).

Finally, we can write our bar graph program. First, here's the part that corresponds to our plan.

```
10   REM  BAR GRAPH PLOTTER
20   REM  ASSUMES DATA IS STORED IN 'DATA' STATEMENTS,
30   REM  WITH A NEGATIVE VALUE MARKING THE END.
40   REM  GOSUB TO INITIALIZE.
50        GOSUB 1000
300  REM  FOR EACH WEEK, COMPUTE BAR LENGTH,
310  REM  THEN PRINT BAR.
320  REM  W  COUNTS NUMBER OF WEEKS WE'VE DONE.
330       LET W = 0
340  REM  START WITH DATA FOR FIRST WEEK.
350       READ S
360  REM  REPEAT WHILE NOT END OF DATA.
370       IF S<0 THEN 470
380           LET W = W + 1
400  REM  SUBRS 2000 AND 3000 ARE AS IN PREVIOUS VERSION.
410           GOSUB 2000
420           GOSUB 3000
430  REM      GET NEXT DATA ITEM.
440           READ S
450           GO TO 360
470  REM  DONE
480       PRINT
490       GO TO 9999
```

Next are three subroutines which provide the details of the operations we call "initialize," "figure out how many $s to print," and "print week number, then bar."

```
1000 REM  SUBR--INITIALIZE.
1010 REM  GET INFO TO FIGURE OUT SCALING FACTOR.
1020      PRINT "HOW MANY CHARACTERS FIT ON ONE LINE";
1030      INPUT L
1040 REM  WE USE UP 10 SPACES FOR WEEK NUMBER.
1050      LET L = L - 10
1060      PRINT "NO DATA VALUE IS GREATER THAN";
1070      INPUT M
1080      PRINT "THANK YOU."
1090      RETURN

2000 REM  SUBR--COMPUTE LENGTH OF BAR FOR
2010 REM         SALES OF S PESOS.
2020 REM  VARIABLES--
2030 REM    L  MAXIMUM LINE LENGTH
2040 REM    M  MAXIMUM SALES VALUE
2050 REM    N  RESULT--BAR LENGTH
2060       LET N = INT(L*(S/M))
2070       RETURN
```

notice provision for printing the week number on the line with each bar

```
3000 REM  SUBR--PRINT BAR OF LENGTH N .
3010      PRINT "WEEK"; W; TAB(10);
3020 REM  C  COUNTS NUMBER OF PESO SIGNS PRINTED SO FAR.
3030      LET C = 0
3040      IF C>=N THEN 3080
3050          PRINT "$";
3060          LET C = C + 1
3070          GO TO 3040
3080 REM  DONE WITH BAR, GO TO NEXT LINE ON PRINTER.
3090      PRINT
3100      RETURN
```

Finally, we enter the DATA statements which give the weekly sales figures. For no particular reason, we put three values in each DATA statement. Remember—the only thing that matters is the *order* of the values, so we could have used one DATA statement for each value, or we could have crammed them all into one. We put the value −1 as the end-of-data marker; we could have used any negative value (see line 370 in the program).

```
5000 REM  SALES DATA TO BE PLOTTED.
5010      DATA 1200.00, 1145.50, 974.27
5020      DATA 822.23,  928.74,  1345.43
5030      DATA 947.84,  826.40,  532.45
5040      DATA 533.90,  425.69,  646.78
5050 REM  END-OF-DATA MARKER=NEGATIVE VALUE.
5060      DATA -1
9999      END
```

Here's a trial run:

```
RUN
HOW MANY CHARACTERS FIT ON ONE LINE? 64
NO DATA VALUE IS GREATER THAN? 1400
THANK YOU
WEEK 1    $$$$$$$$$$$$$$$$$$$$$$$$$$$$$$$$$$$$$$$$$$$$$$
WEEK 2    $$$$$$$$$$$$$$$$$$$$$$$$$$$$$$$$$$$$$$$$$$$$
WEEK 3    $$$$$$$$$$$$$$$$$$$$$$$$$$$$$$$$$$$$$
WEEK 4    $$$$$$$$$$$$$$$$$$$$$$$$$$$$$$$
WEEK 5    $$$$$$$$$$$$$$$$$$$$$$$$$$$$$$$$$$$
WEEK 6    $$$$$$$$$$$$$$$$$$$$$$$$$$$$$$$$$$$$$$$$$$$$$$$$$$$
WEEK 7    $$$$$$$$$$$$$$$$$$$$$$$$$$$$$$$$$$$$
WEEK 8    $$$$$$$$$$$$$$$$$$$$$$$$$$$$$$$
WEEK 9    $$$$$$$$$$$$$$$$$$$$
WEEK 10   $$$$$$$$$$$$$$$$$$$$
WEEK 11   $$$$$$$$$$$$$$$$
WEEK 12   $$$$$$$$$$$$$$$$$$$$$$$$

READY
```

EXERCISES 7 1

1 Write a DATA statement which will supply the values 39, −72, and 149 to the variables X, Y, and Z when the READ statements below are carried out.

```
10   READ X
20   READ Y, Z
```

2 Write a READ statement which will give the values 3.14, 2.7, and 1.86E5 to the variables P, E, and C by reading from the DATA statements below.

```
9990 REM  PI
9991      DATA 3.14
9992 REM            NAPERIAN E
9993      DATA      2.7
9994 REM                        SPEED OF LIGHT (MI/SEC)
9995      DATA                  1.86E5
```

3 What will happen if a user of the bar graph program says there will be no data value greater than 100, then enters a data value of 110?

4 Fix the program so that what happens in Exercise 3 won't happen and so that the user gets a (slightly inaccurate) bar printed out with a special signal to indicate that the bar is too short. The special signal should not mar the overall bar graph's appearance.

5 Which line(s) in the program correspond(s) to the part of the plan that asks if there are more weeks to do?

Section 7 2

RESTORE Politeness

The program we developed in the preceding section has an offensive feature. It forces the user to look through the data values to find the largest value. (We need that to figure out the scaling for the bars.) All of the sales figures are sitting right there in the program, in DATA statements, so why can't the program itself compute the largest value? The answer is not only that it can, but also that it *should.* Nobody likes to do extra work, and a polite program does all it can to save the user effort.

Let's plan to alter the initialize subroutine so that instead of asking for the largest value, it figures out that value itself. Here's how our subroutine can determine the largest value: First, look at the first data value. That's the largest so far. Then, go through the rest of the data items, one at a time, comparing each value to the largest-so-far. If the new item is larger, then that value becomes the largest so far. After we've gone through all the data, the largest so far must be the largest of all.

—finding the largest data item—

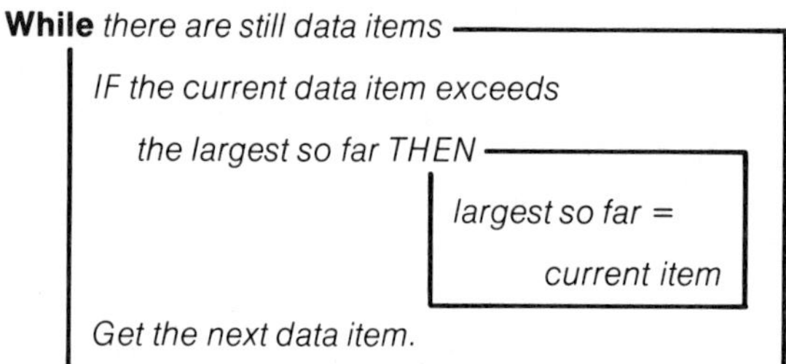

Largest so far = first item
While there are still data items
IF the current data item exceeds
the largest so far THEN
largest so far =
current item
Get the next data item.

Here's our revised version of subroutine "initialize".

```
1000 REM  SUBR--INITIALIZE.
1010 REM  GET INFO TO FIGURE OUT SCALING FACTOR.
1020      PRINT ''HOW MANY CHARACTERS FIT ON ONE LINE";
1030      INPUT L
1040 REM  WE USE UP 10 SPACES   FOR WEEK NUMBER.
1050      LET L = L - 10
1060 REM  SEARCH THROUGH THE DATA TO FIND
1070 REM  THE LARGEST VALUE.
1080      READ S
1090 REM  THE FIRST VALUE IS THE LARGEST SO FAR
1100      LET M = S
1110 REM  WHILE MORE DATA, KEEP LOOKING
1120      IF S <0 THEN 1200
1130 REM      NEW HIGH?
1140          IF S<= M THEN 1170
1150 REM        FOUND NEW LARGEST SO FAR
1160            LET M = S
1170 REM      GET NEXT DATA VALUE
```

```
1180          READ S
1190          GO TO 1110
1200 REM  M  IS THE LARGEST IN ALL THE DATA
1210        RETURN
```

No significant changes are needed in any other part of the program—we're just determining the value of M in a new way. Now when we run the program, it will ask HOW MANY CHARACTERS FIT ON ONE LINE? and will then proceed to go through the data to find the largest value. After that's done, control returns to the main program, and the bar graph can be plotted. Right? But wait a minute! If each time a READ statement gets a value from the DATA statements, it goes on to the next data value. . . and our new version of the subroutine goes through all the data values to find the largest. . . what happens when statements 350 and 450 try to get the data items for the graph? How can statement 350 get the next value when our program has already gone through them all? To find out what happens, let's try the program as it stands now.

```
RUN
HOW MANY CHARACTERS FIT ON ONE LINE? 64
ERROR--OUT OF DATA IN LINE 350
```

So the answer to the question of how the READ in line 350 can get the next data value is that *it can't.*

After our initialization subroutine has gone through the data to discover the largest value, we want to restart the DATA statements. That is, we want to RESTORE the READ-DATA operation so it starts at the beginning of the data again. In BASIC that's accomplished with a RESTORE statement. Adding a line with a RESTORE statement at the end of our initialization subroutine solves our problem, and leaves us with our finished bar graph program.

```
1210 REM  RESTORE TO RE-START THROUGH DATA
1220      RESTORE
1230      RETURN
```

Now when we run it, we get what we expected.

```
RUN
HOW MANY CHARACTERS FIT ON ONE LINE? 64
WEEK 1     $$$$$$$$$$$$$$$$$$$$$$$$$$$$$$$$$$$$$$$$$$$$$$$$
WEEK 2     $$$$$$$$$$$$$$$$$$$$$$$$$$$$$$$$$$$$$$$$$$$$$
WEEK 3     $$$$$$$$$$$$$$$$$$$$$$$$$$$$$$$$$$$$$$
WEEK 4     $$$$$$$$$$$$$$$$$$$$$$$$$$$$$$$$$
WEEK 5     $$$$$$$$$$$$$$$$$$$$$$$$$$$$$$$$$$$$$
WEEK 6     $$$$$$$$$$$$$$$$$$$$$$$$$$$$$$$$$$$$$$$$$$$$$$$$$$$$$$
WEEK 7     $$$$$$$$$$$$$$$$$$$$$$$$$$$$$$$$$$$$$$
WEEK 8     $$$$$$$$$$$$$$$$$$$$$$$$$$$$$$$$
WEEK 9     $$$$$$$$$$$$$$$$$$$$$
WEEK 10    $$$$$$$$$$$$$$$$$$$$$
WEEK 11    $$$$$$$$$$$$$$$$$
WEEK 12    $$$$$$$$$$$$$$$$$$$$$$$$$

READY
```

EXERCISES 7 2

1 What will happen if we put the RESTORE statement at the beginning of the program (say on line 5) instead of at the end of the initialization subroutine?

2 What values will the variables get in the program fragment below?

```
10    READ X, Y, Z
20    DATA 1, 2, 3

40    READ A, B, C, D, E
50    DATA 4, 5, 6, 7, 8
```

3 What values will the variables in the program fragment of Exercise 2 get if we insert a RESTORE statement at line 30?

```
30    RESTORE
```

4 What values will R and S get if we add the READ statement below in addition to the RESTORE statement at line 30 that was added in Exercise 3?

```
60    READ R, S
```

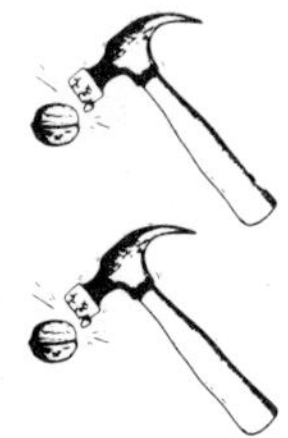

5 The RESTORE statement always goes back to the beginning of the DATA. Write a subroutine which will in effect go back to the third DATA item instead of the first.

6 Write a subroutine that will ask the user which DATA item he or she wants to get, then get ready to READ that one. If the user asks for a number larger than the number of items, print an error message and ask again.

Section 7 3

Strings in DATA

READ statements may be used to put values in string variables as well as numeric variables. Whenever a string variable occurs in a READ statement, this puts the next available DATA item into the string variable. String values and numeric values may be intermixed in DATA statements, but the values must be arranged in the correct order so that the right kind of data goes into the right kind of variable. If your program tries to give a string value to a numeric variable, you'll get an error. String values in DATA statement don't have to be surrounded by quotes (" "), but leading and trailing blanks will be ignored if the quotes are omitted, and some characters can't appear in unquoted strings.

unquoted strings may not contain:
& ' , ! "

We'll make great use of the ability to store string values in DATA statements in Chapter 9. For now, let's just look at an example.

In Chapter 6 we developed a bill-generator program which printed a neat looking bill, given information about the customer, product, unit cost, and quantity. There was one fairly obvious flaw in the program—it could handle just one product per bill. The problem was the same one we faced at the beginning of this chapter—if you're not sure how many products will be purchased (that varies from order to order), it's not easy to get all the information you need before printing the bill. The solution is the same as for the bar graph. By putting the product information in DATA statements, the program can get at it when it needs it, without messing up the printing of the bill.

For example, we could store the information about each order in its own DATA statement. This statement

```
              company        description     product code   quantity  price
5000    DATA DIGITAL SOLUTION, VEEBLEFITZERS, 1200-7A, 144, 1.05
```

provides the data for the first order we processed (see Section 6 2). Now, instead of getting the data with an INPUT statement, we get it with a READ statement.

```
1010    READ C$, D$, P$, Q, P
```

To print a bill for a particular company, say DIGITAL SOLUTIONS, we just start at the beginning of the data and use a READ statement to get the information about an order. If the company C$ is the one we're printing the bill for, DIGITAL SOLUTIONS, then add this into our printed bill. Otherwise, we ignore the data and go onto the next DATA item by carrying out the READ statement again.

To print a bill for another company, we RESTORE the DATA sequence to the beginning and go through the whole process again, this time looking for orders where C$ is the name of the new company. Problem 1 at the end of the chapter gives you a chance to enhance the bill-generator program in this way.

EXERCISES 7 3

1 What values will the variables get?

```
10    READ A$, B$, C$
20    READ X, Y, Z
30    DATA BOB, MARY, ALICE, 18, 23, 21
```

2 What values will the variables get?

```
10    DATA BOB, 18, MARY, 23, ALICE, 21
20    READ A$, X
30    READ B$, Y
40    READ C$, Z
```

3 What values will the variables get?

```
10    READ A$, B$, C$
20    DATA BOB, MARY, ALICE
30    DATA 213-444-9930, 448-26-8823, 414-71-3652
40    READ X$, Y$, Z$
```

4 What values will the variables get?

```
10    READ X$, Y$, Z$
20    DATA 123, 498.2, -298.73
```

5 What values will the variables get?

```
10    READ A$, X, B$, Y
20    DATA 10, 20, 30, FORTY
```

6 What values will the variables get?

```
10    READ A$
20    RESTORE
30    READ X
40    DATA 1972
```

7 What will be printed?

```
10    READ X$, X
20    PRINT X$, X
30    DATA 0123456789000000, 0123456789000000
40    END
```

Section 7 4

Formalities About READ and DATA

A DATA statement has the form

DATA *item, item*. . .*item*

where each *item* is either a number, a string value in quotes, or a string value without quotes. Here are some examples.

```
5000    DATA 1200.00, 1145.50, 974.27
3080    DATA PIZZA
6700    DATA "RODNEY BOTTOMS", 12
```

A READ statement has the form

READ *variable,. . ., variable*

where each variable is either a numeric or a string variable.

Ther RESTORE statement thas this form:

```
RESTORE
```

The sole purpose of a DATA statement is to provide data values which can be obtained by using READ statements. The position of DATA statements in a program is irrelevant to their function, except that the data items are accessed in order. If the computer reaches a DATA statement, it simply goes on to the next statement. The DATA statement has no effect on the computation.

A READ statement causes values to be assigned to the variables in the list following the keyword READ. A string variable may take a value from either a numeric item or a string item in a DATA statement; however, only numbers can be assigned to a numeric variable, Thus, this program will produce an error message when run.

```
10   READ S$, T
20   DATA SYSTEMS, DYNAMICS
9999 END
```

If a string value without surrounding quotes appears as a data item, when the value is assigned to a string variable by a READ statement, any leading or trailing blanks will be removed.

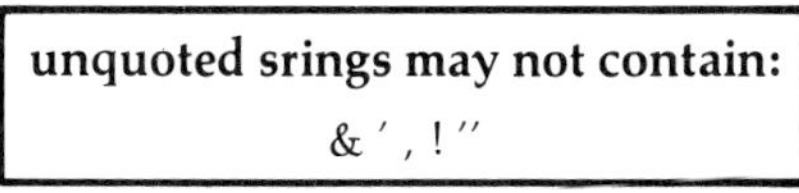
unquoted srings may not contain:
& ' , ! "

```
                                 blank
10   READ A$, B$
20   DATA ***     ,  " *** "
30   PRINT "---" ; A$; "---"; B$; "---"
9999 END
RUN                                blank
---***--- *** ---
READY    no blank
```

The RESTORE statement causes the next READ statement to begin at the first DATA item (that is, the leftmost item in the DATA statement with the lowest line number).

```
10   READ A, B, C, D
20   PRINT A, B, C, D
30   RESTORE <---------
40   READ E, F, G, H
50   PRINT E, F, G, H
70   DATA 1, 2, 3, 4, 5, 6, 7, 8, 9
9999 END
RUN
1              2              3              4
1              2              3              4
READY
```

```
10   READ A, B, C, D
20   PRINT A, B, C, D
40   READ E, F, G, H
50   PRINT E, F, G, H
70   DATA 1, 2, 3, 4, 5, 6, 7, 8, 9
9999 END
RUN
1              2              3              4
5              6              7              8
READY
```

EXERCISES 7 4

1 What will be printed?

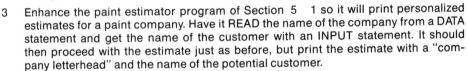

```
                       space
10   DATA " RABBIT ", RABBIT ,"RABBIT "
20   READ A$, B$, C$
30   PRINT B$; A$; C$; B$; C$
9999 END
```

2 What will be printed?

```
10   READ A$, B$, C$, H$
20   PRINT A$; " "; B$; H$; C$
30   DATA CO OP, CO, OP,-
9999 END
```

PROBLEMS 7

1 Using READ and DATA, rewrite the bill generator of Section 6 2. The new version should follow the guidelines described in Section 7 3. In particular, it should allow the bill to have any number of products and should allow the user to specify which company is to billed.

2 The bar graph program of this section prints the bars horizontally. Many people would prefer to see them printed vertically. This can be done by starting with the height of the longest bar (M in the program of Section 7 2) and scanning through (reading) the DATA items. For each DATA item that is less than M, print a blank. For each one that is M or greater, print a "$". Then reduce M by one, move to the next line, and repeat. Continue reducing M down to and including 1. Then the complete vertical-bar graph will be printed. Remember to RESTORE the data at the end of each pass.

3 Enhance the paint estimator program of Section 5 1 so it will print personalized estimates for a paint company. Have it READ the name of the company from a DATA statement and get the name of the customer with an INPUT statement. It should then proceed with the estimate just as before, but print the estimate with a "company letterhead" and the name of the potential customer.

4 Redo Problem 5 14, but, instead of having the user enter the pumpkin weights and contestant names, have your program READ them from DATA statements. ADD a final pumpkin weight of -1 so your program can tell when it has finished READing all the data.

The following six problems demonstrate more techniques for plotting graphs.

5 Use the line printer to make a graph of the function $\sin(x)/x$ from $x = 0$ to $x = 10$, stepping in increments of 0.1. Note: $\sin(x)/x = 1$ when $x = 0$, and all values of $\sin(x)/x$ are in the range -1 to 1.

In plotting graphs like this, it is easier to orient the x-axis down the page rather than across. That way, the program can compute one value of the function, plot it on the current line across the page, and then step to the next value and plot it on the next line, etc.

The only tricky part might be translating values of the function (which lie between -1 and1) to positions on the line to be printed (which we will assume run from column 1 to column 62). To figure out how far across the line to plot a particular value of $\sin(x)/x$, use the **digitizing formula.**

```
LET I = INT(60*(Y + 1)/2) + 1
```

where Y is a value of $\sin(x)/x$ Then I will be in the range 1 to 61 and you can "plot" Y with a PRINT statement

```
PRINT TAB(I); "*"
```

which will put an asterisk in the appropriate position on the line.

> **digitizing formula**
>
> The formula in problem 4 is known as a **digitizing formula**. It converts a Y-value, which lies between −1 and 1, to a positive whole number I, between 1 and 61 (the value 61 arises only in the special case when Y is exactly 1.0). The whole number I is known as the **digital representation** of Y.
>
> A digitizing formula takes numbers from a **continuous range** A to B into whole numbers in a **digital range** 1, 2,. . ., N. The continuous range and the digital range are chosen to suit the problem. The general formula for the digital value I, given the number Y from the continuous range, is:
>
> ```
> LET I = INT(N*(Y−A)/(B−A)) + 1
> ```
>
> It is closely related to the scaling formula we used in the bar graphs of this chapter and the random number formula of Section 2 4. Figure 7 P 1 illustrates how the digitizing formula works.

digitizing formula: $\text{INT}\left(\frac{y-a}{b-a} * n\right) + 1$ — *number of digital levels*

$i = \text{INT}\left(\frac{0.417 - 0.2}{0.85 - 0.2} * 13\right) + 1 = 5$ — *range of y-values*

6 Use the generalized digitizing formula to plot graphs of functions of your choice.

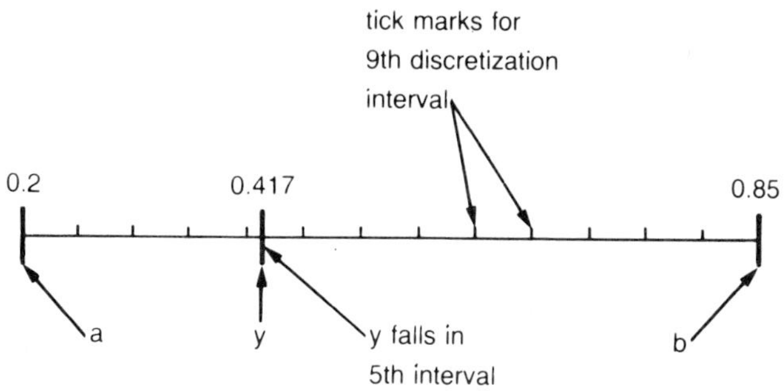

Figure 7 P 1 How digitizing works—the formula lumps all the numbers in the 5th interval into the "digital number" 5

7 Draw axes on your graphs as well as plotting the functions. To do this, you will have to check for two cases: (1) when the plotted point is to the left of the axis on the current line and (2) when it is to the right. At equally spaced intervals, print the appropriate x-value in place of the symbol you are using for the axis which goes down the page. At the bottom of the plot, print indications of the range of y-values covered by the y-axis (across the page). See Figure 7 P 2.

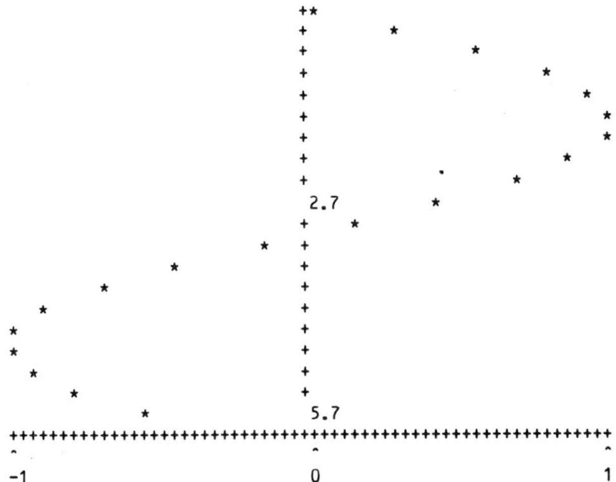

Figure 7 P 2 A plot of the sine function

8 Use the plotting techniques described above to plot the guitar signals of Problems 4 11.

9 Computer engineers frequently deal with an electronic wave form known as a **square wave.** It can be approximated by a sum of natural oscillations know as **sine waves.** The formula below gives this approximation of a square wave. Use the plotting techniques we have discussed in the above problems to show how the approximation gets closer to a square wave as the number of terms in the sum increases. Plot the function using two terms, then four, then six, and finally eight. Assume that all the numbers you will plot will lie between -1.5 and $+1.5$, and plot your approximations to $f(x)$over the range $x = 0$ to $x = 8$.

$$f(x) = \frac{4}{\pi}\left(\sin(x) + \frac{1}{3}\sin(3x) + \frac{1}{5}\sin(5x) + \frac{1}{7}\sin(7x) + \ldots\right)$$

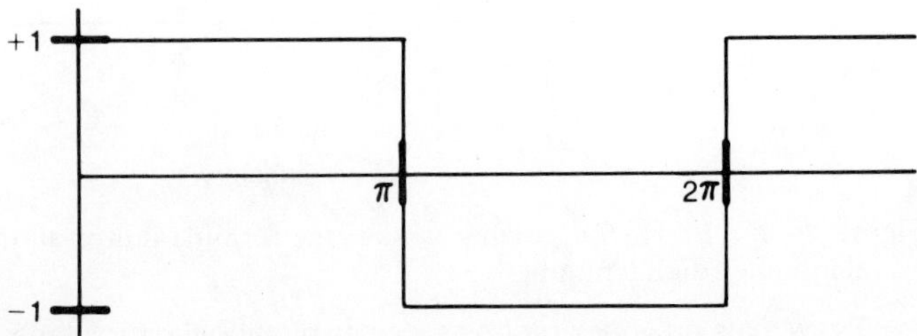

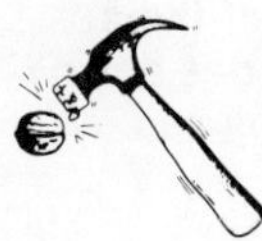

10 A well-known daredevil stunt man plans to jump a canyon on his motorcycle. Assuming that the air drag is proportional to his velocity (k is the proportionality constant), his position after t seconds is given by the following equations:

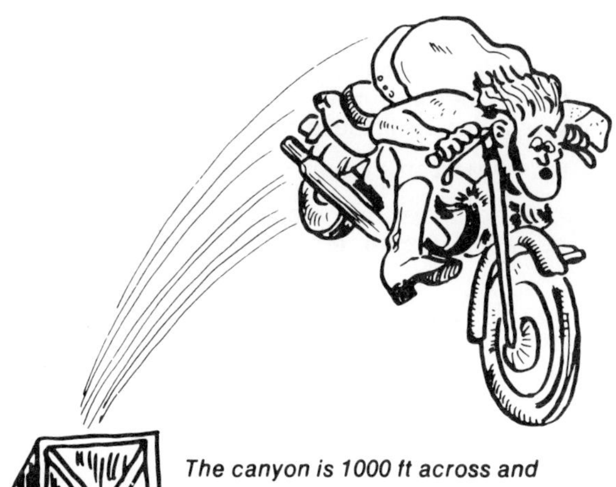

The canyon is 1000 ft across and 100 ft deep. The ramp is 20 ft high in the front and 20 feet long.

$$x = \frac{v_0 \cos \alpha}{k} (1 - e^{-kt})$$

$$= \text{distance}$$

$$y = \frac{-g}{k} t + \frac{1}{k} \left(v_0 \sin \alpha + \frac{g}{k} \right) (1 - e^{-kt})$$

$$= \text{height}$$

$$g = 32.2 \text{ ft/sec}^2$$

$$= \text{acceleration due to gravity}$$

$$v_0 = 330 \text{ ft/sec} = \text{take-off speed}$$

$$\alpha = 45° = \text{angle of take-off}$$

Write a program that writes out his path (x,y, and t) for the cases when k is 0.05, 0.15, and 0.25. Plot the trajectories your program predicts. If he lands on the other side, assume he stops immediately (in a heap).

11 Windows are a source of heat loss during the winter in a typical home. Heat loss can be reduced by installing curtains and drawing them when the sun is down. Unlined curtains cut heat loss through the windows by 20% and lined curtains cut it by 35%.

Write a program which obtains the necessary information from the user (see equations below), and which determines how much money on fuel bills the user will save by installing each type of drape.

cost of heat lost through windows =

total window area in square feet * $\left(\frac{1}{1.13}\right)$ * ← *R-rating for single-pane windows*

(indoor temp - average winter outdoor temp (°F)) *

number of months heat is on * $\left(\frac{8760}{12}\right)$ * ← *hours per month*

heat loss factor = 1.0 for uncovered single-pane glass window
0.8 for unlined curtains
0.65 for lined curtains

1979 fuel prices:	oil heat	$0.0050 per 1000 Btu
	gas heat	$0.0045 per 1000 Btu
	electric heat	$0.0120 per 1000 Btu

data point check your program

heat on for 3 months, 12 windows, average size 2 ft by 3 ft,
indoor temp 70°F, out door temp 40°F, no curtains
cost of heat lost through windows = $18.84
(assuming heat costs $0.0045 per 1000 Btu)

12 Problem 11 investigated the economics of buying curtains to cut fuel bills for heat in the winter. We computed the number of years it would take for curtains to pay for themselves in fuel savings. However, we ignored the effects of accumulated interest on invested capital. The idea is this: if instead of buying curtains, a person puts the money in a savings account, the interest on the money could be used to pay part of

the heating bill. Curtains would be a good investment only if you will save more than you'd earn in interest on the money. Add to the program for Probelm 11 to take this factor into account. Have the user type in the current interest rate and compute the savings on the curtains on a year-by-year basis with the formula

savings = savings on heating costs − interest on invested captial

Reduce the amount of invested capital each year by the amount of savings.Count the number of years until the invested capital goes to zero or less. This gives you the number of years to pay off.

13 Add one more step to the computation of Problem 12. Assume that unlined curtains are $4 per square foot and lined curtains $6 per square foot. Compute the number of years it will take for curtains of each type to pay for themselves in reduced heating costs.

Chapter 8 **More Loops**

Section 8 1

Why So Few?

So far, we've seen three types of loops: the **repeat forever**, the **pretest loop**, and the **posttest loop.** You may wonder why we've restricted ourselves to just those three forms. Since all our loops have been constructed using GO TO and IF-THEN statements, we *could* have made loops with the test in the middle, or with one test at the top and another at the bottom, but we haven't. The reason we haven't is a pragmatic one. Programmers have discovered over the years that loops are trouble spots, places where bugs creep into their thinking, and that the more careful they are in writing loops, the fewer errors they make. By restricting themselves to a few standard forms of loops, they avoid a lot of trouble and confusion.

When you've finished this chapter, you'll be familiar with six types of loops, the three types of loops which you already know about, and you'll learn about **FOR-NEXT loops, process loops,** and **search loops** in this chapter. Almost all the loops you'll ever need to write can be expressed conveniently and efficiently using one of these six constructions, so when you finish this chapter, you'll have the tools you need to write programs of as great a complexity as you care to attempt.

Section 8 2

FOR-NEXT Loops

One type of loop occurs so commonly that BASIC includes a special notation for it. This loop is the *pretest counting loop.* In this sort of loop, a variable (which we'll call the **control variable**) counts up or down in uniform steps from some **initial value** until a **limit** is reached. We already know how to write a loop with those characteristics, as the next program shows.

```
10    REM  PRINT THE SQUARES AND CUBES OF THE FIRST  T  NUMBERS
20         PRINT "HOW FAR DO YOU WANT THE TABLE TO GO";
30         INPUT T
40         PRINT
50         PRINT "NUMBER"; TAB(9); "SQUARE"; TAB(18); "CUBE"
90         LET C = 1
100        IF C>T THEN 9999
110            PRINT TAB(2); C; TAB(10); C*C; TAB(18); C*C*C
120            LET C = C + 1
130            GO TO 100
9999       END
RUN
HOW FAR DO YOU WANT THE TABLE TO GO? 12
NUMBER     SQUARE   CUBE
  1          1        1
  2          4        8
  3          9        27
  4          16       64
  5          25       125
  6          36       216
  7          49       343
  8          64       512
  9          81       729
  10         100      1000
  11         121      1331
  12         144      1728
READY
```

As you can see, the program prints a table of numbers. Line 90 sets the initial value of our control variable (C), line 100 is the pretest, line 120 causes the control variable to increase in steps of 1 each time through the loop, and line 130 is the bottom of the loop. The new notation, the FOR-NEXT notation, allows us to write an equivalent program in a more direct and concise way. Here's the new version of the same program.

```
10    REM  PRINT THE SQUARES AND CUBES OF THE FIRST  T  NUMBERS
20         PRINT "HOW FAR DO YOU WANT THE TABLE TO GO";
30         INPUT T
40         PRINT
50         PRINT "NUMBER"; TAB(9); "SQUARE"; TAB(18); "CUBE"
100        FOR C=1 TO T STEP 1
110            PRINT TAB(2); C; TAB(10); C*C; TAB(18); C*C*C
130        NEXT C
9999       END
```

this statement marks the bottom of the loop

this statement does the work of statements 90, 100, and 120 in the first version

```
RUN
HOW FAR DO YOU WANT THE TABLE TO GO? 12
```

```
NUMBER      SQUARE   CUBE
  1           1       1
  2           4       8
  3           9       27
  4           16      64
  5           25      125
  6           36      216
  7           49      343
  8           64      512
  9           81      729
  10          100     1000
  11          121     1331
  12          144     1728
READY
```

Once you get used to the notation, you'll probably agree that it makes it easier to see at a glance what the loop does. And in complicated programs, it makes it easier to figure out what statements are included in the loop — all you have to do is start with the FOR statement, notice the name of the control variable (C, in this case), then run your finger down the listing until you come to a NEXT statement with the same control variable as the FOR. If your system allows you to indent statements within the loop, as ours does, the loop jumps out at you, making it easier to verify that you've written it properly.

The FOR and NEXT statements don't enable us to do anything we couldn't do before. They just provide a clearer, cleaner, less error-prone way to write pretest counting loops. And we programmers need all the help we can get!

Section 8 3

Formalities About FOR-NEXT Loops

The FOR statement has this form:

FOR *control variable* = *initial value* TO *limit* STEP *step size*

or this form:

FOR control variable = *initial value* TO *limit*

Using the second form has exactly the same effect as using the first form with a *step size* of +1. So we could have written statement 100 in the program in Section 8 2 like this:

```
FOR C=1 TO T
```

instead of like this:

```
FOR C=1 TO T STEP 1
```

The program would have worked exactly the same way. Try it!

The *control variable* is a simple numeric variable (like C or I or T2 or whatever is appropriate). The *initial value, limit,* and *step size* are specified by numeric expressions. For instance, this is a valid FOR statement:

```
FOR I1=R + 1 TO 2*R + 1 STEP G
```

as is this:

```
FOR K=366 TO D2 STEP -1
```

The NEXT statement has this form:

NEXT *control variable*

Every FOR statement must be followed, eventually, by a corresponding NEXT statement, but there may be any number of lines between a FOR and its associated NEXT. The NEXT statement causes the statements between the FOR and NEXT to be repeated with a new value (the *next* value) of the *control variable.*

When the FOR statement is reached in a program, the first thing that happens is that the *control variable* is given the *initial value.* Next, the *control variable's* value is tested against the *limit.* If the control variable exceeds the limit (and the step size is greater than zero), the statements in the loops are skipped, and the computer proceeds from the statement after the matching NEXT statement. The idea here is that the loop is finished when the control variable goes past the limit. Of course, if the step size is negative, going past the limit amounts to becoming less than (rather than greater than) the limit. Therefore, if the step size is negative, the loop is finished when the control variable becomes *less than* the limit.

```
10 REM  FOR-NEXT EXPERIMENT
20      PRINT "INITIAL VALUE";
30      INPUT I
40      PRINT "LIMIT";
50      INPUT L
60      PRINT "STEP SIZE";
70      INPUT S
80      PRINT , "START OF LOOP"
90      FOR C= I TO L STEP S
100          PRINT "CONTROL VARIABLE=";C
110     NEXT C
120     PRINT , "END OF LOOP"
9999    END

RUN
INITIAL VALUE? 1
LIMIT? 3
STEP SIZE? 1
                START OF LOOP
CONTROL VARIABLE= 1
CONTROL VARIABLE= 2   <------  loop from
CONTROL VARIABLE= 3            1 up to 3
                END OF LOOP
```

```
READY

RUN
INITIAL VALUE? 3
LIMIT? 1
STEP SIZE? -1
                START OF LOOP
CONTROL VARIABLE= 3
CONTROL VARIABLE= 2  <------ loop from
CONTROL VARIABLE= 1          3 down to 1
                END OF LOOP
READY

RUN
INITIAL VALUE? 2
LIMIT? 1
STEP SIZE? 1
                START OF LOOP <---- try to loop from
                END OF LOOP         2 up to 1 — no loop
READY
```

If the control variable has not yet reached the limit, the computer performs the statements following the FOR statement up to the matching NEXT. When it gets to the NEXT statement, the control variable goes to its next value (that is, the computer adds the step size to the control variable), and the test of the control variable's value against the limit is repeated. Thus, the computer repeats the loop and changes the value of the control variable again and again until it passes the limit. When the control variable passes the limit, the computer goes down past the NEXT statement and continues from there. The control variable is left with the first value not used, that is, with the first value that passes the limit.

```
10 REM  FOR-NEXT EXPERIMENT
20      PRINT "INITIAL VALUE";
30      INPUT I
40      PRINT "LIMIT";
50      INPUT L
60      PRINT "STEP SIZE";
70      INPUT S
80      PRINT , "START OF LOOP"
90      FOR C=I TO L STEP S
100         PRINT "CONTROL VARIABLE=";C
110     NEXT C
120     PRINT , "END OF LOOP"
130     PRINT "CONTROL VARIABLE="; C
9999    END
                                   ^
                                   |
                            prints value of
                            control variable
                            after loop
```

```
RUN
INITIAL VALUE? 1
LIMIT? 3
STEP SIZE? 1
                START OF LOOP
CONTROL VARIABLE= 1
CONTROL VARIABLE= 2
CONTROL VARIABLE= 3
                END OF LOOP
CONTROL VARIABLE= 4 <------- first unused
READY                        value: 4

RUN
INITIAL VALUE? 3
LIMIT? 1
STEP SIZE? -1
                START OF LOOP
CONTROL VARIABLE= 3
CONTROL VARIABLE= 2
CONTROL VARIABLE= 1
                END OF LOOP
CONTROL VARIABLE= 0 <------- first unused
READY                        value: 0

RUN
INITIAL VALUE? 3
LIMIT? 1
STEP SIZE? 1                 first unused
                START OF LOOP  value: 3
                END OF LOOP  (the initial value was
CONTROL VARIABLE= 3 <------- unused since there is
READY                        no loop that goes from
                             3 up to 1)
```

Although it is legal to specify a step size that is not a whole number, cautious programmers rarely do — the limited accuracy of numbers in BASIC can cause surprises! Here's an extreme example of the kind of trouble you can get into.

```
RUN                          running the same
INITIAL VALUE? 0             experimental program
LIMIT? 1                     as before
STEP SIZE? 0.25
                START OF LOOP
CONTROL VARIABLE= 0
CONTROL VARIABLE= .25   <------- works as expected
CONTROL VARIABLE= .5
CONTROL VARIABLE= .75
CONTROL VARIABLE= 1
                END OF LOOP
CONTROL VARIABLE= 1.25
READY
```

```
RUN
INITIAL VALUE? 0
LIMIT? 1
STEP SIZE? 0.3
                   START OF LOOP
CONTROL VARIABLE= 0
CONTROL VARIABLE= .3  <------ even steps of 0.3 each
CONTROL VARIABLE= .6
CONTROL VARIABLE= .9
                   END OF LOOP
CONTROL VARIABLE= 1.2 <------ first unused value
READY

RUN
INITIAL VALUE? 1000
LIMIT? 1010
STEP SIZE? .0000001
                   START OF LOOP

CONTROL VARIABLE= 1000
CONTROL VARIABLE= 1000
CONTROL VARIABLE= 1000 <---- whoops!
CONTROL VARIABLE= 1000
CONTROL VARIABLE= 1000
CONTROL VARIABLE= 1000
CONTROL VARIABLE= 1000
               .
               .  <---------- we hit the "panic button"
               .
```

The problem here is that when the step size S, which is 0.0000001, is added to the control variable, there isn't enough precision to do the whole addition. Instead, it gets rounded off. When we add 0.0000001 to 1000, we get 1000.00 — no change! As a result, the loop runs on forever because the control variable never passes the limit.

Another surprising thing happens if you try to change the *step size or limit* while the loop is in operation. The surprise is that they don't change. When a FOR statement is encountered, the initial value, limit, and step size expressions are evaluated, and the values obtained are used to carry out the loop — *even if some of the variables which gave those values are changed later in the course of the loop.* Practically speaking, you should avoid altering any variable which appears in the FOR statement within that FOR-NEXT block.

If you want to write a loop with a step size of 1 for the first few iterations and then go to a step size of 2, you'll either have to write two separate loops or use some other loop notation, not the FOR-NEXT notation.

It is illegal to use a GO TO statement to jump into the middle of a FOR-NEXT block — that is, to skip the line that contains the FOR statement itself. The FOR statement sets up the values of the control variable, step size, and limit. To skip that part of the process is to take a chance on those values.

On the other hand, it is meaningful and sometimes useful to jump *out* of a FOR-NEXT block. In Section 8 5 we'll study a kind of loop where jumping out of a

FOR-NEXT block is useful in searching for a particular item within a sequence of values.

FOR-NEXT blocks may be nested — that is, one FOR-NEXT block may lie inside the FOR and NEXT of another block. In that case the inner FOR-NEXT loop is begun and completed anew during each pass of the outer loop. But unless they are wholly nested, FOR-NEXT blocks may not *overlap* one another. (And, of course, that wouldn't make any sense. Try it and see.)

Warning!

A number of older versions of BASIC do not follow the standards with respect to FOR-NEXT loops. Most of these variant versions define FOR-NEXT loops as if they were posttest loops. That means that the statements within the loop will always be carried out at least once, even if the initial value is already past the limit. This obnoxious situation can be avoided in several unappealing ways. One way is to place a statement like this in front of each FOR statement:

IF SGN(*step size*)*(*initial value* – *limit*)> 0 THEN go to the first line after the matching NEXT

But this added statement still doesn't make the program behave like a standard FOR-NEXT loop on some non-standard systems. Remember that the control variable is left with the "first value not used" if the loop is exited normally, and with the "last value used" if exited before completion. If your system leaves the control variable with an unpredictable value, the best solution is to avoid writing programs which depend on the value of the control variable once you've left the loop.

EXERCISES 8 3

1 We said that the *initial value, limit,* and *step size* in a FOR statement have to be **numeric expressions.** In the example in Section 8 2, the FOR statement in line 100 has constants for the *initial value* and *step size.*

```
100   FOR C=1 TO T STEP 1
```

Why is this legal?

2 Which are legal FOR statements?

(a) `FOR I = "START" TO "STOP"`

(b) `FOR I2 = 2 TO 2 STEP 2`

(c) `FOR I = 2, 4`

(d) `FOR K3 = 5*R TO 16∧2 STEP 2`

(e) `FOR 3 TO 5 STEP 1.5`

Use the experimental program to check your answers to each of the questions below. Recall that, in the experimental program, C is the control variable, I is the initial value, L is the limit, and S is the step size.

3 How many times will the computer go through the loop if I is 2, L is 10, and S is 2? if I is 2, L is 10, and S is 3? if I is 3, L is 6.7, and S is 2?

4 What value will the control variable C have when the loop is finished in each of the cases in question 3.

5 How many times will the computer go through the loop if I is 1, L is 8, and S is 1?

6 Insert the statement LET S = C just above the NEXT statement in the experimental program and answer question 4 again.

7 What sequence of values will the control variable C take if I is 5, L is 0, and S is −1?

Section 8 4
The Process Loop

Very often we are called upon to write a program which goes through a sequence of data values, and processes each value in a similar way. We've already seen at least two examples. In Chapter 7 we used DATA statements to store a sequence of values. First, we made a pass through the values to find the largest one. Then we went through them and counted how many fell in each category. Since situations like these arise so often, we use a special notation, the **process loop** notation, in our plans.

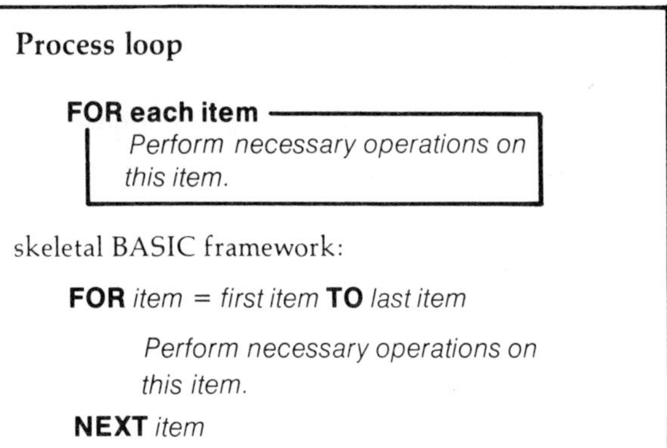

Think of the process loop as a unit. That way, when you need to perform operations on a sequence of values, you won't have to worry about the details of loop control. You can just think, "Process loop," and insert the necessary operations in the framework. What sort of operations will you be filling in? The possibilities are endless. For instance, to find the sum of a group of numbers, you can add each item, one at a time. If you want to find the largest value, you can check each item, one at a time, and determine whether it is the largest seen so far. After the loop has gone through all the items, the largest so far is, of course, the largest of all. To illustrate, let's take this program which forms the framework of the process loop.

```
10    REM  PROCESS LOOP
20    REM  INSERT PRELIMINARIES HERE.
 .
 .
 .
80    REM  LOOP GOES THROUGH ITEMS NUMBER I THROUGH L
90         LET I = 1
100        LET L = 10
110        FOR V=I TO L
120   REM      INSERT NECESSARY OPERATIONS HERE.
 .
 .
 .
200        NEXT V
210   REM  INSERT STATEMENTS TO PRINT ANSWER HERE.
 .
 .
 .
300        GO TO 9999
400   REM  DATA STATEMENTS GIVE THE ITEMS THEMSELVES.
410        DATA -5, 10, 18, -1,  0
420        DATA 17, -6, -9, 23,  2
9999       END
```

Suppose we want the sum of the numbers in the DATA statements. We can insert statements for initializing an accumulator variable for the sum and for adding each successive term to the sum. In the program below we have inserted the necessary preliminaries (lines 30 to 50), the necessary operations (lines 130 to 160), and a statement for printing the answer (line 220).

we're using variable S to accumulate the total of all the items

```
10    REM  PROCESS LOOP
20    REM  INSERT PRELIMINARIES HERE.
30    REM  SUM UP THE ITEMS.
40    REM  AT START, SUM-SO-FAR IS ZERO.
50         LET S = 0
80    REM  LOOP GOES THROUGH ITEMS NUMBER I THROUGH L
90         LET I = 1
100        LET L = 10
110        FOR V=I TO L
120   REM      INSERT NECESSARY OPERATIONS HERE.
130   REM      GET CURRENT ITEM
140            READ C
150   REM      ADD INTO SUM-SO-FAR
160            LET S = S + C
200       NEXT V
210   REM  INSERT STATEMENTS TO PRINT ANSWER HERE.
220        PRINT "SUM OF ALL THE ITEMS IS"; S
300        GO TO 9999
400   REM  DATA STATEMENTS GIVE THE ITEMS THEMSELVES.
410        DATA  5, 10, 18, -1,  0
420        DATA 17, -6, -9, 23  2
9999       END
```

```
RUN
SUM OF ALL ITEMS IS 59
READY
```

Or we can add statements to the framework to make a program which will find the largest number in the list, as shown below.

```
10    REM  PROCESS LOOP
20    REM  INSERT PRELIMINARIES HERE.
30    REM  FIND THE LARGEST VALUE.
40    REM  GET THE FIRST ITEM, THAT'S THE LARGEST-SO-FAR.
50         READ C
60         LET F = C
80    REM  LOOP GOES THROUGH ITEMS NUMBER I THROUGH L
90         LET I = 2 <------ we've already looked at the first item
100        LET L = 10
110        FOR V=I TO L
120   REM      INSERT NECESSARY OPERATIONS HERE.
130   REM      GET CURRENT ITEM
140            READ C
150   REM      IS CURRENT ITEM BIGGER THAN LARGEST-SO-FAR?
160            IF C<=F THEN 200
170   REM        HAVE NEW LARGEST-SO-FAR.
180              LET F = C
200        NEXT V
210   REM  INSERT STATEMENTS TO PRINT ANSWER HERE.
220        PRINT "LARGEST VALUE="; F
300        GO TO 9999
400   REM  DATA STATEMENTS GIVE THE ITEMS THEMSELVES.
410        DATA  5, 10, 18, -1,  0
420        DATA 17, -6, -9, 23,  2
9999       END

RUN
LARGEST VALUE= 23
READY
```

EXERCISES 8 4

What statements would you add to the framework program for the **process loop** to do the following tasks?

1 Find the smallest item in the list.

2 Find the product of all the items in the list.

3 Print the values of all items whose values are less than zero.

4 Find the average of all the items.

5 Find the sum of all items with values greater than zero.

6 Compute the number of items with values greater than zero.

Section 8 5

The Search Loop

Up to now, all our loops have had one exit. That is, there has been just one place the program goes to when the loop is finished. Conventional "structured programming" wisdom has it that this is the only sort of loop that should ever be used. And it is certainly true that it is always possible to write a program in such a way that all loops have just one exit. However, practical experience has shown a common sort of problem which is most naturally expressed with a multiple-exit loop: moving through a sequence of items, looking for one with a particular property. If such an item *is* found, we want to take one action; if such an item is *not found anywhere* in the list of items, we usually need to take some other action.

This sort of problem can be solved with what we call a **search loop.** Just as with process loops, we have a special notation for search loops which we use in our written plans.

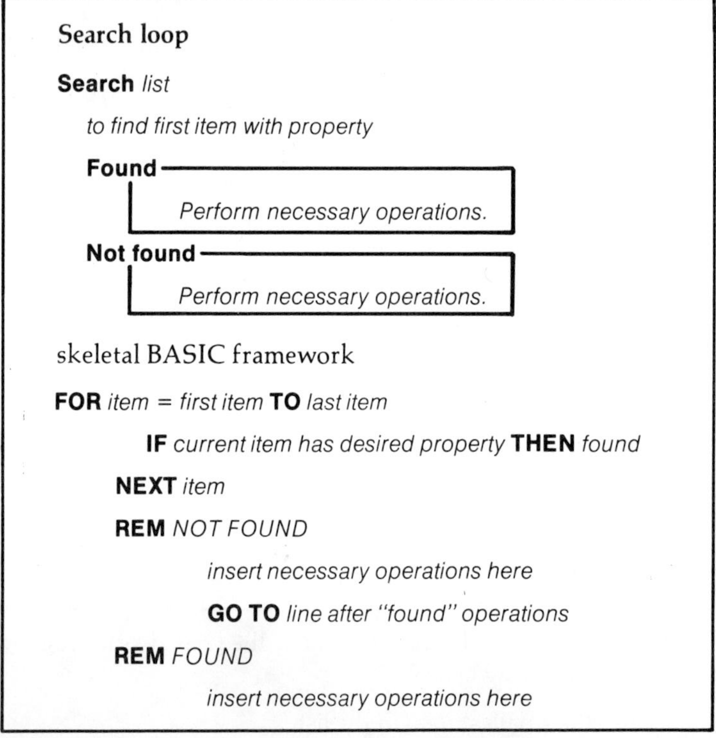

Search loop

Search *list*

to find first item with property

Found

Perform necessary operations.

Not found

Perform necessary operations.

skeletal BASIC framework

FOR *item = first item* **TO** *last item*

IF *current item has desired property* **THEN** *found*

NEXT *item*

REM *NOT FOUND*

insert necessary operations here

GO TO *line after "found" operations*

REM *FOUND*

insert necessary operations here

In the skeletal BASIC framework for the search loop, we put the NOT FOUND section in front of the FOUND section. If the FOR-NEXT loop terminates normally — that is, if the control variable passes the limit — it means we haven't found an item with the desired property. When a FOR-NEXT loop terminates normally, the computer continues with the statement immediately following the NEXT statement, and that is precisely where we've put the necessary operations for the NOT FOUND case. The only way the computer can get to the FOUND statements is by jumping there from the IF-THEN inside the loop.

To see the search loop in action, consider the problem of verifying the authorized users of a computer system. Suppose you are developing a large program and you want to restrict its use to only a few of the people who have access to your computer. You could assign an authorization code (password) to each of these people and have the program start by asking each user for his or her authorization code. If you have listed all the authorization codes in DATA statements within the program, you can write a procedure for searching the list of codes and refusing further access to the program to people who enter codes which aren't in the list.

This part of your program would consist of a search loop and would look like the example below.

```
10   REM  CHECKING FOR AUTHORIZED USERS.
20        PRINT "HELLO. PLEASE TYPE YOUR PASSWORD";
30        INPUT P$
40   REM  THERE ARE 6 PASSWORDS IN THE DATA STATEMENTS,
50   REM  SO WE WANT TO SEARCH THE FIRST SIX ITEMS.
60        LET I = 1
70        LET L = 6
100  REM  SEARCH LOOP STARTS HERE.
110       FOR V=I TO L
120  REM      GET CURRENT ITEM
130           READ C$
140  RE,      IS IT THE SAME AS THE USER'S ENTRY?
150           IF P$=C$ THEN 300
160        NEXT V
200  REM    NOT FOUND
210           PRINT "THAT'S NOT A VALID PASSWORD."
220           GO TO 400
300  REM    FOUND
310           PRINT "WELCOME, FRIEND."
400  REM  END OF SEARCH LOOP
1000 REM  LIST OF VALID PASSWORDS.
1010      DATA PIZZA, RED DOG, MIDNIGHT
1020      DATA HORIZON, SPLASH, GRELB
9999      END

RUN
HELLO.  PLEASE TYPE IN YOUR PASSWORD? RED DOG
WELCOME, FRIEND.
READY

RUN
HELLO.  PLEASE TYPE IN YOUR PASSWORD? RALPH
THAT'S NOT A VALID PASSWORD.
READY
```

—computer authorization—

Get user's authorization code.

Search *valid authorization codes to*

find a code matching user's code.

Found

Welcome user to system

Not found

Inform user of invalid code.

EXERCISES 8 5

What statements would you put in this framework to do the indicated tasks?

```
10    REM  SEARCH LOOP FRAMEWORK.
20    REM  INSERT PRELIMINARIES HERE.
 .
 .
 .
70    REM  THERE ARE 10 ITEMS IN THE DATA STATEMENTS.
80         LET I = 1
90         LET L = 10
100   REM  SEARCH ITEMS I THROUGH L.
110        FOR V=I TO L
120   REM     INSERT TEST FOR "FOUND" HERE.
130   REM     JUMP TO LINE 300 IF FOUND
 .
 .
 .
190          NEXT V
200   REM    NOT FOUND
210   REM       INSERT PROCESSING FOR "NOT FOUND" CASE HERE.
 .
 .
 .
290          GO TO 400
300   REM    FOUND
310   REM       INSERT PROCESSING FOR "FOUND" CASE HERE.
 .
 .
 .
400   REM  END OF SEARCH LOOP
9000       DATA  5, 10, 18, -1, 0
9001       DATA 17, -6, -9, 23, 2
9999       END
```

1 Print the first value less than zero. If no value is less than zero, print NO ITEM LESS THAN ZERO.

2 Print the first value found which is greater than the number the user enters. If no value is found satisfying that criterion, print NO NUMBERS LARGER THAN YOUR ENTRY.

3 Print the position in the list (i.e., 3 if the value is the third one encountered) of the first value that's greater than 10. Print NO NUMBERS EXCEED 10 if the search fails.

4 Print the position in the list of the first value which is equal to the one the user enters. If none found, print NO NUMBERS EQUAL YOUR ENTRY.

Section 8 6

Processing an Inquiry

This section introduces no new features of BASIC. Instead, it serves to review things we've already seen. Treat it as a chance to catch your breath and to assess your progress.

A **word processor** program is a computer program which helps the user create, edit, and print text (like letters, term papers, books, and so on). A large number of word processors are available for computers today, and people have begun running elaborate tests to allow potential customers to compare before they buy. Results from one such set of tests are given in Figure 8 6 1.

Name	*Cost*	*Effort to Learn*	*Ease of Use*	*Mistakes Made*
BI	$ 750	10	2	7
ChangSpell	$ 5000	6	4	6
C-Minch	$ 250	9	6	6
EDI	$ 50	10	1	9
Electric Wand	$ 425	4	8	5
EZ Writer	$ 325	5	7	6
Lindburg	$ 125	9	2	4
Magic Pencil	$ 400	9	4	5
MMM	$ 4250	3	3	6
The Wheel	$ 65	2	9	3
WordStroke	$ 500	9	5	7

Cost: Suggested retail price.

Effort to learn: Time required for subjects to achieve minimal level of competence, on a scale from 1 (least time) to 10 (most time).

Ease of use: Rating based on weighted total number of keystrokes required for 10 simple tasks, on a scale from 1 (hardest to use) to 10 (easiest to use).

Mistakes made: Rating based on weighted total number of command errors made by users during their learning phase, on a scale from 1 (least mistakes) to 10 (most mistakes).

Figure 8 6 1 Results from word processor comparison tests

Our goal here will be to design and create a program which will allow a user to access the results of the tests in a convenient way. Specifically, we'll assume that each user has some limit on how much he or she wants to spend, and has an opinion about how much effort he or she is willing to expend to learn to use the product. We'll ask what those limits are, and then show the data about those word processors which satisfy the user's criteria.

Given what we want to do, the plan is relatively simple to come up with. Basically, it's just a *process loop,* where the process is to see if the current item passes the user's criteria, and, if so, to print a line describing that item.

Ask for cost limit.

Ask for effort-to-learn limit.

PRINT a heading.

FOR *each item*
  IF cost is OK THEN
    IF effort-to-learn is OK THEN
      PRINT all data about this item

Each "item" actually consists of 5 individual pieces of information: the name, cost, effort to learn, ease of use, and mistakes made. The only thing left to do before we can write the whole program is to design the spacing of the output. We can save a lot of time by using a spacing chart (see Figure 8 6 2) to lay out the areas on the line where the data will be printed. Notice how the TAB( ) spacers in the finished program correspond directly to the spacing chart — and we didn't have to waste time fiddling with the TAB( ) values, trying to get the output to look neat.

```
LIST
10   REM  WORD PROCESSOR TEST REPORTER
20   REM    DATA STATEMENTS CONTAIN RESULTS FROM
30   REM    TESTS ON WORD PROCESSOR PROGRAMS.
40   REM    CATEGORIES:
50   REM      NAME -- NAME OF PROGRAM
60   REM      COST -- SUGGESTED RETAIL PRICE
70   REM      EFFORT TO LEARN -- WEIGHTED AVERAGE, 1 TO 10
80   REM                          10 IS HARDEST TO LEARN
90   REM      EASE OF USE -- WEIGHTED AVERAGE OF SAMPLE TEXTS,
100  REM                      10 IS EASIEST TO USE
110  REM      MISTAKES MADE -- WEIGHTED AVERAGE NUMBER OF MISTAKES
120  REM                        MADE IN SAMPLE TEXTS BY EXPERIENCED
130  REM                        USERS. 1 TO 10, 10 IS MOST MISTAKES
140  REM  FIND OUT WHAT CATEGORIES OF ITEMS TO SELECT
150       PRINT
160       PRINT "MAXIMUM COST = ";
170       INPUT CO
180       PRINT "MAXIMUM EFFORT TO LEARN ";
190       INPUT EO
250  REM  PRINT HEADING FOR REPORT
260       PRINT
270       PRINT "WORD PROCESSORS COSTING LESS THAN $"; CO
```

(program continued on page 192)

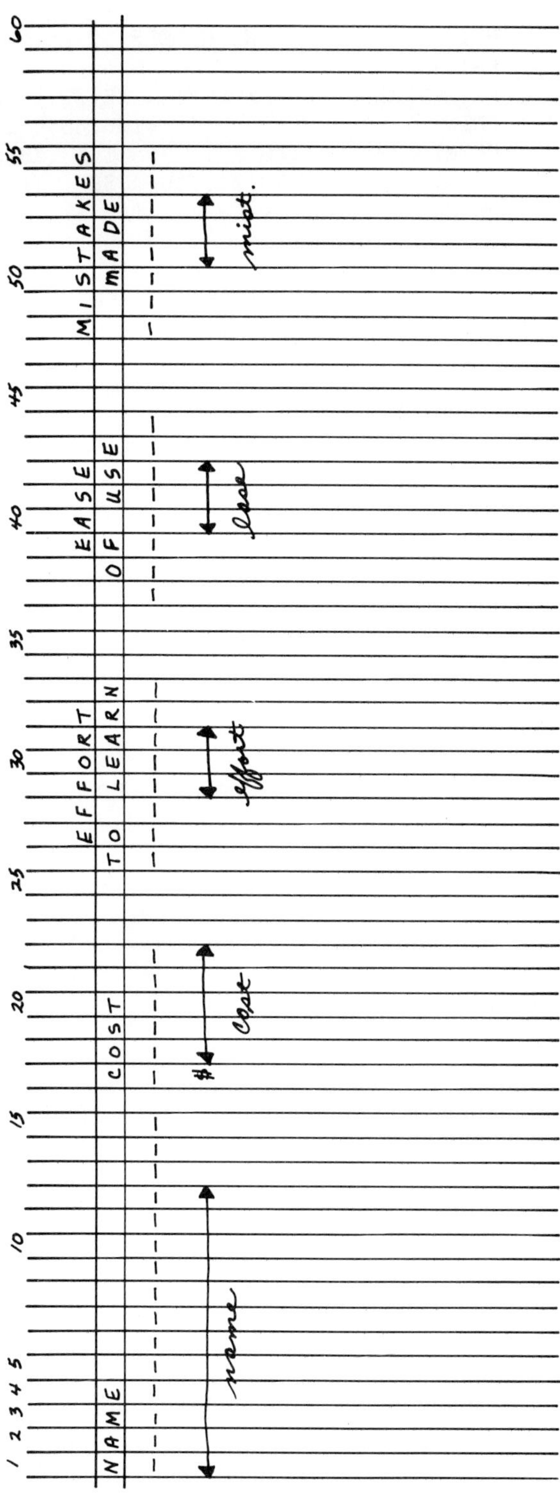

Figure 8 6 2 It saves time and energy to figure out the spacing on paper before completing the code.

```
280        PRINT "      AND NO HARDER TO LEARN THAN "; E0
290        PRINT
300        PRINT TAB(27);"EFFORT";  TAB(39); "EASE";
310        PRINT                    TAB(48);"MISTAKES"
320        PRINT "NAME"; TAB(17); "COST"; TAB(26); "TO LEARN";
330        PRINT        TAB(38);"OF USE"; TAB(50); "MADE"
340        PRINT "---------------"; TAB(17);"------";
350        PRINT    TAB(26); "--------"; TAB(37); "--------";
360        PRINT    TAB(48); "--------"
500   REM  PROCESS LOOP GOES THROUGH ALL 11 WORD PROCESSORS
510        LET I = 1
520        LET L = 11
530        FOR V=I TO L
540   REM     GET CURRENT ITEM
550   REM          NAME, COST, EFFORT (LEARN), EASE (USE), MISTAKES
560           READ W$,   C,    E,               U,          M
570   REM     DOES THIS ONE FAIL THE COST CRITERION?
580           IF C>C0 THEN 800
590   REM     DOES IT FAIL THE EFFORT TO LEARN CRITERION?
600           IF E>E0 THEN 800
610   REM       PASSED ALL CRITERIA, SO SHOW IT.
620             PRINT W$; TAB(17);"$";C; TAB(29);E;
630             PRINT TAB(40);U; TAB(51);M
800        NEXT V
810        PRINT
820        GOTO 9999
1000 REM   RESULTS OF TESTS ON EACH WORD PROCESSOR
1010       DATA BI                  , 750, 10,  2,  7
1020       DATA CHANGSPELL          ,5000,  6,  4,  6
1030       DATA C-MINCH             , 250,  9,  6,  6
1040       DATA EDI                 ,  50, 10,  1,  9
1050       DATA ELECTRIC WAND       , 425,  4,  8,  5
1060       DATA EZ WRITER           , 325,  5,  7,  6
1070       DATA LINDBURG            , 125,  9,  2,  4
1080       DATA MAGIC PENCIL        , 400,  9,  4,  5
1090       DATA MMM                 ,4250,  3,  3,  6
1100       DATA THE WHEEL           ,  65,  2,  9,  3
1110       DATA WORDSTROKE          , 500,  9,  5,  7
9999       END
READY
```

compare with our spacing chart

getting the next item

```
RUN

MAXIMUM COST = ? 450
MAXIMUM EFFORT TO LEARN ? 5

WORD PROCESSORS COSTING LESS THAN $ 450
      AND NO HARDER TO LEARN THAN   5

                            EFFORT     EASE     MISTAKES
NAME               COST    TO LEARN   OF USE      MADE
---------------   ------   --------  --------   --------
ELECTRIC WAND     $ 425       4          8          5
EZ WRITER         $ 325       5          7          6
THE WHEEL         $ 65        2          9          3
```

only three pass the criteria

```
READY
RUN

MAXIMUM COST = ? 750
MAXIMUM EFFORT TO LEARN ? 9

WORD PROCESSORS COSTING LESS THAN $ 750 ← less stringent criteria
     AND NO HARDER TO LEARN THAN   9

                             EFFORT      EASE     MISTAKES
NAME                 COST   TO LEARN    OF USE      MADE
---------------     ------  --------   --------   --------
C-MINCH             $ 250       9          6          6
ELECTRIC WAND       $ 425       4          8          5
EZ-WRITER           $ 325       5          7          6
LINDBURG            $ 125       9          2          4
MAGIC PENCIL        $ 400       9          4          5
THE WHEEL           $ 65        2          9          3
WORDSTROKE          $ 500       9          5          7

READY
```

EXERCISES 8 6

1 Which are valid reasons for using a process loop in the word processor test report program?

(a) We know that no user will ever want fewer than two lines printed.

(b) We always want to go through every item in the list.

(c) We're not looking for the first item that meets the criteria; we want all of them.

(d) The search loop is too complicated to use when you have to figure out the spacing.

2 Modify the plan to include a user specified criterion on the ease-of-use rating instead of the effort to learn rating.

3 Modify the program to include a validity check on the effort-to-learn criterion as shown in this partial plan:

Ask for effort-to-learn limit.

IF effort-to-learn isn't in the range of 1 to 10 THEN

PRINT warning message.

Repeat IF *effort to learn not in range.*

4 Some of these tasks call for a *process loop*, some for a *search loop*. Which calls for which? (If a task seems to require both, name only the search loop.)

(a) Find the largest of a list of numbers.

(b) Find the first occurrence of the name SMITH in a list of names.

(c) Find all items which cost more than $10.

(d) Find the first item whose name appears in the list more than once.

PROBLEMS 8

1 Businesses depreciate capital assets for tax purposes on a year-by-year basis. Write a program which accepts from the user (1) the name of a capital asset, (2) the cost of the asset, (3) the expected life of the asset, and (4) the estimated salvage value of the asset at the end of its expected life. The program should print out a depreciation table using the **straightline depreciation** method. Each year the asset is depreciated by an amount equal to the difference between its cost and its salvage value divided by its expected life. Its book value decreases by that amount each year. Your table should cover the years of expected life for the asset.

```
ASSET:   TRS 80 - LEVEL II
                    COST:   $ 1000
                    LIFE:   5 YEARS
                 SALVAGE:   $ 500

DEPRECIATION TABLE

YEAR     DEPRECIATION  VALUE
 1         $ 100       $ 900
 2         $ 100       $ 800
 3         $ 100       $ 700
 4         $ 100       $ 600
 5         $ 100       $ 500
```

2 Print a table of the value of an annuity on a yearly basis. Accept from the user (1) the amount invested, (2) the annual interest rate, and (3) the number of years desired in the table. Print the value at the end of each year, compounding the interest yearly.

```
AMOUNT INVESTED:       $ 1000
ANNUAL INTEREST RATE: 10%

     YEAR INTEREST     VALUE
      1   $ 100       $ 1100
      2   $ 110       $ 1210
      3   $ 121       $ 1331
      4   $ 133.1     $ 1464.1
      5   $ 146.41    $ 1610.51
```

3 Enhance the program for either Problem 1 or Problem 2 so it prints the actual years (e.g., 1983, 1984, 1985,. . .) instead of just year 1, year 2, year 3,. . . Have the user input the year in which the asset was acquired, and have your FOR-NEXT loop run from that year up to the total number of years desired by the user.

4 Modify the plan and program from Section 8 6 so it asks for (and uses) criteria on all four measures of the word processors (cost, effort to learn, ease of use, mistakes made).

5 Using a collection of items from a consumer magazine, such as ratings of cameras or cars, and basing your plan and program on those in Section 8 6, write a program that shows the user which items meet the criteria he or she enters.

6 Print a table showing the amount owed on an installment loan with monthly payments. Accept from the user (1) the amount of the loan, (2) the annual interest rate (3) the amount of each payment, and (4) the number of payments to be made. Print, on a monthly basis, the current amount owed, the interest paid this month, and the amount paid on the principal this month. Interest is charged on the unpaid balance (current principal) each month.

```
AMOUNT OF LOAN:   $ 1000
ANNUAL INTEREST RATE: 12%
MONTHLY PAYMENT:   $ 47.08
PAYOFF PERIOD:  24 MONTHS

MONTH         INTEREST       PRINCIPAL       CURRENT
                PAID            PAID        PRINCIPAL

  1           $ 10           $ 37.08        $ 962.92
  2           $ 9.63         $ 37.45        $ 925.47
  3           $ 9.25         $ 37.83        $ 887.64
  4           $ 8.88         $ 38.2         $ 849.44
  5           $ 8.49         $ 38.59        $ 810.85
  6           $ 8.11         $ 38.97        $ 771.88
  7           $ 7.72         $ 39.36        $ 732.52
  8           $ 7.33         $ 39.75        $ 692.77
  :              :              :              :
  18          $ 3.17         $ 43.91        $ 272.7
  19          $ 2.73         $ 44.91        $ 228.35
  20          $ 2.28         $ 44.8         $ 183.55
  21          $ 1.84         $ 45.24        $ 138.31
  22          $ 1.38         $ 45.7         $ 92.61
  23          $ .93          $ 46.15        $ 46.46
  24          $ .46          $ 46.62        $ -.16
```

7 Write a program which keeps accepting numbers from the user until a value less than −1,000,000 is entered. Then have your program print the number of values, the largest value, the smallest value, and the range between the largest and smallest value.

8 Write a program which asks the user whether he or she wants a Dutch flag or a French flag. Then, print a version of the appropriate flag, using * for red, + for blue, and blank for white. Use FOR-NEXT loops where appropriate. Is one of the flags easier to create than the other?

```
RUN
DUTCH OR FRENCH? DUTCH

+++++++++++++++++++++++++
+++++++++++++++++++++++++
+++++++++++++++++++++++++




*************************
*************************
*************************

READY
```

9 In the game of "rock, paper, scissors," paper wraps rock (i.e., paper wins over rock), rock breaks scissors, and scissors cut paper. Using a pair of nested FOR-NEXT loops, print out the table of all possible outcomes in the format shown below. To do this, associate a number 1, 2, or 3 with each object (1 for rock, 2 for paper, and 3 for scissors), and select the winner by making appropriate comparisons between the numbers which come up.

```
    ROCK, PAPER, SCISSORS
A TRADITIONAL CHILDREN'S GAME

PLAYER 1  PLAYER 2  WINNER
--------  --------  ------
ROCK      ROCK      TIE
ROCK      PAPER     PLAYER 2
ROCK      SCISSORS  PLAYER 1
PAPER     ROCK      PLAYER 1
             .
             .
             .
```

(Hint for the output: Have a subroutine which, given a number from 1 to 3, will produce a string variable with the value "ROCK", "PAPER", or "SCISSORS".)

10 Write a program which prints out a multiplication table. The size of the table should be determined by a number between 2 and 9 supplied by the user. Your program should print the multiplication table up to that number. For example, if the number is 3, your output should look like that below.

```
*  1  2  3
1  1  2  3
2  2  4  6
3  3  6  9
```

11 Write a program which translates English words into their French equivalents. The idea is to have the corresponding English and French words paired up in DATA statements. Accept an English word from the user, and then use a search loop to find it and its French equivalent. If the word the user entered isn't in your list of words, print an appropriate message. YES↔OUI, NO↔NON, PENCIL↔CRAYON, DOG↔CHIEN, HOUSE↔MAISON.

12 Make your program from problem 11 into a subroutine and test it on at least two different translation problems. (It's the DATA statements that determine what sort of translation is done — English to French, Spanish to German, English to Pig Latin, Greek to Martian, or whatever.) Be sure to RESTORE the data on each entry to the subroutine.

13 Use your subroutine from Problem 12 to accept a number from 1 through 20 from the user and print the English word for the number. Note: The "number" the user enters will be treated as a string by your subroutine, but that's OK, right? 1↔ONE, 2↔TWO,..., 13↔THIRTEEN, 14↔FOURTEEN,..., 20↔TWENTY.

14 Alter the subroutine you created for Problem 13 so it treats the first term in each pair of corresponding terms as a number, and the second term as a string value. Use this new subroutine to convert the numbers 1, 2, 3,..., 20 into the words ONE, TWO, THREE,..., TWENTY, and the numbers 30, 40,..., 100 into THIRTY, FORTY,..., HUNDRED. Have the search loop in your subroutine set the variable E to 0 if it finds the number and to 1 if it doesn't.

> **missing zero:** The number zero was left out of the list intentionally. If the input is zero, your subroutine should set E = 1; otherwise E = 0. This will be important in Problem 15.
>
> 908 = "NINE HUNDRED EIGHT" not "NINE HUNDRED ZERO EIGHT"
>
> 70 = "SEVENTY" not "ZERO HUNDRED SEVENTY ZERO"

15 The subroutine below, given a number between 1 and 999, will produce three numbers: the first digit, the second digit, and the third digit, each a whole number between zero and nine. Use this subroutine and your subroutine from Problem 14 to print English versions of numbers typed by the user. For example, if the user types 823, your program should print EIGHT HUNDRED TWENTY THREE; if 92, then NINETY TWO. (Hint: Use the output from the subroutine below to produce a conversion of the last two digits of the input number to values appropriate for your translator subroutine (from Problem 14) as follows: If the second digit is two or greater, then multiply it by ten and leave the third digit alone. If the second digit is zero or one, then add ten times the second digit to the third digit and set the second digit to zero.)

```
9000 REM  SEPARATE DIGITS
9010 REM    INPUT: N=1, 2, 3,   ... 999
9020 REM    OUTPUT: N1,N2,N3--THE THREE DIGITS OF N
9030 REM    EXAMPLE:    N=823  -=> N1=8, N2=2, N3=3
9040 REM                N=92   -=> N1=0, N2=9, N3=2
9050       DEF FNS(X) = INT(X/10)
9060       DEF FND(X) = X - 10*FNS(X)
9070       LET N1 = FND(FNS(FNS(N)))
9080       LET N2 = FND(FNS(N))
9090       LET N3 = FND(N)
9100       RETURN
```

data validation: An important part of any useful program is the validation of the data. The program should do as much as possible to prevent the user from running the program with incorrect data. When the input is numbers, one way to get the user to check an entry is to print out the entry in words instead of numbers. That way the user has to rethink the entry and may catch an error more easily. This trick and many others are explained in the book, *Humanized Input — Techniques for Reliable Keyed Input,* by Tom Gilb and Gerald M. Weinberg (Winthrop Publishers, Cambridge, MA, 1977).

16 People sometimes like to spell words by turning their pocket calculators upside down. Then some of the numbers look like letters.

number	*letter it looks like upside down*
1	I
3	E
4	h
5	S
6	g
7	L
0	O

Use a search loop in a subroutine to find and print one of the letters I, E, H, S, G, L, or O, depending on whether the input to the subroutine is 1, 3, 4, 5, 6, 7, or 0. If the input is any other number, have the subroutine print an asterisk. Use the subroutine in a program which accepts four one-digit numbers from the user and prints out what word that would look like on a calculator turned upside down.

17 If you get 23 people together and ask them all their birthdays, the odds are a little better than fifty-fifty that two of them will have the same birthday.

Hard to believe? Pick a person. That eliminates one birthday, and the odds that the next person you pick will have a different birthday are about 365/366 (this includes February 29 birthdays — the leap year people). That eliminates two birthdays. The third person will have yet another birthday with a likelihood of about 364/366. For the fourth person the odds are 363/366, and so on.

In the end, the odds that at least two people have the same birthday are the inverse of the likelihood that they all have different birthdays.

$$\text{likelihood of } n \text{ people all having different birthdays} = 1 - \frac{365}{366} * \frac{364}{366} * \frac{363}{366} * \ldots * \frac{367 - n}{366}$$

Write a program which asks how many people are at the party and uses a FOR-NEXT loop to compute the odds that at least two of the people have the same birthday. Use your program to find out how many people it takes to make the odds 90% or better.

Chapter 9 **Menus**

Section 9 1

The Idea

Many of our programs have asked the user to select among alternatives. For example, in our border-town store program in Section 3 5, we gave the user the option of DOLLARS to PESOS versus PESOS to DOLLARS. In the checkbook balancing program (Section 4 4), the user was given the choices CHECK, DEPOSIT, or FINISHED. A great many useful programs interact with the user in this way, allowing a choice among alternatives. Programmers refer to the list of alternatives as a **menu,** and the problem, from the programmer's point of view, is to convert the user's menu selection into a way of getting to the right place in the program to do what the user wants. We need to develop a method of menu selection which requires minimal effort from the user and which is general enough that we can use it over and over in different programs. In this chapter we'll develop a set of subroutines which we'll use henceforth in all menu-selection problems. Once you understand what they do, you can include these menu subroutines in your programs with very little effort. They are prime candidates for inclusion in your **subroutine library.**

> **Notice of intent**
>
> This chapter is a design study—the first versions of the **menu routine** we arrive at are incomplete in one way or another. The job won't be finished until the very end of the chapter. Our goal isn't simply to show you a menu routine—it's to show you how programs are actually developed and written.

During the development of a general method for solving a problem, it's usually a good idea to have some specific applications in mind. So as we go along, we'll work on putting our painting estimator program in its final form.

When we last saw the painting estimator program (Section 5 7), it had the ability to estimate how much paint would be required to paint any given number of walls, and each wall could have any number of windows. The *amount* of paint that's necessary depends almost exclusively on the area to be covered. But the *time* it will take is heavily dependent on the technique being used. Also, when a professional painter makes a bid on a job, the time required to clean the walls before painting has to be included in the estimate. Both considerations are in our plan:

—paint job estimator—

Give introduction.

Ask what technique will be used for painting.

Select *the appropriate time factor:*

- **brush** — *90 minutes per gallon.*
- **roller** — *60 minutes per gallon.*
- **spray gun** — *25 minutes per gallon.*
- **other** — *Ask user how long it takes to apply one gallon.*

select the appropriate time factor based on the technique being used

Thanks to the Tim Collins Painting Service Del Mar, CA

Ask what technique will be used for cleaning.

Select *the appropriate time factor:*

- **sponge** — *20 minutes per 100 sq. ft.*
- **mop** — *5 minutes per 100 sq. ft.*
- **other** — *Ask user how long it takes to clean 100 sq. ft.*

Give instructions for entering walls.

Area = 0 ← at this point in the program, the area "so far" is 0 — we add in the area of each wall, and take away the area of each window later in the program

> *Get width and height of this wall.*
>
> *Area = area + area of this wall.*
>
> *Ask if there are any windows.*
>
> **While** *there are more windows*
>
> > *Get the dimensions of this window.*
> >
> > *Subtract window area from total.*
> >
> > *Ask if there are more windows in this wall.*
>
> ← loop for each window in this wall
>
> *Ask if there are more walls.*

← loop for each wall

Repeat IF *there are more walls*

PRINT estimated time to clean walls.

PRINT estimated time and paint for walls.

PRINT total estimated time.

This program provides a good place to develop a menu system—there are four places where the user is asked to make a selection among alternatives. First, for painting techniques the user must choose BRUSH, ROLLER, SPRAY GUN, or OTHER. Next, for cleaning method, the user has a choice of SPONGE, MOP, or OTHER. The other two selections are between "yes" and "no". Let's begin by seeing what's involved with a selection like the first one.

Since our plan indicates that we want to do something different for each of the four cases, that means we'll need to GO TO the right section of the program based on what the user types in. It makes sense to think about using an ON-GO TO statement to select the right part of the program. That means that we'd like to turn whatever the user types into a number from 1 (for BRUSH) to 4 (for OTHER). Some programmers solve this problem in an impolite way—they force the user to do the translation.

```
1  BRUSH
2  ROLLER
3  SPRAY
4  OTHER
WHICH NUMBER?
```

Besides being unnatural, that method is prone to user error—there's nothing about the number 3 that reminds the user of a spray gun, so the user has to pay close attention no matter how familiar the program might be. Another problem with using numbers in this way is that the entire menu has to be printed out each time a selection is required, to remind the user of which number corresponds to what. On a fast video terminal, that may be OK. On a slow terminal like a Teletype, all the extra printing will drive the user bonkers, sooner or later. We'd like the user to be able to type in a word, like BRUSH, or ROLLER, because that's the natural thing. On the other hand, some users are terrible typists—they would get impatient if they had to type out the whole word ROLLER every time. We might want to accept B for BRUSH, R for ROLLER, S for SPRAY, and O for OTHER, as well as the complete words. It would also be good to allow for common misspellings—anyone who strikes the zero key probably meant to hit the letter O for OTHER.

Up to now, when we've offered the user a choice, our programs have used a series of IF-THEN statements to make the selection, like this:

```
IF A$="BRUSH" THEN 110
IF A$="B" THEN 110
IF A$="ROLLER" THEN 150
IF A$="R" THEN 150
         .
         .
         .
```

When there are more than a couple of options, the IF-THEN sequence technique is too cumbersome and inflexible.

So we have a list of legal responses, and a number associated with each. We can put the responses and their numbers in DATA statements, then use a search loop (à la Section 8 5) to find the response and associated number. If the user enters a response that's not in the list, the search loop will end up at the not found exit, and we can tell the user to try again. Here's our plan.

—menu subroutine—

Get user's reponse.

Set data to beginning of sequence (RESTORE).

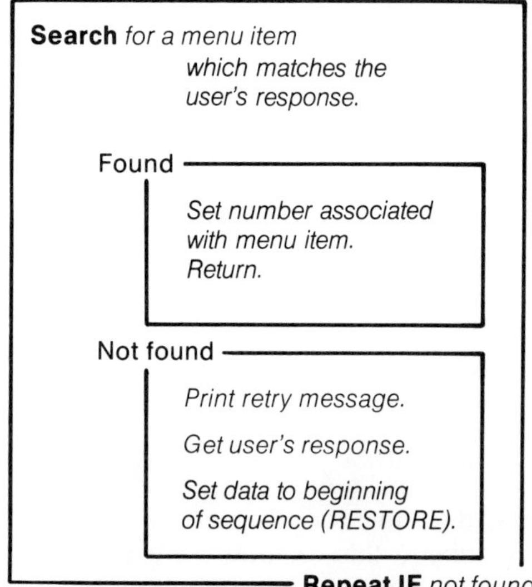
Search *for a menu item which matches the user's response.*
Found
Set number associated with menu item.
Return.
Not found
Print retry message.
Get user's response.
Set data to beginning of sequence (RESTORE).
Repeat IF *not found*

And here's the BASIC version. When the subroutine is called, the value in F9 should equal the number of menu word/number pairs in the DATA statements. We'll write a little program to test the subroutine soon—for now, look to see that the subroutine is simply a search loop which is repeated if the user's response is not on the menu. If a menu item that matches the user's response (U$) is found, then the search loop takes the found exit, and the **class** of that menu item (that is, the number associated with the menu item) has been stored in the variable W9 by the READ statement. If a menu word isn't found, the user is told so, and the search loop is repeated after the RESTORE statement starts the DATA off at the beginning again.

```
            9500 REM  MENU SUBROUTINE
            9520 REM  F9  FINAL LOCATION IN LIST OF MENU WORDS.
            9530 REM  GET USER RESPONSE.
            9540      INPUT U$
            9550      RESTORE
            9570 REM  LOOK FOR  U$  IN MENU--USE SEARCH LOOP.
            9580      FOR I9=1 TO F9
            9590          READ W$, W9<-------------- we read each menu word's
            9600          IF U$=W$ THEN 9710         class number right along
            9610        NEXT I9                      with the word itself
NOT FOUND: ->9620 REM   DIDN'T FIND IT.
            9630          PRINT "SORRY, BUT I DON'T KNOW WHAT ";U$;" MEANS."
            9660          PRINT "PLEASE TRY AGAIN."
            9670          INPUT U$
            9680          RESTORE
            9700          GO TO 9570
    FOUND: ->9710 REM   FOUND IT.  IT'S CLASS W9 .
            9720          RETURN
```

Now let's write a program to test the menu subroutine — just to make sure we haven't forgotten something. To test it, we need to supply the menu words and classes. How about the ones we discussed for the painting estimator?

```
8000  REM  MENU ITEMS FOR PAINTING PROGRAM
8010       DATA BRUSH,1,  B,1  <-- class 1 words
8020       DATA ROLLER,2, R,2
8030       DATA SPRAY,3,  S,3          "zero"
8040       DATA OTHER,4,  O,4,  0,4
                      "oh"
```

Next, we need a simple main program to invoke the menu subroutine and print enough information for us to make sure everything is working OK. All we need is a loop that tells us to enter a word, then a GOSUB to the menu subroutine, then a PRINT statement telling us what class was chosen.

```
10   REM  TEST OF MENU SUBROUTINE
20             PRINT "PAINTING TECHNIQUE=";
30   REM       USE MENU ROUTINE TO GET ANSWER.
50             LET F9 = 9
60             GOSUB 9500
70             PRINT "THAT'S CLASS #"; W9
80             PRINT
90   REM       REPEAT FOREVER
100            GO TO 10
 .
 . <-- menu subroutine is here
 .
9999      END

RUN
PAINTING TECHNIQUE=? B
THAT'S CLASS # 1

PAINTING TECHNIQUE=? SPREY
SORRY, BUT I DON'T KNOW WHAT SPREY MEANS.
PLEASE TRY AGAIN.
? SPRAY
THAT'S CLASS # 3

PAINTING TECHNIQUE=? OTHER
THAT'S CLASS # 4

PAINTING TECHNIQUE=? ROLLER
THAT'S CLASS # 2
          .
          .
          .
```

EXERCISES 9 1

1 Why did we use separate DATA statements for menu items of different classes?

Would it make any difference if items from different classes were put into the same DATA statement, as shown below?

```
8010        DATA BRUSH,1, B,1,  ROLLER,2, R,2
8020        DATA SPRAY,3, S,3,  OTHER,4, O,4 0,4
                                      "oh"  "zero"
```

2 Why do we need the RESTORE statement at the beginning of the subroutine (line 9560)?

3 Write DATA statements to make the menu subroutine work for a checkbook balancing program where the options are CHECK, DEPOSIT, SUBTOTAL, or FINISHED.

4 Write DATA statements to make the menu subroutine work for a hand-held calculator program where the options are +, −, *, /, =, and SQR.

5 What would happen if we had duplicate entries in the DATA statements under different classes? This would be an easy mistake to make if two menu items started with the same letter—we might accidentally list the same shorthand for both items.

```
8010        DATA BRUSH,1,  B,1
8020        DATA BROOM,2,  B,2
```

6 Assuming that the parts of the program which will handle BRUSH, ROLLER, SPRAY, or OTHER will start at lines 120, 150, 190, and 230, write an ON-GO TO statement which will transfer to the right part of the program given W9, the class of the menu item selected by the user.

Section 9 2

Making Multiple Use of the Menu Subroutine

As it stands, our menu subroutine works fine for one menu—it gives the user the choice among BRUSH, ROLLER, SPRAY, and OTHER. But one menu is not enough to cover the problem. Our complete painting estimator program needs to do more. Look again at our plan for the complete program in Section 9 1. After we've figured out what painting technique is being used, we need to know how the walls will be cleaned. That involves giving the user the choice among SPONGE, MOP, and OTHER. Later in the program, we need to ask some YES/NO questions, like "ARE THERE ANY WINDOWS IN THIS WALL?".

Obviously, we will need a group of DATA statements for each menu the program will use.

```
8000 REM  MENU ITEMS FOR PAINTING PROGRAM   \
8010      DATA BRUSH,1,  B,1                 |
8020      DATA ROLLER,2, R,2                 }  first menu
8030      DATA SPRAY,3,  S,3                 |
8040      DATA OTHER,4,  O,4, 0,4           /
```

```
8050 REM   ITEMS 10 THROUGH 16 ARE FOR CLEANING METHOD
8060       DATA SPONGE,1, S,1
8070       DATA MOP,2,    M,2
8080       DATA OTHER,3,  O,3, O,3
8090 REM   ITEMS 17 THROUGH 23 ARE FOR YES/NO QUESTIONS }
8100       DATA YES,1, Y,1, YEP,1, SURE,1              }  third menu
8110       DATA NO,2,  N,2, NOPE,2                     }  S9=17, F9=23
```

Now we're left with the question of how to get the search loop in the menu subroutine to look through just those menu words in the proper section of the DATA statements. The search loop always starts at the beginning of *all* the DATA, but we need a way to get it to start at the right spot, depending on which menu we want to search.

For this we'll need two variables: S9 to tell the menu subroutine where to start searching (that is, at the S9th position with respect to the whole DATA sequence) and F9, as before, to tell it where to stop searching (at the F9th position in the DATA). To get it started searching at the right spot, we simply skip past the first S9-1 menu items. We do this by carrying out S9-1 READ statements. We'll start with the first menu item, read it, then read the second menu item, and so on. After S9 - 1 READs, we're ready to start the search because the next READ statement to be carried out will read the S9th item in the whole menu sequence (that is, the first item within the menu we want to search).

We'll write a subroutine to do all this skipping and use the subroutine to get us to the right place to start searching instead of using the RESTORE statements that we used before (see lines 9560 and 9680 in the menu subroutine—we'll replace them with GOSUB statements).

```
9950 REM   SKIP TO ITEM  S9 .
9960       RESTORE
9970       FOR I9=1 TO S9 - 1
9980           READ W$, W9 ←—— pass over the
9990       NEXT I9            first S9-1 items
9995       RETURN
```

Now that we know *how* to get to the start of the menu we want, we need to put GOSUB statements in our menu subroutine to use skipping subroutine at the right times. Certainly we want one before the search loop starts, and we also need one in the not found section of our search loop in order to restart the search in the right spot.

It's important to keep our written documentation up to date, so before revising our subroutine, let's make the necessary changes to our plan.

> If your version of BASIC handles FOR-NEXT loops in a nonstandard way (i.e., as *post*test loops—see Section 8 3), you will need to add a statement which skips for FOR loop in case S9 is 1. In that case, S9 - 1 is zero, and we want to perform zero READs.
>
> ```
> 9965     IF S9=1 THEN 9995
> ```

> **Menus should be limited:**
>
> The ideas about hierarchically organized programs in which there are at most 7 ± 2 options or things to think about at any one point apply to menus too. The user should never be presented with a choice of more than 8 or 9 options in any one menu, and the options in any one menu should be at the same level of thought. Large choices should be split up into a nested group of menus. Try to make things easy and natural for the user!

—menu subroutine—

Get user's response.

Skip to menu item number S9.

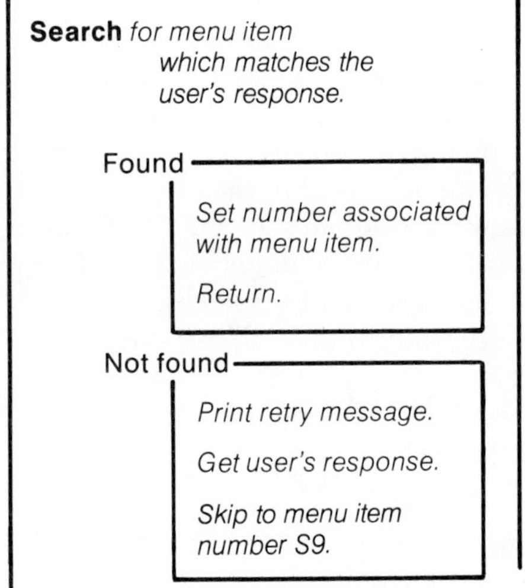
Search for menu item which matches the user's response.
Found
Set number associated with menu item.
Return.
Not found
Print retry message.
Get user's response.
Skip to menu item number S9.
Repeat IF not found

Now we can make the changes to our menu subroutine. We need to add these lines to handle the positioning before searches:

```
9550 REM  SKIP TO ITEM  S9 .
9690      GOSUB 9550

9680 REM      SKIP TO ITEM  S9 .
9690          GOSUB 9950
```

We also need to change the FOR statement:

```
9580      FOR I9=S9 TO F9
```

Then we need to upgrade our test program,

```
10   REM  TEST MULTI-MENU CASE
20        PRINT "PAINTING TECHNIQUE=";
30        LET S9 = 1
40        LET F9 = 9
50        GOSUB 9500
```

```
60        PRINT "THAT'S CLASS #"; W9
70        PRINT
80        PRINT "CLEANING METHOD=";
90        LET S9 = 10
100       LET F9 = 16
110       GOSUB 9500
120       PRINT "THAT'S CLASS #"; W9
130       PRINT
140       PRINT "YES/NO";
150       LET S9 = 17
160       LET F9 = 23
170       GOSUB 9500
180       PRINT "THAT'S CLASS #"; W9
190       GO TO 9999
 .
 .
 .
```

and make sure everything works as we expected.

```
RUN
PAINTING TECHNIQUE=? B
THAT'S CLASS # 1

CLEANING METHOD=? SPONGE
THAT'S CLASS # 1

YES/NO? NOPE
THAT'S CLASS # 2
READY
```

EXERCISES 9 2

1 Why does the FOR-NEXT loop in the skipping subroutine run from I9 = 1 to I9 = S9 − 1 instead of up to I9 = S9?

2 Why do we need to change the FOR statement in the menu subroutine from "FOR I9 = 1 TO F9" to "FOR I9 = S9 TO F9"?

3 Why not change the FOR statement in the menu subroutine to "FOR I9 = 1 TO F9 − S9 + 1"?

4 Write DATA statements for a program which uses two menus.

Menu 1 (user selects desired level of instructions to be printed):

DETAILED
OUTLINE
NONE

Menu 2 (user selects the role he or she wants to play):

EARTHLING
VULCAN
RIGELIAN
KLINGON

What values would have to be given S9 and F9 in order to use your first menu? your second?

5 A program to print form letters might have three modes of operation: NEW LETTER, EDIT LETTER, and TYPE LETTER. Within the EDIT LETTER mode there might be four modes: INSERT LINE, CHANGE LINE, DELETE LINE, and QUIT. Within the TYPE LETTER mode there might be five modes: MARGIN, COPIES, DATA, GO, and QUIT. Write DATA statements for all the necessary menus in this program. In a remark with each group of DATA statements, say what values S9 and F9 would need to use the menu within the group.

6 What happens to the values of W$ and W9 that the skipping subroutine reads?

7 A program to process BASIC statements might have a menu with these items: PRINT, LET, STOP, INPUT, REM, GO TO, IF, END, READ, DATA, GOSUB, FOR, NEXT, DEF, and ON. However, that's too many items for one menu. Divide the alternatives into some logical groups, and design DATA statements to implement the necessary menus.

8 A program to collect statistics on cars might have a menu with these items: BUICK, CADILLAC, CHEVROLET, CHRYSLER, DODGE, FORD, LINCOLN, MERCURY, OLDSMOBILE, PLYMOUTH, and PONTIAC. However, that's too many items for one menu. Divide the alternatives into some logical groups, and design DATA statements to implement the necessary menus.

Section 9 3

Making Our Menu Routine More Polite

As it stands now, our menu routine is impolite in one situation. If the user makes a typing mistake, or has forgotten what the options are, the routine will (politely) say, "SORRY, BUT I DON'T KNOW WHAT *user response* MEANS", and ask the user to type in something else. But what *are* the legal responses? If we're unable to find an entry in our table of menu words for the user's response, then probably the user is having trouble and should be reminded of the allowable responses at that point in the program. Otherwise the user may wind up sitting there trying to guess, getting one "SORRY..." message after another, and getting increasingly mad at the person who wrote the program!

Let's add a feature to our menu routine to cover this problem. If the not found exit is taken in the search loop, we'll print the "I'M SORRY" message, and then have the routine list the allowable responses. How can we do that?

> **problem statement:** print the allowable responses in the menu which is stored from position S9 to F9.

Certainly it wouldn't be hard to print the allowable responses one after the other —we'd need to skip to the S9th menu item and then use a process loop (Section

8 4) to print each menu item. But will that be good enough? Let's start with that and see.

—print allowable menu items—

Skip to menu item S9.

FOR item = menu item S9 TO menu item F9

Read menu item and class number.

Print menu item.

When we implemented our plan in BASIC and tested it, we didn't like what we saw. Implementing "Print menu item" like this:

```
9900     PRINT W$
```

produced output like this:

```
RUN
PAINTING TECHNIQUE=? BRSH
SORRY, BUT I DON'T KNOW WHAT BRSH MEANS.
LEGAL RESPONSES ARE:
BRUSH
B
ROLLER
R
SPRAY
S
OTHER
O
O
```

We decided that it wasn't good enough. It took up too much space, and just seemed offensive on aesthetic grounds. And printing all the menu items in one line is even worse:

```
RUN
PAINTING TECHNIQUE=? BB
SORRY, BUT I DON'T KNOW WHAT BB MEANS.
LEGAL RESPONSES ARE:
BRUSHBROLLERRSPRAYSOTHEROO
```

If we've come this far, we might as well go all the way. The best way to display the legal menu items would be to have all allowable forms that mean the same thing be on one line, and to have forms with different meanings be on different lines. Since the class number associated with each menu item tells the meaning of the menu item (as far as our program is concerned), we can distinguish among menu words by testing the class numbers. As long as the class number is the same, we can keep printing menu items on the same line. As soon as the class number changes, we want to go to a new line.

—print allowable menu items—

Skip to menu item S9.

Current class is unknown at this point.

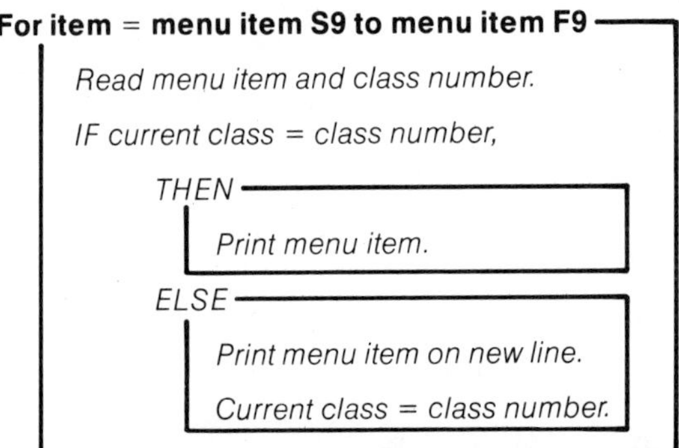

For item = menu item S9 to menu item F9
Read menu item and class number.
IF current class = class number,
THEN
Print menu item.
ELSE
Print menu item on new line.
Current class = class number.

The plan lays out the details and makes it easy to put the subroutine together. There are only two things left to do—insert a GOSUB in our menu subroutine to use the routine which prints all the allowable menu items and write the BASIC code for the new routine. Inserting the GOSUB is not difficult. It obviously goes just after the SORRY message in the not found section.

```
9620 REM    DIDN'T FIND IT.
9630        PRINT "SORRY, BUT I DON'T KNOW WHAT ";U$;" MEANS."
9640        PRINT "LEGAL RESPONSES ARE:";
9650        GOSUB 9800
9660        PRINT "PLEASE TRY AGAIN."
9670        INPUT U$
9680 REM    SKIP TO ITEM  S9 .
9690        GOSUB 9950
9700        GO TO 9570
```

And here's our BASIC version of the subroutine "print allowable menu items".

```
9800 REM  DISPLAY LEGIT RESPONSES FROM  S9  TO  F9  IN MENU.
9810 REM  FIRST, SKIP TO ITEM S9 .
9820      GOSUB 9950
9830 REM  W8  IS LAST CLASS SEEN (USED FOR SPACING).
9840      LET W8 = -999999
9850 REM  USE PROCESS LOOP TO SHOW LEGIT WORDS.
9860      FOR I9=S9 TO F9
9870          READ W$, W9
9890          IS W8=W9 THEN 9920
9895 REM                  NEW CLASS, NEW LINE
9900            PRINT
9905            PRINT W$;
9910            LET W8 = W9
9912            GO TO 9930
9915 REM                  SAME CLASS, SAME LINE
9920            PRINT ", ";W$;
9930      NEXT I9
9940      PRINT
9945      RETURN
```

We've made a number of changes to the menu subroutine since the first version, but we haven't really changed the way it's used. In fact we can still use the same test program we used in Section 9 2. We *have* changed the way the routines handle errors, though. Now the user gets an understandable, helpful, polite response in all situations. It's virtually foolproof as far as the user is concerned. As long as the programmer sets up the menus correctly and sets S9 and F9 to the right values before calling the menu subroutine, things should run smoothly.

```
RUN
PAINTING TECHNIQUE=? SPRY
SORRY, BUT I DON'T KNOW WHAT SPRY MEANS.
LEGAL RESPONSES ARE:
BRUSH, BRUSH, B
ROLLER, ROLLER, R
SPRAY, SPRAY, S
OTHER, OTHER, O, O
PLEASE TRY AGAIN.
? SPRAY
THAT'S CLASS # 3
      .
      .
      .
```

To summarize the whole process in one place, the menu subroutine and all of its necessary subroutines are listed below.

```
9500 REM  MENU SUBROUTINE
9530 REM  GET USER RESPONSE.
9540      INPUT U$
9550 REM  SKIP TO ITEM  S9 .
9560      GOSUB 9950
9570 REM  LOOK FOR  U$  IN MENU--USE SEARCH LOOP.
9580      FOR I9=S9 TO F9
9590          READ W$, W9
9600          IF U$=W$ THEN 9710
9610        NEXT I9
9620 REM    DIDN'T FIND IT.
9630          PRINT "SORRY, BUT I DON'T KNOW WHAT ";U$;" MEANS."
9640          PRINT "LEGAL RESPONSES ARE:";
9650          GOSUB 9800
9660          PRINT "PLEASE TRY AGAIN."
9670          INPUT U$
9680 REM      SKIP TO ITEM  S9 .
9690          GOSUB 9950
9700          GO TO 9570
9710 REM    FOUND IT. IT'S CLASS W9 .
9720          RETURN

9800 REM  DISPLAY LEGIT RESPONSES FROM  S9  TO  F9  IN MENU.
9810 REM  FIRST, SKIP TO ITEM  S9 .
9820      GOSUB 9950
9830 REM  W8  IS LAST CLASS SEEN (USED FOR SPACING).
```

(program continued)

```
9840       LET W8 = -999999
9850 REM   USE PROCESS LOOP TO SHOW LEGIT WORDS.
9860       FOR I9=S9 TO F9
9870           READ W$, W9
9890           IF W8=W9 THEN 9920
9895 REM                      NEW CLASS, NEW LINE
9900             PRINT
9905             PRINT W$;
9910             LET W8 = W9
9912             GO TO 9930
9915 REM                      SAME CLASS, SAME LINE
9920             PRINT ", ";W$;
9930       NEXT I9
9940       PRINT
9945       RETURN

9950 REM   SKIP TO ITEM  I9 .
9960       RESTORE
9970       FOR I9=1 TO S9 4 1
9980           READ W$, W9
9990       NEXT I9
9995       RETURN
```

EXERCISES 9 3

1 With the test program as we have it set up, and the DATA statements for the painting menus, what gets printed if we type PAINT BRUSH in response to the painting technique question?

2 What if we type ROLLER in response to the cleaning technique question?

3 Suppose the DATA statements for a menu have the response classes scrambled. What will happen if the user types a legal response? What if the user types an illegal response?

```
8000 REM   SCRAMBLED MENU-- S9=1, F9=8
8010       DATA HOUSE,1,  CAR,2,   BOAT,3
8020       DATA H,    1,  C,  2,   B,   3
8030       DATA PAD,  1,  AUTO,2
```

4 Suppose the customer you were writing the menu subroutine for didn't like the commas between items when the legal responses get printed out. The customer wants slashes (/) instead. What would you have to change in the progam?

Section 9 4

Using It

Now that we've designed, developed, and tested our menu routine, we can use it to put the finishing touches on our painting estimator program. The BASIC program below is a direct translation of our plan for the painting estimator (see Section 9 1).

Look carefully at the way we use the menu routine to carry out the selection process. The general pattern is

Setup: Print instructions, telling user what the choices are.

Menu: GOSUB to the menu routine to get the class number of the user's response.

Select: Use an ON-GO TO, basing the choice on the class number W9.

Perform: Provide a section in the program to cover each of the options.

The first use of the menu routine is in lines 40 through 250. The instructions to the user are given in lines 40 and 50. Lines 60 through 80 set up and make the call to the menu routine. The ON-GO TO is in line 100. The BASIC statements corresponding to class number 1 (BRUSH) are in lines 110 through 140; those corresponding to class number 2 (ROLLER) are in lines 150 through 170; and so on.

The selection of cleaning method follows the same pattern. The selections between YES and NO are done slightly differently. Since there are only two "classes," 1 corresponding to YES and 2 corresponding to NO, we use a simple IF-THEN instead of an ON-GO TO after we get the class (1 or 2) from the menu routine.

Aside from the use of the menu routine, the program is only a slight elaboration of the version we developed in Section 5 7. It is amazing how much the menu routine improves the program. The program in this section, together with the exercises you have worked in the other sections of this chapter, should provide you with enough guidance to use the menu subroutine effectively.

Happy painting!

```
10   REM  PAINTING ESTIMATOR
20        PRINT "GREETINGS.  I'LL HELP YOU ESTIMATE HOW MUCH PAINT"
30        PRINT "AND HOW MUCH TIME IT'LL TAKE TO PAINT A HOUSE."
40        PRINT "FIRST, HOW WILL YOU APPLY THE PAINT?"
50        PRINT "BRUSH, ROLLER, SPRAY, OR OTHER";
60        LET S9 = 1
70        LET F9 = 9
80        GOSUB 9500
90   REM  SELECT CHOSEN OPTION
100       ON W9 GO TO 110, 150, 190, 230
110  REM    IT TAKES ABOUT AN HOUR AND A HALF TO APPLY ONE
120  REM    GALLON OF PAINT USING A -BRUSH-
130         LET R0 = 90
140         GO TO 300
150  REM    USING -ROLLER- (AND BRUSH IN CORNERS)
160         LET R0 = 60
170         GO TO 300
190  REM    USING -SPRAY- GUN IS FASTEST
200         LET R0 = 25
210         GO TO 300
220  REM    USING SOME -OTHER- TECHNIQUE
230         PRINT "HOW MANY MINUTES TO APPLY ONE GALLON OF"
240         PRINT "PAINT USING YOUR TECHNIQUE";
250         INPUT R0
```

use the first menu (lines 60–70)

be sure to find each part of the plan in the program listing

painting technique (lines 40–250)

(program continued)

```
300  REM  NOW GET CLEANING METHOD
310       PRINT
320       PRINT "HOW WILL YOU CLEAN THE WALLS BEFORE PAINTING?"
330       PRINT "SPONGE, MOP, OR OTHER";
340       LET S9 = 10
350       LET F9 = 16   } use the second menu
360       GOSUB 9500
370  REM  SELECT BASED ON CLEANING METHOD
380       ON W9 GO TO 390, 430, 470
390  REM    WITH A -SPONGE- IT TAKES ABOUT 20 MINS / 100 SQ. FT.
400         LET R1 = 20
410         GO TO 550
430  REM    USING A -MOP- IS FASTEST
440         LET R1 = 5
450         GO TO 550
470  REM    USING SOME -OTHER- METHOD
480         PRINT "ABOUT HOW MANY MINUTES DOES IT TAKE TO CLEAN"
490         PRINT "100 SQ. FT. OF WALL WITH YOUR METHOD";
500         INPUT R1
550  REM  HAVE NECESSARY FACTORS.  GET WALL AREA AS IN SECTION 5  5
560       PRINT "NOW I'LL GET THE DIMENSIONS (IN FEET) OF EACH"
570       PRINT "WALL YOU'RE GOING TO PAINT."
580       LET A = 0
590  REM  NOTE: ALL USES OF THE MENU SUBROUTINES FROM HERE
600  REM        ON USE THE  YES/NO  MENU.  SET THAT UP NOW.
610       LET S9 = 17
620       LET F9 = 23   } use the third menu from here on

700  REM  TOP OF LOOP ON WALLS
705           PRINT
710           PRINT "WIDTH OF THIS WALL=";
720           INPUT W
730           PRINT "AND HOW HIGH IS IT";
740           INPUT H
750           LET A = A + W*H
760  REM      BUT YOU DON'T PAINT OVER WINDOWS...
770           PRINT "DOES THIS WALL HAVE ANY WINDOWS IN IT";
780  REM      USE MENU ROUTINES TO GET YES/NO ANSWER.
790           GOSUB 9500
800  REM      WHILE THERE ARE WINDOWS, KEEP GETTING THEIR SIZE.
810           IF W9<>1 THEN 910
820               PRINT "WIDTH OF THIS WINDOW=";
830               INPUT W
840               PRINT "WINDOW HEIGHT=";
850               INPUT H
860               LET A = A - W*H
870               PRINT "ANY MORE WINDOWS IN THIS WALL";
880               GOSUB 9500
890  REM          BOTTOM OF LOOP ON WINDOWS
900               GO TO 800
910           PRINT "ANY MORE WALLS TO BE PAINTED";
920           GOSUB 9500
930  REM      REPEAT IF MORE WALLS.
940           IF W9=1 THEN 700
```

```
950   REM  AT LAST WE HAVE THE TOTAL AREA TO BE PAINTED IN A
960   REM  IT TAKES ABOUT ONE GALLON OF PAINT FOR 400 SQ. FT.
970        LET F = 400
980        PRINT
990        PRINT
1000       PRINT "IT WILL TAKE ABOUT"; A/100*R1; "MINUTES FOR CLEANING."
1010       PRINT "YOU'LL NEED SOME"; A/F; "GALLONS OF PAINT."
1020       PRINT "IT WILL TAKE ABOUT"; A/F*R0; "MINUTES (";
1030       PRINT INT( (A/F*R0)/60 * 10)/10; "HOURS) TO DO THE PAINTING."
1040       PRINT "AND OF COURSE, AFTER THAT YOU'LL HAVE TO";
1050       PRINT " CLEAN THE EQUIPMENT."
1060       PRINT
1070       PRINT "HAPPY PAINTING!"
1080       GO TO 9999
  .        <-------- the menus go in here
  .
  .        <-------- the menu subroutines go in here
9999       END

RUN
GREETINGS.  I'LL HELP YOU ESTIMATE HOW MUCH PAINT
AND HOW MUCH TIME IT'LL TAKE TO PAINT A HOUSE.
FIRST, HOW WILL YOU APPLY THE PAINT?
BRUSH, ROLLER, SPRAY, OR OTHER? ROLLER

HOW WILL YOU CLEAN THE WALLS BEFORE PAINTING?
SPONGE, MOP, OR OTHER? MOP
NOW I'LL GET THE DIMENSIONS (IN FEET) OF EACH
WALL YOU'RE GOING TO PAINT.

WIDTH OF THIS WALL=? 14
AND HOW HIGH IS IT? 8
DOES THIS WALL HAVE ANY WINDOWS IN IT? YES
WIDTH OF THIS WINDOW=? 2
WINDOW HEIGHT=? 3
ANY MORE WINDOWS IN THIS WALL? YESS <---- ooops!
SORRY, BUT I DON'T KNOW WHAT YESS MEANS.
LEGAL RESPONSES ARE:
YES, YES, Y, YEP, SURE
NO, NO, N, NOPE
PLEASE TRY AGAIN.
? YES
WIDTH OF THIS WINDOW=? 2
WINDOW HEIGHT=? 3
ANY MORE WINDOWS IN THIS WALL? N
ANY MORE WALLS TO BE PAINTED? Y

WIDTH OF THIS WALL=? 24
AND HOW HIGH IS IT? 8
DOES THIS WALL HAVE ANY WINDOWS IN IT? N <---- no windows in the second wall
ANY MORE WALLS TO BE PAINTED? Y
```

(Margin annotations: "first wall" beside the first wall's dialogue; "second wall" beside the second wall's dialogue.)

(program continued)

```
WIDTH OF THIS WALL=? 14
AND HOW HIGH IS IT? 8
DOES THIS WALL HAVE ANY WINDOWS IN IT? N
ANY MORE WALLS TO BE PAINTED? Y

WIDTH OF THIS WALL=? 24
AND HOW HIGH IS IT? 8
DOES THIS WALL HAVE ANY WINDOWS IN IT? Y
WIDTH OF THIS WINDOW=? 2
WINDOW HEIGHT=? 3
ANY MORE WINDOWS IN THIS WALL? Y
WIDTH OF THIS WINDOW=? 2
WINDOW HEIGHT=? 3
ANY MORE WINDOWS IN THIS WALL? N
ANY MORE WALLS TO BE PAINTED? N

IT WILL TAKE ABOUT 29.2 MINUTES FOR CLEANING.
YOU'LL NEED SOME 1.46 GALLONS OF PAINT.
IT'LL TAKE ABOUT 87.6 MINUTES ( 1.4 HOURS) TO DO THE PAINTING.
AND OF COURSE, AFTER THAT YOU'LL HAVE TO CLEAN THE EQUIPMENT.

HAPPY PAINTING!
READY
```

PROBLEMS 9

1 Write a program which a publisher could use to print form letters to authors. First, the program asks for the *name$* of the author and the *title$* of the manuscript. Then the program offers the user the options REJECT and ACCEPT. If the user chooses the ACCEPT option, the letter is printed with the upper lines shown below. The REJECT option causes the letter to include the lower lines in the curly brackets. Of course, *name$* and *title$* are to be filled in with the values the user entered.

DEAR *name$*

THE MANUSCRIPT YOU SENT US, *title$,* IS OF { SUPERIOR / GOOD }

QUALITY, AND WE APPRECIATE THE OPPORTUNITY TO REVIEW IT.

{ WE FEEL / HOWEVER, } THE SUBJECT MATTER { TO BE TIMELY AND APPROPRIATE / DOES NOT SUIT OUR CURRENT NEEDS. }

WE WILL BE { SENDING YOU A CONTRACT / RETURNING IT SOON } UNDER SEPARATE COVER.

SINCERELY,

COLLAPSE OF THE EMPIRE PRESS, INC.

2 Revise the checkbook balancing program of Chapter 4 to use the menu program. Your program should now allow the user to type C, CH, or CHECK for specifying a check and D, DEP, or DEPOSIT for a deposit. Is the new version easier or harder for the *programmer* to understand?

3 Add another option called SUBTOTAL to the checkbook balancing program (Problem 2). When the user selects the subtotal option, the program asks whether a subtotal should be printed after every transaction. If the user answers YES, from then on, the subtotal should be printed after every check and deposit transaction. If the user answers NO, or if the user never chooses the subtotal option, no subtotals should be printed.

4 Upgrade the painting estimator program in at least these two ways. First, add the capability to account for differing wall textures as in Section 5 1. Second, make the program more polite by incorporating this observation: Almost all rooms have an even number of walls (Figure 9 P 1), so if the user says that he or she is finished after an odd number of walls have been entered, it's likely that an error has been made, Third, if there *was* a mistake, the user should be given the opportunity to add in the forgotten wall without typing all the rest in again.

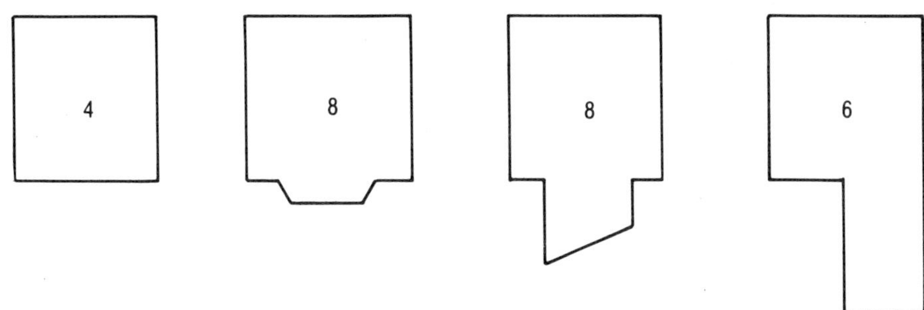

Figure 9 P 1 The number of walls per room is usually even

5 Most states which charge a sales tax use one scheme for fixing the tax on small sales ("small" usually means below $1.00), and another scheme for larger sales. One line in a tax table looks like the next, so the different ways of charging are rarely noticed.

Write a program which computes the sales tax charged on the amount the user enters. If you can't find a tax table for your state, base your program on the 6½% Tax Schedule shown in Table 9 P 1.

Table 9 P 1. 6½% Tax Schedule Used in Santa Cruz County, California, 1979.

To	*Tax*	*To*	*Tax*	*To*
.10	.00	5.15	.33	10.07
.20	.01	5.30	.34	.
.35	.02	5.46	.35	.
.51	.03	5.61	.36	.
.67	.04	5.76	.37	
.83	.05	5.92	.38	
.99	.06	6.07	.39	
1.15	.07	6.23	.40	
1.30	.08	6.38	.41	
1.46	.09	6.53	.42	
1.61	.10	6.69	.43	
1.76	.11	.	.	
1.92	.12	.	.	
.	.	.	.	
.	.			
.	.			

Tax on a purchase of *cost* dollars: If *cost* > $0.99, compute the tax by rounding *cost* *0.065 to the nearest cent. Otherwise, use a search loop to find the *position* of the first item in the DATA statement greater than or equal to *cost.* Knowing the value of *position,* you can easily compute the tax.

```
                          .00 to .10        .21 to .35
                          no tax            2¢ tax
2000        DATA .10, .20, .35, .51, .67, .83, .99
                          .11 to .20                    .84 to .99
                          1¢ tax                        6¢ tax
```

6 Is the state making money, losing money, or breaking even by using a special method for computing tax on small purchases (problem 5)? Compare the special method to the "take 6½% and round" method by computing the total tax charged by each method on the 99 purchases—1¢, 2¢, 3¢, . . . , 99¢. Compute the total tax and average rate for each case. Print a message appropriate to your findings.

> 0.22*0.065 = 0.0143 ← rounds to 1¢, the state charges 2¢
>
> 0.09*0.065 = 0.00585 ← rounds to 1¢, but the state charges 0¢

7 Design and write a program which lets the user produce business cards tailored to his or her needs. The program should offer the user a menu of 5 options, as detailed below. Provide *default values* which the program will use automatically for the variables unless the user indicates different values.

option	*action*
INDENT	Allows user to specify how many spaces to indent before each line of the card is printed.
SKIP	Allows user to specify how many lines to skip after each card is printed.
TEXT	Allows user to change any or all of the 6 lines that make up each card.
PRINT	First ask HOW MANY to print, and then prints them.
QUIT	Tells user how many business cards were created during the run and then stops.

There are 8 important variables in this program. We'll call them *indent, skip,* and *line 1$,. . .,line 6$.* Each is to be given the default value shown below. Unless the user chooses the indent, skip, and/or text options, the cards will be indented 5 spaces, with a skip of one line after each, and they will be CHET SNOW's cards.

> **Default value**
>
> A value which a program will use unless the user takes some action to change it.

variable	*default value*
indent	5
skip	1
line 1$	"C.P. 'CHET' SNOW"
line 2$	"GENERAL MANAGER"
line 3$	"ROBOWASHOMAT"
line 4$	"1600 MAIN ST."
line 5$	"FERNLY, NEVADA"
line 6$	" 89408"

Use your finished program to print a card for Mr. Snow, and to print a few cards for yourself and your friends.

8 Program your computer to behave like a pocket calculator. Implement the opertions +, −, *, /, and =. (The = operation displays the result and then clears the calculator so it can be used for a new problem.) Use the menu program to accept the operators from the user and transfer to the part of the program which does that function.

Here's a typical session:

```
WELCOME TO THE CALCULATOR

VALUE? 3           the "display"
          -->3
OP    ? +
          -->3
VALUE? 2
          -->2
OP    ? =
          -->5
VALUE? 12
          -->12
OP    ? *
          -->12
VALUE 5
          -->5
OP    ? -
          -->60
VALUE? 5
          -->55
OP    ? =
          -->55
VALUE? 0
          -->0
OP    ? QUIT

GOODBYE.
```

9 Don't attempt this problem unless you're interested in the details of pocket calculator design.

The pocket calculator of problem 8 requires the user to enter a value, then an operator, then a value, then an operator, and so on. On a real pocket calculator, you punch any of the keys in any order. (Some orders may not make much sense, but the calculator will do something anyway.) Write a program which mimics the functioning of a simple pocket calculator.

This problem will require a great deal of planning. Begin by figuring out, in detail, what your calculator does for each of these combinations:

 # button then *# button*

 # button then *op button*

op button then *# button*

op button then *op button*

#button: 0, 1, . . . , 9, or *period*
op button: +,−,*,/,=, or *clear*

Simple pocket calculators have two variables. One stores a *current total,* and one contains the value which you see on the face of the calculator. We'll call the second variable *display.*

When the power is turned on, or when the *clear* button is pushed, this happens:

Let *current total* = 0.
Let *display* = 0.

When a *# button* is pushed immediately after an *op button,* this happens:

Let *display* = value of *# button.*

When a # button is pushed immediately after a *# button,* this happens:

Let *display* = *display**10 + value of *# button.*

Actually, the . button is a # button too, and complicates this slightly. After a *period* has been entered, the first # button struck does this instead of what's shown above:

Let *display* = *display* + value of *# button* / 10.

The second *# button* after the period adds 1/100 of its value, and so on.

By including the digits (0, 1, 2, . . . , 9) and the period in your DATA statements from problem 8, you can use the menu routines to interpret each button the user strikes.

Sample session:

"keyboard"	"display"	"keyboard"	"display"
BUTTON? 3		BUTTON? -	
	--> 3		--> 41
BUTTON? 0		BUTTON? 9	
	--> 30		--> 9
BUTTON? +		BUTTON? +	
	--> 30		--> 32
BUTTON? 1		BUTTON? 8	
	--> 1		--> 8
BUTTON? 1		BUTTON? =	
	--> 11		--> 40
BUTTON? =		BUTTON? CLEAR	
	--> 41		--> 0

Table 9 P 2 Snack Foods

snack	serving	calories per serving
POPCORN	1 CUP	65
PRETZELS	5 STICKS	20
CARAMELS	1 OZ.	115
CHOCOLATE	1 OZ.	150
MARSHMALLOWS	ONE	25
HONEY	1 TABLESPOON	65
RYE WAFERS	2 WAFERS	45
PIE	1 PIECE	340
COOKIE	1 COOKIE	120
CUPCAKE	ONE	145
PEACH	ONE	35
PEANUTS	2 TABLESPOONS	220
CRACKER	TWO	35
DOUGHNUT	ONE	125
CAKE	1 PIECE	400

Based on tables in *Nutritive Value of Foods*, U.S. Department of Agriculture.

10 Table 9 P 2 shows the number of calories per serving of common snack foods. Using methods similar to those we used to develop the menu routines, write the program implied by the **scenario** (in box).

Scenario

"Thank heaven for my Flabblaster Diet Control Computer! Here's a picture of a sorry looking me as a 250 pounder. Then my doctor recommended a Flabblaster, and it changed my life.

"Here's how it helped me. I used to snack between meals something awful! My doctor, Teddy, said I didn't have to cut down or go on a diet or anything I just had to type in the name and amount of every snack I had, from morning to night.

"Here I am reaching for some popcorn. . . and now you can see me typing the word POPCORN into the Flabblaster. I don't know if you can see that, but here it's asking me how many CUPS of it I ate. I had two cups. . . and the Flabblaster is telling me that the POPCORN is 130 Calories, and my total so far for the day is 700 Calories. And look at the next thing it shows! That's what made me realize what I was doing to myself, and helped me lose weight for the first time in my life.

```
700 CALORIES OF SNACKS= .2 POUNDS OF UGLY FAT
```

"And here's how I look today, thanks to my Flabblaster!" (jingle)

"You'll get the facts from a Flabblaster! No scolding, no guilt, just the facts."

—Flabblaster Diet Control Computer—
A registered trademark of the General Computronix Corporation.

(Hints: In the menu routines each "item" in the DATA statements consists of a string value (e.g., BRUSH in the painting estimator program) and a number. Here each item will consist of a string value (e.g., POPCORN), another string value (the normal serving, e.g., 1 CUP), and a number (the number of calories). Don't forget, 3500 calories in excess of a balanced diet converts to one pound of ugly fat!)

11 Write a program to help compile baseball statistics. For each player or manager whose name is entered, use the menu subroutines to select the appropriate set of statistics, as shown in Table 9 P 3.

Table 9 P 3 Menu of Baseball Statistics

if the person is a	*ask for*	*compute*
PITCHER	games won, games lost, innings pitched, earned runs allowed	won-lost percentage, earned run average*
FIELDER	times at bat, number of singles, doubles, triples, and home runs	batting average, slugging percentage**
MANAGER	games won, games lost	winning percentage

*To compute an earned run average, take (earned runs allowed/innings pitched)*9
**To compute the slugging percentage, take total bases/times at bat
where
total bases = 1*singles + 2*doubles + . . . +4*homeruns

12 This problem can be done in conjunction with any program you've written that makes use of the menu routines. The goal is to **fine tune** your program, making it as easy to use as possible before you sell it to the general public for Big Bucks.

When you first develop any program, it's likely that although the menu words you choose and the instructions your program gives make perfect sense to you, some of them will be misinterpreted by naive users. Fine tune your program by letting naive users run it and detecting the sorts of mistakes they make.

Each time the user is given a choice from a menu, the program invokes the menu subroutines. Let's call that a **menu session.** During a given menu session, the user might type just one word (if that word is, in fact, in your menu), or the user might have to type a series of words, getting an I'M SORRY, BUT. . . message for each incorrect response. We want to know first, how many menu sessions there have been, and out of those, how many I'M SORRY, BUT. . . messages the user had to face.

But we'd like to know more than that. We'd like to know which option(s) caused most of the I'M SORRY, BUT. . . messages. Within the menu routines, set a variable (we'll call it *user error*) like this:

user error = {
0 —user had no trouble in this menu session.
1 —user go one (or more) I'M SORRY, BUT. . . messages in this menu session.

Eventually, the user types in an acceptable response, and the program selects the option the user wanted. At that point (i.e., within the code corresponding to that option) you know whether the user had trouble getting that option:

IF *user error = 1,*

THEN

Let error in option x = error in option x + 1.

Once you've successfully added this measurement device to your program, fine tune your choice of menu words and user prompts (instructions). Find a volunteer army of naive users, let them use your program (with no coaching from you!), and look at the measurement results. If a particular option caused a lot of trouble, and you don't see why, ask the users what they *thought* the program wanted there.

Chapter 10 **Arrays**

Section 10 1

Arrays

Like many words used in computer programming, the word **array** is taken from everyday English. In English, the word array can be used to mean (in somewhat grandiose language) an impressive series of things: "Stevens Creek Boulevard is an array of used car lots." Perhaps you are more used to hearing the word in a negative sense, as in "This room is in disarray." Disarray means disorder. Array implies *an orderly collection of things.*

In computer programming, the word **array** is used to describe an orderly collection of things, too. In programming, the things in (an) array are variables. Understanding the uses of arrays is one of the keystones of advanced computer programming. There are some close analogies among **variables** (which we've used all along), **DATA statements** (which we've used since Chapter 7), and **arrays** (which, in case you haven't guessed, we're going to use from now on).

Let's begin by reviewing some of the properties of variables and DATA items. Let's restrict our attention to numeric variables, and to DATA items which are numbers. A **variable** has a *name* and a *value.* An item in a **DATA statement** has a *value,* but instead of a name, it has a *position.*

```
530   DATA  7, 22, -1, 128
540   DATA  0, 95,  2, -46
```

The value of the third DATA item is −1. The value of the sixth DATA item is 95. A program cannot change the value of the sixth (or any) DATA item. *You* can retype the DATA statements, and in so doing change the sixth value, but a program can't do that. *There is no statement in BASIC that will change the value of a DATA item.*

```
280   LET V = 12
```

The value of the variable named V is 12 after the LET statement has been carried out. *The value of a variable can be changed by a program (that's why it's called a variable).* Line 290 changes the value of the variable V from 12 to −2.

```
290    LET V = -2
```

The variable V has no position, however. It doesn't come before or after other variables.

Arrays provide a way to combine the features of variables and DATA items. An array is an orderly sequence of variables. Items in an array have a *name,* have a *position,* and a *value which can be changed by a program.*

The number of items in DATA statements is simply the number of items that appear in all DATA statements in the entire program. We have to tell the computer how many items will be in an array, however. We do that with a new statement, the **DIM** (short for DIMension) **statement.** In a DIM statement, we tell the computer the name of the array we want to use, and the number of items we want it to have. For instance

```
20    DIM  A(50)
```

specifies that A( ) is an array, and that we want room for 50 items in it. A( ) is the name of the entire sequence of 50 items. The name of the third item (the third variable) in the array A( ) is A(3). The name of the seventh item is A(7).

The individual items in an array have all the properties of the variables that we've been using all along. For instance, you can put a value into one of the items. Here, line 670 puts the value 17 into the sixth item of the array A( ).

```
670    LET A(6) = 17
```

Line 790 prints the values currently stored in the fourth, fifth, and sixth items.

```
790    PRINT "FOURTH="; A(4); "FIFTH="; A(5); "SIXTH=";A(6)
```

It probably isn't very clear yet how arrays are used in programs, but we hope you can see how they combine the properties of variables and DATA items. They give us the flexibility of both.

EXERCISES 10 1

1 Which statements are true about the variable K2 immediately after this statement is carried out?

```
220    LET K2 = 345
```

(a) It is the 345th variable in the program.

(b) Its name is K2.

(c) Its value is 345.

(d) Its position is determined by other DATA statements.

2 Which statements are true about the third DATA item in line 2900? Assume that this is the first DATA statement in the entire program.

```
2900  DATA 2, -1, 345, 0, 444
```

(a) Its name is DATA.

(b) Its value is 345.

(c) Its the 3rd DATA item.

(d) Its value will change with the third READ.

3 Which statements are true about the array item G(3) immediately after this program reaches line 50?

```
10    DIM G(20)
20    LET G(1) = 2
30    LET G(2) = -1
40    LET G(3) = 345
50    LET G(4) = 0
9999  END
```

(a) It is the third item in the array G( ).

(b) Its value is 345.

(c) Its name is G( ).

(d) Its value is 0.

Section 10 2
Inventory Control

Many stores are switching to computer inventorying schemes. Computers are so inexpensive now that even small businesses can afford to use them for the busywork of keeping track of how many thises and thats are on hand. Let's think about what would be involved in an inventory control program. This is a case where the properties of arrays can be critical to the success of a program. But first, let's try it *without* using arrays.

The most basic requirement is that our program store the quantity on hand of each product in the store. The most direct way to do that is to give each product a number (the 1st product, the 2nd product, etc.), and to put the quantities on hand in a DATA statement so the first value in DATA is the quantity on hand of the 1st product, and so on. Assuming we have 10 different products with the quantities on hand as shown in the DATA statements, this simple program could be used to find out how much the store has of a given product.

```
10   REM  HOW MUCH ON HAND?
20        PRINT "WHICH ITEM";
30        INPUT I0
40        FOR I=1 TO I0
```

```
50        READ Q
60        NEXT I
70        PRINT "ITEM"; I0; " ---"; Q; "ON HAND"
80        GO TO 9999
90        DATA 23, 10, 11,  5, 39
100       DATA  0, 20, 12, 24, 1
9999      END

RUN
WHICH ITEM? 3
ITEM 3  --- 11 ON HAND
READY
```

The program involves using one number (the item number I0) to select one of a list of values. This is sometimes called **indexing.** We used the value 3 as an index; that is, we choose the third value in the DATA statements.

Although our program does store the quantities on hand of the procducts the store sells, it's not a very useful solution to any other part of the inventory control problem. Each time a customer buys a particular item, the quantity on hand should be reduced by one. Each time a shipment arrives, the quantity on hand of the products in the shipment should be increased. As our program stands now, the poor checkout clerk would have to rewrite the DATA statement which contained the quantity on hand for each item a customer bought. And as each shipment came in, the stockroom personnel would have to retype the DATA statements to reflect the increases in quantities on hand. Not only would that be awkward and time consuming, it would be terribly error-prone. Imagine a half-asleep stockroom worker accidentally leaving out one of the DATA items when updating the values. Typing

```
90        DATA 23, 10, 12, 39
                          ↖ oops!
```

instead of

```
90        DATA 23, 10, 12,  5, 39
```

not only "loses" the quantity on hand of the 4th item (5), but throws off all the quantities on hand for all items after the 3rd! There's got to be a better way.

One thing we need is a sequence or list of values, the first value representing the quantity on hand of item 1, the second value the quantity on hand of item 2, and so on. The DATA statements give us that. But in addition, we need some convenient way to *change* the values in the list as the program runs. What we need is an array.

Since in our experimental inventory control programs we assume there are just 10 products for sale in the store, we need an array of size 10. Here's our new experimental inventory control program. Try it.

```
10   REM  INVENTORY CONTROLLER
20   REM  THE ARRAY Q() STORES THE QUANTITY ON
30   REM  HAND OF EACH ITEM.
40        DIM Q(10)
50   REM  START WITH 0 ON HAND FOR EACH ITEM.
60        FOR I=1 TO 10     when I has the value 1, this means LET Q(1)=0
70            LET Q(I) = 0  when I has the value 2, it means LET Q(2)=0
80        NEXT I                  ⋮
```

(program continued)

```
100  REM  START OF MAIN LOOP.
110           PRINT "WHICH ITEM";
120           INPUT I
130           PRINT "CURRENTLY"; Q(I); "ON HAND."
140           PRINT "NEW QUANTITY ON HAND=";
150           INPUT Q(I)
160           PRINT
170  REM      REPEAT FOREVER
180           GO TO 100
9999      END
```

the INPUT operation stores the value the user enters in variable Q(I) (line 150)

```
RUN
WHICH ITEM? 1
CURRENTLY 0 ON HAND.
NEW QUANTITY ON HAND=? 23

WHICH ITEM? 2
CURRENTLY 0 ON HAND.
NEW QUANTITY ON HAND=? 10
        .
        .
        .
WHICH ITEM? 10
CURRENTLY 0 ON HAND.
NEW QUANTITY ON HAND=? 1
```

here we're storing the initial quantity-on-hand of each item, using the same values as in our first inventory program

```
WHICH ITEM? 1
CURRENTLY 23 ON HAND.
NEW QUANTITY ON HAND=? 22
```

now we've started using the program. a customer just bought one item 1.

```
WHICH ITEM? 1
CURRENTLY 22 ON HAND.
        .
        .
        .
```

notice that the quantity-on-hand reflects the sale

```
WHICH ITEM? 8
CURRENTLY 12 ON HAND.
NEW QUANTITY ON HAND? 36
        .
        .
        .
```

a shipment of 24 item 8's just arrived

An array is a collection of variables, each with its own name and value. For example, in our experimental inventory control program, after lines 50 through 80 have been carried out, we can think of the array as looking like this:

Q(1)	0
Q(2)	0
Q(3)	0
Q(5)	0
Q(6)	0
Q(7)	0
Q(8)	0
Q(9)	0
Q(10)	0

When we request item number 1 (line 120 in the program) the computer stores 1 in variable I. In that case line 130 has the same meaning as if we'd written Q(1) instead of Q(I). If the next time around, we request item 2, line 130 will have the same meaning as if we'd written Q(2). By changing the value of I, our program can gain access to each of the values in the array. After our first interaction with the program (where we changed the quantity on hand of item 1 from 0 to 23), the array looked like this:

```
Q(1)    [23] ←— only Q(1) was affected
Q(2)    [ 0]    by our first use of
Q(3)    [ 0]    the program
 .
 .
 .
Q(10)   [ 0]
```

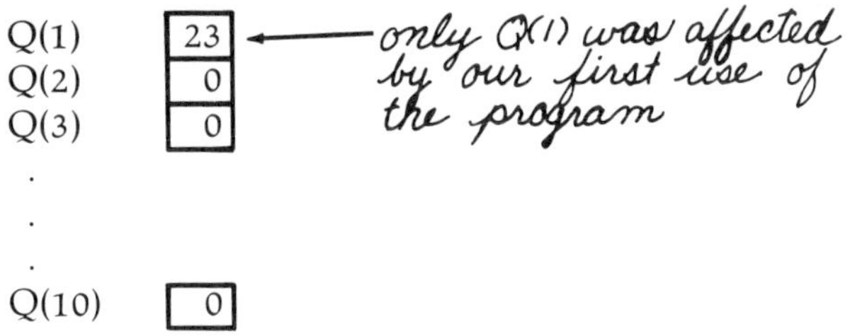

After our first 10 interactions with the program, the array looked like this:

```
Q(1)    [23]
Q(2)    [10]
Q(3)    [11]
Q(4)    [ 5]
Q(5)    [39]
Q(6)    [ 0]
Q(7)    [20]
Q(8)    [12]
Q(9)    [24]
Q(10)   [ 1]
```

We're sure you'll agree that although our program is much more useful than before, it still isn't ready to be turned loose on the world. Certain errors are still too easy to make (what if the stockroom person couldn't add very well and entered 34 as the new quantity on hand?). It still isn't really very polite. But those are minor points which we'll fix later in this chapter. First, it's crucial for you to understand arrays, what they are, and how to use them.

EXERCISES 10 2

1 In order to find the value of the I0th item in the DATA statements, the first experimental program carries out this loop:

```
30      FOR I=1 TO IO
40          READ Q
50      NEXT I
```

What does the loop do?

(a) It reads each item in the DATA statements, storing only the one we want in Q.

(b) It reads successive items from the DATA statements, stopping after it has read a total of I0 items.

(c) It reads successive items from the DATA statements, stopping after it has read the first item whose value is I0.

2 In order to find the value of the Ith item in the array we called Q( ), the second experimental program does which of these?

(a) It reads successive value from the array, stopping after it has read a total of I0 items.

(b) It skips over the first I0 − 1 array positions, then takes the next value, and then skips to the end of the array (the 10th position).

(c) It gives the name of the array, followed by a subscript value in parentheses. The subscript value is the one stored in variable I.

3 This DATA statement gives a sequence of five values.

```
DATA 1, 3, 5, 7, 9
```

The array A( ) gives a sequence of five variables called A(1), A(2), A(3), A(4), and A(5). The variables have the values shown.

A(1)	A(2)	A(3)	A(4)	A(5)
1	3	5	7	9

Assume that the DATA statement appears in a program, and the array A( ) has been declared (in a DIM) and filled with the values by the program. If a phrase below is true of the DATA statement, write "DATA" beside it. If it is true of the array, write "array" beside it.

(a) The program can access the value 3 without having accessed the value 1.

(b) The fourth item in the sequence of values is 7.

(c) The program could change the value 9 to the value 10.

(d) By retyping parts of the program, the second and third values could be reversed.

(e) The program itself could reverse the second and third values.

4 Rewrite the second experimental program so that before the user types in anything, the array stores the values 23, 10, 11, 5, 39, 0, 20, 12, 24, and 1 instead of all zeros (as the programs stands).

Section 10 3

More About Arrays

Now that you've had an introduction to arrays, let's look at some general rules for using arrays and DIM statements. Then, we'll show how more complex arrays can be set up for a program.

The DIMension statement is written in the form of a list of one or more array declarations.

DIM *array declaration, array declaration, . . ., array declaration*
where each *array declaration* has one of the forms
letter (whole number)
or
letter (whole number, whole number)

The second form of the *array declaration* is for arrays with two subscripts, the more complex type of array which we'll discuss a little later.

Each array declaration names an array—that's what the *letter* is for. In Minimal BASIC the name of an array must be a single letter (A is all right; A2 is not). Each array declaration also specifies the number of subscripts (one or two) that the array will have and the values those subscripts may take—that's what the *whole number* is for. For example, the DIMension statement

```
DIM A(25)
```

sets up an array named A whose subscript must be a number between 0 and 25, inclusive. We think of the array as a list of variables, indexed by a subscript: A(0), A(1), A(2), A(3), . . ., A(24), A(25)

> **Is A(0) or A(1) the first variable in the array?**
>
> In Minimal BASIC normally the first variable in an array is the one with subscript 0. However, in some cases it's more convenient to have the variable with subscript 1 be the first. In that case you may insert this statement in your program, somewhere before any DIM statements:
>
> *line number* OPTION BASE 1
>
> and the first variable in any array will be the one with subscript 1. It's a rare case when you need to worry about the OPTION BASE statement—if you don't want to use array position 0, you don't have to, even if it's there.

The whole numbers in a DIMension statement must be exactly that; they cannot be numbers with fractions, nor can they contain computations, like addition or subtraction. An array may be DIMensioned only once.

The DIMension statement

```
DIM B(7), C(12)
```

sets up two arrays:

B(0), B(1), B(2), . . .,B(7) and
C(0), C(1), C(2), C(3), . . ., C(12)

A subscript which indexes one of the variables in an array must, of course, be within bounds. The array B in the DIMension statement above contains only the variables, B(0) through B(7). It doesn't make sense to index B(8), B(15), or B(−3) because they don't exist. Therefore, when we are using one of the variables in B, the subscript must be between 0 and 7, inclusive. If the subscript isn't a whole number, it is automatically rounded to the nearest whole number. The statements

```
10    DIM B(7)
20    LET N = 10
30    LET B(N/3) = 1
40    LET B(N/6) = 2
```

have the effect of putting the value 1 into B(3) and the value 2 into B(2) because N/3 is 3.33333 (which rounds off to 3) and N/6 is 1.66667 (which rounds off to 2).

Warning!

If you put a subscript after a variable, but you haven't declared an array with that name in a DIM statement, BASIC will assume that you want an array anyway. In effect, it automatically puts that variable in a DIM statement and sets the upper bound(s) at 10. This can have surprising effects if you don't want an array. For example, you might mistakenly write

```
A(1 + B)
```

and find that your program sets up an array named A instead of multiplying A by the sum 1 + B.

You will do both yourself and anyone else who reads your program a favor if you list all arrays you use in DIM statements.

As we saw in Section 10 1, arrays are needed when you want to be able to index a list of values which must be changed as the program is running. When the values remain constant throughout the program's history, you can use DATA statements and count to the Nth value when you need it. However, the counting process complicates the program and can be avoided by storing the list of values in an array. Then, to index the Nth value, you simply use N as a subscript. Because indexing is automatic with arrays, they are often used to store tables, even when the information in the tables never changes.

A case of this nature comes up in writing a program to print the expected stopping distance, given the speed of a car (Table 10 3 1).

TABLE 10 3 1 Stopping-Distance Table

speed (mph)	10	20	30	40	50	60	70	80	90	100
stopping distance (feet)	50	60	120	180	250	330	430	550	690	820

stopping distance: The information in the table presented here was obtained from the owner's handbook for a BMW 2002. It assumes average road conditions and includes a one-second reaction time.

The table contains entries for ten different speeds, so we need an array with ten variables. We would like to be able to index the array by speed, but that causes problems, because of the gaps in the table (no entry for 12 mph, 27 mph, etc.). However, if we think of the speeds in units of 10 mph, then there are no gaps (1 ten, 2 tens, 3 tens, etc.) Based on this observation, we divide the given speed by 10 to get a subscript in the appropriate range. If the speed is 40 mph, then 40/10 is 4, and the fourth entry in the table tells us the stopping distance for 40 mph. The program below uses this indexing technique to print the correct stopping distance when the user enters the speed of the automobile.

```
10    REM  PROGRAM TO PRINT STOPPING DISTANCES ON REQUEST
20         DIM D(10)
30    REM  SET UP THE TABLE OF STOPPING DISTANCES
```

```
40          FOR I=0 TO 10
50              READ D(I)
60          NEXT I
70    REM   GET SPEED FROM USER
80          PRINT "WHAT IS YOUR SPEED (IN MPH)";
90          INPUT S
100         PRINT "STOPPING DISTANCE AT"; S; "MPH IS"; D(S/10); "FEET."
110         GO TO 9999
1000        DATA 0, 50, 60, 120, 180, 250, 330, 430, 550, 690, 820
9999        END

RUN
WHAT IS YOUR SPEED (IN MPH)? 52
STOPPING DISTANCE AT 52 MPH IS 250 FEET.
READY
```

the standards say that subscript expressions are rounded.

if this program doesn't seem to work right on your computer, check your manual. your system might use INT(S/10) instead.

Try the stopping distance program on your computer. Notice how it rounds off the subscript to select the nearest entry when the user enters a speed like 48 mph. Another subtlety is the extra entry in the table for zero mph.

This is mostly a precaution. We don't really expect people to enter speeds of zero, but someone might innocently enter a speed of 4 mph and get a nonsensical answer if we had not put 0 in D(0).

The table of stopping distances has only one line of information, but most tables have several. A **windchill table,** for example, gives temperatures for equivalent cooling conditions based on wind speed and air temperature. In Table 10 3 2 you can see that when the wind is blowing at 15 mph and the air temperature is 10°F, the chilling effect is like that of an air temperature of four degrees below zero. In order to write a program which uses this table to print out windchill temperatures when the user types in wind speed and air temperature, it is convenient to use an **array with two subscripts.** You can think of an array with two subscripts as a table of variables with several lines. The number of lines in the table is given by the first whole number in the array declaration. The second number in the declaration gives the number of variables per line.

Table 10 3 2 Windchill Temperatures

		temperature (°F)					
		0	5	10	15	20	25
wind (mph)	5	0	5	10	15	20	25
	10	−9	−4	1	9	14	18
	15	−18	−11	−4	1	9	16
	20	−26	−17	−9	−2	5	12
	25	−36	−26	−17	−8	0	9

> **windchill:** The information in table 10 3 2 was obtained from the work of R.G. Steadman which appeared in the *Journal of Applied Meteorology,* Volume 10 (1971), pp. 674–683. His figures measure heat loss for a person clothed adequately to maintain thermal equilibrium. For exposed flesh, the windchill temperatures would be considerably lower. Your TV weather personality usually gives the more dramatic "exposed flesh" figures.

The statement DIM A(3,5) sets up a table of variables like this:

A(0,0)	A(0,1)	A(0,2)	A(0,3)	A(0,4)	A(0,5)
A(1,0)	A(1,1)	A(1,2)	A(1,3)	A(1,4)	A(1,5)
A(2,0)	A(2,1)	A(2,2)	A(2,3)	A(2,4)	A(2,5)
A(3,0)	A(3,1)	A(3,2)	A(3,3)	A(3,4)	A(3,5)

As you can see, the first subscript tells which line the variable is in, and the second subscript tells which position it's in on the line (or which column of the table it's in).

The program below is almost identical to the stopping distance program except that it uses an array with two subscripts to store the multilined windchill table. The values are placed in the array by a sequence of READ statements controlled by a doubly nested FOR-NEXT loop. The inside loop reads a single line of the table, from column to column, while the outside loop moves from line to line. This sequence of READs is relatively complicated, but it is a very common type of operation.

Just as the stopping-distance program had an entry for zero speed in case someone entered a very low speed, the windchill program has an extra line in its table to cover the possibility of someone entering a small wind speed. Another similarity between the two programs is the indexing trick. The wind speeds and temperatures jump in units of five, so we divide the given values by five to put them in the correct range for subscripts.

```
10    REM  WIND CHILL PROGRAM
20    REM  SET UP WIND CHILL TABLE.
30         DIM C(5,5)
40         FOR W=0 TO 5
50             FOR T=0 TO 5
60                 READ C(W,T)
70             NEXT T
80         NEXT W
90         PRINT "WHAT IS THE TEMPERATURE";
100        INPUT T
110        INPUT "WHAT IS THE WIND SPEED";
120        INPUT W
130        PRINT "THE WIND CHILL TEMPERATURE IS"; C(W/5, T/5)
140        GO TO 9999
1000 REM   VALUES FOR WIND CHILL TABLE.
1010 REM   NOTE EXTRA LINE FOR ZERO WIND SPEED.
1020       DATA  0,   5,   10,   15,   20,   25
1030       DATA  0,   5,   10,   15,   20,   25
1040       DATA -9,  -4,    1,    9,   14,   18
```

```
1050     DATA -18, -11,  -4,   1,   9,  16
1060     DATA -26, -17,  -9,  -2,   5,  12
1070     DATA -36, -26, -17,  -8,   0,   9
9999     END

RUN
WHAT IS THE TEMPERATURE? 21
WHAT IS THE WIND SPEED? 19
THE WIND CHILL TEMPERATURE IS 5
READY

RUN
WHAT IS THE TEMPERATURE? 26
WHAT IS THE WIND SPEED? 18
THE WIND CHILL TEMPERATURE IS 5
READY
```

EXERCISES 10 3

1 Which are legal Minimal BASIC DIMension statements?

(a) `10 DIM A(21)`
(b) `10 DIM B(25, 25)`
(c) `10 DIM M(200), S(200)`
(d) `10 DIM Z(0:127)`

2 Which are legal Minimal BASIC DIMension statements?

(a) `20 DIM A2(209`
(b) `20 DIMENSION C(12)`
(c) `20 DIM E(128, 5)`
(d) `20 DIM F(10), F(20), F(30)`

3 Given that the array L( ) was set up with this DIM statement,

```
10       DIM L(12)
```

which of the following assignment statements are legal? Assume that F has the value 5 and G has the value 2.

(a) `130 LET K = L(1)`
(b) `130 LET L(F) = L(F) + 1`
(c) `130 LET K = L(F*G + 3)`
(d) `130 LET L(G) = "END OF DATA"`

4 Given that the array C( ) has the values shown in the "before" picture, fill in the values C( ) will have after these statements are carried out.

```
1310     LET P = C(1) + C(3)
1320     LET C(P) = C(P) + 1
```

	before		*after*
C(1)	1	C(1)	
C(2)	2	C(2)	
C(3)	4	C(3)	
C(4)	8	C(4)	
C(5)	15	C(5)	

5 What does the stopping distance program print out if the user types in 58 mph? 55 mph?

6 If the user types in 120 mph, the stopping distance program will either halt with an error message or behave very strangely. Why? How can the program be altered to prevent this?

7 What happens if the user of the windchill program types in −10 degrees?

8 If the nesting of the FOR-NEXT loops in the windchill program is reversed (that is, if the statements in lines 0040 and 0050 are interchanged and the statements in lines 0070 and 0080 are interchanged), then the windchill values are put in the wrong places in the table. If the programmer had made this mistake, what would the program print if the user typed in a wind speed of 10 and a temperature of 20?

Section 10 4
Inventory Control Revisited

In Section 10 2 we developed a "bare bones" inventory control program. There our main goal was to show how arrays could be used to store a large number of values which can change during the running of a program. Let's return to the idea of an inventory control program, and see how we can make our program more useful. We'll take one step toward practicality here—the problems at the end of this chapter suggest more improvements.

Our program in Section 10 2 did nothing but store and change a value (the quantity on hand) for each product. It didn't reflect the varying uses different sections of the store would make of an inventory control system. At the checkout counters the clerks would enter information telling which item was being purchased. They would never care how many of that item were on hand, and they would never want to *add* to the quantity on hand. In the stockroom the use would be different—the stockers would add to the quantity on hand for each item which arrived in a shipment, but they would probably never care how many were on hand. And the people who do the ordering would want to know how many of a given item were on hand, but wouldn't make any other use of the system. One way we can improve our program is to tailor it to these specific uses. That way, when, for example, the stockroom people use it, it will make sense to them, and they'll be less likely to make errors.

Of course, a company will want to know more about each product than the quantity on hand. At the very least, they will want to know the price of each item. No doubt you can think of more things, like the cost (how much the company paid for

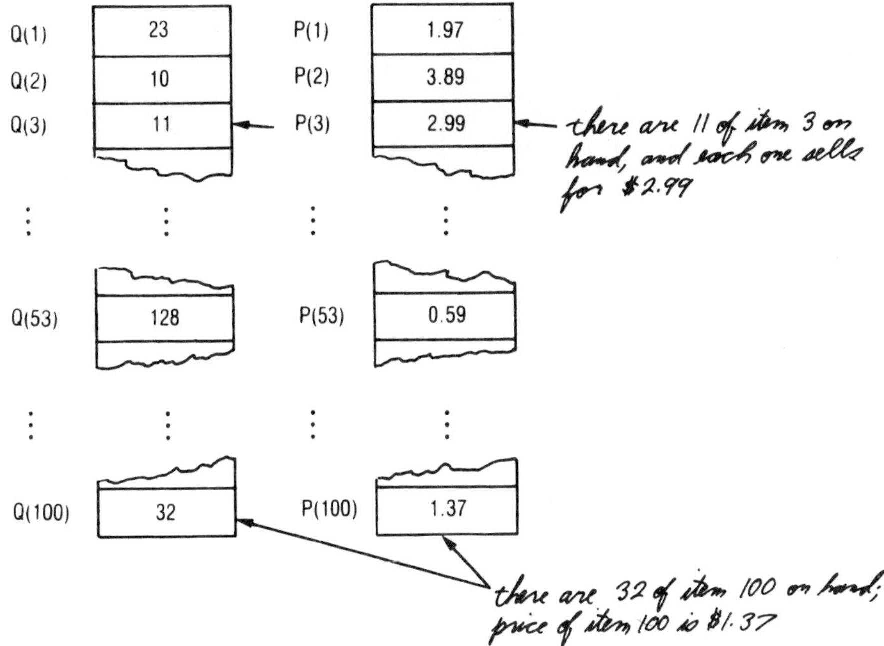

FIGURE 10 4 1 Storing two pieces of information about each item

the item), the manufacturer, spoilage date (for perishables), average number sold per month, etc. The method we'll use to store the price as well as the quantity on hand can be used to store at most any piece of information you think a store would want to keep in its inventory records. Let's work on this part of our revision first.

In our program in Section 10 2 we used an array Q( ) (quantity) to store the number of each item on hand. We'll do the same here. Thus, for item number I, the variable Q(I) will contain the number of that item on hand. If we can use an array to store the quantity on hand, we can also use an array to store the price of each item. Now, in addition to the array Q( ), we'll have an array P( ) (price). For item number I, Q(I) will store the quantity on hand of item I, and P(I) will store the price of item I (Figure 10 4 1).

Our other refinement to the inventory control program will be to take into account the three different types of uses. We'll call the three different uses **checkout, inquiry,** and **restock.** In the **checkout** mode the clerk enters the item number of each purchased item. Our program will print the price of that item, and then subtract one from the quantity on hand.

In the **inquiry** mode the person will enter an item number, and the program will print the price and quantity on hand of that item.

In the **restock** mode the person will enter the item number, the program will ask how many of that item came in the shipment, and what the price is (since it will probably be higher than for the last shipment). Given the user's responses, the program will store the new price in P(I), and add to the quantity on hand.

Here's our plan.

—inventory control—

For each item I:

LET Q(I) = 0

LET P(I) = 0

Ask clerk for mode of operation.

Select *the desired mode:*

checkout

Ask for item number; store it in I.

PRINT price of item I.

Subtract one from quantity on hand.

inquiry

Ask for item number; store it in I.

PRINT price and quantity of item I.

restock

Ask for item number; store it in I.

Ask for number in shipment,

Ask for price.

Store price as new price of item I.

Add number in shipment to quantity on hand.

Repeat forever

```
10    REM  INVENTORY CONTROL PROGRAM.
20    REM  THE ARRAY  Q( )  STORES THE QUANTITY ON HAND
30    REM    OF EACH ITEM.  FOR INSTANCE, Q(15) IS  THE
40    REM    QUANTITY ON HAND OF ITEM 15 .
50    REM  THE ARRAY P( )  STORES THE PRICE OF EACH ITEM.
60    REM  WE HAVE 100 ITEMS.
70         DIM Q(100), P(100)
80    REM  AT FIRST, WE DON'T KNOW ANYTHING, SO SET ALL
90    REM    INFORMATION TO  0 .
100        FOR I=1 TO 100
110            LET Q(I) = 0
120            LET P(I) = 0
130        NEXT I
140   REM  GET READY TO USE THE MENU ROUTINES.
150        LET S9 = 1
160        LET F9 = 14
200   REM  MAIN LOOP:
210            PRINT
220            PRINT "CHECKOUT, INQUIRY, RESTOCK, OR QUIT";
230            GOSUB 9500
240            ON W9 GO TO 1000, 2000, 3000, 9999
```

```
1000 REM        CHECKOUT OPTION.
1010            PRINT "ITEM # =";
1020            INPUT I
1030 REM        SINCE THE STORE JUST SOLD AN ITEM  I ,
1040 REM          NOW HAVE ONE FEWER ON HAND.
1050            LET Q(I) = Q(I) - 1
1060            PRINT "ITEM "; I; TAB(12); "---$"; P(I)
1070            GO TO 4000

2000 REM        INQUIRY OPTION.
2010            PRINT "ITEM #";
2020            INPUT I
2030 REM        SHOW CURRENT QUANTITY ON HAND.
2040            PRINT "ITEM #";I; "PRICE =$"; P(I);
2050            PRINT   TAB(25); Q(I); "ON HAND."
2060            GO TO 4000

3000 REM        RESTOCK OPTION.
3010            PRINT "ITEM # =";
3020            INPUT I
3030            PRINT "HOW MANY CAME IN";
3040            INPUT S
3050 REM        ADD TO THE QUANTITY ON HAND.
3060            LET Q(I) = Q(I) + S
3070            PRINT "WHAT PRICE";
3080            INPUT P(I)

4000 REM      REPEAT FOREVER
4010          GO TO 200

8000 REM  MENU WORDS FOR INVENTORY PROGRAM.
8010      DATA CHECKOUT,1, CHECK,1,   CH,1,  C,1
8020      DATA INQUIRY,2,  INQUIRE,2, IN,2,  I,2
8030      DATA RESTOCK,3,  STOCK,3,   R,3,   S,3
8040      DATA QUIT,4,     Q,4
 .
 .  <-------- the menu routines go in here
 .
9999      END
READY

RUN

CHECKOUT, INQUIRY, RESTOCK, OR QUIT? RESTOCK
ITEM # =? 1
HOW MANY CAME IN? 12
WHAT PRICE? 0.65

CHECKOUT, INQUIRY, RESTOCK, OR QUIT? INQUIRE
ITEM # =? 1
ITEM # 1 PRICE =$ .65      12 ON HAND.

CHECKOUT, INQUIRY, RESTOCK, OR QUIT? CHECK
ITEM # =? 1
ITEM # 1    ---$ .65
```

(program continued on page 240)

```
CHECKOUT, INQUIRY, RESTOCK, OR QUIT? I
ITEM # =? 1
ITEM # 1 PRICE =$ .65      11 ON HAND.
```

EXERCISES 10 4

1 Look at Figure 10 4 1. If I has the value 53, what are the values of Q(I) and P(I)? If I is now changed to 100, what are the values of Q(53) and P(53)?

2 The restock option in the inventory control program asks the clerk for the price of the newly arrived items. Suppose there are 126 cans of French-cut green beans on hand, with a listed price of $0.39 per can. Now a shipment of 32 cans of French-cut green beans comes in, and the clerk enters them into the system and indicates a price of $0.41 per can. From now on, how much will a customer be charged for one of the newly arrived cans? For one of the original cans?

3 As the inventory control program stands now, there's no way to account for losses from inventory due to theft, spoilage, or breakage. Make a plan for an additional option called "adjust" which first asks the user for a password, and, if the correct one is entered, allows the user to change the values stored for any item. If the user doesn't know the right password, he or she is, no doubt, Up to No Good, so do something drastic.

4 Would it be possible to do the inventory program using a two-dimensional array to store the Quantity on hand and the Price of each item instead of using two one-dimensional arrays? If so, how? If not, why not?

PROBLEMS 10

1 Here are instructions for knitting a scarf:

Using No. 9 needles, cast on 64 sts.
row 1 and all odd rows up to 19: k across
row 2 and all even rows up to 20: p across
row 21 - 100: k4, p2 across, end k4
row 101 and all odd rows up to 119: p across
row 102 and all even rows up to 120: k across

Write a program which carries out the knitting instructions by

(a) printing a + for every "knit"
(b) printing a – for every "purl"
(c) going to a new line for each new row.

2 The bar graph program described in Section 7 2 depends on the sales figures having been placed in DATA statements. This is a dangerous practice for naive users. Protect such users by revising the program so it uses an INPUT statement to get the values to be plotted. In addition, ask the user for a brief heading, and print it above the bar graph.

3 Make two further improvements to the bar graph plotter (Problem 2). Ask the user which character to use for the bars (we used "$" before), and another character to use to show the average value. Have your program compute the average, and put the special character in each line at the position corresponding to the average. That way, someone looking at the finished bar graph can quickly see which bars are above and which are below the average length.

4 If your version of BASIC allows arrays of string variables (see Section 16 1) redo the inventory control program from Section 10 4, now adding a third array which holds product names. At the beginning of the program, set all the names to "?". During a RESTOCK operation, if the name of the item is "?" ask for the correct name. During CHECKOUT, print the name along with the price.

5 Design and write a program which keeps accepting batting averages until either 20 have been entered or the user gives a negative number for a batting average. Then have your program print the averages, one per line, with a * beside those which are lower that average of all the batting averages entered.

6 The Boss Tweed clothing store has computerized its inventory operations. It sells twenty different styles of suits. Each style has been assigned a number from 1 to 20. At the start of the day there are 10 suits of each style in stock. Each time a salesperson unloads a suit on a customer, the word SOLD followed by the appropriate style number is typed at Boss Tweed's computer terminal, and the computer updates the quantity on hand of that particular style. If a salesperson claims to have sold a suit when, in fact, there were none of that style on hand, the computer prints a message congratulating the salesperson for Super Salesmanship. In addition, it prints a message suggesting that someone might want to order some more suits of that style.

When the manager wants to check on supplies, she types SHOW ME, and the computer prints the number of suits of each style that are in stock.

Write a program to handle Boss Tweed's inventory control needs. Make up enough test data to ensure that you have tested every combination of options.

7 Your company is considering building a new plant in one of the eleven Western states. The president has written to each state asking for their business tax rates. Your job is to write a program which will analyze the tax rates and produce an official-looking document the president can use to impress the stockholders.

Your program will be used like this: As each letter comes in, the president's secretary will type an abbreviation for the state and then the tax rate. Some states might not respond promptly, so your program might not have a rate for every state by the time the secretary types DONE.

After receiving a DONE message, your program prints a fancy heading, then one line for each of the eleven states. Each of these lines starts with the abbreviation for the state, and continues with one of several things. If no tax rate was entered for the state, your program prints NO REPLY. Otherwise, the next thing on the line is the tax rate. If that tax rate is lower than the average of all the rates that were entered, it is followed by

*****LOWER THAN AVERAGE*****.

Use the menu routines for dealing with the state abbreviations. Store the rates in an array so your program can compute the average before printing. Be sure that when your program computes the average, it ignores states that didn't respond to the president's letter.

Eleven Western States

Arizona	AZ	New Mexico	NM
California	CA	Oregon	OR
Colorado	CO	Utah	UT
Idaho	ID	Washington	WA
Montana	MT	Wyoming	WY
Nevada	NV		

8 Revise the checkout option in the inventory control program to make it more useful to the checkout clerks. The sample sales slip that follows shows the features to be added. Notice that now the program stays in the checkout mode until the clerk is completely through taking care of a customer. Use the sales tax routine from Problem 9 7.

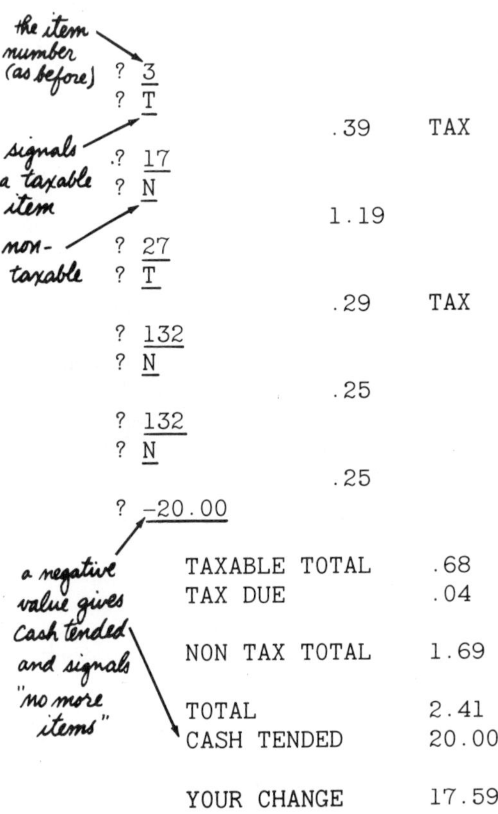

WISELY SUPER MARKET
the item number (as before)
? 3
? T
.39 TAX
signals a taxable item
? 17
? N
1.19
non-taxable
? 27
? T
.29 TAX
? 132
? N
.25
? 132
? N
.25
? -20.00
a negative value gives cash tended and signals "no more items"
TAXABLE TOTAL .68
TAX DUE .04
NON TAX TOTAL 1.69
TOTAL 2.41
CASH TENDED 20.00
YOUR CHANGE 17.59
---THANK YOU FOR SHOPPING WISELY---

9 Revise the INQUIRY option in the inventory control program. Allow the user to keep getting information about specific items until he or she enters a negative item number. Then have your program go through the records and compute the total value of the stock on hand.

10 The table shown below may be used for computing tax due for a person whose income is from $4500 to $5000, and who has no more than 6 exemptions. Using the technique we used in the windchill factor program (Section 10 3), write a program which tells the user how much tax he or she will owe. If the user enters an income or number of exemptions outside the range covered by the table, print a message directing the user to the IRS.

TAX TABLE

Income	*Exemptions* 1	2	3	4	5	6
4500-4549	565	430	326	218	116	18
4550-4599	565	430	326	218	116	25
4600-4649	581	444	342	224	130	32
4650-4699	589	451	350	241	137	39
4700-4749	597	459	358	249	144	46
4750-4799	606	463	366	256	151	53
4800-4849	614	474	374	264	159	60
4850-4899	622	482	382	271	166	67
4900-4949	630	490	390	279	174	74
4950-4999	638	497	398	286	181	81

11 The inventory control program has a major flaw which would prevent it from being used commercially. How can a person using the program know what item number goes with a given product? A grocery store has thousands of items. There's no way the employees could memorize the number of each item, and looking them up would be too slow. However, each item has a UPC number right on it. That should be used to identify a product.

UPC symbol

The **Universal Product Code** (UPC) serves as an identifying number for (presumably) every product that will ever be sold in large quantities. The bars provide a machine readable form of the numbers on the UPC symbol. There are two main parts to the code, a Manufacturer identifier, and a Specific product identifier. The 51000 on the symbol above identifies the Campbell Soup Company. The 01261 is Campbell's code for a 10¾-oz. can of Cream of Mushroom Soup.

Revise the inventory control program so items are identified by their UPC instead of by their array subscripts as before. Add two more pieces of information about each item—the manufacturer code and the specific product code.

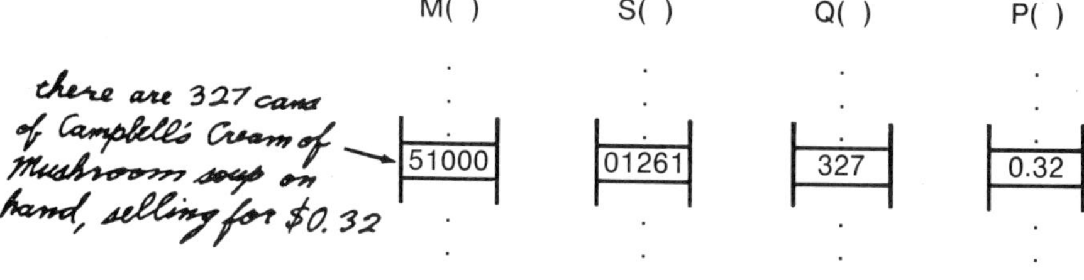

Use a **search loop** (Section 8 5) to find the information about an item, given the two parts of its Univeral Product Code.

Test your program by entering information about some of products in your kitchen. Simulate using some of them up (checkout) and buying some more (restock).

12 In order to find the records for a specific item, the program of Problem 11 looks at each successive array position until it finds the one with the desired manufacturer code and specific product code. If there are many thousands of items in the arrays, this can take a long time.

When you look a person up in the phone book, you use a different scheme. Since the names are in alphabetical order, you can skip over huge chunks of names without worrying that you've missed the one you want.

If all the items in an array are in order, the **binary search method** can be used to find a specific item quickly. It's called a **binary search** because at each step it eliminates about ½ the alternatives from consideration.

Assume the array M( ) contains *n* items, M(1) through M(*n*), with the items in increasing order. To find the position of an item with value *m*, the binary search method (plans shown below) first looks at the middle of M( ). If that's the right one, the search is over. If the desired item *m* is greater than the middle item, the search continues, but is confined to the last half of M( ). If the desired item is less than the middle item, the search continues in the first part of the array.

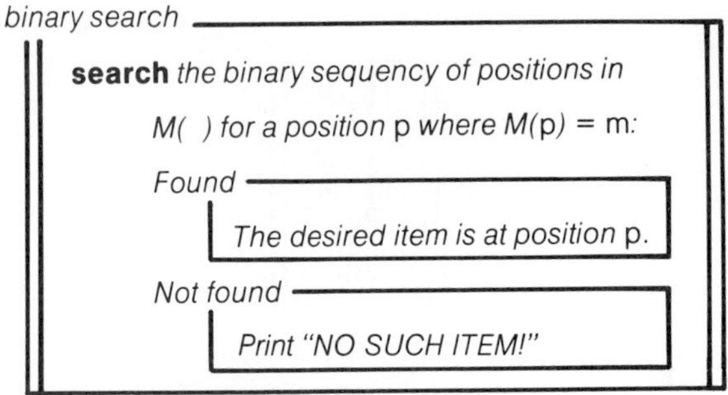
binary search
search the binary sequency of positions in
M( ) for a position p where M(p) = m:
Found
The desired item is at position p.
Not found
Print "NO SUCH ITEM!"

binary sequence of positions

LET low = 0.

LET high = n + 1.

LET p = (low + high)/2
Select *based on the relative values of M(p) and m:*

M(p) < m
The next region to search is between p and high, i.e., LET low = p.

M(p) > m
The next region to search is between low and p, i.e., LET high = p.

M(p) = m or low ⩾ high
The search is over.

Repeat until *the search is over*

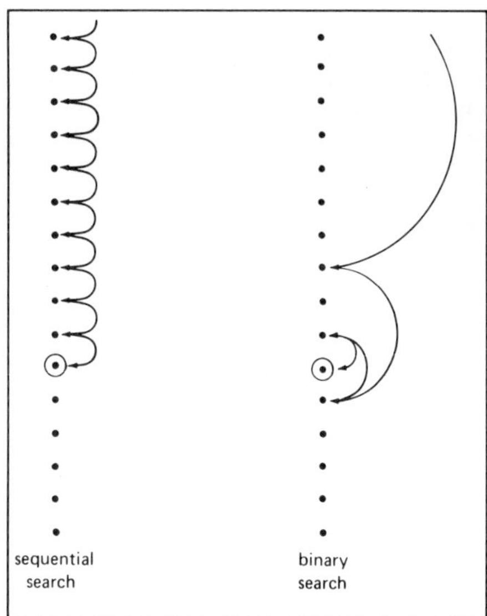

Refine the plans for the binary search method, and write a program which uses it to find values in an array of manufacturer codes. Be sure the array is in order to begin with! Have your program print the number of positions it looked at before it found each item. Compare the binary search to methods used in Problems 4 4 and 8 4.

13 Re-revise the inventory control problem. Use the more realistic technique described in Problem 11, and search for items using the fast search method of Problem 12. Be sure the items are stored in order!

14 Over the years, the qualifications for being a recognized guru have become more refined. In one modern certification test, scientists record the potentials induced in a 10-by-10 sheet of polystyrene by the meditations of candidate gurus. If a candidate is able to cause some point on the sheet to have a voltage greater than twice the average voltage over the 10-by-10 grid, he passes the first phase of the test. Otherwise he is labeled a sham and sent away in disgrace.

Aging guru radiates potential

In the second, more rigorous, phase of the test, the pattern of points having above average potential is plotted, and if the pattern is balanced, with no more large values appearing to the left than to the right, at the top than at the bottom, the candidate is welcomed into the Brotherhood of Enlightened Guhury.

Write a program which carries out the first phase of the test and prints an appropriate message. For those candidates who pass the first phase (and for *only* those candidates), print the pattern of voltages they induced. Print a blank at spots which were of average or below average voltage; print * at spots of above average potential.

Make up some data, or perform the measurements yourself on a guru of your acquaintance.

15 Write a program to list all the prime numbers between 1 and 1000. To compute these numbers, use the algorithm below, which is known as **Eratosthenes' sieve.**

(a) Make a list of all the consecutive integers you are interested in, starting from 2.

(b) Mark off all the multiples of 2 (they can't be primes).

(c) Find the next integer remaining in the list beyond the one whose multiples you just marked off, and mark off *its* multiples (they can't be primes).

(d) Repeat step c unless the integer whose multiple you just marked off is the square root of the largest integer in the list; that is, the square root without its fractional part. (This termination condition depends of the fact that the two factors in a product can't both exceed the square root of the product.)

Keep track of which numbers are still on the list by initializing an array of 1000 positions to 1 (for "on the list") and then crossing the number *n* off the list by changing the *n*th value in the array to 0.

Chapter 11 **Putting It All Together**

Section 11 1

Politeness, Portability, and Program Design — Loops, Arrays, and Subroutines

Programming is not easy. It's fun, but not easy. You've probably had fun learning about the ANSI Minimal BASIC programming language. (You've seen the whole language now.) No doubt there have been some frustrating times when the machine didn't treat you right, when things went wrong that you couldn't explain. Don't feel bad; it happens to everyone.

Computer systems just aren't very polite. They're getting better, but they're still terribly rude. There are lots of details to go wrong, and it's almost impossible for the designer of a large system to catch all of them and give you an understandable message.

Computer systems *could be better,* though. That's why the issue of **politeness** is so important. All the time you spend making your programs polite and helpful to the user is worthwhile, even if you're the only user. A polite program will save you time in the long run.

Even when you think you're the only user, it often turns out, especially with good programs, that other people want to use them. This is where **portability** comes in. The person who wants your program usually has a different computer system from yours. If you've depended on a lot of special features of your system, like strings with 4000 characters or special kinds of whole numbers, or long variable names, etc., then your program probably won't work on someone else's computer. That leads to a lot of work in revision or rewrite. So even though it is frustrating to stay within the restrictions of Minimal BASIC, the effort can pay off. Let it be a challenge to you. You can do a great deal more in Minimal BASIC than most people give it credit for, with not too much difficulty. There are things you can't do in a practical way, but try Minimal BASIC first. If that doesn't work, explain in your documentation why you used an extended feature; and in your program, *mark it.* Then anyone revising your program to make it work elsewhere can find the hard spots quickly.

Steps in program design

1 **define the problem**
figure out what we really want the program to do

2 **make a plan**
consider alternative solutions to the problem, select one, and write an overall, higher-level plan

3 **refine the plan**
work out the solution in detail

4 **code the refined plan**
write the BASIC statements corresponding to each part of the refined plan

5 **verify that the program works properly**
debug the program so there are no error messages, make sure each subpart does what the refined plan says, and make sure the program solves all aspects of the original problem

6 **put on finishing touches**
make sure it's polite, easy to use, and portable; write documentation telling how the program works; write instructions for its use

You've learned all of Minimal BASIC. You've learned how to keep your programs manageable in size, even though they do a lot of work, by using **loops, arrays,** and **subroutines.** You've learned many programming techniques, and you've learned **program design** from the ground up (or maybe we should say, from the top down!).

Now that you've come this far, you must have realized that the ideas of program design do actually make a difference in how long it takes to write a program, and how good the program will be when you're done. However, you must have also realized that they are an *outline* of the process, not gospel which must be followed mindlessly. Writing good programs is hard. By now you are beginning to have a feeling for when you really understand a problem. This is an important ability, one that develops slowly with time. Use it to guide you in your work. If you really do understand what you want to do, but are not sure about the details, you will find that taking the top-level processes all the way through step 5 before you begin with the intimate details of the subparts will be useful. As you work with the top level, you will see aspects of what the subtasks must do that will help you as you go back to refine and develop the subtasks. When you're creating a large program which will be used by many people, you will find that the users discover things which you couldn't have foreseen, and you'll take these new ideas, improvements, and further refinements back to step 1, following all the steps of design as you fine tune the program. In this sense, program design is a process that's never done.

The more programming you do, the more you will come to understand the wisdom of Murphy's Law. Buried in its humorous pessimism is a message — we must take great pains to detect places in our thinking that could (that is, *will*) cause things to go wrong.

Murphy's law

Anything that *can* go wrong *will* go wrong.

It's time to put all the things you've learned together. In this chapter, we'll see an example using all the ideas you've learned to create a substantial useful program. We'll go through the statement of the problem itself (processing questionnaires), plan our solution method, and devise a coding and testing strategy, all the way to the finishing touches.

Section 11 2

The Problem

Paragraph 3 of Section 2 of Article 1 of the Constitution of the United States of America requires an "enumeration of the people" to be made every ten years. Interestingly, this brief clause (and Congress' elaborations) has had a major impact on the development of computers and the data processing industry. This "enumeration," which originally was envisioned solely as a means for determining how many representatives each state would have, grew and grew until it became the census we know today.

Originally the census was counted completely by hand. By the late eighteen hundreds, the combination of growing population and more elaborate census questions was causing nightmares for the Census Office. It was no longer possible, using conventional hand sorting and counting, to complete the analysis of census data before it was out of date. The analysis of data from the census of 1880 was still going on in 1887! The Census Office held a competition, and of the three top entries, one using punched cards and an electrical tabulating scheme was chosen (Figure 11 2 1). It was an invention of Herman Hollerith (who liked to think of himself as the first "statistical engineer"). Hollerith's company (the Tabulating Machine Company) later was combined with others to form the Computing-Tabulating-Recording Company, which was later renamed International Business Machines Corporation, now, of course, known as IBM.

The effect of the massive data compilation tasks of the Bureau of the Census again had a major effect in the early 1950s. On June 14, 1951, the Bureau of the Census took delivery of the world's first commercially available digital computer, the UNIVAC, built by the Eckert-Mauchly Computer Corporation. (IBM didn't jump into the digital computer market for another couple of years. As late as 1954 it was estimated that, in the long run, not more than 50 private companies could justify buying a computer!).

Processing a questionnaire that has hundreds of questions on it, and which is distributed to millions of people, is *still* a large data processing job. Not because the programs are particularly hard to write, but because of the physical bulk of the answer forms, the time required to put the answers in machine readable form, the time it takes to compute the desired statistics, and the time required to print the results in all of the required formats.

In this chapter we'll develop a program for processing responses to questionnaires. First, we have to **define the problem.** We want to write a program which will analyze responses to a questionnaire. But what does that mean? We need to decide what sorts of questions there will be, how many there might be, what sorts of analyses we want to perform, and how we'd like the results presented.

Figure 11 2 1 A user at the console of one of Herman Hollerith's electric tabulating machines. When the user lowers the pins, they go through holes in the card he is now holding and plunge into cups of mercury to establish electrical contacts. (Facts from *A Computer Perspective*, Charles and Ray Eames, Harvard University Press, 1973. Photo from the Library of Congress.)

Some questionnaires have extremely general questions, like "What is your opinion of Indonesia?" Questions like that require analysis by humans, and there's not much our program could do with them. So we'll ignore them. Fortunately, most questionnaires consist of a list of multiple-choice questions. Here are some typical questions from a questionnaire we helped analyze.

1 What is your age?
   a under 15
   b 15 to 18
   c 19 to 21
   d 22 to 25
   e 26 to 30
   f 31 to 40
   g 41 to 60
   h over 60

2 Are you
   a male
   b female

3 How many years have you lived in your present town?
   a less than one
   b 1 to 2
   c 2 to 4
   d more than 4

4 Where do you meet new people? (Please choose *one.*)
   a class
   b party
   c through friends' introductions
   d through work
   e bar
   f other ______

The first three questions are easy to handle. But the fourth can cause trouble. Through experience, we've found that no matter how much you say things like "Please choose one even though you may meet people in more than one setting. Mark the dominant way you meet new people," some 10% of the responses will have more than one answer marked. In fact, in one recent survey we did, about 2% of the respondents marked both male and female for their sex, and about 4% marked neither. In order to write a useful program for questionnaire analysis, you have to realize that things like this will happen. The program *must* be able to cope with this type of data. Otherwise the user will be forced to spend a great deal of time fixing up the input to the program.

Another thing we'll need to think about is what analyses our program should do. Certainly we'll want a breakdown of how people answered each question on the questionnaire, perhaps something like this:

Question 1 What is your age? *(number of responses)*

a	under 15	32	25.6%
b	15 to 18	23	18.4%
c	19 to 21	27	21.6%
d	22 to 25	14	11.2%
e	26 to 30	16	12.8%
f	31 to 40	8	6.4%
g	41 to 60	2	1.6%
h	over 60	0	0.0%
	no response	3	2.4%

(percentage choosing answer d)

In addition, we'd like to be able to study patterns in the responses. For instance, we might want to know if men and women answered some questions differently. Here's a typical **cross tabulation** (as such analyses are called).

57 people answered "female" to Question 2.

Their answers to Question 4 were

a	class	11	19.298%
b	party	8	14.035%
c	through friends	16	28.07%
d	through work	7	12.281%
e	bar	5	8.772%
f	other	6	10.526%
	no response	4	7.018%

By obtaining a similar breakdown showing how those who answered "male" to Question 2 responded to Question 4, we can see if there are significant differences in where men and women say they meet new people.

Another problem we face is how the data will be entered from the returned questionnaires. We want a method that is fast (doesn't require much typing), understandable (so not too many mistakes are made), and consistent (so the program won't have to be too large to be practical).

The last major area of concern we can think of is exactly how the person using our finished program will interact with it. It seems likely that there will have to be several different phases to using the program. At first, the user will surely have to enter some information about the questionnaire; for example, how many questions are in it. Then the user will have to enter each response. Somehow the user will have to specify what analyses to perform, unless all possible ones are done automatically.

We can't think of any more big questions, so it's time to start making decisions.

EXERCISES 11 2

1 The questionnaire problem is the most involved we've dealt with so far. To keep the explanations within bounds, we've made strict definitions of the terms on the left. To make sure you don't get confused going through the development of the questionnaire program, draw lines to match each term with its definition.

a	questionnaire	A	a person who has marked answers to a questionnaire and turned it in for processing
b	respondent	B	a person who makes up a questionnaire
c	response	C	a possible answer which has been marked by a respondent
d	answer	D	a set of answers given by one respondent
e	possible answer	E	one of the list of alternatives given after a question on a questionnaire
		F	one of the questions on a questionnaire
		G	a list of questions which will be duplicated and given to people for them to answer

> **Technical terms**
>
> In this chapter the terms
>
> **questionnaire**
> **respondent**
> **response**
> **answer**
> **possible answer**
>
> are used *strictly* as technical terms for specific aspects of the problem. See Figure 11 2 2 for definitions.

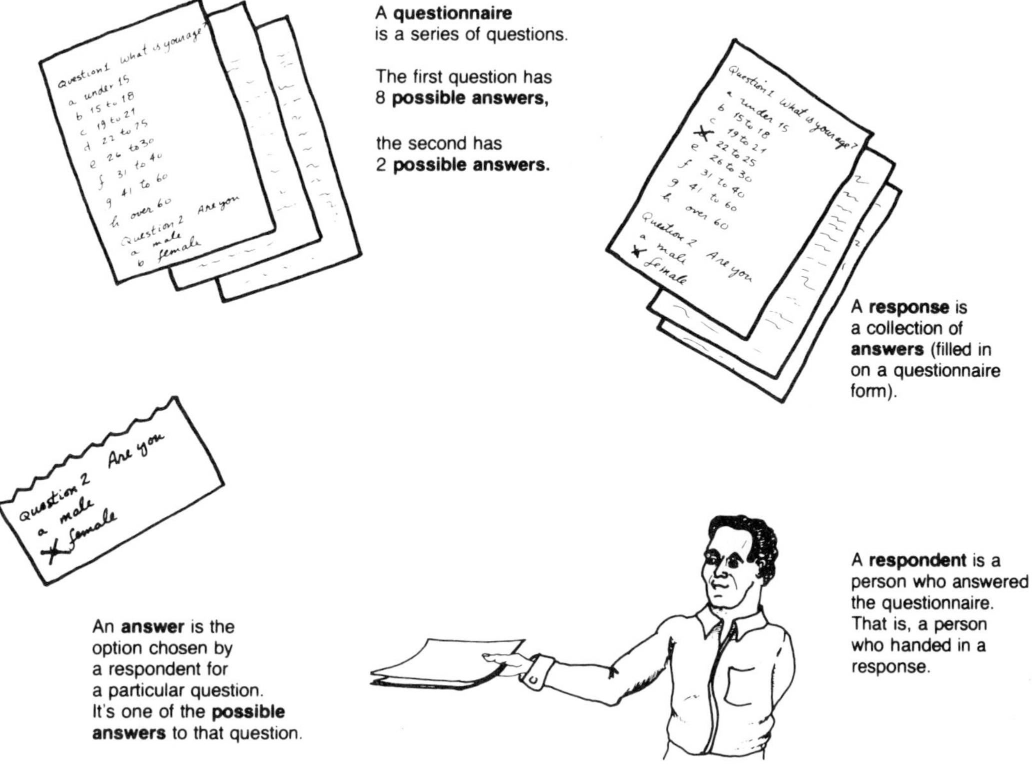

A **questionnaire** is a series of questions.
The first question has 8 **possible answers,**
the second has 2 **possible answers.**
A **response** is a collection of **answers** (filled in on a questionnaire form).
An **answer** is the option chosen by a respondent for a particular question. It's one of the **possible answers** to that question.
A **respondent** is a person who answered the questionnaire. That is, a person who handed in a response.

Figure 11 2 2

Section 11 3

The Plan

The most important decision we have to make is how questionnaire responses will be stored by our program. Once we decide that, we'll know how the user should enter the responses into the computer, and we'll know what sort of data the program will have to analyze.

Our intention is to create a general program — one which will be useful for analyzing a range of different questionnaires. Since the number of questions varies from questionnaire to questionnaire, it seems only reasonable to use an array to store the answers that make up a response, with a variable, say N, telling how many spots in the array are being used.

> **Important note**
>
> Just because you store some value within your program as a number *doesn't* mean the user of your program has to think of the data as numbers. You can have the user enter the values as words or letters, and use our menu subroutines to convert the words or letters into numbers. Similarly, for output, you can translate the numbers you use internally back into words or letters.

In Minimal BASIC the only type of array that is available is numeric. That means we'll store the answers as numbers.

The next decision we need to make is whether our program will have to store all responses to the questionnaire in memory at once, or whether the analyses we want can be made "on the fly," with just one response in memory at a time.

In order to make this decision, we need to have a better idea of what has to happen to make the analyses we want. We thought of three different types of analyses. We want to compute the number of responses, but that's easy, no matter which way we go. We want a **breakdown** of how each question was answered. And we want to be able to do **cross tabs.**

> **What's going on here?**
>
> At this point, we're beginning the planning of our questionnaire program. We know what analyses of the responses the program will have to make, and we're thinking about how the raw data should be handled by the program. The "on the fly" method has the advantage that it places no restriction on the number of responses the program will be able to handle, since just one response would be kept in memory at a time. The "gather all responses in memory" method has the advantage that it allows more complicated analyses to be made. For the next few pages, we'll be deciding between the two methods. We'll think about the "on the fly" method first because it would be best if our program could handle any number of responses. However, we'll find that it won't do.

Let's see how we might compute a breakdown of answers "on the fly." We need to know, for each question, how many people gave each possible answer. We can build up that information in a two-dimensional array. Figure 11 3 1 shows the array as it might look in the midst of analyzing the questions shown in Section 11 2.

How do the numbers get into the array? Well, suppose the program is accepting the next response. The user types in the answer given for the first question. Suppose it's 2. Our program simply adds 1 to the value stored in the array corresponding to question = 1 and answer = 2. Then the program asks for the answer to question 2, adds 1 to the appropriate place in the second column, and so on. After all the

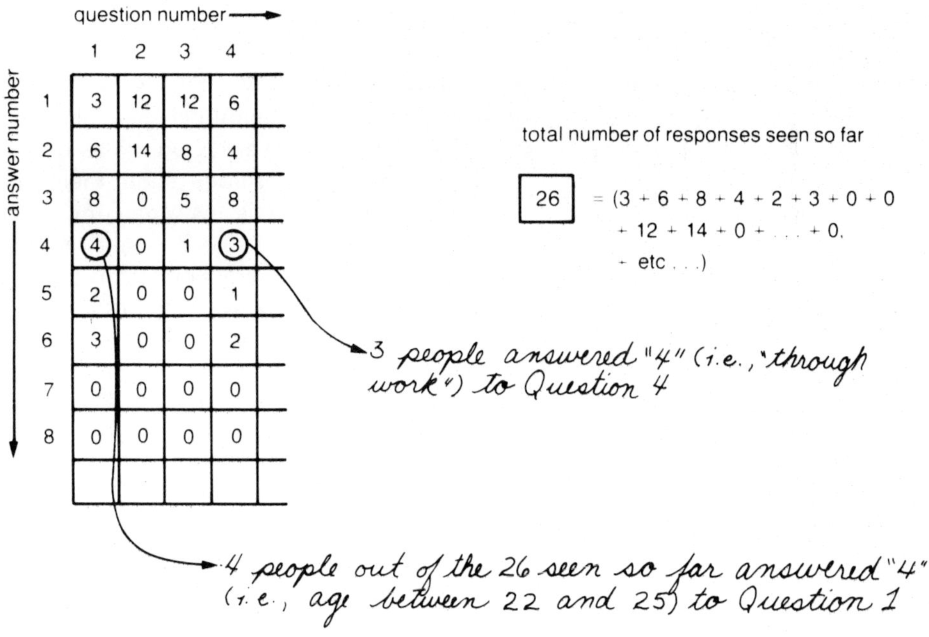

Figure 11 3 1 Doing the computation "on the fly." A two-dimensional array holds running totals of the number of times each answer was given to each question. Ultimately, we decide against this method.

responses have been entered, the column under each question number gives the breakdown of how that question was answered by all the respondents. To get the percentages, we divide each total by the number of responses.

Computing the breakdown of answers to each question is similar in the case where we store all the responses in memory. The only difference is that our program gets the individual answers from memory, not directly from the user.

So far in our thinking, it looks like the method for making the computations "on the fly" is the best, because we can do all the analyses in either case, but storing all the responses in memory at once will limit the number of responses our program can handle. However, there's one more type of analysis left to consider — cross tabulations.

A **cross tabulation** involves two questions at once. We choose an answer to a particular question — say Answer 4 to Question 6, for example. We call the particular question the **basis question** and the chosen answer the **basis answer.** Then we ask the question, "Of all the people who marked Answer 4 to Question 6, what was the nature of their responses to Question 14?" Or, more generally, "Of all the people who marked the basis answer to the basis question, what was the distribution of their answers on a selected **analysis question?**" In Section 11 2 we gave an example of finding out how females answered Question 4. In that case the basis question is number 2 ("Are you (a) male or (b) female?"), the basis answer is 2 ("female"), and the question we're analyzing is Question 4. We can compute the breakdown of answers to the analysis question the same way do the standard breakdown of answers. The only difference is how now we don't count *all* the responses, just those which answered "2" to Question 2.

At this point the "on the fly" method falls apart because there are just too many possible cross tabulations. Certainly the user won't want every possible cross tabulation computed in every questionnaire, but which ones will be wanted? Since we don't know, our programs has to be *able* to compute them all. How many possible cross tabulations are there? Let's see. If there are N questions on the questionnaire, and there can be A different answers to each question, then there are N*A different combinations of basis questions and basis answers. For each of those, we have to be able to analyze N − 1 other questions (it doesn't make sense to do a cross tabulation in which the question being analyzed is the same as the basis question, so we get N − 1 instead of N). And for each of those, we need to store a count of how often each of up to A different answers was given. In all, then, we need to be able to store N*A*(N − 1)*A different values. Unless you have a computer with a huge amount of memory, this severely limits how big N and A can be. Suppose, for example, the questionnaire has twelve different questions on it, and some of the questions have 10 different possible answers. We'd need to store 12*10*11*10 or 13,200 different values. The computer we're using doesn't have that much room in memory. Besides, we have the feeling that the program would be inordinately complicated to write, and might take too long to run.

Limits

Every computer system has limits. The two major limits are
— the amount of memory available
— the speed of operation

The questionnaire problem is the first we've covered which is likely to bump against the limits of your computer system. Until now we haven't had to worry about such things, but the limits can affect the questionnaire program in these two ways: The amount of memory your system makes available limits the number of responses the finished program will be able to store at once. If that's too small, our program won't be of much use. The speed of operation of your system is almost certainly more than adequate for the questionnaire program, but it's possible that an extremely slow system could cause trouble for a skilled typist who is entering the responses. If the system can't process the input fast enough, the user may try to type the next answer too soon, and the computer will give an error message. If that happens too often, the user will get extremely frustrated and decide to do the analysis some other way.

Before we abandon the "on the fly" method, we'd better make sure that doing cross tabulations will be easier if we use the other method. Thinking about it a bit, we see clearly that it will be. Our program will need to be able to do just one cross tabulation at a time. If the user wants another, all the responses are still sitting in memory, and our program can pass through them again, computing the new cross tabulation.

The only thing preventing us from settling on the "all responses stored in memory" method is the question of how many responses the program will be able to handle. If only a few (say ten or twenty), our program won't be of much use. Before we go to the trouble of making a detailed plan, we need some way to get a rough estimate of how many responses our finished program will handle. Let's work on that.

Let's suppose the questionnaire has no more than 12 questions on it. We can use a two-dimensional array to store the responses, with the first subscript being the respondent's number and second the question number. Let's call the array Q (Questionnaire). Then, for example, array element

Q(47, 6)

will store the answer the 47th respondent marked on Question 6. The experimental program shown on the following page can be used to get a rough estimate of how many responses our program will be able to handle at one time. Of course, the result is applicable to our particular system only, but since ours is relatively small, your system will probably be able to handle at least as many responses.

```
10    REM  EXPERIMENTAL PROGRAM--ABOUT HOW MANY RESPONSES
20    REM    WILL WE BE ABLE TO HANDLE AT ONE TIME?
30    REM  ASSUME FINISHED QUESTIONNAIRE PROGRAM ITSELF
40    REM    WILL TAKE UP ABOUT AS MUCH ROOM AS ARRAY  P()
50         DIM P(250)
60    REM  KEEP CHANGING THE NEXT  DIM  STATEMENT
70    REM    UNTIL WE GET  AN OUT OF MEMORY  ERROR.
100        DIM Q(50, 12)
110        PRINT "OK!"
9999       END

RUN
OK!
READY

100        DIM Q(75, 12)
RUN
OK!
READY

100        DIM Q(100, 12)
RUN
OUT OF MEMORY IN LINE 100
READY
100        DIM Q(90, 12)
RUN
OK!
READY
```

of course, this is just a wild guess at this point. We know the statements in our finished program will take up some space, but we don't know exactly how much before we write it...

changing line 100 to correspond to storing 75 responses (each with answers to 12 questions)

our program probably won't be able to handle 100 responses

our estimate is that we'll be able to handle 90 responses at a time

> Although 80 or 90 responses might be enough for most questionnaires you're likely to process, obviously sometimes you'll have more. If you do have more, don't fear.
>
> - You can do the analysis in bunches of 90 (see Problem 11).
> - Section 15 2 tells how to revise this program to make it handle 6 times as much response data, still in standard BASIC.
> - Section 18 2 tells how to expand it to handle as much data as you'd ever have, using an external storage medium like tape or disk.

Ninety responses seems enough, so (finally) we can adopt the "keep all responses in memory at once" scheme.

Before we plunge into the heart of the planning process, let's stop and look at what we've done, and what we haven't done. We *have* chosen the way our program will deal with the raw questionnaire responses. We *have* made sure that our chosen method will work with all the different analyses we require. We *have* made an estimate of how much data our program will be able to handle, and we *have* made sure that it will be useful. We *have not* written any part of the finished program. We *have not* made detailed plans of any part of the program. In other words, we *haven't done anything we might regret later.* The more time you spend at the beginning, making sure you know what you're doing, and checking out your ideas, the less time you'll have to spend at the terminal trying to get your program to do what you want.

Let's begin our detailed plan by thinking about what the user of our program will need to be able to do. Since our program will be used on a variety of different questionnaires (but only one at a time, of course), the user will have to be able to inform the program about the questionnaire he or she wants to process. The program needs to know how many questions are in the questionnaire, and (perhaps) the number of legal answers to each question. Let's call this phase **initialize.**

Of course, the user needs to be able to enter the answers from the responses. Let's call this phase **add.**

The user needs to be able to have the program show the data it has so far, so the data can be checked for accuracy. Let's call this the **verify** phase.

If the user discovers an error, he or she has to be able to correct it, so we'll need a **change** phase.

The user needs to be able to call for the standard breakdown of how each question was answered. Let's call that the **standard report.**

The user has to be able to request a specific **cross tabulation** computation.

And finally, the user may want to **quit** using our program.

When our program is in use, there will be a cycle of activity — the user selects one of the phases, the program carries it out, the user selects another phase, the program carries it out, etc. There are several advantages to this sort of organization beyond the fact that it does what we want the program to do. For one thing, it makes it easy to think of the overall program as a number of relatively independent subparts. The more we break a problem into meaningful subparts, the less we have to keep in mind as we work on the details, and the fewer mistakes we'll make. Another advantage is that we already know how to do the part that involves asking the user what phase of the program he or she wants — our menu subroutines (Chapter 9) do just that.

As we draw out our plan, we'll think in greater detail about what each of the phases of the program will have to do.

EXERCISES 11 3

As things stand now, the person who uses our program to analyze a questionnaire will enter a number representing the answer to each question on each response. The exercises refer to the responses shown on page 260. The questionnaire being analyzed is the brief but representative one given in Section 11 2.

—questionnaire analysis program—

PRINT greeting to user.

Ask user what phase *he or she wants*

initialize

Get N, the number of questions.

Get anything else we need to get started.

So far, have 0 responses in memory.

add

Get answers to Questions 1 through N.

Add one to the number of responses in memory.

Repeat IF *more responses*

verify

PRINT all responses (along with number of the response so user can identify each one).

change

Ask which response user wants to change.

Accept and store new answers for that response.

standard report

FOR Question=1 TO N

Go through all the responses, counting the number of occurrences of each answer to this question.

PRINT breakdown of answer to this question, including percentages.

cross tabulation

Ask user for basis question, answer to basis question, and which question to analyze.

Go through all the responses, selecting those responses in which the answer to the basis question is the right one, then count the occurrences of each answer to the question we're analyzing.

PRINT number of responses which answered the basis question with the basis answer, and breakdown of answers to the question we analyzed.

Repeat

quit

Stop.

response number	*answer to* Q1	Q2	Q3	Q4
1	1	2	3	1
2	4	1	1	6
3	2	2	2	3
4	2	2	3	3

1 (a) Is the third respondent male or female?
  (b) How old is the second respondent?
  (c) How long has the first respondent lived in her present town?

2 (a) What is the total number of responses?
  (b) What is the number of questions?
  (c) What is the number of possible answers to Question 2?
  (d) What is the number of possible answers to Question 3?

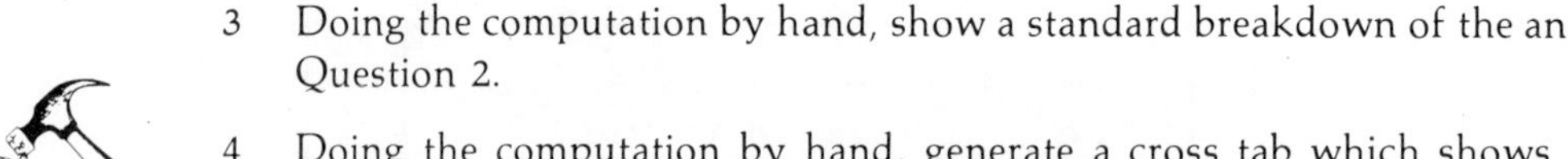

3 Doing the computation by hand, show a standard breakdown of the answers to Question 2.

4 Doing the computation by hand, generate a cross tab which shows how respondents who said they were females answered Question 1.

Section 11 4

Refining the Plan

Now that we have an overall plan, we can start thinking about the details. Let's begin by figuring out what the major variables in our program should be. Figure 11 4 1 shows our first pass at that.

Next, let's take our plan and think through what should happen at each point. Let's start by taking the user's point of view.

The user will have a questionnaire in hand, with a bunch of responses to it. The first thing the user has to do is tell our program something about the questionnaire. Let's think in terms of the four-question questionnaire we used in Section 11 2. Certainly the user will have to enter a value for N, telling how many questions there are, but what else might our program need? Looking over the four questions, we notice that there is a different number of possible answers to each. The first question has eight possible answers, the second has only two, and so on. Perhaps that would be of use. We're not sure at this point. We'll write ourselves a note, and if it turns out that some other parts of the program will need this information, we can return and add it in to the **initialize** phase.

Next, the user will select the **add** phase. The program knows that there are four questions (N=4), so it can ask for the answer to each of the four, then go on to the next response. Let's imagine what could go wrong. What if the user accidentally enters a 3 as the answer to Question 2? Certainly that will make the analysis incorrect if the answer stays that way. On the other hand, we do have both **verify** and **change** phases, so the user could be expected to catch the error later. Then again, if

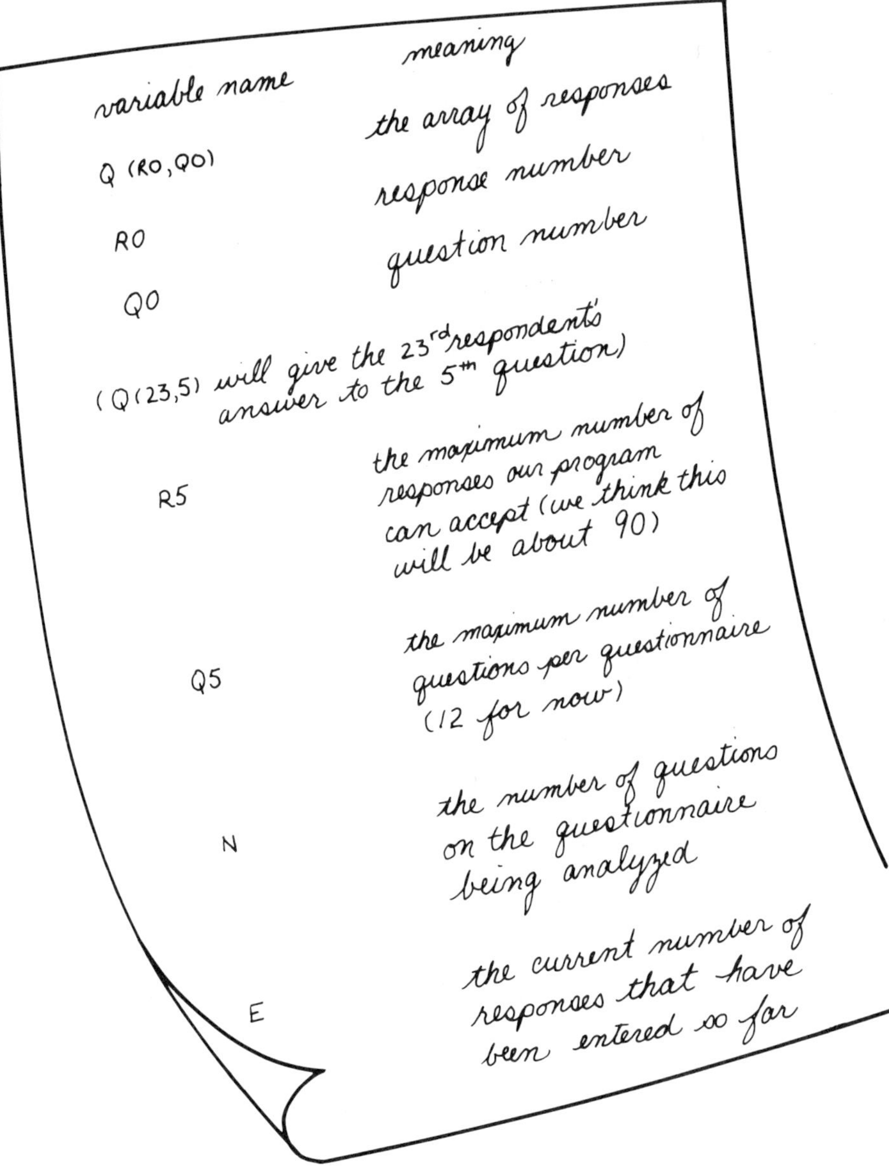

variable name
meaning
Q (RO,QO)
the array of responses
RO
response number
QO
question number
(Q(23,5) will give the 23rd respondent's answer to the 5th question)
R5
the maximum number of responses our program can accept (we think this will be about 90)
Q5
the maximum number of questions per questionnaire (12 for now)
N
the number of questions on the questionnaire being analyzed
E
the current number of responses that have been entered so far

Figure 11 4 1 Preliminary choices of variable names

the program stored the number of possible answers to each question (as we proposed above), it could immediately tell that a mistake had been made. That seems like it would be a real advantage for the user. Entering a large number of responses is going to be a laborious task, and any help our program can give will be well worthwhile. Let's have the initialize phase also ask for the number of possible answers to each question (Figure 11 4 2).

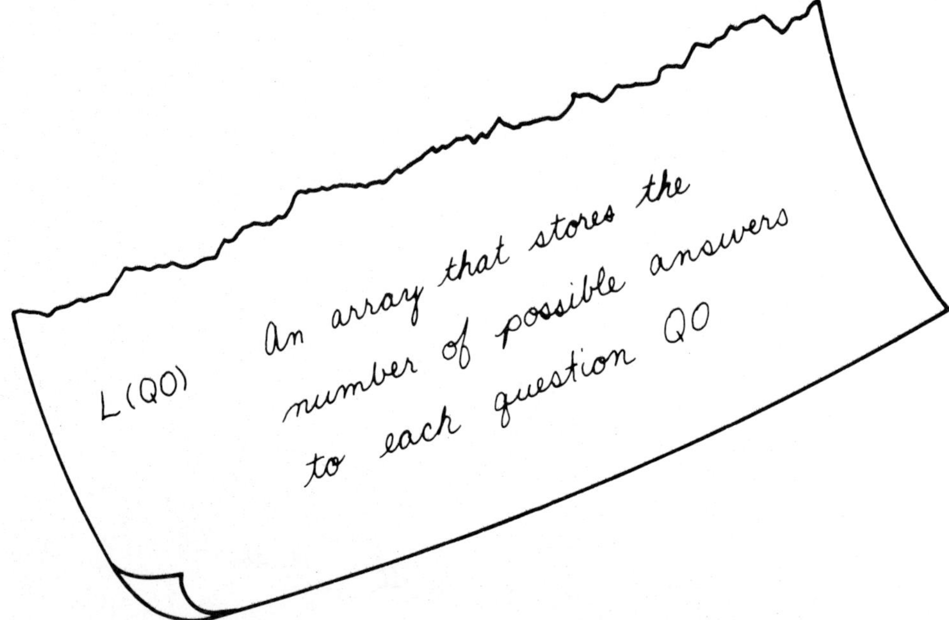
L(QO)
An array that stores the number of possible answers to each question QO

Figure 11 4 2 An addition to our list of variables

What else can happen during the **add** phase? Well, what is the user going to do if more than one answer is marked for one of the questions on a response? Or if one of the questions isn't answered at all? Why don't we reserve the answer 0 for either of those cases?

We need some quick way to decide if the user wants to enter more responses, or wants to quit the add phase. In our plan it looks like we were thinking of having the user answer YES or NO to a question like WANT TO ENTER MORE RESPONSES?—but that will require a lot of extra typing. Instead, let's have our program test the answer to Question 1, and if it's less than 0, that'll mean the user wants to quit the add phase.

The **verify** phase seems easy — we just have our program print out all the responses it's been given so far. We know there are N questions per response, and there are E responses so far, so no trouble there. We will have to have the program number each response as it prints it, so the user can refer to a specific response in the **change** operation.

In the **change** phase the program will ask the user which response should be changed, and then will ask for new answers for that response. As it gets the answers, the program will check them to make sure none of them are too big (as we plan to do in the add phase), and then will store them in the array Q(,), writing over the old answers for that response.

When the user selects the **standard report** option, the program will generate the breakdown of answers to each question in turn. Let's refine that part of our plan.

To generate the breakdown of answers to a particular question, we need to pass through all responses, counting the number of times each possible answer was given to that particular question. That suggests using an array to keep the counts, with the first position in the array storing the number of times the first answer to the question has been counted, and so on. Let's call that array H( ) — for histogram (Figure 11 4 3).

> **histogram:** a bar graph which shows the number of occurrences of each of several different values.
>
> Although our array H( ) is obviously not a bar graph, it contains exactly the same information as a bar graph. That is, it represents a histogram of all the respondents' answers to a particular question.

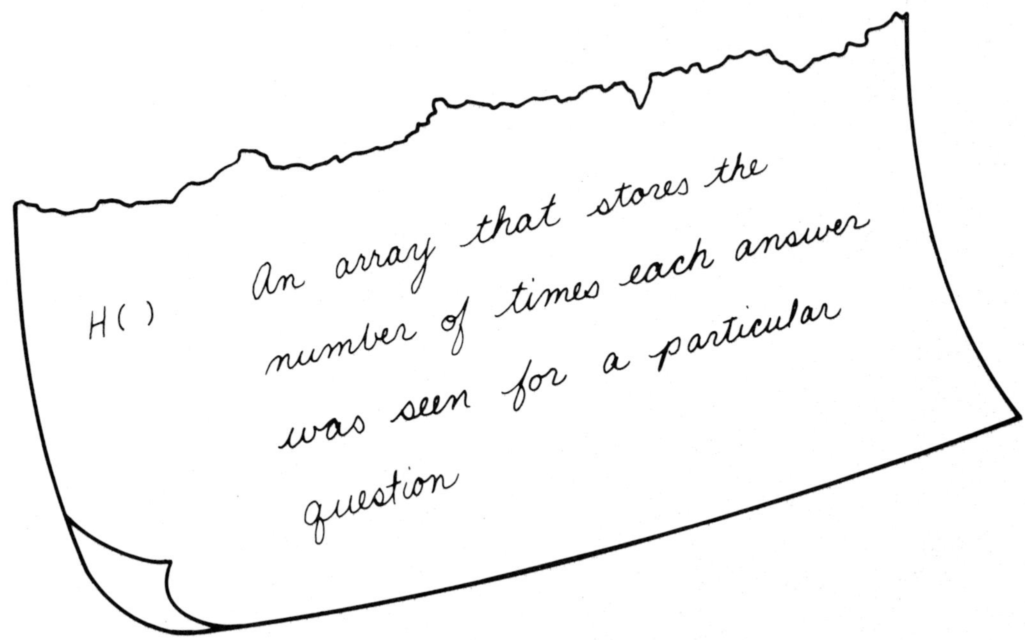

H( )
An array that stores the number of times each answer was seen for a particular question

Figure 11 4 3 Yet another variable we'll need

—standard report—

PRINT heading.

For *each question Q0=1* **to** *N*

> *Set the counting array H( ) to 0.*
>
> **For** *each response R0=1* **to** *E*
>
> > *Count the answer to Q0 in response R0 by adding 1 to H*(answer).
>
> *PRINT breakdown for question Q0.*

RETURN to menu loop.

The **cross tabulation** option is next. There the user has to tell the number of the basis question, the answer to the basis question, and the number of the question to be analyzed. Then the program has to go through all the responses, testing to see if the basis question is answered the right way. If not, the program just goes on to the next response. If so, the program has to count the answer to the question we're analyzing. This is very similar to the inner loop in the standard report option, and we'll use the array H( ) again to keep the running counts. The only real difference is that here we'll have to keep count of another thing, namely, the number of responses that satisfied the criterion on the basis question. We need that to compute the percentages in the breakdown properly.

There's almost nothing to the **quit** option. If we want, we can have our program print out some snappy phrase to the user, then skip to the END statement to stop the program.

Now that we've got a fairly good idea of what we're doing, we can start translating our ideas into BASIC.

EXERCISES 11 4

1 Assuming that you'll be analyzing responses to the questionnaire given in Section 11 2, what values should these variables be given?

(a) N

(b) L(1)

(c) L(2)

2 Assuming that you'll be analyzing responses to the questionnaire given in Section 11 2, what values should these variables be given?

(a) E

(b) L(N)

(c) L(3)

Use the data shown at the beginning of Exercises 11 3 to answer the next two exercises.

3 Look at our plan for the standard report option. When Question 2 is being analyzed (i.e., when Q0 has the value 2), what values will be in H(1) and H(2)

(a) just before the loop over each response begins?

(b) when "Print breakdown for question Q0" is reached?

4 Look at our plan for the standard report option. When Q0 has the value 3 (i.e., when we're analyzing the third question), what positions in the histogram array H( ) will be affected by "Count the answer to question Q0 by adding 1 to H*(answer)*"?

Section 11 5

The Program and Making it Work

Now we're ready to start writing some BASIC. By looking at our plan, we can make a reasonable choice of what order to do things in. We'll want to code and test in a top-down order so that at each step we will be adding another feature to already tested parts of the developing program. Look back at the plan in Section 11 3 and see if you agree that:

- all modules depend on the menu selection process
- the add module can't work before the initialize module is working
- the verify, change, standard report, and cross tab modules can't work before the add module is there to get responses.

Thus, the natural order to code the program is to begin by declaring the arrays and giving the key variables their starting values (the number of responses stored, the maximum number of responses we can handle, etc.) Then we'll proceed to code the menu selection loop and test it, write the add module and test it, then do the same with the remaining modules. Finally, we'll test the completed program. Since the quit option depends on nothing but the menu routines, we can do it anytime we feel like it.

We'll begin by writing a few REMarks that remind us of the uses of the main variables and arrays. Then we'll declare the arrays (in a DIM) and initialize some of the variables.

```
10    REM  QUESTIONNAIRE ANALYSIS PROGRAM
20    REM  VARIABLES--
30    REM    Q(R0,Q0)   ARRAY OF RESPONSES
40    REM    R0  RESPONSE NUMBER (R0=23 MEANS 23RD RESPONDENT)
50    REM    Q0  QUESTION NUMBER
60    REM    N   NUMBER OF QUESTIONS IN THE QUESTIONNAIRE
70    REM    Q5  THE MAXIMUM NUMBER OF QUESTIONS ALLOWED
80    REM    E   THE NUMBER OF RESPONSES CURRENTLY STORED
90    REM    R5  THE MAXIMUM NUMBER OF RESPONSES
100   DIM Q(90,12), L(12), H(10)
110   LET R5 = 90 <-- we're still hoping 90 responses will fit — we'll see!
120   LET Q5 = 12
130   LET E = 0 <-- no responses Entered so far
```

Next, we'll install the main loop that gets the option from the user. We'll need to use the menu subroutines for that, so we'd better dig out our notes and drawings and plans **(documentation)** for them. (Refer to Chapter 9.) From our notes, we see that we need to do several things to use the menu subroutines. First, of course, we have to copy the subroutines themselves. Second, we have to include DATA statements which give the words the menu expects from the user. Third, we have to assign values to the variables S9 and F9, telling which section of the DATA statements to use. Fourth, we have to include a subroutine call (a GOSUB) to the main menu subroutine.

We can begin by writing the DATA statements which give the words our program will accept for the 7 different options or phases our program provides the user.

```
9400 REM   MENU WORDS FOR QUESTIONNAIRE PROGRAM
9410       DATA INITIALIZE, 1,  INIT, 1,  I, 1
9420       DATA ADD, 2,  A, 2
9430       DATA VERIFY, 3,  V, 3
9440       DATA CHANGE, 4,  C, 4
```

(program continued on page 266)

```
9450        DATA STANDARD, 5,  REPORT, 5,  S, 5
9460        DATA CROSS, 6,  TAB, 6,  T, 6
9470        DATA QUIT, 7,  Q, 7
```

Next, we can copy in the menu subroutine themselves. Perhaps there is an easy way to do this on your system (see Appendix A). Or maybe you'll just have to type them all in, copying from a previous listing (Chapter 9). At any rate, at least we don't have to work out all the details — we've done that before. The menu subroutines occupy lines 9500 through 9980.

The menu words we entered ("INITIALIZE" through "Q") occur in positions 1 through 17 in the DATA statements. Knowing that, we're ready to set up the part of our questionnaire program that asks the user what phase or options he or she wants. The only time our program will use the menu subroutines is to get the user's choice of initialize, add, verify, etc. That means we can give values to S9 and F9 once and for all. If other parts of the program used the menu routines with a different menu, lines 140 through 160 would have to be within the major loop. (If that doesn't make sense, be sure to look back at our plan at the end of Section 11 3.)

```
140  REM  MENU WORDS ARE ITEMS 1 TO 17 IN DATA STATEMENTS
150       LET S9 = 1
160       LET F9 = 17
500  REM  TOP OF LOOP OVER THE FIRST SIX OPTIONS
510  REM  GET USER'S CHOICE OF WHAT TO DO
520       PRINT
530       PRINT "YOUR COMMAND";
540       GOSUB 9500
550  REM                INIT  ADD  VERIF CHNGE  REPRT TABS  QUIT
560       ON W9 GO TO 1000, 2000, 3000, 4000, 5000, 6000, 7000
```

We chose the line numbers in the ON-GO TO using this thinking: Each of the seven options is an independent subpart, and having them start with line numbers that end in a lot of zeros makes them sound important. We don't really know how long any of them are going to be yet, but surely we've left enough room by having each line number a thousand greater than the last.

After adding one more statement, namely

```
9999        END
```

we're done with everything except the seven modules that carry out the seven different options. It's time to test what we've entered so far. By adding a few lines that print information telling where in our program we are, we can make sure we copied the menu subroutines properly, and that our overall framework doesn't have any obvious errors in it. For example, we could (temporarily) add statements like these:

```
1000        PRINT "INITIALIZE OPTION"
1010        GO TO 500

2000        PRINT "ADD OPTION"
2010        GO TO 500
              .
              .
              .
```

Let's plunge ahead and start working on the modules that carry out the options. Let's start with an easy module, to build confidence. As we present the code for the modules, be sure to look back to our overall plan (Section 11 3) and to reread our elaborated plan for that module (Section 11 4).

The **quit** option is the easiest by far.

```
7000 REM  MODULE 7--QUIT
7010      PRINT
7020      PRINT "THANK YOU FOR YOUR PATRONAGE!"
7030      GO TO 9999
```

Next let's work on the **initialize** module. Our plans show that first we need to get a value for N (the number of questions). Certainly our program should check the value the user enters — if it's greater than the value of Q5, our program won't work. Then we're supposed to get the number of possible answers for each of the N questions. (Why do we need that? So we can check the answers the user types in during the add phase.) Suddenly we realize that there is going to be a lot of checking for legal values going on. We have to check N against Q5; we have to check each answer against the number of possible answers; in the cross tabulation module, we'll have to check the basis question and the question to be analyzed to make sure neither is greater than N; and no doubt there are more. Why don't we back up a minute and plan some sort of limit checker subroutine that we can use in all these places?

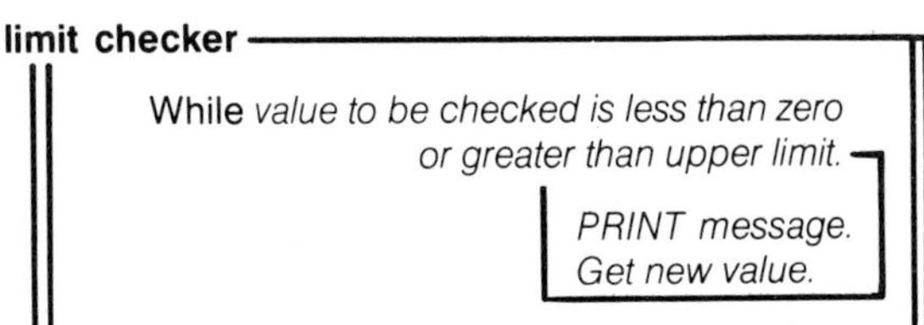

limit checker
While value to be checked is less than zero or greater than upper limit.
PRINT message.
Get new value.


```
9100 REM  LIMIT CHECKER SUBROUTINE
9110 REM    0   ASSUMED LOWER LIMIT
9120 REM    L9  UPPER LIMIT
9130 REM    V   VALUE TO BE CHECKED
9140      IF V<0 THEN 9160
9150      IF V<=L9 THEN 9210
9160 REM    ILLEGAL VALUE
9170        PRINT "BUT THE VALUE CAN'T BE MORE THAN"; L9
9180        PRINT "PLEASE TRY AGAIN.  VALUE=";
9190        INPUT V
9200        GO TO 9140
9210 REM    HAVE LEGIT VALUE  V
9220        RETURN
```

To use our new limit checker, we assign the upper limit value to the variable L9, put the value to be checked in V, and call the subroutine. On return from the subroutine, we're guaranteed that the value in V is less than or equal to the limit in L9.

At last we can write the BASIC statements for the first module.

```
1000 REM  MODULE 1--INITIALIZE
1010      PRINT
1020      PRINT "HOW MANY QUESTIONS IN YOUR QUESTIONNAIRE";
1030      INPUT V
1040 REM  CHECK LIMITS
1050      LET L9 = Q5
1060      GOSUB 9100
1070      LET N = V
1080      PRINT "NOW GIVE ME THE HIGHEST NUMBERED"
1090      PRINT "ANSWER FOR EACH QUESTION."
1100      FOR Q0=1 TO N
1110         PRINT "QUESTION"; Q0;
1120         INPUT L(Q0)
1130      NEXT Q0
1140      PRINT "THANK YOU."
1150 REM  NOW WE KNOW ALL WE NEED TO ABOUT THE QUESTIONNAIRE
1160 REM  REPEAT MENU LOOP
1170      GO TO 500
```

Next, let's work on the second module — **add.** Our plan calls for this module to keep accepting responses until the user types −1 as the answer to Question 1. As we think about it, though, there's another situation in which we want to stop accepting data. Our array Q(,) has room for no more than R5 responses, so we'd better check that there's room left before we accept the next response. After making that addition to our plan (not shown here), we can write the code for the add module.

```
2000 REM  MODULE 20--ADD NEW DATA
2010      PRINT
2030      PRINT "CURRENTLY WE HAVE"; E; "RESPONSES."
2040      PRINT "TO STOP ENTERING DATA, TYPE -1 AS THE RESPONSE"
2050      PRINT "TO QUESTION 1."
2060 REM  WHILE ANSWER ISN'T NEGATIVE, KEEP STORING RESPONSES.
2070      PRINT "QUESTION 1 ";
2080      INPUT V
2090      IF V<0 THEN 2500
2100 REM    CHECK VALIDITY OF RESPONSE
2110        LET L9 = L(1)
2120        GOSUB 9100
2130 REM    MAKE SURE THERE'S ROOM
2140        LET E = E + 1
2150        IF E<=R5 THEN 2180
2160          PRINT "SORRY--NO ROOM FOR ANY MORE RESPONSES."
2170          GO TO 2500
2180        LET Q(E,1) = V
```

we deal with the first answer separately since it's also used to signal "no more data" (handwritten note pointing to line 2070)

```
2190 REM     GET REST OF THIS RESPONSE
2200         FOR Q0 = 2 TO N
2210             PRINT "QUESTION"; Q0;
2220             INPUT V
2230             LET L9 = L(Q0)
2240             GOSUB 9100
2250 REM         HAVE A VALID RESPONSE, FILL IT IN
2260             LET Q(E,Q0) = V
2270         NEXT Q0
2280 REM     MOVE ON TO THE NEXT RESPONSE
2290         PRINT
2300         PRINT "NEXT RESPONSE"
2310         GO TO 2060
2500 REM   USER WANTS TO (OR HAS TO) QUIT
2510       PRINT
2520       PRINT "WE NOW HAVE"; E; "RESPONSES STORED."
2530 REM   RETURN TO MENU LOOP
2540       GO TO 500
```

getting answers to questions 2 through N

How will we test the add module? Well, what's it supposed to do? It is supposed to get and store responses until the user types −1 as the answer to Question 1. So if, for example, we enter two responses, we should find that E, the variable we use to store the number of responses that have been entered, has the value 2, and that the first two "rows" of the array Q(,), which stores responses, are filled with the values we entered. Line 2520 will show us the value of E, so we can check that by running the add option. The verify option will let us check that the answers are getting stored correctly, so let's do that next. Then we can test the add and verify options in conjunction.

There's nothing tricky about module 3 **(verify)**, except perhaps for spacing the output so it's legible. One sure way to get into trouble when you're printing out columns of values is to think you can figure out the PRINT statements in your head as you're typing. Figure 11 5 1 shows what we came up with.

```
3000 REM   MODULE 3--DISPLAY DATA FOR VERIFICATION
3010       PRINT
3020       PRINT "HERE'S THE DATA SO FAR."
3030       PRINT "RESP"; TAB(6);
3040       FOR Q0=1 TO N
3050           PRINT "Q"; Q0; TAB(4*Q0 + 6);
3060       NEXT Q0
3070       PRINT
3080       FOR R=1 TO E
3090           PRINT R; TAB(7);
3100           FOR Q0=1 TO N
3110               PRINT Q(R,Q0); TAB(4*Q0 + 7);
3120           NEXT Q0
3130           PRINT
3140       NEXT R
3150       PRINT
3160 REM   GO BACK TO MENU LOOP
3170       GO TO 500
```

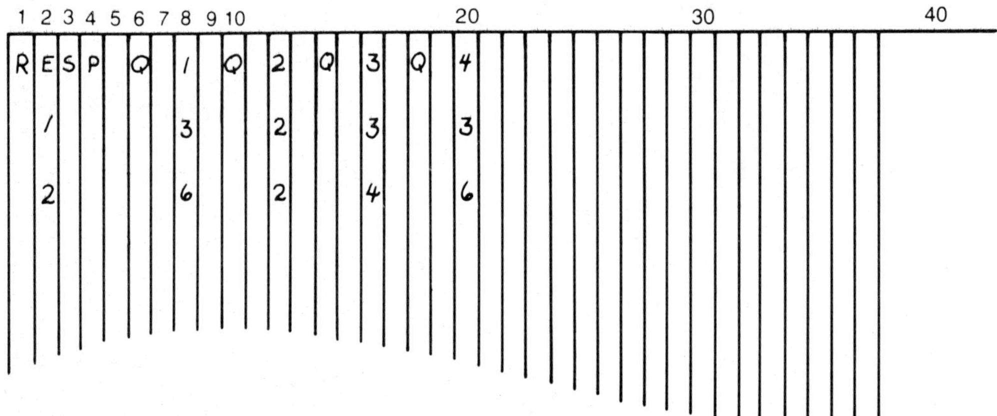

Figure 11 5 1 Figuring out the spacing for the verify option

Considerations: We want to use the TAB operator to line up the columns. Otherwise an answer greater than 9 would throw off the spacing on the rest of that line. The column for Question 1 starts in position 8; that for Question 2 starts in position 12 = 8 + 4*1; that for Question 3 starts in position 16 = 8 + 4*2; and so on. So, if after printing the answer to Question Q0, we TAB to position 4*Q0 + 8, we'll have close to what we want. The added complication is this: in minimal BASIC, positive numbers are preceded by a blank when they're printed. Taking that into account, we want to move to position 4*Q0 + 8 − 1 after printing the Q0th answer. See line 3110 in the program.

Now we can test the add and verify options.

```
RUN

YOUR COMMAND? INITIALIZE

HOW MANY QUESTIONS IN YOUR QUESTIONNAIRE? 4
NOW GIVE ME THE HIGHEST NUMBERED
ANSWER FOR EACH QUESTION.
QUESTION 1 ? 8
QUESTION 2 ? 2
QUESTION 3 ? 4
QUESTION 4 ? 6
THANK YOU.

YOUR COMMAND? ADD

READY FOR RESPONSE DATA.
CURRENTLY WE HAVE 0 RESPONSES.
TO STOP ENTERING DATA, TYPE -1 AS THE RESPONSE
TO QUESTION 1.
QUESTION 1 ? 3
QUESTION 2 ? 2
QUESTION 3 ? 3
QUESTION 4 ? 3
```

```
NEXT RESPONSE
QUESTION 1 ? 6
QUESTION 2 ? 3
BUT THE VALUE CAN'T BE MORE THAN 2
PLEASE TRY AGAIN. VALUE=? 2
QUESTION 3 ? 4
QUESTION 4 ? 5

NEXT RESPONSE
QUESTION 1 ? -1

WE NOW HAVE 2 REPONSES STORED.

YOUR COMMAND? V

HERE'S THE DATA SO FAR.
RESP Q 1 Q 2 Q 3 Q 4
 1     3   2   3   3
 2     6   2   4   5

YOUR COMMAND? QUIT

THANK YOU FOR YOUR PATRONAGE!
READY
```

here we see our limit checker subroutine working properly. there are only 2 possible answers to the second question (male/female)

E is getting the right value

Verify

just as we entered them, so everything looks OK.

the Quit option seems to work OK.

The **change** option, module 4, follows easily from our plan.

```
4000 REM  MODULE 4--ALLOW USER TO CHANGE AN ERROR
4010      PRINT "CHANGE WHICH RESPONSE";
4020      INPUT V
4030      LET L9 = E
4040      GOSUB 9100
4050      LET E1 = V
4060      PRINT "PLEASE GIVE THE CORRECT ANSWERS."
4070      FOR Q0=1 TO N
4080          PRINT "QUESTION"; Q0;
4090          INPUT V
4100          LET L9 = L(Q0)
4110          GOSUB 9100
4120          LET Q(E1,Q0) = V
4130      NEXT Q0
4140 REM  GO BACK TO MENU LOOP
4150      GO TO 500
```

using the limit checker subroutine

To test the change option, we enter the same data as before, and try changing a few answers.

```
YOUR COMMAND? CHANGE
CHANGE WHICH RESPONSE? 2
PLEASE GIVE THE CORRECT ANSWERS.
QUESTION 1 ? 6
QUESTION 2 ? 2
QUESTION 3 ? 3
QUESTION 4 ? 6
```

(program continued on page 272)

```
YOUR COMMAND? V

HERE'S THE DATA SO FAR.
RESP Q 1 Q 2 Q 3 Q 4
 1     3   2   3   3
 2     6   2   3   6
```

now the changed answers are stored for response 2

Now that we've entered and tested all the parts they depend upon, we can concentrate on the hard modules — standard report and cross tabs.

The logic for the **standard report** module is worked out (see the plans in Section 11 4). Looking back over our plan, we notice something. We want to add one to

H(*answer*)

to count the number of occurrences of *answer.* But what values can *answer* have? The possible answers to Question Q0 are 1, 2, . . ., L(Q0). But if the respondent gave no answer at all, or if the respondent marked more than one of the possible answers, we decided to have the user enter a zero. What worries us is the 0. Up to now, we'd been thinking that the first position in our arrays would be position 1. (More precisely, we hadn't been thinking about it at all, or we wouldn't have gotten into trouble here. Everything we've coded so far assumes that the arrays start at position 1. We count the number of responses from 1 up through E; the questions are numbered 1 through N.) In Minimal BASIC, arrays start with position 0 unless a statement like

```
5       OPTION BASE 1
```

appears. But if we let one array start with position 0, *all* the arrays start at 0. If we do that, our program will waste space in Q(,), unless we rewrite the modules we've already done. An unpleasant pair of alternatives. We don't want to waste any space because that will mean fewer responses can be stored. We don't want to rewrite the modules we've already done because they make sense the way they are (and it would be extra work for us). Instead, let's keep 1 as the first position in our arrays, and offset the value *answer* when we use H( ). That is,

use H(1) to store the number of 0 answers
use H(2) to store the number of 1 answers
use H(3) to store the number of 2's

.
.
.

use H(*answer* + 1) to store the number of occurrences of *answer.*

> To see how much space we'd waste by starting arrays at position 0 but storing values only at positions 1 and above in Q(,), do Exercise 6.

With that consideration, we're ready to do all aspects of the standard report option except the spacing of the output. Figure 11 5 2 shows the spacing chart we made.

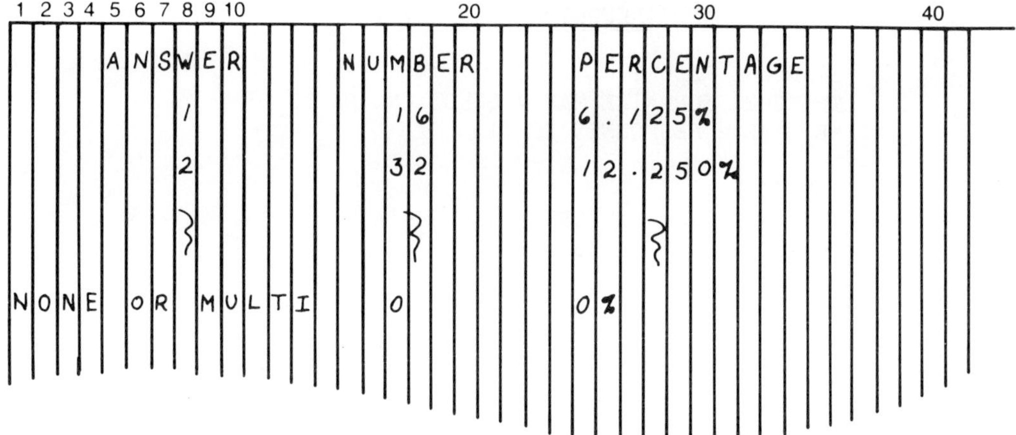

Figure 11 5 2 Planning the format for printing the standard report. We translate this into BASIC using TAB( )'s to get to the proper column for each value.

```
5000 REM  MODULE 5--GENERATE STANDARD REPORT
5010      PRINT
5020      PRINT "STANDARD REPORT"
5030      PRINT "THE QUESTIONNAIRE HAS"; N; "QUESTIONS ON IT."
5040      PRINT "WE HAVE"; E; "RESPONSES TO IT."
5060 REM  FOR EACH QUESTION, COMPUTE NUMBER OF TIMES
5070 REM    EACH POSSIBLE ANSWER WAS CHOSEN.
5080 REM  THEN PRINT TOTALS AND AVERAGES.
5100      FOR Q0=1 TO N
5110 REM      H() IS USED TO TOTAL ANSWERS.
5120          FOR I=0 TO L(Q0)
5130              LET H(I+1) = 0
5140          NEXT I
5150          FOR R0=1 TO E
5160              LET H(Q(R0, Q0) + 1) = H(Q(R0, Q0) + 1) + 1
5170          NEXT R0
5200          PRINT
5205          PRINT "QUESTION"; Q0
5210          PRINT TAB(5); "ANSWER"; TAB(15); "NUMBER";
5220          PRINT TAB(25); "PERCENTAGE"
5230          FOR I=1 TO L(Q0)
5240              PRINT TAB(8); I; TAB(17); H(I+1);
5250              PRINT TAB(25); H(I+1)/E*100; "%"
5260          NEXT I
5270          PRINT "NONE OR MULTI"; TAB(17); H(0+1);
5280          PRINT TAB(25); H(0+1)/E*100; "%"
5290      NEXT Q0
5300      PRINT
5310      PRINT "END OF STANDARD REPORT"
5320 REM  GO BACK TO MENU
5330      GO TO 500
```

Now we can test the standard report option, using the same data we used to test the other parts of the program.

```
YOUR COMMAND? REPORT

STANDARD REPORT
THE QUESTIONNAIRE HAS 4 QUESTIONS ON IT.
WE HAVE 2 RESPONSES TO IT.

QUESTION 1
     ANSWER     NUMBER     PERCENTAGE
         1         0         0 %
         2         0         0 %
         3         1         50 %
         4         0         0 %
         5         0         0 %
         6         1         50 %
         7         0         0 %
         8         0         0 %
NONE OR MULTI      0         0 %

QUESTION 2
     ANSWER     NUMBER     PERCENTAGE
         1         0         0 %
         2         2         100 %
NONE OR MULTI      0         0 %

QUESTION 3
     ANSWER     NUMBER     PERCENTAGE
         1         0         0 %
         2         0         0 %
         3         2         100 %
         4         0         0 %
NONE OR MULTI      0         0 %

QUESTION 4
     ANSWER     NUMBER     PERCENTAGE
         1         0         0 %
         2         0         0 %
         3         1         50 %
         4         0         0 %
         5         0         0 %
         6         1         50 %
NONE OR MULTI      0         0 %

END OF STANDARD REPORT
```

The final planning, coding, and testing of the cross tabulation option follows the same pattern.

```
6000 REM  MODULE 8--CROSS TABULATION COMPUTATION
6010      PRINT
6020      PRINT "PLEASE SEE INSTRUCTIONS BEFORE USING."
6030      PRINT "BASIS QUESTION:";
6040      INPUT V
6050      LET L9 = N
6060      GOSUB 9100
```

```
6070        LET B = V
6080        PRINT "ANSWER TO BASIS QUESTION:";
6090        INPUT V
6100        LET L9 = L(B)
6110        GOSUB 9100
6120        LET A = V
6130        PRINT "QUESTION TO BE ANALYZED:";
6140        INPUT V
6150        LET L9 = N
6160        GOSUB 9100
6170        LET Q = V
6200 REM    CO   COUNTS NUMBER WHO ANSWERED  A  TO QUESTION  B
6210 REM    H()  ACCUMULATES PATTERN OF ANSWERS TO  Q
6220        LET CO = 0
6230        FOR I=0 TO L(Q)
6240            LET H(I+1) = 0
6250        NEXT I
6260 REM    GO THROUGH ALL RESPONSES, SKIP THOSE WHICH DON'T
6270 REM      ANSWER  A  TO QUESTION  B
6280        FOR RO=1 TO E
6290            IF Q(RO, B)<>A THEN 6330
6300 REM          GOT ONE, SO COUNT IT.
6310              LET H(Q(RO, Q) + 1) = H(Q(RO, Q) + 1) + 1
6320              LET CO = CO + 1
6330        NEXT RO
6340        PRINT CO; "PEOPLE RESPONDED"; A; "TO QUESTION"; B
6350        PRINT
6360        PRINT "THEIR ANSWERS TO QUESTION"; Q; "WERE"
6370        PRINT TAB(5); "ANSWER"; TAB(15); "NUMBER";
6380        PRINT TAB(25); "PERCENTAGE"
6390        FOR I=1 TO L(Q)
6400            PRINT TAB(8); I; TAB(17); H(I+1);
6410            PRINT TAB(25); H(I+1)/CO*100; "%"
6420        NEXT I
6430        PRINT "NONE OR MULTI"; TAB(17); H(0+1);
6440        PRINT TAB(25); H(0+1)/CO*100; "%"
6450        GO TO 500
```

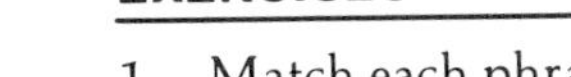

EXERCISES 11 5

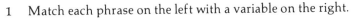

1 Match each phrase on the left with a variable on the right.

A	the maximum number of questions per questionnaire	a	V
B	the maximum number of responses that can be stored	b	Q5
C	the (actual) number of questions in the questionnaire being analyzed	c	RO
D	the number of responses currently stored	d	R5
		e	E
		f	N
		g	L9
		h	QO

2 Write the names of each module (**add, verify**, etc.) which changes the value of each of the variables described below.

(a) the maximum number of questions per questionnaire

(b) the maximum number of responses that can be stored

(c) the (actual) number of questions in the questionnaire being analyzed

(d) the number of responses currently stored

(e) any element in the array of responses Q(,)

3 Which line(s) in the final version of the Standard Report module carry out the part of the plan (Section 11 4) which says, "Count the answer to Question Q0 by adding 1 to H(*answer*)"?

4 Write PRINT statements which will give the spacing shown below. The first statement should print the headings. The line which prints the data values contains the variables Y (which gives the Year), P (rainfall in the sPring), U (rainfall in the sUmmer), A (rainfall in Autumn), and W (rainfall in Winter). It will be repeated as often as needed.

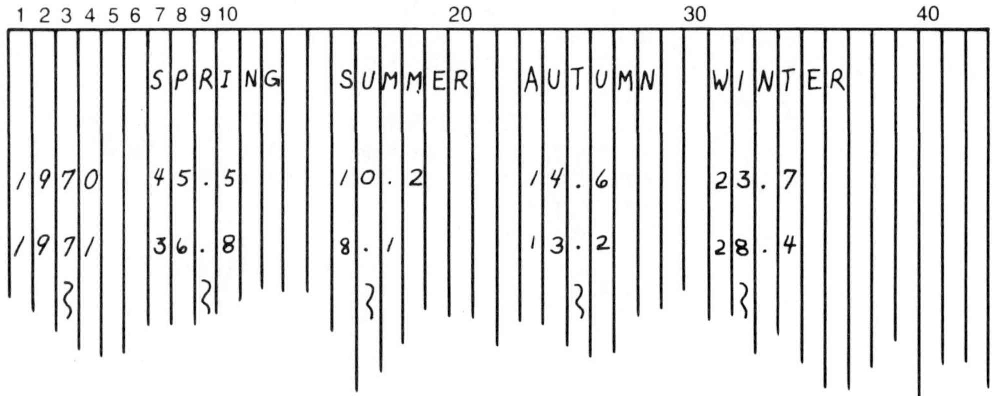

5 Sketch the line spacing chart which corresponds to these PRINT statements.

```
2330    PRINT TAB(28); "LOAN PAYMENT SCHEDULE"
2340    PRINT
2350    PRINT TAB(56); "NEW"
2360    PRINT TAB(2); "DATE"; TAB(13); "PAYMENT";
2370    PRINT TAB(25); "PRINCIPAL"; TAB(39); "INTEREST";
2380    PRINT TAB(54); "BALANCE"
```

6 The questionnaire program uses the two-dimensional array Q(,) to store responses. Q(R0, Q0) is used for values of R0 from 1 through E, and for values of

Q0 from 1 through N. If the array subscripts start at 0 instead of 1, space is taken by some array variables the program never uses. How many such variables will there be?

7 We were taken by surprise when we were writing the code for the standard report module. We had been thinking that all arrays would start with position 1, and then discovered that our plan called for using H(0) to count the number of times respondents gave either no answer or multiple answers. If we had been more scrupulous in following the **steps in program design** we outlined in Section 11 1, we wouldn't have been caught napping. In which of these ways did our use of the design principles break down?

(a) We didn't completely **define the problem.** In Section 11 2 we mentioned that we'd have to do something about the "no answer or multiple answer" case, but we didn't make any decision. We just let it slide.

(b) We didn't adequately **refine the plan.** In Section 11 4 we decided to let a 0 value represent a "no answer" or multiple answer, but we didn't detail how that case would be treated by each of the modules.

(c) We weren't taking enough care to **ensure that the program would work properly.** In Section 11 5 we started testing our partially completed program. But our test data contained no 0 answers!

Section 11 6
Finishing Touches

We have a few more tasks to complete before we're done with our questionnaire analyzer program. We should play with it a while, looking for ways to make it easier to use. We should write up a description of how it works, and of any tricks or complicated things we did, and add this to our notes and plans. And we should write a set of instructions telling how to use our program. The description of how we wrote the program is called **documentation,** and will be of use to us (or some other programmer) in the future, when some change or repair to the program is needed. The material telling the user how to use the program (called the **instructions,** or perhaps **user documentation**) should be made available to anyone who plans to make use of our effort. In a commercial setting, the documentation would be kept "in house," available to programmers. The instructions might be printed up in three-color-cover glossy booklets, and sold along with the program.

The instructions will start with a paragraph or two which will tell what the program can do, in very general terms. Then there should be a more detailed description telling what characteristics the program assumes any questionnaire has (for example, we assume each question can have only one answer), and what sequence of events the user will go through to analyze a specific questionnaire.

There should be a section which covers all aspects of each of the seven options the program gives the user — initialize, add, verify, change, standard report, cross tabulation, and quit. The box on page 279 shows what we might write for the add option.

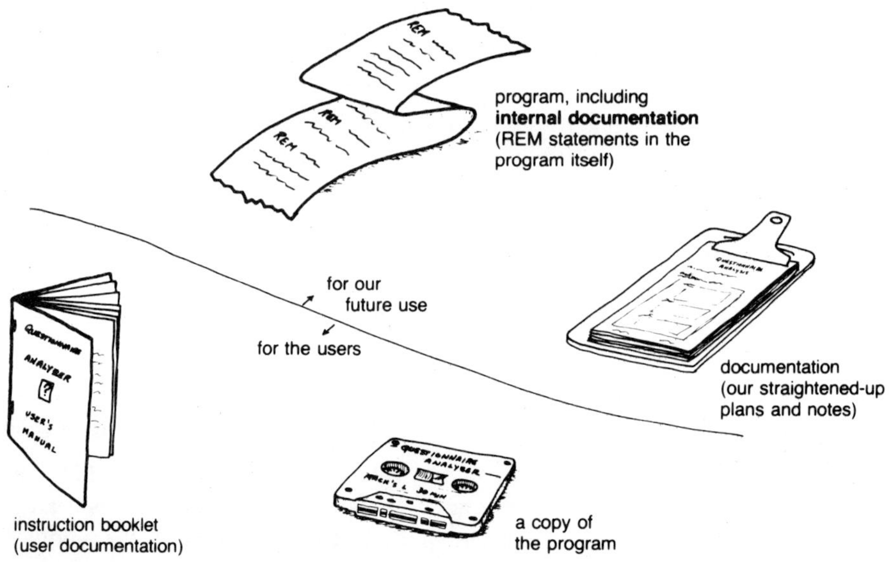

The other six options must be written up in the same format, with the headings *equivalent names, purpose, what you'll see, what you do, what the computer will do, notation to use,* and *what to do if you make a mistake.* These instructions, along with a general description at the beginning of the user documentation, will make it possible for a person totally unfamiliar with the program to use it effectively.

Section 11 7
Postscript

In this chapter we've gone through the entire history of the development of a useful program. While the questionnaire program is our most involved so far, it's not terribly complicated compared to most programs frequently used by the general public. Certainly, though, it is long by the standards of textbook programs. And you've had to expend a good deal of effort following through it.

Not only does the questionnaire program illustrate the history of developing a real-life program; in a sense, it also illustrates the history of computing. We've produced a solution to a problem that has been a driving force in the development of computers. Using Minimal BASIC, we've come up with a program whose capabilities would have been unthinkably advanced in the days of Herman Hollerith. Although Hollerith's tabulating machine (Figure 11 2 1) helped speed the process of analyzing questionnaires, it still required a lot of physical work. To perform a cross tab, huge stacks of punched cards were run through a card sorter machine, then each card from each category (each card which had the basis answer to the basis question) was placed in the tabulating machine by hand. A machine which had the characteristics of our questionnaire program would have seemed like a gift from the gods in those days!

ADD option

equivalent names; ADD, A

purpose: To enter answers from one or more responses.

what you'll see: When you type A or ADD, the program will respond with this message:

READY FOR RESPONSE DATA
CURRENTLY WE HAVE *xx* RESPONSES
TO STOP ENTERING DATA, TYPE −1 AS THE RESPONSE
TO QUESTION 1.

what you do: Type the answer to each question. After all the answers from a response have been entered, the computer automatically goes on to the next response. You may then type the answers to that response. Keep entering responses until you want to quit. At that time answer Question 1 with any negative number.

what the computer will do with the answers: The answers making up a response will be stored under an automatically assigned response number.

If you enter the Add phase more than once, the new responses will be entered at the end of those entered previously — none will be wiped out.

notation to use: If the respondent has chosen no answer, or has marked more than one answer to a particular question, type a zero (this will be treated appropriately by the Standard Report and Cross Tabulation options). Otherwise type the number which identifies the chosen answer.

what to do if you make a mistake: If you have not yet hit the "return" button, you may correct any typing error in the normal manner. Otherwise finish the response, then type a −1 for Question 1 of the next response. This will get you out of the Add phase (temporarily). The computer will print the message

WE NOW HAVE *xx* RESPONSES.

Immediately enter the Change phase, and re-enter all the answers for response number *xx*. Then go back into the Add phase and continue entering responses.

Alternatively, you can make a note of your mistake and fix it later using the Change option.

Here are some things we've seen in this chapter:

1 Programs intended for use by the general public tend to be long and involved, even if the basic computation is fairly straightforward. The complexity is caused by the need for extreme measures to protect users from making mistakes, and by the need to provide ways to correct errors that users make in spite of these extreme measures.

2 Many practical programs consist mainly of data acquisition, correction, and display where the amount of data involved far outweighs the size of the program. Much of the programmer's concern is with coping with the mass of data rather than with sophisticated mathematical analysis. (Hence the term "data processing.")

3 Designing the output format is usually easier than making sure the input the user supplies is valid.

4 If your program is successful, the people who use it will come to you asking for changes, and you'll need to be able to figure out what the program does to alter it. Therefore, always keep your original plans and notes filed with a copy of the program. (One of the best places to keep your notes is right in the program itself — as REMarks.)

5 If people can't easily figure out how to use your program, they'll find some other way to handle their problem. Therefore, write the user documentation as carefully and completely as you write the program.

6 Big programs are constructed piece by piece, using the same programming techniques that you've learned for small programs. The only difference is that there are more pieces in a big program.

PROBLEMS 11

1 The most common statistical analysis consists of computing the **range, mean,** and **standard deviation** of a collection of data values. The **mean** is the average value. The **range** and the **standard deviation** are both measures of the spread of the values. Two sets of numbers might have the same average value and still be quite different, so knowing something about how spread out the values are gives you more information about what to expect when you look at individual values.

Write a program which accepts a series of numbers from the user, and which prints the largest value, the smallest value, the range, the mean, and the standard deviation of all the numbers.

range = (largest value − smallest value)

n = the number of data values

mean = sum of values/n

$$\text{standard deviation} = \sqrt{\frac{\text{sum of (values)}^2 - \frac{\text{(sum of values)}^2}{n}}{n-1}}$$

Note: The "sum of (values)²" is computed by squaring each value and summing. The "(sum of values)²" is computed by summing the values and then squaring the total. Plan your program carefully — no arrays are needed.

Test your program on at least these three sets of data. Try to get a feeling for what the range and standard deviation tell you about the data values.

data set 1	*data set 2*	*data set 3*
1	0	20
2	0	1
3	0	1
4	0	1
5	55	1
6	0	1
7	0	1
8	0	1
9	0	1
10	0	27

2 Use the questionnaire program to analyze the results of a questionnaire you've made up.

Write a report describing your experiences with the program. Keep track of the time you spend using the program, and compare it to doing the analysis by hand. What do you think is the best feature of the program? The worst? In what ways would you make the program easier to use?

3 As tax time draws near, depreciation figures are needed. The idea behind depreciating an asset is to show its value as long as the item is used. The **declining balance method** is one way to calculate depreciation. An item bought the first half of the month in January would be depreciated the entire year; an item bought the last half of January would have only 11 months' depreciation. Use the 1st through the 15th and the 16th through the last day of the month for determining depreciation for that month. The rate is found by taking the useful life (e.g., 5 years), dividing it into 1 and getting a decimal answer (e.g., 1/5 = 0.20), and then doubling the rate (e.g., 0.20 × 2 = 0.40). If the item is used instead of new, use 1½ times the rate (e.g., 0.20 × 1½ = 0.30).

Input Data Items:

accounting code	a 6-digit code
date acquired	yr mo day
useful life	# years
cost	original cost
type	new/used

the balance declines by 40% each year

Output Sketch:

YEAR	COST	ACCUMULATED DEPRECIATION AT BEGINNING OF YEAR	BOOK VALUE AT BEGINNING OF YEAR	RATE	DEPRE-CIATION FOR YEAR	BOOK VALUE AT END OF YEAR
1975	$10,000	----	$10,000.00	40%	$4,000.00	$6,000.00
1976		$4,000	6,000.00		2,400.00	3,600.00
1977		6,400	3,600.00		1,400.00	2,160.00
1978		7,840	2,160.00		864.00	1,296.00
1979		8,704	1,296.00		518.40	777.60

Complete the output design, make a plan, and write and test the program to calculate depreciation by the declining balance method.

4 Write a program which people can use to visualize the effects of inflation. Your program should accept values for the base (starting) year, the number of years, and the rate of inflation (as a percentage). If R stores the inflation rate in percent, a product which cost *x* dollars this year will cost *x**(1 + R/100) dollars next year. If the purchasing power of a dollar is *y* this year, the purchasing power next year will be *y*/(1 + R/100). Apply the formulas once per year to track the effects of inflation over a long period.

Use this spacing chart to design your output.

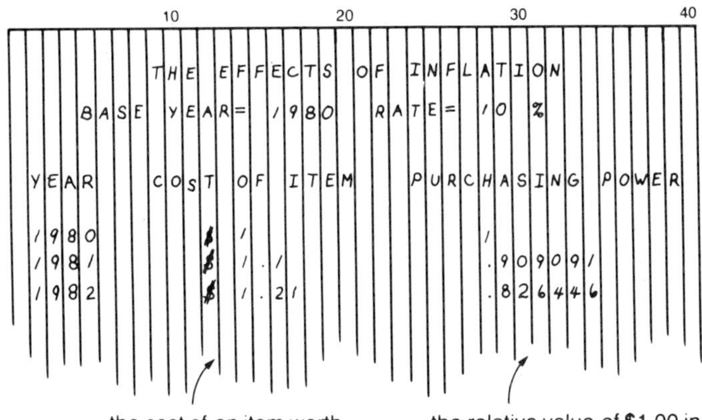

5 The rate of inflation is rarely the same from year to year. Revise the program from problem 4 to take this into account. First, your program should accept up to 20 rates of inflation, one for each successive year, starting with the base year. Then, it should print the results in a form similar to that above, but with an additional column which shows the rate of inflation for each year.

6 Create a program which a weather bureau could use to generate printed reports of a month's high and low daily temperatures. Your program should offer the user the following five options:

phase	*action*
Accept	The program asks for the month and year. Then for each day of the month, it asks for and stores six values: today's high, today's low, record high, year record high was recorded, record low, year record low was recorded.
Verify	The program asks for the day, and then shows the six values it has stored for that day.
Change	The program asks for the day, and then allows the user to enter new values for the six items stored for that day.
Report	The program generates a report like this:

```
                    ----------NOVEMBER 1982----------

      11   1 82          HIGH          52
                         LOW           23

      11   2 82          HIGH          71 *
                         LOW           38

   *(BEATS RECORD OF 70 SET IN 1926)

      11   3 82          HIGH          73 *
                         LOW          -10**

    *(BEATS RECORD OF 68 SET IN 1932)
   **(BEATS RECORD OF -8 SET IN 1908)

      11   4 82          HIGH          59
                         LOW           28

            .             .             .
            .             .             .
            .             .             .
```

Quit	The program stops.

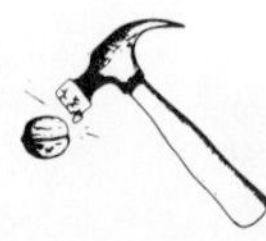

7 Turn the questionnaire program into a package that would be of use to a computer dating service. Make no changes to the questionnaire program except those required by item c below.

To use the questionnaire program for computer dating, do these things:

(a) Devise a questionnaire which, besides asking the person's sex, asks about his or her likes and dislikes. A sample question might be this:

Going to the movies
1 I hate to go to the movies, and never go.
2 I rarely go to the movies.
3 On occasion, I go to the movies.
4 I like to go to the movies.
5 I adore movies, and go all the time.

(b) Keep written records showing each respondent's name and address along with the number of his or her stored response.

(c) Add a module called **match** to the questionnaire program which first asks which respondent to match (that is, asks for the number of the respondent you want to find dates for). The program then goes through all the stored responses to find the three most compatible respondents of the opposite sex.

If respondents *x*'s answers to the questionnaire are $a_1, a_2, \ldots, a_n$ and respondent *y*'s answers are $b_1, b_2, \ldots, b_n$ the **compatibility** between *x* and *y* is given by

$$C_{xy} = \frac{a_1 * b_1 + a_2 * b_2 + \ldots + a_n * b_n}{\sqrt{a_1^2 + a_2^2 + \ldots + a_n^2} * \sqrt{b_1^2 + b_2^2 + \ldots + b_n^2}}$$

(d) Write documentation which describes the module you added.

(e) Write user documentation which tells the people in the computer dating service exactly how to use your program.

8 The computer dating version of the questionnaire program described in Problem 7 has a problem. If one person is particularly compatible, he or she will receive matches with three others, but may be listed as a good date for *many* respondents. The whole thing could get out of balance with almost everybody trying to date a few compatible people. Here's one way to prevent that.

Store a "pseudo answer" along with each response. When a response is entered, have the add module automatically enter 0 for the pseudo answer. Each time the match module pairs two respondents, add one to their pseudo answers. Have the match module skip respondents who already have participated in three matches, that is, who already have their full allotment of three dates.

Using some test data, evaluate the effects of this "fix." Does it cause some other kind of problem?

9 Turn the questionnaire program into a package that can be used to grade multiple-choice tests. In analogy to the array L( ), which stores the largest possible answer to each question, add an array C( ), which stores the correct answer to each question. Add a module (option) called **grade** to the program. The grade module should compute the number (and percentage) of correct answers made by each successive respondent.

10 Revise the questionnaire program so the user enters answers by giving a letter instead of a number. This change will affect input and output operations, but nothing else. Use the menu routines to translate letters the user enters into numbers for internal use. Write a subroutine for use in output which takes an answer number and looks up the corresponding letter in the DATA statements used for the input translation.

11 As it stands, the questionnaire program can process no more responses that will fit in memory at once. However, it can be used to analyze a much larger set of responses by doing the job in chunks. Figure 11 P 1 and 11 P 2 show how it can be done. Plan, write, and test the finalizer program suggested by the figure.

12 You are the conscientious owner of a pizza restaurant. You want to serve only the freshest toppings on your pizza. You're willing to go to the produce store every day, but you don't want to waste money buying vegetables that won't be used before they spoil. You've noticed that for some reason, early in the week, mushrooms and tomatoes are left over, while at the end of the week, green peppers and avocados are left over. You decide to study the pattern so you can buy produce more efficiently. You want to bring your microcomputer into the store to collect statistics that'll help you buy the right amount of each spoilable item each day. Of course, the key to success lies in the writing of the program.

Design a program which assembles statistics showing the pattern of pizzas ordered each day of the week. Design your program so it can be used without change for arbitrarily many weeks (use the "on the fly" method which we considered but rejected in Section 11 3). *(Problem continued on page 286)*

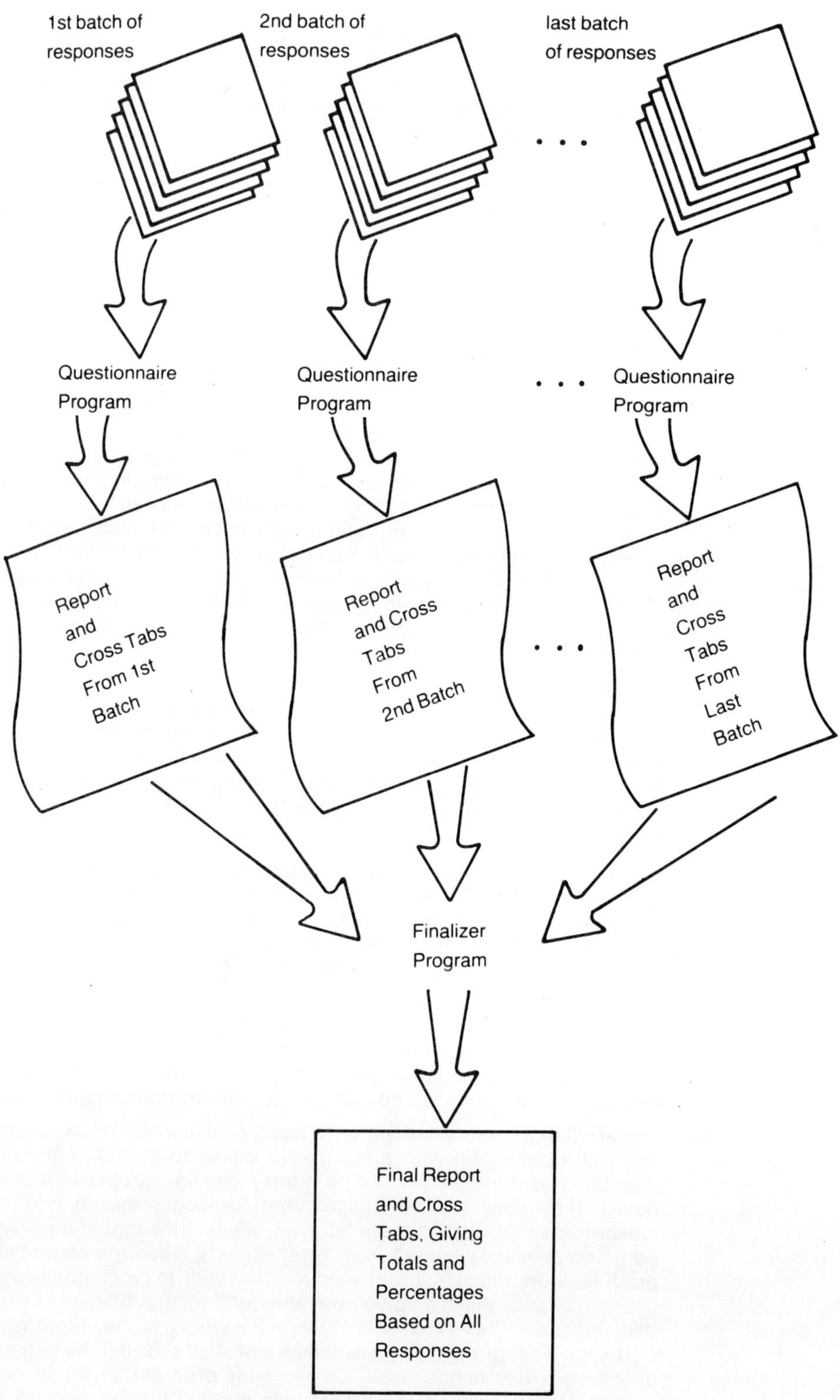

Figure 11 P 1 The grand scheme

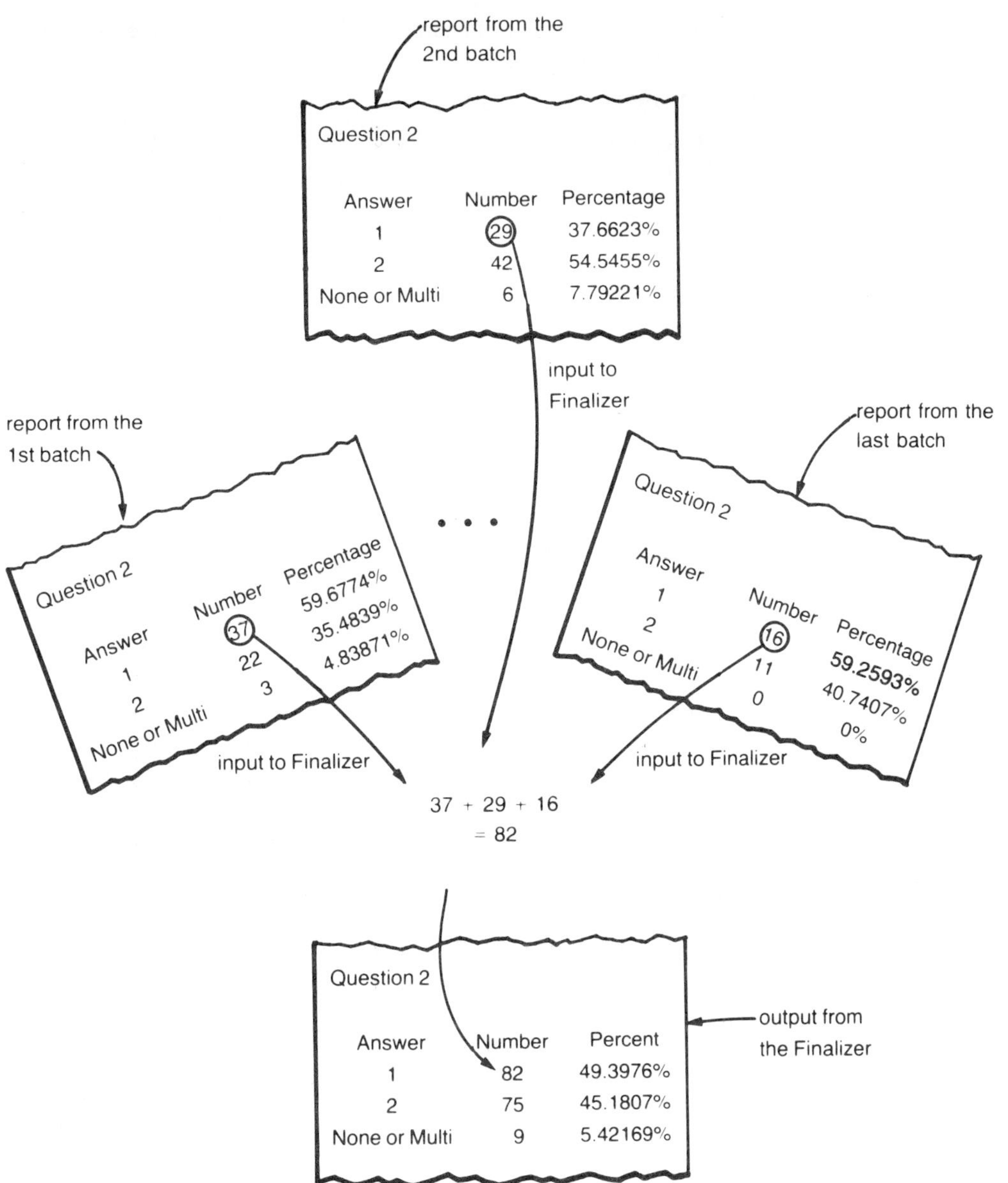

Figure 11 P 2 Assembling the final report from the reports from each batch of responses. The user enters the totals for each answer from the individual reports (and ignores the percentages). The finalizer combines the totals, computes the percentages, and prints a report summarizing all responses. The finalizer does the same thing to print cross tab reports, given the totals for the given cross tab from each batch of responses.

In the NORMAL mode your program should ask the user to enter the toppings used for each pizza that's sold:

```
TOPPING USED?

ARTICHOKE HEARTS
AVOCADOS
ENDIVE
GREEN PEPPERS
MUSHROOMS
OLIVES
ONIONS
PINEAPPLE
TOMATOES

WHICH?
```

If instead of one of those options, the user types WORKER, your program should offer a different set of alternatives:

```
DAY
REPORT
RESTART
NORMAL

WHICH?
```

The DAY option accepts the day of the week (at the beginning of each working day, you'll use this option to tell the program what day it is).

The REPORT option causes the program to print out the latest statistics showing how much of each topping has been sold on each day of the week. You'll use this to plan your shopping trips.

The RESTART option allows you to re-enter the statistics in case you've had a power failure and the program and statistics were wiped out.

The NORMAL option sends the program back into its normal mode of operation, asking for the toppings used on each pizza.

Now that you know the basic techniques of programming, you're ready to start finding your own way through the huge maze of possible uses of computers. Part II provides entrances to four different computing areas. To help you choose which topics you want to cover next, here's a description of the material in the next four chapters.

Chapter 12, Limitations of Computers, will get you thinking about the possible uses and abuses of computers in our society. Since most people associated with computing have rosy views of the future of computers, we've tried to provide an appropriate number of counter-balancing ideas.

Chapter 13, Simulation, introduces you to using computers to help understand complex real-world systems. You now have enough background to create computer simulations, and Chapter 13 shows an example of the hard part — choosing which aspects of the real system to associate with which program constructs.

Chapter 14, Putting Things in Order, should interest two categories of student. The first section of Chapter 14 shows a method for putting an array of values in order (this is called **sorting** an array). The second section describes common uses of sorting. These sections will be of interest if you intend to use computers in the business world.

The last two sections of Chapter 14 provide an introduction to the idea of the analysis of algorithms. They show that not all programs are created equal, that the input/output behavior of a program doesn't tell the whole story. The quicksort algorithm is of practical interest. The understanding of how it works and why it is so much faster than the method given in Section 14 1 will be of interest if you intend to go into computer science.

Chapter 15, Packing and Pointing, shows a number of data manipulation techniques which will be of interest to those who need to get the most out of their computers. This includes those who have their own microcomputers as well as people who plan to become professional programmers. (To cover all of Chapter 15, you will need to have gone through Sections 14 1 and 14 2.)

PART 2

Applications of Standard BASIC

Chapter 12 **Limitations of Computers**

Section 12 1

Rock Piles

This is the computer age, so they say. Man couldn't have gotten to the moon if it hadn't been for computers. Computers are giant brains, capable of making flawless, logical decisions in incomprehensibly small fractions of a second. Computers are controlling us, dehumanizing us. "Computer designed" means "better." Computers never make mistakes and they never go on strike. You put data into a computer and it gives you the answers. Computers draw pictures (see cover) and write music; computers play chess; computers control airplanes and missiles; they keep tabs on your every credit transaction, phone call, and suspicious move. Computers respond to spoken requests with smooth-tongued, seemingly pragmatic but actually borderline psychotic, logic. Computers will free us from drudgery; computers will enslave us.

Perhaps these media notions about computers seem hopelessly at odds with the view of computers you have seen in this book. All our examples, and all the programs you've written, have solved very specific, well-defined problems. On the other hand, most of the media statements about computers concern their use (or potential use) on massive, hard-to-define problems. Certainly you're aware that no computer systems exist today with the capabilities of HAL (in the movie *2001*), Colossus (in the movie *Colossus: The Forbin Project*), or Ira (in the TV series *Wonder Woman*). But it's not so easy to say that such systems will *never* exist. What *are* the limits to what computers can do? In discussing questions like this, we are probably in the same position as cave men discussing whether someone could reach the moon if he made a pile of rocks big enough. Each time someone figured out how to add another rock to the pile, people could see that progress had been made. But the rock-pile builders never got high enough to even *discover* the problems they would have to solve (weightless rocks are hard to keep in place, and it's hard to get good workers in a vacuum). Eventually, people *did* get to the moon, so the goal wasn't impossible; the techniques were just inadequate.

We may be in an analogous situation today with respect to creating an "artificial intelligence". Probably the goal is achievable, but we're not close enough yet to understand what the really tough obstacles are, and if the problem is solved, it will probably involve some as-yet-unimagined technique.

In this chapter we'll describe some limits and limitations of computing as we understand it today. That is, we'll be discussing masonry, not space flight.

Section 12 2

The Combinatorial Explosion

There's no denying that computers can do some things much faster than people can. A computer can *add* a list of numbers much faster than you can even *read* the values. If we're not careful, this can lead us to overestimate the capabilities of computers.

Suppose for some reason we wanted to write a program which would play tic-tac-toe. We all know how to play, and if you've played very much, you probably know how to play so that you never lose. Once we settle on a way to represent the board, and to communicate moves to the computer, the only problem left is how our program will choose its moves. Here's one idea: Have the computer figure out all possible outcomes of each move available to it, and then select a next move which leads only to ties and wins for the computer. This scheme will produce an unbeatable tic-tac-toe program. Certainly it doesn't play the way we do — for instance, we use a rule of thumb that says to always play in a corner on the second play if the first play was in the middle — but it will never lose. It does a lot of extra work, but since "the computer is lightning fast," that's OK.

The brute force method

Compute all possible situations.
Select the one which solves the problem.

Our proposed tic-tac-toe program uses the **brute force** method. It computes all possible results of each move, and selects the move which leads only to wins and ties. It works in this case for three reasons:

1 We know how to compute all possible results of each move.

2 We know how to tell if we've won, lost, or tied.

3 There aren't very many possibilities.

Given our success with this problem, and with blind faith in the speed of computers, we might be led to assume that this proves that computers will be able to do almost anything. Obviously board games like checkers, chess, and Go fit the same pattern, and if you could specify how to recognize a work of art, you could have the computer go through all possible pictures, selecting works of art. The possibilities are endless. Except for one problem. The catch in the brute force method is item number 3.

There aren't very many possibilities

It turns out that in most problems there are vastly too many possible situations for even the fastest computer to deal with *all* of them.

Let's analyze this seemingly simple idea: Create a beautiful picture by having the computer display all possible black-and-white pictures made of (say) 20 rows and 20 columns of dots. Since we're not sure how to define what makes a picture beautiful, we'll just sit in front of the screen and hit the "panic" button when we see a nice picture.

Our problem seems easy to solve. Each of the 20*20 = 400 spots can be either white (no character there) or black (we'll put a "*" there). Here's a program which solves a small version of the problem. It's easy to imagine expanding the program to handle the 20-by-20 case.

```
10 REM  TEENY FORM OF THE ART PROGRAM.
20      FOR A1=1 TO 2
30          FOR B1=1 TO 2
40              FOR A2=1 TO 2
50                  FOR B2=1 TO 2
60 REM                  PRINT FIRST ROW.
70                      IF A1>1 THEN 100
80                        PRINT " ";
90                        GO TO 110
```

A1	B1
A2	B2

```
100                       PRINT "*";
110                     IF B1>1 THEN 140
120                       PRINT " "
130                       GO TO 150
140                       PRINT "*"
150 REM                 PRINT SECOND ROW.
160                     IF A2>1 THE 190
170                       PRINT " ";
180                       GO TO 200
190                       PRINT "*";
200                     IF B2>1 THE 230
210                       PRINT " "
220                       GO TO 240
230                       PRINT "*"
240 REM                 PRINT BLANKS TO CLEAR SCREEN
250                     FOR B=1 TO 5
260                         PRINT
270                     NEXT B
280                  NEXT B2
290             NEXT A2
300         NEXT B1
310     NEXT A1
9999    END
```

Before we bother expanding the program, let's estimate how long it might take to look over all of the 20-by-20 black-and-white dot pictures. Let's suppose that we have a fast computer system and are willing to look at 100 pictures each second. How long should we expect to be at the screen picking out beautiful patterns? Let's see how many pictures there are.

There are 2 pictures when we use one dot position
4 pictures when we have two dot positions
8 pictures when we have three dot positions
16 pictures when we have four dot positions
.
.
.
2^n pictures when we have n dot positions
.
.
.
2^{400} pictures when we have a 20-by-20 grid of positions.

We look at 100 pictures each second. Using the facts that there are 60 seconds per minute, 60 minutes per hour, 24 hours per day, 365 days per year, and 100 years per century, we can use this BASIC statement to see how many centuries it will take.

```
PRINT (2^400)/100/60/60/24/365/100; "CENTURIES"
 3.17099E90 CENTURIES
```

over 3×10^{90} centuries

(this may not work on your system. the standards require numbers up to $\times 10^{38}$, our system provides more)

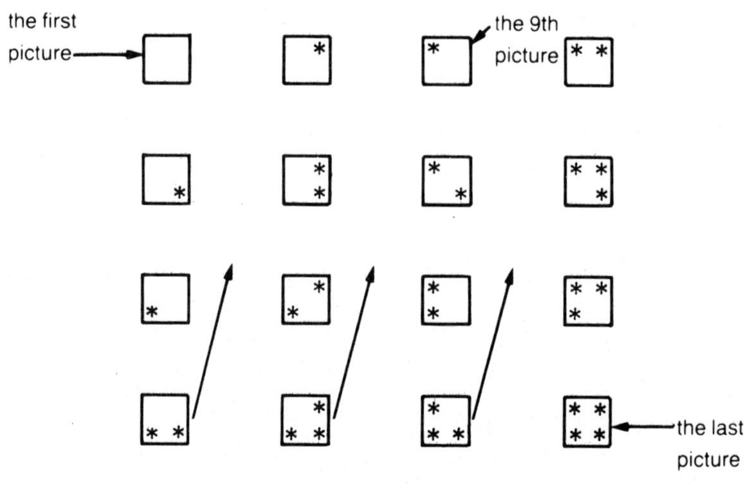

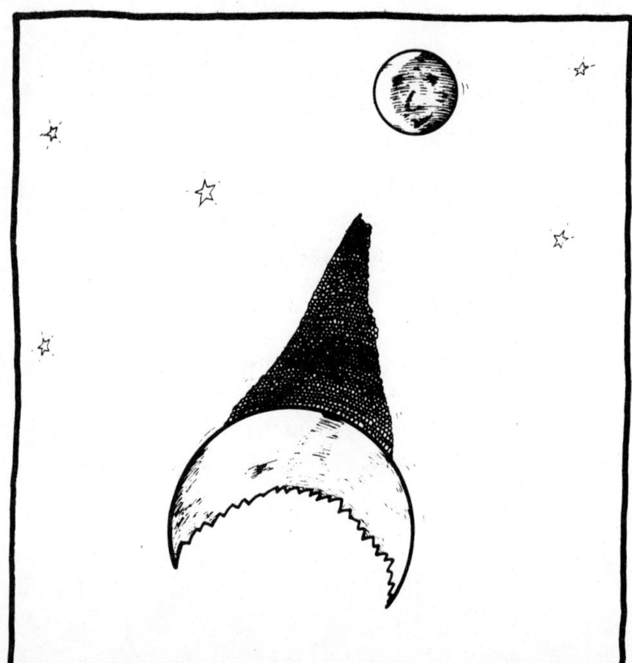

Needless to say, that's a long time. It's unimaginably longer than the age of the universe!

Unavoidable fact of life

the biggest, fastest computer

assumption 1: that the whole world could be made into one giant computer with individual components about the size and weight of protons

assumption 2:	that each component of the giant computer can process one little black or white spot on one of the 20-by-20 dot pictures we've been discussing in the time it takes light to travel across the diameter of a proton (6.67E − 24 sec.)
fact 1:	400 dots in a 20-by-20 dot picture
fact 2:	2^{400} = 2.59E120 different 20-by-20 black-and-white dot pictures
fact 3:	1.07E123 dots to process in order to look at all of the pictures
data:	mass of Earth = 6.00E24 kg mass of proton = 1.7E − 27 kg diameter of proton = 2E − 15 m speed of light = 3.00E8 m/sec one century = 3.15E9 sec
conclusion:	It would take the world's biggest, fastest computer more than a billion billion billion billion centuries to look at all of the 20-by-20, black-and-white dot pictures.
moral:	Sometimes the biggest and fastest is not enough.

There's nothing special about the problem we chose. It sounds simple, it doesn't seem (at first glance) to be particularly large, and yet it cannot be solved using the brute force method, *no matter how fast your computer is.* If we analyzed the number of possibilities in the game of chess (or checkers or Go), or the number of possible newspaper articles, or the number of possible rain-cloud patterns over the Western United States, we'd get similar astronomically large numbers.

Of course, we haven't proved that these problems are impossible to solve. We've just proved that having a super-fast computer isn't any cure-all. In these cases, doing something crude very fast isn't any better than doing something crude slowly — neither solves the problem.

Very hard problems

It is clearly impossible to examine all of the 20-by-20 dot-pictures, but it *may* be possible to look at all of the "beautiful" pictures by finding some way to automatically select a reasonably sized subset of the total collection of pictures which includes all the beautiful ones. In other words, it is still possible that someone may solve the "beautiful picture" problem by finding a clever way to avoid the brute force method.

However, there *are* problems, seemingly reasonable and easily stated, which *cannot* be solved by the world's biggest, fastest computer — even if you let it run for a billion billion years. Such a problem is described in an article by Larry J. Stockmeyer amd Ashok K. Chandra, "Intrinsically Difficult Problems," *Scientific American*, May 1979, pages 140–159.

EXERCISES 12 2

1 Suppose you were able to write a subroutine which returned a number telling how beautiful a given dot picture was. Then you wouldn't have to watch the pictures go by yourself. Suppose you ran the "beautiful picture" program with your subroutine on a super-computer which could generate and analyze a billion pictures each second. How long would it take to discover the most beautiful 20-by-20 dot picture?

2 A color TV picture is made up of about 512 × 512 ≅ a quarter million dots. Each dot is made up of some combination of three colors of various intensities. Each "picture" lasts about a thirtieth of a second. Within a millionth of a percent, what percent of all possible TV pictures have been viewed by someone, somewhere, up to this moment? (Hint: You can make the estimate in your head.)

3 We said it was "easy to imagine" expanding our program to handle 20-by-20 pictures. There are two limitations in Minimal BASIC which would get in our way, however. What are they?

Section 12 3

Nobody's Perfect

What's one-third plus one-third plus one-third? What's five billion plus one, minus five billion? If you make these computations in BASIC, the results may not be what you'd expect. Try it.

```
10      PRINT 1/3 + 1/3 + 1/3; " =1?"
20      PRINT (5000000000 + 1) - 5000000000; " =1?"
9999    END
RUN
 .999999 =1?
  0  =1?
READY
```

these may be different on your system depending on # of significant digits carried and details of the arithmetic routines

What's the trouble? Well, since the "boxes" that BASIC uses to store values are of fixed, limited size, any part of a value that won't fit gets lots. On our system each variable has just enough room to hold about 6 decimal digits, so the result of dividing 1 by 3 is

.333333	333333333333. . . (*the rest is lost*)

And, of course, when you add 0.333333, 0.333333, and 0.333333, you don't get 1, you get 0.999999. A similar problem happens when we add 1 to 5 billion. The answer we expect, 5000000001, can't be stored in its entirety, and the 1 at the end is lost.

Can this limited accuracy cause trouble? Or is it just a quirk that we needn't worry about? Yes, it can cause trouble; and no, it isn't just a cute, endearing little quirk.

No matter how perfect it may look, each component is slightly off.
If you're lucky, the errors will tend to cancel.
If you're not, look out!

Occasionally the seemingly tiny inaccuracies can jump up and bite you when you're least expecting it. In some computations, the errors, though each is small, can compound themselves.

A few years ago a clever but unscrupulous computer programmer used this fact to bilk a bank's customers out of a small fortune. Our unworthy programmer had written the program the bank used to compute the monthly interest earned by each account. For example, if at the start of the month an account had $100.00 in it, and accounts earn 5.25% yearly interest, at the end of the month it would have earned 100*0.0525/12, or $0.4375, in interest. But bank accounts are kept in dollars and cents, which means that something has to be done with the $0.0075 (three quarters of a cent). Here's where our devious programmer made his move. Instead of rounding the interest earnings off to the nearest cent, he wrote the program so it credited the customer's account with

```
INT(0.4375*100)/100
```

that is, with 43¢ instead of 44¢. What about the three quarters of a cent that was left over? Well, the unprincipled cad had the program tuck that away in a special account — his own. Notice how insidious this is — the totals all balance, and each customer's account is so close to being right that no one notices a thing! To discover how much money the wicked fellow made in an average year, do problem 2 at the end of this chapter.

The bank scheme worked because no one missed the small amounts being taken, but after a large number of transactions, they added up to a large amount. Similarly, in long mathematical calculations, small errors caused by the limited accuracy of computer arithmetic can accumulate and cause large errors in the final answer. In fact, the "noise" can be so large that it overwhelms the good data in the answer and makes the result complete nonsense.

It's important to understand that in cases like this, the computer isn't exactly doing anything wrong; it's just not doing what you might expect if you assume that numbers in BASIC work like mathematical numbers. Most of the time, things work out OK, but occasionally, you get caught by the limited accuracy. Moral: Just because something comes out of a computer, it isn't necessarily right.

EXERCISES 12 3

1 What will happen if this program is run on a BASIC system which has 6-place accuracy?

```
10      FOR C=1000000 TO 2000000
20      NEXT C
30      PRINT "DONE"
9999    END
```

2 Experiment with your BASIC system to see how many of the sums like (1/2) + (1/2), (1/3) + (1/3) + (1/3),. . .,(1/*n*) + (1/*n*) +. . .+ (1/*n*) come out to exactly 1.

Section 12 4
Where's It All Going?

In this section we're talking about things that nobody knows very much about. We're asking questions, not laying out "facts." You won't agree with everything we say — we're suggesting some *starting points* for thinking about the effects of computers and computer technology on our society.

A further note of warning: Our observation is that most people involved with computers are optimistic about the possible uses and effects of computers on our society. So are we. But since we believe in looking at both sides of every picture, here we've tried to concentrate more on the side that we feel receives less attention. Possibly you will feel that we're being slightly negative. We do feel that computerization isn't something that should be taken for granted.

The computer revolution has been roaring along for something like a third of a century. At every step there have been attempts to understand where it's all going. Let's begin our attempt at prognostication by humbly noticing that in the past, good people making a serious effort have been way off base.

SOME OLD PREDICTIONS

In 1962 the Center for the Study of Democratic Institutions prepared a report which received quite a bit of attention. It had the provocative title *Cybernation: The Silent Conquest.* It did a thorough job of projecting the effects of computerization on broad aspects of our society: the effects on the average person's leisure time (supposed to increase radically), the depersonalization of the individual, and the predicted undermining of democracy and capitalism. The main conclusion of the report was that the forces which led companies and government agencies to computerize their operations (efficiency, tighter control of operations, and more "rational" decision-making capabilities) were so strong and appealing that (put crudely) the computers would take over before anyone would realize what happened. And once in place, the computers could not be removed without causing collapse.

In some ways that all sounds plausible. But the effects haven't been as drastic as the report predicted (not yet, at least), probably because the authors' assumptions about the capabilities of computer technology were extravagant. Listen.

"In twenty years [i.e., by now!]. . . most people will have had to recognize that, when it comes to logic, the machines by and large can think better than they, for in that time good thinking computers should be operating on a large scale" (p. 44).

"There is every reason to believe that. . . machines will be available outside the laboratory that will do a credible job of original thinking, certainly as good thinking as that expected of most middle-level people who are supposed to 'use their minds'"(p. 9).

Later we'll see how the authors might have arrived at such an over optimistic prediction. But before that, here's one last prediction from the report. At this very moment you are disproving it!

"There will be a small, almost separate society of people in rapport with the advanced computers. These cyberneticians will have established a relationship with their machines that cannot be shared with the average man. . . Those with the talent for the work probably will have to develop it from childhood and will be trained as intensively as the classical ballerina'' (pp. 44–45).

That last prediction seems positively ludicrous twenty years later, in the days of $500 computers you can buy in shopping centers all over the nation! In the days of ''hobby computers,'' video game computers, pocket calculators, and computers in even the smallest businesses...

Where might the authors have gotten such a distorted view? For one thing, in 1962 computers *were* tremendously expensive, were not widespread, and were much harder to use. But probably the main sources of this view were the fantastic predictions made by people who were working in the computer area at that time.

The Jan–Feb 1958 issue of *Operations Research* contained the article ''Heuristic Problem Solving: The Next Advance in Operations Research,'' by Herbert A. Simon and Allen Newell. In that article they predicted that within 10 years (by 1968!) a computer would be world chess champion; a computer would discover and prove a new, important mathematical theorem; computers would write aesthetically pleasing music; and most psychological theories would be expressed as computer programs.

Needless to say, none of their predictions came true within their allotted 10 years. In fact, none came true within *20* years. Our personal hunch is that none of the predictions — except possibly the one on chess — have much chance of being fulfilled by 1988 (30 years).

CAN WE DO BETTER? SHOULD WE TRY?

If precise predictions seem doomed to failure, what's the use? Well, the predictions above do have grains of truth in them. Computers *have* pervaded our society, and it may be too late to do without them, as the first report perceived. Certainly *some* psychological theories are expressed in information-processing terms (e.g., in cognitive psychology). So there may be some hope. In a carefully thought-out prediction there will be *some* truth. But more importantly, a careful look at where things seem to be heading can suggest things to worry about while there's still time to change them.

> It seems that every time the forces of technology come up with a widely applicable new gadget, it sneaks into our society rather quietly at first. Four rough stages are identifiable. In the first phase, people who already have an interest in the gadget start using it and talking about it. In the second phase, people starting with no commercial or personal interest gradually learn of the gadget, become interested in it, and make the decision to indulge on the basis of fairly personal, close to home, factors. Will it make my life easier, more fun, richer? How much does it cost? Will my spouse agree to spend our money for it? What can I do with it? (The home/personal computer movement seems to be in the second phase right now.) For gadgets which gain mass acceptance, the second phase snowballs into a third phase in which so many people have the gadget that it becomes an accepted part of the *good life*, and people who otherwise might not even have dreamed of having the gadget get one simply because everyone else has one — it's the thing to do. Once the third stage is well established, and millions and millions of people own and use the gadget, the full effects of the gadgets start to be felt throughout the whole society. In the mature, fourth phase, all the little side effects which were ignored, unnoticed, or ruled insignificant by early owners come to light — side effects which may well *be* insignificant for each individual, but which when multiplied by millions and millions of users make up a new set of problems and changes in our society as a whole.

The introduction, gradual acceptance, and ultimate effects of the automobile, television, the pill, disposable food and drink containers, the Xerox machine, etc., provide ample evidence of the process. Until rather recently, the side effects of technological advances have been ignored or at worst grouchily tolerated — taken as signs of *progress*. In a growth oriented society, in fact, the side effects of one gadget may be welcomed as providing openings for yet more gadgets which, in soothing the side effects of established gadgetry, cause yet more side effects, opening room for more gadgets, and so on in the infinite loop. In the last decade, however, it has become clear that we are starting to bump against the limits, that some of the flexibility is going out of the system. We no longer appear to have the natural resources, the energy (both physical and mental), or the space to withstand continuing waves of radical, unforeseen changes.

One solution we can rule out is that of simply stopping technological change. We needn't spend time trying to evaluate whether that would be a good thing to do — it simply seems to be impossible, given our current circumstances. Some people have tried, and failed miserably — one of the more colorful attempts was that of the Luddites. Ned Lud lived in Nottingham, England in the early 1800s. He and his fellow stocking weavers felt threatened by the introduction of mechanized looms. What makes us remember the Luddites was the way they expressed their concern — they stomped into the local mills and destroyed the looms. It's a sign of our society's attitudes about the inevitability of technological change that the Luddites are now thought of as buffoons.

If we as a society have neither the desire nor the ability to stop technological change, and we no longer have the ability to cope smoothly with rapid, radical, unanticipated change, what can we do? Perhaps we can develop ways to anticipate side effects of new technologies and try to gently guide their development away from potentially harmful outcomes.

Well, that sounds nice, but how in the world can we do it? Maybe if the very people who are involved with a new gadget would take a little time to think about possible effects instead of concentrating solely on the commercial development and personal use of the gadget, maybe if the early users would make a little effort to observe the effects of the new gadget on themselves and their families, maybe if the first owners would make an effort to get people talking about the possibilities, maybe that would be an important first step.*

TRENDS IN HARDWARE

Let's begin with something relatively easy — the trend in computer hardware. While research continues in efforts to build ever faster, more powerful computers, the trend which will almost certainly have the biggest effect on the largest number of people is the production of moderately fast, moderately powerful computers which are smaller and less costly. If we include computers which serve special-purpose tasks, then we're surrounded already. There are computers in sewing machines (to control "zig-zig" and other stitches), microwave ovens, television tuners, traffic light controllers, automobiles, pocket calculators, children's toys, pocket chess players, cassette tape players, thermostats, pinball machines, "memory" typewriters, telephones, and on and on. This tendency to redesign existing products, using digital electronic devices to make the new versions smaller, lighter, and more versatile, will continue. The electronics industry is a roaring success, and there is no end in sight to the improvements in hardware. At least no end is in sight with regard

---

*From *Kilobaud* #5, May 1977, page 10. Reprinted by permission of *Kilobaud Microcomputing Magazine*.

to the strictly technical problems involved. We suspect that because of the *rising* costs of software (so far, at least, it takes people to write programs, and their labor keeps rising in cost), at some point in the future, hardware will represent such a small portion of the total cost of a computer sytem that there will be less motivation for designing newer, less costly hardware.

Computers have been in widespread use in large companies, universities, and governmental agencies for some 15 to 20 years. The trend toward broader uses of computers by these groups will continue. A current favorite for large corporations is **distributed processing.** A distributed system consists of a number of computers (usually all but a very few being terminals with some limited computing power) hooked together. Using a distributed system, a secretary can enter a draft of a letter and edit it, or enter and edit records, or scan through a small number of records at an individual terminal, relying on the computer in the terminal for these tasks. Once the material is acceptable, it can be sent to the main computer(s) where it is stored in a way that allows other users of the distributed network to access and modify it. Or an engineer might use one of the small computers for simple calculations while sending larger programs to be processed by a larger machine. Even in large businesses which could afford the largest computers, then, there is a trend toward smaller, more personalized computing. Helping people to communicate may be more valuable than performing specialized computations with tremendous speed.

HOME COMPUTERS

While the use of digital electronics to improve common household items and the use of computers by business and government are interesting topics, we think there's a chance that the most noticeable changes in our society could come from another source — the inexpensive general-purpose computer. The home computer, personal computer, small business computer: the potential seems enormous. For instance, a family could build up a library of useful programs (games, record keeping, educating the kids, making computations to help plan woodworking projects, etc.) Families could further increase their computers' capabilities by trading programs and data bases with others. (What else can you think of?)

The potential for home computers seems enormous. But let's not confuse *potentialities* with *actualities.* Even though inexpensive home computers are available, and are being purchased in large numbers, and even though they have the *potential* for individual self-expression, that doesn't mean they'll be used that way. When television was first being developed, there were glowing predictions about the great boost to people's ability to communicate with each other. The idea was that people could use it to send messages to their friends and relatives, making a vast improvement over talking on the phone. Instead, it has turned out that most people simply watch slick professional programs, just as most people read newspapers and books written by strangers rather than sharing their own writings with their friends. Perhaps it will turn out the same way with home computers. Instead of writing programs tailored to their own life and interests, people will (in the large) simply buy mass-produced programs. Already, telephone-linked networks of home computers provide a sort of electronic bulletin. Will these catch on? Will special-interest groups (say, model railroaders or stamp collectors) trade information by sending data through the mails? Or will most people be content buying mass-produced battle games for their computers?

> Virtually all home computers come equipped with BASIC systems. So many small computers have been sold in the last few years that BASIC is now almost certainly the world's most widely available computer language.

WHAT AFFECTS NEW USES OF COMPUTERS?

Now let's turn to a slightly different question. What factors determine what new products will appear in the next few decades? You might expect that the rise of inexpensive computers would lead to the introduction of really revolutionary new products. But so far, it seems the major use has been to make slight improvements to existing product lines. The only really different product has been games which are played on the family TV. We can think of several interpretations of this.

One interpretation is that computers aren't much good for anything beyond what's been done already — that small, inexpensive computers are capable of nothing much more than games and controlling sewing machines. This seems unlikely. Surprising new uses for computers are bound to come along.

Another interpretation we feel we can reject is that new products are developed only to fill preexisting needs. Attractive products, especially when backed by good promotion, have a way of creating their own necessity.

Why have certain products come on the market before other, possibly more interesting, applications? We think there are several explanations. First, there is little **risk** in producing new versions of established products. Almost everyone in the country is familiar with watches, sewing machines, and TVs. Every year large numbers of these items are sold, so a new product which offers some advantage (cost, weight, accuracy, flexibility) is assured a ready market. Also, people are more likely to accept computers in the guise of sewing machines — everyone knows what a sewing machine does, so there's not much fear of the unknown to be overcome. This also explains why the first major new products have been games. It's common knowledge that children and young people accept new things readily, and that children like games. The risk involved in producing an exciting, really new sort of game is less than the risk associated with trying to get set-in-their-ways grown-ups to learn something really new.

We can also surmise that markets in which there is **heavy competition** will tend to adopt new products early, since even a slight advantage can make a large difference in sales. Again, the game market fits.

Other factors come to mind. There's the "what *can* be done is what *will* be done" syndrome. For instance, if you have a pocket calculator which computes trigonometric functions like sine and cosine, there is probably a switch on your calculator which you set to specify how you're going to enter angles — in *degrees, radians,* or *grads.* Now the unit *grad* (1/100 of a right angle) is used by surveyors, but probably not by too many other people — we had to look in an unabridged dictionary to find a definition of the term. The capability of computing angles in grads almost certainly wasn't introduced because of demand from the marketplace, or due to competition, or because someone decided it would be a wonderful new product. Someone realized that it would be easy to add grads to pocket calculators (you need a three-position switch instead of a two-position switch and an extra indicator on the display), so they did — whether anybody really needed them or not. What *can* be done *will* be done. Similarly, since computers have been used in business (to do accounting, word processing, record keeping, etc.) for years, the newer, less expensive microcomputers were immediately put to these traditional tasks.

The last factor we can think of which influences the introduction of innovative computer applications is the time it takes to assimilate new ideas. Here's an example. Even though it seems clear that eventually, small special-purpose computers will be used to control energy-efficient heating and cooling systems in houses, it will probably be quite a while before this is widespread. It takes some 10 years to train new architects, and most good architects who are already trained are busy — probably too busy to stop working and learn what they would need to know to make effective use of microcomputers. In addition, as yet there are few if any construction workers with the skills needed to install and test such devices. Each specialized group has its own **lag time.**

The factors we've discussed have this in common: They suggest a slow but steady infiltration of computers into our lives. At first, they will sneak into our homes in the guise of small improvements to familiar products. The young will be the first to accept them in unfamiliar forms. By the time really innovative products become widely available (say, 10 to 20 years), people will be so accustomed to having computers around that they won't put up much resistance.

WHAT MIGHT IT BE LIKE IN A HEAVILY COMPUTERIZED SOCIETY?

If our thinking is right, then in the next decade or two we'll have another Stage 4 situation (when all the little effects start to add up). The little effects of everyone having, using, and depending on computers will add up to have a big effect on our society and lives. But what might those big effects be? And will they be predominantly good, bad, or neutral? No one can say for sure. Certainly *we* don't know. But we're not above making a few wild guesses.

Our first wild guess is that computers and the computer industry will assume a power and economic importance equal to or greater than that of today's automobile industry. The automobile has a tremendous effect on our everyday lives. We suspect that computers will have effects as broad reaching (but certainly each specific effect will be different from those caused by the automobile). Let's see if we can back up our first wild claim.

Right now the automobile forms the backbone of the private sector of the United States' economy. (Automobile manufacturers, tire makers, oil companies, gas stations, auto mechanics, insurance companies, road builders, scrap iron dealers, on and on.) Because of its tremendous economic impact, the automobile affects national and local politics (globally, we are at the mercy of foreign oil; locally, we fight over where new roads should go). The automobile affects our lives in an incredible panorama of ways (smog, noise, where we live, where we shop, who our friends are, how we date and mate). The automobile industry is so important to the well-being of the country that the government is specifying in greater and greater detail what the industry may do. If restrictions continue to be applied to the automobile industry (as it seems they will and must), and if computer-related industries continue their astonishing rates of growth, then in the next decade or two, computer-related industries will displace the automobile industries from their current ruling position. In the next decades government planners will notice a number of advantages to the computer industries — the disadvantages, whatever they may prove to be, will be glossed over at first. Computers don't use gasoline. Computers keep getting smaller, so the amount of raw materials required to build computers of a given power will *shrink*. Neither do computers, once built and in operation, need to consume much raw material. Wider use of video terminals will save a good portion of the massive amounts of paper used today. The largest amounts of labor and money will be spend on software, and this will provide lots of jobs with little requirement for expensive physical plants. All these advantages are bonuses to the traditional advantages of better organization and control.

Imagine the effects of replacing our economic reliance on the automobile with a similar reliance on computers. Perhaps we will come to ignore countries with rich natural resources like oil and instead concern ourselves with countries with abundances of cheap labor. (Even today, many of the computer components are constructed in labor-rich places like Korea, Taiwan, Singapore, Mexico, and Hong Kong.) On the other hand, if software becomes, as we suspect, the largest part of the business, small countries with imagination could compete effectively on the world market without becoming industrialized in the traditional sense.

Let's move from the economic sphere into the broader question of how widespread reliance on computers might alter a society's patterns of behavior. We'll be concentrating on the idea that excessive reliance on computers might result in a **loss of flexibility.**

In a given culture there are limited numbers of ideas, methods, and ways of doing things. The larger and more diverse this pool of techniques, the better a culture can adapt to change. One possibility is that as a culture gives up more of its traditional personal and societal functions to computers, people will tend to stop thinking about and inventing new ways to do things, and the pool of ideas will stagnate. This seems more likely to occur if people adopt the attitude that when something is computer controlled, it can't be changed, so there's no reason to think about it. Some of this is seen today*: "I'm sorry you think your bill is wrong, madam, but we can't do anything about it. It's on the computer." Not all such statements are simply excuses for poor business practice. Huge programs can be very expensive to change, and not every eventuality can be foreseen by the original programmers. There is also this: Out of all possible ways to set up a new club, business, or governmental organization, probably those which seem easiest and least expensive to computerize will be selected. Eventually, these ways will be accepted as the natural way to do things, with more imaginative (perhaps more human) methods being ignored. The cost of writing the necessary programs may become the determining factor in what is attempted. Alternatives involving nonelectronic methods may not even be thought of in a world where one's fancy can be quickly turned into a video screen reality.

Here's an extreme example of the possible effects of loss of flexibility! Suppose an enemy had a secret weapon that disrupted digital electronics, so that when the weapon was turned on, errors popped up in all the computers in the country. It seems likely that over a few weeks the country would fall into chaos. People would stop working when paycheck after paycheck didn't show up. No one could buy anything with a credit card (and probably most transactions will be electronic within a decade or two). The logistics of buying and bringing food into the major cities would be overwhelming. Cars and trucks with computer-controlled ignitions wouldn't run. The key thing is that we couldn't simply revert to doing things the way we did before computerization — those ways will have been forgotten; parts,

*For example, see T.D. Sterling, "Consumer Difficulties with Computerized Transactions: An Empirical Investigation," *Communications of the ACM*, May, 1979, pp. 283–289.

tools, and plans won't be available. Automated assembly lines wouldn't work, and even if skilled workers still existed, the plants weren't designed for human labor. If all the computers in the country suddenly became unusable, we could be reduced to a pretechnological barter society — if large-scale riots and looting could be prevented.

Scenario

The sky fills with satellites. For months, nothing happens, and people start to relax. Then, without further warning, computers and digital devices all over the country start malfunctioning in subtle ways.

The satellites contain particle beam generators. They blanket the country with streams of a newly discovered subatomic particle which has a high-interaction cross section with silicon crystals. The particles pass harmlessly through most materials, but interact with silicon, imparting tiny amounts of energy. The energy level is so small that it causes no gross physical effects, but is large enough to disrupt the delicate internal workings of digital devices.

Chaos reigns.

–The End–

Our final wild guess about the fuzzy, computerized future concerns changes in human values. "When a new machine comes along that can do something we're used to thinking of as a human job, the ultimate response is to deny that that ability has much to do being human. [We'd]. . . imagine that before the development of writing, people assumed that remembering things was a basic, important part of being human."* Devices such as the domesticated horse, the steam engine, and the internal combustion engine have served to reduce the image of a "strong man" from an exceptionally valuable worker to a sex object. And in the Old West they made the change in image wrought by a machine explicit: "They called the Colt 44 the 'Equalizer' because it eliminated the thing that made some people 'better' than others, namely, their hand-to-hand fighting skills. Physical strength was no longer the 'measure of a man'.

"Right now we tend to think of 'intelligence' as a uniquely human property, and to reward people who use logical thinking to get ahead." We suspect that as computers take over our everyday, routine, repetitive tasks — as we turn to them for the answers to simple arithmetic problems and logical deductions — the ability to do such things will no longer matter to us and will no longer enter into our estimates of a person's worth. "When everybody has their own computer, it won't make any difference if you can make simple logical deductions faster than your competitor — their computer will be their IQ Equalizer. And as a consequence, other aspects of being human will be the ones we value most."

IN CONCLUSION

We don't pretend to have guessed all the changes that reliance on computers will bring, nor even to have guessed right in the few that we mentioned. Perhaps people

---

*Quotes are from *Home Computers: 2^{10} Questions & Answers, Vol, 2: Software*, page 173, 1977, and are reprinted courtesy of dilithium Press, 30 N.W. 23rd Pl., Portland, OR 97210.

The rock builders' defenses are breached

will be freed from petty routines and will find ways to lead richer lives. Perhaps we will come to feel enslaved by a rigid, tightly organized, totally efficient state computer system. We don't know. But if people pay attention to what's going on, and think about the possible consequences of new technologies, we might avoid stumbling into an unpleasant situation only to find that it's too late to do anything.

PROBLEMS 12

1 Write a program which accepts the number of hours you're willing to spend sitting at the screen, and which gives the size of the largest dot grid you could go completely through in that time. Assume (as in Section 12 2) you can look at 100 pictures per second.

2 The unscrupulous programmer of Section 12 3 receives

amount in cents – INT *(amount in cents)*

on each monetary transaction. On the average, this will be half a cent on each account each time the interest is posted.

Write a program which figures out how much money the dirty trickster makes a year, given the number of accounts and the number of times interest is posted each year. (A medium-sized bank or savings and loan might have 8000 accounts.)

TOPICS FOR DISCUSSION

1 We don't know if the rock-pile builders existed or not. Suppose they did. Then we could think of the Tower of Babel as their monument. The technologies developed by them made it possible for the Egyptians to build the Great Pyramids. And the idea of a culture undertaking a gargantuan task as a symbol of their greatness was one of the motivations for our own Great Pyramid — putting a Man on the Moon. Is it conceivable that some future society will undertake the construction of an Artificial Intelligence as a massive, somewhat impractical, societal monument? Does the Japanese government's national goal of a fifth-generation machine fit this idea?

2 Each section in this chapter has a rock-pile builders drawing. Discuss the analogies between the drawings and the material in the text around them. Propose some drawings of your own.

3 Write brief descriptions of all the movie computers you can think of (a few are mentioned in Section 12 1). In what ways are they similar? How do they differ? Do you think they are based on present-day computers? Or do you think they are more like human characters with funny ways of talking, and with certain character flaws?

4 What is wacky about this argument? "If a computer came with a built-in multiply unit but no divide unit, there would be no way you could do division. It might look like you could divide *x* by *y* by going through all possible *z's* and stopping when you find one that satisfies the equation

$$x = y*z$$

but since there are so many possibilities, it would take too long to be practical." (Hint: How else could you do division?)

5 Discuss the differences between the properties of the numbers in BASIC and the properties of the numbers we're familiar with in everyday life. How can these differences lead people astray? Is there any limit to the number of decimal places of accuracy in everyday numbers?

6 If you had the opportunity to turn one everyday, repetitive task over to a personal computer, what task would you choose? How would it change the way you live? How hard do you think it would be to write the necessary program for your application?

7 Do you agree with the four-phase description of the way new technological gadgets infiltrate? Does it explain anything? Try to identify such phases in the adoption of some gadget like television, garbage compactors, pocket calculators, or the "pill".

8 Make a collection of cartoons about computers and their effects. What attitudes are common to many of the cartoons? Do the portrayals seem accurate to you? Do any of the drawings look like the computer you're using? Can any of the cartoons be treated as predictions or warnings as well as humor?

9 If you or one of your friends has a computer, think about why it was purchased, what you *thought* you could do with it, and what you're *actually* doing with it. How has it changed your life? Has it altered the amount of time you spend watching TV? reading books? doing homework? being outdoors? How would society change if everyone had one?

10 If there's a computer store near you, find out what they offer. See if you can find out how much of their business is in actual computer hardware versus books and magazines versus programs.

11 Do you think our warning about possible ill effects of mass computerization and our discussion of **loss of flexibility** makes sense? Or do you think we're just latter-day Luddites who would make similar complaints about anything that wasn't around when we were kids?

From *Finite State Fantasies*, 1976, page 48. Reprinted courtesy of Matrix Publishers, Inc., 30 N.W. 23rd Pl., Portland, OR 97210.

12 There is a school of thought that holds that all things can be explained by the laws of physics. Although this may seem reasonable on the surface, there are many problems in which the laws of physics are of no practical benefit. For example, starting with a description of the state of the universe sometime prior to 1966, including a description of the physical state of all people's brains, their genetic char-

acteristics, the phase of the moon, etc., it *might* be possible to accurately predict the writing of the song "The Fool on the Hill." However, it seems safe to say that no reasonable person would undertake to do such a prediction in that manner.

There is another school of thought which holds that there is nothing going on in the human mind that cannot be explained on the basis of the principles of information processing, that is, the principles on which computers are based. It is possible that this is correct in principle, but impossible to apply in the same sense that the laws of physics give us little aid with the "The Fool on the Hill." It is also possible that the principles of information processing will be of great benefit in explaining the nature of intelligence, just as the laws of physics help us explain physical phenomena.

Our question is, in what ways do these schools of thought seem reasonable and in what ways do they seem extravagant?

Chapter 13 **Simulation**

Section 13 1
Models

If you're in a city planning department, and you're asked to pick the best spot for a new shopping center, you can't very well proceed by building a shopping center in every possible location and seeing which one causes the fewest problems. If you're a large company building a new airplane, you can't very well design it by building a bunch of full-sized multimillion dollar airplanes and seeing which ones don't crash. If you're in the forest service, and you're asked the best place to build fire breaks, you can't very well set the forest on fire to see which way the fire will spread the fastest.

Instead, people build models, make trial runs, test things out on a small scale before committing large amounts of time and money. In some fields, modeling techniques have been developed which work extremely well. Wind tunnels make very accurate predictions about the behavior of new airplane shapes. Classical mathematical methods allow exceptionally accurate predictions of spacecraft trajectories. Sometimes we don't have a guaranteed method for predicting the behavior of a system, but through past experience people have built up a "feeling" for how it works. In the last few decades, computers have been used to make models of a tremendous variety of real-world situations, and so have been used to guide decision making in a broad range of fields.

There are two main classes of computer models: **structural models** and **aggregated models.**

A **structural computer model** has a direct correspondence between parts of the program and physical subparts of the real object. For example, a structural model of a bridge might have a collection of variables in the program for each separate member of the bridge (specifying that member's length, weight, shape, material, etc.), and other variables which specify how the various members are hooked together. By accepting values for the forces placed upon the bridge by traffic and wind loads, and using the equations civil engineers have developed for predicting the effects of forces and shears on girders, the program could derive the deflection of every point in the bridge.

In other cases the system we want to study may have so many subparts, or may involve such complex interactions among its subparts, that a manageable structural model is virtually impossible to create. For example, if you want to study the effects of governmental policy changes on the economy of the United States, it wouldn't be reasonable to have variables detailing the buying and selling characteristics of each person in the US. Instead, an **aggregated model** would be used, one which deals with gross measurements on the system, not with individual transactions. For instance, you might have variables giving the percentage of unemployed people, the average wage of certain job classes, the average costs of a few important raw materials, and so on. Notice the difference—you can't touch a percentage like you can touch part of a bridge—the percentage of people out of work is a **measurement** on (a property of) the system we want to study. An aggregated model is a little farther from reality than a structural model, but since there *is* a real underlying process (the buying and selling patterns of all the people in the society), we hypothesize (read "hope") that measurements on the whole system will be related in orderly ways, and that we can study and model those instead of worrying about each individual economic transaction.

If your goal is to produce a rigorous scientific theory of the behavior of some system, aggregated models have a number of questionable features. But they can be used to suggest experiments which can lead to deeper understanding. On the other hand, if your goal is to take some action (say, alter some governmental policy), aggregated models can provide a basis for sound decision making.

In this chapter we'll illustrate the creation, testing, revision, and use of an aggregated model. The situation is imaginary, but the principles involved are universal.

Section 13 2

A Specific Model—Musca Obscura

To: Dr. Melissa Lancaster
Dept. of Disease Control
National Institute
Bethesda, Maryland
USA

From: Sr. Ramón Bernal
Prisión Federal
Santa Cerveza, Maryland
SA

Dear Melissa,

I write this without any certain knowledge that it will ever reach you. Perhaps I am writing only for my own sanity, searching for some way to understand what has happened to me and my group. In times like these, a shred of historical perspective may serve to help me cope with the present.

When I last spoke with you (it seems like decades!), I had just opened a laboratory on the outskirts of Santa Cerveza. If only I could have foreseen the consequences! But I must put self-pity aside...

We had been in business only a few weeks when we received a visitor from the government. El Presidente wanted to improve his image... wanted us to do a scientific study for him. After several hours of conversation, we proposed doing a study of the fly population in rural parts of the country. In due course this was approved, and a specific village was selected. We sent observers out, and they returned with a few hundred flies, and a report indicating that the village was indeed infested with flies. We took it as our job, nay, our *civic duty,* to investigate methods of controlling the flies. Our plan was to study the sample flies, create a computer simulation of their population dynamics, and so compare different control techniques.

El Presidente

For a while, things went very well. We received special permission to use the state library, and were able to identify the flies as *musca obscura.* All that was known about this species was that it had a life cycle of 21 days, from egg to larva to pupa to adult to death from old age. We confirmed this figure in our laboratory, and further found that one adult female produced about 400 eggs. Given unlimited quantities of the right food, the eggs passed through the larva and pupa stages to become adults in about eight days. We further discovered that only the larval stage is highly dependent on food—adult males ate not at all, while some females ate small quantities of food during their egg-laying periods.

Beginning in the spirit of "small steps for tiny feet," we designed the simplest computer model we could imagine. We hypothesized that as long as we considered fairly long periods of time, and large numbers of flies, we wouldn't have to distinguish among the various stages of the *musca obscura* life cycle. Since we were interested in the total number of flies in the population, and the only thing that seemed to affect that was the current size of the population and the amount of food available, we tried to write down meaningful expressions involving those variables. If my memory serves me well (and I must say, with the rations we've been subsisting on, my mind isn't properly described as "clear"), we began with

$$\text{flies}_{\text{tomorrow}} = \text{flies}_{\text{today}} + \text{today's new adults} - \text{today's deaths}$$

$$\text{food}_{\text{tomorrow}} = \text{food}_{\text{today}} - \text{food eaten today} + \text{today's new food}$$

Yes, I think that's it. At any rate, then we argued over each of the terms. We supposed that the number of new adults was a function of the current number of flies and the amount of food available for the larva. But *what* function? To begin with, we took the simplest that seemed reasonable, namely, multiplication.

$$\text{today's new adults} = a{*}\text{flies}_{\text{today}}{*}\text{food}_{\text{today}}$$

That seemed reasonable since if there were no $\text{flies}_{\text{today,}}$ then even if there was $\text{food}_{\text{today}}$(or vice versa), there would be no new adults. The *a*, of course, was a proportionality constant which we'd have to determine.

Now let's see. As I recall, we decided that since adult flies basically don't eat, that "today's deaths" would simply be proportional to $\text{flies}_{\text{today}}$.

$$\text{today's deaths} = b{*}\text{flies}_{\text{today}}$$

Our biggest disputes came in determining the "today's new food" term. Now we knew that flies ate (more precisely, *larvae* ate) specific types of rotting waste matter. The question was how much waste matter was scattered about the village each day? We sent a crew back to the village to get an estimate of how much manure, rotting food, etc. the villagers and their animals produced each day. It brings a smile to my mind (but not, I regret, to my sad, pale face) to recall the reaction of the workers to our request. Clearly, they thought us some manner of perverts!

While the crew was in the field, we set about estimating the proportionality constants *a* and *b*.

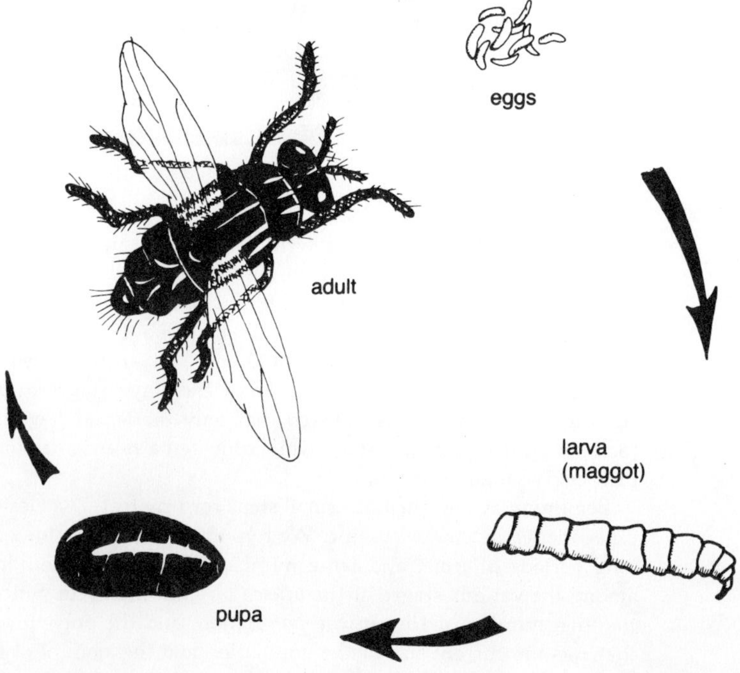

Figure 13 2 1 The *musca obscura's* life cycle. Based on "Control of Domestic Flies," Leaflet 2504, University of California, Division of Agricultural Sciences.

$$\text{flies}_{\text{tomorrow}} = \text{flies}_{\text{today}} + a^*\text{flies}_{\text{today}}{}^*\text{food}_{\text{today}} - b^*\text{flies}_{\text{today}}$$

$$\text{food}_{\text{tomorrow}} = \text{food}_{\text{today}} - \text{food eaten today} + \text{today's new food}$$

involves a proportionality constant c *involves a constant d*

We began by writing a skeletal simulation program, one which had just enough detail to allow us to experiment with it. Then we attempted to establish reasonable values for the constants by matching conditions we could create in the laboratory with settings of the program.

—musca obsucra simulator—

Ask user for constants and initial conditions.

PRINT headings.

For each day in the simulation

- *Compute each term.*
- *Use equations to get tomorrow's flies and food.*
- *PRINT current state of affairs.*

```
10    REM   MUSCA OBSCURA MODEL
20    REM   VARIABLES--
30    REM     F0  --NUMBER OF FLIES
40    REM     F1  --AMOUNT OF FOOD (IN GRAMS)
100         PRINT "A=";
110         INPUT A
120         PRINT "B=";
130         INPUT B
140         PRINT "C=";
150         INPUT C
160         PRINT "D=";
170         INPUT D
180         PRINT "INITIAL NUMBER OF FLIES=";
190         INPUT F0
200         PRINT "INITIAL AMOUNT OF FOOD=";
210         INPUT F1
220         PRINT "FOR HOW MANY DAYS SHOULD THE";
230         PRINT " SIMULATION BE RUN";
240         INPUT L
300   REM   PRINT HEADINGS AND INITIAL STATE.
310         PRINT
320         PRINT "******************************************"
330         PRINT "MUSCA OBSCURA"
340         PRINT TAB(10); "A="; A; TAB(20); "B="; B
350         PRINT TAB(10); "C="; C; TAB(20); "C="; C
360         PRINT
370         PRINT TAB(3); "DAY"; TAB(10); "FLIES";
380         PRINT TAB(20); "FOOD (GRAMS)"
390         PRINT "----------------"; TAB(20); "------------"
400         PRINT TAB(3); 0 ;TAB(10); F0; TAB(20); F1
```

print headings (lines 300–400)

(continued)

```
1000 REM   CARRY OUT THE SIMULATION FOR L DAYS.
1010       FOR D0=1 TO L
1500           LET F0 = F0 + A*F0*F1 - B*F0
1550           LET F1 = F1 - C*F1*F0 + D
1600 REM       DISPLAY TODAY'S STATE OF AFFAIRS
1610           PRINT TAB(3); D0; TAB(10); F0; TAB(20); F1
1660       NEXT D0
1700       PRINT
1710       PRINT
9999       END
```

carry out the simulation

if it seems strange to have fractional flies, add a statement LET F0 = INT(F0) here

notice all the "gaps" in line numbers to allow easy addition of later details

```
RUN
A=? 0
B=? .2
C=? 0
D=? 0
INITIAL NUMBER OF FLIES=? 1000
INITIAL AMOUNT OF FOOD=? 0
FOR HOW MANY DAYS SHOULD THE SIMULATION BE RUN? 8

****************************************
MUSCA OBSCURA
          A= 0        B= .2
          C= 0        C= 0

   DAY    FLIES       FOOD (GRAMS)
------------------    ------------
   0      1000        0
   1      800         0
   2      640         0
   3      512         0
   4      409.6       0
   5      327.68      0
   6      262.144     0
   7      209.715     0
   8      167.772     0

READY
```

with b = 0.2, the flies die off too fast

```
RUN
A=? 0
B=? .1
C=? 0
D=? 0
INITIAL NUMBER OF FLIES=? 1000
INITIAL AMOUNT OF FOOD=? 0
FOR HOW MANY DAYS SHOULD THE SIMULATION BE RUN? 8
```

```
*******************************************
MUSCA OBSCURA
            A= 0        B= .1
            C= 0        C= 0

   DAY      FLIES       FOOD (GRAMS)
-------------------- -------------
   0        1000        0
   1        900         0
   2        810         0
   3        729         0
   4        656.1       0
   5        590.49      0
   6        531.441     0
   7        478.297     0
   8        430.467     0

READY
```

looks about right

We began with the death rate constant, *b*. Since it takes about 8 days to reach adulthood, and the entire life cycle is about 21 days, the adults live about 13 days. If we had a large population of adults, some would have 13 days to live, some 12, . . . , some 1, and some would have just died. So the average adult fly would have 6½ days to live (see Exercise 2).

That meant that if no new flies were born, about half the existing flies would die after 6 or 7 days. That gave us a way to estimate *b*. We ran our skeletal program with 1000 flies, no food, and with *a*, *c*, and *d* equal to zero. Then we adjusted *b* until about half the flies died after 6 days.

Next, we concentrated on the "today's new adults" term. We had preliminarily set that at

$$a*\text{flies}_{\text{today}}*\text{food}_{\text{today}}$$

but as we thought about it, we saw a flaw with that formulation. We had seen that one female could produce about 400 surviving offspring, given an unlimited amount of food. But our expression would predict that one fly could produce an unlimited number of offspring! It seemed more reasonable to us that the number of offspring was proportional to the amount of food available up to a certain point, and then constant no matter how much excess food was available. The question was, what should the cutoff point be? In other words, how much food did one fly need during its lifetime?

This provided us an opportunity to turn back to our laboratory. We weighed an amount of food, placed one fly egg in it, and then weighed the food remaining after we removed the adult several weeks later. We found that (on the average), one fly used about 10 grams of waste material. That gave us the cutoff point. Now our plan for computing "today's new adults" was

compute amount of food available per fly

use that figure or 10 grams, whichever is smaller

today's new adults = a*(the figure above)*$\text{flies}_{\text{today}}$.

Now we were left with the task of determining *a*. We knew that, given unlimited food, one fly produced 400 offspring during her adult lifespan of 13 days. That gave us a way to set *a*. We would provide lots of food, set "today's deaths" to zero (by setting *b* to zero), start with 2 flies (one male, one female), then adjust *a* until we got a total of about 400 flies after 13 days. Since it took 8 days for the eggs to become adults, that meant that one pair of adults would produce 400 new adults (assuming, again, unlimited food) in about 21 days. By setting up that situation in our model, we could determine a reasonable value for *a*.

—determining today's new adults—

Compute food available per fly (call that F2).

IF *F2 is greater than 10 grams per fly,*

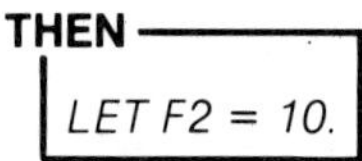

Today's new adults = a**F2*flies*$_{today}$.

```
1020 REM        COMPUTE FOOD PER FLY
1030            LET F2 = F1/F0
1040            IF F2<=10 THEN 1060
1050              LET F2 = 10
1060 REM        TO GIVES TODAY'S NEW ADULTS
1070            LET TO =  A*F2*F0

1500            LET F0 = F0 + TO        -B*F0
```

—experimenting to determine a reasonable value for a—

```
RUN
A=? .029
B=? 0
C=? 0
D=? 100
INITIAL NUMBER OF FLIES=? 2
INITIAL AMOUNT OF FOOD=? 10000000
FOR HOW MANY DAYS SHOULD THE SIMULATION BE RUN? 22

*******************************************
MUSCA OBSCURA
          A= .029    B= 0
          C= 0       C= 0

   DAY    FLIES      FOOD (GRAMS)
------------------   ------------
   0      2          1E+07
   1      2.58       1.00001E+07
   2      3.3282     1.00002E+07
   3      4.29338    1.00003E+07
   4      5.53846    1.00004E+07
   5      7.14461    1.00005E+07
   6      .
```

```
7          .          1.00012E+07
           .          1.00013E+07
           70.6783    1.00014E+07
15         91.175     1.00015E+07
16         117.616    1.00016E+07
17         151.724    1.00017E+07
18         195.724    1.00018E+07
19         252.485    1.00019E+07
20         325.705    1.0002E+07
21         420.16     1.00021E+07
22         542.006    1.00022E+07
```

looks OK

Several days later, we got around to worrying about the "food eaten today" term. Some members of the group argued that the amount of food eaten was dependent both on the number of flies and on the amount of food. They said that if there was very little food, the flies might have trouble finding it. They wanted the term to involve the product of $flies_{today}$, and $food_{today}$. It was my position that if there was anything flies did well, it was to find rotting matter in which to lay their eggs. I agreed that the amount of food eaten did depend on the amount of food available, but only to the extent that the flies couldn't eat more food than the amount of $food_{today}$. It brings me a nostalgic melancholy to think of the hours we spent over coffee in our intricate, passionate arguments. In the end, I prevailed, and we modeled the "food eaten today" term thusly:

We knew that a fly uses about 10 grams of food during its 21-day life span, hence we first computed

$$\frac{10}{21} * flies_{today}$$

Then, since no matter how many flies there were, they could eat no more than $food_{today}$, we took the "food eaten today" to be the minimum of the two values.

```
1200 REM        T3  GIVES FOOD EATEN TODAY
1210            LET T3 = C*F0 <------ C = 10/21 = 0.496
1220            IF T3<=F1 THEN 1250
1230 REM          CAN'T EAT MORE THAN IS THERE!
1240              LET T3 = F1
1250 REM
                              food eaten today
1550            LET F1 = F1 - T3        + D
```

Finally, we had established all the terms except "today's new food." Fortunately, our crew returned in a few days. The brought back an estimate that something like 20 kilograms of waste matter was being produced each day. They also brought back an inordinate number of bills for drinks at the cantina, but that's another matter. When pressed for an estimate of the amount of waste matter lying around in the village (as opposed to the amount *added* each day), they said it must have been well over a hundred kilograms. Excitedly, we ran our model, inserting the new parameters.

According to our model, the village was supporting a population of over 40,000 flies! No wonder the government thought there was a problem. Now, of course, that was only our model's prediction. The question was, did that conform to reality? When we asked the field crew, they were incredulous. How did *they* know how many flies there were? How did you count flies—they keep moving! We rephrased the question. There were about 400 people and animals in the village. Did it seem reasonable that there were about 100 flies per inhabitant? "Yes," they said. We were jubilant!

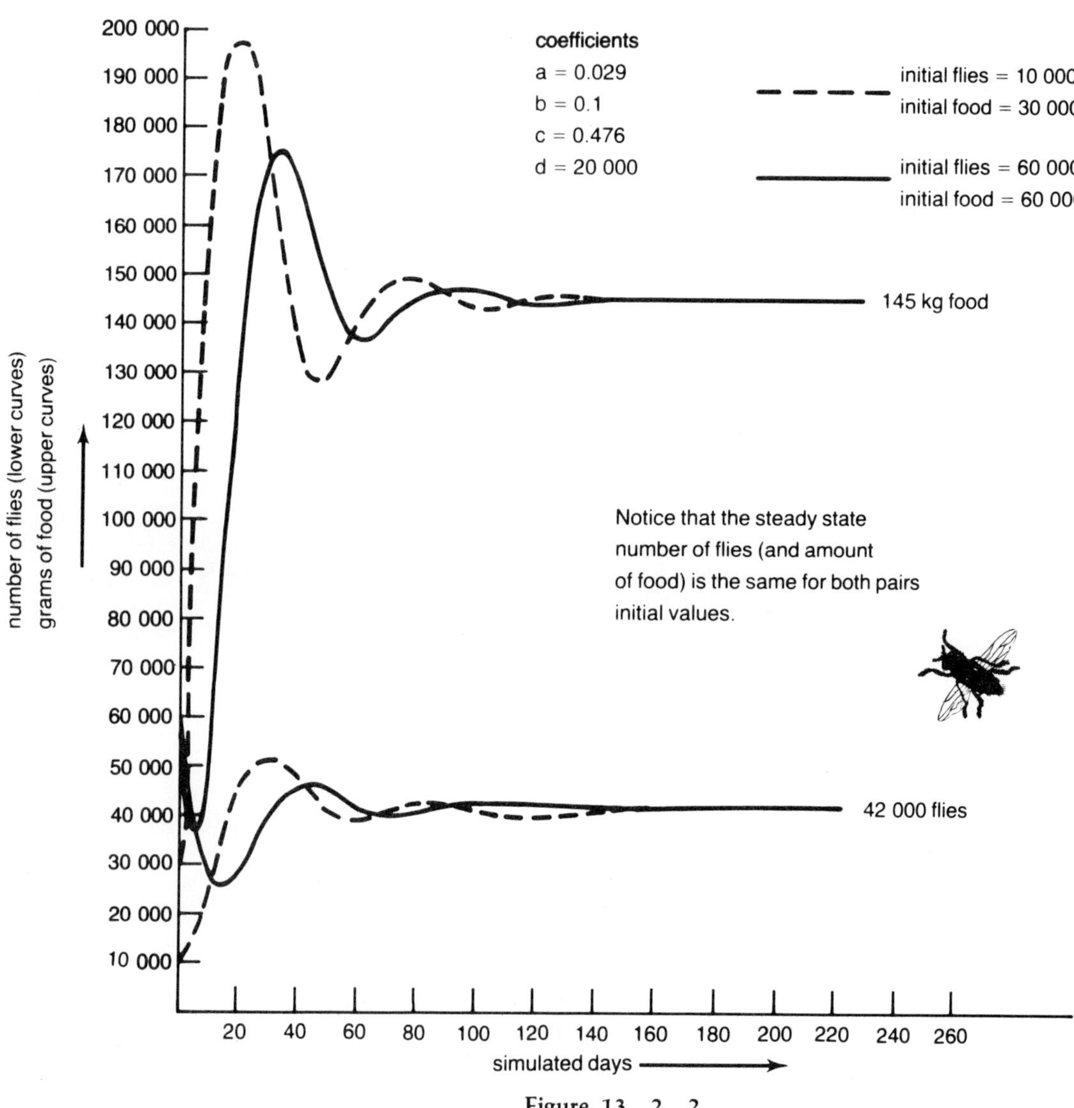

Figure 13 2 2

Of course, being scientists, we knew we weren't done with our basic model just yet—we had to make sure that the reasonable predictions we were getting weren't caused simply by a fortuitous choice of parameters. We felt that the values we'd chosen for the constants were reasonable, but if we were (say) 10% off in a parameter, would that radically change the model's behavior? Our spirits were bolstered further after we found that small changes in *a* and *b* had only slight effects on the projected number of flies. Perturbations (slight changes) to *c* and *d* had more substantial effects on the projected number of flies, but not enough to worry about. As I recall, a 10% change in *c* or *d* had a corresponding 8 or 9% change in the fly population. Of course, had any minor parameter changes had a marked effect, we would have been suspicious of the model, and would at least have had to devote substantial amounts of time in an effort to determine that a parameter as accurately as possible.

I sent a letter to El Presidente, informing him our initial investigations had gone exceptionally well, and that we were ready to begin evaluating alternative methods of controlling the flies.

EXERCISES 13 2

1 The researchers determined the coefficient *b* first. That seems reasonable, since according to their model, the only thing that causes flies to die is old age—no other factors or terms enter in. As the program stands, was it necessary for them to set *a*, *c*, and *d* to zero to study the *b* term in isolation?

2 The researchers determined that the average adult fly has 6.5 days to live. They reasoned that in a large constant population of flies, some had just been born, so would have 13 days to live; an equal number had been born yesterday, so would have 12 days to live; an equal number had been born two days ago, so would have 11 days to live; and so on. Verify that for a population of 1400 flies, the average time left to live is 6.5 days.

3 Figure 13 2 2 shows that for two different sets of initial values (initial flies = 10,000, initial food = 30,000; and initial flies = 60,000, initial food = 60,000), after a while the predicted number of flies and the predicted amount of food is the same. That's true for a very wide range of initial values. Is it true for *every* set of initial values?

4 By running the model with the coefficients used by the researchers, but varying *a* by 10% plus and minus, estimate the dependence of the model's predictions on the exact value of *a*. Should the researchers have spent time getting a more exact value for *a*?

Section 13 3

Using the Model

Sr. Bernal's letter continues:

Now that we had developed a basic model, our work entered a new phase. In this phase we wanted to hypothesize a variety of control methods, express each in turn in BASIC, and explore the effects on the simulated fly population.

It seemed clear to us that the only reasonable long-range way to keep the flies under control would be to cut down on the food supply through improved sanitation. Perhaps the government would want to pay for periodic waste removal. In that case we needed to know how often the village would need to be cleaned to keep the flies under control. Or, possibly, the government would be willing to provide airtight refuse containers, coupled with an advertising campaign to convince the villagers to be more careful with refuse. In that case we needed to know how much the inhabitants would have to do—would they have to run around cleaning up after every dog in town, or would putting kitchen wastes in the imagined containers be enough?

In either situation the control mechanism would work by altering our term *d*, "today's new food." To simulate our second scenario, we needed only to cut down *d*. We picked cutting the fly population to about 10,000 as a goal, and adjusted *d* until the simulation met that goal. We found that *d* could be no larger than 5000 grams a day. That is, the inhabitants (and dogs, cats, and goats) would have to cut down from producing 20,000/400 = 50 grams of fly food a day to under 12.5 grams each. According to our field crew, that seemed possible, if people would learn to put waste matter in

sealed containers. In fact, they thought that even if the dogs, cats, and goats continued their current waste removal practices (none), the goal could be reached, since the worst problem seemed to be kitchen refuse.

Blissfully ignorant of what was to come, we then turned to the "periodic cleanup" scenario. We hypothesized that a squad of Federales could reasonably be expected to be able to collect 80% of the refuse in town every few weeks. But when we made the necessary alterations to the model, we found that doing so didn't help the fly situation at all!

We added these lines to implement periodic cleanups.

```
211         PRINT "CLEANUP HOW OFTEN";
212         INPUT CO

1570 REM        IF TIME FOR CLEANUP, REMOVE 80% OF FOOD.
1580            IF INT(DO/CO)<>DO/CO THEN 1600
1590              PRINT "CLEANUP..."
1595              LET F1 = INT(.2*F1)
```

skip the cleanup unless CO goes into DO an even number of times

It seemed clear what the reason was: Cleaning up the refuse caused flies to die off. But when the flies died off, food continued to build up until there was so much food lying around that the fly population zoomed up again (Figure 13 3 1). We tried having the soldiers remove *all* of the food every so often (a feat which, no doubt, would be impossible in practice), and even that didn't help. It appeared that the refuse would have to be cleaned up too often to be practical. It only made sense to have the inhabitants of the village cut down on the amount of wasted matter that was strewn about.

We wrote a nicely phrased report recommending the airtight garbage container and advertisement campaign approach, and sent it to our superiors in the government. We felt pleased with our work.

The government was furious when they read our report. "Fools!" they said. "We'll be the laughing stock of the world! All modern countries use insecticide sprays to control flies! Rewrite your report."

We slouched around the laboratory for a few days, wondering how we could have forgotten about spraying. Fortunately, it wouldn't require much work to simulate spraying. In fact, the changes to our program were almost exactly the same as those required to simulate the cleanup. Every so often, the number of flies would be reduced by 80%.

We made these changes:

```
211         PRINT "SPRAY HOW OFTEN";
212         INPUT SO

1570 REM        IF TIME TO SPRAY, REMOVE 80% OF FLIES.
1580            IF INT(DO/SO)<>DO/SO THEN 1600
1590              PRINT "SPRAY..."
1595              LET FO = INT(.2*FO)
```

compare to the "cleanup" version

We found that spraying once every two weeks was ineffective (see Figure 13 3 2). The problem was that killing 80% of the flies allowed the amount of food to build up, which led to a rapid increase in flies.

Spraying once a week actually did reduce the fly population, but the amount of food that built up was so huge that if the spraying was skipped for a week, there would

coefficients
a = 0.029
b = 0.1
c = 0.476
d = 20 000

clean up once
every two weeks

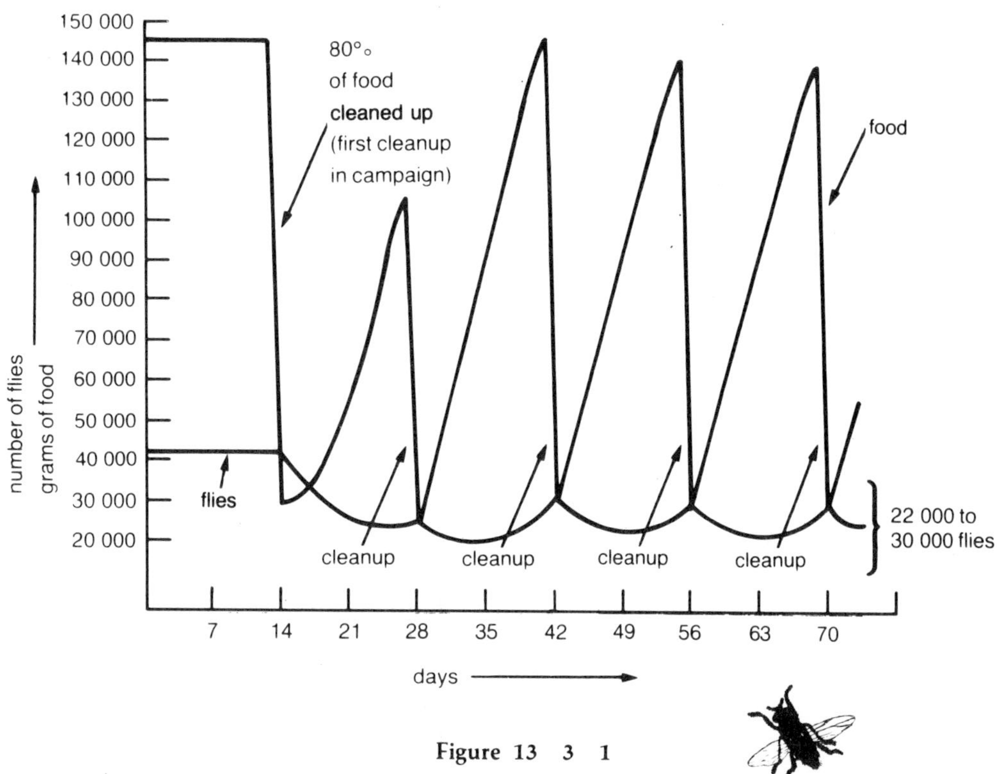

Figure 13 3 1

be an enormous explosion in the fly population. Besides, all the rotting matter would pose a serious health hazard (see Figure 13 3 3).

We rewrote our report, adding our predictions about the effects of spraying, and, as carefully as possible, noting that the build-up of waste matter was of serious concern. We still felt that the best way to control the flies was to control the amount of garbage lying around.

I had the unfortunate task of presenting our new report to our superior. I sat nervously in an uncomfortable chair in front of his huge gleaming wooden desk. After he finished the last page, which included our warning about waste build-up, he stared at me in silence for almost a minute, his face getting redder and redder. I started squirming, wondering what the matter was. At last he broke his silence.

"Idiot!" he began. "If you ever went out of your stinking laboratory, you would know what the youngest peasant knows, that manure *rots!* The Colonel bought the spray machines a month ago. All we lack is the television cameras to cover the ceremonies. And you can't even write a decent report! Here we are, doing a great service to the people. . . and you want to make us look like fools. Out of my sight!"

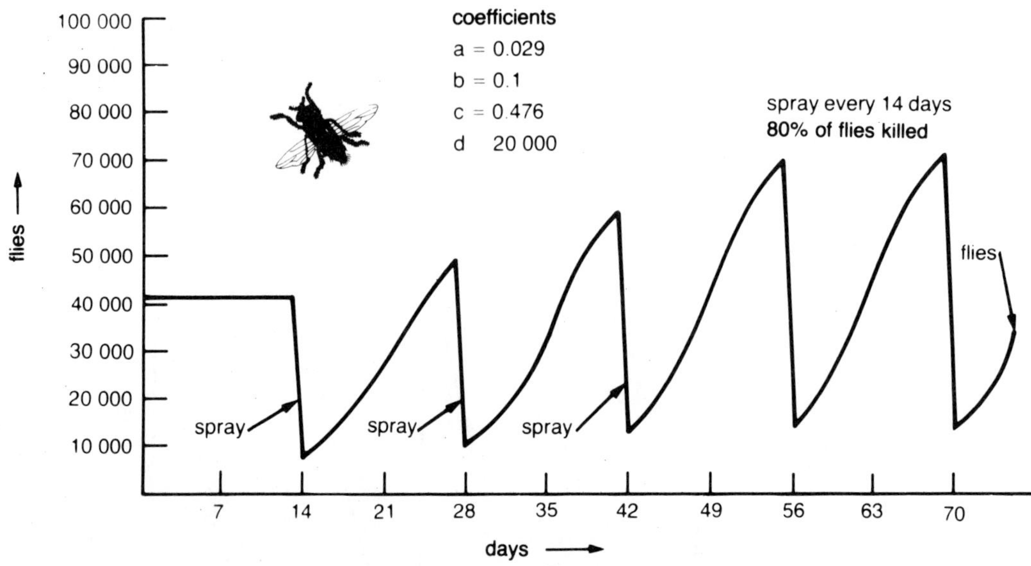

Figure 13 3 2a Flies only — see Figure 13 3 2b for food

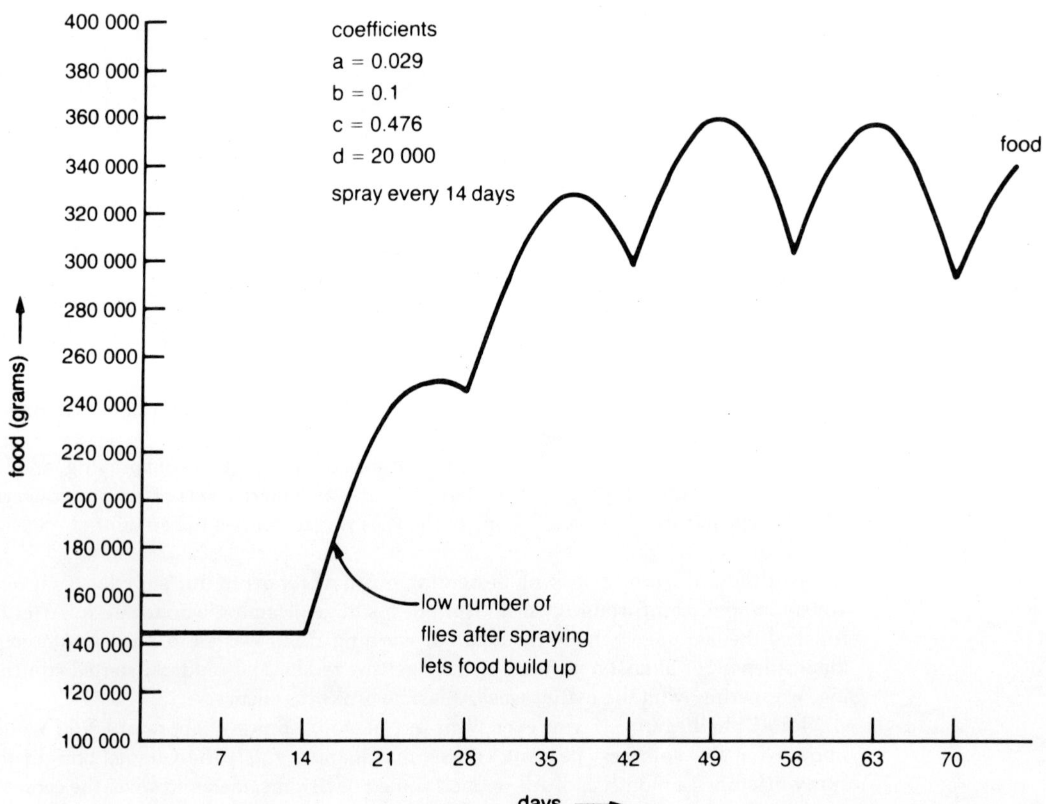

Figure 13 3 2b Food

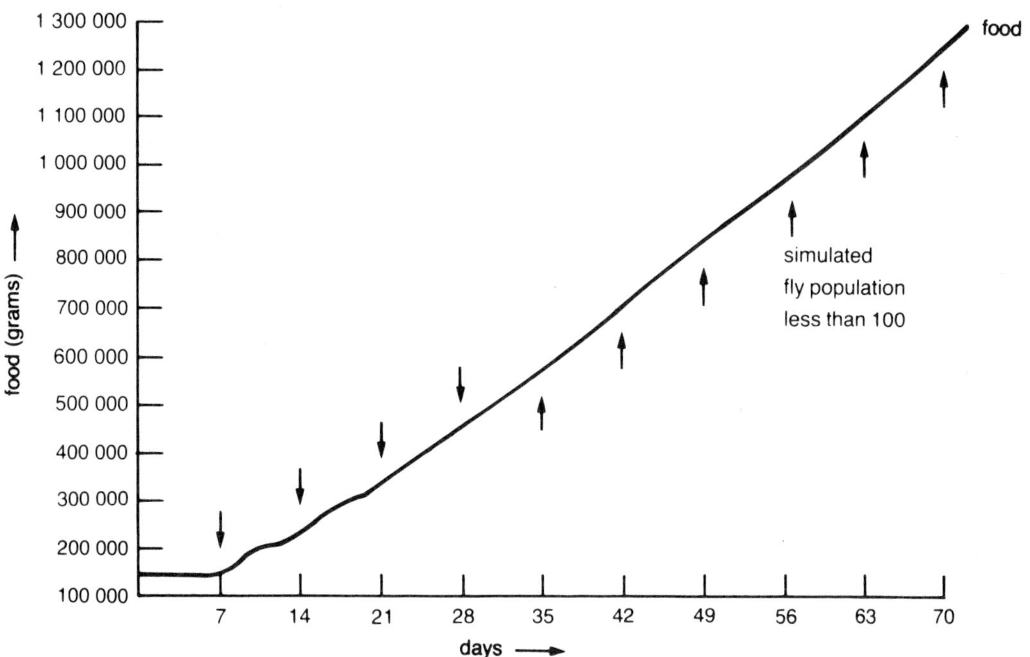

Figure 13 3 3 Food keeps building up when 80% of the flies are killed each week

EXERCISES 13 3

1 Match the phrase on the left with the expression on the right. Refer to the most recent form of the simulation program, including the cleanup and spraying additions.

A	the greatest amount of food that can be eaten today, no matter how many flies there are	a	F1
		b	FO
B	the number of flies	c	F2
C	the proportion of flies in the larva stage	d	10
D	the frequency of cleanups	e	A*FO*F1
		f	CO
		g	Not represented in the model

2 Match the phrase on the left with the expression on the right. Refer to the most recent form of the simulation program, including the cleanup and spraying additions.

A	today's deaths	a	F1
B	today's new food	b	FO
C	the amount of food	c	D
D	the frequency of spraying	d	SO
E	the number of drinks the field team bought at the catina	e	B*FO
		f	B*F1
		g	Not represented in the model

3 What would you do to simulate cleaning 90% of the waste from the village once every three weeks?

4 Change the program as per exercise 3. Simulate cleaning up once every three weeks, and plot the predictions on graph paper. Do the changes seem to make matters better or worse? Why do you think that is?

Section 13 4

Predict/Test/Refine/Predict/Test/Refine/...

Sr. Bernal's letter concludes:

Since all other progressive countries had scientific teams in their villages, we were allowed to go along to observe the fly-spraying program. We were sternly warned not to say anything, however.

The Federales sprayed the village amid much fanfare. Of course, there were many dead flies lying around for the TV cameras to hover over. The ceremonies finished, everyone from the government packed up and left. We stayed behind to compare what actually happened with the predictions we'd generated with our model.

After a week, a noticeable number of flies were around, and after two weeks, there were as many, if not more, flies as there had been before the spraying. The village leaders called the Federales, asking them to spray again. Hoping to get back in the good graces of the government, we pointed out that our report has said that weekly spraying would be necessary.

With surprisingly few grumbles, the Federales set up a weekly spraying program. For a while, things seemed to be going well. The fly population varied roughly in agreement with our model. But unlike in our model, the "food" supply didn't grow all that fast—some did decompose just as our superior back in Santa Cerveza had said, plus an intriguing variety of worms, sow bugs, dung beetles, and other creatures broke it down. We decided that our model needed another term to account for the natural decline in food supply due to these factors.

We were calmly discussing alternative ways of modeling the food decay when we noticed an argument outside the cantina. The sergeant in charge of the spraying program was yelling at one of the Federales who did the spraying. An ancient Indian woman was yelling at the sergeant. A young woman with one baby on her back and another in the crook of her arm was yelling at the old woman. And the soldier was shrugging his shoulders at the same time he shook his open hands back and forth. Through the din, we heard the word "moscos" ("flies"), so we walked over to see what was going on.

It took a while to figure out what was being said by whom, but I think it was something like this. The old woman was yelling at the sergeant, complaining that the spray had killed all the spiders in her house. The spiders used to catch flies, and now her house was full of flies. The young woman was telling her grandmother (the old woman) to stop causing trouble and come home. The sergeant was accusing the soldier of getting lazy and missing too many flies on the weekly sprayings, because the town was getting full of flies again. The soldier was swearing on his mother's honor that the entire village had been thoroughly sprayed. He insisted that the flies were becoming immune to the spray. This, of course, piqued our scientific curiosity. There seemed little hope of interjecting any calm into the four-part yelling contest, so we went back to the cantina and began discussing what data we should try to gather.

By the time the next spraying was due, it was obvious to everyone that something was wrong. There seemed to be more flies in the village than before the spraying began! And when we followed the Federales around and watched the spraying it was clear that they were right—the spray killed only a fraction of the flies. We took some samples of flies in all life stages and went back to our laboratory in Santa Cerveza.

We split up into two groups. One group took our simulation program and played around with the parameters, trying to see if they could find settings that would lead to the behavior we had observed in the village. They reported that the only thing they could imagine was that the flies bred much faster than we'd thought.

The other group studied the flies we'd brought back. But our original data still looked good. It took about 8 days for the flies to go from eggs to adults, and each female laid about 400 eggs in her life. Finally, we tested the insecticide. Most of the flies seemed unaffected by it. How could that be? We sent a field crew out to a different village, one deeper in the jungle, one which had no fly-control program. They returned with a few thousand maggots and eggs. When they turned into adults we tested the spray on them. All but about one percent died. We allowed the survivors to breed, and tested the spray on the adult offspring. Most of them were unaffected!

Now we had an idea of what was happening. Apparently, in the initial population of flies, there was a small percentage of mutants, flies which were immune to the insecticide. Naturally, as the nonmutants were killed off, that left more food for the mutants, and they would be the only ones increasing in population. Eventually, most of the flies in the village would be ones descended from the initial small number of mutants, and the flies in the village would appear to have become immune to the spray.

This required a major alteration of our model. Now we'd need *two* fly populations. As far as we could tell, the only important way the two populations varied was their susceptibility to the spray.

```
10    REM    MUSCA OBSCURA MODEL--TWO TYPES OF FLIES
20    REM    VARIABLES--
30    REM      F0  --BLACK HEADED FLY POPULATION
35    REM      W0  --WHITE HEADED FLY POPULATION
40    REM      F1  --AMOUNT OF FOOD (IN GRAMS)
100          PRINT "A=";
110          INPUT A
120          PRINT "B=";
130          INPUT B
140          PRINT "C=";
150          INPUT C
160          PRINT "D=";
170          INPUT D
180          PRINT "INITIAL NUMBER OF BLACK FLIES=";
190          INPUT F0
191          PRINT "INITIAL NUMBER OF WHITE FLIES=";
```

(continued)

```
192       INPUT W0
200       PRINT "INITIAL AMOUNT OF FOOD=";
210       INPUT F1
211       PRINT "SPRAY HOW OFTEN";
212       INPUT S0
220       PRINT "FOR HOW MANY DAYS SHOULD THE";
230       PRINT " SIMULATION BE RUN";
240       INPUT L

300  REM  PRINT HEADINGS AND INITIAL STATE.
310       PRINT
320       PRINT "*******************************************"
330       PRINT "MUSCA OBSCURA"
340       PRINT TAB(10); "A="; A; TAB(20); "B="; B
350       PRINT TAB(10); "C="; C; TAB(20); "C="; C
360       PRINT
370       PRINT TAB(3); "DAY"; TAB(10); "BLACK";
380       PRINT TAB(20); "WHITE"; TAB(30); "FOOD (GRAMS)"
390       PRINT "----------------------------";
395       PRINT TAB(30); "------------"
400       PRINT TAB(3); 0 ;TAB(10); F0; TAB(20); W0;
410       PRINT TAB(30); F1
1000 REM  CARRY OUT THE SIMULATION FOR  L  DAYS.
1010      FOR D0=1 TO L
1020 REM      COMPUTE FOOD PER FLY
1030          LET F2 = F1/(F0 + W0)
1040          IF F2<=10 THEN 1060
1050            LET F2 = 10
1060 REM      T0 GIVES TODAY'S NEW ADULTS
1070          LET T0 = A*F2*F0
1080 REM      WHITE FLIES BREED SIMILARLY
1090          LET T1 = A*F2*W0
1200 REM      T3  GIVES FOOD EATEN TODAY
1210          LET T3 = C*(F0 + W0)
1220          IF T3<F1 THEN 1250
1230 REM        CAN'T EAT MORE THAN IS THERE!
1240            LET T3 = F1
1250 REM
1500          LET F0 = F0 + T0      - B*F0
1520 REM      WHITE FLIES BREED AND DIE WITH THE SAME
1525 REM        CONSTANTS (A, B, C, AND D) AS BLACK FLIES.
1530          LET W0 = W0 + T1  - B*W0
1550          LET F1 = F1 - T3  + D
1570 REM      IF TIME FOR SPRAY, WIPE OUT 80% OF FLIES.
1575 REM      (SPRAY AFFECTS BLACK FLIES ONLY)
1580          IF INT(D0/S0)<>D0/S0 THEN 1600
1590            PRINT "SPRAY..."
1595            LET F0 = INT(.2*F0)
1600 REM      DISPLAY TODAY'S STATE OF AFFAIRS
1610          PRINT TA(3); D0; TAB(10); F0; TAB(20); W0;
1620          PRINT TAB(30); F1
1660      NEXT D0
1700      PRINT
1710      PRINT
9999      END
```

We were excited to see that our refined model's output matched what had happened in the village (see Figure 13 4 1). We decided to try our periodic cleanup and "tight garbage can" schemes with the new model. While the changes were being made to our new model, foolishly, I called our superior to tell him what we'd found.

Thinking back, I see that I should have waited... Or perhaps I should simply have gone back to the village and tried to talk the Federales into something... I don't know, maybe I should have just taken the first flight out of the country. I do know that what I did had unfortunate consequences.

Apparently, no one in the village had told our superior that the flies were back. When I told him of the wondrous success of our new version of the model, he was irate! Why didn't we tell him that spraying wouldn't work in the first place! The government was a laughing stock! They couldn't even spray flies right. I tried to explain that any simulation has to go through a number of cycles of prediction, testing, and refinement, that it wasn't unusual for the first model to be deficient in a number of unforeseen ways. I tried to calm him down, but to no avail.

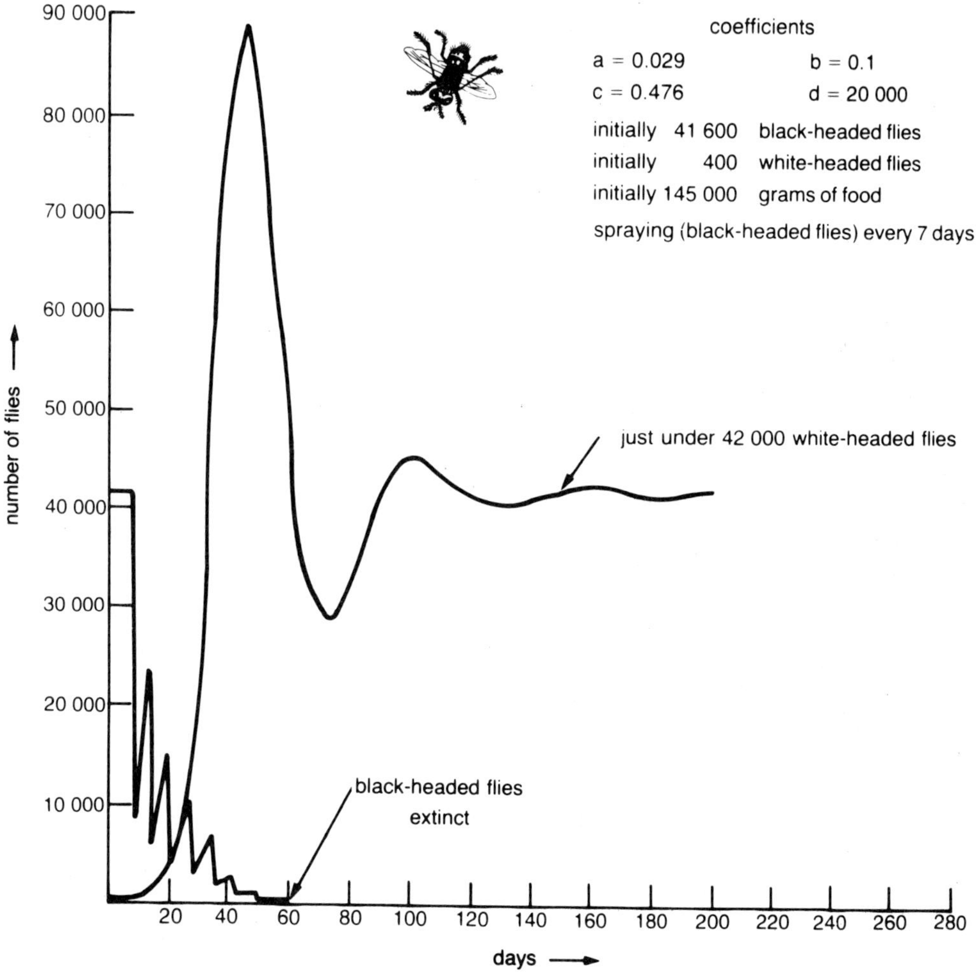

Figure 13 4 1a The black-headed flies are wiped out; the white headed flies prosper

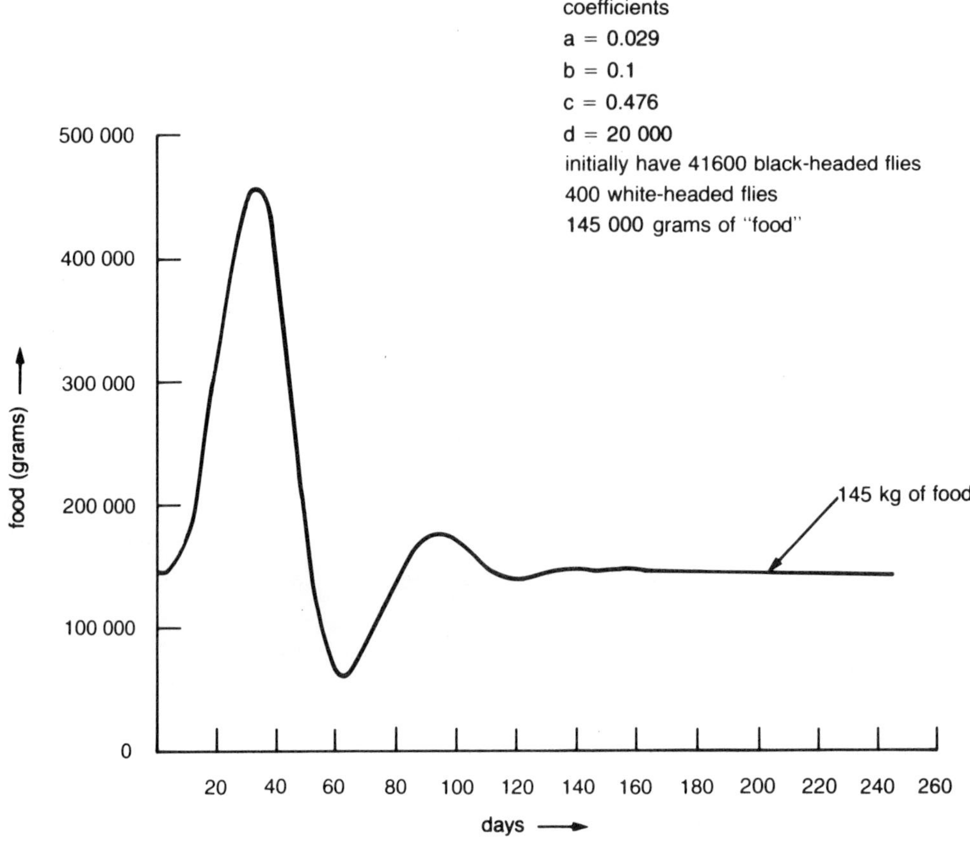

Figure 13 4 1b Food reaches steady state as white-headed fly population stabilizes

I hope this does reach you. Bribing the guards to get paper and to mail this has cost me all my personal effects, so I won't be able to try again. Surely El Presidente will calm down and let us out of here one day. I look forward to returning to the laboratory. I only hope it will be soon.

Yours scientifically,

Ramón Bernal

EXERCISES 13 4

1 Suppose that the "white-headed" flies (the ones that are immune to the spray) breed more slowly than the "normals," so that for the white-headed flies, the constant a is lower. How would you change the program to implement different a's for the two types of flies?

2 Which of these changes would correspond to modeling the decay of the food supply (due to rot, bugs, worms, and all other causes except flies) by 5% a day?

(a) change line 1550 to

```
1550          LET F1 = F1 - T3
```

(b) change line 1210 to

```
1210          LET T3 = C*(F0 + W0)*0.95
```

(c) change line 1550 to

```
1550          LET F1 = F1 - T3 - 0.05*F1 + D
```

and add these lines

```
1551          IF F1<0 THEN 1560
1552            LET F1 = 0
```

(d) change line 1550 to

```
1550          LET F1 = F1 - T3 + D + 0.05*F1
```

PROBLEMS 13

> **Bunnies:** Each adult female has an average of 6 litters a year. Each litter contains an average of 6 babies. A female rabbit is ready to become a mother at age 6 months. Rabbits live to be 7 years old.
>
> Famous rabbits: Peter, Bugs, Br'er, and Welsh.

1 Simulate the growth and prosperity of the family of Adam and Eve Rabbit. Your program should first ask

```
HOW MANY BUNNIES?
```

Then have it use the formula below to simulate the rabbit population from month to month. Keep the simulation going until the desired number of bunnies is met or surpassed. Then print the time (number of months) required to produce that number of bunnies from the original pair

$$\text{bunnies}_{\text{next month}} = \text{bunnies}_{\text{this month}} *(1 + 1.5)$$

average number of baby bunnies per month per adult

This simulation contains a number of simplifying assumptions: All bunnies live forever; there's no limit to the food supply; there are no enemies; and babies are treated as adults right away.

2 The rabbit simulation in problem 1 gives exaggerated results. Bunnies do multiply rapidly, but not *that* fast.

Add more realism to the bunny simulator by taking into account the time it takes before a baby rabbit can have bunnies of her own. Formulas are given below. Before you use the formulas (assignment statements) to write your program, work through some examples by hand to make sure you understand how they keep track of the number of 1-month-old babies, 2-month-old babies, . . . , and turn 5-month-old babies this month in $\text{adults}_{\text{next month}}$.

$\text{babies1} = \text{adults}_{\text{this month}} * 1.5$

babies2 = babies1

babies3 = babies2

babies4 = babies3

babies5 = babies4

$\text{adults}_{\text{next month}} = \text{adults}_{\text{this month}} + \text{babies5}$

> The **escape velocity** is the speed at which a small object (say, a spacecraft) must move away from the surface of a massive object (say, the moon) in order to be able to escape the gravitational pull of the massive object. If a spacecraft attempts to leave a planet at a speed less than the escape velocity, it won't make it.
>
> The escape velocity is given by the expression
>
> $$v_{\text{escape}} = \sqrt{\frac{2*G*M}{R}}$$
>
> where M is the mass of the object being escaped from, R is its radius, and G is the **gravitational constant.** As the mass increases and the radius decreases, the escape velocity increases. A **black hole** is an astronomical object for which the escape velocity exceeds the speed of light. By doing the next two problems, you'll be able to discover how incredibly dense black holes must be.

3 Write a program which asks the user for a radius (in meters) and which tells how much a black hole with that radius would weigh. This is given by

$$\text{M (in kilograms)} = \frac{c^2*R}{2*G}$$

> c (the speed of light) is 3×10^8 meters per second
> G (the gravitational constant) is 6.673×10^{-11}

> A black hole the size of a marble (radius = one centimeter) would have to weigh at least 6.7×10^{24} kilograms.

4 Write a program which asks the user for a mass (weight) in kilograms and tells how large a black hole with that mass could be.
This given by

$$\text{R (in meters)} = \frac{2*G*M}{c^2}$$

> The mass of the earth is 5.983×10^{24} kilograms.
> The mass of the sun is 1.97×10^{30} kilograms.

5 Simulate flipping a fair coin. If RND gives a value less than 0.5, print T (tails); otherwise, print H (heads). After a user-selected number of tosses, have the program

print the total number of heads, the total number of tails, the number of tosses, and the percentage of heads and tails.

6 Randomness is a tricky thing. In a short run of trials, it can be extremely hard to tell a fair coin from a biased one. Design a program which flips two coins, one fair (like the one in problem 5) and one biased. To simulate the biased coin, print T if RND gives a value less than 0.45, and print H otherwise.

It won't be much fun to watch your program flip the coins if you know which one is fair. Have your **program** flip the fair coin to decide whether all the fair coin tosses will be printed to the left and all the biased coin tosses to the right, or vice versa. When your program starts, it should ask the user how many tosses to do. After it's done that many, have it ask the user to guess which coin was the fair one. Print an appropriate message depending on whether the guess was right.

```
HOW MANY FLIPS? 6

T     H
T     T
T     H
H     H
T     H
T     T

WHICH ONE WAS THE FAIR COIN (LEFT OR RIGHT)? RIGHT

YOU'RE RIGHT!
```

7 Write a program which simulates fleas on a dog. Perform the simulation for several different values of the parameters and see what happens (for some values, the fleas die out; for some they overwhelm the poor dog; for some they reach an uncomfortable compromise with the dog). For each set of parameter values, print out the flea population each minute for a total of 60 simulated minutes.

variable	*meaning*	*typical value*
fleas	The total number of fleas on the dog this minute.	50
scratch	The number of scratches the dog makes this minute.	10
scr rate	The number of scratches the dog makes per minute per flea.	.1
tired	The maximum number of scratches the dog can make each minute.	20
new fleas	The fraction of flies born or hopping on the dog each minute.	.2
dead fleas	The fraction of fleas which die or jump off the dog each minute.	.1

Equations:

scratch = (*scr rate***fleas*) or *tired* (whichever is less)

$fleas_{\text{next minute}} = fleas + new\ fleas*fleas - dead\ fleas*fleas - scratch$

8 Alter the final, two-types-of-fly program to simulate periodic cleanup of waste matter in the village (as in Section 13 3). Then simulate reducing the amount of waste made available each day. Compare the results of these two control methods to the predicted results of spraying (Figure 13 4 1a). According to the simulations, were the researchers right when they thought that the best fly-control method would be to reduce the amount of waste lying around the village (the air-tight-garbage-can method)?

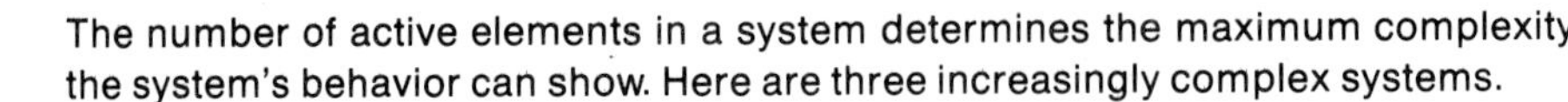

9 The number of active elements in a system determines the maximum complexity the system's behavior can show. Here are three increasingly complex systems.

System 1: $x_{next\ time} = a$

System 2: $x_{next\ time} = b^* x_{this\ time} + c$

System 3: $x_{next\ time} = d^* x_{this\ time} + e^* y_{this\ time} + f$

$y_{next\ time} = g^* x_{this\ time} + h^* y_{this\ time} + i$

> **system:** anything we tend to view as a whole (as a "thing"), but which we understand to have subparts.

System 3 is capable of doing anything that System 1 is capable of. That is, if you choose the constants *d, e, f, g, h,* and *i* properly, you can create a version of System 3 which does exactly what System 1 does, no more and no less. (Of course, those values would be $d = 0, e = 0, f = a, g = 0, h = 0$, and $i = 0$.) Similarly, System 2 can do anything System 1 can do, and System 3 can do anything System 2 can do. But, of course, System 2 can do more than System 1, and System 3 can do more still. Figure 13 P 1 shows a number of system behaviors. Each graph represents a plot of the successive values taken by $x_{this\ time}$ as time goes by. Some of the system behaviors can be done by all three Systems, some only by Systems 2 or 3, and some only by System 3. And one of the behaviors can't be done by any of the three systems.

> *a, b, . . ., i* represent constants. Fixing the value of the constants in System 1, 2, or 3 determines a **particular system.**
>
> $x_{next\ time} = a$
>
> describes a whole range of particular systems.
>
> $x_{next\ time} = 1$
>
> is one of them.
>
> (It's also a particularly *boring* system, but that's another matter.)

Write a program and use it to determine which of the behaviors shown in Figure 13 P 1 can be done by which of the three systems. Your program should first ask, "Which system?" Then it should ask for values for the constants needed for the chosen system. Then it should ask for the value that $x_{this\ time}$ (and, in the case of System 3, $y_{this\ time}$) should begin with. Finally, it should print the value of $x_{this\ time}$ for a user-selected number of time steps. By running the program and giving different values to the constants, discover which behaviors can be done by which systems. Each time you start working on a different behavior, start by seeing if you can get System 1 to do it. If you can, there's no need to test Systems 2 and 3—you know they can do it. Note: The constants *a, b,. . ., i* may be any legal BASIC number, including negative ones.

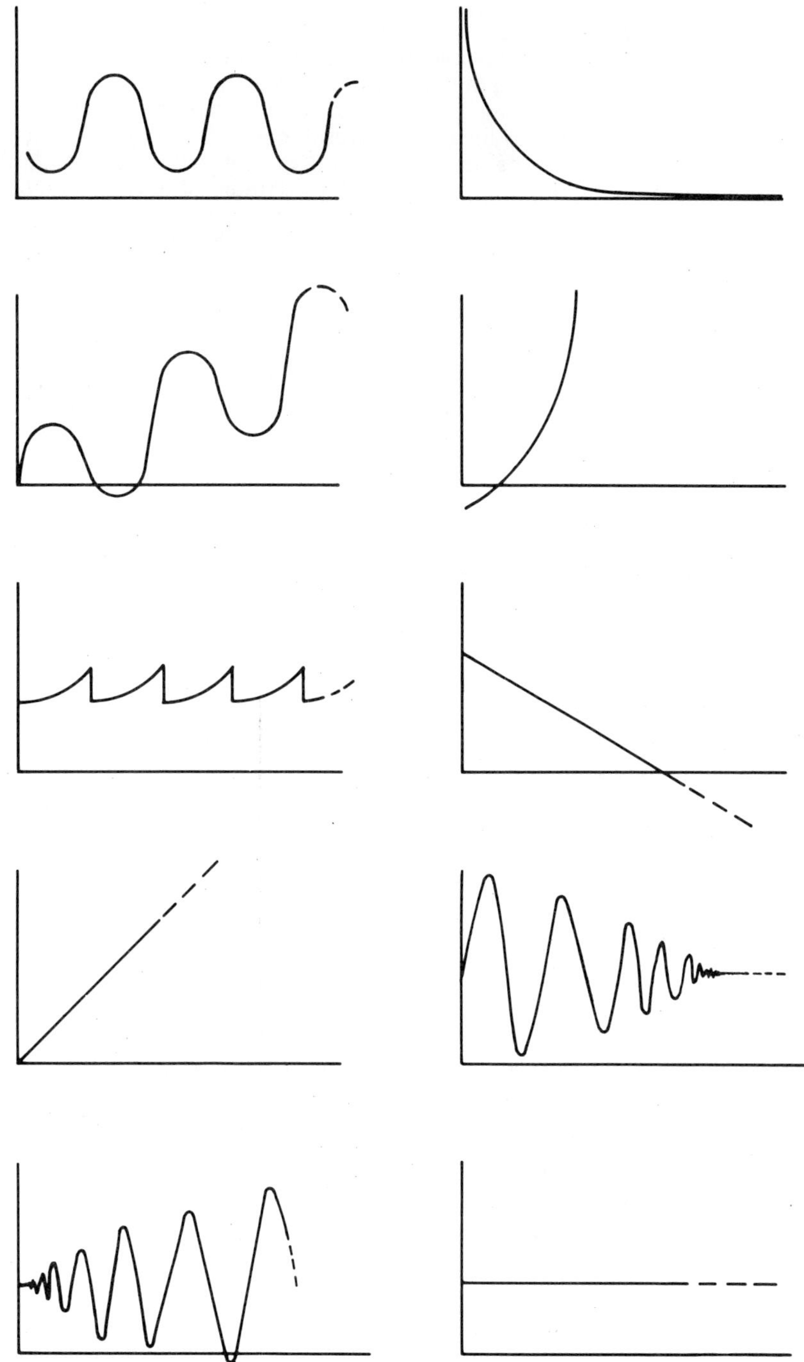

Figure 13 P 1 Some system behaviors. In every case the horizontal axis represents time, the vertical axis represents the value of $x_{\text{this time}}$, and the curves show the shape obtained by drawing a line between successive points produced by the program described in problem 9.

10 Don't get the idea that simulations like the one we covered in this chapter provide easy, accurate, guaranteed solutions to every situation in the world. Besides the fact that a simulation might not contain all of the important factors, there are other treacheries lurking in the method. One of the trickiest is understanding the effect of changing the time scale of your simulation. Look at the formula we provided in problem 1. We estimated the growth constant 1.5 by reasoning that each pair of bunnies produces an average of 6*6 = 36 babies a year. Dividing that by the number of months in a year and the number of bunnies in a pair gave 1.5 as the average number of new bunnies per existing bunny per month.

Now suppose we use the same logic to estimate the growth factor when the basic time step is 3 months instead of 1 month. We'd get 36/(2*4)=4.5, so our formula would be

$$\text{bunnies}_{\text{next season}} = \text{bunnies}_{\text{this season}} *(1 + 4.5)$$

So far, so good. However, the two formulas don't give the same prediction for the total number of rabbits at the end of one year!

Write a program and run it to show this effect. Plot the number of bunnies predicted per time unit by each method. Instead of drawing a smooth curve through the points, draw straight lines from point to point. Can you see what's going on? It's exactly the same situation as this: If you have money in the bank earning compound interest at a yearly rate of 5%, if the interest is compounded each week instead of each month, you'll have more money at the end of the year.

No completely general solution to this problem is known; that is, there's no general way to adjust the growth factors to take into account shifts of time scale. That means when you're creating a simulation, you must take great care to choose a time unit which is natural for the real-world system you're modeling. And you must take great care to compare your results against real data. And you should be on the lookout for effects caused solely by your choice of time step.

The classical **prey-predator equations** have this form

$$\text{prey}_{\text{tomorrow}} = \text{prey}_{\text{today}} * (1 + a) - c*\text{prey}_{\text{today}} *\text{predator}_{\text{today}}$$

$$\text{predator}_{\text{tomorrow}} = \text{predator}_{\text{today}} *(1 - b) + d*\text{prey}_{\text{today}} * \text{predator}_{\text{today}}$$

where

- a is the rate at which the prey increase in isolation
- b is the rate at which predators decrease with no prey to eat
- c is the rate at which predators eat the prey
- d is the rate at which predators increase due to eating prey

and we add the restriction that the number of prey or predators can't be less than zero.

Choose one of the situations given in problems 11 through 13 and, in that context, do the following:

- Design and write a program which uses the prey-predator equations to simulate the situation.
- Choose a variety of initial numbers of prey and predators.
- For each run of your program, draw a graph of the two populations over time.
- Make small changes in the four parameters to see what effect that has on the general shapes of the graphs.
- Find settings of the parameters which lead to extinction of both the prey and the predators.

- Find a setting of the constants that leads to extinction of only the predators. What happens to the prey population in that case?
- Explore ways of controlling the two populations. Is it ever possible to limit the number of predators by removing some of the prey? Vice versa?
- Discuss your results. Think about factors which affect the system in real life but which aren't considered in your simulation.

11 Prey = rabbits, predators = wolves. Rabbits eat grass (which is in such bountiful supply that it needn't enter into the simulation) and multiply rapidly in isolation. Wolves eat rabbits and increase in numbers the more rabbits they eat. The wolves have no other source of food, so in the absence of rabbits, the wolves die off.

Time step in the simulation: one month

Constants to try: $a = 0.1$ $c = 0.0001$
$b = 0.05$ $d = 0.000001$

12 Prey = deer, Predators = wolves, added complexity = hunters. The deer have plenty of food (bushes, young tree branches, vegetables from people's gardens, . . .). Deer reproduce at a rate of 1 to 2 babies per mother per year. Wolves eat the deer (no rabbits or other food in this godforsaken wilderness), and it doesn't take very many deer to allow the wolves to increase in numbers. However, if in any month there is at least one wolf per ten deer, the local hunters become irate and kill half the wolves.

Time step: one month
Constants: $a = 0.08$ $c = 0.00005$
$b = 0.05$ $d = 0.00001$

13 Prey = radio listeners, predators = radio commercials. Radio station XERB, which broadcasts in Mexico from just across the California border, has an incredibly powerful transmitter and can potentially be heard by some 30 million people. The number of listeners increases rapidly when there are no ads. If a company buys an ad on XERB, the ad brings in more business increasing the company's ability and desire to buy more ads. But the more ads there are, the more listeners the station loses. A classical prey-predator situation!

Time step: one week
Constants: $a = 0.025$ $c = 0.00005$
$b = 0.1$ $d = 5 \times 10^{-9}$

Chapter 14 **Putting Things in Order**

Section 14 1
A Sorting Algorithm

Historically, the one job computers have been used the most for is this: Given an array of data, rearrange the data items so they are in order. This task is called **sorting** an array. It occurs everywhere computers are used. Businesses need to sort data to produce reports. The telephone company needs to sort data to produce telephone directories. Universities need to sort data to produce class lists, grade reports, and class time schedules. Psychologists do sorting to rank order their data. Even the BASIC system you're using has to put data in order — the statements you enter are kept in order by line number.

Because sorting is of such tremendous practical value, it has been studied by many people, and there are lots of solutions to the problem. Some are better than others. In this section we'll develop a method which is easy to understand and which results in a very short BASIC program. Later in this chapter we'll develop another method which is very widely used because, in most cases, it requires much less computer time.

Figure 14 1 1 shows a typical array of data. How can we put the data in order? One possibility is this: We look through the array, find the smallest value, and put it at the beginning. Now we know that the first position in the array has the proper value. Since the first position has the smallest value in it, we don't need to consider it any more. We look from the second spot in the array through to the end

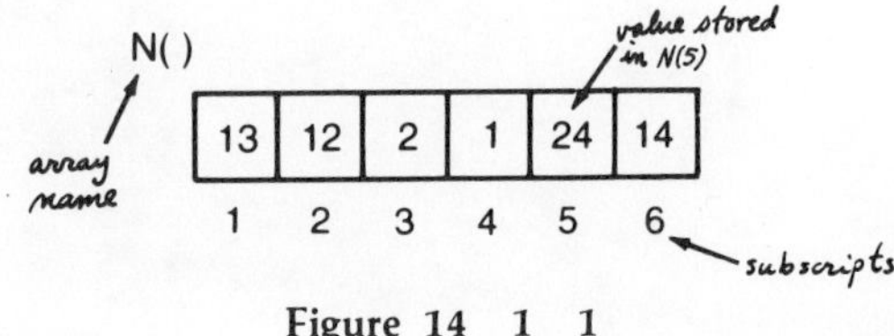

Figure 14 1 1

and find the smallest value. It belongs in the second position (that is, at the beginning of the region we looked through), so we stick it there. Now we know that the first *two* values are right, so we can ignore them from now on. We move on to the third position in the array, find the smallest value from there to the end, and so on until we've gone through the entire array.

There's only one tricky part. When we move a data item into the leftmost position of the region we're working on, what do we do with the value that started out there? Certainly we don't want to lose it! On the other hand, what about the memory cell where we found the smallest item? We don't want to leave a copy of the smallest value there, and we can't leave it empty, so we'll put the value that used to be at the beginning there. Figure 14 1 2 shows an example.

Problem statement: Given an array N( ) of data values, rearrange the data so the items are in increasing order.

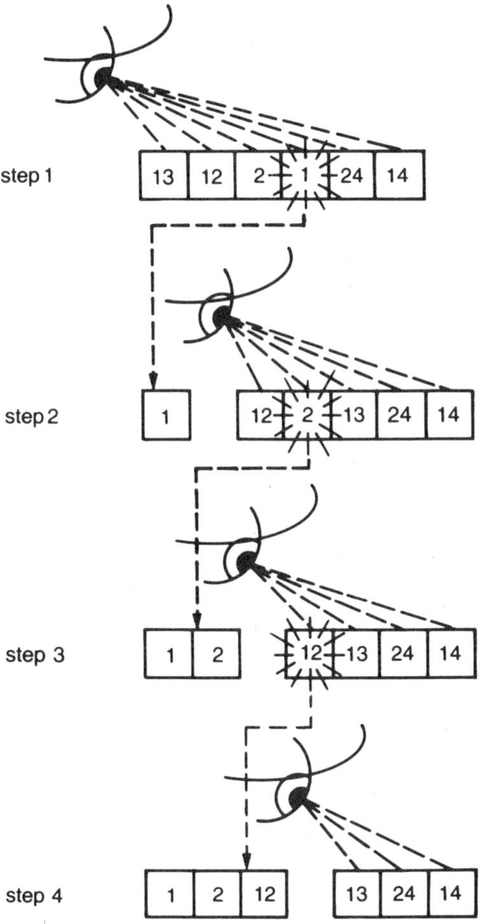

Figure 14 1 2 Our strategy for putting the values in order

Now that we have a rough idea of what we want to do, let's turn it into a plan.

FOR *Left = position 1, 2, . . . TO the end of the array*

Find the position of the smallest value from Left to the end of the array.

Swap the value in position Left with the smallest value.

Let's translate our plan into BASIC. We'll write it as a subroutine, starting in line 7000. We'll assume that a subroutine we'll put at line 7100 performs the subtask of locating the smallest value in the remainder of the array.

```
7000 REM    CLEARSORT
7010        FOR LO=1 TO Z
7020 REM        MAKE N(LO) BE SMALLEST VALUE OF N(LO),...,N(Z)
7030            GOSUB 7100
7040 REM        P  IS POSITION OF SMALLEST VALUE.
7050            LET NO = N(LO)     }
7060            LET N(LO) = N(P)   } notice the use of the
7070            LET N(P) = NO      } "temporary" variable NO here
7080        NEXT LO
7090        RETURN
```

Before going on to plan and code the subproblem, let's go over the main part of the subroutine to make sure everything is OK. Looking back at Figure 14 1 2, and comparing our drawing of what should happen with the plan and BASIC program, everything seems all right. When LO is 1, we find the smallest value in the entire array; what about when LO is Z, though? That means there's only one value to look through to find the smallest. It wouldn't hurt anything to look at one value, but it's a waste of time (see Figure 14 1 3). We might just as well change line 7010 to

```
7010        FOR LO=1 TO Z - 1
```

We're left with the subproblem: "Find the position of the smallest value from Left to the end of the array." But we've done things like that before (see Section 8 4), using a process loop.

—Find position of smallest value—

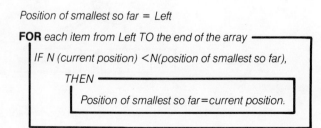

Position of smallest so far = Left

FOR *each item from Left TO the end of the array*

IF N (current position) <N(position of smallest so far),

THEN

Position of smallest so far=current position.

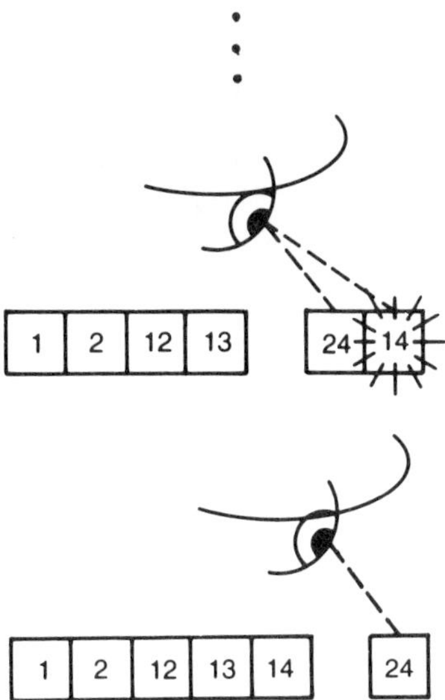

Figure 14 1 3 When there's just one array position left, there's no need to look at it — it has to be in the right place already

Turning the subproblem into BASIC is straightforward. We made these choices for BASIC variables, all of which are used to refer to positions in the array N( ).

name in plan	*BASIC variable used*
Left	L0
end of the array	Z
position of smallest so far	P
current position in the array	L1

```
7100 REM  SUBR--COMPUTE POSITION OF SMALLEST VALUE
7110 REM        IN  N(L0), N(L0+1),...,N(Z)
7120 REM  L0  IS POSITION OF SMALLEST-SO-FAR
7130      LET P = L0
7140      FOR L1=L0 + 1 TO Z
7150          IF N(L1)>=N(P) THEN 7180
7160 REM        HAVE NEW LOW.
7170            LET P = L1
7180      NEXT L1
7190      RETURN
```

Now we have a general-purpose sorting routine, one which we can insert into any program which needs it. The only restrictions on it are that it sorts the values in an array called N( ), and the last position in the array to be sorted is stored in memory cell Z. If you need to sort two different arrays, you'll have to transfer the values to be sorted into N( ) before calling the sorting routine.

Here's a small program we wrote to test this sorting technique, which we refer to as Clearsort.

if you want to test more than 100 numbers, just change this (line 20)

get the values (lines 50–90) · *sort them* (lines 100–110) · *show the result* (lines 120–150)

```
10   REM  TEST CLEARSORT
20        DIM N(100)
30        PRINT "HOW MANY VALUES DO YOU WANT TO SORT";
40        INPUT Z
50        PRINT "PLEASE GIVE ME THE VALUES."
60        FOR I=1 TO Z
70            PRINT "N("; I; ")=";
80            INPUT N(I)
90        NEXT I
100       PRINT "HERE GOES!"
110       GOSUB 7000
120  REM  SHOW SORTED ARRAY.
130       FOR I=1 TO Z
140           PRINT N(I)
150       NEXT I
160       PRINT
170       GO TO 9999

7000 REM  CLEARSORT
7010      FOR L0=1 TO Z - 1
7020 REM      MAKE N(L0) BE SMALLEST VALUE OF N(L0),...,N(Z)
7030          GOSUB 7100
7040 REM      P  IS POSITION OF SMALLEST VALUE.
7050          LET N0 = N(L0)
7060          LET N(L0) = N(P)
7070          LET N(P) = N0
7080      NEXT L0
7090      RETURN
7100 REM  SUBR--COMPUTE POSITION OF SMALLEST VALUE
7110 REM          IN N(L0), N(L0+1), ..., N(Z)
7120 REM  L0 IS POSITION OF SMALLEST-SO-FAR
7130      LET P = L0
7140      FOR L1=L0 + 1 TO Z
7150          IF N(L1)>=N(P) THEN 7180
7160 REM        HAVE NEW LOW.
7170            LET P = L1
7180      NEXT L1
7190      RETURN
9999      END

RUN
HOW MANY VALUES DO YOU WANT TO SORT? 10
PLEASE GIVE ME THE VALUES.
N( 1 )=? -1
N( 2 )=? 16
N( 3 )=? 14
N( 4 )=? -2
N( 5 )=? 11
N( 6 )=? 5
N( 7 )=? 5
N( 8 )=? 5
N( 9 )=? 22
N( 10 )=? 9
```

scrambled

```
HERE GOES!
-2
-1
 5
 5
 5
 9
 11
 14
 16
 22

READY
```

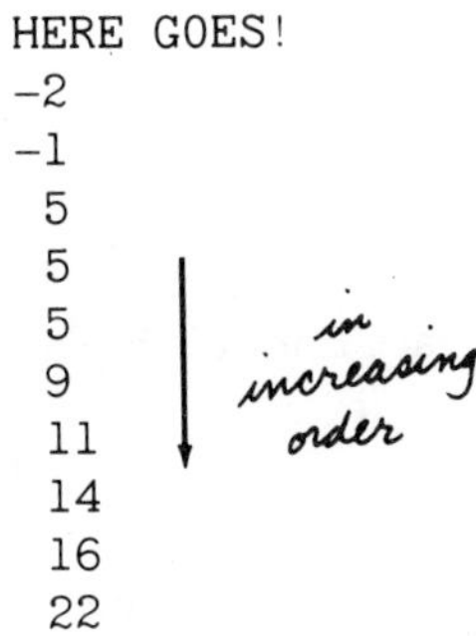

> **Confession**
>
> We made up the name **CLEARSORT** for this sorting method. We think it is the easiest sorting method to understand.
>
> A more widely accepted (and more unwieldly) name for this method is the "Linear Selection with Exchange Sort."
>
> See the problems for descriptions of other sorting methods, including the **bubble sort,** the **distribution sort,** and the **insertion sort.**

EXERCISES 14 1

1 Look at our *plan* for Clearsort. Are we doing too much work? What if the value in position Left is already the smallest value from Left to the end of the array? Then there's no need to swap it with itself, is there?

2 Look at our *plan* for "find the position of the smallest value from Left to the end of the array". Will the plan still work if we start position of smallest so far at the end of the array instead of at position Left?

3 Look at our *program* for "Find the position of the smallest value from Left to the end of the array". Notice that the process loop starts with element L0+1. Why is it OK to skip looking at position L0?

4 How many times will statement 7150 be carried out by our program if we have it sort this array?

1	3	5	4	3	2

Can you think of a formula which tells how many times line 7150 will be carried out, given the length of the array?

5 Look carefully at the "compute position of smallest value from N(L0) through N(Z)" subroutine. What value (what position) does it return if L0 is 1, Z is 7, and N( ) looks like this:

N(1)	N(2)	N(3)	N(4)	N(5)	N(6)	N(7)
4	4	4	4	4	4	4

Section 14 2
Variations

In actual practice, there are two important variations of the sorting process. First, very often it is people's names that must be put in order, not just numbers. That is not easy to do in standard Minimal BASIC, but is very easy to do with a common extension to BASIC (details are given in Chapter 16). In the other variation there are several values stored about each item, and you want to put the items in order of one of the values.

In Chapter 10 we touched on inventory control programs. And in Problem 10 9 we described a realistic one. We stored four pieces of information about each item — the manufacturer code, the specific product code, the quantity on hand, and the retail price. Depending on exactly what you want to know about the stock on hand, you might want a list of each item in order of any one of the four pieces of information. Let's study the case in which we want to put the items in order of the manufacturer code. Figure 14 2 1 shows a sample collection of data. Figure 14 2 2 shows what would happen if we ran our Clearsort routine on array M( ). Obviously we've forgotten something!

Running Clearsort on the array M( ) puts the manufacturer codes in order all right, but it leaves the three other pieces of information alone. Before, M(1), S(1), Q(1), and P(1) all referred to the same item. Now M(1) is the lowest manufacturer code, and has no relationship to S(1), Q(1), and P(1). We've destroyed an important structure that was in the original data.

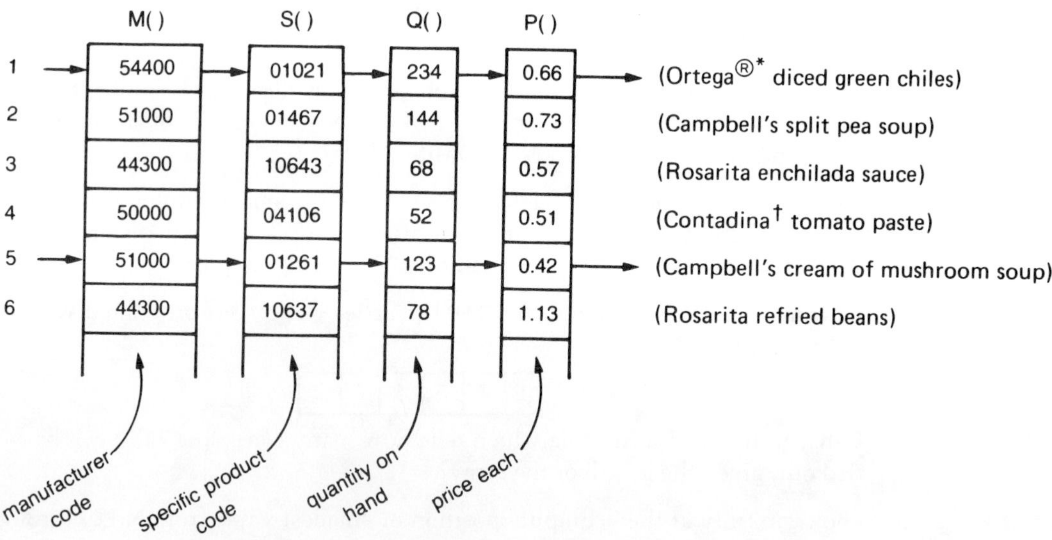

Figure 14 2 1 Some typical inventory data

*Ortega® is a trademark of Heublein, Inc.

†*Contadina* is a registered trademark of Carnation Company.

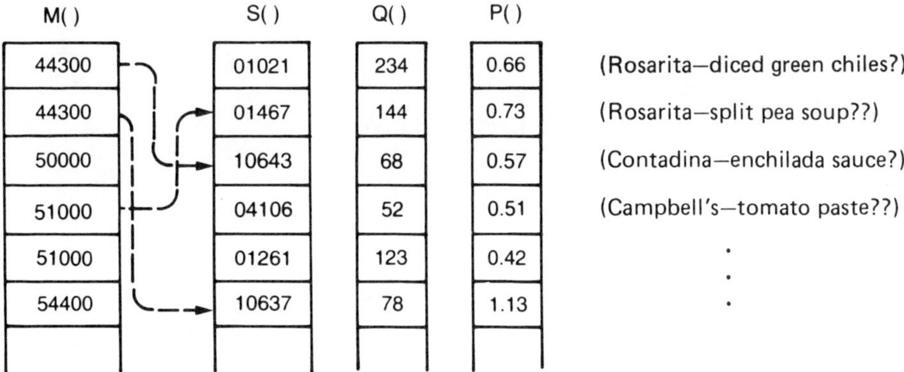

Figure 14 2 2 After running Clearsort on the array M( ). The relationship among the four values about each item has been lost!

How can we sort the items in order of the manufacturer numbers and yet not destroy the relationship among all four arrays? There are two ways. One way involves an auxiliary array, and is covered in Section 15 4. The method we'll use here uses only the data arrays, but involves rearranging all of them (not just the one that determines the order).

What's wrong with Figure 14 2 2? M(1) doesn't go with S(1). M(2) doesn't go with S(2). We can solve the problem with one simple change to Clearsort. Every time Clearsort says to swap two values in M( ) [see lines 7040 through 7070 in the Clearsort subroutine in the previous section], we'll make the same swap in S( ), Q( ), and P( ). That way, we'll keep related information together. If we ensure that the four pieces of information about each item stay together at each step of the Clearsort algorithm, then we can be sure that the related pieces will be together after the entire sorting process. With these changes, Clearsort looks like this:

```
7000 REM  CLEARSORT--MULTIPLE ARRAY VERSION
7010      FOR LO=1 TO Z - 1
7020 REM      MAKE M(LO) BE SMALLEST VALUE OF M(LO),...,M(Z)
7030          GOSUB 7100
7040 REM      PO  IS POSITION OF SMALLEST VALUE.
7050          LET MO = M(LO)
7051          LET M(LO) = M(PO)      } swap M(LO) with M(PO)
7052          LET M(PO) = MO
7053          LET SO = S(LO)
7054          LET S(LO) = S(PO)      } swap S(LO) with S(PO)
7055          LET S(PO) = SO
7056          LET QO = Q(LO)
7057          LET Q(LO) = Q(PO)      } swap Q(LO) with Q(PO)
7058          LET Q(PO) = QO
7059          LET P1 = P(LO)
7060          LET P(LO) = P(PO)      } swap P(LO) with P(PO)
7061          LET P(PO) = P1
7080      NEXT LO                    Notice the changes of
7090      RETURN                     variable names in
                                     this version.
```

(program continued)

```
7100 REM  SUBR--COMPUTE POSITION OF SMALLEST VALUE
7110 REM         IN M(L0), M(L0+1), ..., M(2)
7120 REM  L0 IS POSITION OF SMALLEST-SO-FAR
7130      LET P0 = L0
7140      FOR L1=L0 + 1 TO Z
7150          IF M(L1)>=M(P0) THEN 7180
7160 REM        HAVE NEW LOW.
7170            LET P0 = L1
7180      NEXT L1
7190      RETURN
```

We changed P to P0 because now we have an array called P. In standard Minimal BASIC, you can't have a numeric variable and an array with the same name.

The only change necessary to the subroutine that Clearsort uses to find the position of the smallest value in the part of the array under consideration is to refer to M( ) instead of N( ). Using the revised program, we get the results we wanted.

```
10    REM  TEST CLEARSORT--MULTIPLE ARRAY VERSION
20         DIM M(100), S(100), Q(100), P(100)
30         PRINT "HOW MANY VALUES DO YOU WANT TO SORT";
40         INPUT Z
50         PRINT "PLEASE GIVE ME THE VALUES."
55         PRINT TAB(10); "MANUF.  SPECIFIC QUANT. PRICE"
60         FOR I=1 TO Z
70             PRINT "ENTRY"; I; TAB(10);
80             INPUT M(I), S(I), Q(I), P(I)
90         NEXT I
100        PRINT "HERE GOES!"
110        GOSUB 7000
120   REM  SHOW SORTED ARRAY.
130        FOR I=1 TO Z
140            PRINT M(I); TAB(10); S(I); TAB(20);
145            PRINT Q(I); TAB(30); P(I)
150        NEXT I
160        PRINT
170        GO TO 9999
 .
 .  <-- the modified version of Clearsort goes here
 .
9999        END

RUN
HOW MANY VALUES DO YOU WANT TO SORT? 6
PLEASE GIVE ME THE VALUES.
```

```
                   MANUF.   SPECIFIC  QUANT.   PRICE
ENTRY 1        ? 54400, 01021,      234,      0.66
ENTRY 2        ? 51000, 1467,       144,      0.73
ENTRY 3        ? 44300, 10643       68,       0.57
ENTRY 4        ? 50000, 4106,       52,       0.42
ENTRY 5        ? 51000, 1261,       123,      0.42
ENTRY 6        ? 44300, 10637,      78,       1.13
HERE GOES!
 44300         10643       68          .57
 44300         10637       78         1.13
 50000         4106        52          .42
 51000         1261        123         .42
 51000         1467        144         .73
 54400         1021        234         .66

READY
```

in order of Manufacturer

EXERCISES 14 2

1 Could we have gotten the same result if, instead of doing multiple swaps, we'd used the original version of Clearsort to put M( ) in order, then used it to put S( ) in order, then Q( ), and, finally, P( )?

2 Draw a diagram of the information stored about item number 1 after the first pass through the loop in the main Clearsort routine. That is, what will M(1), S(1), Q(1), and P(1) be? After this point, under what conditions will the values in M(1), S(1), Q(1), and P(1) be changed by the Clearsort routine?

Section 14 3

Two Programs Which Do the Same Thing Can Be Different

> **Warning:**
>
> If you're going through this book on your own, be prepared to spend as much mental effort on this section as you spent on the first three chapters. (It'll be worth it.)

There's more than one way to skin a cat. And there's more than one way to put a bunch of numbers in order. As we mentioned at the start of this chapter, sorting is a much studied, much solved problem. At least a hundred different sorting methods (some, we'll admit, are just tiny variations of others) have been proposed and tested. They all do the same thing — you give them an array of numbers, and they return the array with the numbers in order. But the various methods do differ in some ways. Some take more computer time than others. Some require more memory than others. Some require tremendously complex programming. Some have funny names. Some are **stable,** meaning that two equal values will be left in the same relative order after the sort. Some are appropriate when all the data values fit into memory at once; some are appropriate when the data is on external storage devices. And so on. There are numerous factors to take into account when you're trying to choose the best sorting method for a particular situation.

In this section, to demonstrate how different two programs which do the same thing can be, we'll develop a program for **Quicksort.** Quicksort was first introduced in 1960 by C.A.R. Hoare. It is a method of tremendous practical use. It's an unstable method, appropriate when the data to be sorted as in memory (as opposed to being on disk or tapes). And, in most cases, it is the fastest method. We'll expand on this after we develop the program.

Quicksort is interesting in that the program follows the same philosophy we use in the process of programming: To solve a big problem, break it down (in a reasonable way) into smaller subproblems. Then solve the subproblems using the same "divide and conquer" approach.

How can we break the problem of sorting the values in an array into reasonable subproblems? Here's one way.

Look at the array of values shown in Figure 14 3 1. It has a very interesting property. The value 32 is in position 6 in the array. All the values to the left of position 6 are less than 32, and all the values to the right of position 6 are greater than 32. That tells us something, if we think about it. If *all* the values to the left of the 32 are less than 32, and *none* of the values to the right are less than 32, there's no need to look to the right of the 32 to figure out where the values on the left should go. (Agreed?) No values from the right need be moved to the left of the 32, no values from the left need be moved to the right of the 32, so the 32 will stay right where it is, in position 6, and we can sort the values in positions 1 through 5 as a separate, completely independent subproblem (Figure 14 3 2).

The same thing applies to the values on the right. Since they're all greater than 32, and there are no values greater than 32 anywhere else in the array, they can be put in their final positions by making comparisons among just themselves. That is, sorting the values in positions 7 through 10 is another separate, independent subproblem (Figure 14 3 3).

At this point you may be asking yourself, "So what?" After all, it was just a fluke that the array we chose could be divided that way. Most arrays of data aren't like that. For instance, if we'd been given the data in the order shown in Figure 14 3 4, we couldn't have divided it into neat, independent subproblems.

But if the array isn't in that form to begin with, we can rearrange it until it *is,* and then solve the two subproblems. Not only that, but we can solve the subproblems using the same method. First, rearrange the array until it is **partitioned** (divided) into two independent subproblems, and then solve the subproblems. And that's the idea of the sorting technique called Quicksort.

Perhaps you are wondering, "If we keep dividing the problem up into subproblems, how will we ever get done?" Well, each subproblem is guaranteed to be smaller than the problem it came from. Thus, eventually, we'll get very small subproblems, ones we can solve easily. The easiest subproblem is the one with *no* values left to sort. If the part of the array we're working on gets partitioned at the very left, then the left subproblem has no items in it. That's easy to do: you just don't do anything, and you're done. The same thing applies if we wind up with a subproblem that has only one data value in it. Just leaving it alone does the job. Each

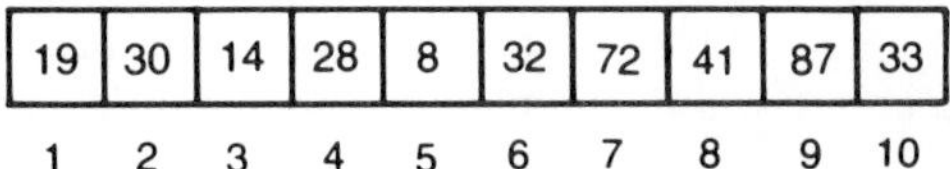

Figure 14 3 1

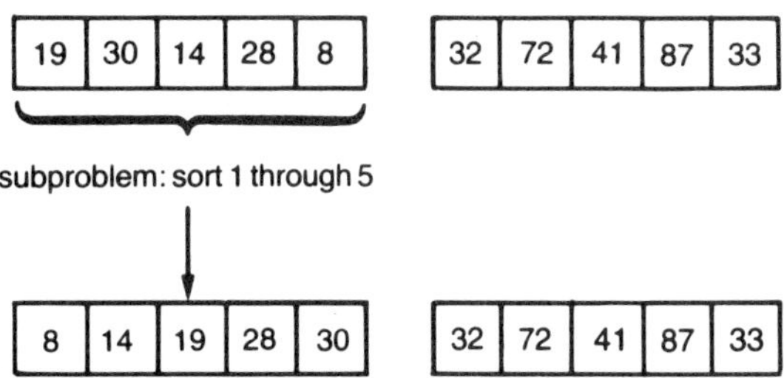

Figure 14 3 2

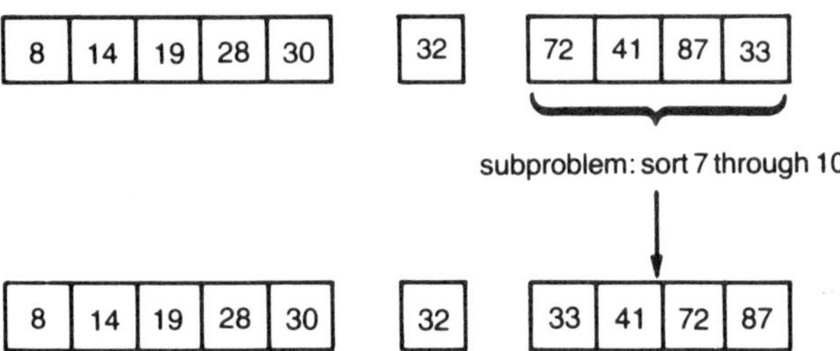

Figure 14 3 3

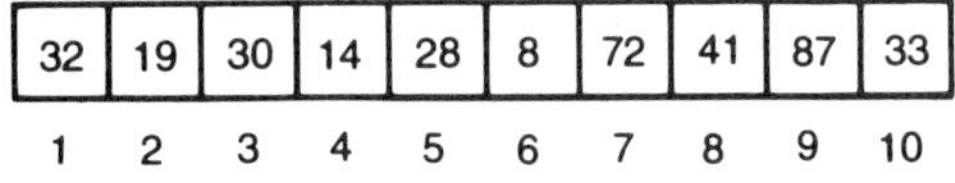

Figure 14 3 4

subproblem has the form "sort the values from Left to Right in the array", so if, for some subproblem, Left isn't less than Right, we can just go on to the next subproblem, because this one is already finished.

Here's our plan.

To sort an array N( ), with data values from position 1 to position Z, call Quicksort with Left = 1 and Right = Z. At the beginning there are no subproblems yet.

—Quicksort, (Left, Right)—

IF *Left < Right*

THEN

Partition the array from position Left to position Right, with P giving the position of the partitioning element.

Set up the left subproblem (from Left to P − 1).

Set up the right subproblem (from P + 1 to Right).

Get the next subproblem.

Repeat unless *there were no more subproblems*

We're left with two issues to resolve before we can finish our plan. First, exactly how do we "partition the array from Left to Right", and second, how do we "set up" and "get" a subproblem? Let's start with the first question.

We want to "partition the array from position Left to position Right". What does that mean again? It means that all values to the left of some spot in the array (we'll call that spot the **partition point**) are less than (or equal to) the value in the partition point (the **partition value**), and all the values to the right of the partition point are greater than the partition value. We know that we can't assume that the array is partitioned already. Worse, we don't know where the partition point will be, or what the partition value is. We have to start somewhere, so we'll just arbitrarily decide that the leftmost value in the array, that is N(Left), will be the partition value. (Other choices are possible, and some may be better in some cases — see the discussion in Section 14 4.) Now that we know the partition value, we need to find a way to find the partition point, and to make sure the array is properly partitioned.

Figure 14 3 5 shows a typical array to be partitioned. Let's begin by choosing two variables, L1 and R1. We'll come up with a method that guarantees that

every item to the left of position L1 ≤ partition value

and

every item to the right of position R1 > partition value

Certainly we can start L1 off with the value Left + 1, since the only value to the left of position Left + 1 is the partition value itself. But perhaps the value in position Left + 1 is OK, too. We'd better look at it to see. If it is OK, then we can increase L1, and have a look at the next position to the right. In fact, we want to search the array, starting at position Left + 1, looking for the first item that's *not*

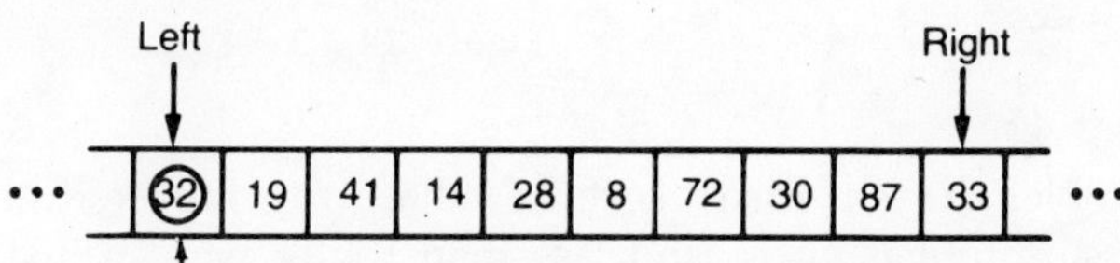

Figure 4 3 5 We plan to rearrange the values in the positions from Left to Right so this value lies at the partition point less than or equal to the partition value. Once we've found that, we know the largest value we can give to L1. (See Figure 14 3 6.)

Since we've increased L1 as far as possible, there's nothing to do but work on R1. Before we've looked at anything, we don't know if there are any items greater than the partition value at all, so we'd better start with R1 equal to Right. Now we can search the array (moving from right to left) for the first value that's not OK. Once we've found that, it tells us the smallest value we can give to R1, and still have our rule

every item to the right of position R1 > partition value

be true. (See Figure 14 3 7.)

What should we do now? We have to do something, because the partition value should be put to the right of the value 30. . .but left of the value 41. Obviously that's impossible as things stand. (A program could recognize this situation by testing the relative values of L1 and R1.) We can solve our immediate problem by swapping the value in position L1 (41) with the value in position R1 (30). And *then* (see Figure 14 3 8) L1 can start moving right again!

This time L1 gets blocked at the position with the value 72, so we give R1 a try again. R1 gets stopped when it's at the position with the value 8 (see Figure 14 3 9). *Now,* unlike the last time that L1 and R1 were blocked, we have found the partition point. (Our program can tell that this is the case by simply testing to

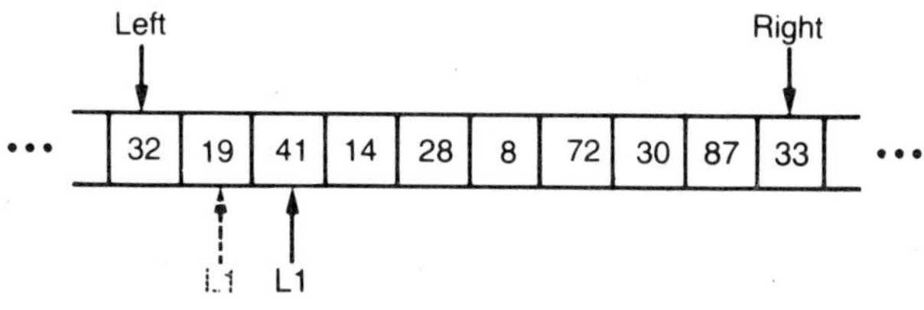

Figure 14 3 6 We move L1 right as long as it's true that "every value to the left of L1 ⩽ partition value"

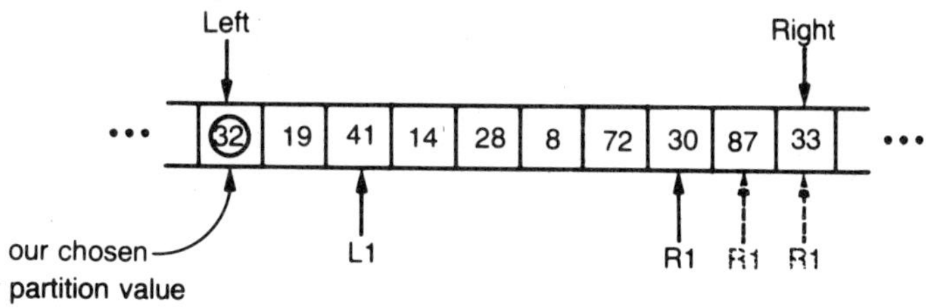

Figure 14 3 7 We move R1 to the left as long as it's true that "every value to the right of R1 is OK (greater than the partition value)"

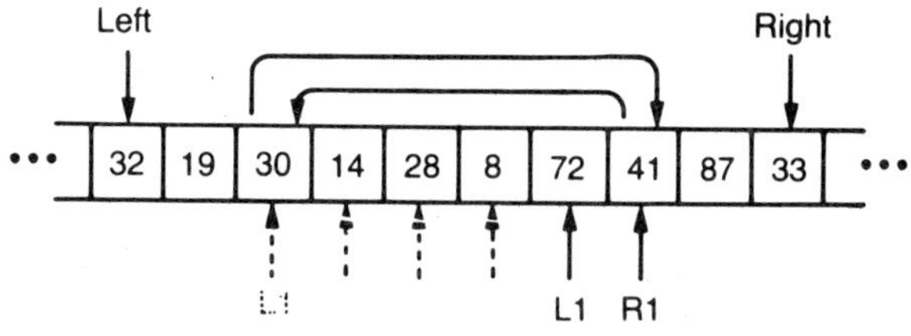

Figure 14 3 8 We swap the 41 with the 30, then let L1 move right again

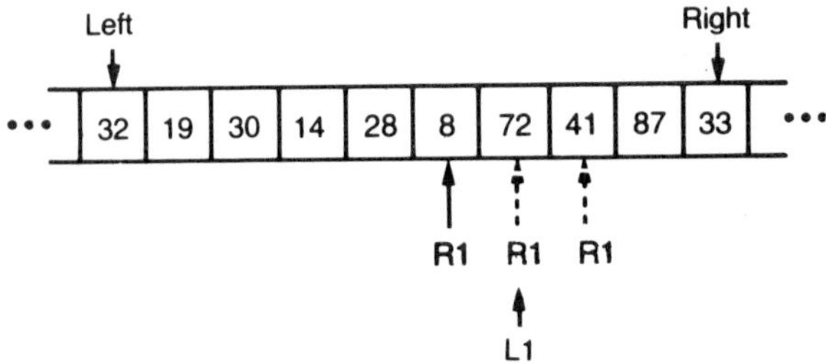

Figure 14 3 9 R1 moves left again

see if L1 and R1 have crossed, that is, if L1 is greater than R1.) If it's not clear to you why we know that when L1 and R1 have crossed, R1 gives the partition point, be sure to compare the rule about L1

every item to the left of position L1 ⩽ partition value

with the rule about R1 and the definition of the partition point.

Once we know the partition point, we can finish partitioning the array by swapping the partition value (it's in N(Left), don't forget) with the value that happens to be in the partition point (we know that that value belongs to the left because L1 is past it).

Here's our plan for "partition the array from Left to Right".

LET the partition value = N(Left).

LET L1 = Left + 1.

LET R1 = Right.

Search *(moving right) from L1 to Right*
to find the first position i *where* N(i) > *partition value.*
not found —
LET L1 = Right + 1.
found —
LET L1 = i.

Search *(moving left) from R0 to Left + 1*
to find the first position j where N(j) ⩽ *partition value.*
not found —
LET R1 = Left.
found —
LET R1 = j.

IF L1 and R1 haven't crossed,
THEN —
Swap N(L1) with N(R1).

Repeat unless *L1 and R1 have crossed*

LET Partition point = R1.

LET N(Left) = N(R1).

LET N(R1) = partition value.

```
6200 REM  SUBR--REARRANGE SO ARRAY IS PARTITIONED.
6210 REM  CHOOSE LEFTMOST ITEM AS PARTITION VALUE.
6220      LET V = N(L0) <------- L0 is Left
6230      LET L1 = L0 + 1
6240      LET R1 = R0 <--------- R0 is Right
6250 REM  TOP OF LOOP--KEEP ADJUSTING UNTIL PARTITION
6260 REM  IS DETERMINED.
6270 REM      MOVE RIGHT--SEARCH LOOP.
6280          FOR I=L1 TO R0
6290              IF N(I)>V THEN 6340
6300            NEXT I
6340 REM        NOT FOUND OR FOUND (BOTH COME HERE).
6350              LET L1 = I
6360 REM      MOVE LEFT--SEARCH LOOP.
6370          FOR J=R1 TO L0 + 1 STEP -1
6380              IF N(J)<=V THEN 6440
6390            NEXT J
6440 REM        NOT FOUND OR FOUND (BOTH COME HERE).
6450              LET R1 = J
6460          IF L1>R1 THEN 6520 <---- have L1 and R1 crossed?
6470 REM        SWAP N(R1) WITH N(L1) TO "UNBLOCK"
6480            LET T = N(L1)       }
6490            LET N(L1) = N(R1)   } "unblock" L1 and R1
6500            LET N(R1) = T       }
6510                        GO TO 6250 <---- L1 and R1 haven't crossed, so Repeat
6520 REM  DONE PARTITIONING, PUT PARTITION VALUE IN PLACE.
6530      LET N(L0) = N(R1)
6540      LET N(R1) = V
6550      RETURN
```

(Margin notes: lines 6270–6350 "move L1 right search loop"; lines 6360–6450 "move R1 left search loop")

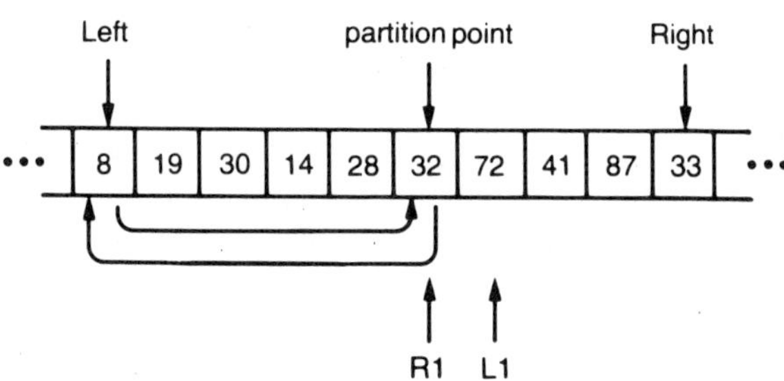

Figure 14 3 10 After swapping N(Left) with N(R1), the array is partitioned; the final value of R1 is the partition point.

Now where do we stand? Looking back at our overall plan for Quicksort, we see that we've figured everything out except how to set up and get subproblems. Let's work on that now.

Our array N( ) stores the values that are to be put in order, so we can specify a subproblem simply by telling what region of the array we're to work on. And we need just two numbers to specify a subregion of the array, namely, the position of

If you're cursed with a version of BASIC which doesn't follow the standards concerning FOR-NEXT loops, you'll have to add some lines to the routine to get it to work properly.

If your BASIC always insists on going through FOR-NEXT loops at least once, regardless of the starting and ending values, you'll need.

```
6275            IF L1>R0 THEN 6340
```

and

```
6365            IF R1<L0+1 THEN 6440
```

If your BASIC doesn't leave the FOR-NEXT control variable with the "first value not used" as per the standards, you'll have to treat the *not found* case separately, like this:

```
6310 REM        NOT FOUND
6320              LET L0 = R0 + 1
6330              GO TO 6360
6340 REM        FOUND
6350              LET L0 = I
```

and

```
6400 REM      NOT FOUND
6410            LET R1 = L0
6420            GO TO 6460
6440 REM      FOUND
6450            LET R1 = J
```

the leftmost element and the position of the rightmost element. The problem is that we can have a number of subproblems waiting to be done at a given point in time. We need a method which will let us store and retrieve a number of pairs of numbers. Our solution is to store the numbers specifying subproblems in two arrays: one array to store the left end of the subproblem, one for the right end. And we'll need a variable which tells how many subproblems are stored in the arrays. Suppose D tells how many subproblems we have, L( ) stores the left ends, and R( ) stores the right ends. Then to store the left subproblem from Figure 14 3 11 (namely, "sort the array from position 1 through position 5"), we add 1 to D (since we now have another subproblem), and store the value 1 (the leftmost position) in L(D), and the value 5 in R(D).

After storing the right subproblem, the arrays are as shown in Figure 14 3 12.

To get a subproblem, we take L(D) as the Left end, R(D) as the Right, subtract one from D (since now we have one less subproblem left to do), and carry out the Quicksort process.

We're almost done, but there is one last consideration. How large will the arrays L( ) and R( ) have to be? It turns out that if we're not careful, the arrays which store the subproblems can take up as much room as the array which stores the data! That would be terrible, because it would severely restrict the size of problems our

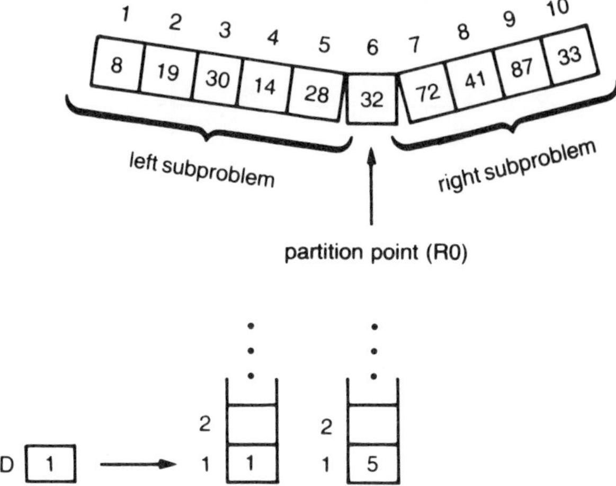

Figure 14 3 11 The first subproblem, sorting from position 1 through 5, is stored in L( ) and R( ); D indicates that there is one subproblem to do.

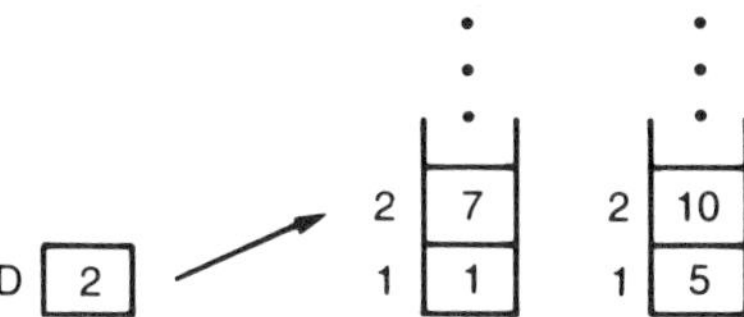

Figure 14 3 12 After adding the right subproblem, D indicates that we have two subproblems to do

sorting method could be used on. If, on the other hand, we make sure that when we set up the left and right subproblems, we do it so that the program will always work on the *shortest* subproblem first, small subproblems will quickly be completed and removed from the arrays, so L( ) and R( ) need not be very big. In fact, they need be no larger than INT($\log_2$(Z + 1)). We won't worry here about why that's so. At any rate, it means that we don't waste much space storing subproblems, as Figure 14 3 13 indicates.

Finally, we can finish our program for Quicksort. Compare our BASIC statements carefully with our plan. Notice that we've used two subroutines for setting up the subproblems. Remember that our partitioning subroutine returns the partition point in R1, so the left subproblem is from L0 (Left) up to R1 − 1, and the right subproblem is from R1 + 1 up to R0 (Right).

```
6000 REM  QUICKSORT
6010 REM  IS THIS SUBPROBLEM DONE?
6020      IF LO>=RO THEN 6130
6030 REM    PARTITION BETWEEN  LO  AND  RO
6040        GOSUB 6200
6050 REM    NOW WE'RE LEFT WITH TWO SUBPROBLEMS.
6060 REM    WE WANT TO DO THE SMALLEST FIRST, SO
6070        IF R1 - LO<RO - R1 THEN 6110
6080          GOSUB 6600
```

(program continued on page 356)

Z	int ($\log_2$ (Z + 1))
10	3
100	6
1,000	9
10,000	13
100,000	16
1,000,000	19

to sort this many values — L( ) and R( ) must be this big

Figure 14 3 13

```
6090          GOSUB 6650
6100          GO TO 6130
6110          GOSUB 6650
6120          GOSUB 6600
6130 REM  GET NEXT SUBPROBLEM (IF ANY)
6140      IF D=0 THEN 6190
6150        LET L0 = L(D)
6160        LET R0 = R(D)
6170        LET D = D - 1
6180            GO TO 6010
6190      RETURN
```

if D is 0, there are no subproblems left to be done

have another subproblem, so Repeat

.
. ← *the partition subroutine goes here*
.

```
6600 REM  LOAD LEFT SUBPROBLEM
6610      LET D = D + 1
6620      LET L(D) = L0
6630      LET R(D) = R1 - 1
6640      RETURN
6650 REM  LOAD RIGHT SUBPROBLEM
6660      LET D = D + 1
6670      LET L(D) = R1 + 1
6680      LET R(D) = R0
6690      RETURN
```

remember: R1 is the partition point when we get here

To test our Quicksort routine, we can use the same test program we used for Clearsort (see the last program listing in Section 14 1), but we need a few additions. Quicksort requires the two subproblem arrays, and we need to start D at zero to indicate that before we start, there are no subproblems yet.

```
10   REM  TEST QUICKSORT
20        DIM N(100)
30   REM  QUICKSORT NEEDS TWO (SMALL) ARRAYS
40   REM    TO HOLD SUBPROBLEMS.
```

```
50         DIM R(6), L(6)
60         PRINT "HOW MANY VALUES DO YOU WANT TO SORT";
70         INPUT Z
80         PRINT "PLEASE GIVE ME THE VALUES"
90         FOR I=1 TO Z
100            PRINT "N("; I; ")=";
110            INPUT N(I)
120        NEXT I
130        PRINT "HERE GOES!"
140   REM  TO START QUICKSORT, WE SET LO (LEFT) AND
150   REM    RO  (RIGHT).
160        LET LO = 1
170        LET RO = Z
180   REM  AND THERE ARE NO SUBPROBLEMS YET, SO
190        LET D = 0
200        GOSUB 6000 <------ call Quicksort
210   REM  SHOW SORTED VALUES.
220        FOR I=1 TO Z
230            PRINT N(I)
240        NEXT I
250        PRINT
260        GO TO 9999
  .
  .    <------------ Quicksort subroutines go here
  .
9999     END

RUN
HOW MANY VALUES DO YOU WANT TO SORT? 10
PLEASE GIVE ME THE VALUES
N( 1 )=? -1
N( 2 )=? 16
N( 3 )=? 14
N( 4 )=? -2
N( 5 )=? 11
N( 6 )=? 5
N( 7 )=? 5
N( 8 )=? 5
N( 9 )=? 22
N( 10 )=? 9
HERE GOES!
-2
-1
 5
 5
 5
 9
 11
 14
 16
 22

READY
```

EXERCISES 14 3

1 Here's an array that's in our special, partitioned form.

9	7	2	12	84	13	14
N(1)	N(2)	N(3)	N(4)	N(5)	N(6)	N(7)

(a) What is the partition point?

(b) What is the partition value?

(c) What is the left subproblem?

(d) What is the length of the right subproblem (how many values does it involve sorting)?

(e) What is the sum of the lengths of the two subproblems plus twice your age?

2 Here's an array of values we'd like to partition.

67	24	94	104	62	68	74
N(4)	N(5)	N(6)	N(7)	N(8)	N(9)	N(10)

Assuming the partition value is 67,

(a) for what value(s) of L1 is it true that

every item to the left of position L1 is less than or equal to the partition value

(b) for what value(s) of R1 is it true that

every item to the right of position R1 is greater than the partition value

3 Redo exercise 2, but now assume that the partition value is 104.

4 We translated "L1 and R1 have crossed" as the test L1> R1 in our BASIC version of the "partition" operation. Why do we know that L1 and R1 will never be *equal* at that point (line 6450)?

5 Stare at line 6070 in the main Quicksort subroutine for a while. If the left subproblem is smaller than the right subproblem, which statement is carried out next, 6080 or 6110?

6 Suppose we get to line 6110 in the main Quicksort subroutine. Which subproblem gets set up first, the left or the right? One of those will be gotten first by lines 6150 through 6170. Which one?

7 Based on line 50 in the test program, and on Figure 14 3 13, what is the maximum number of data items the program can sort?

Section 14 4

Clearsort vs. Quicksort

It took us much longer to develop Quicksort. The Quicksort routines are more complicated than those of Clearsort. Is it worth it? Let's see how the two compare when we use them to sort the same values.

Here's our plan for a program to compare Clearsort with Quicksort.

—compare two sorting methods—

Find out how many values the user wants to sort (call that Z).

Generate Z random numbers, and store them in positions 1 through Z in two arrays (one to sort, one to keep a copy of the original problem).

Run Quicksort, allowing the user to time how long it takes.

Set up the original problem again.

Run Clearsort, allowing the user to time how long it takes.

Here's the BASIC version of our plan.

```
10   REM  COMPARE CLEARSORT WITH QUICKSORT
20   REM  N() AND M()--VALUES TO BE SORTED (M() IS A COPY)
30        DIM N(250), M(250)
40   REM  L() AND R()--ARRAYS TO HOLD QUICKSORT SUBPROBLEMS
50        DIM L(8), R(8)
60        PRINT "HOW MANY RANDOM NUMBERS TO YOU WANT TO SORT";
70        INPUT Z
80   REM  FILL ARRAY WITH RANDOM VALUES IN THE RANGE 0...999
100       FOR F=1 TO Z
110           LET N(F) = INT(RND*1000)
120           LET M(F) = N(F)
130       NEXT F
140  REM  SHOW NUMBERS BEFORE SORTING.
150       PRINT "BEFORE:"
160       GOSUB 1000
170  REM  CARRY OUT QUICKSORT ON THE VALUES IN N()
180       PRINT "START QUICKSORT";
190       INPUT A$
200       LET D = 0
210       LET LO = 1
220       LET RO = Z
230       GOSUB 6000
240       PRINT "DONE"
250       PRINT "SORTED VALUES:"
260       GOSUB 1000
270  REM  COPY  M()  INTO  N()  SO CLEARSORT SORTS
280  REM    EXACTLY THE SAME PROBLEM AS QUICKSORT.
290       FOR I=1 TO Z
300           LET N(I) = M(I)
310       NEXT I
320  REM  CARRY OUT CLEARSORT ON  N()
330       PRINT "START CLEARSORT";
340       INPUT A$
350       GOSUB 7000
360       PRINT "DONE"
370       PRINT "SORTED VALUES:"
380       GOSUB 1000
390       GO TO 9999
```

Handwritten annotations:
- *generate a random sorting problem* (lines 80–130)
- *Quicksort and show result* (lines 170–260)
- *wait for user to get his or her watch ready* (→ line 190)
- *set up the original problem again* (lines 270–310)
- *Clearsort and show result* (lines 320–380)
- *wait for user to get ready* (→ line 340)

(program continued)

```
1000 REM  PRINT A TABLE OF THE  Z  VALUES IN  N(),
1010 REM    TEN TO A ROW.
1020      FOR I=1 TO Z
1030          LET I0 = I - INT((I-1)/10)*10
1040          PRINT TAB(5*I0); N(I);
1050          IF I0<10 THEN 1080
1060 REM        START A NEW LINE.
1070            PRINT
1080      NEXT I
1090      PRINT
1100      PRINT
1110      RETURN
  .
  .
  .
9999      END
```

notice how we made the spacing look "pretty" (lines 1020–1070)

← Quicksort subroutines

← Clearsort subroutines

Here's a sample run.

```
RUN
HOW MANY RANDOM NUMBERS DO YOU WANT TO SORT? 50
BEFORE:
      377  733  127  379  878  21   201  695  42   579
      711  892  228  129  304  117  705  788  549  288
      805  482  992  134  861  125  97   766  428  763
      981  803  993  154  628  35   433  219  540  19
      3    484  953  338  591  352  287  44   657  302

START QUICKSORT?
DONE
SORTED VALUES:
      3    19   21   35   42   44   97   117  125  127
      129  134  154  201  219  228  287  288  302  304
      338  352  377  379  428  433  482  484  540  549
      579  591  628  657  695  705  711  733  763  766
      788  803  805  861  878  892  953  981  992  993

START CLEARSORT?
DONE
SORTED VALUES:
      3    19   21   35   42   44   97   117  125  127
      129  134  154  201  219  228  287  288  302  304
      338  352  377  379  428  433  482  484  540  549
      579  591  628  657  695  705  711  733  763  766
      788  803  805  861  878  892  953  981  992  993

READY
```

← the sorting problem

we hit the "return" key here, and measure how long it takes for the "DONE" message to appear.

same end result, but Clearsort takes much longer on this problem

The results of our tests are shown in Figure 14 4 1. We happen to be using a particularly slow computer, so if you reproduce the tests on your system, you'll probably find that the times you measure are less than ours. But the relative sizes will be the same. As you can see, when we were sorting 10 values, Clearsort took less time (6 seconds) than Quicksort (9 seconds). But after that, Quicksort is, well,

Z	time for Quicksort (seconds)	time for Clearsort (seconds)
10	9	6
20	19	25
50	57	159
100	129	696
150	231	1722
200	358	3520
250	457	5398

← that's right — almost an hour!

Figure 14 4 1

quicker. And the ratio between them keeps increasing, so that by the time we're sorting 250 values, Clearsort takes more than ten times as long as Quicksort (Figure 14 4 2). Imagine what the difference would be if we'd had the patience to run the test with 1000 values!

We seem to have proved that our Quicksort routine is faster than our Clearsort routine. Or have we? We've tested them on just one particular arrangement of the data values. Is Quicksort faster than Clearsort on every arrangement of data values? No! It turns out that Quicksort is superior for almost every arrangement of data values, but (given the exact form of our partition subroutine), Quicksort is virtually as slow as Clearsort when the data values are in order (or "almost" in order) to begin with! Perhaps you can imagine why. If the data values are in order, the partition point is always at position Left, and so the left subproblem will be empty. That means that the right subproblem is almost as big as the original problem — i.e., our "divide and conquer" approach degenerates into "sliver and struggle." If you want to observe this, just change line 110 in our test program to

```
110            LET N(F) = F
```

Then the array will be in order to begin with, and our Quicksort routine will flounder.

When we first introduced Quicksort, we mentioned that it was of tremendous practical value. And, in actual situations, it certainly can happen that the array to be sorted is almost in order (say, for example, you're adding a few new values to the end of a sorted array, and now want to put the array in order again). Does that mean that you pay a penalty for using Quicksort? No, because there's an easy way to make Quicksort run fast if you know (or suspect) the array is almost in order already. All we have to do is change our partition subroutine so it chooses a value near the middle of the subproblem for the partition value, instead of the leftmost value. We could do that by adding these statements to our "partition" subroutine.

```
6210 REM  CHOOSE MIDDLE VALUE AS PARTITION VALUE
6220      LET V = N( (LO+RO)/2 )
6221      LET N( (LO+RO)/2 ) = N(LO)
```

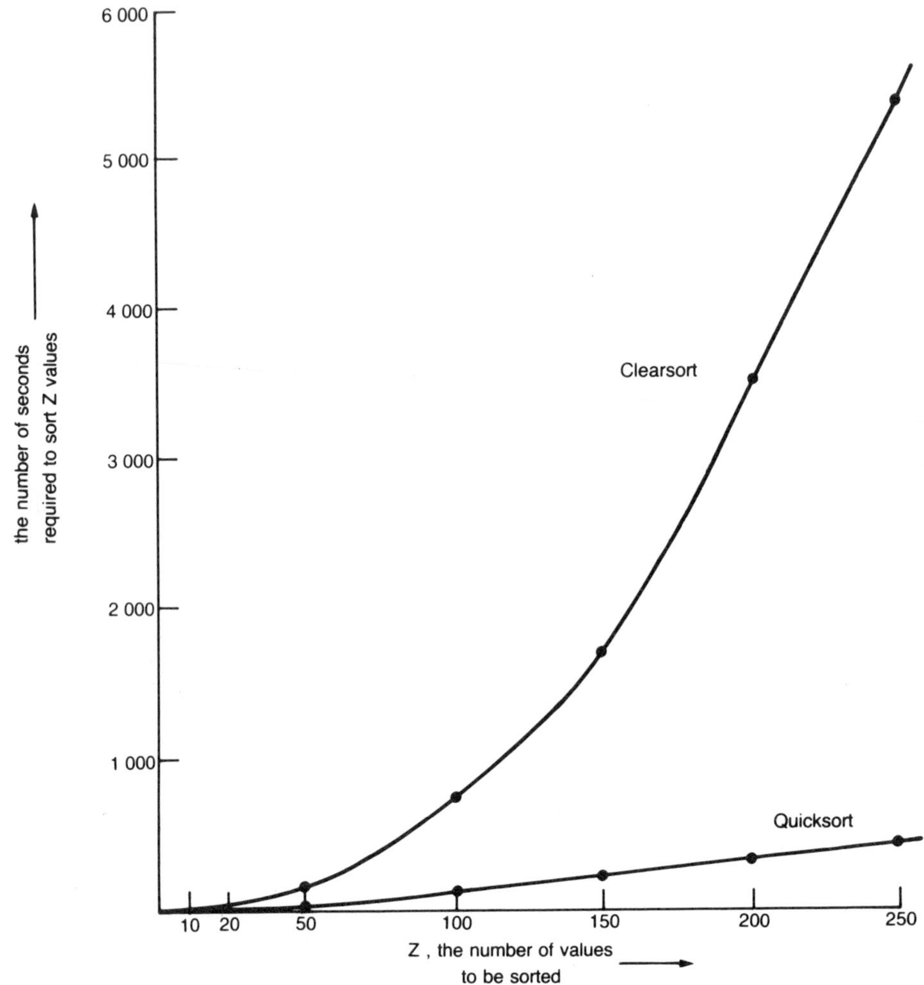

Figure 14 4 2

That is, before we start, we swap the value in the middle with the leftmost value, then go on exactly as before (try it). Of course, now there's *another* particular order of the array that Quicksort does poorly on, but it doesn't occur very often (see exercise 5).

Clearsort and Quicksort do the same thing. You give them an array of values, and they put the values in order. Clearsort is relatively easy to write and debug; Quicksort relatively hard. The program for Clearsort is shorter than the program for Quicksort, and, in addition, Quicksort uses a little bit of auxiliary storage (to hold the subproblems). Clearsort has the advantage that the time to sort any array of a given length is constant. Quicksort runs lightning fast on almost every arrangement of values, but slowly on a few, so the time required to sort a given-length array is variable. (However, since even in the worst case, Quicksort is no slower than Clearsort, this isn't much of a plus for Clearsort.) In most practical cases, Quicksort is the hands-down winner.

A true story

system involved: a Road Design System (RDS) used to aid civil engineers in laying out dirt roads in mountainous forest lands.

sorting involved: sorting elevation measurements by distance (along the surface) to a given reference point; sorting measurement records by elevation for plotting.

The two sorting subproblems should have been only a small part of the total effort. When we got the system, a sorting technique similar to Clearsort was being used. The sorting subroutine was changed to the one described in problem 9 (Quicksort with a slight wrinkle).

The *total* computer time required to produce an average road design decreased by 45% with Quicksort. This had a major impact on the total throughput of the entire computer system on which RDS was being used, since RDS runs account for about one-third of the total use of the computer system (dual UNIVAC 1108's).

Amazing, but true!

EXERCISES 14 4

1 Why didn't we include a line like this in our test program?

```
85        RANDOMIZE
```

2 In which situations would you choose Quicksort, in which Clearsort?

(a) When your program will be used every day for years to put the points scored by each player on a basketball team in order.

(b) When you're in a terrible hurry, and you need a program that you'll use just once to put about 50 people in order of their heights.

(c) When you're working for a company that makes telephone directories for cities all over the free world.

(d) When you're in a terrible hurry, and you need a program that you'll use just once to put about 10,000 people in order of their weight.

We'll say that Quicksort **totally and completely flounders** when every time it partitions the values it's working on, one of the subproblems is empty (i.e., the partition point turns out to be Left or Right).

3 If the partition routine chooses the Leftmost value as the partition value, for which arrays does Quicksort totally and completely flounder?

(a) | 5 | 4 | 3 | 2 | 1 |

(b) | 1 | 2 | 3 | 4 | 5 |

(c) | 3 | 2 | 4 | 5 | 1 |

(d) | 2 | 4 | 1 | 3 | 5 |

4 Redo exercise 3, but assume the value in position INT((Left+Right)/2) is now used as the partition value.

5 Suppose we take the numbers 1, 2, 3,. . . , 20 and mix them up in all possible ways. When we run Quicksort on them, it totally and completely flounders on two of the arrangements. How many other arrangements of the numbers are there?

For more information about sorting see:

Donald E. Knuth, *The Art of Computer Programming, Vol. 3, Sorting and Searching* (Reading, Mass.: Addison-Wesley, 1973).

Harold Lorin, *Sorting and Sort Systems* (Reading, Mass.: Addison-Wesley, 1975).

PROBLEMS 14

1 Have a contest to see who can write the fastest sorting routine. Here are some rules you can choose from:

The number of values to be sorted is

-less than 5
-less than 10
-exactly 100
-between 100 and 200
-more than 1000 and less than 10,000

The values to be sorted will be

-in a scrambled order
-almost in order
-in reverse order
-told to everyone before you start working on your programs
-given out only when everyone is ready to make their bid for glory

The data values will be

-from 1 to 10
-from 1 to 10,000
-from 1 to 9E10
-from −9E10 to +9E10
-people's names

You may use no more than

-50 lines of BASIC (not counting REM statements)
-one array (the one which contains the values to be sorted)
-5 variables besides the array to be sorted
-2 hours to design, develop, and test your routines

Figure 14 P 1 A badge for the winner

2 Revise the Clearsort routines so they put the values in increasing or decreasing order, depending on the value in variable C. If C is 0, sort them in increasing order; otherwise put them in decreasing order. Be sure to include enough test runs to prove that your routines work properly.

3 Write a subroutine which carries out the sorting method shown in Figure 14 P 2.
This method is called **distribution sorting,** and, in the rare case when it's applicable, it's extremely fast. Discuss its speed and its limitations.

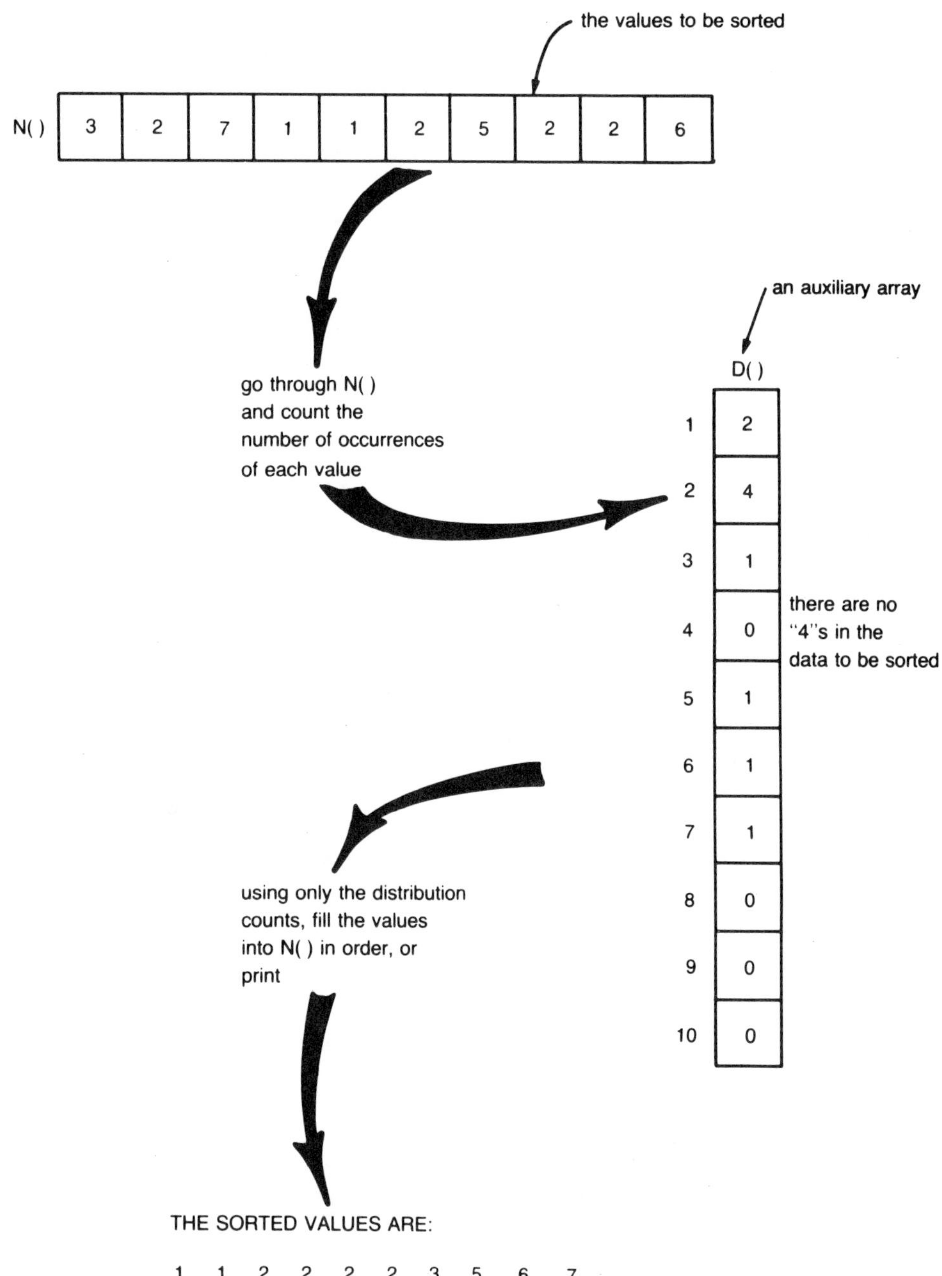

Figure 14 P 2 Distribution sorting

> Two ways to use Clearsort to order two different arrays M( ) and S( ):
>
> - Put *two* copies of the Clearsort routines in your program: one which operates on M( ), one which operates on S( ).
> - First, have your program copy the values in M( ) into the corresponding positions in N( ), run Clearsort, then copy the sorted values from N( ) back into M( ). Second, do the same for the values in S( ).

4 If each numeric variable has only 6 digits of accuracy, you can't store a telephone number in a single variable. But, by using two or three variables, you can. For example, by using one array to store area codes, one for the "exchange," and one for the remaining four digits, we can store complete phone numbers (Figure 14 P 3).

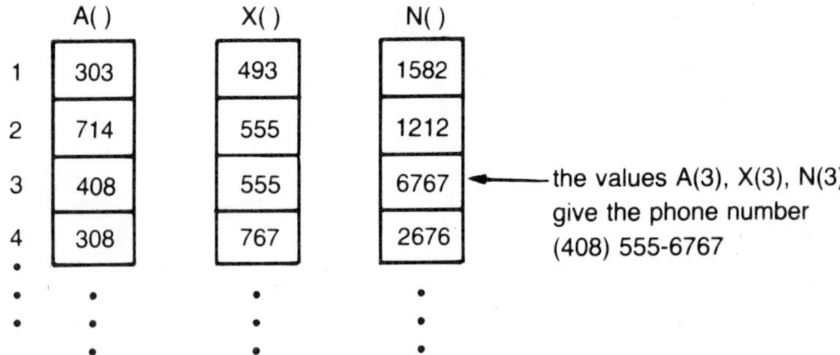

Figure 14 P 3 Using three arrays to store a list of phone numbers

Using the method described in Section 14 2, we can put the phone numbers in order of any one of the three parts without losing track of which Area code goes with which Exchange with which Number, but that won't complete the job of putting the items in order of the complete number. Write a program which does.

(Hint: If you use Clearsort three times in a row, once on each of the three different arrays, each time keeping the three parts of the phone number together, you'll do the job. You need to figure out what order to do the sorts in — it matters greatly!)

5 When the array to be sorted is almost in order to begin with, both Clearsort and Quicksort go through a lot of wasted effort. If a collection of information is kept in order and updated by adding a few new values at the end and then sorting the entire collection, the array will be almost in order. In that case the **insertion sort** is a good choice.

Pretend you're holding a hand of cards. To put them in order, you start with the second card from the left, and put it in order with respect to the card on its left. Next, you take the third card, and put it in the proper place among the cards to its left. And so on (Figure 14 P 4).

Of course, an array isn't quite as easy to handle as a hand of cards. Instead of just slipping the next card into position among the cards to its left, in the computer case, we'll have to slide some values to the right to make room for the value we want to insert.

Here are two successive refinements of the insertion sort algorithm.

FOR each position h *from 2 through Z*

> *Look to the left to find the place to insert N*(h).
>
> *Slide the values in between* h *and the place you want to insert N*(h) *to make room.*
>
> *Insert* N(h).

```
FOR each position h from 2 through Z
    LET v = N(h).
    Search positions l=h−1, h−2, down to 1 to find the first place where
    N(l) ≤ = v.
        not found
            LET s = 1.
    found
        LET s = l + 1.
    FOR l=h, h−1, DOWN TO s+1
        LET N(l) = N(l−1).
    LET N(s) = v.
```

Write a subroutine which carries out the insertion sort, install it in a test program like the one we used to test Clearsort in Section 14 1, and make sure it works.

Figure 14 P 4 Putting the fourth card in place; the fifth card (2) will be inserted next

6 Using your insertion sort subroutine from problem 5 and your choice of either Clearsort or Quicksort, devise a test program and use it to compare the sorting methods.

Try at least these test cases:

N(1)=1, N(2)=2,. . .,N(100)=100	(in perfect order)
N(1)=1,. . .,N(99)=99, but N(100)=50	(one out of order)
N(1)=1,. . .,N(98)=98, but N(99)=50, N(100)=50	
N(1)=100, N(2)=99,. . .,N(100)=1	(reverse order)

7 In a **bubble sort,** the program passes through the data repeatedly, interchanging pairs of values which are out of order. When a pass is completed in which no interchanges were necessary, the array is in order. Obviously, if the array is already in order, this is a fast method. Write a test program which lets you compare a bubble sort with Clearsort. Try to describe in English those cases in which bubble sort is slower than Clearsort.

8 If the version of BASIC you are using allows arrays of string values, do problem 4, but add an additional array N$( ) which stores the person's name associated with each phone number. [See Section 16 2 first.]

While the next three problems (9, 10, and 11) may at first glance appear a little picky, if you do them, you will have turned the version of Quicksort we presented in Section 14 3 into the world's best general-purpose sorting method (as of this writing).

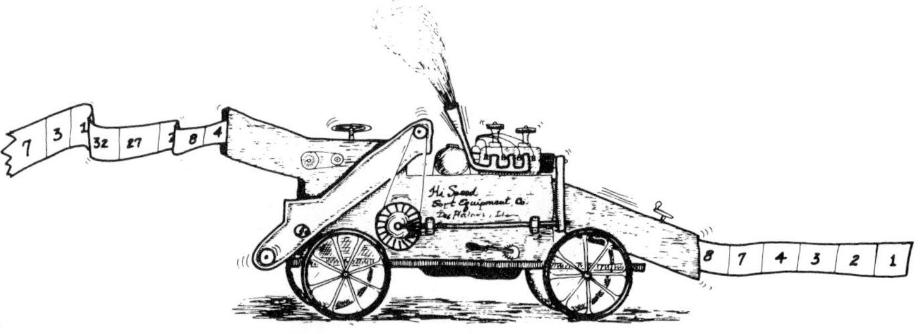

9 If there happen to be very many equal values in the data we're sorting, the version of Quicksort in Section 14 3 has a problem. We can dramatize it by looking at this extreme case:

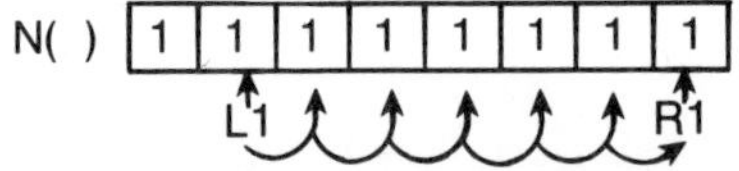

Look at the partition process (Section 14 3). If L1 keeps moving right until a value *strictly larger* than the partition value is discovered, our version of Quicksort flounders. As you can see in the extreme case above, L1 will be moved all the way to the right, forcing the partition point all the way to the right, which makes the left subproblem very large, and the right very small (namely, empty). That's terrible — the more nearly even-sized the left and right subproblems are, the faster Quicksort runs. And time is money, as they say.

This problem can be circumvented in a way that might, at first, seem odd. If we stop L1 when it reaches a value which is greater than or *equal to* the partition value, and we continue to stop R1 when it reaches a value that's less than or equal to the partition value, we'll be able to create equal-sized subproblems, and so, speed up the sorting. Why should that seem odd? Well, if you look at the partition algorithm, you'll see that stopping L1 before it has crossed R1 means that N(L1) and N(R1) will be swapped with each other before we continue moving L1 and R1. In the extreme case above, that means we'll be swapping 1 with 1, and that seems like an obvious waste of time. However, doing a few "obviously dumb" swaps in order to obtain more even-sized subproblems turns out to be a very good deal.

Altering the partition algorithm involves two small changes. First, we change the first *search* criterion in the partition algorithm to

Search (moving right)
to find the first position *i* where N*(i)* ≥ partition value

And the second change is... Well, if we told you the second change, there wouldn't be any point to this problem, would there?

(Hint: Is it possible that as the partition algorithm stands in Section 14 3, two successive passes through the "Repeat unless L1 and R1 have crossed" loop might needlessly compare certain positions in the array to the partition value more than once? And is it just possible that doing that would cause trouble when we make the first change we described above?)

10 Figure 14 4 2 shows that Clearsort is very expensive sorting method to use. However, Figure 14 4 1 shows that statement to be too strong, for there are *some* cases in which Clearsort is actually faster than Quicksort, namely when there are very few items to be sorted. The same thing is true of the insertion sort method (problem 5). And insertion sort has the added feature of being very fast if the array it's given to sort is almost in order.

As Quicksort stands (Section 14 3), it decides that a subproblem is done if it involves sorting no more than one value (see the plan and lines 6010 and 6020 in the subroutine). However, the partitioning process guarantees that once a subproblem has been identified, all of the values in that subproblem belong somewhere within the range of array positions making up the subproblem. And *that's* true no matter what the size of the subproblem. So, if we decided to say that as far as Quicksort is concerned, a subproblem is done if it contains no more than (say) 10 values, we'd know that although the array (probably) wasn't completely in order, all of the values were *close* to the positions they should be in. And if all the values are close to where they should be, the array is almost in order. As soon as a subproblem is almost in order, we can turn the rest of the work over to insertion sort, and it will finish it faster than any other method could.

Adding the ideas we've just outlined to the version of Quicksort described in Problem 9 gives the current world's fastest general-purpose sorting method.

Note: These ideas are R. Sedgwick, "Quicksort," *Stanford Computer Science Report, 75-492,* May 1975.

Problem 11 is for fanatical sorting speed freaks only.

11 The optimum subproblem size at which Quicksort should give up varies from computer system to computer system. Set up a sequence of tests in which you compare the time required to sort large arrays of random values by versions of Problem 10 Quicksort with different subproblem limits. The optimum size will probably be in the range from 5 to 15.

12 Read the article "Meansort" by Dalia Motzkin, in the *Communications of the ACM,* Volume 26, No. 4, April 1983, pages 250-251, and report on it to your class.

Chapter 15 **Packing and Pointing**

Section 15 1

Giving Symbols Meaning

When your computer is adding numbers together, it doesn't make any difference whether the numbers stand for dollars or inches or oranges or pounds. The only meaning the BASIC system attaches to numbers is their mathematical meaning, in the context of arithmetic (addition, subtraction, etc.) and comparison (less than, greater than, etc.). By the same token, the BASIC system doesn't know any more about the character strings you've stored in string variables than it takes to copy and compare them. This is at once a blessing and a curse. It's a curse because we're not protected from writing ridiculous programs. Any fool knows you don't find the number of fruits you have by multiplying the number of apples by the number of oranges, but a momentary lapse of attention or a typing error can turn + into *, and the program certainly won't warn us. On the other hand, it's a blessing because it gives us tremendous freedom in how we interpret and use the numbers and symbols in our programs.

When you design a program, you must choose a way to represent the information you want to process in terms of numbers or strings — that's all that's available. It's up to you, the programmer, to keep the meanings straight. The meanings of different numbers within the same program can vary widely. In the painting estimator program (Chapter 2), some of the numbers stand for gallons of paint, others for square feet of wall surface, and still others for the porosity of the wall surface. In the menu routines in Chapter 9, numbers stand for different alternatives ("BRUSH", "ROLLER",. . .). Even when the meaning seems totally obvious to us, as in

```
HOW MANY QUESTIONS ARE ON YOUR QUESTIONNAIRE?
```

it doesn't have anything to do with BASIC. BASIC would be just as happy to print

```
HOW MANY A4708*6 ARE IN YOUR VLECH?
```

The computer simply *prints* the characters. It's up to the programmer and user to choose and interpret the meaning appropriately. But you know that.

In this chapter we'll move beyond the straightforward assignments of meaning to numbers we've used so far. We'll look at an example of using one number to represent several others (it's a space-saving technique called **packing**). We'll look at an example of using a bunch of separate numbers to stand for one huge number. And we'll look at an example of using numbers not to represent quantities, but to keep track of groups of other data values (an organizational technique called **pointing**).

Section 15 2
Packing and Unpacking

We've been thinking of a number as a single entity, but we could just as well think of it as a sequence of separate digits. From this viewpoint a numeric variable is a container for six separate digits rather than a container for a single six-digit number. When you need to store a lot of one-digit numbers and you find yourself running out of space in the computer's memory, this new point of view comes in handy. It allows us to store six times as many numbers in the space available.

There is no automatic way to store, say, the number 7 into the third digit of the variable V. But we can use our knowledge of arithmetic to work out a way to do it as well as a way to retrieve a specific digit from a variable. The trick is to remember what each digit in a number stands for. Take the number 347521 for example. The "3" in the 100,000's place, the "4" in the 10,000's place, and so on down to the "2" in the 10's place and the "1" in the 1's place. In other words, "347521" stands for

	3	100,000's
plus	4	10,000's
plus	7	1,000's
plus	5	100's
plus	2	10's
plus	1	1's

Each of the numbers on the right is a power of 10: 100,000 is 10 ^ 5, 10,000 is 10 ^ 4, and so on down to 1, which is 10 ^ 0. Therefore, if we want to build the number 347521 out of its individual digits, we can write the expression

```
3*10^5 + 4*10^4 + 7*10^3 + 5*10^2 + 2*10^1 + 1*10^0
```

Now suppose we want to extract a particular digit from the number stored in the variable V. To be specific, let's extract the last digit. We have to do it with the arithmetic operations available in BASIC, and if you cast around for an idea, you might realize that the last digit in any number is the *remainder* when you do long division by 10.

In BASIC we can do long division by using the INT operator. The quotient Q in dividing V by D is

```
LET Q = INT(V/D)
```

That makes the remainder (by the checking formula)

```
LET R = V - D*Q
```

> in case you haven't done long division since fifth grade:
>
> Q remainder R
> D)V
>
> V is the **dividend** (the number you are dividing into), D is the **divisor** (the number you are dividing by), Q is the **quotient** (the number you get when you make the division), and R is the **remainder** (what's left over after the last subtraction).
>
> V = D*Q + R ← you use this formula to check the long division

This gives us the tool we need to extract the last digit from the number stored in the variable V.

> The last digit in the number stored in the variable V is the value stored in R by the statements below:
>
> ```
> 8200      LET Q = INT(V/D)
> 8210      LET R = V - D*Q
> ```

So much for the last digit. What about the other ones? It turns out they're not too much harder to extract. The trick is to shift the number to the right enough decimal places to put the digit we want into the last digit position. Then we use the technique we've already devised to extract the last digit. Shifting the number is simply a matter of dividing by a power of 10, again using long division (the INT operator). If we want to extract the second digit from the six-digit number 347521, we first shift it four places to the right

```
LET V = INT(347521/10000)
```

and then extract the last digit by our standard procedure. If we want to extract the fifth digit, we shift it one place

```
LET V = INT(347521/10)
```

and extract the last digit in what's left.

In general, if want to extract the Pth digit from a six-digit number stored in the variable V, we shift it 6 − P places to the right and then extract the last digit. We shift it, of course, by dividing (long division) by 10 ^ (6 − P).

```
8200 REM  ROUTINE FOR EXTRACTING THE P8-TH DIGIT FROM V
8210      LET V8 = INT(V/10^(6-P8))
8220      LET D8 = INT(V8/10)
8230      LET D8 = V8 - 10*D8
8240      RETURN
```

> We use the unusual names with the "8" suffix to avoid conflicting with other variables which might be used in any program which uses this routine.

This procedure for extracting a particular digit from a number is known as **unpacking.** In addition, we need a way to *store* a digit into a particular spot in a variable. Then we'll be able to use our memory space more efficiently when we need to handle lots of one-digit numbers. Storing a digit into a particular position within a variable is known as **packing.** The basic idea is to add the digit into the right spot by first multiplying it by the correct power of ten. For example, if we want to put a 5 into the fourth digit of 347021, we add 5*100 to 347021. If we want to put a 4 into the second spot in 307521, we add 4*10,000. In general, if we want to put the digit D into the Pth position of the six-digit number V, we

```
LET V = V + D*10^(6 - P)
```

But this works only if the Pth digit in V is a zero. If it's any other number, then D will get added to that number, and we won't get what we want.

To get the procedure to work correctly, no matter what digit is already stored in the Pth spot in V, we have to first zero out the Pth digit of V. We can do this by extracting the Pth digit and then subtracting. But we have to subtract from the correct position within V, and we do this by multiplying the digit we extracted by a power of ten. Suppose we have the number 347521 and we want to change the third digit to a 9 instead of a 7. We first extract the 7, then multiply it by 1000 and subtract. That leaves a zero as the third digit. Finally, we add 9*1000 to the result.

$$349521 = 347521 - 7*1000 + 9*1000$$

Or, in a slightly condensed form,

$$349521 = 347521 + (9 - 7)*1000$$

From these observations we get the following packing procedure.

```
8300 REM  PUT THE DIGIT  R  INTO THE P8-TH POSITION OF V
8310      GOSUB 8200
8320      LET V = V + (R - D8)*10^(6-P8)
8330      RETURN
```

remember: this subroutine extracts the P8th digit and returns it in variable D8

Try the packing and unpacking procedures. Make sure that they work and that you understand why they work. This is a sophisticated example of using numbers in BASIC to represent another type of information, namely sequences of digits. Of course, a number is, in a sense, a sequence of digits, but in order to use it as a sequence of *separate* digits, we have to make some special provisions.

In the questionnaire program (Chapter 11) we needed to store lots of one-digit numbers which represented answers to questions. With a long questionnaire and many people responding, space in the computer's memory was critically short. This is a good place to use our packing and unpacking procedures. However, there is an additional complication in this problem. Say we have a questionnaire with 20 questions and 200 people responding. In our original program we would have used an array

```
DIM Q(200, 20)
```

to store the responses.

Now we'll store six responses per variable instead of only one. That way we can store 20 responses in only four variables instead of twenty, and we can use a much smaller array.

```
DIM Q(200, 4)
```

When we store the answer to a question, we first have to figure out which variable to store it in. Say we are dealing with respondent number 147. We'll store his or her first 6 responses in the variable Q(147,1) the next 6 in Q(147,2), the responses to questions 13 through 18 in Q(147,3) and the last two responses in Q(147,4). (See Figure 15 2 1.) What we need is a general procedure for storing answer A to the Q0th question answered by respondent number R0.

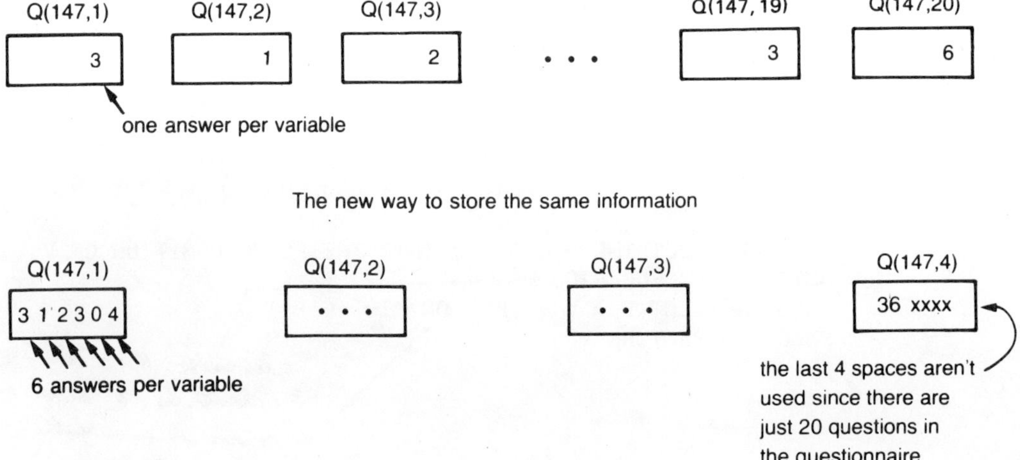

Figure 15 2 1 The old and new ways of storing responses

Basically, it's a matter of quotients and remainders again. For respondent number R0 we have four variables to store responses in: Q(R0,1), Q(R0,2), Q(R0,3), and Q(R0,4). The answer to question number 1 goes in the first digit of Q(R0,1), the answer to question number 2 in the second digit of Q(R0,1), and so on up to question number 6. Then the answer to question number 7 goes in the first digit of Q(R0,2). For question number Q0, we find out which variable to use by computing the quotient of Q0 divided by 6 (long division again): INT(Q0/6). Then the position within that variable is the remainder in the same division: Q0 − 6*INT(Q0/6). Taking into account that the packed words and digit positions start at one instead of zero, we come up with the following procedures to store and extract responses to questions.

```
8000 REM  EXTRACT ANSWER TO QUESTION  Q0  BY
8010 REM    RESPONDENT NUMBER  R0
8020      LET V9 = INT((Q0-1)/6) + 1 } get the right packed word
8030      LET V = Q(R0, V9)
8040      LET P8 = Q0 - 6*(V9 - 1)   figure out which position we want
8050      GOSUB 8200   unpack it
8060      LET A = D8
8070      RETURN
8100 REM  STORE ANSWER  A  TO QUESTION  Q0  BY
8110 REM    RESPONDENT  R0
8120      LET V9 = INT(Q0/6)  } get the packed word as it is now
8130      LET V = Q(R0, V9)
8140      LET R = A
8150      LET P8 = Q0 - 6*V9 ← where do we want to put the answer?
8160      GOSUB 8300 ← pack it
8170      LET Q(R0, V9) = V ← put the finished product
8180      RETURN                in the response array
```

Deciding to go to the trouble of packing and unpacking small values in single variables is a fair amount of work, and it's not something you'd do frivolously. However, when the program you're working on hits the limits of the machine you're using, as did our questionnaire program, there may be no choice in the matter. By packing six answers where we could fit only one before, now our program can store six times as many answers in the same amount of memory. This makes a big increase in its usefulness.

EXERCISES 15 2

1 V is the dividend, D the divisor, Q the quotient, and R the remainder. None has a fractional part. Write a BASIC assignment statement which computes

(a) the quotient, given the dividend and the divisor.

(b) the remainder, given the dividend and the divisor.

(c) the divisor, given the quotient, the dividend, and the remainder.

2 Write a program which uses the "extract the P8th digit" subroutine to print each digit of any whole number the user enters. For example:

```
NUMBER=? 327
 327 = 0  0  0  3  2  7
```

3 Devise a test for whether a given value is a whole number. Add it into the "put the digit R into the P8th position" subroutine, so it prints a warning message if V is not a whole number.

4 In our packing and unpacking examples, all the numbers involved were positive. Does that matter? Suppose the number we're trying to unpack is negative. What value does this program print?

```
1000    LET V = -123456
1010    LET P8 = 4
1020    GOSUB 8200
1030    PRINT "THE"; P8; "-TH DIGIT IS"; D8
1040    GO TO 9999
  .
  .     the "extract the P8th digit" routine goes here
  .
9999    END
```

5 We worked out procedures for packing and unpacking one-digit numbers. What if you wanted to pack and unpack two-digit numbers? How many could you pack into one variable?

6 Write a procedure for extracting two-digit numbers packed into variable V.

7 Write a procedure for packing two-digit numbers into a variable.

8 Suppose the possible answers to our questionnaire had been a and b instead of 0, 1, 2, 3,. . . , and 9. How could we continue to use our one-digit packing and unpacking routines for questions with this type of answer?

9 It seems that with only the two possible answers a and b instead of ten possible answers, we should be able to pack more answers into one variable than before. How many do you think will fit?

Section 15 3

Big Numbers

If you have a pocket calculator, it may well give you more digits of accuracy than your BASIC system does. Some calculations need to be accurate to more than 6 decimal digits — certainly 6 digits of accuracy wouldn't be enough for the accounting department of a large company. Is it possible to get more accuracy? Sure. Let's write a program which computes *really* big numbers. Did you ever wonder how many different ways there are to shuffle a deck of cards? That's a big number, for certain. It requires many more than 6 digits to represent exactly.

How many ways are there to shuffle (rearrange) a deck of cards? Let's see. . . Suppose we start with our hands empty. There are 52 choices for the first one we pick up. Now there are 51 cards left in the pile. We choose one of those as the second card. We had 52 choices for the first card, and for each choice, there are 51 choices left for the second card, so there must be

```
52*51
```

different ways to put two cards in order. Continuing with this line, we see that after the choice of second card, we have 50 choices for the third card, so there must be

```
52*51*50
```

ways to put three cards in order. And so on, until we see that there must be

```
52*51*50*49*...*3*2*1
```

different ways to put a deck of cards in order. How big a number is that? Unimaginably big. But not too big for us to estimate (see experiment), or, by using special methods, to compute with complete accuracy.

```
10      LET W = 52
20      FOR H=51 TO 1 STEP -1
30          LET W = W*H
40      NEXT H
50      PRINT W; "WAYS TO SHUFFLE."
9999    END

RUN
 8.06582E+67 WAYS TO SHUFFLE.
READY
```

note: this may not work on your system. You may get an "OVERFLOW" message when W gets too big.

The way we'll compute it is to use an array to store the digits of the number. That way, instead of being limited to the accuracy of numeric values on your system, we can be accurate to as many digits as we have spaces in our array. Of course, there's a penalty for choosing our own idiosyncratic way to represent numbers — we'll have to write a program to do the multiplication because the BASIC * operator works only on BASIC numbers. Let's look at a few cases to see what our program will have to do. Since we want to multiply 52 times 51 times 50 times... times 2 times 1, the multiplier (that is, the number we're multiplying *by*) can be represented in the normal way, and stored in an ordinary numeric variable. The product, on the other hand, quickly develops into a number with too many digits for an ordinary variable. We'll have to store it in an array.

Our program will have to be able to multiply a small number stored in an ordinary variable times a big number stored in an array. Doing such a multiplication is pretty much like doing multiplication by hand, and the hard part of writing the program is in figuring out exactly what we do when we do multiplication by hand. The example below details the individual steps in multiplying 3 times 1280.

```
 1280
   ×3
 ----
    0        3 times 0 is 0
   4         3 times 8 is 24 — write down the 4 and carry the 2
  8          3 times 2 is 6 — add the carry of 2
 3           3 times 1 is 3 — no carry here
 ----
 3840
```

In doing the multiplication by hand, we sometimes have to carry a digit from one position to the next and sometimes we don't. This is a minor inconsistency which would complicate the program if we followed our hand process exactly. We can describe the process in a more consistent way if we view the no-carry case as a zero-carry. That way we'll always have a carry to add in, but sometimes we'll be adding zero (which is equivalent to no carry at all). For each digit in the number we are multiplying, we do the multiplication, add the carry, write down the last digit in the result, and carry the rest into the next place.

Doing multiplication

Start out with carry = 0.

FOR each digit in the number being multiplied, starting at the right,

Multiply the digit by the multiplier.
Add the carry.
Extract the last digit.
Figure out the new carry.

This procedure works fine until we get to the last digit. Even then we're OK as long as there's no carry left over. If there *is* a carry left over, we have to do something with it. Here again we can simplify the program by making the process more consistent. We'll assume the number being multiplied has enough leading zeros to handle any carry that might be left over. Essentially, this amounts to assuming that there will be no carry left over when we get to the last digit. We do a little extra work when we continue the multiplication across the extra leading zeros, but the program is easier to describe without the special cases.

```
0006894
      7
-------
      8     7 times 4 is 28, plus carry of 0 is 28−8 carry 2
     5      7 times 9 is 63, plus carry of 2 is 65−5 carry 6
    2       7 times 8 is 56, plus carry of 6 is 62−2 carry 6
   8        7 times 6 is 42, plus carry of 6 is 48−8 carry 4
  4         7 times 0 is 0, plus carry of 4 is 4−4 carry 0
 0          7 times 0 is 0, plus carry of 0 is 0−0 carry 0
0           7 times 0 is 0, plus carry of 0 is 0−0 carry 0
-------
0048258
```

There is one more worrisome point which turns out to be easy to handle: What if the multiplier has more than one digit, like in 37 times 4821? In doing this by hand, you would do 7 times 4821 first, then 3 times 4821, then add the results together with the second one shifted over one place.

```
  4821
    37
------
 33747
14463
------
178377
```

You may find it a little surprising that you can do it all at once using 37 as the multiplier instead of 7 first, then 3 — as long as you keep things straight. At least, we found this a little surprising when we first thought of it, but it allows us to use the same procedure as before, even when the multiplier has several digits. The carries get long sometimes, but nothing gets lost.

```
0004821
     37
-------
      7     37 times 1 is 37, plus carry of 0 is 37−7 carry 3
     7      37 times 2 is 74, plus carry of 3 is 77−7 carry 7
    3       37 times 8 is 296, plus carry of 7 is 303−3 carry 30
   8        37 times 4 is 148, plus carry of 30 is 178−8 carry 17
  7         37 times 0 is 0, plus carry of 17 is 17−7 carry 1
 1          37 times 0 is 0, plus carry of 1 is 1−1 carry 0
0           37 times 0 is 0, plus carry of 0 is 0−0 carry 0
-------
0178377
```

The procedure we've been using forms the heart of our program to compute the number of ways to shuffle a deck of cards. We can use the tricks from Section 15 2 on packing and unpacking to extract the last digit and figure out the carry. All that's left is to decide how we want to number the digits in the array where we store the big number.

There are two problems in numbering the digits: how many should there be, and should we number them from left to right or right to left? We don't know when we write the program how many digits there are in the big number we're trying to compute. So we have to guess. Let's try 100 digits first. Next, we need to decide which way to number the digits. We normally think of them as being numbered from left to right because that's the way we write them down, but we have to work with them from right to left in figuring the products so it might be better to number them in that direction. But then we'd have to print them out in the reverse order, so maybe we should number them from left to right to make the printing more natural.

It's a toss-up. We choose left-to-right numbering: digit 100 is the last digit on the right, digit 99 the next to last, and so on. Using this scheme, we find the plan for our program falls out easily. We've added some extra output so we can see the product as it builds up in the array.

```
Store 52 in the array (that's 0 0 0. . .0 5 2).
FOR M = 51, 50, 49,. . ., 2, 1
    PRINT the big number in the array.
    PRINT "TIMES"; M: "IS".
    Compute M times the big number in the array.
PRINT the final result.
```

```
Compute M times the big number in the array
    Start with carry = 0.
    FOR each digit numbered 100, 99, 98,. . ., 2, 1
        Multiply M times the digit and call the product V.
        Add the carry to V.
        Extract the last digit of V and store it into the array
              (last digit of V = V − 10*INT(V/10)).
        Compute the carry (carry = INT(V/10)).
```

The program is then a simple translation of the plan into BASIC. We have two subprograms, one to compute the product of M times the big number stored in the array (as we've indicated in the description above) and one to print the number in the array. In the print routine we've gone to the trouble of skipping over leading zeros because they would be distracting in the output. Other than that, there should be nothing surprising in the program if you understand the description we've gone through.

```
100  REM  COMPUTING THE NUMBER OF WAYS TO ARRANGE
110  REM  A DECK OF CARDS.
120       DIM A(100)
130       LET N = 100
140  REM  STORE 52 IN  A()    (AS A BIG NUMBER)
150       FOR D=1 TO  N-2
160           LET A(D) = 0
170       NEXT D
180       LET A(N-1) = 5
190       LET A(N)   = 2
200  REM  COMPUTE THE PRODUCT 52*51*50*...*2
210       FOR M=51 TO 2 STEP -1
220  REM      PRINT INTERMEDIATE RESULTS
230           GOSUB 1000
240           PRINT "TIMES"; M; "IS"
250  REM      COMPUTE  M  TIMES THE NUMBER IN A()
260           GOSUB 2000
270       NEXT M
280  REM  PRINT FINAL RESULT
290       PRINT
300       PRINT "THE NUMBER OF WAYS TO SHUFFLE "
310       GOSUB 1000
320       GO TO 9999

1000 REM  PRINT  A()  WITHOUT LEADING ZEROS.
1010      LET F = 1
1020      IF A(F)<>0 THEN 1100
1030          LET F = F + 1
1040          GO TO 1020
1100      FOR D = F TO N
1110          PRINT A(D);
1120      NEXT D
1130      PRINT
1140      PRINT
1150      RETURN

2000 REM  COMPUTE  M  TIMES THE NUMBER IN A()
2010      LET C = 0
2020      FOR D=N TO 1 STEP -1
2030          LET V = M*A(D) + C
2040          LET A(D) = V - 10*INT(V/10)
2050          LET C = INT(V/10)
2060      NEXT D
2070      RETURN
9999      END
```

```
RUN
 5  2

TIMES 51 IS
 2  6  5  2

TIMES 50 IS
 1  3  2  6  0  0

TIMES 49 IS
 6  4  9  7  4  0  0

TIMES 48 IS
 3  1  1  8  7  5  2  0  0

TIMES 47 IS
 1  4  6  5  8  1  3  4  4  0  0

                     .
                     .
                     .
TIMES 3 IS
 4  0  3  2  9  0  8  7  5  8  5  4  7  1  9  3  9  2  8  5  8
 3  0  3  1  8  4  2  8  2  0  1  8  8  3  4  8  7  6  4  4  7
 5  2  7  2  0  4  4  1  6  3  8  9  1  2  0  0  0  0  0  0  0
 0  0  0  0  0

TIMES 2 IS
 8  0  6  5  8  1  7  5  1  7  0  9  4  3  8  7  8  5  7  1  6
 6  0  6  3  6  8  5  6  4  0  3  7  6  6  9  7  5  2  8  9  5
 0  5  4  4  0  8  8  3  2  7  7  8  2  4  0  0  0  0  0  0  0
 0  0  0  0  0

THE NUMBER OF WAYS TO SHUFFLE
 8  0  6  5  8  1  7  5  1  7  0  9  4  3  8  7  8  5  7  1  6
 6  0  6  3  6  8  5  6  4  0  3  7  6  6  9  7  5  2  8  9  5
 0  5  4  4  0  8  8  3  2  7  7  8  2  4  0  0  0  0  0  0  0
 0  0  0  0  0

READY
```

It's not very common to need to compute a number accurate to over 50 decimal places. But it is fairly common to find companies whose profit statements are full of 7- or 8-digit figures (some in red ink!). If you find yourself in a situation where you need more than 6 places of accuracy, the idea of using more than one variable to store what you think of as a single number can be a salvation if you have to adhere to Minimal BASIC.

EXERCISES 15 3

1 Suppose you could make one shuffle each second, and that by some fluke, each shuffle produced a new ordering of the cards (i.e., you never accidentally wind

up with an ordering you've had before). How long would it take to produce all possible orderings? Write a small program that gives a rough answer (to the accuracy of normal BASIC numbers) in centuries.

2 Normally, when we do multiplication by hand, we multiply each digit in the multiplicand by each digit in the multiplier, getting one row for each digit in the multiplier. Then we add it all up. Effectively, we calculate like this:

(4000 + 800 + 20 + 1)*7 + (4000 + 800 + 20 + 1)*30

```
  4821
    37
 33747
14463
178377
```

In our program we multiply each digit in the multiplicand by the entire multiplier, which means we're calculating it like this:

(4000 + 800 + 20 + 1)*37

Fill in the missing line in this argument to show that the two methods result in the same value.

```
4821*37 = (4000 + 800 + 20 + 1)*7 + (4000 + 800 + 20 + 1)*30
        = 4000*7 + 800*7 + 20*7 + 1*7 + 4000*30 + 800*30
          + 20*30 + 1*30
        =
        = (4000 + 800 + 20 + 1)*37
        = 4821*37
```

3 There's a simple way we could have known that we'd need no more than 68 digits in the array we used to store the developing big number. What is it?

4 Describe in plain English what line 2050 in the "compute M times the number in A( )" subroutine does.

5 Each year about 128 college basketball teams participate in the NCAA playoffs. After the final game, the teams could be ranked in order from best to worst. How could you use our program to compute the number of different possible results, with complete accuracy?

Section 15 4

Sorting by Pointing

In Section 14 2 we sorted four arrays: M( ), S( ), Q( ), and P( ). Array elements with the same subscript value contained inventory information about the same product. M(I), S(I), Q(I), and P(I) stored the manufacturer's code, specific product code, quantity on hand, and price of item I. To sort them in order of the manufacturer's code, we applied the Clearsort routine, altering it so each time that it called for two values to be switched, all four corresponding entries were moved together. In the commercial computing world, where there may be thousands of items to be sorted, and where there may be many pieces of information about each item, sorting by this method is a very costly proposition. All you really want is to know what order the items go in — if you knew that, it wouldn't make any difference if the items were actually in that order in the arrays. But if the items aren't in order in the arrays, how can a program tell what order they go in?

The current position of a particular item is given by the array subscript of the four pieces of information about that item. Given the state of affairs in Figure 15

4 1, knowing the array subscript value 6 is sufficient to tell the position of the Rosarita refried beans item. The value 6 serves to identify the item, and we say that the value 6 is a **pointer** to the item. If we knew the subscript value of the item which comes first in order of the manufacturer's code, that is, if we had a **pointer** to the first value, that would be enough to print the first value out, or to change part of the information. If we had a pointer to the item which goes in each position in the ordering, then we could easily access the items in the desired order. And obviously, it will require less effort to deal with pointers (subscript values) than it would to move entire assemblages of information around.

We'll solve the problem by adding another array, an array of pointers, called a **directory** (or **index**). Instead of moving the items themselves, we'll confine all the movement to the directory. Now the problem of putting the items in order of the manufacturer codes is replaced by the problem of putting the pointers to the items in the proper order. Figure 15 4 2 shows what we want to achieve. Figure 15 4 3 shows the way this is usually drawn. Once we understand that we're dealing with pointers, we don't care about the actual subscript values when we think about the problem; we just think in terms of pointers.

Once we put the directory in the right order, we can do anything we were able to do with our old method. We simply refer to the items through the directory. For instance, to print the first item:

```
PRINT M(L(1)), S(L(1)), Q(L(1)), P(L(1))
```

To print the second item in the ordered list, we do

```
PRINT M(L(2)), S(L(2)), Q(L(2)), P(L(2))
```

and so on. When we write programs that access the ordered information, we don't need to know or care that in this particular case, L(1) has the value 3. All we need to

	M( )	S( )	Q( )	P( )	
1	54400	01021	234	0.66	(Ortega®* diced green chiles)
2	51000	01467	144	0.73	(Campbell's split pea soup)
3	44300	10643	68	0.57	(Rosarita enchilada sauce)
4	50000	04106	52	0.51	(Contadina† tomato paste)
5	51000	01261	123	0.42	(Campbell's mushroom soup)
6	44300	10637	78	1.13	(Rosarita refried beans)

Figure 15 4 1 The items we want to sort

*Ortega® is a trademark of Heublein, Inc.
†*Contadina* is a registered trademark of Carnation Company.

L( )		M( )	S( )	Q( )	P( )
3	1	54400	01021	234	0.66
6	2	51000	01467	144	0.73
4	3	44300	10643	68	0.57
2	4	50000	04106	52	0.51
5	5	51000	01261	123	0.42
1	6	44300	10637	78	1.13

Figure 15 4 2 The directory shows that item 3 comes first, item 6 comes second, and so on.

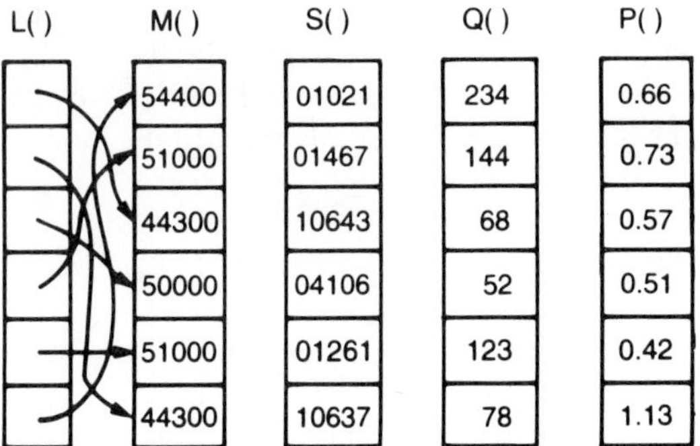

Figure 15 4 3 The directory contains pointers to the items

know is that (assuming we shuffled the directory properly) L(1) is a pointer to the first item, L(2) is a pointer to the second item, and so on. L(1) is really a subscript for the other arrays. M( ), S( ), Q( ), and P( ) hold data — L( ) holds subscripts.

The value of such a directory should be clear. Now we need to figure out how to create it. Surprisingly, doing so requires only a minor change to any usual sorting method. First, when the sorting method requires comparing two values, we refer to the values through the directory instead of directly as before. Second, when the sorting method indicates that we need to switch two items, we just move the corresponding entries in the directory and leave the items themselves alone. That's all there is to it. It's as if believing in the idea solves the whole problem!

We start by filling the directory with a pointer to each item. An easy way to do that is to let L(1) = 1, L(2) = 2,. . .,L(Z) = Z. When the sorting algorithm says to exchange M(L(3)) with M(L(1)), we interchange L(3) with L(1) instead. After the swap, M(L(3)) is what M(L(1)) used to be and vice versa. When the sort procedure is finished, the directory indicates the proper ordering for all the items, and we've avoided moving any of the items.

The program below uses Clearsort, and it's very similar to the version in Section 14 2. We need to add a DIM statement for the array L( ) — the directory. We also need to initialize the directory. That's done in lines 101 through 104. We need to change all references to M(I) to M(L(I)). And when we want to print the items out in order, we change M(I) to M(L(I)), S(I) to S(L(I)), and so on.

```
10    REM  SORTING-BY-POINTING VERSION OF CLEARSORT
20         DIM M(100), S(100), Q(100), P(100)
25    REM  THE ARRAY OF POINTERS (DIRECTORY) IS  L()
26         DIM L(100)
30         PRINT "HOW MANY VALUES DO YOU WANT TO SORT";
40         INPUT Z
50         PRINT "PLEASE GIVE ME THE VALUES."
55         PRINT TAB(10); "MANUF.  SPECIFIC  QUANT.  PRICE"
60         FOR I=1 TO Z
70             PRINT "ENTRY"; I; TAB(10);
80             INPUT M(I), S(I), Q(I), P(I)
90         NEXT I
100        PRINT "HERE GOES!"
101   REM  INITIALIZE DIRECTORY.
102        FOR I=1 TO Z
103            LET L(I) = I
104        NEXT I
110        GOSUB 7000
120   REM  SHOW SORTED ARRAY.
130        FOR I=1 TO Z
140            PRINT M (L(I)); TAB(10); S(L(I)); TAB(20);
145            PRINT Q(L(I)); TAB(30); P(L(I))
150        NEXT I
160        PRINT
170   REM  SHOW FINAL STATUS OF DIRECTORY
180        PRINT "POSITION IN DIRECTORY    'POINTER'"
190        FOR I=1 TO Z
200            PRINT TAB(9); I; TAB(27); L(I)
210        NEXT I
220        PRINT
230        GO TO 9999

7000 REM   CLEARSORT--SORTING BY POINTING
7010       FOR L0=1 TO Z - 1
7020 REM       MAKE  M(L(L0)) BE SMALLEST OF M(L(L0)),....,M(L(Z))
7030           GOSUB 7100
7040 REM       P0  IS POSITION OF SMALLEST VALUE.
7050           LET T0 = L(L0)
7051           LET L(L0) = L(P0)
7052           LET L(P0) = T0
7080       NEXT L0
7090       RETURN
7100 REM   SUBR--COMPUTE POSITION OF SMALLEST VALUE
7110 REM        IN M(L(L0)),....,M(L(Z))
7120 REM   L0  IS POSITION OF SMALLEST-SO-FAR
7130       LET P0 = L0
7140       FOR L1=L0 + 1 TO Z
7150           IF M(L(L1))>=M(L(P0)) THEN 7180
7160 REM          HAVE NEW LOW.
7170              LET P0 = L1
7180       NEXT L1
7190       RETURN
9999       END
```

Compare to the version in Section 14 2.

(program continued on page 386)

```
RUN
HOW MANY VALUES DO YOU WANT TO SORT? 6
PLEASE GIVE ME THE VALUES.
              MANUF.  SPECIFIC  QUANT.  PRICE
ENTRY 1     ? 54400, 01021,    234,     0.66
ENTRY 2     ? 51000, 01467,    144,     0.73
ENTRY 3     ? 44300, 10643,    68,      0.57
ENTRY 4     ? 50000, 04106,    52,      0.51
ENTRY 5     ? 51000, 01261,    123,     0.42
ENTRY 6     ? 44300, 10637,    78,      1.13
HERE GOES!
 44300        10643       68          .57
 44300        10637       78         1.13
 50000        4106        52          .51
 51000        1261        123         .42
 51000        1467        144         .73
 54400        1021        234         .66
POSITION IN DIRECTORY      'POINTER'
             1                 3
             2                 6
             3                 4
             4                 5
             5                 2
             6                 1

READY
```

There's another interesting advantage to this scheme. Suppose we need to refer to the items in two different orders; say, sometimes we want them in order of manufacturer codes, and at different points we want them in order of price. By creating *another* directory and putting it in order based on price, we can effectively have the items in two orders at once. If we want the first in order of manufacturer codes, we use L(1). If we want the first in order of price, we use the pointer in the first position in the other directory! (See Figure 15 4 4.)

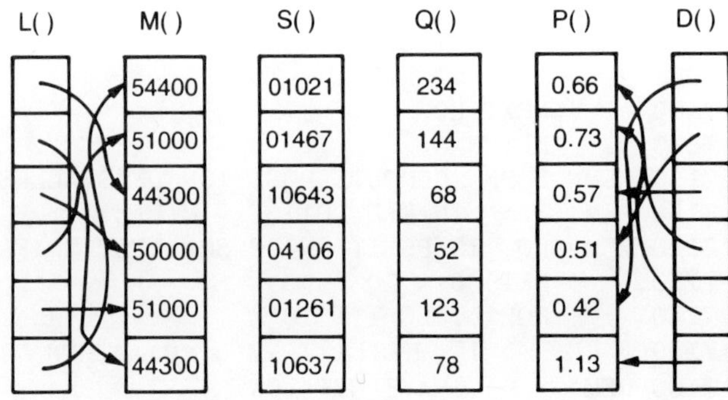

Figure 15 4 4 Directory L( ) points to the items in order of the manufacturer code; directory D( ) points to the items in order of price; the items themselves are still in their original positions in the four arrays.

EXERCISES 15 4

1 Based on the information in Figures 15 4 2 and 15 4 3, draw the rest of the pointers from phrases on the left to expressions on the right.

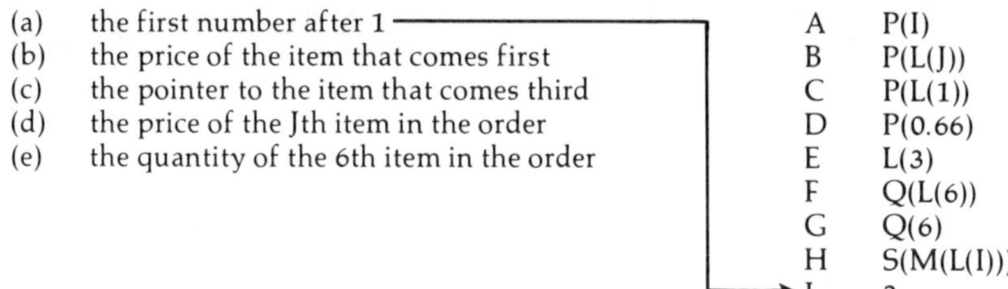

(a) the first number after 1
(b) the price of the item that comes first
(c) the pointer to the item that comes third
(d) the price of the Jth item in the order
(e) the quantity of the 6th item in the order
A P(I)
B P(L(J))
C P(L(1))
D P(0.66)
E L(3)
F Q(L(6))
G Q(6)
H S(M(L(I)))
I 2

2 If there are Z items in the arrays which store the detailed information about specific items, what range of values must a variable used as a pointer be able to take? Given that numeric variables have 6-digit accuracy, what's the maximum number of items you could have and still be able to use the index sort method?

3 Once you have sorted the directory, you can use it to print the items in order of increasing manufacturer code, as the program shows. How could you use the very same directory to print the items in decreasing order?

4 Suppose you want to use the index sorting method to put the items in order of *decreasing* price, so the most expensive comes first. As Figure 15 4 4 shows, using D( ) as a directory and doing the sorting on P(D( )) puts the index in increasing order of price, so something will have to be changed. Your friend hits on the bright idea of starting the directory off upside-down, that is with

$$D(1) = N, D(2) = N - 1, \ldots, D(N - 1) = 2, D(N) = 1$$

Will this trick work?

5 Assume as per Figure 15 4 4 that you have two directories — one which points to the items in order of increasing manufacturer code, and one which points to the items in order of increasing price. Write a plan for a program which finds all items which occur in the same position in both orderings. (For example, suppose Ortega® diced green chiles come 3rd in order of manufacturer code and 3rd in order of price.) Print the manufacturer code, special product code, and position in the order of any and all such items. If no items are found meeting the criterion, print a message to that effect after the program has checked all N positions.

PROBLEMS 15

1 Folk wisdom has it that you don't get something for nothing. If you pack 6 single-digit values into one variable, you appear to get something for nothing, namely the 5 other variables you would have needed had you stored the 6 values the normal way. What's the price? Well, one type of price is that the program is larger and takes more effort to write. But when you're thinking of storing many thousands of single-digit values as we are in the questionnaire program, the small growth of the program and the small additional effort seem well worth it. But there's another price we have to pay for gaining the extra room. The program will run more slowly, because the previously simple

processes of storing and retrieving values from memory are now more complex, involving multiplying, raising to powers (for shifting), additions, and taking INT( ). Thus, we've traded space (in memory) for time.

Create a program you can use to estimate how much longer our packing scheme requires. First, the program should ask the user how many iterations to go through. Then the program should print a message announcing that it is beginning "NORMAL STORING AND RETRIEVING". For each iteration the user requested, in this phase the program should store and retrieve a value from each of six different variables. (LET A1 = A1 will store and retrieve a value from variable A1.)

As soon as all the iterations are finished, the program should print a message, so the user can record the length of time it took.

In the second phase the program prints "PACKED STORING AND RETRIEVING"; then, for each iteration the user requested, the program stores (using our "put the digit R into the P8th position of V" subroutine) and retrieves a value from each of the 6 possible positions in a single variable.

Once the program is working properly, use it to make an accurate estimate of the cost in time of using the packing-and-unpacking method.

2 On some small computer systems, the packing-and-unpacking method will cause a noticeable delay. Usually the most time-consuming part of the whole operation is computing the proper power of ten. Both the packing (8300) and the unpacking (8200) subroutines compute 10 ^ (6 − P8). There's no need to compute the powers of ten from scratch each time. Instead, you could fill an array with the powers of ten you'll need (10^0, 10^1, . . ., 10^5) at the beginning of the program, and then have the packing and unpacking routines look up the appropriate power of ten in the array when needed.

Alter the packing and unpacking routines to reflect this change, and analyze the effects on performance using the timing program from problem 1.

In Minimal BASIC, when you print a digit, it's surrounded by blanks.

```
PRINT 1; 2; 3; 4; 5
 1  2  3  4  5
```

Here's a subroutine that'll print a digit with *no* spaces around it.

```
8700 REM  PRINT THE DIGIT  V  WITH NO SPACES
8710      ON V+1 GO TO 8720, 8740, 8760, . . . , 8880, 8900
8720        PRINT "0";
8730        RETURN
8740        PRINT "1";
8750        RETURN
8760        PRINT "2";  }
8770        RETURN      }
 .
 .
 .
8880        PRINT "8";
8890        RETURN
8900        PRINT "9";
8910        RETURN
```

continue the pattern to fill in the rest of the subroutine

If there's no simpler way (see Section 17 2) to print a digit with no spaces around it on your system, you can use the subroutine to do problems 4, 5, 7, 8, and 9.

3 Alter the questionnaire program (Chapter 11) so it packs six answers per variable and thus has room for six times as many answers.

Doing this will require only minor changes to the questionnaire program. Of course, you'll have to install the four subroutines we developed in Section 15 2. Other than that, all you have to do is replace each reference to the response array Q(,) with an appropriate use of either the "extract answer to question Q0 by respondent R0" or the "store answer A to question Q0 by respondent R0" subroutine.

4 Revise the big-number program (Section 15 3) so it prints the big numbers in a more usual form. When people write large numbers, they usually group the digits by threes, and put either a comma (in the USA), a period (in Europe), or a space (engineers) between groups.

Note: Even though you'll have to print the big number from left to right, and the digits are grouped from right to left, it's still possible to group them properly, since you know the digit number of each digit you're about to print.

80,658,175,170,. . .,277,824,000,000,000,000

5 Use the idea of the big-number program to print a table of powers of whatever number the user chooses. For example, if the user chooses powers of 2, your program should produce this:

```
POWERS OF 2
  0    1
  1    2
  2    4
  3    8
  4    16
  5    32
  6    64
  7    128
  8    256
  9    512
 10    1 024
 11    2 048
 12    4 096
 13    8 192
 14    16 384
 15    32 768
 16    65 536
 17    131 072
 18    262 144
 19    524 288
 20    1 048 576
 21    2 097 152
 22    4 194 304
 23    8 388 608
 24    16 777 216
  .          .
  .          .
  .          .
```

6 Write a program which prints the quotient of two whole numbers as a decimal fraction.

```
WHAT IS M? 9
WHAT IS N? 7
```

```
M/N IS:
1 . 2  8  5  7  1  4  2  8  5  7  1  4  2 ← we hit the "panic button" here
```

The user will have to hit the panic button to stop the program, because there's an infinite number of digits in any decimal fraction. (That's true even if in some cases, like 4/5, all the digits after the first few are 0's.)

(Hint: The trick to this problem is to figure out how long division works. You can get the number in front of the decimal point by computing

```
LET W = INT(M/N)
```

To get the first digit after the decimal, use the formulas

```
LET R = M - N*W
LET D = INT(10*R/N)
```

For the next digit, update R to be the remainder in the division indicated in the last formula above, and re-apply the process.)

7 The output from the division program (Problem 6) isn't very easy to read. The spaces between the digits make it look strung out. Long decimal fractions are often printed in groups of 5 digits, with spaces separating the groups:

1. 28571 42857 14285. . .

Modify the division program to use the more legible format.

8 Modify the division program (Problem 7) so the user first selects the number of decimal places to be printed, then enters a series of M/N problems.

```
HOW MANY DECIMAL PLACES? 12
WHAT IS M? 9
WHAT IS N? 7

M/N IS: 1. 28571 42857 14

WHAT IS M? 29
WHAT IS N? 8

M/N IS: 3. 62500 00000 00
```

9 Write a program which adds two decimal fractions of a specified length.

```
HOW MANY DECIMAL PLACES? 12
WHAT IS M? 9
WHAT IS N? 7
M/N IS: 1.28571 42857 14

WHAT IS M? 29
WHAT IS N? 8

M/N IS: 3. 62500 00000 00

THE SUM IS: 4. 91071 42857 14
```

(Hint: Use the division program from Problem 8. Store the digits of the divisions in two arrays. After you've completed both divisions, add them together, doing the carries as in Section 15 3.)

10 Do Problem 14 4, only now use the index sorting method (with Clearsort, *not* Quicksort) to order the telephone numbers.

11 A **cross-reference dictionary** consists of multiple orderings of information. Add an employee-number piece of information to the phone-number information of Problem 14 4 (or an employee-name field, if arrays of strings are allowed in your version of BASIC), and use the index sort several times to put the items in order by both the phone numbers *and* and the employee numbers (or names). Print the sorted lists side by side on the page, with the list in order of employee numbers on the left, the list in order of phone numbers on the right.

```
EMPLOYEE    PHONE                    PHONE       EMPLOYEE
********************                 ***********************

2329      204 476 8882               202 384 4444      6708
3467      408 321 2209               204 476 8882      2329
3468      408 321 1340               303 468 9972      1281
4211      415 484 6418               408 321 1340      3468
4800      415 483 3848               408 321 2209      3467

  .         .   .   .                  .   .   .         .
  .         .   .   .                  .   .   .         .
  .         .   .   .                  .   .   .         .
```

BASIC was developed in 1965 at Dartmouth College by John G. Kemeny and Thomas E. Kurtz. Since that time it has been implemented in a number of slight variations on an enormous number of different computers. Until very recently there had been no agreement on a standard form of BASIC, so programs written in "BASIC" on one computer system might very well not run properly on the "BASIC" provided on another system. Most versions of BASIC, even ones defined before the American National Standards Institute issued their standard for Minimal BASIC, will run the programs shown in the first two parts of this book.

It has proved difficult to agree on standards for more advanced features because so many different versions of "BASIC" are already in existence. The versions of such non-Minimal features as string operators, long variable names, and multiline statements which we show in Part III are based on the American National Standards Institute's document X3J2/82-17, "Draft Proposed American National Standard for BASIC". In most cases, we also show common variants. You will probably have to refer to the manual for the specific version of BASIC that you're using to discover the exact forms to use on your computer. If your goal is to produce portable programs, you should stick to Minimal BASIC as much as is possible, because we suspect it will be several years before the new standards are widely implemented. Even after standards for these enhancements are accepted, programs written purely in Minimal BASIC will be able to run without alteration on the widest range of computer systems.

PART 3

Enhancements to BASIC

Chapter 16 **The String Enhancement**

Section 16 1

String Operators, Arrays of Strings

In Minimal BASIC, string values and variables are available, but no operations can be made on them. You can store string values (using LET, INPUT, or READ statements), you can PRINT them and you can test for equality or inequality of two strings, but that's all. In addition, to ensure portability, string values may be no more than 18 characters long.

In the proposed standard string enhancement, a variety of operations on strings is provided, you can make any sort of test between two string values you wish (=, >, <, >=, <=, <>), and string values may be up to 132 characters in length.

Just as in Minimal BASIC, string variables are identified by a letter followed by a dollar sign, Thus,

A$, B$, and Z$

are all valid names for string variables (But, see Section 19 1). Unlike in Minimal BASIC, however, we may have arrays of string values. For instance,

```
90        DIM R$(25)
```

declares that the array R$( ) will hold up to 26 string values, from R$(0) up to R$(25).

Before we get into any of the details, let's think about what operations we would like to perform on string values. String values are sequences of arbitrary characters. Here we'll put quotes (" ") around the characters in a string so it's obvious what string we mean, but remember that quotes are not always required in BASIC. Here's a typical string value:

```
"FARNSWORTHY J. C."
```

and here's another:

```
"SMITH CARLOTTA"
```

Certainly, one thing we might want to do is tell if one string value comes before another in alphabetical order. That's what the relational operators do. For instance,

```
330        IF "FARNSWORTHY J. C." < "SMITH CARLOTTA" THEN 500
```

will transfer control to line 500 because the first string does indeed appear before (i.e., is less than) the second in alphabetical order.

Quotes

When the meaning is obvious, BASIC doesn't require a string to be surrounded by quotes. The only places where it's obvious are in DATA statements and as replies to INPUT statements. These two forms are equivalent:

```
9000       DATA "PIZZA", "SALAD"
9000       DATA  PIZZA,   SALAD
```

When we're dealing with numeric values, we're accustomed to using operators like +, *, /, and −. But they don't make sense when we have string values—who knows what "FARNSWORTHY" multiplied by "SMITH" means? Instead, we need operators that are appropriate for dealing with text. We need to be able to tack two strings together to form a longer string. We need to be able to tell how long a string is. And we need to be able to break a string into smaller pieces. The operators shown in Table 16 1 1 provide these capabilities.

Rules for comparing strings

First, compare the leftmost characters of the two strings. If they are not the same, then one comes before the other alphabetically, and the test is decided. If the leading characters *are* the same, then the characters in the next position are compared. This process continues until some difference is found, or (if the strings are actually the same) the ends of the strings are reached. If the two strings are not of the same length, the shorter one is treated as if blanks had been added to its right end—enough blanks to make the strings the same length. The only question remaining is what happens when the two characters being compared are weird ones like "+"and "*", or "2" and "B"? We all know that "A" comes beore "B", but what about "2"? Here the order is given by the ASCII code. According to ASCII, the numbers come before the letters, so "2" comes before "B".

The string operators shown in Table 16 1 1 follow this convention: If the result of applying the operator is a string value, the operator's name ends with a $. This rule is violated only in the case of the concatenation and substring operators.

To explain the ORD( ) and CHR$( ) operators, we need to fill in a little background. All data values in BASIC are actually stored in a common internal form.

Table 16 1 1 Standard String Operators and Functions

operator	*meaning*	*example*
st_1 & st_2	concatenate; tack two strings together	"ABC" & "DEF" has the value "ABCDEF"
st (*n*:*l*)	the substring consisting of positions *n*, *n* + 1,. . . , *l* of string *st*.	if S$ is "ABCDEF" then S$(3:5) is "CDE"
CHR$(n)	the character corresponding to the internal numeric value given by *n*; typically 0⩽*n*⩽127; see ORD( ).	CHR$(65) is "A"
LEN(*st*)	the number of characters in the string value *st*; the length of *st*.	LEN("") is zero. IF S$ has the value "711 SUNSET" then LEN(S$) is 10.
LTRIM$(*st*)	the string value obtained by removing all lead blanks from *st*.	LEN (LTRIM$(" a")) is one.
ORD(*ch*)	the internal numeric code for the (single) character value *ch*; see CHR$( ).	ORD("A") is 65
POS (st_1, st_2)	First position within st_1 where a substring equal to st_2 begins; if st_2 doesn't occur in st_1 then POS (st_1, st_2) returns zero.	POS("Pizza", "zz") is 3 POS("Doe, John", ",") is 4 POS("xxx", ":") is 0
RTRIM$(*st*)	the string value obtained by removing all trailing blanks from *st*.	
STR$(*n*)	the string corresponding to the numeric value of *n*; like what PRINT *n* would show, but no leading or trailing blanks; see VAL( )	STR$(132.3) is "132.3" STR$(−5/2) is "−2.5"
UCASES$(*st*)	the string obtained by raising all lower case letters in *st* to upper case	UCASE$ ("Robin") is "ROBIN"
VAL (*st*)	the numeric value corresponding to the string *st*; see STR$( )	VAL ("132.3") is 132.3

Note: *st* means any expression whose value is a string value.
n and *l* mean any expression with numeric value.
ch means any expression whose value is a string of length one.
The first character in a string value is in position 1.

That is, the computer memory is capable of storing information only as some sequence of 1s and 0s. It is up to the program which uses the information to interpret the pattern of 1s and 0s in the appropriate way. The same pattern in memory can mean different things depending on which way the program using it chooses to interpret it. The ORD( ) operator interprets the pattern as a number—the CHR$( ) operator interprets the pattern as a character. Now it happens that the ASCII (American Standard Code for Information Interchange) code specifies not just the order of characters, but also the specific patterns of 1s and 0s used to represent each character in the computer's memory. So, if you know that you're doing, you can use

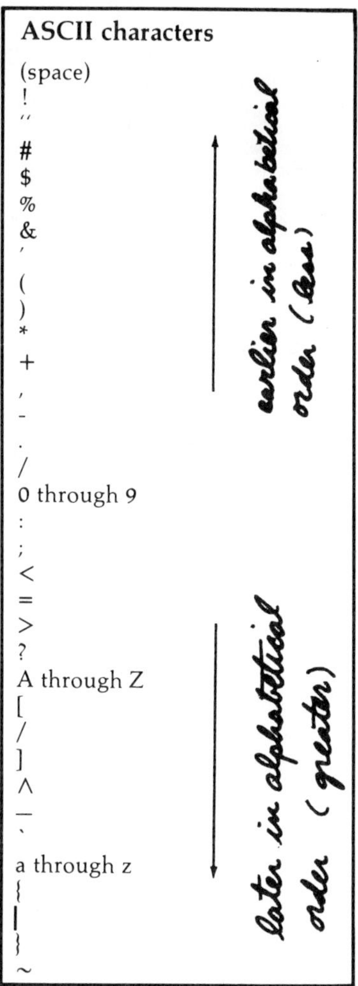

the CHR$( ) and ORD( ) operators to do things like code and decode spy messages, or, more commonly, change lower-case letters to upper case or vice versa. The subroutine shown below converts the character stored in C$ to upper case if it was a lower-case letter to begin with. Otherwise it leaves C$ alone.

```
10   REM  TEST THE CONVERT SUBROUTINE
20        PRINT "CONVERT WHAT CHARACTER";
30        INPUT C$
40        GOSUB 2000
50        PRINT "THE CONVERTED VERSION IS "; C$
60        PRINT
70        GO TO 20
2000 REM  CONVERT THE CHARACTER IN  C$  TO UPPER CASE
2010 REM    IF IT'S A LOWER CASE LETTER, OTHERWISE
2020 REM    LEAVE IT BE.
2030      IF C$>"z" THEN 2090
```

(program continued on page 398)

```
2040        IF C$<"a" THEN 2090
2050 REM      IT'S NOW LOWER CASE.  CONVERT TO UPPER
2060 REM      BY REMOVING THE ASCII OFFSET  A
2070          LET A = ORD("a") - ORD("A")
2080          LET C$ = CHR$( ORD(C$) - A )
2090        RETURN
9999        END
```

```
RUN
CONVERT WHAT CHARACTER? a
THE CONVERTED VERSION IS A

CONVERT WHAT CHARACTER? B
THE CONVERTED VERSION IS B

CONVERT WHAT CHARACTER? *
THE CONVERTED VERSION IS *

CONVERT WHAT CHARACTER? q
THE CONVERTED VERSION IS Q
            .
            .
            .
```

The substring operator can be used both on simple string variables and on array elements. For instance, suppose the array N$( ) holds a collection of product names. This process loop will print all the names which start with the letters M through Q. Don't be confused by the row of parentheses in line 930. The expression N$(I)(1:1) can be thought of like this: N$(I) specifies a string, then the substring operator (1:1) takes the first character of that string.

```
            .
            .
            .
910        FOR I=1 TO NO
920 REM        F$ IS THE FIRST LETTER OF THE I-TH PRODUCT NAME
930            F$ = N$(I)(1:1)
940            IF F$<"M" THEN 980
950            IF F$>"Q" THEN 980
960 REM            THIS NAME PASSES
970                PRINT I, N$(I)
980        NEXT I
            .
            .
            .
```

Some older versions of the string enhancement use a plus sign [+] instead of an ampersand for the concatenation operator. Also, many versions provide three substring operators [LEFT$, RIGHT$, and MID$] instead of the single standard substring operator. These operators are described in Table 16 1 2, and the equivalences between them and the standard substring notation are explored in Exercise 3.

Table 16 1 2 Common variant substring operators

operator	*meaning*	*example*
LEFT$(st,n)	the first n characters of st	LEFT$("YES",1) is "Y"
RIGHT$(st,n)	the last n characters of st	RIGHT$("WARSAW",3) is "SAW"
MID$(st,n,l)	the substring of length l beginning with the nth character in st	if B$ has the value "MONTUEWEDTHU", then MID$(B$,4,3) is "TUE"

EXERCISES 16 1

1 The box titled **ASCII characters** shows that both the comma and the space characters come earlier (are less than) any of the letters. Using that box and the **rules for comparing strings** box, put these strings in order.

```
"SMITH, JOHN"
"SMITHY,JOAN"
"SMITH  JEAN"
```

2 Which statements are true?

(a) CHR$(ORD(X$)) is the same as X$ whenever LEN(X$)=1.

(b) X$(1: N/2) & X$(N/2 : LEN(X$)) is the same as X$ no matter what value X$ has, as long an N is 0 or greater.

(c) X$(1:LEN(X$)) is the same as X$, no matter what value X$ has.

(d) VAL(STR$(N)) is always 1 unless N is 0.

3 Write an expression using the proposed standard subset operator which is equivalent to

(a) RIGHT$(A$,L)

(b) LEFT$(A$,L)

(c) MID$(A$,S,F)

Section 16 2

Putting People's Names in Order

The string enhancement is virtually indispensable when you're writing any kind of advanced business program. And it fits into Minimal BASIC very naturally. Here's an example of using the string enhancement features to do a common problem.

Let's write a program which will (1) get a list of people's names in standard Last, First Middle format; (2) put the list in alphabetical order; and (3) print the ordered list of names in the more socially acceptable First Middle Last format. We'll use a slightly altered version of subroutine Clearsort from Section 14 1 to do the sorting. If you have a lot of names to sort, and you care about how long it takes, subroutine Quicksort (Section 14 3) could be used.

—people's names—

INPUT names until END OF DATA.

Clearsort *the array of names.*

FOR each name in the sorted array

> Convert *to First Middle Last form.*
>
> *PRINT converted name.*

The only tricky part is converting a name from this form

```
"SMITH, ALVY RAY"
```

to this form

```
"ALVY RAY SMITH"
```

And that's not very tricky. Here's the plan for that step. The BASIC statements corresponding to the plan are in lines 420 through 510. To make sure you see how line 510 works, carry it out by hand for a few cases.

—put a name in First Middle Last form—

Search *the name for the first comma.*

Not found: PRINT error message.

Found: PRINT everything to the right of the comma, then a blank, then everything to the left of the comma.

```
10   REM  ACCEPT NAMES, PUT THEM IN ORDER.
100  REM  THE ARRAY  N$()  HOLDS THE NAMES.
110       DIM N$(100)
120  REM  GET UP TO 100 NAMES, STOP IF "END OF DATA"
130       FOR NO=1 TO 100
140           PRINT "LAST, FIRST MIDDLE=";
150           INPUT L$, F$
160           IF L$="END OF DATA" THEN 300
170           LET N$(NO) = L$ & "," & F$
180       NEXT NO
190  REM  OUT OF ROOM
200         PRINT "SORRY--NO MORE ROOM."
210         PRINT "FIRST 100 NAMES USED."
300  REM  HAVE ALL THE NAMES.
310       LET Z = NO - 1
320  REM  SORT THEM.
330       GOSUB 7000
400  REM  NOW PRINT EACH NAME IN POLITE FORM.
410       FOR N1=1 TO Z
420  REM        FIND COMMA, INVERT AROUND IT.
```

we have to put the comma in ourselves

if your BASIC doesn't conform to the standards concerning FOR-NEXT loops, you may need
220 LET Z = 100
230 GO TO 320

```
430             LET S$ = N$(N1)
440             FOR P=1 TO LENS(S$)
450                 IF S$(P:P)="," THEN 500
460               NEXT P
470   REM         NO COMMA FOUND!
480                 PRINT "GROSS ERROR--NO COMMA IN "; S$
490                 STOP
500   REM         FOUND THE COMMA, IT'S AT POSITION  P
510                 PRINT S$(P+1:LEN(S$)); " "; S$(1:P-1)
530         NEXT N1
540         PRINT
550         GO TO 9999

7000 REM    CLEARSORT--MODIFIED TO WORK ON STRING VALUES.
7010        FOR L0=1 TO Z - 1
7020 REM        MAKE N$(L0) BE SMALLEST VALUE OF N$(L0), ..., N$(Z)
7030            GOSUB 7100
7040 REM        P  IS POSITION OF SMALLEST VALUE.
7050            LET T$ = N$(L0)
7060            LET N$(L0) = N$(P)
7070            LET N$(P) = T$
7080        NEXT L0
7090        RETURN

7100 REM    SUBR--COMPUTE POSITION OF SMALLEST VALUE
7110 REM          IN  N$(L0), N$(L0+1), ..., N$(Z)
7120 REM    L0  IS POSITION OF SMALLEST-SO-FAR
7130        LET P = L0
7140        FOR L1=L0 + 1 TO Z
7150            IF N$(L1)>=N$(P) THEN 7180
7160 REM          HAVE NEW LOW.
7170              LET P = L1
7180        NEXT L1
7190        RETURN
9999        END

RUN
LAST, FIRST MIDDLE=? SMYTH, CALVIN K
LAST, FIRST MIDDLE=? SMYTHE, SALLY MAY
LAST, FIRST MIDDLE=? SMITH, JAMES
LAST, FIRST MIDDLE=? SMITH, JANE
LAST, FIRST MIDDLE=? SMITH, ALVY RAY
LAST, FIRST MIDDLE=? LANGSFORD, RAYMOND
LAST, FIRST MIDDLE=? END OF DATA,
RAYMOND LANGSFORD
ALVY RAY SMITH
JAMES SMITH
JANE SMITH
CALVIN K SMYTH
SALLY MAE SMYTHE

READY
```

Search S$ for a comma (→ 440–450)

Not Found: (→ 470)

Found: (→ 500)

Clearsort changed to work on string values. (7000–7190)

Compare to the version in Section 14 1

look at line 150 in the program to see why we typed a comma here (→ END OF DATA,)

EXERCISES 16 2

1 Which of these subroutines removes all leadings blanks from the string in N$?

(a)
```
8710   IF N$(1:1)<>" " THEN 8740
8720     LET N$ = N$( LEN(N$):LEN(N$) )
8730     GO TO 8710
8740   RETURN
```

(b)
```
8710   IF N$(1:1)=" " THEN 8740
8720     LET N$ = N$(1:LEN(N$))
8730     GO TO 8710
8740   RETURN
```

(c)
```
8710   IF N$(1:1)<>" " THEN 8740
8720     LET N$ = N$(2:LEN(N$))
8730     GO TO 8710
8740   RETURN
```

2 Line 510 in the people's names program does three things. It removes the comma (which is at position P) from the name, it reverses the name so the Last name comes last, and it prints the name. Write three lines which do the three operations one at a time, with the same end result.

3 Generalize the technique used to find the (first) comma in the string S$ to create a subroutine which returns (in numeric variable P) the starting position of the first occurrence of the string T$ in the string S$. If T$ doesn't occur in S$, P should be 0.

4 If your version of BASIC provides the POS( ) operator (see TABLE 16 1 1), you don't need the search loop we used to find the comma in the people's names program. Write a LET statement which will give the variable P the value 0 if the string S$ has no comma, and gives the position of the (first) comma in S$ if there is (at least) one. Revise the people's names program to use your LET statement.

PROBLEMS 16

1 Write a program which you can use to print birthday greetings to your friends. Use the idea shown below, or think up one of your own.

Happy Birthday program: First your program should ask for a person's name. Then it should print a fancy pattern like this:

```
H
HA
HAP
HAPP
HAPPY
HAPPY
HAPPY B
HAPPY BI
HAPPY BIR
HAPPY BIRT
HAPPY BIRTH
HAPPY BIRTHD
HAPPY BIRTHDA
HAPPY BIRTHDAY
HAPPY BIRTHDAY WANDA JUNE!
```

2 Write a program which asks for a string, and which then prints the original string and the same string backwards. Write the part which reverses a string as a subroutine.

> **palindrome:** a word or phrase which reads the same forward as backward.
> A palindrome: "Madam, I'm Adam."
> Not a palindrome: "Able was I ere I saw Chicago."

3 Write a program which detects palindromes. Blanks, punctuation marks, and capitalizations don't count in determining palindromes, so when you type in a phrase to be tested, type just the letters. Here are some phrases you can use to test your solution.

RADAR
TOOHOTTOHOOT
PIZZA
(Hint: Use the subroutine from problem 2.)

4 Revise the palindrome program from problem 3. Add a preprocessor subroutine which removes blanks and punctuation marks from the phrase being tested. Here are some phrases you can use to test your new version.

A MAN,A PLAN,A CANAL:PANAMA!
WARSAW WAS RAW, YES SIR!
POOR DAN WAS IN A DROOP.

5 Revise the inventory control program in Section 10 3 so that in addition to storing the quantity on hand and price of each item, a product description is stored. In the checkout mode the product description should appear to the left of the price, so the customer has a list of what was bought with the price of each. In the inquiry mode print the item number, product description, quantity on hand, and price. In the restock mode, when the user enters the item number, print the product description, and ask the user if that's the right item. If so, go on as before. If not, loop back to get the right item number.

6 Revise the program at the end of Section 14 2 so that in addition to the Manufacturer code, specific product code, quantity on hand, and price of each item, a product description (a string value) is stored. Revise clearsort so it orders the items in increasing order of their product descriptions.

7 Combine your solution to Problem 6 with the ideas in Problem 10 9 to create a realistic, useful inventory control system for a grocery store. In addition to the checkout, inquiry, and restock modes, add a report mode which prints out a listing of all items in order of their product descriptions.

8 The Boss Tweed Clothing chain does an enormous amount of direct mail advertising, and has been getting a lot of complaints from people who have received multiple copies of its glossy four-color flyer. Boss Tweed has discovered that one of their big problems is that the format of people's names they buy varies from mailing list to mailing list. Even though the program they use checks for duplicate names, it doesn't help much because it tests for an exact equality of names. If one version of a name differs just by a space or a period, their program thinks the names are different.

Write a subroutine which makes a "soft" comparison between two names. It should put the two names into a standard form before making the test for equality.

Write a program to test your subroutine. It should decide that these strings represent the same name

```
PHILIP K NERDLY
PHILIP K. NERDLY
PHILIP     K.     NERDLY
```

but differ from this

PHILIPA K NERDLY

> **note:**
>
> If you think it would be more reasonable to solve Boss Tweed's problem by comparing street addresses instead of names, do it that way. The subroutine will be exactly the same.

9 Increasingly, computer systems are being used by people who have no background in computers or programming. Bank tellers, sales personnel, used car dealers, and cooks suddenly find themselves face to face with computer terminals. If you write a program for use by such people, you'll find that the less restrictive your program is, the easier time the totally naive user will have, and the more likely you'll get another programming job.

Write a subroutine which asks the user for a number, and which returns the value of what the user typed. Design your subroutine so it accepts at least these cases:

user response	*action*
1	return the value 1 to the main program
+1	return the value 1
$1.00	return the value 1
1	tell the user you don't understand that, and ask for another response
1.0.	tell the user you don't understand, and ask for another response
50¢	return the value 0.5

(Hint: INPUT the user response as a string, then try to put it in a standard form. If it can be put in your standard form, use the VAL( ) operator to extract the value.)

10 Write a subroutine which asks a totally naive user for a date, and which interprets the response if possible, and asks for another response if not. Accept at least these cases:

user response	*action*
1/12/1984	accepted; Month = 1, Day = 12; Year = 1984
9/31/82	print "THAT DATE DOESN'T EXIST! TRY AGAIN PLEASE"
9 30 82	accepted; Month = 9; Day = 30; Year = 1982
8-2-12	accepted; Month = 8; Day = 2; Year = 2012

(Hints: Use the date checker subroutine from Section 6 2 to tell whether a particular date exists. Assume that any user response which gives a year number less than 40 means 2000 plus that number. Assume that any user response which gives a year number less than 100 and greater than or equal to 40 means 1900 plus that number. Assume that any user response which gives a three-digit year number is in error. Assume that any four-digit year number means that year.)

11 Write a program which could be used to print the results of a mile race. In the first phase it should accept runners' names and their times. Once all the names and times have been entered, it should begin the report-generation phase. In this

phase, first the entries are displayed in order of times (winner first), then the entries are displayed in alphabetical order of the runners' names. The second format should include the runner's name, time, and finishing position.

12 Write a program that accepts names of states or abbreviations of names of states and that returns the official U.S. Post Office abbreviations for each state named. If an abbreviation is undecipherable, print an appropriate message. Unless you feel like doing more, just have your program deal with the 11 western states.

user response	*action*
NEVADA	print "THE OFFICIAL USPO ABBREVIATION IS NV"
MONT.	print "THE OFFICAL USPO ABBREVIATION IS MT"
C.	print "SORRY, I DON'T KNOW WHICH STATE YOU MEAN."

11 western states	
Arizona	AZ
California	CA
Colorado	CO
Idaho	ID
Montana	MT
Nevada	NV
New Mexico	NM
Oregon	OR
Utah	UT
Washington	WA
Wyoming	WY

(Hint: This problem can be as hard as you want to make it. It would be best to do it in stages. In the first stage accept only a correctly spelled state name or the official USPO abbreviation. In the next stage accept those plus anything that matches the first few letters of just one state (i.e., "CAL" matches just "CALIFORNIA", but "C" matches two western states). If you want to go on, start by trying to figure out why "WSHNGTN" seems "closer" to "WASHINGTON" than any other name. Then program your idea.)

13 Write a program which accepts a body of text, on line at a time, and determines which words appear in the (entire) text, and the number of times each word appears. you may assume that not more than 300 different words will appear in the text. If your program finds more, have it give an error message and quit. Otherwise your program should quit when it gets the line

```
END OF DATA
```

Once your program has accepted its last line, have it print each different word it found, the number of occurrences of each word, the total number of different words, and the total number of characters in the text.

Note: If your version of BASIC provides a LINPUT or INPUT LINE feature (Section 18 8), use it to gather the text. Otherwise have the user enclose each line in quotes so you don't get into trouble with commas in the text.

14 Redo Problem 13, but have your program produce a concordance instead of an unordered list of the words it found in the text.

> **concordance:** an alphabetical list of all the words in a text along with the number of occurrences of each word.

Chapter 17 **PRINT and INPUT Enhancements**

Section 17 1

Free Form INPUT

One big problem with using the INPUT statement in Minimal BASIC is that if the user types a comma when you don't expect it, it causes the user's response to be broken into parts. Also, on some systems, if the user just hits the return key without typing anything else, an error message appears. This may not be what you would like. In both these cases, you might like to have more control over how a user's input is handled. This is made possible via the line input enhancement.

standard form

  LINE INPUT *string-variable*

other common forms

  LINPUT *string-variable*

  INPUT LINE *string-variable*

Check your manual to see which form you can use with your version of BASIC. When a LINE INPUT statement is used, everything the user types up to the first carriage return (or until no more characters will fit in the *string variable*) is put into the *string variable*. Notice that, unlike with a regular INPUT statement, here only a *single* string variable is specified.

In the examples, assume the program is carrying out this line:

```
120    LINE INPUT R$
```

if the user types	*R$ gets this value*
CHANDLER, RAYMOND↲	"CHANDLER, RAYMOND"
NICK DANGER↲	"NICK DANGER"
↲	""
1, 2, 3, ..., INFINITY↲	1, 2, 3, ..., INFINITY"

↵ denotes the carriage return character

One other problem you may have with the Minimal BASIC INPUT statement is this: What if you don't *want* your program to print a question mark before accepting a response from the user? In Minimal BASIC there's no way to avoid it, but the enhanced INPUT statement provides a way. By including an explicit PROMPT, the normal question mark is eliminated.

standard form
INPUT PROMPT *quoted-string* : variable-list

other common form
INPUT *quoted-string;* variable-list

For instance, when this statement is carried out,

```
130     INPUT PROMPT "Password:" : p$
```

the user will see

```
Password:
```

on the screen, with no question mark.

EXERCISES 17 1

1 Using the line input enhancement, write a subroutine which puts the message

```
HIT <RETURN> TO GO ON?
```

starting at column 40, then waits until the user strikes the return key.

2 Using the line input and prompt enhancements, revise your solution to Exercise 1 so the question mark doesn't appear.

Section 17 2
Formatted Output

Most of the time the PRINT statement gives us what we want. We can use it to print numbers we've computed and intersperse them with commentary. However, there are some times when the PRINT statement doesn't give us what we really would like to see on the printed page. For example, the PRINT statement puts spaces around numbers. That works out fine most of the time because it separates one number from the next. It's annoying when we need to jam the numbers next to each other for some reason or to separate them by some nonblank symbol. Printing calendar dates is a familiar example. If we have the month, day, and year stored in the variables M, D, and Y, we might like to print them in the form

```
10/27/80
```

But if we used the PRINT statement

```
PRINT M; "/"; D; "/"; Y
```

we would get

```
10 / 27 / 80
```

— too strung out. In situations like this we need more control over the printing process.

The **PRINT USING** statement is provided to fill this need. With this statement the programmer describes the format of the line exactly as it should appear when it is printed, and the computer uses the description when it does the printing. Things like spacing, number of decimal places in numbers, and whether or not to print leading zeros can be specified in the description of the line.

The standard PRINT USING statement comes in two forms:

PRINT USING *quoted string* : *formatted PRINT list*

or

PRINT USING *statement label* : *formatted PRINT list*

You will probably find that the version of BASIC you use provides one or the other. In the first form, the *quoted string* following the word USING provides a description of how the values in the *formatted PRINT list* should appear. In the second form, the *statement label* following the word USING must be the line number of an IMAGE statement. An IMAGE statement looks like this:

IMAGE : *unquoted-string*

The unquoted string in the IMAGE statement serves the same purpose as the quoted string in the first form of the PRINT USING statement.

The *formatted PRINT list* is just like the lists of things to be printed we're used to putting in PRINT statements except for two restrictions. First, successive items must be separated by commas (no semicolons allowed except possibly at the very end). And second, no TAB( ) spacers may appear.

Let's follow through a few examples of the first form. Once you understand the basic idea — that the quoted string is providing a sort of picture (or image) of how the values should be printed on a line, you will probably be able to decipher your manual. (You *will* need the manual for your specific version of BASIC, since we are unaware of *any* existing version of BASIC which completely follows the standards!)

The quoted string in a PRINT USING (or the unquoted string in an IMAGE statement) contains a sequence of characters which have a one-to-one correspondence with the character positions on the line which will be printed by the statement. The string tells in detail how the values in the formatted PRINT list should be printed. It specifies not only where the values should be printed, but also how such things as leading zeros and commas in large numbers should be treated. Table 17 2 1 shows the characters which have special meanings for PRINT USING. All other characters appear verbatim in the printed line, so a PRINT USING like this which contains no special characters in its quoted string, and which has an empty formatted PRINT list simply prints the quoted string.

Example 1

```
PRINT USING "Nothing special to do." :
```

output:

```
Nothing special to do.
```

The special characters #, %, and * are used to specify fields in which either numeric (if the matching item in the formatted PRINT list is numeric) or string (if the matching item is a string value) values will be printed. A **field** is made up of a contiguous sequence of special characters. In the next example, all the characters except the two exclamation points (which are printed verbatim) make up a single field. The field has space for five digits to the left and two to the right of the decimal point, and a PRINT USING will always fit the matching numeric value into that space. Trailing zeros are printed. With the # character, leading zeros are replaced by spaces.

Table 17 2 1 Characters with special meaning in PRINT USING formats

character	*meaning*
<	left justify following field
>	right justify following field
*	position for a character or digit — if digit, then if this position would be a leading zero, print * instead.
#	position for a character or digit — if digit, then if this position would be a leading zero, print a space instead.
%	position for a character or digit — if digit, then if this position would be a leading zero, print it.
$	floating dollar sign — position just to left of leading digit or sign (if any is present)
,	optional comma — print only if digit position immediately to left is filled with a digit.
.	decimal point for a real number
−	place a sign only if the value is negative.
+	print a + sign if the value is positive, a − sign if negative.
^	position for exponent in E-notation for a number

Note: Any other character (e.g., a letter, a digit, a parenthesis, etc.) which appears inside a format string is to be printed verbatim.

Example 2

```
PRINT USING "!#####.##!": 7
```

output:

```
!     7.00!
```

Now we can get to the case we started worrying about — printing dates in a uniform format. The / characters in the PRINT USING below are not special characters, so they will be printed verbatim. In addition, they serve to delimit the fields for the month, day, and year.

Example 3

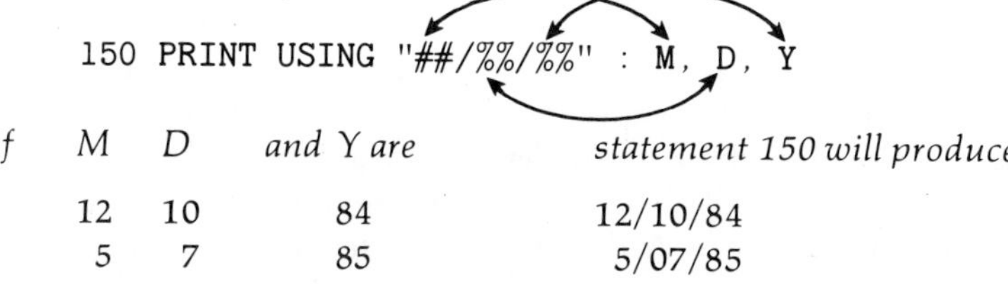

if	*M*	*D*	*and Y are*	*statement 150 will produce*
	12	10	84	12/10/84
	5	7	85	5/07/85

The format string "##/%%/%%" specifies a field of 8 characters. The # and % signs indicate that digits will be filled in at the corresponding positions. The # character means that if the digit assigned to the corresponding position would be a leading zero, print a space instead. The % sign means that if the digit assigned to the corresponding position would be a leading zero, go ahead and print it. This explains why the second example has a one digit month, but a two digit (07) sequence for the day.

Example 4

```
5010 PRINT USING "Total Due $*,***.##": T2
```

if T2 has the value	*statement 5010 will produce*
1.25	Total Due $****1.25
3456.00	Total Due $3,456.00

Example 5

```
5030 PRINT USING "Total Due $#,###.##": B
```

if B has the value	*statement 5030 will produce*
1.25	Total Due $1.25
3456.00	Total Due $3,456.00
−55	Total Due $−55.00

Example 6

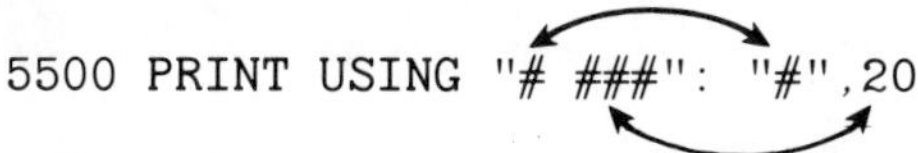

```
5500 PRINT USING "# ###": "#",20
```

will print the line

```
#  20
```

EXERCISES 17 2

1 Using the manual for your version of BASIC, look up the form of PRINT USING you have available. Does it require that the format string appear in an IMAGE statement?

2 Using your manual, look up the special characters which have meaning in PRINT USING format strings. How many of them are the same as the standard ones shown in Table 17 2 1?

PROBLEMS 17

Redo a problem from an earlier chapter, but use PRINT USING to improve the appearance of the printed output. Here are some suggestions:

Chapter 3 Problem 13
Chapter 4 Problem 3
Chapter 4 Problem 4
Chapter 5 Problem 8
Chapter 5 Problem 9
Chapter 5 Problem 10
Chapter 6 Problem 1
Chapter 6 Problem 11
Chapter 6 Problem 13
Chapter 7 Problem 1
Chapter 7 Problem 3
Chapter 8 Problem 1
Chapter 8 Problem 2
Chapter 8 Problem 3

Chapter 18 **The Files Enhancement**

Section 18 1
What's Here

In the first edition of this book, we described three typical versions of the files enhancement. Those three versions were radically different from each other. We said "Let's hope that when ANSI defines standards for the file enhancement, they can make order out of the chaos." Today we have a proposed ANSI standard which does, in one way or another, incorporate most of the capabilities of many of the pre-existing file enhancements. But we know of no existing version of BASIC which implements the proposed standards. That means the version you are using almost certainly is different from the proposed standards. We are in the uncomfortable position of writing about a feature (the files enhancement) which is in flux. Probably in four or five years, many versions of BASIC will conform to the ANSI standards. But you have to write programs before then. So, in the next two sections of this chapter, we cover three typical existing versions of the files enhancement. You will have to pay close attention to the manual for your version of BASIC to make sure which file enhancements are appropriate for your situation. Good luck.

Section 18 2
Typical Forms

All computer systems except the most tiny come with some form of i/o device which can be used as additional memory. Perhaps the system you're using has cassette tape recorders hooked to it. Perhaps it has floppy disks, or fixed-head disks or disk packs, or large magnetic tape units, or bubble memory, or magnetic card memory. These devices have four characteristics in common. They provide a large amount of storage compared to the computer's regular (main) memory. They provide a permanent (well, at least long-term) method of storing information. They are much cheaper per data value stored than the computer's main memory. And they are much slower than the computer's main memory.

In problems like inventory control (Section 10 4) or questionnaire analysis (Chapter 11), there are two main reasons for utilizing a peripheral memory device. Most computers today lose whatever is stored in their main memory when the power is turned off. Most inventories and questionnaire responses involve too much data to consider typing it all in again each time you want to use the program. That might mean that either you leave the inventory program with the inventory data in the computer 24 hours a day, never turn the power off, and never use the computer for anything else — or, you store the data (and program, but that's another story) on some peripheral device like tape or disk. That way, you can turn the computer off, or can run other programs — without affecting the data for the inventory. When you want to use it again, you just read it into the computer's main memory from the peripheral device.

The second reason for using peripheral memory devices is to overcome the limitations imposed by the size of main memory. For instance, in our questionnaire program (Chapter 11) we were limited to handling something like 90 responses at a time — no more would fit. By storing the responses on a peripheral device, we will be able to deal with an almost unlimited number of responses. Of course, there's a price to pay — our program will run much more slowly because getting a data value from a peripheral device can take thousands of times as long as getting a data value from the computer's main memory.

Storing programs

Here we're concentrating on using peripheral devices to store data values. Of course, these devices are also used to store programs so you don't have to type them in each time you want to use them. But on most systems there are very convenient ways to store programs. See Appendix A.

Data stored on devices like disks and magnetic tape is organized into groups called **files.** There are two main sorts of file organizations. A **stream file** consists of a sequence of values, with no other organization. For example, the stream of characters that a program sends to a printer has no underlying organization, as far as the computer system is concerned. The other type of file consists of a number of individual records, where a **record** is an organized collection of **fields.** Each field is a data value.

Typically, many different files can be stored on a given device. When your program wants to access data in some file, it must be able to specify which one it wants. Thus, there is a way to **name** files. Almost always, a file is named by giving a string value, often in a form like this:

```
"RESPONSE.DAT"
```

The substring after the period is called an **extension,** and may refer to the type of file. Here we're imagining that the file "RESPONSE.DAT" consists of DATa giving questionnaire RESPONSEs.

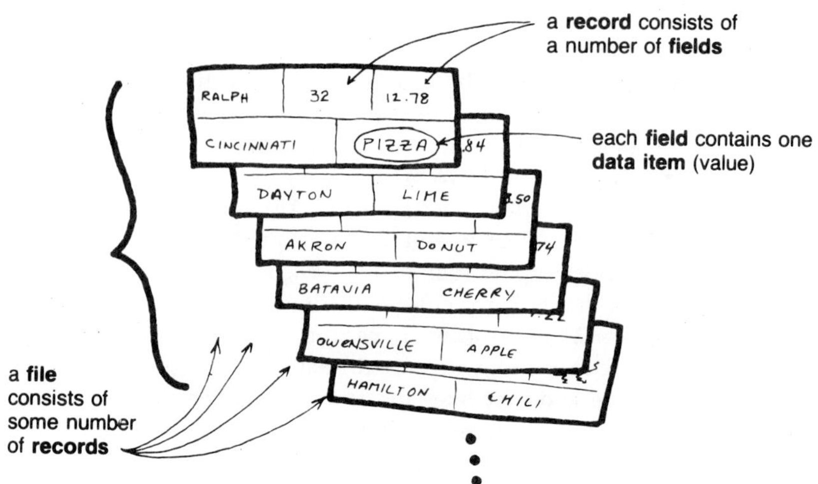

Figure 18 2 1 Files, records, fields, values

Besides being able to identify a particular file, our programs need to be able to create new files, read values from existing files, put data into existing files, wipe out files we don't want any more, and change the name of a file.

Also associated with a file is an **access method.** That is, a way for programs to read and write values from and to the file. The two major categories are **sequential** and **random access.** If the peripheral device is a tape recorder, then data values are necessarily stored sequentially — one after another. If the device is some sort of disk, then any storage location (choose one at random) can be accessed about as easily as any other, and a **random access** organization is possible. Any device which can handle random access files can also handle sequential files. Some devices, like tape recorders, can handle sequential files only. The proposed standards use the term **relative file** for what we call random access file. The standards also describe **keyed files** in which a given record can be identified by a string value (the key) as well as by record number.

The rest of this section shows how the common file operations are done on the two types of files (sequential and random access) on three popular versions of BASIC. CBASIC (sold by Digital Research, Inc.) is used on many commercial microcomputers. BASIC-PLUS (sold by the Digital Equipment Corporation) is used on a large number of time-shared computer systems. HP-45 BASIC is used on a popular line of desktop computers manufactured by the Hewlett-Packard company. In Table 18 2 1 not every file-related command available in each of the three versions is shown — some, especially BASIC-PLUS, provide a bewildering array of subtly different options. We show enough to do most normal tasks, however.

Let's try to make sense of Table 18 2 1. We'll go over each of the tasks, explaining them in more detail, and adding a few notes.

In all three file enhancements (CBASIC, BASIC-PLUS, and HP-45 BASIC) there are two different ways to refer to a specific file. First, there is the **external file name** (see entry 1 in the table). This is a name that is used by the operating system of the computer to keep track of files — it's not part of BASIC. In addition, there is an **internal designator** (a number) which is used within your BASIC program to refer to a

Table 18 2 1 Three Versions of the File Enhancement

	task	CBASIC	BASIC-PLUS	HP-45 BASIC
1	name a file	"*device*:*name*.*extension*" *device* is a letter (A,. . . ,P) which specifies a particular disk drive or tape unit *name* is from 1 to 8 characters *extension* is from 1 to 3 characters *device*: and .*extension* are optional examples: "B:FAMILY.DAT" "MENU.BAS" "TEMP"	"*device*:*name*.*extension* [*proj*, *programmer*] <*protection*>" *device* consists of an abbreviation for a peripheral device (e.g., MT for mag tape, DF for disk drive) followed by a digit from 0 to 7 specifying which such device *name* is from 1 to 6 characters *extension* is from 1 to 3 characters *proj* is a number from 1 to 254 giving the "project number" *programmer* is a number from 1 to 254 giving the "programmer number" *protection* is a number from 1 to 63 specifying who may access and alter the file (e.g., if *protection* is 60, only the owner may access the file, where the "owner" is anyone who knows *proj* and *programmer* *device*: , .*extension*, [*proj*, *programmer*] and <*protection*> are optional examples: "MT2:FAMILY.DAT [44, 2]<40>" "MENU.BAS<16>" "TEMP"	"*name*: *msus*" *name* is from 1 to 6 characters *msus* is a mass storage unit specifier, which identifies an i/o device in detail *msus* is optional examples: "FAMILY" "DATA:T15" "MENU:Y7"

Table 18 2 1 Three Versions of the File Enhancement (Cont.)

2	gain access to an existing sequential file called "RESP", use internal designator 1	OPEN "RESP" AS 1	OPEN "RESP" FOR INPUT AS FILE 1	ASSIGN # 1 TO "RESP"
3	gain access to an existing random access file called "RAND" with record length 200	OPEN "RAND" RECL 200 AS 2	OPEN "RAND" FOR INPUT AS FILE 2 DIM #2, A$(1000)=200	ASSIGN #2 TO "RAND"
4	gain access to an existing sequential file named "NAMES" if one exists already; otherwise create a new file with that name	FILE "NAMES"	OPEN "NAMES" AS FILE 3	70 ON END #3 GO TO 2000 80 ASSIGN #3 TO "NAMES" . . . 2000 CREATE "NAMES", 20, 32 2010 GO TO 80
5	gain access to a file called "INTS", creating it if it doesn't already exist; wiping out all the records in it if it does already exist	CREATE "INTS" AS 4	OPEN "INTS" FOR OUTPUT AS FILE 4	PURGE "INTS" CREATE "INTS", 100 ASSIGN #4 TO "INTS"
6	change the name of the file "RESP" to "CURS"	CLOSE 1 (if currently OPEN), then LET F = RENAME ("CURS", "RESP")	NAME "RESP" AS "CURS"	RENAME "RESP" TO "CURS"
7	read the next record from file #1 (a sequential file)	READ #1; *list*	INPUT #1; *list*	READ #1; *list*
8	read record number R0 from random access file #2	READ #2, R0; *list*	LET *var* = A$(R0)	READ #2, R0; *list*
9	write the next record on sequential file #3	PRINT #3; *list*	PRINT #3; *list*	PRINT #3; *list*
10	write record number 74 on random access file #2	PRINT #2, 74; *list*	LET A$(74) = *value*	PRINT #2, 74; *list*
11	detect whether a READ operation on a sequential file has just read the end-of-file mark.	IF END #3 THEN 4000	ON ERROR GOTO 3000 plus 3000 IF ERR=11 THEN 4000 3010 RESUME	ON END #3 GO TO 4000

Note: In some places we had to continue on to the next line to make the examples fit on the page. Be sure to type OPEN "RAND" RECL 200 AS 2 all on one line when you enter it, though.

Table 18 2 1 Three Versions of the File Enhancement (Cont.)

	task	CBASIC	BASIC-PLUS	HP-45 BASIC
12	detect the end of a random access file	the form above (IF END) may be used if sequential READs are being performed on the random access file; otherwise the program must keep track of how many records are currently in the file	DIM statement gives maximum number of records available (see entry 3 above)	ON END #3 GO TO 5000
13	terminate use of file with internal designation 2, leaving it intact for later use	CLOSE 2	CLOSE 2 (If the file is sequential, the program must place an end-of-file mark at the end, like this: PRINT #2; CHR$(26))	ASSIGN #2 TO *
14	wipe out file #3 (external name "NAMES"), wiping out all the data in it, and leaving no record of its existence	DELETE 3	KILL "NAMES"	ASSIGN #3 TO * (if open) PURGE "NAMES"
15	go back to the beginning of a sequential file with external name "QUESTS" and internal designator 7	CLOSE 7 then OPEN "QUESTS" AS 7	CLOSE 7 then OPEN "QUESTS" FOR INPUT AS FILE 7	ASSIGN #1 TO * ASSIGN #1 TO "QUESTS"

Notes: Each of the forms shown is a BASIC statement, and appears preceded by a line number in an actual program.

In all cases the internal designator (and the record number) may be specified by a numeric expression; thus, if F has the value 2, entry 9 could be written as

PRINT #F + 1; *list*

list is a list of expressions like those that appear in READ, INPUT, or PRINT statements in Minimal BASIC (except that TAB( ) may not be included).

var means a BASIC variable of the appropriate type.

value means a single expression of the appropriate type.

Information on CBASIC is from *CBASIC: A Reference Manual*, Software Systems, 1977.

Information on BASIC-PLUS is from *BASIC-PLUS Language Manual*, Digital Equipment Corporation, 1972.

Information on HP-45 BASIC is from *Hewlett-Packard System 45B Desktop Computer Operating and Programming*, Hewlett-Packard Desktop Computer Division, 1979.

specific file. The first step in using a file in any of the three versions is to set up a correspondence between an external file name and an internal designator. In all three versions, part of the external file name can tell which specific device the file will be (or is already) stored on. You will have to refer to a local expert or the manual for your specific computer system to determine what to do with the *device* part of external file names. If your goal is to use a file to store data for a BASIC program, the *name* (and *extension*) part of an external file name can be chosen at will — as long as you don't accidentally choose a name someone else has used for a file of their own. The external file name does not tell whether the file will be used in the sequential or the random access mode — if the device can perform random accesses, the program may treat a file in either fashion.

Entries 2 through 5 in the table show ways of hooking external file names to internal designators. In all cases except CBASIC entry 4, the internal designator is specified directly as part of the statement which makes the hookup. Once a statement like

```
100    ASSIGN #1 TO "RESP"
```

has been carried out, further references to the file RESP are made by giving not the name (RESP) but the internal designator (in this case, 1). The exception is in CBASIC. The statement

```
100    FILE "NAMES"
```

hooks the file called NAMES to the next available internal designator. Thus, if two files with designators 1 and 2 had already been opened by the time line 100 was reached, NAMES would be assigned the internal designator 3. In CBASIC the internal designator is a number from 1 to 20; in BASIC-PLUS a number from 1 to 12; in HP-45 BASIC a number from 1 to 10.

On some systems creating a new file consists of nothing more than recording the name of the file (e.g., NAMES) and setting aside a little space on the peripheral device. As the program sends data to the file, every so often more space will be needed, and it is allocated at that time. Other systems are less flexible, and the ultimate size of the file is fixed when it is created. HP-45 BASIC reflects the latter case. Notice the CREATE statements in entries 4 and 5 (in the HP-45 column). The first number after the file name tells how many records to allocate for the file. The second number (if one appears) tells the number of characters per record. Thus,

```
2000   CREATE "NAMES", 20, 32
```

creates a file called NAMES and sets aside space for 20 records, each of length 32. If the second number is left out, a record size of 256 is assumed. Further, on the HP-45, each record is filled with delimiting markers. Thus, if you create a large file on a slow device, it may take the system quite a while to "create" a file. In CBASIC systems, on the other hand, creating a file is fast; but every so often, as the file fills up, you may notice a delay as another block of space is allocated to your file. Each system not only has its own way of expressing the file operations, it also has its own quirky personality!

On most systems all files, whether the user thinks of them as sequential or as random access, are stored in a uniform manner. Thus, it is usually possible to treat a given file in either manner. From that point of view, it's not reasonable to call a *file* sequential — it's the *access* method that's either sequential or random access.

Let's discuss using a **sequential file.** Entries 2, 4, and 5 show ways of obtaining access to a sequential file. A sequential file, like any other file, consists of some number of records. Unlike in a random access file, however, each record can be of a different length. Given an existing sequential file, each read operation (entry 7) accesses the next record. If you are at the end of a sequential file (see entry 11), each successive write operation (entry 9) puts a new record on the file. (If you start writing into a newly created file or an empty file, you are at the end of file to begin with.) It's OK to think of the fields in a record in a sequential file as being separated by commas, with records being separated by carriage returns. Here's a simple example of creating, writing into, and reading from a sequential file.

CBASIC

```
10      CREATE "MAIL" AS 1
20      PRINT #1; "NAMES AND CITIES"
30      PRINT "NAME=";
40      INPUT N$
50      IF N$="END OF DATA" THEN 100
60          PRINT "CITY=";
70          INPUT C$
80          PRINT #1; N$, C$
90          GO TO 30
100     CLOSE 1
110     OPEN "MAIL" AS 1
120     READ #1; M$
130     PRINT M$
140     IF END #1 THEN 200
150     READ #1; N$, C$
160         PRINT N$; TAB(33); C$
170         PRINT
180         GO TO 150
200     CLOSE 1
9999    END
```

BASIC-PLUS

```
10      OPEN "MAIL" FOR OUTPUT AS FILE 1
20      PRINT #1; "NAMES AND CITIES"
30      PRINT "NAME=";
40      INPUT N$
50      IF N$="END OF DATA" THEN 100
60          PRINT "CITY=";
70          INPUT C$
80          PRINT #1; N$ C$
90          GO TO 30
100     PRINT #1; CHR$(26)
101     CLOSE 1
110     OPEN "MAIL" FOR INPUT AS FILE 1
120     READ #1; M$
130     PRINT M$
140     ON ERROR GO TO 2000
150     READ #1; N$, C$
160         PRINT N$; TAB(33); C$
170         PRINT
180         GO TO 150
2000    IF ERR=11 THEN 4000
2010    RESUME
4000    CLOSE 1
9999    END
```

HP-45 BASIC

```
10      CREATE "NAMES", 100
15      ASSIGN #1 TO "NAMES"
20      PRINT #1; "NAMES AND CITIES"
30      PRINT "NAME=";
40      INPUT N$
50      IF N$="END OF DATA" THEN 100
60          PRINT "CITY=";
70          INPUT C$
80          PRINT #1; N$, C$
90          GO TO 30
100     ASSIGN #1 TO *
110     ASSIGN #1 TO "NAMES"
120     READ #1; M$
130     PRINT M$
140     ON END #1 GO TO 200
150     READ #1; N$, C$
160         PRINT N$; TAB(33); C$
170         PRINT
180         GO TO 150
200     ASSIGN #1 TO *
9999    END
```

To the user, all three versions look the same:

```
RUN
NAME=? JASON
CITY=? ALBANY
NAME=? SUSAN
CITY=? CINCINNATI
NAME=? END OF DATA
NAMES AND CITIES
JASON                               ALBANY

SUSAN                               CINCINNATI

READY
```

After the program is finished, the file MAIL will still exist, and the three records that were created will still be there for later use. Figure 18 2 2 illustrates the operation of the programs.

From the programming end, there are a number of small differences in the programs.

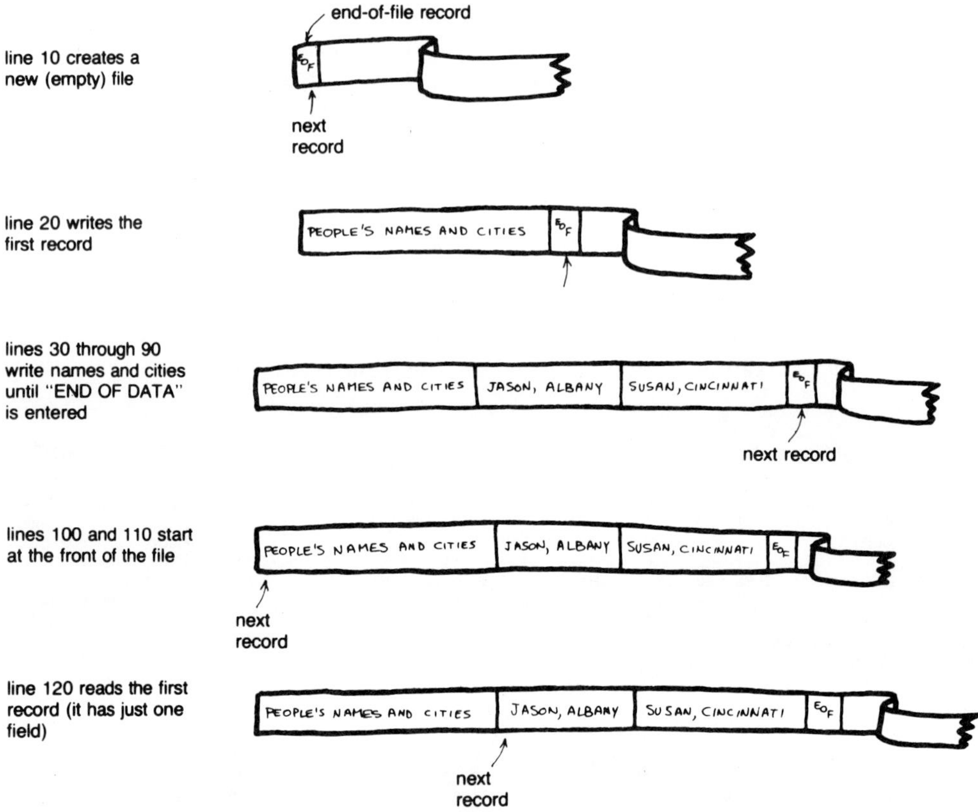
end-of-file record
line 10 creates a new (empty) file
next record
line 20 writes the first record
PEOPLE'S NAMES AND CITIES
lines 30 through 90 write names and cities until "END OF DATA" is entered
JASON, ALBANY
SUSAN, CINCINNATI
next record
lines 100 and 110 start at the front of the file
line 120 reads the first record (it has just one field)

Figure 18 2 2 Illustrates the operation of the programs

Notice that in all three cases, the statement which determines when the loop reading the values from the file (lines 150 through 180) terminates is *not in the loop.* This is unlike anything we have seen before, and is a very peculiar situation in programming. The statements

```
140    IF END #1 THEN 200          (in CBASIC)
140    ON ERROR GO TO 2000         (in BASIC-PLUS)
140    ON END #1 GO TO 200         (in HP-45 BASIC)
```

mean, "If at any time, an end of file is reached on file #1, transfer to line 200," or equivalently, "whenever and wherever." (Actually, the BASIC-PLUS statement is more general, since it transfers to line 200 "whenever and wherever" *any* error condition occurs.) Statements with this "whenever" property are sometimes called **declarative conditionals,** sometimes **demons.** Using them carelessly can make a program hard for a human to understand, since the statement which terminates a loop can be arbitrarily far away in the program! Try to keep them close to the place they are used, so a person reading your program has a chance at figuring out why what appears to be an infinite loop actually isn't.

The differences in the three versions of the file enhancement are more pronounced in the case of **random access files.** In a random access file each record is of the same length. That's required so the computer system can easily compute the actual place on the device to go to when you want to read or write a particular record. In all three versions, records are identified by a number. In BASIC-PLUS the first record is record number 0. In the other two versions the first record is record number 1. In CBASIC and HP-45 BASIC any field substructure within a record may be used (it just depends what you give for *list* in the READ and PRINT statements — entries 8 and 10). In BASIC-PLUS the fields are set by the DIM statement you use when you're defining the file (entry 3).

In CBASIC, random access files are typically used in this way: First, the file is created as a random access file with the desired characteristics (RECL *reclen* creates records of length *reclen* characters in CBASIC). Then the file is filled with data sequentially (entry 7). Now, using random access reads and writes, any record in the file can be read or altered, without affecting any of the records around it, and in any order.

In HP-45 BASIC the process of filling a random access file is more natural, but at the same time, more limited than in CBASIC. It is more limited because you must specify the total size of the file at the time of creation. It is more natural because you may fill the records in any order whatsoever, and if for some reason your program retrieves a record that has not yet been filled, it simply looks like an end-of-file. That means that an

ON END # *file number* GO TO *line*

statement can be used to recover from the mishap.

In BASIC-PLUS, random access files are disguised as a form of array (and, in fact, are called "virtual arrays" instead of files in the manuals). A special form of the DIM statement is used to declare the maximum number of records that will ever be in the file, the field structure, and the record length. For instance,

```
DIM #2, A$(10000)=200
```

specifies that file #2 is random access, that it has one field per record (that field is a string field called A$), that there will never be more than 10,000 records in the file, and that the record length is 200 (that is, no string value in any record will have more than 200 characters).

To access a specific record in CBASIC and HP-45 BASIC, an expression whose value is the desired record number is placed in the READ or PRINT statement (entries 8 and 10). In BASIC-PLUS only one field of one record can be dealt with at a time — the record number is given in parentheses after the field name. For example,

```
80    LET A$(R0 + 1) = "THURSDAY"
```

stores the string "THURSDAY" in field A$ of record R0 + 1.

Expanding a file

Even if you must set the size of a file when you create it, all is not lost if it fills up. You can write a program which creates new, larger file with a temporary name, then copy the old file into the new one, then wipe out the old, small file, and, finally, give the old name to the new file.

Here's an example of using random access files. It gives an indication of how random access files could be used in the checkout phase of the inventory control problem. The UPC code is sent to our program. The program searches a file (here sequentially, but a faster, random access-based method could be used) to find the record number where information about that product is kept. Then the description and price of that product are retrieved from the random access file and printed on the customer's sales slip. Finally, the numeric field which gives the quantity of that product on hand is reduced by one. (See Figure 18 2 3.)

The UPC value is obtained by line 200. Then we look for that value in the file UPC, counting its position. If an entry is found that matches the UPC code we're looking for, the search loop exits to line 260. If no such entry is anywhere in the file UPC, we get to line 2000.

CBASIC

```
.
.
.
100         OPEN "UPC" AS 1
110         OPEN "PRODS" RECL 30 AS 2
200         INPUT U
210         IF END #1 THEN 2000
220         LET R = 0
230         READ #1; U0
240              LET R = R + 1
250              IF U<>U0 THEN 230
260 REM     FOUND IT--RECORD NUMBER  R
270         READ #2, R; D$, C, Q
280         PRINT D$; TAB(21); C
290         PRINT #2, R; D$, C, Q - 1
300 REM     REWIND "UPC"
310         CLOSE 1
320         OPEN "UPC" AS 1
330         GO TO 200
2000 REM    SEARCH LOOP FAILED.
2010        PRINT "NO SUCH UPC CODE!"
.
.
.
```

BASIC-PLUS

```
.
.
.
100         OPEN "UPC" FOR INPUT AS FILE 1
110         OPEN "PRODS" FOR INPUT AS FILE 2
120         DIM #2, D$(5000)=20, C(5000), Q(5000)
200         INPUT U
210         ON ERROR GO TO 2000
220         LET R = -1
230         READ #1; U0
240              LET R = R + 1
250              IF U<>U0 THEN 230
260 REM     FOUND IT--RECORD NUMBER  R
280         PRINT D$(R); TAB(21); C(R)
290         LET Q(R) = Q(R) - 1
300 REM     REWIND "UPC"
310         CLOSE 1
320         OPEN "UPC" FOR INPUT AS FILE 1
330         GO TO 200
2000        IF ERR<>11 THEN 2090
2010 REM    SEARCH LOOP FAILED
2020        PRINT "NO SUCH UPC CODE!"
.
.
.
```

HP-45 BASIC

```
.
.
.
100         ASSIGN #1 TO "UPC"
110         ASSIGN #2 TO "PRODS"
200         INPUT U
210         ON END #1 GO TO 2000
220         LET R = 0
230         READ #1; U0
240              LET R = R + 1
250              IF U<>U0 THEN 230
260 REM     FOUND IT--RECORD NUMBER  R
270         READ #2, R; D$, C, Q
280         PRINT D$; TAB(21); C
290         PRINT #2, R; D$, C, Q - 1
300 REM     REWIND "UPC"
310         ASSIGN #1 TO *
320         ASSIGN #1 TO "UPC"
330         GO TO 200
2000 REM    SEARCH LOOP FAILED
2010        PRINT "NO SUCH UPC CODE!"
.
.
.
```

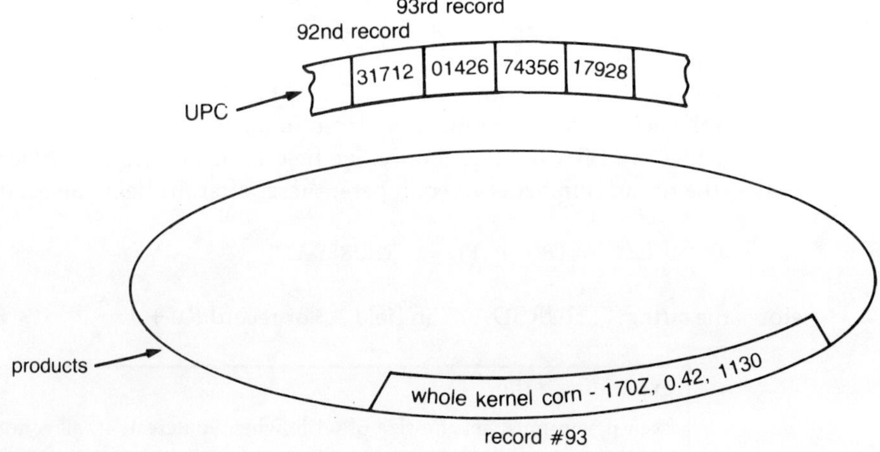

Figure 18 2 3 The (small) sequential file UPC is searched to find the position of the desired item on the (large) random access file PRODUCTS

Once the UPC value is found, we use the counter R to access the appropriate record in the random access file containing the product information. Lines 270 through 280 get the information from record number R and print the product description and cost on the customer's sales slip. Line 290 changes the quantity-on-hand field on the file, making it one less than its old value.

Perhaps the file enhancement on your system is different still. The three versions we've covered here are very common ones, but there are many variations on the theme. The general ideas are the same, but the specific forms of the statements used to perform the needed operations vary radically. If you keep the principles in mind as you read the manual for your specific version of the file enhancement, you should be able to make sense of it.

EXERCISES 18 2

1 At the bottom of the main loop in the "UPC" program (lines 300-320) we rewind the file UPC. Why?

2 Using the manuals for your computer system and for your version of BASIC, make a duplicate of Table 18 2 1, filling in the details for your particular case.

3 Rewrite the "names and cities" sequential file program for your particular version of BASIC.

4 Rewrite the UPC program (which uses random access files) for your system.

Section 18 3
A Revision of the Questionnaire Program

In Chapter 11 we developed a program which analyzes responses to questionnaires. It had inconvenient limitations which we can fix by using files. In Chapter 11 the program could store only 80 or 90 responses in memory at once, and if there were more responses than that, the analysis had to be carried out a batch at a time. If we revise the program so it stores the responses in a file, the number of responses will be limited only by the capacity of the peripheral device the file is on. Cassette tape storage devices have room for something like 100,000 characters (obviously this depends on the length of tape in the machine); floppy disks have room for several hundred thousand characters per diskette; rigid disks have room for millions of characters. That means that our revised program will be able to handle a huge number of responses instead of fewer than 100. Of course, there'll be a slight penalty — the revised program will take longer to run (remember that it can take thousands of times longer to get a value from a file than from the computer's main memory — perhaps a few thousandths of a second versus a few millionths of a second per value).

Before we get into the details, let's think about how our new version will differ. Before we can do that, we need to know whether we'll be using a random access file organization or a sequential one, since that will have a major effect on what we have to do. If we have a random access device to use, the changes to our program will be relatively minor. We could organize the file just like the array Q( ) we used in Chapter 11. Then we'd change all assignments to Q( ) into PRINT statements to the file, and change statements that access values in Q( ) into READ statements that get the appropriate value from the file. The initialize section would be more complex: it would have to create the file if it didn't exist already.

Even though using sequential files to upgrade the questionnaire program will be a bit more work, we'll do that because it will demonstrate so many points about using files. Here we'll show just the hard parts. We'll change the initialize, change, and add modules. The other parts — standard report, cross tabulations, verify, and quit — should be relatively easy once you see what we do in the three parts we cover.

The overall idea is this: As our program gathers responses from the user, it appends them at the end of a sequential file. After all the responses have been entered, to perform an analysis (say, the standard report), the program will start at the beginning of the file and read in each response, one at a time, building up a histogram just as in Chapter 11. Since the add, verify, standard report, and cross tabulation modules already deal with one response at a time, one after another, they will not require major revision. On the other hand, the change operation is essentially a random access one — you want to correct just those responses that are in error, not each one in order. We have some major work to do to convert the change option to sequential files. Similarly, the initialize option is radically different from before. Before, we assumed that the program would keep running until the entire analysis process was completed. That meant that each time the program was run, it started out with no data at all. Now we will have the advantage of being able to work on a questionnaire for a while, then quitting if we get tired or need the computer for something else. We'll be able to restart the questionnaire program whenever we feel like it without losing the data we'd entered before.

In addition to the changes required to make our basic algorithm from Chapter 11 work with sequential files, there is another consideration we need to think about. Computers break, people make mistakes, tape and disks develop bad spots, the power goes off now and then, and in general, it's possible that while our program is accessing, creating, or changing a file, something horrible could happen which would destroy the integrity of our data. The first line of defense is to keep fairly recent copies of all the files your program needs. A secondary defense is to build in a way to recover from small disasters. For example, if the power goes out after our program has written the answers to the first few questions for a particular response to the file, when we restart the program and try to read in the responses, the program will reach an unexpected end of file since that response wasn't completed. We'll have to think of some reasonable way to recover from such occurrences.

We'll use CBASIC file operations in our sample programs. Refer to Table 18 2 1 for help in translating to your particular version.

Let's start by figuring out how the questionnaire responses will be placed in our sequential file. As much as is practical, we'll want to mimic the format of the program in Chapter 11, and we'll use the same variable names, where feasible. So each response consists of one answer to each of the N questions. When we need to, we'll store a response in memory in a one-dimensional array Q( ). Q(1) gives the answer to the first question, Q(N) gives the answer to the last question. (We'll never have more than one response in memory at a time.) Let's use the variable R0 to indicate

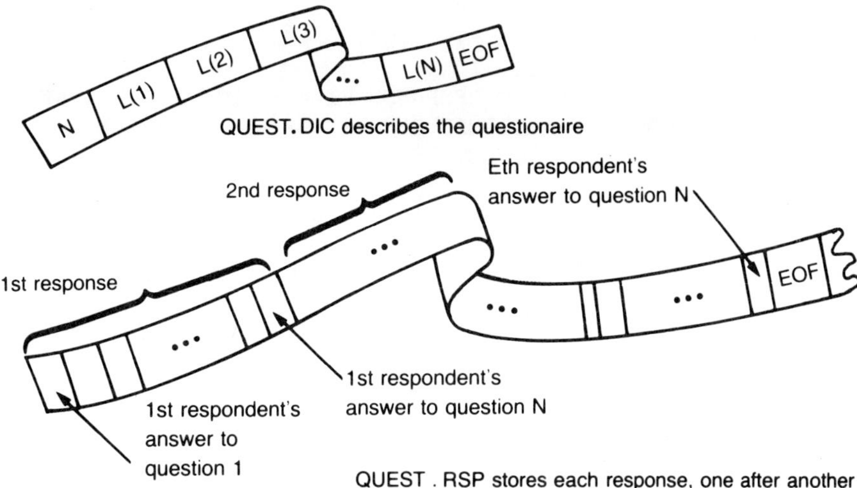

Figure 18 3 1 The two sequential files used by the revised questionnaire program

which response would be accessed next if we did a READ (or would be written next if we did a PRINT). Remember that in Chapter 11 we used an array L( ) which stored the number of legal answers to each question. If we now want a program which we can shut off and restart, we need to store the information about the questionnaire on a file too, not just the responses. So we don't get confused, let's store the values of N and L(1),. . . , L(N) in another sequential file. Let's call it QUEST.DIC since it contains a dictionary of values needed to process the questionnaire results. Let's call the file that will hold the responses QUEST.RSP. Figure 18 3 1 shows the organization we plan to use.

Let's begin working on the details of the new program by figuring out what the Initialize module should do.

There are two possible cases when the program starts running. Either the user intends to start work on a questionnaire, or else the questionnaire is partially entered and the user wants to return to work on it. In the first case neither QUEST.DIC nor QUEST.RSP will exist. In the second case they will. We can use that fact to figure out what to do. If the files don't exist, our program should ask the user to describe the questionnaire, that is, to give values for N and L(1),. . .,L(N). If the files do exist, our program should get the values of N and L(1),. . .,L(N) from QUEST.DIC and then give the user the choice of add, change, verify, standard report, cross tabs, or quit.

Here's what we came up with for the initialize module:

```
1000 REM  INITIALIZE MODULE--CARRIED OUT ONCE EACH TIME
1010 REM    PROGRAM IS RUN.
1020        IF END #1 THEN 1200
1030        FILE "QUEST.DIC"
1040 REM  IF WE GET HERE, THE FILE EXISTS ALREADY, SO
1050 REM    READ THE PARAMETERS DESCRIBING THE QUESTIONNAIRE.
1070        READ #1; N
```

(program continued on page 426)

```
1080      FOR Q0=1 TO N
1090          READ #1; L(Q0)
1100      NEXT Q0
1110 REM  OPEN THE RESPONSE FILE, INDICATE THAT WE'RE
1120 REM    POSITIONED BEFORE THE FIRST RESPONSE.
1130      OPEN "QUEST.RSP" AS 2
1140      LET R0 = 1
1150 REM  WE'RE DONE WITH THE DICTIONARY FILE, SO...
1160      CLOSE 1
1170 REM  GO TO MAIN MENU LOOP TO START PROCESSING.
1180      GO TO 1800
1200 REM  "QUEST.DIC" DIDN'T EXIST, SO WE'RE STARTING
1210 REM    WORK ON A BRAND NEW QUESTIONNAIRE."
1220      PRINT
1230      PRINT "HOW MANY QUESTIONS ARE IN YOUR QUESTIONNAIRE";
1240      INPUT N
1250      PRINT "NOW GIVE ME THE HIGHEST NUMBERED"
1260      PRINT "ANSWER FOR EACH QUESTION."
1270      FOR Q0=1 TO N
1280          PRINT "QUESTION"; Q0;
1290          INPUT L(Q0)
1300      NEXT Q0
1310      PRINT "THANK YOU."
1320 REM  PUT THE PARAMETERS INTO "QUEST.DIC"
1330      PRINT #1; N
1340      FOR Q0=1 TO N
1350          PRINT #1; L(Q0)
1360      NEXT Q0
1370      CLOSE 1
1380 REM  CREATE A FILE TO STORE RESPONSES.
1390      CREATE "QUEST.RSP" AS 2
1400      LET R0 = 1
```

Next, let's turn to the add module. In order to add a response, we have to get the answers to each of the N questions from the user. We have to print each answer at the end of QUEST.RSP to store it. The only major difference from the add module in Chapter 11 is that now before we start adding responses, we'll have to make sure we're at the end of file.

```
2000 REM  MODULE 2--ADD NEW DATA
2001 REM  MAKE SURE "QUEST.RSP" IS AT END OF FILE.
2002      GOSUB 8000
  .
  .
  .
2250      PRINT #2; V
  .
  .
  .
2320      PRINT #2; V
  .
  .
  .
```

—revised questionnaire analysis program—

PRINT greeting to user.

IF QUEST.DIC exists,

THEN

> *READ values for N and L(1), . . . ,L(N) from it.*
>
> *Open QUEST.RSP.*
>
> *LET R0=1 to indicate that we're ready to read or write the first response.*
>
> *Close QUEST.DIC.*

ELSE

> *Create QUEST.DIC*
>
> *Ask the user for values for N and L(1), . . . ,L(N).*
>
> *PRINT the values on the file QUEST.DIR.*
>
> *Create a file called QUEST.RSP.*
>
> *LET E = 0 since we have no responses yet.*
>
> *LET R0 = 1 to indicate that we're ready to PRINT the first response on QUEST.RSP.*
>
> *Close QUEST.DIC.*

Ask user what phase he or she wants

> *Add:*
>
> *Verify:*
>
> *Change:*
>
> *Standard report:*
>
> *Cross tabulation:*

Repeat

Quit:

> *Close QUEST.RSP.*
> *Print goodbye message.*

Figure 18 3 2 Our revised plan. (Compare to the plan in Section 11 3.) Now the Initialize phase is out of the main menu loop, and is elaborated to distinguish the case when the user is beginning work on a new questionnaire from the case when the user is returning to do some more work on an old questionnaire. Notice that now we've added a variable R0 which will keep track of which response will be read or printed next on the sequential file QUEST.RSP. This variable will be used in the Add and Change options.

Except for the lines shown above, the add module is the same as in Chapter 11. The "Make sure QUEST.RSP is at end of file" subroutine must read values from the file until it reaches the end. While it's doing that, we'll have it count the number of responses in the file so far.

```
8000 REM  MAKE SURE "QUEST.RSP" IS AT THE END OF FILE
8010      IF END #2 THEN 8150
8020 REM      KEEP READING ONE RESPONSE AFTER ANOTHER
8030 REM      UNTIL WE HIT END OF FILE (NEED TO READ
8040 REM      THIS WAY SO WE CAN COUNT # OF RESPONSES
8050 REM      ALREADY STORED)
8060          FOR Q0=1 TO N
8070              READ #2; Q(Q0)
8080          NEXT Q0
8090          LET R0 = R0 + 1
8100          GO TO 8020
8150 REM  HIT END-- SINCE  R0  INDICATES NEXT RESPONSE,
8160 REM    THE TOTAL # OF STORED RESPONSES IS ONE LESS.
8170      LET E = R0 - 1
8180      RETURN
```

Figure 18 3 3 shows the effect of adding a response.

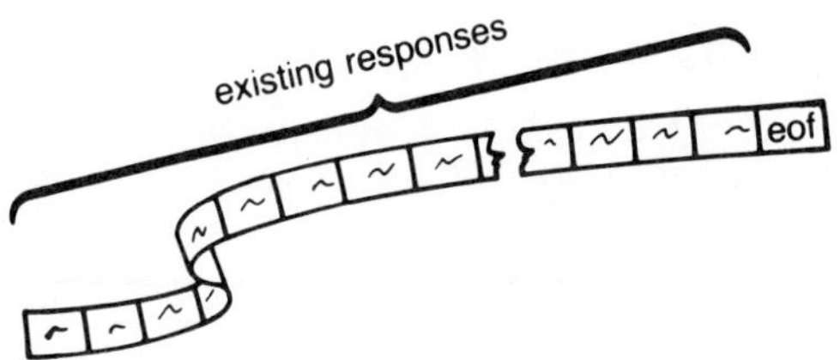

No matter where the program is in the file at this point (i.e., no matter what value R0 has), the subroutine starting at line 8000 will read until the end of the file, and give the appropriate values to R0 and E.

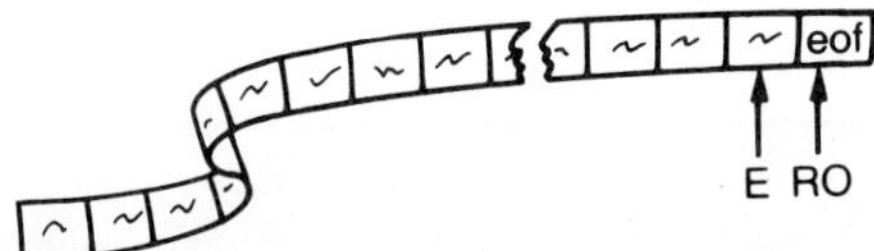

Then the print statements in lines 2250 and 2320 add a new response (that is, N answers) to the end of the existing responses.

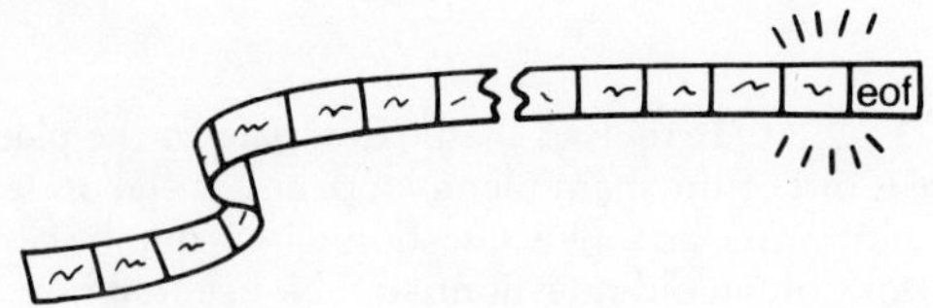

Figure 18 3 3 The add option adds new responses to the end of QUEST.RSP

The last module we'll update here is the change module. It's primary purpose is to allow the user to correct erroneous answers. It's an awkward and time-consuming process to make changes to a large sequential file. The user will save time overall if he or she does all the corrections at one sitting, and in increasing order of response numbers. That is, the best way will be to run the verify option, mark all the mistakes, and then use the change option to go through correcting them in order.

So far we've made it sound as if we intend to make changes to the file QUEST.RSP itself. But that's not possible. You can add to a sequential file, but you can't go back and change something in the middle. Instead, we'll have to make a new, corrected copy of the file.

Here's our plan:

—change module—

Create a new file QUEST.TMP for responses.

Rewind QUEST.RSP (start at the beginning).

WHILE *response user wants to change (E1) is greater than or equal to 0.*

IF E1 > = R0

THEN

Copy all responses from R0 through E1 − 1 from QUEST.RSP to QUEST.TMP.

Get correct answers from user.

Put correct answers on QUEST.TMP.

Skip over response on QUEST.RSP.

LET R0 = E1 + 1.

ELSE

PRINT "Too late to correct"; E1.

PRINT "You'll have to change again."

Copy all responses from R0 to E from QUEST.RSP to QUEST.TMP.
Rename QUEST.RSP as QUEST.RBK.
Rename QUEST.TMP as QUEST.RSP.

This change process is illustrated in Figure 18 3 4.

Now that we've worked out what we want to do in the change mode, we notice that is has a useful side effect. It makes a backup copy of the responses. That is, after the user goes through a change operation, there are *two* files of responses, one a corrected version of the other. Now if catastrophe strikes and there's a power failure while the program is accessing QUEST.RSP, all is not lost. When the computer system is ready to be used again, the user can see if QUEST.RSP is intact, and if it's not, can revert to using QUEST.RBK. If only we also had a backup copy of QUEST.DIC, we'd feel reasonably safe. But that's easy to get; we just need to add a few statements to the initialize module (see exercise 5).

Before you look over the BASIC version of our new change option, be sure to follow through Figure 18 3 4.

First, the Change option creates a new (empty) file called QUEST.TMP

The data as it stands

eof

eof

QUEST. RSP

QUEST.TMP

The user wants to change response #3, so we copy the first two responses from QUEST.RSP to the end of QUEST.TMP

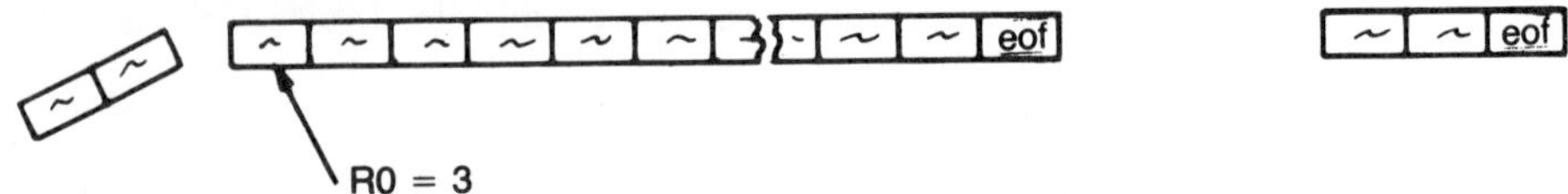

We accept new answers for response #3, tack them at the end of QUEST.TMP, and skip over the third response on QUEST.RSP

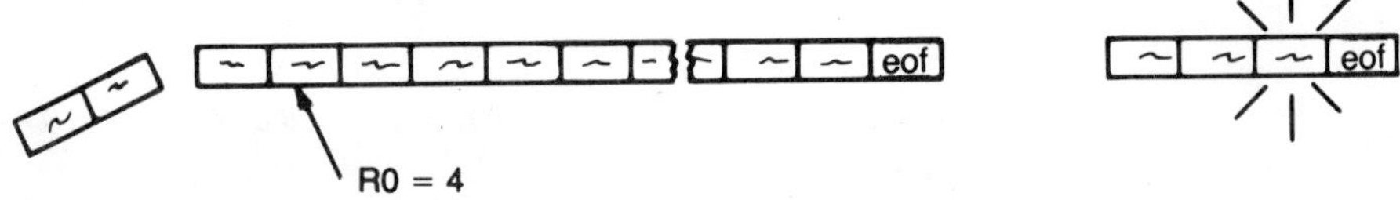

Next, the user wants to change the 7th response, so we copy responses 4 through 6 to QUEST.TMP

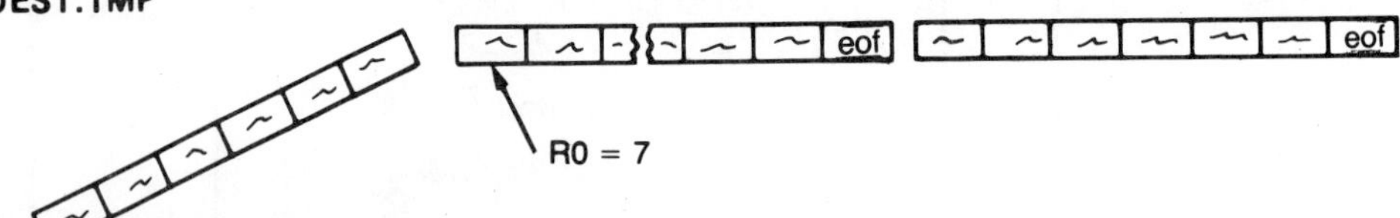

We accept new answers for response #7, print them at the end of QUEST.TMP, and skip over the 7th response on QUEST.RSP

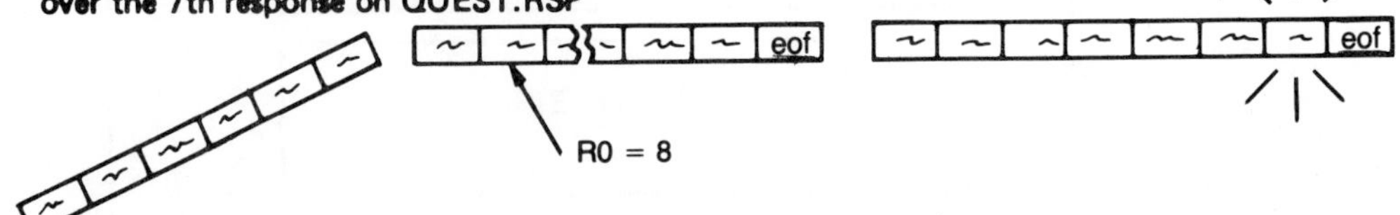

After all changes have been made, we copy the rest of QUEST.RSP to QUEST.TMP, and then rename the files so that QUEST.RSP is the changed version, and the old version of the data is called QUEST.RBK

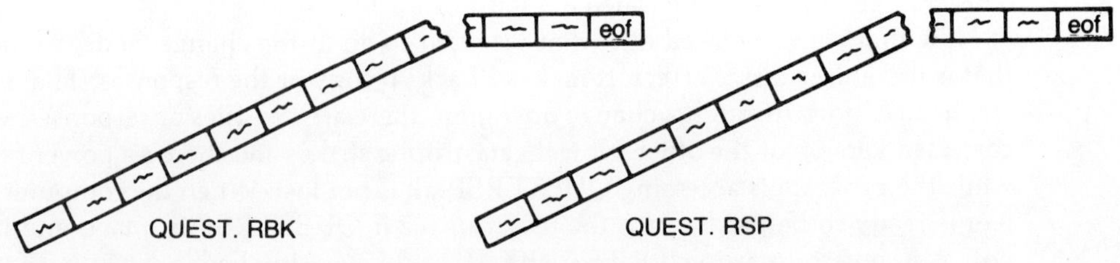

Figure 18 3 4 The change process, showing what happens when the user makes changes to responses #3 and #7.

Gaining access to QUEST.RBK

There are two ways to gain access to QUEST.RBK. Either your computer's operating system provides a simple way, or you can write a small BASIC program to rename files. For example, in the CP/M operating system, to wipe out QUEST.RSP and then rename QUEST.RBK, we would type

```
ERA QUEST.RSP
REN QUEST.RSP=QUEST.RBK
```

If you have to write a BASIC program to do it, in CBASIC it would look like this:

```
10    OPEN "QUEST.RSP" AS 1
20    DELETE 1
30    LET F = RENAME("QUEST.RBK", "QUEST.RSP")
9999  END
```

[Handwritten note, arrow pointing to "QUEST.RSP" in line 30: this file is given the name on the left]

No matter which way you do it, next time you run the questionnaire program, you'll be using the backed-up copy.

```
4000 REM  MODULE 4--ALLOW USER TO CHANGE ERRORS.
4010 REM  THE ALTERED FILE OF RESPONSES WILL BE PUT
4020 REM  IN A TEMPORARY FILE.  AFTER ALL CORRECTIONS
4030 REM  HAVE BEEN MADE, THE TEMPORARY FILE WILL
4040 REM  BECOME THE FILE USED BY THE PROGRAM, AND
4050 REM  THE ORIGINAL FILE WILL BE LEFT AS A BACKUP.
4060      CREATE "QUEST.TMP" AS 3
4070 REM  "REWIND" QUEST.RSP (START AT THE BEGINNING)
4080      GOSUB 8200
4090 REM  KEEP CHANGING RESPONSES UNTIL USER GIVES
4100 REM    A NEGATIVE RESPONSE NUMBER.
4110      PRINT "CHANGE WHICH RESPONSE (<0 TO QUIT)";
4120      INPUT E1
4130      IF E1<=0 THEN 4500
4140 REM      IF WE'RE ALREADY PAST THE DESIRED
4150 REM        RESPONSE, TOO BAD.
4160          IF E1<R0 THEN 4400
4170 REM        COPY UP TO THE DESIRED ONE.
4180            FOR R1=R0 TO E1 - 1
4190                FOR Q0=1 TO N
4200                    READ #2; V
4210                    PRINT #3; V
4220                NEXT Q0
4230            NEXT R1
4240            PRINT "PLEASE GIVE THE CORRECT ANSWERS FOR ";
4245            PRINT "RESPONSE NUMBER"; E1
4250            FOR Q0=1 TO N
4260                PRINT "QUESTION"; Q0;
4270                INPUT V
4280                LET L9 = L(Q0)
4290                GOSUB 9100
4300                PRINT #3; V
4310            NEXT Q0
```

[Handwritten note, bracket beside lines 4190–4220: copy response number R1]

[Handwritten note, arrows to lines 4280 and 4290: remember: we check each answer to make sure it's legitimate (see Chapter 11)]

(program continued on page 432)

```
4320 REM        DONE GETTING CORRECT VERSION, SKIP OVER
4330 REM          RESPONSE E1 ON OLD QUEST.RSP
4340            FOR Q0=1 TO N
4350                READ #2; V
4360            NEXT Q0
4370 REM        NEXT RESPONSE IS NOW E1 + 1
4380            LET R0 = E1 + 1
4390            GO TO 4440
4400 REM        ELSE CASE--WE'RE PAST DESIRED SPOT.
4410            PRINT "SORRY, BUT IT'S TOO LATE TO CORRECT";
4420            PRINT "RESPONSE"; E1
4430            PRINT "(YOU'LL HAVE TO RUN -CHANGE- AGAIN.)"
4440 REM    BOTTOM OF WHILE LOOP
4450        GO TO 4100
4500 REM  DONE WITH ALL CORRECTIONS ON THIS PASS.
4510 REM  FINISH COPYING RESPONSES FROM QUEST.RSP.
4520      FOR R1=R0 TO E
4530          FOR Q0=1 TO N
4540              READ #2; V
4550              PRINT #3; V
4560          NEXT Q0
4570      NEXT R1
4580 REM  NOW MAKE THE NEW COPY THE RESPONSE FILE, THE
4590 REM  OLD COPY THE BACKUP.
4600      CLOSE 2, 3
4610      LET F = RENAME("QUEST.RBK", "QUEST.RSP")
4620      LET F = RENAME("QUEST.RSP", "QUEST.TMP")
4630      OPEN "QUEST.RSP" AS 2
4640      LET R0 = 1
4650 REM  DONE WITH CHANGE OPTION, RETURN TO MENU LOOP.
4660      GO TO 1800
```

the file on the right is given the name on the left

Problem 4 gives hints for completing the renovation project.
What have we seen here?

- By using files, it's possible to do problems which are too large to fit in the computer's main memory all at once.
- By using files, it's possible to write programs which can be stopped and then rerun without losing data you entered before.
- When you choose to use files, it's probably because you're dealing with a large amount of data. In that case you will want to take extra measures (like making backup copies) to ensure that you don't lose a lot of work if something bad happens.

EXERCISES 18 3

1 N stores the number of questions on the questionnaire. E stores the number of responses entered so far. If the end of file mark counts as a record, how many records are in the file QUEST.DIC? How many are in QUEST.RSP?

2 Suppose that when we were entering the details of a new questionnaire, terrorists blew up a power plant, and our computer system ground to a halt. That is, suppose the program was stopped when it was somewhere in line 1280, 1290, or 1300.

(a) What would be the state of the file QUEST.DIC?

(b) What would be the state of the file QUEST.RSP?

Suppose we ran the questionnaire program again when the power came back on, having made no changes to the files in the meantime.

(c) What would the program do?

(d) Does that seem reasonable, or will it cause us grief?

3 If the user is in the change module, and corrects response number 12, then response number 21, then asks to change response number 6, our program refuses to do so (see lines 4400 through 4420). Instead of just refusing (which seems impolite, after all), why didn't we have the program jump back to line 4060 and start over again from the front?

4 We didn't show the BASIC version of subroutine 8200. It's supposed to "rewind" the file QUEST.RSP, that is, to start at the beginning of the file. Write subroutine 8200. Remember that the variable R0 gives the number of the next response on the file, so be sure your subroutine leaves an appropriate value in R0.

5 If you're using some sort of tape recorder to store sequential files, it will be more efficient (in time) to have the change option write QUEST.TMP on another tape drive from the one you're using to read QUEST.RSP. In CBASIC if A: and B: are the device names of two tape machines, we'd change the file names to A:QUEST:TMP and B:QUEST.RSP if the temporary file was to be written on machine A:. In addition, we'd like to make a backup copy of QUEST.DIC so that one tape would be a complete backup for the other. What would you add to the change option to accomplish backing up QUEST.DIC as well?

PROBLEMS 18

The first three problems are very useful when a large number of people use the same computer system.

1 Write two programs which maintain an **environment file.** The environment file has these data items:

- today's date (month, day, year)
- today (i.e., Monday, Tuesday,...)
- the name of the operator on duty
- the phone number to call if you're having trouble
- the building and room number to go to if you want help with a program

The first program will be used by one person (presumably the operator who's on duty). It asks for values for each of the items in the file, and stores the updated file.

The second program will be used by an user. It simply reads the environment file and displays the data on the screen. When the user has read the items, he or she hits the return key and the program stops, letting the user go on with his or her work.

2 Write two programs which maintain a **message file.** A message file is most useful when it keeps the messages in a last in-first out order. That way, someone who didn't get around to reading the messages yesterday can catch up by staying at the terminal a bit longer. Someone who wants just the most recent messages gets them right away, and then terminates the program.

The first program accepts today's messages, writes them to a new file, and then appends the previous messages after the new ones. So that the file doesn't get too long, it throws away any messages after the first (say) 200. Finally, it renames the new file so program two can find it.

The second program is used by anyone who wants to see the messages. It opens the message file and displays the first (most recent) message. It asks the user if he or she wants to go on to the next message or quit. If the user reads all the messages in the file, when the program reaches the end-of-file, it should print a polite statement to that effect, and quit.

3 Upgrade the message-file handling system of problem 2 so it keeps a date with each message. When the first program is used to add today's messages, it throws away all messages that are more than two weeks old (instead of simply limiting the total number of messages as before). The second program should have an added feature which lets the user request messages from a specific date.

4 Finish the final version of the questionnaire program by revising the standard report and cross tab modules and tying the modules together. Here's a plan for the standard report module. The same idea (reading one response into memory at a time) can be used for the cross tab module.

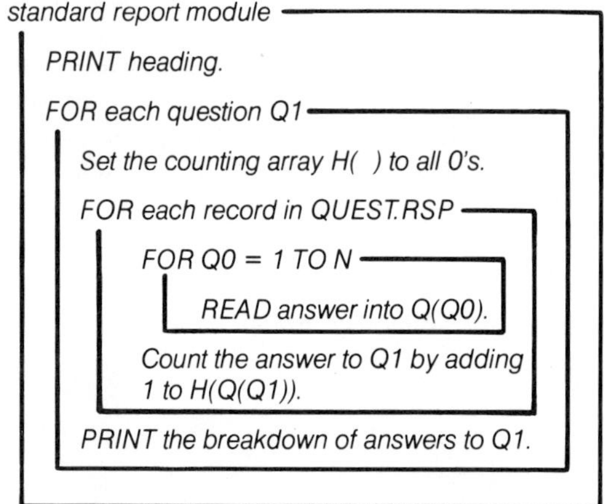

> Problems 5 and 6 require putting a file in order.
>
> If your system has a peripheral device which is capable of random access (say, a floppy disk drive), you can sort values in a file by using a slight variation of either of the sorting techniques covered in Chapter 14 or the index sort in Section 15 3. Only two records are brought into memory at a time to be compared or switched. If the file contains many records, this technique will be very slow. On the other hand, it has the benefit of being easy to program.
>
> If your system is capable only of sequential access, you will need some sort of merge program to order the records in a file. One is described in problem 7.

5 Write a program which could be used to print the results of the Boston Marathon. In the first phase the program accepts runners' names and elapsed times. In the second, report-generation phase, the program orders the file and prints the records in two different ways: by increasing elapsed time, and in alphabetical order.

6 Redo Problem 16 14, but now put no limit on the number of different words that will appear in the concordance.

7 **External sorting.** Suppose two files contain sorted entries.

file 1: $r_1 r_2 \ldots r_n$ where $r_i \leqslant r_{i+1}$

file 2: $s_1 s_2 \ldots s_m$ where $s_i \leqslant s_{i+1}$

Then we can merge the two files into one file of n + m sorted entries by the following procedure.

```
READ item1 (first value on file 1).
READ item2 (first value on file 2).

While not at end of file on file 1 and
      not at end of file on file 2
    IF item1 ≤ item2
    THEN
        PRINT item1 onto file 3.
        READ item1 (next value on file 1).
    ELSE
        PRINT item2 onto file 3.
        READ item2 (next value on file 2).

IF not at end of file on file 1
    THEN
        Copy rest of file 1 to file 3.
IF not at end of file on file 2
    THEN
        Copy rest of file 2 to file 3.
```

Using this type of merge and four files, we can sort as many entries as we like without using much computer memory. (The sorting techniques we discussed in Chapter 15 required all the entries to be stored in an array.) This type of external sorting method is known as a balanced merge. We use four files and assume that two of them contain an equal number of sections, a section being a collection of sorted entries. We make a first pass by merging the first section of one of the files with the first section of the other file, and writing the merged result on a third file. Then we merge the second section of one file with the second section of the other file and write the result on file number four. We keep merging sections with sections, alternating where we write the newly merged sections between files three and four, until we run out of sections. (If one file contains more sections than the other, we simply split the remaining sections: half go onto file three and the other half onto file four.)

At the next stage we repeat the same process, but this time we are reading from files three and four and writing onto files one and two. As we continue this merging process, alternating the read files and the write files, the sections get longer and longer until, finally, all the entries are merged into one section which is the sorted file.

Implement a balanced merge and test it on two files which, at the beginning, each has 100 sections of one entry per section.

Chapter 19 **Enhanced Names, Lines, and Functions**

Section 19 1

Longer Variable Names

One thing that makes programming in BASIC difficult is that you cannot give variables names that tell you what they are being used for. It is much easier to understand a program like the one on the right.

```
      .                              .
      .                              .
      .                              .
180   PRINT "AMOUNT=";         180   PRINT "AMOUNT=";
190   INPUT C                  190   INPUT CHECK
200   LET B = B - C            200   LET BALANCE = BALANCE - CHECK
210     .                      210     .
        .                              .
        .                              .
```

The reason Minimal Basic limits variable names to a single letter or a letter followed by a digit is twofold. It makes the job of writing the program which interprets BASIC programs easier, and (as is most often the case) if the BASIC program is contained in memory in its original form while it is being carried out, the shorter names take up less space in memory.

The new standards allow variable names which begin with a letter followed by from none up to 30 letters, digits, and/or underbar characters. If the variable is a string variable, it must end with a dollar sign. No variable name may have more than 31 characters in it. CapiTaliZation doesn't matter, so the variable name Pizza is the same as pizza.

```
amount
bank_balance
DAYS_THIS_MONTH
number_of_customers
PRIMO$
regnent_idea$
```

A number of versions of BASIC allow variables names almost like the ones specified by the new standards. For instance, in CBASIC (sold by Digital Research, Inc.), the only difference is that the underbar character is replaced by a period. Thus, these are legal variable names in CBASIC:

```
new.balance
DAYS.THIS.MONTH
Number.of.customers
```

In large program the advantage of being able to give variables meaningful names is overwhelming.

Section 19 . 2
Multistatement Lines

In some versions of BASIC it is possible to put more than one statement on one line in your program. Usually a colon is used to separate statements. For example, these three lines in Minimal BASIC

```
80    REM  START ROW AND COLUMN AT 0
90         LET RO = 0
100        LET CO = 0
```

could be written like this:

```
80    LET RO = 0 : LET CO = 0 : REM  START ROW AND COLUMN AT 0
```

In our opinion, putting more than one statement on a line always makes the program harder to read. It also makes the program harder to change.

Section 19 3
Multiline Statements

Sometimes a statement is just too long to fit on one line. For instance, in Section 6 3, in our subroutine which tests dates, we have these three lines:

```
8120          IF M>6 THEN 8140
8130          ON M   GO TO 8400, 8200, 8400, 8300, 8400, 8300
8140          ON M-6 GO TO 8400, 8400, 8300, 8400, 8300, 8400
```

We had to split the ON-GO TO statement into parts because we couldn't fit it on one line. In the standard form of multiline enhancement, you put an ampersand at the physical end of the first line, and put another ampersand at the beginning of the continuation line. Using that, we could have written the test like this:

```
8130        ON M GO TO 8400, 8200, 8400, 8300, 8400, 8300, &
&                      8400, 8400, 8300, 8400, 8300, 8400
```

Other versions of BASIC use different notations. For instance, in CBASIC, you place a back slash character (\ ) to indicate that a line continues to the next. In MicroSoft BASIC and in DEC BASIC-PLUS, you hit the key called LINE FEED instead of the return key to signal that the statement is continued on the next line.

Section 19 4
Logical Operators

There have been a number of cases in which we used more than one IF-THEN statement, one after the other, to perform a complicated test. For example, in Section 5 3, in the program which performed a statistical analysis of pay rates, we had to check to make sure the pay rate was in the range from $0.00 up to $6.99. We did it this way:

```
250         IF P<0 THEN 2000
260         IF P>=7 THEN 2000
```

where 2000 was the line number we wanted to go to if P was out of range.

The new standards provide three operators that can be used to put complex, multipart tests in a single IF-THEN statement. These three operators are AND, OR, and NOT.

We can rewrite the test shown above, using the OR operator, like this:

```
250         IF P>0 OR P>=7 THEN 2000
```

The OR operator always appears between two relations. It means "if the first relation is true, or if the second relation is true, or if both are true, then true; otherwise false."

The AND operator always appears between two relations. An expression involving the AND operator is true if both relations are true, and the expression is false otherwise. For instance, this IF-THEN will transfer control to line 1010 if P is greater than 0 and N$ has the value "CONTINUE".

```
800         IF P>0 AND N$="CONTINUE" THEN 1010
```

The NOT operator always appears in front of a relation. It reverses the value of the relation—if relation *rel* is true, NOT *rel* is false; and vice versa.

Relations may involve combinations of uses of the logical operators. Parentheses should be used to make the meaning clearer. For instance, this IF-THEN statement goes to line 3300 if F$ has the value "END OF DATA" or if P is not the range from 0 to 7.

```
IF (F$="END OF DATA") OR NOT (P>=0 AND P<=7) THEN 3300
```

Section 19 5
Multiline Functions

Minimal BASIC requires all function definitions to be one-liners.

```
100      DEF FNY(X) = S*X - 1

110      DEF FNG(A) = EXP(-(X - A)*(X - A))/F2

120      DEF FND = INT(6*RND)
```

These functions have one parameter (or none) and provide a convenient shorthand for arithmetic expressions. More general functions are available as an enhancement. These definitions may have many lines and may specify more than one parameter. When these multiline functions are available, they are sometimes used in place of subroutines because they make it easier to get the necessary information in and out of the routine.

For example, suppose you are writing a program which frequently needs to compute the positive part of a number. (The positive part of a number is the number itself if it is positive and zero if it is not. This function comes up in income tax forms where the form says, "Take the number on line 37 or zero, whichever is larger.") We could express the function as a subroutine, as shown below; but then, every time we want to compute the positive part of a number, we have to store the number in the variable X, the GOSUB 8000, then retrieve the positive part of X from P.

```
8000 REM  POSITIVE PART ROUTINE
8010 REM  INPUT:  X
8020 REM  OUTPUT: P
8030      IF X<0 THEN 8060
8040        LET P = X
8050        GO TO 8070
8060        LET P = 0
8070        RETURN
```

Using a multiline function, we can express the same idea and not have to use the variables X and P to communicate with the subroutine.

```
8000 REM  POSITIVE PART FUNCTION
8010      DEF FNP(X)
8020        IF X<0 THEN 8060
8040          LET FNP = X
8050          GO TO 8070
8060          LET FNP = 0
8070      END DEF
```

Multiline functions are invoked in the same way as ordinary functions.

`LET Y = FNP(X)`	puts positive part of X into Y
`LET T = FNP(0.03*G - 100)`	puts positive part of 3% of G less 100 into T
`PRINT FNP(0.25*G - 3000)`	prints positive part of .25*G−3000

The definition heading (first line) is as shown in the example: the keyword DEF, function name, and parameter list (*x, y, z,* . . .). The standards allow zero or more parameters, with the individual parameters separated by commas. The heading line is followed by an arbitrary number of lines containing ordinary BASIC statements, as in a subroutine. When execution reaches an END DEF statement, the computer transfers back to the place where the function was invoked. The value returned is the last value assigned to the function name in the function. For instance, in the positive part function FNP, either line 8040 or 8060 gives the value to be returned.

Warning: Do not use the name of the function as an ordinary variable; you only assign values *to* it.

Our positive part function FNP computes the larger of its argument and zero. It's a restricted form of the maximum function which computes the larger of two given numbers.

```
8100 REM  MAXIMUM FUNCTION
8110      DEF FNM(X,Y)
8120        IF X<Y THEN 8150
8130          LET FNM = X
8140          GO TO 8160
8150          LET FNM = Y
8160      END DEF
```

A multiline function can compute a string value. In this case, the function name ends with a dollar sign:

```
8200 REM  CONVERTING 0,1 TO TRUE, FALSE
8210      DEF FNL$(B)
8220        IF B=0 THEN 8050
8230          LET FNL$ = "TRUE"
8240          GO TO 8260
8250          LET FNL$ = "FALSE"
8260      END DEF
```

Multiline functions do not completely replace subroutines because a function computes a single value. Subroutines, on the other hand, are often used to compute a collection of values, usually stored in an array but sometimes stored in a few different variables. The sorting routines of Chapter 14 fall into the first category. They return an array of values. The subroutine for computing subtotal, tax, and total in Section 6 2 falls into the second category. It returns its values in three separate variables.

Chapter 20 Enhanced Control Structures

Section 20 1
Selection

Historically, BASIC has been a language with a paucity of control structures: IF-THEN, ON-GO TO, FOR-NEXT, GO TO, and GOSUB were the only ones, even in many so-called Extended BASICs. The new proposed standards call for a luxuriant array of new control structures to be available in all but Minimal BASIC. If the BASIC you are using provides any of these extended control structures, they are definitely worth learning, since they can give real help in making programs more understandable. If they are available for your version of BASIC, start by revising some of your earlier programs. Both the **block IF-THEN-ELSE** and the **SELECT** structures have forms very close to the plan notation, so it should be easy to rewrite programs from the same plan you used before. Only this time, it will be easier.

In Minimal BASIC, the IF-THEN statement has this form:

IF *relation* THEN *line number*

Traditionally, most versions of BASIC have allowed this enhancement as well:

IF *relation* THEN *imperative*

where *imperative* is a simple statement (e.g., a LET, a PRINT, a STOP, a READ; not a compound statement like FOR or IF).

The new standards allow the forms above, plus more.

IF *relation* THEN *line number* ELSE *line number*
IF *relation* THEN *imperative* ELSE *imperative*

plus the other two variations on the theme. So, these one-liners are all legitimate:

```
110  IF A>0 THEN 200 ELSE PRINT "Invalid Invalid Invalid"
250  IF K$="END" THEN STOP ELSE 5000
396  IF P1<12 THEN PRINT P1; ELSE PRINT P1
```

The new standards also provide for Fortran-77 style **block IF-THEN-ELSE.** The ELSEIF and ELSE blocks are optional:

IF *relation* THEN
  if-block
ELSEIF *relation* THEN
  if-block
ELSE
  if-block
END IF

The block IF-THEN-ELSE is an extremely useful construct. Here are some examples:

```
10  IF R=1 THEN
20     PRINT "ONE OF THE ";
30     LET C = C + 1
40  END IF

110 IF F$="TAIL" THEN
120    PRINT
130    PRINT
140    PRINT "End of Data"
150    LET C = 0
160 ELSE
170    PRINT F$
180    LET C = 1
190 END IF

220 IF I=1 THEN
230    PRINT "ONE ";
240    LET T(K) = 1
250 ELSEIF I=2 THEN
260    PRINT "TWO ";
270    LET T(K) = 1
280 ELSE
290    PRINT "MANY ";
300    LET T(K) = -1
310 END IF
```

Perhaps the most elaborate of the proposed new standard control structures is the **SELECT** statement. Let's begin with an example:

```
1000  SELECT CASE C$
1010    CASE "A", "a"
1020      REM  ADD
1030           GOSUB 4000
1040    CASE "D", "d"
1050      REM  DELETE
1060           GOSUB 5000
1070    CASE ELSE
```

```
1080        REM  INVALID RESPONSE
1090             PRINT "Please try again"
1100             LET E = 0
1110    END SELECT
1120    REM
```

In this example, if the string variable has the value A or a, then the first CASE block will be carried out, and after line 1030 is completed, line 1120 will be done next. If C$ has the value D or d, lines 1050 and 1060 will be carried out. If C$ has any value other than A, a, D, or d, lines 1090 through 1100 will be executed. The SELECT construct implements a selection of one block from many.

The SELECT statement can be based on a numeric or a string expression, and the individual CASE blocks can be selected on the basis of one or more constants or relations. The example above is based on a string value (C$), and the first two CASE blocks contain implied tests against two different constants. The value of C$ is used in conjunction with all the cases listed in all CASE blocks in the SELECT construct to select which block of statements should be executed. Only one CASE block is selected each time the SELECT statement is carried out. It is illegal for more than one CASE block to match a given select value.

Here's an example of a SELECT statement which bases the selection on a numeric value.

```
2500    SELECT CASE N + 1
2510      CASE IS < 0
2520        PRINT "ERROR: Count Invalid"
2530        STOP
2540      CASE 0
2550        PRINT "Re-start"
2560        LET C = 0
2570        GOSUB 8500
2580      CASE 1 TO 99
2590        LET C = C + N
2600      CASE ELSE
2610        LET C = 0
2620        GOSUB 8450
2630    END SELECT
```

In this example, the range of CASE test expressions is shown. In the first block (lines 2510 through 2530), the test is a relation. This case will be selected if the select value (N+1) is less than zero. The second block is the numeric analog of the ones we saw in the first example. It is selected only if N+1 has the value 0. The third CASE block (lines 2580-2590) is an example of a range of constants. The third block is selected if N+1 satisfies 1 <= N+1 <= 99.

The new SELECT statement is excitingly close to the plan notation for selection we've used throughout this book. It will allow programs to match plans more closely, which will be a big aid to clarity.

Section 20 2

Looping

The proposed standards require that all standard versions of BASIC except Minimal BASIC include a looping construct which can be used to create the loops we introduce in Chapters 3-8. This construct is called the **DO Loop.** Here's the form of what is called a *repeat forever loop* in Chapter 3:

```
300  DO
310      PRINT "Don't Panic! ";
320  LOOP
```

Notice that no explicit GO TO is needed. The LOOP statement marks the bottom of the loop, the DO statement marks the top.

The *repeat until loop* (Section 3 3) is created by adding a condition to the LOOP statement.

```
100   DO
110     PRINT
120     PRINT "WHAT'S YOUR NAME";
130       .
 .        .
 .        .
 .        .
220     PRINT "ANSWER 'Y' TO TRY AGAIN: ";
230     INPUT A$
240   LOOP UNTIL A$<>'Y' <----------
```

Notice how much more like our plans this construct is, compared to the "IF A$='Y' THEN 100" form of loop bottom. The actual line numbers involved are irrelevant to our thinking.

The *pretest,* or *while, loop* (Section 5 1) is created by adding a condition to the DO statement.

```
120     PRINT "DOES THIS WALL HAVE ANY WINDOWS 'Y' OR 'N' ";
130     INPUT A$
140     DO WHILE A$='Y' <----------
150        PRINT
 .         .
 .         .
 .         .
310        PRINT "ANY MORE WINDOWS 'Y' OR 'N'";
320        INPUT A$
330     LOOP
 .         .
 .         .
 .         .
```

The DO loop construct consists of a DO statement which serves as the top of the loop, a LOOP statement which serves as the bottom of the loop, and a block of statements in between which make up the body of the loop. **Loop conditions** may be added to the DO statement (pretest) or to the LOOP statement (posttest). A **loop condition** has one of two forms:

WHILE *condition*

or

UNTIL *condition*

As you can tell from the English meanings of WHILE and UNTIL, a WHILE causes the loop to continue if the *condition* is true and an UNTIL causes to loop to terminate if the *condition* is true.

For those cases like the search loop (Section 8 5) where a single loop exit point is not appropriate, there is a new statement, the **EXIT DO** statement, which does what it says. It causes the computer to go to the first statement after the LOOP statement of the innermost DO loop.

Appendices

Appendix A **The World BASIC Lives In**

The exact procedure you must go through to use BASIC varies from computer system to computer system. Here we'll indicate some common forms of the process, with the goal of helping you understand the manual for your specific system, or what your local expert tells you to do.

Most large computer systems first require you to enter an account number and (perhaps) a password. This serves to assign the charges to the right party, and to ensure that someone (shudder) is not trying to use an account not assigned to him. Since most computer systems make a number of languages available for use, the next thing you will have to type is probably

```
BASIC
```

From that point on, you should be dealing with a BASIC system like that described in this book. You can enter, change, LIST, and RUN programs.

When you're finished, typically, you type

```
BYE
```

to so indicate. At that point the system may well print a number of lines giving an accounting of the amounts of its resources that you used, perhaps the time of day, perhaps some other marginally useful information. At that point you can turn the terminal off, or turn it over to the person waiting in line behind you.

Local Expert

Most small systems are more casual. On some, in fact (for example, the IBM PC), all you have to do to "get into BASIC" is to turn on the power, leaving the diskette door open. Others may be casual and yet complicated. For example, with versions of BASIC like CBASIC (one of seven versions of BASIC we used in writing this book), entering and running a program is a three-part process. First, you use a program called a **text editor** to create a program. Then you invoke a program called CBASIC which operates on the text file the text editor creates to produce an intermediate form of your program. Finally, you invoke a program called CRUN which takes the intermediate form and acts it out. If you discover an error, you must stop your program (by hitting the panic button), use the text editor to change the program, call on CBASIC again, and finally use CRUN to carry out the new version.

A picture of your computer

In books like this, the authors usually include a bunch of pictures of computers, terminals, and printers. They hope if they include enough pictures, one of them will be like your computer system. We've decided that isn't good enough. No, we're going that extra step. Showing a computer *like* yours isn't good enough for us. *We've decided to show your computer itself!*

Instructions:

1 Cut a hole in this page, following the dotted line.
2 Walk to within about 10 feet of your computer.
3 Hold this page in front of your eyes.

Cut-out this region

Figure A 1 1 A picture of your computer. Identify the keyboard, the printer or CRT screen (or both), the computer itself, and any storage devices (tapes, floppy disks, etc.) Look closely at the keyboard, and find the return key and the key marked control (or CTRL).

SAVING A PROGRAM FOR LATER USE

On all but the very smallest computer systems there is a way to save and retrieve BASIC programs. Usually this requires giving a name to the program. Suppose you are entering a program that computes gas mileage, and you want to save it so you can use it again without retyping it. Here's one common way to accomplish this.

First, get into BASIC. Next, you specify that you want to enter a new program, and that you want it called GAS.

```
NEW GAS
```

Next, you enter the program. No doubt you will run it to make sure it works properly.

```
RUN
```

When you're satisfied with the program (or you have to quit working on it), you type

```
SAVE
```

This will store a copy of the lines you typed, under the name GAS. When (a few hours or a few days later) you want to use the program again, you enter BASIC, and then type

```
OLD GAS
```

If all went well, when you now type

```
LIST
```

you'll see the program you SAVEd before.

On small computers that use cassette tape for storage, the process is similar. (The keyword OLD may be replaced by CLOAD, for Cassette LOAD; the keyword SAVE may be replaced by CSAVE.) Of course, you must be sure the right tape is in the machine!

On all large systems and most small ones, there is a command which causes the system to display the names of all the programs (files) you have saved. Within the DEC BASIC-PLUS system, you type CAT (short for CATALOG). In CDC BASIC you type CATLIST. In the CP/M system (CBASIC), you type DIR (for DIRectory). In MicroSoft BASIC you type FILES. In addition, there is a command which will wipe out a program you no longer wish to keep. See your reference manual or local expert.

INCORPORATING PART OF ONE PROGRAM IN ANOTHER

Suppose you have a file called MENU available which contains the menu routines from Chapter 9. You're writing a new program, but you want to include the menu routines without having to retype them. Here's how you can do that on three different systems. We assume the new program will be called PAINT1, and that you will want to save it after entering it.

DEC BASIC-PLUS	CDC BASIC	CBASIC (CP/M)
"get into" BASIC OLD MENU RENAME PAINT1 –add your new statements to the routines from MENU– SAVE time passes any time you want to run your program, get into BASIC, then type OLD PAINT1 RUN	"get into" BASIC OLD,PAINT1=MENU –add your new statements to the routines from MENU– SAVE time passes any time you want to run your program, get into BASIC, then type OLD,PAINT1 RUN	use the text editor to create a file called "PAINT1.BAS" Put the line %include MENU in the program exactly where you want the menu routines to appear in the finished version. When you're through with the editor, type CBASIC PAINT1 any time you want to run your program, type CRUN PAINT1

WHAT'S REALLY GOING ON HERE, ANYWAY?

BASIC is a **computer language.** A computer language is an abstract idea, not a physical thing. The ANSI standards for Minimal BASIC tell what properties legal Minimal BASIC programs have, so, in that way, they define the language. The number of different legal Minimal BASIC programs is infinite.

When you run a BASIC program on a computer, what does that mean? It means the computer does what the program says to do. Each BASIC statement has two collections of information associated with it. First, there is a description of the **legal forms.** For example, the first LET statement is legal, but the second is not.

```
10    LET A = 23

10    LET A BE 23
```

In addition, there is a description of the **meaning** of the statement. You can describe the allowable forms of LET statements without ever mentioning what they mean. A LET statement's meaning is, "Evaluate the expression to the right of the = and store the resulting value in the variable named to the left." What or who carries out the command? It's another program, one which accepts the characters that make up your BASIC program as input, and causes various appropriate actions to occur in the computer system, based on the exact nature of your program. How can a program cause actions (such as changing a value in memory, or causing a particular pattern of bright spots to appear on a screen) in a computer?

In most systems there are several levels of programs involved in actually getting something to happen. Your BASIC program as we've said, is interpreted by another program which breaks down the meanings you've expressed into terms closer to the primitive operations of the computer. In some cases this second-level program works by sending sequences of commands to yet other programs. But eventually, through however circuitous a path, the meaning of your program is expressed as a sequence of primitive machine operations. For many people who are interested only in software, an explanation like "a pattern of 1s and 0s gets sent to the processor, and is used to turn on and off a bunch of little switches which control the way other patterns of 1s and 0s are allowed to flow over the multitudinous wires connecting the various circuit components" is enough. It seems to be saying something, but contains so many unfamiliar words that they can't quite think of another question, so they say "I see" with the emphasis on the second word, in a grave and serious voice, and change the subject. But we suspect, if you've read this far, that you're made of sterner stuff.

Let's back up and try again. The question that needs answering here is this: When you write a program, you give a list of commands (BASIC statements). If your program is written properly, the meanings of the statements combine to cause actions in the computer system that solve you problem. *You* know what a LET statement is supposed to mean, but must some part of the computer system know what it means in the same sense? We think not, as the paragraphs below attempt to show. Instead, there is a hierarchy of agreements among people involved with each aspect of the computer system. The agreements prevent the patterns that convey meaning from one human to another from being destroyed. That's all.

The more often a program has been used, the more likely the errors in it will have been discovered and fixed. The operating system is in constant use by everyone. The BASIC processor is used very frequently by many people. The program you just entered has never been used by anyone. If something is wrong, where do you think you should look first, second, third, fourth, fifth,...?

Most current computer languages are based on a simple model of computer hardware. This model has three interconnected, intercommunicating parts, plus the user.

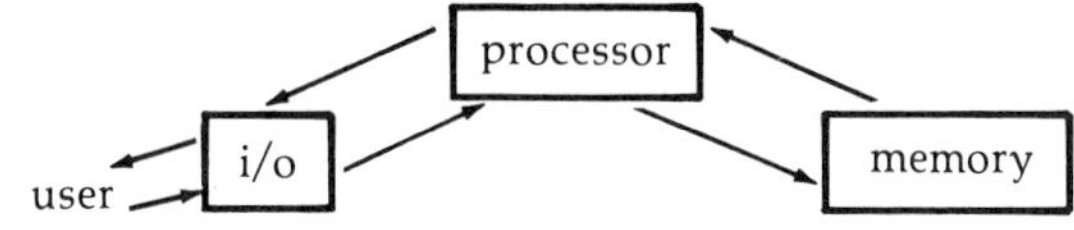

Both programs and data are stored in **memory.** Each program statement lies passively in memory until it is brought into the **processor** to be acted out. GO TO, IF-THEN, GOSUB, RETURN, and ON-GO TO statements determine which line of the program should be processed next. The LET statement changes data values in memory. INPUT and PRINT statements cause values to be brought from or sent to the **input/output** (i/o) **devices.**

hardware: those parts of a computer system you can touch; actual physical devices; e.g., the wires, cases, keyboards, screens, tape machines, integrated circuit chips, boards,...

software: those parts of a computer system you can't touch; programs and data values.

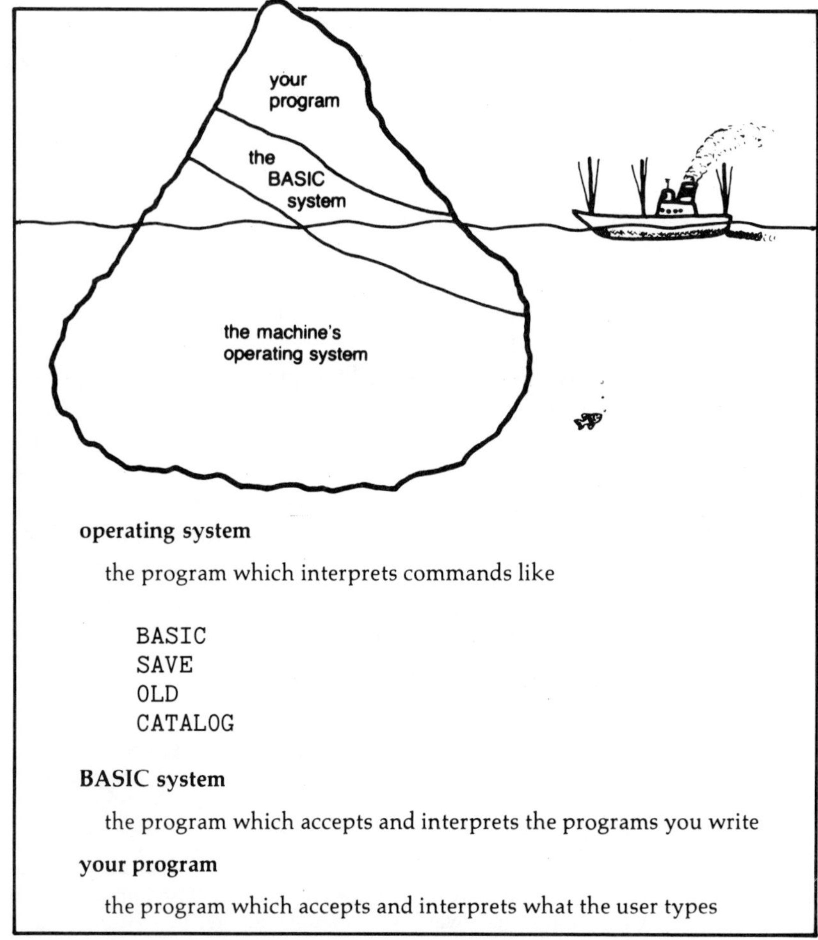

operating system

the program which interprets commands like

```
BASIC
SAVE
OLD
CATALOG
```

BASIC system

the program which accepts and interprets the programs you write

your program

the program which accepts and interprets what the user types

> On many computers (and almost all current-day micro-computers), if you enter a program and then shut the power off, your program is lost. Where, you might ask, did it go?
>
> Suppose your name is spelled out in the array of lights on the side of the Goodyear blimp. One minute your name is there, and in the next, when the power to the lights is turned off, your name is gone.
>
> Wherever your name went is the same place your program went.

When we write a program that interacts with a user, it's as if we've invented a simple computer language. For example, in the inventory control problem (see Section 10 3), the language we invented has three keywords (CHECKOUT, INQUIRY, and RESTOCK). In addition, there's a fixed set of rules about when and where the user may type numbers. In some cases these numbers mean quantity on hand; in others, the numbers mean price. That is, the numbers have these meanings to the user. Do they have a "meaning" to our program? When the program asks for a price, it prints the string PRICE; when it prints out a Price, the value is preceded by the string PRICE. The programs treats numbers consistently, that's all. If a number was entered after the word PRICE, it will never be printed after the strings ITEM # or QUANTITY — it will appear only after PRICE. If the user wants to think that the program "understands" the difference between prices of things and the quantity on hand, that's fine. In fact, it is only the person who *wrote* the program who must understand the difference, not the program itself.

The process we went through to write the inventory control program is analogous to the process the people who wrote your BASIC system went through. We decided what CHECKOUT should mean, and wrote the lines of BASIC that do it. Similarly, they knew what LET should mean, and wrote a program to do just that whenever their program comes across a LET statement in *your* program.

So far, we've got a two-step process. The user thinks he or she is programming in the inventory control language, but we know that our BASIC program just does certain things to make it look like RESTOCK means something. We think we're programming in BASIC, but the people who wrote our BASIC system know that their program just does certain simple things to make it look like LET statements and GOTO statements and REM statements mean something.

This all sounds very tidy. We have a series of translations, each providing more detail, until the actual meaning of the program is expressed as primitive machine operations. But why should we suspect that the primitive machine operations are any different? In fact, the individual machine language instructions, although expressed as strings of 1s and 0s instead of letters, are directly analogous to keywords like LET or RESTOCK! The machine designer thinks in terms like this: "Let's see. . . this instruction's code is 10101001, and it's supposed to be a MOVE. How can I hook up these circuit components so when 10101001 is in here, that lets the 1s and 0s over here flow along some wires into there. . ."

And why stop there? The circuit designer has to design circuits that will let the machine designer think he is manipulating patterns of 1s and 0s. But as far as the circuit designer is concerned, those aren't *really* 1s and 0s; in fact, they are simply electrical signals. The circuit designer cleverly manipulates his devices so the signals are kept within certain bounds, thus enabling the machine designer to safely think of the signals as 1s and 0s.

Now, the solid state physicists and electrical engineers who developed the techniques the circuit designer uses know that the circuit designer isn't *really* dealing with electrical signals. They know that, in fact, the circuit designer is dealing with the shifts in quantum state of multitudes of subatomic particles.

And *we* know that the words (electron, meson, quantum state) that physicists use to describe the basic operations of the universe are simply metaphors and models they've made up as they try to make order of their experimental findings.

So: The universe fools the physicists into thinking they're dealing with subatomic particles; the physicists fool the circuit designers into thinking they're dealing with electrical signals; the circuit designers fool the machine designers into thinking they're dealing with 1s and 0s; the machine designers fool the system programmers into thinking the basic unit of meaning is the primitive machine instruction; the system programmers fool us into thinking the unit of meaning is BASIC statements like LET, IF-THEN, and so on; we fool the user into thinking the computer understands what RESTOCK means; and everybody lives happily ever after.

The End

Appendix B **Glossary**

algorithm directions for doing something; more formally: a collection of rules which, when carried out, solve a specified problem in a finite number of steps

alphanumeric alphameric (see **character**)

ANSI Minimal BASIC a computer language defined in standards maintained by the American National Standards Institute, Inc.

array a collection of variables, individual members of which may be referenced by a single identifier followed by a numeric value (the **index** or **subscript**)

argument a value which serves as an input to a **subprogram**

bit a binary digit (0 or 1)

bug an error; a statement or pattern of statements which causes an error

character

numeric character: a decimal digit; one of 0 1 2 3 4 5 6 7 8 9

alphabetic character: a capitalized letter; one of A B C D E F G H I J K L M N O P Q R S T U V W X Y Z

alphameric: a numeric or alphabetic character (in some literature, this term is synonymous with character)

other character: anything not mentioned above that you can find: < > ^ # = * % ? ! a b c, etc.

code

noun: the text of a program, i.e., the lines of the programs as opposed to the plan or idea of the program.

verb: to write BASIC statements; to translate a plan into BASIC

compiler a program which translates the statements of a program into the lower-level language appropriate for a computer — compiling a program makes it possible for the computer to carry out the program, but does not in and of itself carry out the program.

computer a machine which can perform arithmetic operations, make logical decisions, and perform other symbol manipulation tasks by automatically following the instructions in a computer program

debug to locate and remove **bugs**

default a value or condition which is assumed unless explicitly overridden

defined having a value; having been specified; for instance, a variable is **defined** once it has been given a value by a LET, INPUT, or READ statement

directory a collection of pointers ordered by some aspect of the data values being pointed to; an **index**

dirty trick a statement or sequence of statements used for an obscure or devious purpose

disk a **random access i/o device** containing one or more spinning magnetic storage surfaces

documentation information prepared for humans describing a program or collection of related programs

element one of a collection of things; an **array element** is one specific variable chosen from the collection of variables that make up the array

executable statement a statement which is a command that causes the computer to take some immediate action (contrast with **specification statement**); assignments of any kind (LET, INPUT, READ), transfer of control of any kind, input/output of any kind.

function a **subprogram** which returns a single value, references to which may appear within expressions (functions are either built-in or are specified in a DEF statement); an **operator** (functions and operators are mathematically equivalent, but in the computing field, **function** is used to describe operators which are invoked by giving the name, then the arguments (if any) in parentheses. **Operator** describes a function which is invoked by placing the arguments around the symbol, as in 3*2)

higher-level language a computer language which allows commands to the computer to be expressed in a form closer to normal human language than is allowed by machine language; BASIC, COBOL, FORTRAN, LISP and PASCAL, are examples of **higher-level languages.**

host the underlying computer system (hardware and operating system); a portable program is one which works properly even when installed on different hosts

identifier a name (of a **simple variable,** an **array**, a **function**)

I/O device equipment which reads or writes data on an input or output medium

I/O medium material used for storing data (e.g., computer paper, 80-column card, magnetic tape, floppy diskette)

index

noun: a label which identifies one of a group of items; an **array subscript;** a **directory**

verb: to point out members of a collection (usually a collection of **array elements**)

initialize to prepare for a process to begin; to give starting (initial) values to variables

interpreter a program which carries out a BASIC program by performing machine operations appropriate to the meaning of each BASIC statement it comes to

key in sorting, the values which determine the sorted arrangement are called the **keys**

keyword a sequence of characters making up a distinguishing part of a statement; for example: PRINT, IF, REM, LET

line a line number followed by a statement

loop

noun: a sequence of statements that's repeated over and over

verb: to branch back to a previously performed statement

menu a list of choices the user is asked to choose from

mnemonic

adjective: aiding memory

noun: a word chosen to help you remember something; if you name a variable B for "Balance," then B is a mnemonic

module a collection of statements which is a logical subunit of an overall program; a **subroutine**

operating system a program which supervises the running of all programs on the computer system

operator one of + − * / or ^; see **function**

pack to place what the programmer thinks of as several values in a single variable

parameter an **identifier** used to specify the form and type which an **argument** to a subprogram will have; for instance, X is a **parameter** in this function definition

```
20   DEF FNR(X) + INT(X + 0.5)
```

pointer an array subscript; a variable which stores an array subscript

polite easy, understandable, and natural to use (e.g., a **polite** program)

portable able to be used without change on many different computer systems

precision the degree to which a value discriminates between measured quantities; a value correct to two digits is more *precise* than one correct to only one digit since the first discriminates among a hundred possibilities, the second among only ten

program a sequence of instructions which tell a computer to do something; a sequence of lines, where each line consists of a line number and a BASIC statement, with the highest-numbered line containing END

program fragment part of a **program,** used to illustrate some particular point

program stub a simplified form of a module, used during preliminary testing of a developing program

programmer a person who creates **programs**

random access i/o device an i/o device whose read/write head can move in a nonsequential way, thus making the data retrieval time almost independent of the location of the data on the i/o device (e.g., **disk**)

record a set of data items treated as a unit

recursive self-referential; a **recursive** subprogram is one which includes a reference to itself

routine a **program,** or a logical subpart of a program; a **module;** a subroutine

selection part of a program which results in one action being taken next, to the exclusion of other possible actions

sentinal a value which appears among data values and which serves not as data but to mark a position (such as the end of the data)

simple variable a variable which is not part of an **array**

specification statement a **statement** which causes no action to be taken but which provides information for the computer; a DIM statement or an OPTION BASE statement

statement a single BASIC command

statement label a line number

structured programming an approach to programming which leads to understandable, correct computer programs

subprogram a subsidiary part of a program; a subroutine or function

subscript a value designating a particular element of an array

subscripted variable an **array;** an array **element**

system any thing thought of as having subparts

test

noun: a condition (e.g., C < = 4)

verb: to verify that a program or module works properly

type the interpretation given a stored data value, i.e., numeric or string

unpack to remove one or more values from a packed value (see **pack**)

user a person who interacts with a finished program

user friendly polite

verbose overly wordy; generating excessive output

Appendix C BASIC MiniManual

The purpose of this reference manual is to provide a concise description of the programming language Minimal BASIC as specified in the American National Standards document X3.60–1978. Look here if you need to know the precise form or meaning of a BASIC statement.

PROGRAM FORM

program a sequence of lines; the last line must be an END statement.

line begins with a line-number followed by a keyword; details of a command follow the keyword; lines over 72 characters long may not be accepted by some BASIC systems.

line-number a sequence of one to four digits, not all zeros; line-numbers in a program must all be distinct, ignoring leading zeros (i.e., 0020 is considered to be the same as 020 or 20), and must increase statement by statement.

keyword one of the following:

DATA	INPUT	RANDOMIZE
DEF	LET	READ
DIM	NEXT	REM
FOR	ON	RESTORE
GOSUB or GO SUB	OPTION BASE	RETURN
GOTO or GO TO	PRINT	STOP
IF (always with THEN)		

In Minimal BASIC, keywords must be surrounded by blanks except that the blank following a keyword is not needed at the end of a line. However, few BASIC systems hold you to this restriction.

CONSTANTS

numeric constant one of four possible forms:

		examples
integer	*sdd...d*	327 −2 +54
decimal	*sdd...d.dd...d*	−2.002 .625
scaled decimal	*sdd...d.dd...dEsdd*	6.0238E23 6.63E−34
implicit decimal	*sdd...dEsdd*	602E21 −16E−20

where *s* stands for an optional sign (+ or − 1)
and *d* stands for a digit (0,1,2, up to 9).
No spaces may be imbedded within numeric constants.

string constant a sequence of none or more characters enclosed in quotation marks (quotation marks may not be imbedded in string constants)

examples

"BETTY JO"
"#$%*&"
"513-44-6A"
""

All Minimal BASIC systems will accept numeric constants with up to six digits plus up to two digits in the scale factor, and string constants with up to 18 characters, not counting the quotes.

A **scale factor** of the form E*sdd* in a numeric constant shifts the decimal point to the right if the sign is positive, left if negative.

Numeric constants or string constants may be used in DATA, IF, LET, and PRINT statements. String constants in PRINT statements may be as long as will fit on a line.

Quotation marks may be omitted in string constants in DATA statements and in responses supplied for INPUT statements. When the quotation marks are omitted, leading and trailing blanks are ignored, and the string may not contain ampersands, apostrophes, commas, exclamation points, or quotation marks. If a null string (one with zero characters) is listed in a DATA statement, quotation marks must be used. Additionally, integer numeric constants may be used in DIM statements, and any type of numeric constant may be used in FOR, NEXT, and DEF statements.

VARIABLES

simple variable one of three forms:

		examples
numeric variable:	*a*	X T I N
numeric variable:	*ad*	S3 A0 I8
string variable:	*a*$	S$ U$

where *a* is a letter (A, B, . . . , Z)
and *d* is a digit (0, 1, 2, . . . , 9)
No space is allowed betweeen *a* and *d* or *a* and $.

array element one of two forms:

		examples
numeric variable:	*a(s)*	R(3) R(2*N−1) Z(SQR(X)*N)
numeric variable:	*a(s,s)*	X(5,3) A(M,N) B(M−1,12)

where *a* is a letter and *s* is a numeric expression called a **subscript.**

Variables are used to store numbers or strings of characters. In general, variables may be used wherever constants may be used (except in a DIM statement, where only constants may be used to set the size of the array).

Minimal BASIC provides arrays only for storing numeric values, but many versions of BASIC provide some sort of string-array feature. The same name may not be used for a simple variable and an array; however, a numeric variable name and a string variable name may use the same letter (e.g., A and A$ are separate variables, one numeric and one a string variable). There may not be one-dimensional and two-dimensional arrays with the same name.

EXPRESSIONS

numeric expression a sequence of numeric constants, variables, function-references, and/or parenthesized subexpressions separated by the arithmetic operators for addition (+), subtraction (−), multiplication (*), division (/), and exponentiation (∧); a sign (+ or −) may precede the expression.

string expression a string constant or variable.

Except when parentheses indicate otherwise, exponentiations come first in the evaluation of numeric expressions, then multiplications and divisions, and finally additions and subtractions.

In the absence of parentheses, a sequence of successive additions and/or subtractions is normally performed left to right. However, the computer may perform the operations in some other order as long as the results are mathematically equivalent. For example, the expression A + B − C may be evaluated as (A + B) − C or as A + (B − C), but the expression A − B − C would always be evaluated as (A − B) − C. The same rule holds for sequences of successive multiplications and/or divisions, and for exponentiations.

0 ^ 0 = 1, by BASIC fiat.

FUNCTION REFERENCES

function reference one of two forms:

with argument: *f(e)*

without argument: *f*

where *f* is a function name

and *e* is a numeric expression.

function name the name of a supplied function or FN*a*, where *a* is a letter. Function references may appear wherever variables may appear.

Minimal BASIC provides only functions with numeric arguments and numeric values. Some versions of BASIC provide functions which compute string values and which may take string arguments. This goes for user-defined functions as well as supplied functions.

User-defined functions must be defined with a DEF statement before they are referenced (i.e., the first reference must be in a higher-numbered line than the DEF statement). Some versions of BASIC allow functions to have more than one argument.

The terms **function** and **operator** are more or less synonymous in this book, as in mathematics. However, most computer scientists distinguish between them because of the difference in syntax (functions get their arguments enclosed in parentheses after the function name; operators are generally placed between their arguments or operands) and because in some programming languages, functions are allowed to have effects besides the returning of a value.

SUPPLIED FUNCTIONS

In the function-reference prototypes below, *x* stands for a numeric expression.

ABS(*x*)	the **absolute value** of *x*; if *x* is positive or zero, then ABS(*x*) is the same as *x*; if *x* is negative, then ABS(*x*) is the value of *x* with its sign changed to *plus*.
ATN(*x*)	the trigonometric **arctangent** of *x*; the value of ATN(*x*) is always between $-\pi/2$ and $+\pi/2$ radians (not degrees). To compute the arctangent in degrees, use the expression 720*ATN(*x*)/ATN(1) or 180*ATN(*x*)/3.14159.
COS(*x*)	the trigonometric **cosine** of *x*; the value of *x* must be expressed in radians. If *x* is in degrees, use the expression COS(*x**ATN(1)/45) or COS (*x**3.14159/180). If *x* is in grads, use the expression COS(*x**ATN(1)/50).
EXP(*x*)	the **exponential** function; the number *e* (2.71828..., from natural logarithms) raised to the power *x*.
INT(*x*)	the **largest whole number not greater** than *x*; INT(3.9) is 3; INT(3.2) is 3; INT(−3.9) is −4; INT(−3.2) is −4. INT(*x*+0.5) is the value of *x* rounded off to the nearest integer.

LOG(x)	the **natural logarithm** of x; the value of x must exceed zero. If you want the log base 10, use the expression LOG(x)/LOG(10).
RND	delivers a **random number;** 0 <=RND <1. This is a uniform variate; i.e., one number between zero and one is as likely to come up as another. If you want to choose with equal likelihood from the numbers 1, 2, 3,. . .N, use the expression INT(N*RND) + 1.
SGN(x)	the **signum** of x; +1 if x is positive 0 if x is zero −1 if x is negative
SIN(x)	the trigonometric **sine** of x; the value of x must be expressed in radians. If x is in degrees, use the expression SIN (x*ATN(1)/45) or SIN(x*3.14159 /180).
SQR(x)	the **square root** of x; SQR(x) >= 0; the value of x must not be negative.
TAN(x)	the **tangent** of x; the value of x must be expressed in radians. If x is in degrees, use the expression TAN(x*ATN(1)/45) or TAN(x*3.14159/180).

BASIC STATEMENTS

the LET statement

Let $v = e$

where v is a variable and e is an expression.

The expression e is evaluated and its value is assigned to the variable v. If e is a numeric expression, then v must be a numeric variable. If e is a string expression, then v must be a string variable.

Some versions of BASIC permit the programmer to omit the keyword LET. This is primarily for the convenience of people who are accustomed to programming in other programming languages, especially FORTRAN. Omitting the keyword from the LET statement results in a nonstandard, hence nonportable, program.

the INPUT statement

INPUT v, v,. . .v

where each v is a variable (there must be at least one variable v in the list).

For each variable in the list, the computer waits for the user to supply a value for the variable from the terminal; the user terminates each list of supplied values by striking the return key. Different values within a list of supplied values are separated by commas. Values for the variables must be supplied in the order that the variables are listed in the INPUT statement.

Subscripts for array elements in the list of variables are evaluated *after* values have been assigned to the variables to the left in the list.

A value supplied for a variable must be a numeric constant if the variable is numeric. Any value supplied for a string variable will be treated as a string constant. Any invalid values will cause the computer to wait for valid values to be supplied.

If a response to an INPUT statement contains invalid data, too many data items, or too few data items, the entire INPUT response can be retyped. Some systems may provide an opportunity to correct parts of the response — the standards require that the user also be able to retype everything.

The quote marks may be omitted from values supplied for string variables. If the quotes are omitted, leading and trailing blanks are ignored, and there are some restrictions on the characters which may be used in the string. Specifically, none of the following characters may be included in an unquoted string: &',!"

Unquoted string
may not have: &',!"

the READ statement

READ *v, v,...v*

where each *v* is a variable.

The variables in the list are assigned values sequentially from values supplied in DATA statements.

The DATA statements in a program determine a sequence of values which are used one by one as needed to supply values for variables in READ statements as the READ statements are carried out.

The rules for supplying values in DATA statements and the rules for assigning these values to variables in READ statements are the same as those for INPUT statements except that invalid values or a dearth of values are treated as errors.

the DATA statement

DATA *c, c,..., c*

where each *c* is a constant.

The collection of DATA statements in a program as a whole determines a sequence of values to be used as needed by READ statements.

Quotation marks may be omitted from string constants; if so, leading and trailing blanks are ignored and there are some restrictions on the characters which may be used in the string (see INPUT statement or string constant).

If the computer reaches a line number containing a DATA statement, it goes to the next line with no other effect.

the RESTORE statement

RESTORE

Regardless of how many READ statements have been performed, the sequence of values determined by the DATA statements is restarted from the beginning for subsequent READs.

the PRINT statement one of three forms:

PRINT
PRINT *e s e s*. . .*e*
PRINT *e s e s*. . .*e s*

where each *e* is an expression or a tab of the form TAB(*n*), *n* is a numeric expression, and each *s* is a comma or semicolon; any of the *e*'s may be omitted. Each expression is evaluated and printed with spacing determined by the separators *s* and the tabs; if the PRINT statement does not end with a separator, subsequent printing will begin on the next line.

the printing of numbers Every BASIC system defines two integers to determine the format of printed numbers; the number-width *d* and the scale-width *e* (*d* is at least 6 and *e* is at least 2). Let *x* stand for the number to be printed. Then there are four cases:

integer: If *x* can be expressed as a whole number with *d* or fewer digits, then it is printed like an integer constant with as many digits as actually needed (no leading zeros).

decimal: If *x* can be expressed like a decimal constant with *d* or fewer digits and a decimal point, then it is printed in that manner. Leading zeros are always omitted and trailing zeros after the decimal point may be omitted.

scaled decimal: All other numbers are printed in the scaled decimal notation with exactly *d* digits, one before the decimal point and $d-1$ after the decimal point, some of which may, of course, be trailing zeros. The sign is not omitted from the scale factor.

If the sign of *x* is positive, the number is printed with a leading blank; otherwise it is printed with a leading minus sign. A trailing blank is printed after each number.

the printing of strings String values are printed verbatim, with no additional blanks. Of course, the string value itself may contain blanks in any position.

spacing Commas, semicolons, and tabs in print lists are used to control spacing as follows:

comma: move to the next **print zone.**

semicolon: no spacing.

TAB(*n*): move to column *t* = INT(*n*−*m**INT((*n*−1)/*m*) + 0.5)

where *m* is the number of print positions the BASIC system allows on a line; exception: if moving to column *t* would require backspacing, move to column *t* in the next line. Note: **Columns** are print positions on the line, numbered from 1 to *m*. Column *t* is column *n* rounded to the nearest integer and reduced modulo *m* until it is in the range 1 to *m*. If *t* is zero or less, it is set to one and an error may be signaled.

print zone Every BASIC system divides the print-line into a fixed number of print zones of equal size. The size of the print zones (except possibly for the last one on the right, which may be smaller) is large enough to accommodate a number printed in scaled decimal notation.

Each expression or string in a PRINT statement is known as a **print item,** in particular a **numeric print item** or a **string print item.**

If the printing of a **numeric print item** would cause printing beyond the right-hand margin, the item is printed at the beginning of the next line.

If the printing of a **string print item** would cause printing beyond the right-hand margin, then as much as possible of the string is printed on the current line, and the rest is printed at the beginning of the next line.

the IF-THEN statement

IF *e r e* THEN *s*

where each *e* is an expression, *r* is a relation, and *s* is a line number.

If the value of the first expression stands in the relation *r* with the second expression, then the computer goes to the statement at line *s*; otherwise the computer goes to the next statement after the IF-THEN.

The **relation r** is one of:

= *(equals)*

<> *(not equal to)*

<= *(less than or equal to)*

< *(less than)*

>= *(greater than or equal to)*

> *(greater than)*

If the expressions are string expressions, then *r* must be either *equals* or *not equal to*. Some versions of BASIC support the ordering or collating relations for strings (*less than*, etc.), but Minimal BASIC does not.

Equality between two string expressions holds only when both strings consist of identical sequences of characters, leading and trailing blanks included.

the GOTO statement one of two forms:

GOTO *s*

GO TO *s*

where *s* is a line number. The computer goes to the statement at line number *s*.

the ON-GO TO statement one of two forms:

ON *e* GOTO *s,s,. . .s*

ON *e* GO TO *s,s,. . .s*

where *e* is a numeric expression and each *s* is a line number. The expression is evaluated and rounded to the nearest integer *n*; the computer goes to the *n*th line number in the list. If the expression rounds to a number less than one or greater than the number of line numbers in the list, an error condition occurs.

the FOR statement one of two forms:

FOR *v* = *b* TO *e*

FOR *v* = *b* TO *e* STEP *i*

where *v* is a simple numeric variable called the **control variable,** and *b, e,* and *i* are numeric expressions.

the NEXT statement

NEXT *v*

where *v* is a simple numeric variable, the **control variable.**

FOR and NEXT statements occur in pairs:

FOR statement

.

.

.

NEXT statement

The sequence of statements beginning with a FOR statement and proceeding up to the first NEXT statement with the same control variable is known as a **FOR-NEXT block** or a **FOR loop.** A FOR-NEXT block becomes **active** when its FOR statement is encountered.

The execution of a FOR-NEXT block proceeds as follows:

1 The expressions *b, e,* and *i* are evaluated. We will refer to the values of these expressions as the *initial value,* the *limit,* and the *increment,* respectively. If STEP *i* is omitted, the *increment* is 1.

2 The control variable is given the *initial value.*

3 If the value of the control variable is not beyond the *limit* (i.e., if (*v* − *limit*)*SGN (*increment*) <= 0), then the computer performs the statements in the FOR-NEXT block after the FOR statement and up to the NEXT statement. If the control variable has passed the limit, then the computer goes to the statement after the FOR-NEXT block.

4 When the NEXT statement is reached, the *increment* is added to the control variable and the process described in step 3 is repeated.

When the control variable passes the *limit,* the FOR-NEXT block **terminates normally** and becomes **inactive;** otherwise it remains **active** until a FOR statement with the same control variable is encountered.

When a FOR-loop terminates normally, the control variable retains the first unused value in the sequence generated by starting with the *initial value* and repeatedly adding the *increment.*

Because of the possibility of rounding errors in adding the *increment* and comparing against the *limit,* the number of iterations through the loop may not always be what the programmer expects, especially when the *increment* is a negative number with a fractional part.

FOR-NEXT blocks may be nested one inside another, but they may not be interleaved. There may be as many as ten FOR-NEXT blocks active at any one time. Minimal BASIC systems *may* allow more than ten active blocks, but if you want your program to be portable, don't count on it.

the GOSUB statement one of two forms:

GOSUB *s*

GO SUB *s*

where *s* is a line number. The computer transfers to line *s*. The GOSUB statement is a returnable GOTO statement used in conjunction with the RETURN statement for subroutine linkage.

the RETURN statement

RETURN

The computer transfers to the first statement after the most recently executed GOSUB statement. As many as ten GOSUB statements may be executed before any RETURNs are performed. Some versions of BASIC permit even greater depth in the nesting of GOSUB-RETURN pairs.

the DEF statement one of two forms:

DEF FN*a*(*p*) = *e*

DEF FN*a* = *e*

where *a* is a letter (A, B,. . .Z), *p* is a simple numeric variable known as the **parameter,** and *e* is a numeric expression. The DEF statement sets up a function with the name FN*a*, whose value when referenced is the value of *e* when *p* is replaced by the value of the argument in the function reference.

The first reference to a function must be in a higher-numbered line than the DEF statement which defines the function.

The expression in a DEF statement may refer to *previously defined* functions.

Some versions of BASIC permit functions with string values, functions with string expressions as arguments, more than one parameter, and/or multi-line functions.

A function reference must provide an argument if a parameter is specified in the DEF statement for the function and must not supply an argument if the DEF statement does not specify a parameter. If the computer reaches a line number containing a DEF statement, it goes to the next line with no other effect.

the DIM statement

DIM *d*, *d*,. . .*d*

where each *d* is an **array declaration.**

array declaration one of two forms:

a(*n*)

a(*m*,*n*)

where *a* is a letter (A, B, up to Z) known as the **array name** and *m* and *n* are integer numeric constants known as the **subscript limits.**

A DIM statement sets up the arrays named in the declarations. The array elements in these arrays have one or two subscripts as indicated in the array declarations, and their subscripts may not exceed the limits specified in the declarations.

If the computer reaches a line number containing a DIM statement, it goes to the next line with no other effect.

An array may be dimensioned only once in a program. Arrays which do not appear in DIM statements automatically have a bound of ten on their subscripts and have one or two dimensions according to their first use in the program.

There may not be one-dimensional and two-dimensional arrays with the same name.

the OPTION BASE statement one of two forms:

OPTION BASE 0

OPTION BASE 1

Specifies the lower bound (zero or one) for all array subscripts in the program. Array subscripts start at zero unless an OPTION BASE 1 statement precedes the first DIM statement in the program. If the computer reaches a line number containing an OPTION BASE statement, it goes to the next line with no other effect.

the RANDOMIZE statement

RANDOMIZE

Generates a new unpredictable starting point for the random number function RND.

In the absence of a RANDOMIZE statement, the RND function will always generate the same sequence of "random" numbers.

Some BASIC systems without access to some unpredictable random element may require the user to supply a random value to be used in starting the sequence.

the REM statement

REM *r*

where *r* is any sequence of characters, possibly empty. The REM statement has no effect on the computation but is used to annotate the program.

If the computer reaches a line number containing a REM statement, it goes to the next line with no other effect.

the STOP statement

STOP

Terminates execution of the program.

the END statement

END

Terminates execution of the program. There must be exactly one END statement in a program, and it must have the highest line number in the program.

Appendix D Answers to Exercises

This appendix contains answers to virtually all odd-numbered exercises from Chapters 1 through 18.

ANSWERS TO EXERCISES 1 2

1
```
10    PRINT "FIELDING MELLISH"
20    PRINT "1309 KIRKWOOD DR."
30    PRINT "FT COLLINS, CO"
40    END
LIST
```

3
```
10 PRINT
20 PRINT
30 PRINT
40 END
LIST
```

or

```
10 PRINT "    "
      etc.
```

ANSWERS TO EXERCISES 1 3

1 There will be a blank line printed between the 1 and the 2.

3 You can leave out the quotes around the numbers (1, 2, and 3).

ANSWERS TO EXERCISES 1 4

1
```
10    PRINT 1+2+3+4+5+6+7+8+9+10
20    END

RUN
 55
READY
```

3 You may have found that PRINT \$23.49 − \$14.23 − \$5.00 doesn't work. You can't put dollar signs in numbers.

```
10   PRINT 23.49 - 14.23 - 5.00
20   END

RUN
 4.26
READY
```

ANSWERS TO EXERCISES 1 5

1 The program on the left prints

```
HELLO          THERE.
```

The program on the right prints

```
HELLO THERE.
```

It's the old print zone trick. The comma in the first program causes the computer to skip to the second print zone, leaving a bunch of spaces between the two words. The semicolon in the second program keeps the computer from printing on the next line, even though there are two PRINT statements in the program.

3 The following program prints a "banner" to mark the columns 01, 02, 03,. . .39. Then it uses a PRINT statement with asterisks to mark the beginning of the first two print zones.

```
10   PRINT "000000000111111111122222222223333333333"
20   PRINT "123456789012345678901234567890123456789"
30   PRINT "*", "*"
40   END

RUN
000000000111111111122222222223333333333
123456789012345678901234567890123456789
*             *
READY
```

Since the first asterisk is in column one and the second is in column 15, we deduce that our print zones are 14 columns wide.

5 The information in PRINT statements gets printed out when you RUN the program. The information in REM statements doesn't get printed when you RUN the program, only when you LIST the program.

ANSWERS TO EXERCISES 1 6

1 N, V7, and K are numeric variables. N$ and M$ are string variables. The others are not legal variable names in Minimal BASIC.

3
```
10  REM  NAME AND AGE PRINTER
20       PRINT "WHAT'S YOUR NAME";
30       INPUT N$
40       PRINT "YOUR AGE";
50       INPUT A
60       PRINT N$; " IS"; A; "YEARS OLD."
99       END

RUN
WHAT'S YOUR NAME? ANN MARIE
YOUR AGE? 19
ANN MARIE IS 19 YEARS OLD.
READY

RUN
WHAT'S YOUR NAME? ELIZABETH ROBERTS
YOUR AGE? NONE OF YOUR BUSINESS
?INVALID DATA--RE-ENTER
?
```

the system won't (can't) put a string value in a numeric variable. It gives an error message, then prints another question mark and waits for the user to enter the correct type of value

You may have had trouble with the spacing. When the computer prints numbers, it automatically puts spaces around them. We'll get into this in more detail later.

ANSWERS TO EXERCISES 1 7

1 There are *two* things wrong. First, to INPUT two values into variables X and Y, the proper form is INPUT X *comma* Y. Second, in standard BASIC, every program must have an END statement.

3
```
10  REM  COMPUTE THE YEAR YOU WERE BORN
20       PRINT "WHAT'S YOUR AGE";
30       INPUT A
40       PRINT "WHAT YEAR IS IT NOW";
50       INPUT Y
60       PRINT "IF YOU ARE"; A; "AND IT'S"; Y
70       PRINT "YOU MUST HAVE BEEN BORN ABOUT"; Y - A
99       END
```

5
```
10  REM  SLEEP SCHEDULE LAST WEEK
20       PRINT "MONDAY", "6:30 AM", "11:00 PM"
30       PRINT "TUESDAY", "7:00 AM", "10:00 PM"
40       PRINT "WEDNESDAY", "9:00 AM", "2:30 AM"
50       PRINT "THURSDAY", "11:30 AM", "8:30 PM"
60       PRINT "FRIDAY", "6:30 AM", "4:00 AM"
99       END
```

7 Even though it's sometimes difficult, it's usually worth the effort to think up reasonable names which remind you of the way you're using a variable rather than to settle for random names. In this case you might use W for pencils (Writing instruments), P1 for pizza (the 1 looks a little like an I—PIzza), and P0 for popcorn (the zero looks like an "oh" – POpcorn). Of course, there are lots of other reasonable choices.

ANSWERS TO EXERCISES 2 1

1 Add the statement PRINT "IN FEET" between line 80 and line 90. To make things completely clear, you might also want that statement between line 100 and line 110.

3 Yes. Everywhere the variables F and T are used (lines 140 and 150) replace them by 400 and (90/400), respectively.

5 N is still 1.0 in line 30.
N gets the value −2.5 in line 40.
N is still −2.5 in line 50.

ANSWERS TO EXERCISES 2 2

1 X will be 5 and Y will be 4.

3
```
LET C = C + 1
```

5
```
LET S = S^2/2
```

or

```
LET S = S*S/2
```

7 A will have the value 25 and B the value 15. Notice that their values have been "swapped". A started out with 15, and B with the value 25.

ANSWERS TO EXERCISES 2 3

1 (a) `LET F = (X - Y)/2`

(b) `LET F = 5*X + 1/(X - 1)`

(c) `LET F = A*(B - C)^2`

(d) `LET F = (A*Z + B)/(C*Z + D)`

(e) `LET F = ((X + Y)/2)*(A^3/(X*Y))`

(f) `LET F = X - (A*Y - B)`

ANSWERS TO EXERCISES 2 4

1 (a) 4 (b) 4 (c) 2 (d) 3 (e) 3 (f) −1

3 `INT(ABS(X))*SGN(X)`

5 whole feet: INT(X/12); inches left over: X − 12*INT(X/12)

7 `LET X = 2*RND + 1.5`

ANSWERS TO EXERCISES 2 5

1

```
10   REM  EXPERIMENT TO TEST ADDITION
20        PRINT "ENTER TWO NUMBERS WITH A COMMA BETWEEN THEM"
30        INPUT X, Y
40        PRINT X; "+"; Y; "="; X + Y
9999      END
```

Most of the test cases in (a)−(f) are pathological cases which run into the limits of accuracy on a Minimal BASIC system. In particular (b) should come out to exactly one; (c) should be 1.0E29; and (d) should have several unexpected digits (we expected the answer to be .000001). Depending on the accuracy of the numbers in your system, (a), (e), and (f) may have been strange too.

3 The expression 1.9*10^1.7 requires the computer to do an exponentiation to raise 10 to the power 1.7, then a multiplication to get the result. The "number" 1.9E1.7 is meaningless in BASIC because the scale factor must be a whole number. You can't shift the decimal point 1.7 places — only a whole number of places.

ANSWERS TO EXERCISES 2 6

1

```
RUN
WHAT DO YOU WANT? 123456789012345678
123456789012345678  <-- 18 characters is OK
READY

RUN
WHAT DO YOU WANT? 1234567890123456789
INVALID DATA--RE-ENTER  <-- 19 characters is too long
?                           (on our system)
```

3 c, d, and e should have a Q marked beside them. None should be marked with X. (It's always OK to enclose a string value in quotes when you enter it.)

ANSWERS TO EXERCISES 3 2H

1 It wouldn't have made any difference because a REM statement has no effect on the computation. However, if you were reading the program and trying to understand it, your eye would be drawn to the remark in scanning the repetition, and this could be an aid to understanding.

ANSWERS TO EXERCISES 3 2V

1 It wouldn't have changed the printed output because a REM statement has no effect on the computation. The computer simply goes on to the next statement. However, on some systems the timing would be affected because it takes the computer some small amount of time to pass by the REM statement. The extra time will be immeasurable on almost all BASIC systems. (Do exercise 2 and find out.)

Even though it doesn't affect the computation, it can be an aid to understanding for a person reading the program because it draws attention to the remark as you scan the repetition.

ANSWERS TO EXERCISES 3 3

1 The user would have to type Y instead of YES to keep the program going.

3
```
10    REM  MULTIPLICATIONS FOREVER
20         PRINT "TYPE IN TWO NUMBERS, ";
30         PRINT "SEPARATED BY A COMMA"
40             INPUT X, Y
50             PRINT X; "*"; Y "="; X*Y
60             GO TO 20
9999       END
```

ANSWERS TO EXERCISES 3 4

1 b, d, f, and g are OK. The numeric variable A in the first IF-THEN statement is compared to the string "YES" — illegal. There is no condition expressed in c. The condition in e is illegal because strings can be compared only for equal or not equal in Minimal BASIC.

3
```
1     REM  COMPOUND INTEREST ON $1000
2          LET P = 1000
10    REM  REPEAT A TASK  R  TIMES
           .
           .  ←——— copied directly from the program in Section 3 4
           .
```

```
110  REM  WILL BE DONE  R  TIMES
200       LET P = P + 0.015*P
980       LET C = C + 1
           .
           .   <——copied from Section 3 4
           .
1010 REM  FINISHED
1100      PRINT "COMPOUNDED INTEREST ON $1000"
1110      PRINT "FOR 12 MONTHS AT 1.5% PER MONTH:",
1120      PRINT "$"; P - 1000
9999      END
```

5

get R, the largest number, from user.
Start the counter C at 1.
Start the sum S at 0.

```
┌──────────────┐
│  S = S + C   │
│  C = C + 1   │
│              │
└──── Repeat IF C<R
```

PRINT the sum S.

ANSWERS TO EXERCISES 3 5

1

```
10   REM  ADD OR MULTIPLY
20        PRINT "TYPE IN TWO NUMBERS SEPARATED BY A COMMA"
30        INPUT X, Y
40        PRINT "DO YOU WANT + OR *";
50        INPUT A$
60        IF A$<>"+" THEN 90
70          LET R = X + Y
80          GO TO 100
90          LET R = X*Y
100       PRINT X; A$; Y; "="; R
9999      END
```

3 A good program is designed to handle a wide variety of reasonable responses. This program could be improved a little bit by inserting a test for additional reasonable answers,

```
175      IF A$ = "PESOS" THEN 300
```

thus giving a multiple condition on the selection of alternative. To make the program really polite requires a great deal more work, however. Situations like this are the topic of Chapter 9, where a solution to the "politeness on input" problem is presented. Regarding the round-off to cents, it should (see problem 2 4 and excercise 2 4 2a).

5 The program prints the lines from Aesop regardless of the wishes of the user. The programmer has made an error in line 40. It should have been either one of the following:

```
40       IF A$<>"AESOP" THEN 90
```

or

```
40       IF A$="MOTHER GOOSE" THEN 90
```

ANSWERS TO EXERCISES 4 1

1 Plan, refine, code, and debug. Don't count on the process going smoothly. Refinements change the plan; code changes the refinements (and the plan too, sometimes); results from the program, if they seem outlandish or even just slightly unrealistic, change the plan, refinements, and/or code; and debugging can affect any of the other stages of development. The best you can do is to stay organized throughout the process and keep good notes.

3 A **portable program** is one which will run on several computer systems with a minimum of changes. Writing in a standardized language like Minimal BASIC helps, but it's not a complete solution. Nevertheless, it is important to strive towards portability because good, useful programs have a tendency to travel around much more than you expect when you write them.

5 When a program is finished, tested, and debugged, it goes into use. If it is a program of any size beyond the toy program level, it is almost certain to have bugs remaining it it. When these bugs show up, a user will complain and the program has to be fixed. That's program maintenance. Sometimes making modifications to the program to meet new requirements is lumped with maintenance, but it probably should be called program **enhancement**.

ANSWERS TO EXERCISES 4 2

1 It saves time in the long run. You think of alternatives that weren't obvious in the beginning. Special cases come to mind that have to be covered. You can make decisions about which cases to cover and which can safely be let go. Planning improves your chances of writing a correct program. Planning almost always leads to a clearer program.

3 It's not really accounted for, but the user should be told that he or she can correct checks by entering the amount that was entered incorrectly again, but as a deposit instead of a check. Then the incorrect amount will be added back onto the balance, and the check can be re-entered. Vice versa for deposits entered incorrectly.

ANSWERS TO EXERCISES 4 3

1 **—balance a checkbook—**

Get old balance.

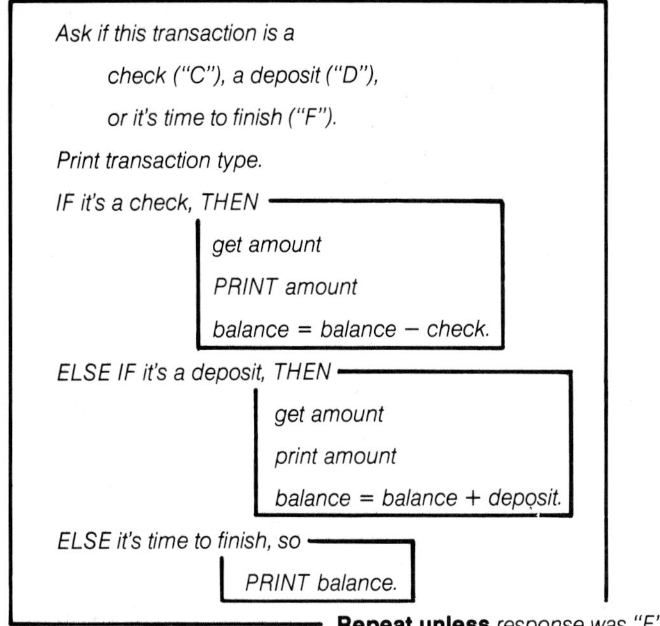

Ask if this transaction is a
check ("C"), a deposit ("D"),
or it's time to finish ("F").
Print transaction type.
IF it's a check, THEN
get amount
PRINT amount
balance = balance − check.
ELSE IF it's a deposit, THEN
get amount
print amount
balance = balance + deposit.
ELSE it's time to finish, so
PRINT balance.
Repeat unless response was "F"

3 **—do addition or multiplication—**

Get two numbers.

Ask which operation.

IF "+" THEN

add the numbers.

ELSE

multiply the numbers.

Print the numbers, the operation, and the result.

ANSWERS TO EXERCISES 4 4

1 The REMark at the beginning of the program gives a person reading the program (or looking for the listing in a stack of dusty old listings) a good idea of the general purpose of the program.

3 Add the following statements after the *repeat unless* box:

Skip a line.

Print farewell message.

ANSWERS TO EXERCISES 4 5

1 It means that the sequence of messages and values the program prints out doesn't correspond to that dictated by our plan. It means the program, she don't work right.

3 By viewing the program as an object of scientific study, a black box almost, you can divorce yourself from what you *think* it does and try to find out what it *really* does. You need to keep notes on the behavior you observe in the program because you may be checking a lot of things, and you will forget small details which seem irrelevant, but which turn out later to be crucial.

5 You should constantly check the plan against the program in the debugging stage to make sure you coded what you planned to code.

7 Line 170 is in error. If the user response wasn't C, the program should then test to see if the response was D. Instead, the program skips the test at the top of the deposit option. The correct version is

```
170          IF A$<>"C" THEN 300
```

ANSWERS TO EXERCISES 4 6

1 How do you feel when your BASIC system says

```
UNRECOGNIZED STATEMENT          ?
```

3 If the user types a negative number, it gets added backwards into the running balance. The user has probably made a mistake and the program should account for this. One reasonably simple solution is to test for negative inputs, warn the user, and allow him or her to re-enter the number. The plan below shows what to do with checks. A similar thing can be done with deposits.

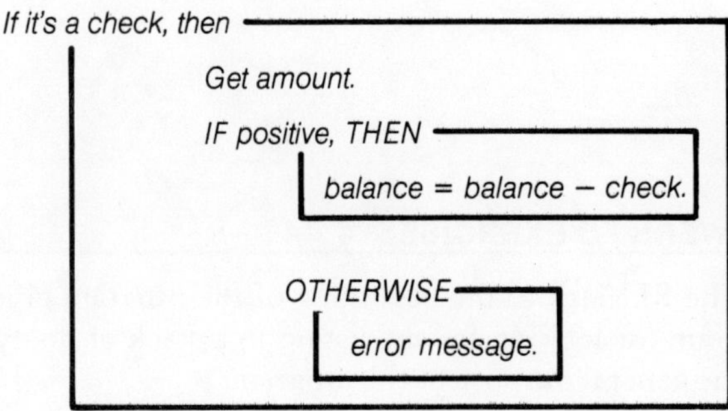

ANSWERS TO EXERCISES 4 7

1 ANSI Minimal BASIC

ANSWERS TO EXERCISES 5 1

1 Since the posttest loop travels through the body at least once, we were assuming that the user would have at least one check or deposit to enter. This seems reasonable. Most people wouldn't bother to run the program if they hadn't written any checks.

3 The first two don't print Y the last time through the loop. The one on the right always prints Y, even the last time through.

5 Using the ABS function would protect the user from subtracting negative wall space. However, it would be better to detect negative dimensions as the user enters them. They are likely to be errors, and the user should be warned.

7 A posttest loop would work well in this case. No user would run the program unless there was at least one wall to paint, so it makes sense to go through the loop at least once.

ANSWERS TO EXERCISES 5 2

1 Move line 430 (the transfer to the top of the loop) up to line 375 and change 500 to 380 in line 330. In the plan this amounts to taking the PRINT statement out of the loop and putting it just before the end.

3 The lines numbered in the two-hundreds give the instructions for entering the data. The lines preceding the two-hundreds correspond to "ask for the starting mileage" in the plan.

5 **—batting average—**

PRINT instructions.

No "at bats" or "hits" at this point.

Start with game 1.

While *there are more game left*

> *Add "at bats" and "hits" for this game to totals.*
>
> *PRINT current average.*
>
> *LET game = game + 1.*

```
10    REM  BATTING AVERAGE
20    REM  VARIABLES--
30    REM    A = AT-BATS IN A GAME     T = TOTAL AT-BATS
40    REM    H = HITS IN A GAME        S = TOTAL HITS
50    REM    G = GAME NUMBER
60    REM  INSTRUCTIONS
70         PRINT "TYPE IN THE NUMBER OF AT-BATS AND HITS ";
80         PRINT "FOR EACH GAME."
90         PRINT "TYPE IN  -1  FOR AT-BATS WHEN YOU'RE DONE."
100        PRINT
110   REM  INITIALIZE TOTALS
120        LET T = 0
130        LET S = 0
140        LET G = 1
200   REM  GET DATA AND PRINT AVERAGES
210        PRINT "AT-BATS FOR GAME"; G
220        INPUT A
230        IF A<0 THEN 9999
240             PRINT "HITS";
250             INPUT H
260             LET T = T + A
270             LET S = S + H
280             IF T=0 THEN 320
290               PRINT "CURRENT AVERAGE:";
300               PRINT INT(1000*S/T + .5)/1000
310               GO TO 340
320   REM         SPECIAL CASE FOR PLAYER WITH NO AT-BATS YET.
330               PRINT "NO AT-BATS YET THIS SEASON"
340             PRINT
350             LET G = G + 1
360             GO TO 200
9999      END
```

any more games? (lines 210–230)
add to totals (lines 240–270)
print current average (lines 280–330)
rounds to traditional three digits (line 300)
we don't want to compute S/T if T is zero. (line 320)

7 To do this, you would have to keep track of the mileage between stops, and this would require another variable. Let's call it B. Then we would set B equal to starting mileage R0 in line 290, just before the loop starts, and set it equal to current mileage R1 in line 425, just before the end of the loop. Instead of printing (R1 − R0)/T, we print (R1 − B)/T.

ANSWERS TO EXERCISES 5 3

1 Lines 270 through 1020 make up the selection.

2 `ON K GO TO 100, 200, 100, 200, 100, 200`

ANSWERS TO EXERCISES 5 4

1 `ON K GO TO 400, 600, 600, 500, 600`

ANSWERS TO EXERCISES 5 5

1 Two building blocks (IF-THEN and pretest loop) in sequence.

3 If-then and pretest loop in sequence with posttest loop nested inside the pretest loop.

5 Two posttest loops in sequence.

ANSWERS TO EXERCISES 5 6

1 If the list is of an unpredictable size, then arrange for one special value to be a quitting signal or ask the user to tell you, before each input, whether there is any more data. If the list is of a fixed size, have the computer count them off and ask for the items one by one. If the size would be well known to the user (without having to make a special effort to count), have the user type in the number of items in the list, then count off the items as they are typed in.

3 The user might think there are *no* interesting shows so you have to allow for that possibility.

—best Friday shows—

PRINT instructions.

Ask if there are any interesting shows.

While *there are interesting shows,*

> *Get name of show.*
>
> *Ask if any more.*

ANSWERS TO EXERCISES 5 7

1 **—sum a list of numbers—**

Start with sum = 0.

Ask if any numbers.

While *more numbers*

> *Get number.*
>
> *Add to sum.*
>
> *Ask if any more.*

PRINT sum.

3 **—compute sum or product of two given numbers—**

Ask which, sum or product?

Get the two numbers.

IF sum, THEN

LET S = sum of numbers.

ELSE

LET S = product of numbers.

PRINT numbers, operation, and result.

ANSWERS TO EXERCISES 6 1

1 According to experimental data on short-term memory, the upper limit is about nine. However, because different people have different limitations, and problems have different levels of difficulty, it's best to keep the number of subtasks under seven. The most important criterion is that the subtasks must be chosen on the basis of some logical decomposition of the problem, not random chopping of the problem into pieces.

3 Get up. Perform ablutions. Get dressed. Eat breakfast. Gather needed materials. Travel to work.

ANSWERS TO EXERCISES 6 2

1 (a) module 3—print bill; (b) module 1—get data; and module 3—print bill.

3 When the number, rounded to two decimal places, is zero in the second decimal place (like 23.40), the computer prints only one place.

5 In Minimal BASIC, all positive numbers are preceded by a space when printed. We can't avoid it.

ANSWERS TO EXERCISES 6 3

1

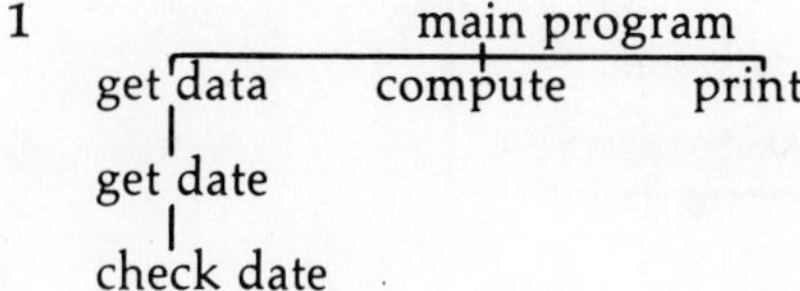

3 Line 8420 gets carried out if the year is legit, the month is January, March, May, July, August, October, or December, and the day is between 1 and 31, inclusive.

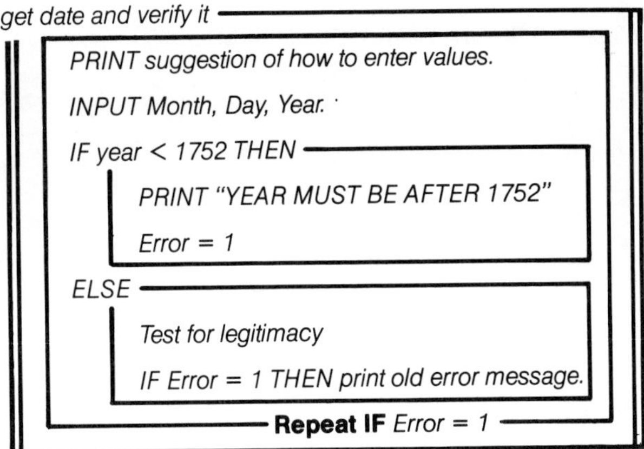

get date and verify it
PRINT suggestion of how to enter values.
INPUT Month, Day, Year.
IF year < 1752 THEN
PRINT "YEAR MUST BE AFTER 1752"
Error = 1
ELSE
Test for legitimacy
IF Error = 1 THEN print old error message.
Repeat IF Error = 1

ANSWERS TO EXERCISES 6 4

1 Only the first one (120 GOSUB 9000) is correct.

3
```
100     LET X = A
110     LET Y = B
120     GOSUB 9000
130     PRINT M2
 .
 .
 .
```

5 The MAX-MIN subroutine expects to find its input values in X and Y. The program fragment sends the input to the subroutine in M1 and M2. (This is doubly bad because M1 and M2 happen to be the output variables used by the subroutine.) The program will print the larger of whatever values happen to be in the variables X and Y.

ANSWERS TO EXERCISES 6 5

1
```
                                  tax to nearest cent
100    PRINT "$"; FNC(8.5*0.59) + FNC(0.06*8.5*0.59)
                  price to nearest cent
```

3
```
10     DEF FNC(V) = FNR(100*V)/100
```

5
```
10     REM  TABLE OF DOUBLING PERIODS
20          DEF FNR(X) = INT( X + .5 )
30          DEF FNT(R) =              <-- from Exercise 4
100         PRINT "INTEREST RATE", "YEARS TO DOUBLE"
110         LET P = 5
120         PRINT "     "; P; "%" , "      "; FNR(FNT(P/100))
130            LET P = P + 1
140            IF P<=12 THEN 120
9999        END
```

(program continued on page 484)

```
RUN
INTEREST RATE YEARS TO DOUBLE
     5 %             14
     6 %             12
     7 %             10
     8 %             9
     9 %             8
     10 %            7
     11 %            7
     12 %            6
READY
```

ANSWERS TO EXERCISES 6 6

1 The parameter must be a simple name. It cannot be an expression like V + 1.

3
```
10    DEF FNN(N) = INT(RND*N + 1)
```

5 D is the parameter; it will take on whatever value is given as the argument when the function is used. D1 and D2 are numeric variables from the program where the function is defined. When the function is used, D1 and D2 must have values, and those values will be used in computing the value of the function.

7 It prints 20 12 32.

ANSWERS TO EXERCISES 7 1

1
```
30    DATA 39, -72, 149
```

3 The computer will try to print past column L. Since L is the last column that will fit on a line (assuming the user answered the INPUT question correctly), the remaining $-signs in the bar being printed will go onto the next line.

5 Lines 360 and 370. 370 contains the actual test.

ANSWERS TO EXERCISES 7 2

1 The RESTORE statement wouldn't do any good at the beginning of the program because the DATA sequence always starts at the beginning. It's only after some READ statements have been carried out that RESTORE has any effect.

3 X = 1; Y = 2; Z = 3; A = 1; B = 2; C = 3; D = 4; E = 5.

5 The idea is to go back to the beginning by using a RESTORE statement, then skip past the first two DATA items by reading the first two DATA items into a "dummy" variable.

```
7000 REM  SET UP TO READ THIRD DATA ITEM
7010      RESTORE
7020      READ D, D
7030      RETURN
```

ANSWERS TO EXERCISES 7 3

1 A$ = "BOB"; B$ = "MARY"; C$ = "ALICE"; X = 18; Y = 23; Z = 21.

3 A$ = "BOB"; B$ = "MARY"; C$ = "ALICE"; X$ = "213-44-9930"; Y$ = "448-26-8823"; Z$ = "414-71-3652".

5 The value which should go into Y is a string, but a string will not go into a numeric variable. The computer stops with an error condition.

7 0123456789000000 1.234567E + 14.

ANSWERS TO EXERCISES 7 4

1

```
RABBIT RABBIT RABBIT RABBITRABBIT
  B$     A$     C$     B$    C$
```

ANSWERS TO EXERCISES 8 3

1 A **constant** is an example of a **numeric expression.** Review Section 2 3 if you are confused.

3 Why are you looking here? Run the programs on your computer to get the answers.

5 and 7 —ditto—

ANSWERS TO EXERCISES 8 4

1 Change the relation in line 160 of the last example to "greater-than-or-equal-to".

3

```
120  READ C
130  IF C>=0 THEN 200
140    PRINT C
```

5

```
20   LET S = 0
 .
 .
 .
120  READ C
130  IF C<=0 THEN 200
140    LET S = S + C
 .
 .
 .
210  PRINT "SUM OF POSITIVE ITEMS="; S
```

ANSWERS TO EXERCISES 8 5

1
```
120   READ C
130   IF C<0 THEN 300
 .
 .
 .
210     PRINT "NO ITEM LESS THAN ZERO"
 .
 .
 .
310     PRINT "FIRST NEGATIVE ITEM:"; C
```

3
```
120   READ C
130   IF C>=10 THEN 300
 .
 .
 .
210      PRINT "NO NUMBERS EXCEED 10"
 .
 .
 .
310      PRINT "THE NUMBER IN POSITION"; V;
320      PRINT "IS THE FIRST TO EXCEED 10"
```

ANSWERS TO EXERCISES 8 6

1 b, c

3
```
190          INPUT E0
200          IF E0>10 THEN 220
210          IF E0>0  THEN 250
220  REM        ILLEGAL VALUE
230             PRINT "EFFORT TO LEARN IS FROM 1 TO 10"
240             GOTO 180
250  REM   PRINT HEADING FOR REPORT
```

ANSWERS TO EXERCISES 9 1

1 We used separate DATA statements for items of different classes because we thought it made the data easier to understand. It doesn't make any difference to the computer if items of different classes are in the same DATA statement. They can even be scrambled up as long as the correct class number always comes right after each menu item.

3
```
8000 REM  MENU ITEMS--BANK BALANCE PROGRAM
8010      DATA CHECK,1,    C,1, CHK,1
8020      DATA DEPOSIT,2,  D,2, DEP,2
8030      DATA SUBTOTAL,3, S,3, SUB,3, CURRENT BALANCE,3
8040      DATA FINISHED,4, F,4, FIN,4, END,4, DONE,4
```

5 The search loop finds the *first* occurrence of an item in the menu. Therefore, with the DATA statements shown in the exercise, the program would treat all B entries as BRUSH entries.

ANSWERS TO EXERCISES 9 2

1 If it ran up to I9 = S9, the first item in the desired menu would already be read, and the menu subroutine would start searching with the second item. As a result, any user who typed in the first item on the menu would be out of luck.

3 The range from 1 to F9 − S9 + 1 would work OK. The only thing that matters is the *number* of values for I9 within the range. The actual values of I9 aren't used and are irrelevant. However, it is easier and makes the program clearer to control the number of iterations with the range from S9 to F9 than with the range starting at 1, even though both ranges make the loop go through the same number of iterations and therefore have the same effect.

5
```
8000 REM  FORM LETTER MENU-- S9=1, F9=3
8010      DATA NEW LETTER,1, EDIT LETTER,2, TYPE LETTER,3
8020 REM  EDIT LETTER MENU-- S9=4, F9=7
8030      DATA INSERT LINE,1, CHANGE LINE,2,
8040      DATA DELETE LINE,3, QUIT,4
8050 REM  TYPE LETTER MENU-- S9=8, F9=12
8060      DATA MARGIN,1, COPIES,2, DATA,3, GO,4, QUIT,5
```

You might have been more conscientious than we were and put in alternative spellings for the menu items. If so, your values for S9 and F9 will be different.

7 We divided the statements into three groups: I/O, CONTROL, and OTHER. You can see how we classified each statement by looking at the DATA statements below. This is not the only way to classify the statements, of course, so your answer may be different.

```
8000 REM  STATEMENT CATEGORY MENU-- S9=1, F9=3
8010      DATA I/O,1,  CONTROL,2,  OTHER,3
8020 REM  I/O MENU-- S9=4, F9=7
8030      DATA PRINT,1,  INPUT,2,  READ,3,  DATA,4
8040 REM  CONTROL MENU--  S9=8, F9=13
8050      DATA GO TO,1,  GOSUB,2,  FOR,3  NEXT,4,
8060      DATA IF,5,  ON,6
8070 REM  OTHER MENU-- S9=14, F9=18
8080      DATA REM,1,  DEF,2,  STOP,3,  END,4,  LET,5
```

ANSWERS TO EXERCISES 9 3

1 It treats PAINT BRUSH as an invalid response, prints out all the legal responses, and gives the user another chance.

3 The program will work as usual whenever the user types a legal response. An illegal response will send the computer to the "print legal responses" subroutine (as usual), and all the legal responses will be printed out. However, instead of printing all responses of the same class on one line, the responses will get printed on separate lines. This is because the routine which prints them stays on the same line only as long as consecutive menu items have the same class number.

ANSWERS TO EXERCISES 10 1

1 b, c

3 a, b

ANSWERS TO EXERCISES 10 2

1 b

3 (a) array
(b) array, DATA
(c) array
(d) array, DATA
(e) array

ANSWERS TO EXERCISES 10 3

1 a, b, and c are legal. d is not.

3 a and b are OK. c is not because it attempts to index L(13), which doesn't exist. d is illegal.

5 A speed of 58 mph results in a subscript of 58/10 or 5.8. Since subscript values are rounded to the nearest whole number in Minimal BASIC, the program will return D(6), or 330 (feet). Similarly, if the user types 55, the program will respond with an answer of 330. (Rounding x to the nearest whole number means computing INT(x + 0.5).)

7 Disaster. The subscript value will be -2, and the lowest numbered position is 0. The program should be rewritten to test for inputs that will lead to illegal, out-of-bounds subscripts. It should politely tell the user that it can't handle the entered value.

ANSWERS TO EXERCISES 10 4

1 If I has the value 53, then Q(I) is Q(53), which has the value 128 in Figure 10 3 1. Similarly, P(I) is 0.59. Changing the value of I doesn't do anything to Q(53), so Q(53) is still 128. Similarly, P(53) is still 0.59.

3 Assume the password is "PIZZA".

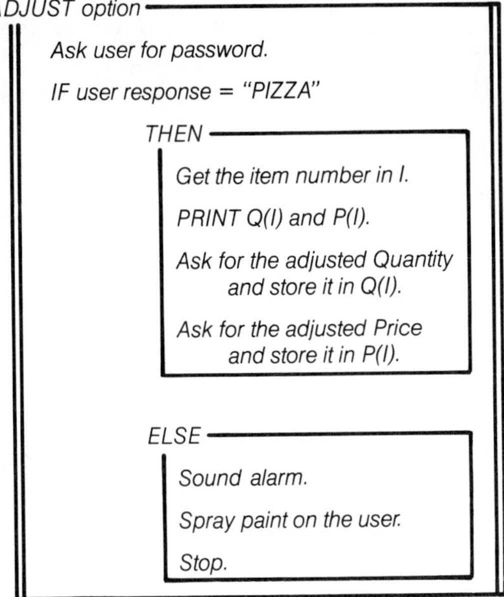
ADJUST option
Ask user for password.
IF user response = "PIZZA"
THEN
Get the item number in I.
PRINT Q(I) and P(I).
Ask for the adjusted Quantity and store it in Q(I).
Ask for the adjusted Price and store it in P(I).
ELSE
Sound alarm.
Spray paint on the user.
Stop.

ANSWERS TO EXERCISES 11 2

1 (a) G
(b) A
(c) D
(d) C
(e) E

ANSWERS TO EXERCISES 11 3

1 (a) female (the value 2 entered for the answer to question 2 by the third respondent means the second possible answer, which you can see from the original question in Section 11 2 is "female".)
(b) 22 to 25
(c) 2 to 4 years

3 Question 2 — Standard Report

male	1	25%
female	3	75%

ANSWERS TO EXERCISES 11 4

1 (a) 4 (Since there are 4 questions in the questionnaire.)
(b) 8 (Since there are 8 possible answers to the "What is your age?" question.)
(c) 2

3 (a) H(1) and H(2) will both be 0 since at that point the program hasn't looked at any of the responses yet.

(b) H(1) will have the value 1 since one response (response number 2) lists 1 as the answer to question 2.

H(2) will have the value 3 since three responses give the answer 2 to question 2.

ANSWERS TO EXERCISES 11 5

1 A b Q5
B d R5
C f N
D e E

3 Line 5160

```
5160      LET H(Q(R0,Q0) + 1) = H(Q(R0,Q0) + 1)  +  1
```

answer (under H(Q(R0,Q0)); the bias we add to avoid using H(0) (pointing to each + 1 inside the parentheses); the 1 we add to record another occurrence of answer (pointing to the final + 1)

5

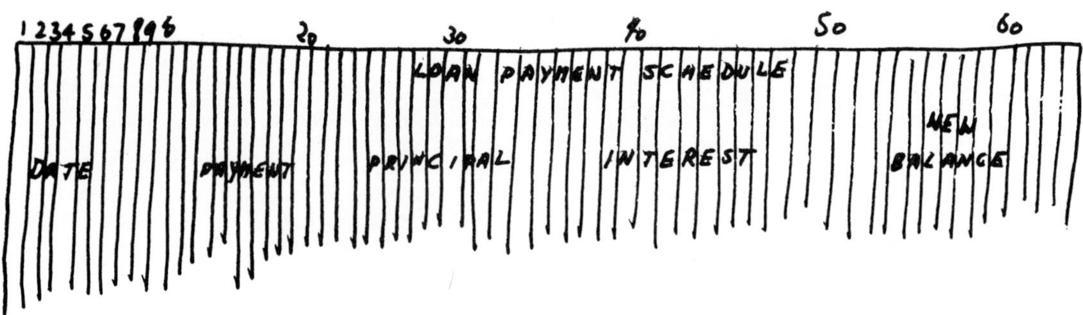

7 a, b, and c

ANSWERS TO EXERCISES 12 2

1 3.17098E83 centuries — still completely out of the question.

3 In our teeny version of the "beautiful picture" program, we used one FOR-NEXT loop for each picture position, and we used one variable for each position. In a 20-by-20 picture, we'd need 400 variables and 400 nested FOR-NEXT loops. In standard BASIC there are only 286 numeric variables, and FOR-NEXT loops may be nested to a depth of only 10.

To expand the program, we could store the picture in a 20-by-20 array, and generate the different pictures by making changes to the values in the array. No problem to write the program, but it would still take many, many times the age of the universe to *run* it.

ANSWERS TO EXERCISES 12 3

1 The program is an infinite loop! The FOR-NEXT loop will never terminate since the final value (2000000) will never be reached. To six places of accuracy, 1000000 + 1 is 1000000.

ANSWERS TO EXERCISES 13 2

1 Well, they didn't *have* to do it that way, but it seems like the clearest way to do it. They did need to force all the terms except the one involving *b* to zero to study the "today's deaths" term in isolation, and setting *a*, *c*, and *d* to zero certainly accomplishes that. But so would setting *d* to zero, giving *a* and *c* any values whatever, and starting off with no food. That would make the food variable F1 stay at zero, and that, in turn, would make all terms except today's deaths be zero no matter how long the program was run.

3 No. If there were no flies to begin with, none would ever be born, so no matter how long the program ran, the number of flies would be zero. For all other reasonable initial conditions, after a while, the predicted number of flies and amount of food would be the same as in Figure 13 2 2. (We don't consider starting with a negative number of flies to be a reasonable initial condition.)

ANSWERS TO EXERCISES 13 3

1 A a
B b
C g
D f

3 There are two things to do. First, the line which simulates the cleanup should be changed from

```
1595        LET F1 = INT(0.2*F1)
```

to

```
1595        LET F1 = INT(0.1*F1)
```

since if 90% of the waste is cleaned up, only one tenth of it remains.

Second, when you run the program, you should answer the CLEANUP HOW OFTEN message with 21.

ANSWERS TO EXERCISES 13 4

1 If we use the variable A0 for *a* for the "normal" flies, and A1 for *a* for the "mutants," the following changes will accomplish the task.

```
100        PRINT "A  FOR THE BLACK FLIES=";
110        INPUT A0
111        PRINT "A  FOR THE WHITE FLIES=";
112        INPUT A1

1070           LET T0 = A0*F2*F0
1090           LET T1 = A1*F2*W0
```

In addition, the headings should be changed to reflect the differences between the two types of flies (lines 340 and 350).

ANSWERS TO EXERCISES 14 1

1 Well, there's no need to swap it with itself, but we'd have to add an additional statement to test for that case. Since in a large array that's in jumbled order, this case will happen rarely (if at all), the program would probably waste more time making the test than it would switching N(Left) with itself now and then.

3 Since we started position-of-smallest-so-far with the value L0 (Left), there's no need to compare N(L0) with itself.

5 It returns the value 1. Look at line 7150. As the REMark in the next line indicates, it causes the routine to notice only "new lows". If a value is equal to the old smallest value, that's not a "new" low. Do you think we should have described the subroutine this way?: "Compute the position of the first occurrence of the smallest value lying in N(L0) through N(Z)."

ANSWERS TO EXERCISES 14 2

1 No, certainly not. If we'd done that, we would have scrambled the information totally. M(1) would be the lowest Manufacturer code, S(1) the lowest Specific product code, Q(1) the lowest Quantity on hand, and P(1) the lowest Price. We would have lost the relationship among the pieces of information for each item.

ANSWERS TO EXERCISES 14 3

1 (a) 4

(b) 12

(c) "Sort the values from position 1 through position 3."

(d) 3

(e) 6 + twice your age (*not* 7 + twice your age — the partition value is in place already).

3 (a) Positions 4, 5, 6, 7, 8, 9, and 10.

(b) Position 10.

5 If the left subproblem is smaller, line 6110 will be carried out next. The left subproblem goes from position L0 to position R1 − 1. The right subproblem goes from R1 + 1 to R0.

left subproblem shorter than right subproblem

is the same as

R1 − 1 − L0 *less than* R0 − (R1 + 1)

which is the same as

R1 − L0 < R0 − R1

7 100

ANSWERS TO EXERCISES 14 4

1 In the absence of a RANDOMIZE statement, the random number operator spews out the same sequence of numbers each time the program is run. That way, when we run the test on 100 numbers, the first 50 will be the same numbers (in the same order) as when we ran the test on 50 values. We thought that since Quicksort can take a different length of time on the same-sized array, depending on the initial order of the values, it would make the most sense to test the effects of increasing the size of the array if the first part of the problem was the same. What do you think?

3 a and b

5 There are 20 ways to choose the value we put in N(1). That leaves 19 different values we can put in N(2), and so on. That's

20*19*18*. . .*2*1 − 2

or, using the common notation for factorial,

20! − 2

Our trusty computer estimates that as

2.43290E18, or

2,432,900,000,000,000,000 or so. Quite a few.

ANSWERS TO EXERCISES 15 2

1 (a) `LET Q = INT(V/D)`

(b) `LET R = V - D*INT(V/D)`

(c) `LET D = (V - R)/Q`

3

```
8300 REM  PUT THE DIGIT  R  INTO THE P8-TH POSITION OF  V
8301      IF INT(R)=R THEN 8310
8302        PRINT "WARNING: R HAS A FRACTIONAL PART."
8303        PRINT "IN PACK ROUTINE--R="; R; "P8="; P8
8310      GOSUB 8200
8320      LET V = V + (R - D8)*10^(6 - P8)
8330      RETURN
```

5 Three.

7 Let's assume we have the extract routine from exercise 6, and that it starts at line 9200. Then to pack the value R into the P8th pair in V,

```
9300 REM   PUT THE VALUE  R  INTO THE P8-TH PAIR OF  V
9310       GOSUB 9200
9320       LET V = V + (R - D8)*100^(3 - P8)
9330       RETURN
```

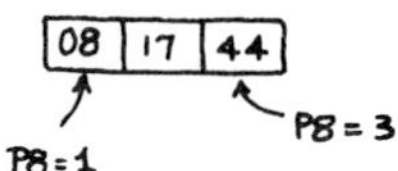

9 There are 10^6 different 6-digit decimal patterns to play with, from 000000 to 999999. The question is, "How many patterns are required to store x answers, each of which can be either of two values?" It takes two different patterns to store one answer, four to store two, eight to store three, . . . , and 2^x to store x. Now we need to know how large x can be before 2^x uses up all million patterns. Whipping out our pocket calculator, we see how many times we can multiply two by itself without exceeding a million. Unless we made a mistake, that's 19, so you could store 19 answers per variable.

Here's another way to figure it out. We need to find the largest x which satisfies this inequality:

$2^x <= 10^6$

Therefore,

$x \log(2) <= 6 \log(10)$

Using BASIC, we compute

```
LET X = INT(6*LOG(10)/LOG(2))
```

and discover that, as before, we can fit 19 answers per variable.

If you figured that you could fit three per decimal digit, so 18 in all, count that right and congratulate yourself for not going to all the work we did.

three answers require 8 patterns	
000	0
001	1
010	2
011	3
100	4
101	5
110	6
111	7

ANSWERS TO EXERCISES 15 3

1

```
100 REM  ESTIMATE HOW LONG IT WOULD TAKE TO
110 REM  MAKE ALL POSSIBLE SHUFFLES.
120 REM  FIRST, ESTIMATE THE # OF DIFFERENT ARRANGEMENTS.
130      LET W = 52
140      FOR H=51 TO 1 STEP -1
150          LET W = W*H
160      NEXT H
170 REM
180 REM  NOW FIGURE OUT HOW MANY CENTURIES IT WOULD
190 REM  TAKE AT 1 SHUFFLE EACH SECOND.
200      LET C = W/60/60/24/365/100
210      PRINT "IT WOULD TAKE"; C; "CENTURIES!"
9999     END
```

if this part tries to compute a number that's too big for your system, just do this part (lines 120–170), *and finish the estimate by hand* (lines 180–210)

3 If we'd just looked at the experiment at the start of the section, we could have seen that the answer was going to be about 8.1E67...

5 Of course, the REMark statements and the PRINT statements should be changed to reflect the different use of the program. Aside from those, the only changes would be in lines 110 through 210. We'd need a much bigger array, maybe for as many as a thousand digits. We'd need to start the array off with the value

```
000...0128
```

and the FOR loop starting in line 210 should go from 127 down to 2 instead of from 51 down to 2.

ANSWERS TO EXERCISES 15 4

1

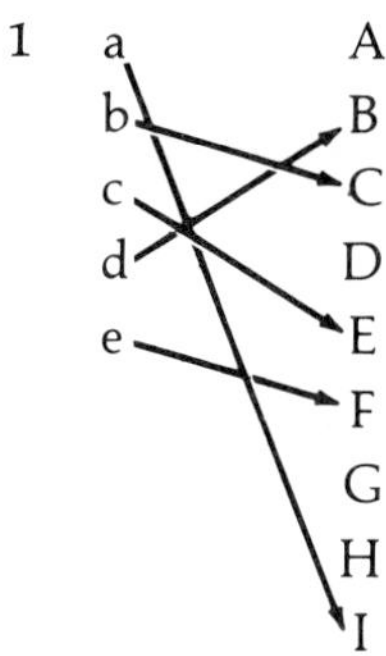

3 Print the item pointed to by L(Z) first, then the one indicated by L(Z − 1), and so on, finishing with L(2) and L(1).

```
FOR I=Z TO 1 STEP -1
    PRINT M(L(I)); S(L(I)); Q(L(I)); P(L(I))
NEXT I
```

5

```
Number found = 0:
For position = 1 to Z
    If L(position) = D(position) then
        Number found = number found + 1.
        Print M(L(position)), S(L(position)),
            and position.
If number found = 0 then
    Print "None found".
```

ANSWERS TO EXERCISES 16 1

1 From earliest ("least") to latest ("greatest") they are

```
"SMITH  JEAN"
"SMITH ,JOHN"
"SMITHY,JOAN"
```

3 (a) `A$( LEN(A$) - L + 1 : LEN(A$) )`

(b) `A$( 1 : L )`

(c) `A$( S : S + F - 1 )`

ANSWERS TO EXERCISES 16 2

1 Only subroutine c works. The other two not only don't remove all leading blanks from N$, they go into infinite loops in certain cases. For example, if N$ *doesn't* start with a blank, subroutine b never stops! Can you see what case makes a similar thing happen in subroutine a?

3

```
8700 REM  FIND THE FIRST OCCURRENCE OF  T$  IN  S$
8710 REM  P  RETURNS EITHER THE STARTING POSITION
8720 REM     OF  T$  OR 0 (IF IT DOESN'T APPEAR IN  S$ )
8730      FOR P=1 TO LEN(S$) - LEN(T$) + 1
8740         IF S$( P : P + LEN(T$) -1 )=T$ THEN 8790
8750        NEXT P
8760 REM    NOT FOUND
8770          LET P = 0
8780          RETURN
8790 REM    FOUND
8800          RETURN
```

ANSWERS TO EXERCISES 17 1

1
```
9000 REM  WAIT FOR USER TO READ SCREEN BEFORE CONTINUING
9010      PRINT TAB(40); "HIT <RETURN> TO GO ON";
9020      LINE INPUT R$
9030      RETURN
```

ANSWERS TO EXERCISES 18 2

1 We have to rewind the sequential file UPC each time because if we didn't, our program wouldn't be able to locate a UPC value lower than the one before.

ANSWERS TO EXERCISES 18 3

1 There are N + 2 records in QUEST.DIC and E*N + 1 in QUEST.RSP. (See Figure 18 3 1.)

3 Because in that case the corrections the user entered for responses 12 and 21 would be lost.

5 You would need to add statements which create a backup file for QUEST.DIC, and then print the values of N and L(1), . . . , L(N) on it.

Appendix E **Index**

Appendix F Guide to BASIC Commands

action	typical forms	my system
Getting the hardware ready	turn the power on insert the system diskette turn the switch on the terminal to ON-LINE or REMOTE type a Log-in message like <u>HELLO</u> or <u>LOGON</u> type a password	
Getting into the BASIC system (See Appendix A for more options)	type <u>BASIC</u> <u>LOAD BASIC</u> or <u>CLOAD BASIC</u>	
To stop a running program (the "panic button")	hold the CONTROL key down and hit the <u>C</u> key hit the key marked ESC hit the key marked BREAK	
Editing a line before you've hit RETURN		
Delete previous character	hit one of these keys BackSpace DELete RUBOUT hold the CONTROL key and hit one of these <u>H</u> <u>X</u> <u>U</u>	
Delete entire line (so you can start it over)	hold the CONTROL key and hit <u>U</u> or maybe <u>X</u>	

action	typical forms	my system
Wipe out an existing program so you can enter a new one	NEW CLEAR SCRATCH SCR	
To start running a program you've entered	RUN	
To look at a program you've entered	LIST	
To look at part of a program (from line 100 through 250)	LIST 100 TO 250 LIST 100,250 LIST 100-250	
To delete a portion of a program		
To delete (say) line 120	120	
To delete (say) lines 125 through 150	DELETE 125 TO 150 DELETE 125,150 DELETE 125-150	
To renumber a program		
Renumber all lines so they will have line numbers 10, 20, 30,. . .	RENUMBER RENUM REN	
Renumber lines which now have numbers 200 and greater, so they'll start at 500 and go in steps of 10 (so they'll be 500, 510, 520,. . .)	RENUMBER 200 TO LAST AT 500 RENUMBER 200,500,10 RENUM 500,200,10 REN 500,200	
To save a program called "MILES" so you can use it again later	SAVE "MILES" SAVE MILES	
To get a previously saved program	LOAD "MILES" OLD MILES	
To get out of the BASIC system and return to the computer's operating system	BYE SYSTEM MONITOR CONTROL-C	

Appendix G **Quick Reference Index**